Sweethearts

Sweethearts

The Timeless Love Affair
–On-Screen and Off–
Between Jeanette MacDonald and
Nelson Eddy

SHARON RICH

INTRODUCTION BY JON EDDY

DONALD I. FINE, INC.

New York

Library of Congress Catalogue Card Number: 94-071105
ISBN: 1-55611-407-9

Manufactured in the United States of America

10 9 8 7 6 5 4 3 2 1

Designed by Irving Perkins Associates

Acknowledgements

This book has been twenty years in the making—exactly half my life. First, thanks must go to Blossom Rock, whom I met as a teenager and whose friendship steered me into the MacDonald/Eddy story. Who knew then where the early tidbits of data she told me would lead?

Thanks are also due to Diane Goodrich, whom I met next in the search for clarification of the story. Since she knew the Nelson angle and I was learning Jeanette's side of it, we had a lot of notes to compare. For several years we had a great working relationship.

After Diane and I parted ways professionally, I was lucky to meet Judy Burns and T. A. Long, who were willing to interview those who would not have spoken to me otherwise. (It should be noted that early on I did know Gene Raymond casually as a friend of Blossom's, also I spoke with Jeanette's secretary a few times, and managed to get a few comments out of the usually tight-lipped Ted Paxson.) Judy had an extensive interview with Gene Raymond to hear his side of the story, plus a shorter conversation with Ann Eddy at Nelson's grave site.

In the last few years I struck out on my own, interviewing everyone I could find who was still alive, then I put this book together, trying to make sense of the hundreds of interviews and thousands of pages of letters that were sent to me from people all over the world. Here I must stop and thank my family for their years of tolerance: my father, whom I regret did not live to see this book's publication; my eternally patient mother; my two sisters Arlene and Julie; the McIntyre and Lefkowitz families; my husband Jake and my daughter Juliet, who has grown up sharing her mother with Jeanette and Nelson.

Special thanks must also be given to Dot "Little Dorothy" Dillard, who was an invaluable source of data and very helpful with editing, and to Ann Argo, who enthusiastically helped me with any research tasks I needed done.

Nearly thirty people I interviewed spoke only with the agreement that they remain anonymous—you know who you are and I thank you. The following people (alive and dead) granted interviews or important data, or help, either to me or to my research associates, and can be acknowledged: Lew Ayres, Brad Ballentine, Rose Bampton, Richard Barclay, Hilda Barrows, Rose Brasch, Joan Bice, Sister Mabel Bishop, Zepha Bogart, DeWitt Bodeen, Bernard Brown, Nancy Brown, Clarence Bull, Carol Burnette, Charles Cagle, Al Caiazza, Bino Cameron, Leah Campion, Kay Carbone, Ken Carpenter, Noble Kid Chissell, Marie Collick, Olga Collins, Iron Eyes Cody, Bob Connolly, Hans Conried, Doug Cramer, Billy Canniels, Poppy Delmando, Marc Cole Desmond, Cleo Dorman, Eleanor Knowles Dugan, Douglas Dumbrille, Irene Dunne, Buddy Ebsen, Jon Eddy, Robert Eddy, Rose Fefercorn, Susanna Foster, Fred Foy, Rose Friedland, Herbert Gahagan, Elsa Dik Glass, Marie Gerdes, Sam Gill, Ruth Gordon, Naomi Gottlieb, Sunny Griffin, Bob Grimes, Reverend Richard Halverson, Margaret Hamilton, Roseanne Hanna, Lynn Hereford, Charles Higham, Ken Hollywood, Jackie Hoover, Margaret Hovey, Mildred Hudson, Pat Hudson, Betty Jaynes, Mrs. Claude Jarman, Sr., Helen Jepson, Jean Johnson, Shirley Johnson, Allan Jones, Allan Joslyn, Eva Justice, Garson Kanin, Larry Kiner, Leonard Knazik, Mickey Knazik, Miliza Korjus, Miles Krueger, Audrey LaGanke, Chic LaGanke, Frank Laric, Elsa Lanchester, Olwen Lewis, Myrna Loy, Ida Lupino, Norma Nelson McDaniel, Truley McGee, Harper McKay, Donald McLellan, Lois Maher, Rouben Mamoulian, Sam Marx, Mildred Miller, Betty Monroe, Rita Morrow, Doris Mundinger, Maryon Murphy, Kay Neal, Susan Nelson, Margaret O'Brien, Scot O'Brien, Tim O'Sullivan, Shirley Jean Otto, Marvin Paige, Cecilia Parker, Dorothea Parsons, Theodore Paxson, Arnold Peasley, Brent Perry, Carol Stothart Perkins, Fred Phillips, John Pickard, Perry Pickering, Walter Pidgeon, Malcolm Poindexter, Jr., Malcolm Poindexter, Sr., Carolyn Power, Eleanor Powell, Randall Pratt, Ronald Reagan, Sandy Reiss, John Ritchie, Jr., Nancy Ritchie, Jeanie Rushing, Carol Russell, Anna May Ryder, Mary Sale, Richard Sale, Joe Sampson, Regina Schindel, Irving Schneider, Jim Schwartz, Esther Shipp, Natalie Simpson, Margo Slaughter, Sarah Smith, Regina Sokol, Milo Speriglio, Rise Stevens, Bob Stern, Herbert Stothart, Jr., Teresina Sullo, Bill Sutherland, Florence Thomas, Tony Thomas, Bill Thornton, Lawrence Tibbett, Jr., William Tuttle, Theodore Uppman, Lou Valentino, Ruth Van Dyke, Winston Van Dyke, Woody Van Dyke III, Jean Warren, Shirley Weinger, Richard Wells, Dick Weston, Betty White, Meredith Willson, Bette Wilmot, Darryl Winston, Anne Wood, Phyllis Woodbury, Marshall Wright, Monti Wylie.

Also, Ned Comstock at the USC Doheny Library (where what remains of Nelson's personal collection is housed), the staff at the Library of the Academy of Motion Pictures Arts and Sciences, U.C.L.A. special collections, Billy Rose

Library at Lincoln Center, Los Angeles Hall of Records, New York Public Library, Philadelphia City Hall, and Temple University.

I'm certain there are names I've missed, and I apologize for any omissions. Also, I need to thank the hundreds of fans who've written me with their experiences; thank you for your support and imput.

Thanks also to my editor Jason Poston, to Production Director Larry Bernstein, and to Don Fine, for your wholehearted enthusiasm and support.

—Sharon Rich

Contents

Introduction
by Jon Eddy

Jeanette MacDonald and Nelson Eddy were the most beloved movie stars of their era. Between 1935 and 1942 they made eight films together, most of them blockbusters that earned millions of dollars for Metro-Goldwyn-Mayer Studios. Each was a musical star in his own right, but once they sang their first duet on-screen they achieved instant immortality. Audiences of the Depression years were mesmerized by their romantic chemistry, the epitome of timeless love. Their faithful fans saw each film dozens of times—and still wanted more. They were uncaring of the few critics who found the movie plots sentimental or corny. What mattered was the on-screen intimacy, the way Nelson unconsciously caressed Jeanette's fingers, his blatant adoration when she walked into his view, her seductive child/woman quality, their haunting duets that were imprinted forever in the listener's memory. Jeanette's and Nelson's fame spread across the globe; soon they were Hollywood's top box office stars in China, Australia, Europe and South America.

As singers they had a powerful impact in other ways. They bridged the gap between classical singing and movies, and inspired thousands of young people to seek careers in opera or show business—a handful of names would include such diverse stars as Beverly Sills, Joan Sutherland, Mario Lanza, Carol Burnett and Betty White. As concert artists, MacDonald and Eddy were as popular as today's rock stars; they needed bodyguards and police escorts and broke attendance records everywhere. Nelson, who additionally had a weekly radio series, was the highest paid singer in the world for over a decade.

From day one the fans were convinced theirs was a love affair off-screen. When they married other people, MGM was deluged with thousands of stunned, irate letters. As the years passed most fans felt something had gone awry in their lives, for the on-screen chemistry never changed. Did they love each other or hate each other? The point was argued for decades, when their film careers ended suddenly and inexplicably, when they died prematurely—and even now, some thirty years after their deaths. What is not disputed is the continuing loyalty of their fans, unwavering with the passage of time. At this writing there are at least four fan clubs around the world. New fans are being made daily, thanks to the release of their films on video.

The astonishing thing about Nelson Eddy is that while he was a public figure whose influence stretched over an entire generation, he was also a man who guarded his private life almost to a fault. Why? He was not devious by nature, so what were the secrets he guarded so carefully?

There were a number of them. First, hard as it may be for some to believe—myself included—I am the son of Nelson Eddy.

Then there was Jeanette MacDonald, who was in fact the love of his life. I never met her, but I was privy to one conversation about her. During the 1960s Nelson was giving an interview in his dressing room in the Palmer House in Chicago, in the presence of his accompanist Theodore Paxson and the columnist of a local newspaper. I saw the color drain from Nelson's face when he was asked about Jeanette; he had a longing in his voice and expression as he spoke about her. The change in him was startling enough to indicate that she meant something to him. After the interview I asked Ted Paxson about Jeanette and Nelson, and after a silence he said: "That's a story that can't be written in our lifetime."

I never pressed for a closer relationship with Nelson, not wishing to embarrass a fine man. In that I felt I was a better son by respecting his privacy.

There are so many self-proclaimed experts who claim to know everything about Nelson and Jeanette. In *Sweethearts* Miss Rich allows the reader to make his own decision about their relationship, and that decision is based on detailed and collaborated fact, not what some people wish had occurred. With skill and caring the author relates the personal tragedy of two star-crossed lovers who as "America's Singing Sweethearts" brought happiness to millions all over the world, but who were never destined to find it for themselves.

—Jon Eddy

1

October 17–22, 1943

As the sun was setting, Jeanette and Nelson went to their favorite spot over-looking Lake Tahoe, where they performed a sentimental wedding ceremony. Jeanette sang "Indian Love Call," a song they'd made famous, then they knelt together and promised to love, honor and cherish each other forever. Their vows were performed without witnesses and without a clergyman. They were re-newing the pledge of love they'd exchanged eight summers before in 1935, at this very place, while filming their second movie together, *Rose Marie*.

But now it had to be done in secret because legally and in the public eye, each was happily married to someone else. A series of incredible events had prevented their wedding from ever taking place and had hurtled them into lifestyles from which they now could not extricate themselves. By necessity they lived double lives—a rollercoaster ride with moments of great passion countered by even longer stretches of agonizing separation. Sometimes the burden was too difficult to bear; they'd battled back from numerous breakdowns and suicide attempts during their years together.

That was why now in the final days of 1943, they needed to get away from the world and reaffirm their love and their faith in a God they trusted to somehow, someday, make things right for them.

Jeanette took a ring off her finger and handed it to Nelson. It was a stunner—an emerald surrounded by diamonds that had cost him $40,000 in 1935. Some-times she wore it in public on her wedding finger—more often on a chain around her neck. "Your dear life is bound to me forever," Nelson said as he slipped the ring back onto her finger and kissed her.

They returned to their "honeymoon" cabin, Nelson tenderly calling Jeanette "my wife." After dinner, they discussed several topics, including the state of their careers, then retired to their separate rooms. Recently, they had been keeping things on a "spiritual" level, because intimacy brought with it such a devastating letdown when they were forced to part. "The physical has always been the least important for us," Jeanette claimed. But their willpower would not hold out much longer.

Nelson kept a diary in which his impassioned writings reveal a man quite different than his public ever knew. He told Jeanette that the diary was her "insurance"—something she could always treasure in case anything ever happened to him. The following entry, dated December 3, 1943, chronicles their trip to Tahoe. The writing style is typical of Nelson's personality, alternately Victorian and sexually graphic:

> Three whole days and nights we had been together, satisfied with our kisses, happy just being in love, but with our goodnight kisses, little sweetheart, did you know how desperately I was longing to keep you with me? Your bedroom became a symbol, and I knew that one night soon I must step across the threshold and reclaim my wife . . . But there was no hurry, I loved your delicacy, your sensitivity about it all . . . content just to be with me. And then one evening I came and found you looking at an album of stills—our work—and suddenly you were facing me, speaking my name, so gently, so sweetly, I almost wept. And it was at that moment that I knew I would never have the strength to leave you alone this night.
>
> I dreamed it would be like this. But this night you were intoxicating beyond my fondest dreams—so wonderful—how I wanted to forever keep your lips to mine . . . And then you said, "You're making me dizzy—" But dearest, this is just what I wanted you to say . . . did you know I understand all your secrets so well? . . . I loved the hard way you were trying to keep repressed your rising emotions. We had been together three whole days and nights without allowing this to happen—it was all the sweeter for the waiting. I crossed with you to your bedroom door—do you remember? And suddenly I knew that I had to make you give me an invitation. Not by one word had you given me any sign that you wanted me in that bedroom with you—no, your delicate lady-like manner never would—so that's why I wanted to make you. I stooped to kiss you and found you powerless to utter a word —you were at the breaking point. And then I said goodnight, hoping, oh how I was hoping, you wouldn't disappoint me. I felt your numb little fingers cling to mine, and you whispered my name . . . with joy in my heart I lifted my darling in my arms and carried her to my own bedroom and gathered you in heaven's own earthly bliss. And dearest, did you know you were a very intoxicated little girl? . . . The curve of your white little breast . . . that intimate glorious part of you . . . that magic evening . . . I remember telling you that you belonged to me—that I would never let you go.

Oh my darling, what a mistress for a man's home. I closed my eyes and imagined you presiding at my table when we entertain our friends. How proud I shall be. In all the world there never will have been a man so proud.

At the end of the self-styled honeymoon Nelson and Jeanette went their separate ways. With renewed urgency they tackled the matter at hand: how could they finally free themselves from the disaster they'd made of their lives?

Nelson as he looked when he arrived in Hollywood, 1933.

2

Love at first sight

In late 1933 Nelson Eddy was thirty-two years old but he'd already learned to put a sturdy clamp on his emotions. He was a serious concert and operatic singer whose career was starting to take off. Now the critics compared him to Lawrence Tibbett and predicted that he might topple Tibbett off his throne as America's greatest baritone. Nelson took advantage of every opportunity afforded him, determined to be successful and disgustingly rich. No personal sacrifice was too dear, not even in romance. At just the hint of a relationship becoming serious, he abruptly broke it off. If Nelson couldn't bear to do it himself, his mentors or his mother intervened on his behalf. Music became Nelson's emotional outlet, his passion, his mistress. Marriage was something he might consider years down the road, and even then it would never be to a "career girl."

This attitude of strict mental celibacy ruled his early years, but Nelson at heart was a romantic. Someday, he dreamed, he'd have a loving wife and children. A great believer in fate, he was willing to wait for his great love. He didn't know how or when she would appear in his life, but he had a sixth sense about it.

How did he describe his dream girl? "Beautiful, and she's alive! A woman is attractive if she has vitality. A woman either has it or she hasn't. If she lacks that spark or the zest for living, nothing else she might have would interest me." He added, "She is very, very tolerant and she'll have to put up with an awful lot of nonsense from me. I'm a sensitive person and prone to be egotistical and self-centered. She is not just a sweet girl who says 'yes' and she's not a fighting girl

5

who says 'no.' She's smart enough to kid me along, knows my moods and keeps me guessing. In general, she is so gorgeous, so beautiful, so wise, so gentle and understanding, so cultured, so full of life, that when I did find her, she wouldn't have me."

That girl materialized sooner than he'd expected. One morning in the fall of 1933, he wandered onto an MGM sound stage. Still a novice in Hollywood, he often visited movie sets to learn more about filmmaking. He heard a lovely soprano voice singing, and followed the sound. It was a sweet, lilting voice. He found himself trying to get a better look at the singer. She was laughing at some joke and she whirled around. Their eyes met for a moment, then she turned away.

Nelson stood stunned. There she was! Thirty-one years later he would recall in an interview his first glimpse of movie star Jeanette MacDonald: "She was stunning and startlingly beautiful. She would take your breath away."

She was in costume, in period dress and a blonde wig, as the Merry Widow. He didn't introduce himself to her. He stood in the shadows and watched her for some time, then left. He made it a point to find out everything he could about her.

A few days later Nelson was formally introduced to Jeanette at a party given at the home of Mr. and Mrs. Frank Lloyd. Lloyd was a film director, responsible for the hits *Cavalcade* (1933) and the upcoming *Mutiny on the Bounty* (1935).

Jeanette had received an invitation to attend the Lloyds' dinner party. Mrs. Lloyd included a handwritten note, which read:

> I have a small dinner party Wednesday evening, friends you know and like. Among them will be a new concert singer, Nelson Eddy. Both Frank and I liked him when we met him last week. He seems so lost out here, we thought it would be nice to have him meet some of our friends. I do hope you and Bob can come.

"Bob" referred to Robert Ritchie, Jeanette's business manager. They were publicly engaged and rumored to be secretly married, though it was an open relationship and on shaky ground these days.

The morning of the party Jeanette phoned Mrs. Lloyd to inform her that Bob was unable to attend, so she would come alone. The two women briefly discussed Nelson Eddy. To her friend's surprise, Jeanette seemed predisposed to dislike him. "I have heard that he is very much of a bore in spite of his voice. I know the studio has him under contract, and I hope that doesn't mean I ever have to work with him. These concert males are always so annoying, and their temperaments are truly out of this world. Besides, this one doesn't know a thing about acting, and is obviously so inexperienced that he would certainly ruin any chance I might have for a hit picture. So dear, all I ask is, please keep him away from me as much as you can."

On the fateful evening, Jeanette was driven to the party by her chauffeur. Once at the Lloyds' house, she was seized with a sudden fear and almost told her driver to go on. Feeling "utterly ridiculous," she ignored her impulse and instead made her grand entrance, every inch the prima donna.

At the dinner table, Jeanette kept looking around for Nelson, who was late. Mrs. Lloyd finally ended the suspense by informing Jeanette that Nelson had phoned; he was held up at the studio and would arrive after dinner.

"Why, how rude!" Jeanette replied loudly. "He's just what I expected him to be. He's only concerned with himself. I'm going to enjoy putting him in his place."

Mrs. Lloyd was intrigued. "You know, dear, it would be very amusing to some of us, if it should turn out that this is the one man who could put you in your place."

"No man has ever done that yet," Jeanette retorted, "and no man ever will.

Nelson would later carry this portrait of Jeanette in his wallet.

They're all easily forgotten." She looked around the table at her friends' husbands and said with a coy smile, "Besides, all the men I am fond of are already married. So I'll just go right on being Jeanette MacDonald."

After dinner, the group retired to the music room, where Jeanette sang a Stephen Foster song. Mid-number, Nelson finally arrived. He stood enraptured, listening to her. "She was a vision or an angel—I wasn't sure which," he later told his mother. "She was dressed in a flowing gown of pale lavender chiffon and walked toward me with grace and dignity in every step." Nelson took Jeanette's hand, but could barely speak coherently. "I remember the first time I actually met her, I was tongue-tied and didn't know how to act," he later admitted.

Jeanette's recollection was also vivid. "He was a big, awkward hunk of man, very shy. He made me feel uncomfortable because all he did was look at me. He stood there, trying to talk, but kept stuttering, and couldn't finish a sentence. Everyone was watching us. I wanted to walk away, but found I couldn't. There was something about him—his eyes. They haunted me, there was a such a sadness to them."

Nelson was finally able to speak, praising Jeanette's singing voice. The guests heard her mumble a nervous "Thank you," and she uneasily pulled out of his grasp. Shortly afterwards, Jeanette decided she had to leave. But, ironically, when she called her chauffeur she learned that her car had broken down. Nelson gallantly offered to drive her home. Jeanette refused, preferring to call a cab. Nelson grabbed her arm roughly and said, "Miss MacDonald, I am going home now and you are going with me. We did meet at a mutual friend's house, and that should be recommendation enough. Unless, of course, you don't trust your friends."

"I was angry enough to slap him," Jeanette recounted. "This man was fresh as well as rude." But to her amazement, she said instead, quite graciously, "Thank you, shall we go now?"

On the ride home they sat in stony silence. Nelson felt cheated somehow; was he wrong about her? Why was her angelic voice in such contrast to her cool indifference? Despite his disappointment Nelson stepped from the car and politely escorted Jeanette to her door. "Please forgive me if I seemed forward tonight," he said, "but I've been snubbed no end out here, and I have only a very few friends who understand. I don't know why, but it hurts to find you like all the others—only I don't believe you are like the others. Somehow I feel I can tell you that I've never been so lonely and lost as I am out here, and I want my release from MGM. I'm doing nothing there, you know, and I could go out on more tours."

Earlier in the evening Nelson had mentioned a Los Angeles concert date coming up on November 21. Jeanette said suddenly, "Can I come to your concert? I don't have a ticket, but maybe you could get one for me. I would love to come, if you don't mind."

Nelson at first doubted her sincerity, then deciding she really meant it, opened his wallet and handed her a front row ticket. "Every one except those couple of friends I told you of has turned down my tickets. I've tried to give them away on the lot, but nobody wants them."

Before going inside, Jeanette said, "I wouldn't demand a release from the studio if I were you. You never can tell what the future holds."

When Nelson returned to his car he found she had dropped a lace handkerchief on the seat. His first impulse was to return it, but on second thought he took it home and put it away in a special box for mementos. It was the first of many treasures he would collect over the years.

Jeanette didn't bother to mention to anyone that she in fact knew all about Nelson Eddy. She'd previously heard him sing a few years earlier. She was at the apartment of her older sister, Blossom MacDonald Rock. While Blossom was sitting on the couch reading the paper, Jeanette was hanging over her shoulder chattering away. Suddenly her hand shot out to prevent Blossom from turning the page. Jeanette stopped talking and studied the photo of a handsome-but-sad-eyed man. The singer's name was Nelson Eddy. Blossom asked whether she knew Nelson. "No," Jeanette replied, "but there's something about his eyes." Jeanette was drawn to the man in the picture. She had to hear him sing, and attended the concert. Blossom later recalled that her sister "raved" about Nelson's looks and his voice.

There are those who suggest that Nelson and Jeanette became friends during their Philadelphia days. Certainly they had at least one mutual acquaintance, Catherine Littlefield. Baritone Wilbur Evans claimed they'd met; Malcolm Poindexter, Jr. (currently a TV newscaster in Philadelphia) spoke of a school chum's claim that Nelson and Jeanette sang together on Jeanette's front porch at the Arch Street house. A ninety-year old man, "Captain Bud," insisted Nelson had been romantically involved with Jeanette and had gotten her pregnant, but she aborted the child. In 1993, sixty-eight year old Robert Eddy claimed at a party to be the son of Jeanette and Nelson. When interviewed later he denied it, insisting he'd been "having some fun and it was all a joke." He explained that he was distantly related to Nelson, but not as a son. Jeanette and Nelson themselves insisted repeatedly over the years that they officially met at a party in Hollywood. No other substantiation to prove otherwise has ever come to light. At any rate, Nelson's name was never mentioned again once Jeanette's own career took her away from the East Coast. The man whose eyes and voice had haunted her was presumably forgotten.

Until, ironically, they ended up under contract at the same movie studio in 1933. For months they did not meet, as Jeanette signed her contract while on an overseas concert tour. When she returned home, she plunged into production of *The Cat and the Fiddle* with Ramon Novarro as co-star. Meanwhile, Nelson did two film walk-ons and concertized around the Los Angeles area.

Blurbs in the trades planted by MGM insisted that Jeanette MacDonald and Nelson Eddy were being teamed for various film projects throughout 1933. In truth, Nelson had heard of Jeanette MacDonald, but he had never seen her nor any of her films prior to 1933. He was too busy with his career to attend movies, and as a serious operatic singer he tended to frown on the kind of bubbly screen musicals in which Jeanette appeared.

On the afternoon of October 25, 1933, just prior to their meeting, Nelson performed at a studio luncheon in honor of the Secretary of the Navy. Jeanette heard him sing there, though she herself was not on the program. By the time they formally met at the Lloyd dinner some days later Jeanette had educated herself all about Nelson Eddy and had thoroughly convinced herself that there was no way she'd ever fall under his spell.

███ On November 9, 1933, Jeanette and Nelson sang for the first time together (though not a duet) on a radio program. It was a national hookup in celebration of the birthday of MGM actress Marie Dressler.

The month of November was a hectic one for Jeanette. She was working on two films simultaneously. She had supposedly completed *The Cat and the Fiddle*, and had started work on *The Merry Widow* with Maurice Chevalier. But the studio was unhappy with *Fiddle* and recalled the cast and crew to film a new ending. The *Widow* production was fraught with problems as well; Chevalier, who had made three other films with Jeanette, no longer wanted to work with her. Producer Ernst Lubitsch, slated also to direct, was still haggling with Metro over money and technically wouldn't sign on as director till the end of the month.

On November 21, Nelson sang with the Los Angeles Philharmonic. The program began promptly at 8:15. At precisely 8:40, there was a disturbance in the theater. A woman came hurrying down the aisle and slunk into a seat in the front row. How and why this woman managed to enter the auditorium mid–number Nelson didn't know, but he was furious. He stopped singing and glared at the culprit a moment. Being nearsighted and without his glasses, he had to squint to recognize her. By now a buzz was going through the audience as others whispered, "Jeanette MacDonald!" Nelson called out to Jeanette, "It's a good thing you're pretty!" and laughed along with the audience. The concert continued without further mishap. Nelson sang unusually well that evening and was called back for fourteen encores. "She inspired me so much that night I couldn't believe it," Nelson told his mother, "especially since I didn't even know her." One critic wrote: "Nelson Eddy gave a performance of two-and-a-half hours' duration. Probably, many of the audience would have remained for another hour, so insistent was the applause."

After this concert Nelson purchased his first gift for Jeanette, a gold charm bracelet. This first charm was a clock, with the hands reading 8:40, the exact time she'd barged into his concert.

The very next day, November 22, Jeanette insisted that Bob Ritchie drive her to San Francisco so she could catch Nelson's concert there. A pattern had begun;

Jeanette was to attend Nelson's performances whenever possible over the years, sometimes sitting in the audience, but more often listening backstage where she had privacy from curious and speculative stares.

By the end of November, Nelson began visiting Jeanette regularly on *The Merry Widow* set, watching her with an intensity that unnerved her and blew her concentration. One day at lunch he demanded to take her out. She refused but he was adamant. They left the studio for a small, nondescript Italian restaurant nearby. Jeanette watched Nelson wolf down a huge plate of spaghetti while she was barely able to choke down a bite.

Nelson finally opened up to her about his disappointment with Hollywood. He had signed a six-month option that expired in December 1933. Despite studio head Louis B. Mayer's promises, no film roles, except for bit parts, had been forthcoming. Nelson had decided to let the contract lapse and to return full-time to his concert career, with a major tour beginning in January 1934.

To his surprise, once again Jeanette warned Nelson not to make a hasty decision about abandoning Hollywood. He felt encouraged and, before returning her to the set again, he asked her out for a date. He was surprised when

One of the first shots of Nelson and Jeanette together. He's sporting the mustache he grew for his walk-on role in *Student Tour* (1934).

she declined. She was surprised when he refused to accept her answer. Jeanette was fast learning that Nelson was extremely persistent. If she wasn't free tonight, what about tomorrow night? Or the next night? Or the next? She finally tried to walk away from him but he grabbed her wrist and wouldn't let go. Nelson was six feet tall, big boned, and strong. Jeanette, just under five-five and of delicate build, was no physical match for him. She finally gave in, agreeing to attend a party with him at the home of silent film star-turned-opera singer, Doris Kenyon. Ignoring Nelson's triumphant grin, Jeanette returned to work, nursing a bruised wrist.

Though apparently confused by her personal feelings for Nelson, Jeanette wasn't ready to put him out of her life. On the contrary—she took action to make certain he'd be very much in the picture. She went to her boss, Louis B. Mayer, and requested that Nelson be co-starred with her in her next film, *Naughty Marietta*. Despite others who claimed responsibility for the teaming of MacDonald and Eddy, it was Jeanette MacDonald herself who not only suggested such an arrangement, but persuaded the unenthusiastic Mayer to make Nelson a star.

Some of Jeanette's followers have insisted that tenor Allan Jones should have made *Naughty Marietta*, and Jones himself said that although the studio wanted him, he couldn't break his stage contract with the Shuberts. (Jones finally arrived at MGM to star in the 1935 Marx Brothers hit, *A Night at the Opera*. However, as late as the 1960s, Jeanette insisted that she had handpicked Nelson to be her co-star.

Mayer hadn't been impressed with Eddy's original screen test, saying, "He's too pretty and he can't act." He only agreed to hire Nelson in the first place at the insistence of Ida Koverman, his gal Friday, who had a nose for spotting talent.

Now Jeanette insisted that Nelson be tested for *Naughty Marietta*, reminding him: "All my other co-stars are either old enough to be my father or queer." She pleaded with Mayer until he finally agreed. Mayer had a soft spot in his heart for Jeanette; it was understood that if Nelson's test was any good at all, Mayer would allow him to co-star with Jeanette.

■ The night of Doris Kenyon's party—their first real date—Jeanette nervously dressed, wanting to impress both Nelson and "his crowd." Her own dream in life since childhood was "to be a grand opera star, and buy a gold bed and a pink limousine for mother." She had been offered operatic roles in Europe, but never in the United States. In 1933, there was still a hugh chasm between the opera world and the motion picture industry, with Opera looking down its nose on films as a bastardized form of burlesque. No doubt this discrimination stemmed in part from the fact that opera stars had thus far bombed in Hollywood.

Until this time Jeanette's films were primarily musical comedy, and most of them were directed by the deliciously risqué director Ernst Lubitsch. Lubitsch had the skill to bring out Jeanette's unique qualities on screen: she had a natural feel for comedy, and a childlike innocence in her mingled with her seductive charm. It didn't hurt her popularity that she usually ran around the screen half-clothed, earning her the nickname "The Lingerie Queen." To the Hollywood crowd Jeanette and her operetta voice were considered highbrow; to the opera world she was an insult. And these were the people she was meeting this night.

Nelson arrived at the house before Jeanette finished dressing. He met her older sister Blossom, and their mother Anna MacDonald, with whom Jeanette lived. Nelson liked Blossom's down-to-earth sense of humor, and the two of them clicked right from the start. But for Nelson and Anna, it was instant mutual dislike. According to Blossom, her mother and Nelson sat and stared daggers at each other until Jeanette descended from the bedroom.

An in-depth description of Doris Kenyon's party was given years later by an old friend of Nelson's, Sybil Thomas. (Sybil Thomas was married a number of times, but for simplicity's sake, she is referred to by the name she used while giving interviews in the mid-1970s.) Sybil was a wealthy Philadelphian who had first met Nelson back around 1916, and had helped him out financially on a number of occasions. Sybil had recently come to visit Nelson in Hollywood; she eventually settled there and remained a confidant of Nelson's throughout his life.

This was Sybil's first meeting with Jeanette, and she was curious to meet the girl who had obviously smitten Nelson so completely.

Sybil's first impression of Jeanette was that she was very out of place in this crowd. She was dressed "like a gypsy, with no clothes-sense at all. There were bows everywhere." Sybil noted with surprise that Nelson seemed unaware of Jeanette's fashion failings, as he usually had a very discerning eye.

Jeanette was snubbed by hostess Doris Kenyon, her friend Ann Franklin (mid-divorce from director Sidney Franklin) and most of the others at the party. Nelson was pulled away by a group of women, and that was the last Jeanette saw of him. Shaken by the reception accorded her, Jeanette finally decided to leave. She tried to sneak out unnoticed, but Nelson spotted her and grabbed her before she reached the sidewalk. He forced her to look at him and demanded to know what was wrong. When he saw that she was close to tears he took her by the arm and marched her back into the house, bellowing loudly for Doris. Everyone stopped dead in their tracks and just stared. Jeanette, acutely embarrassed, tried unsuccessfully to hide behind Nelson and pull her hand from his grip. Nelson angrily accosted Doris for all to hear. "I don't like the way you've been treating my friend." He overrode her attempts at explanation, booming, "I'm sure you feel you owe Miss MacDonald an apology."

Doris mumbled an apology; a devastated Jeanette accepted. Then Nelson loudly explained that they both had an early call and they left together.

In the car Jeanette apologized for making such a bad impression on his friends. "Forget it!" Nelson told her. "I'm just sorry we came. If I'd known they were going to be so rude, I never would have brought you there." He attempted to salvage the evening, suggesting that they take a drive down to the beach. Jeanette declined. He headed toward her house in silence, then he said, "It doesn't matter what they think of you, you're more beautiful and talented than any of them."

At this, Jeanette burst into tears. Nelson tried to comfort her, but she was inconsolable. Not only was the first date a disaster, but these people had hit her where it hurt most; she had wanted to badly to be accepted in the opera world. Nelson held her to him and stroked her hair. "I wanted to crush her to me and kiss away her tears," he later related. He handed her a handkerchief and listened quietly as she talked about her goals as a singer. It was the first time Nelson had understood that she was as driven about her career as he was about his.

When they pulled up to her house, Jeanette thanked him for being so kind and started to leave. Nelson reached out and kissed her. She had to fight to get out of his arms and retreat to the house. When she did, she found her disapproving mother waiting up to hear the outcome of the evening. Jeanette greeted her happily with these words: "Oh, mama, I had the most *wonderful* evening."

Nelson also lived with his mother. Isabel Eddy was very concerned when her son didn't arrive back home until after midnight; Nelson had spent hours driving aimlessly through the Hollywood Hills, wondering at the intensity of his feelings for this girl he'd just met. The very next day he invited her home to meet Isabel. Jeanette dined with them that night. After the meal she wandered over to the organ, saw a piece of music on the rack, sat down and began to sing and play it softly—Wagner's "Song to the Evening Star." When she finished, she looked up to see Nelson's eyes filled with tears. "I'm sorry, Nelson, does that song have some memory?" she asked quietly.

Wordlessly Nelson picked up her hands and held them to his lips. Finally he answered, "Yes, dear, it had a memory, but now it has another. I shall never forget your singing it tonight."

He drove Jeanette home. "Before, when I kissed her she had always just been tender and sweet but this night she really returned my kiss, for the first time—and not because she wanted to either—she just could no longer help it," Nelson wrote years later. "Never shall I forget how timid she was—and how little and submissive she seemed in my arms— and how frightened I was at what was happening to me. That was the moment I knew it was something divine and something that would live throughout the ages."

He left her on her doorstep and once again drove aimlessly. "He did not understand himself," his mother later explained. "He was facing the fact that this girl's friendship had become the most important thing in his life, that he must never be without it. He drove for hours that night fighting the confused fear that he loved her."

By the next morning Nelson Eddy had made up his mind. Less than a week after their first date he asked Jeanette MacDonald to marry him.

3

"I don't believe
in true love"

Jeanette turned down Nelson's marriage proposal. The relationship had moved too quickly for her. "He was the first thing that ever happened to me against which I felt completely helpless," she said years later. "It was too strong a force— I was frightened by it."

She explained to Nelson that she still wanted to be friends with him, but in the meantime there were many things in her life that needed sorting out, including her relationship with Bob Ritchie. Nelson was extremely upset over her rejection. It didn't help matters that his mother reminded him he shouldn't have gotten involved with a "career girl" to begin with.

Then Nelson was summoned to the studio to test for the role of Captain Richard Warrington in *Naughty Marietta*. He felt his test was lousy, and he was surprised to learn that the role was his. Nelson was still unaware that Jeanette had anything to do with his finally landing a starring role. Before accepting the part, Nelson felt he had to clear the air and find out where he stood with her.

He reminded her how inexperienced he was in films, and he said he would understand if she demanded another leading man, even though he felt the part suited him. To his surprise she asked, "Did someone tell you I might be difficult to work with?" When he admitted that, yes, he'd heard as much, Jeanette said bitterly, "You want the part, but you're afraid to work with me, is that it? I might ruin your chances being the awful prima donna I am? I could steal every scene from you. I could insist you have few close-ups and I could rage around screaming that I wouldn't sing duets with you." Then she said: "I'll ask the studio to give you the part of Captain Dick, and I'll refuse to play Marietta. There are other singers on the lot that can be teamed with you. It's too good a role for you to miss out on and you'll make good no matter who works with you."

The beaming Nelson apologized for hurting her feelings, then asked if she thought she could put up with him as her co-star, because he wanted very much to work with her. To his delight, she said yes.

███Nelson's friends were surprised when he agreed to renew his MGM contract in December. With Jeanette's input Nelson negotiated a contract carefully swayed in his favor; he was allowed four months off each year for his concert work (starting with the January 1934 tour), and the studio received no percentage of any of his earnings from concerts, recordings or radio. Mayer was indifferent to Nelson's demands because he didn't think "the chowderhead" would make it in films. Within a year the studio mogul would be tearing his proverbial hair out, cursing Nelson for getting away with contractual murder. As it turned out, *Naughty Marietta* was filmed on two extensions of this contract.

On January 4, 1934, the trades announced that Jeanette MacDonald and Nelson Eddy would be starring together in the Victor Herbert operetta, *Naughty Marietta*. Production was to begin when Nelson returned from his previously scheduled cross-country tour in May.

███Jeanette stayed in touch with Nelson while he was on tour, and managed to attend at least three of his local concerts. Nelson was careful to keep things on a friendly, platonic level with her. If she needed time to sort out her life, he'd give her all the time she wanted. It was worth it to him because, in the end, he knew she would be his.

For his appearance in Santa Barbara on January 8, 1934, Jeanette showed up unexpectedly. A young boy standing outside the theater was trying to sell two autographed photos of Nelson. He wanted $5 apiece, but the always thrifty Jeanette talked him down to $2. She bought a photo, took it home, and stashed it in her own box of mementos. After the concert and reception in his honor, Jeanette went to Nelson's hotel room to speak privately with him. She found him sprawled out in a chair. He apologized for being so exhausted, but if she'd give him a minute to rest, he'd love to take her out somewhere.

Jeanette said, "Never mind that. If you don't get right to bed you'll catch cold. A singer should never go anywhere when exhausted, you know that." He watched, amazed, as she suddenly unbuttoned his shirt and helped him remove it. She sternly ordered him into the shower. When he returned, she tucked him into bed. She called room service and a light meal was delivered with some wine. Nelson, amused at her maternal airs, asked suggestively, "Don't we get to do *anything* at all?"

She was embarrassed by his innuendo, and finally she told him they'd see each other tomorrow. Nelson was agreeable to this, and despite his intentions to sit up and talk with her awhile he fell asleep.

Jeanette left him and checked into a room of her own. She was unable to sleep, trying to sort out her feelings. She had no desire to fall in love with Nelson or anyone else. Her attitude toward romance was aptly summed up in an interview she'd given recently: "I don't believe in true love. I can't possibly guarantee that my love will last for years and years, and I don't believe anyone else can. It's all nonsense. A human being can't care for just one person exclusively and forever. And . . . I don't believe there's any love that you can't get over if you want to. All broken hearts could be cured, if people would just start getting romantic about somebody else."

She decided that when morning came she would inform Nelson that their relationship, such as it was, was over. But she lacked the courage to tell him to his face. Instead, she slipped a note under his door to please stop bothering her. Then she returned to Los Angeles.

■■■During the spring of 1934, Nelson crossed the United States and Canada on tour, giving fifty concerts in a total of twenty-six cities. He traveled by train, his preferred method of travel for concert tours during his entire career. He'd tried flying once, from Los Angeles to San Francisco for his January 3, 1934 concert, but had gotten so airsick he wasn't sure he could go on. He sat resting his head on the dressing room table, trying to regain his composure. In the end he sang, not willing to lose the night's pay.

Jeanette, meanwhile, was still busy at the studio. Metro was unhappy with *The Cat and the Fiddle* and called for yet a third ending to be shot, this time in three-strip Technicolor. She again had to stop work on *The Merry Widow* for about a week. *The Cat and the Fiddle*'s failings were not in the production values, nor in the tuneful Jerome Kern score, nor even in the story line. (The film managed to sneak in under the wire before implementation of the censorship code, which would have found the plot unacceptable due to the fact that the lead characters live together without benefit of marriage.) The main problem, rather, was the lack of chemistry between Jeanette and her co-star Ramon Novarro. Novarro, the original screen Ben Hur, had a pleasant singing voice and good looks. Even with a heavy Mexican accent he should have weathered the transition from silent films to talkies. But he made a fatal error by incurring Mayer's wrath. He was caught in a homosexual scandal, which the studio paid to cover up. Mayer made no secret of his feelings about gays—he "put up" with them, but if they got caught, they were subject to the "Mayer treatment."

Just as Mayer manipulated films to elevate actors to stardom, so he utilized them to ruin careers as well. It is common Hollywood lore that Mayer ruined the career of silent heartthrob John Gilbert by manipulating the sound quality of his voice in his first talkies, making him sound high-pitched and effeminate. Over the years, the seemingly benign Mayer destroyed others as well.

Novarro received the Mayer treatment. He was placed in a few unsuitable films, including *Cat and the Fiddle*, calculated to showcase him badly. (This is the way the vindictive Mayer ran MGM for many years.) The overdone, effeminate makeup and resulting bad press did the trick; by 1935 Novarro was effectively washed up in Hollywood. In 1968 his name once again hit the headlines in a homosexual scandal when he was murdered by two men who stuffed a large, solid gold dildo—a gift from Rudolph Valentino—down his throat, suffocating him.

The Cat and the Fiddle was finally released in February 1934 and enjoyed a modest success. Critics were divided. The New York *World-Telegram* declared that Jeanette was "more attractive than ever," and felt the film was "by far the most tuneful, charming and thoroughly entertaining operetta the screen has offered in years." *Variety* found annoying discrepancies in the continuity: "The heroine shows up at the last minute to play the leading role in the show-within-a-show and save it, even though the heroine is just a music student and, as far as the picture tells, has never before appeared on a stage . . . There are times when Miss MacDonald and Novarro seem to be of dual height, other times when Novarro looks about an inch taller, still others when he's two or three heads above the former Chevalier leading lady." Another critic described Novarro as a "Mexican Peter Pan," while the *Herald-Tribune* summed up, "The plot hasn't really been worth all the trouble."

The Merry Widow looked more promising. It was planned as a big-budget "Class A production" (according to Mayer), utilizing the famous trio of director Ernst Lubitsch and co-stars Maurice Chevalier and Jeanette MacDonald. This team had proved a winning combination over at Paramount Studios; two of their three films together had won Oscar nominations for Best Picture, and all were immensely popular at the box office.

Now Mayer had lured the three artists to his lair to try his hand with the team. He was determined to outdo Paramount. With executive producer Irving Thalberg at the helm, *Widow* was initially scheduled to be shot in Technicolor. A press release to this effect was issued on December 12, but by the end of January 1934, the idea of color had been dropped. *The Merry Widow* had now been in production, off and on, for three months already, with no product. What the problems were exactly is unknown, but during the month of February, Jeanette took off on vacation to New York, accompanied by her dog and her manager, Bob Ritchie. She arrived in time to catch Nelson's Town Hall recital the afternoon of February 18.

As of January 1934, Jeanette's personal relationship with Ritchie had changed. Nelson was Ritchie's first rival for Jeanette's affection, and Jeanette informed Ritchie that she would continue to see him. Ritchie went along with it, continuing his own practice of dating others. Jeanette felt great loyalty to Ritchie because he'd given up his career to manage hers. They'd been together since 1928; much of the time it was a long-distance affair, with little intimacy except through letters. Ritchie kept a little black book with names and dates of women he slept with. Jeanette's name has forty slashes next to it, and no dates recorded except their first time. If his tally is accurate, it would indicate they were intimate forty times over all the years they were together.

In March Jeanette returned to Los Angeles and resumed work on *Widow*, which dragged off and on in production until mid-August. Depending on the source, the final cost of the film ranged between $1,605,000 and $2,640,000. Whatever the sum, it was an outrageous budget for any film in 1934. Some of the expense, aside from the ten months of production, was due to the fact that four separate versions of the film were shot: domestic, English, French and Belgian— all four containing slight alterations in scenes and emphasis. The French version, entitled *La Veuve Joyeuse*, had an entirely different supporting cast, with Jeanette the only American.

Jeanette had personal problems with her leading man, Maurice Chevalier. The famous Frenchman had been an overnight success in America with his first Paramount film here, the silent *Innocents of Paris* (1929). In his next picture, and first talkie, *The Love Parade*, he received top billing over Jeanette, who was making her debut. She too shot to stardom, and over the next four years her popularity rose while Chevalier's declined. By the time *The Merry Widow* went into production Jeanette's name was equally billed, although Chevalier's name still came first. (Grace Moore—Chevalier's first choice for the widow—was unwilling to give up top billing, so she was replaced by Jeanette.)

In May 1934, Nelson returned from his tour and once again marked time, waiting for Jeanette to finish her film so they could begin *Naughty Marietta*, which was now pushed back to June. He told an interviewer, "I was a sensitive sort of person when I came here. But things are different now. When I first came here, I used to report at the studio at 9:30 every morning. Then I'd sit around and wait for something to happen. One day an executive saw me and asked what I was doing there so early. I told him I had reported every morning at that hour. He laughed. 'Go out and play golf,' he said. 'When we want you we'll send for you.' "

With *Widow* dragging on into July, Nelson was awarded an interim assignment, his third bit role, in a "B" picture called *Student Tour*. This college musical boasted an interesting cast including Betty Grable, Jimmy Durante and Charles Butterworth, but it suffered from a mediocre script. Nelson, in a mustache, sang one number, "The Carlo," and even had a few lines of dialogue. (Jeanette supposedly cried when she saw his mustache, making him promise never to grow one again. He never did.) *Student Tour* was considered a showcase for Nelson, and he played himself. His role called for him to give a nervous dancer some reassurance about her performance and to sing at a party. His singing was excellent, and his characteristic gawky, naive, caring quality came across well in his one scene, which somewhat upgraded his status at the studio. But his mannerisms while singing were grossly exaggerated and melodramatic, straight from the opera school of overacting. The difference between his acting skills in this film and his next (after coaching by Jeanette) was monumental.

Nelson saw little of Jeanette early in the year as she was wrapped up in her film work, and on the rare occasions that she was seen in public it was usually with Bob Ritchie. Nelson's name was linked in the trades with actresses Cecilia Parker and Joan Marsh; more often he attended concerts and parties with his mother. But he hadn't given up on Jeanette. Bob Ritchie was frequently in Europe on business, and Nelson took advantage of his absence to go out with her. The first known photos of them together were taken during mid-1934, while he sported his mustache for *Student Tour*. Nelson also invited Jeanette home for meals with his mother, Isabel, so they could get better acquainted.

Isabel Eddy was devoted to her son. A single parent, she had sacrificed much to help Nelson pursue his career, and she was his greatest fan. Nelson commented in an interview about Isabel, "She strung along with me when I was struggling along, and now I'm sticking by her . . . Who is the loveliest woman in Hollywood? My mother. Nelson was indifferent to the remarks that he was a mama's boy. In general they got along famously, except when Isabel also took it upon herself to interfere with her son's private life.

Before Isabel's first meeting with Jeanette, Nelson had issued an ultimatum. It seemed that each time he brought home a date to meet her, Isabel sent the girl out on some errand, and she never returned. "I never minded before," Nelson told Isabel, "but this one better not have an errand to do or you're in trouble."

Isabel liked Jeanette but she was wary of her. When her son continued to date Jeanette, month after month, Isabel figured she'd better do some checking-up on the girl. What she discovered wasn't exactly pleasant: Jeanette was an ambitious career gal with a bad reputation; her marital status was nebulous—even worse, it was rumored that she was the mistress of Louis B. Mayer. Isabel tried to pass on her findings to her son, who brushed her off. "I don't care what she did before I met her," he said. "She's everything I ever wanted in a woman."

Nelson had struck up a friendship with Clark Gable during the shooting of *Dancing Lady*, in which Nelson had filmed his first bit role. Gable was aware of Nelson's interest in Jeanette, and he, too, tried to warn him against her. Nelson refused to listen. He'd developed an idealized image of Jeanette and was not interested in being told that it was unrealistic.

Nelson's angelic picture of Jeanette was furthered when he escorted her to the annual studio picnic. Each year Mayer liked to have a get-together for the crews and stars alike. He rented part of Catalina Island, which was a couple hours' boat ride from the San Pedro Harbor, and treated his "family" to a blissful day. (The following year, the ever-frugal Mayer decided to cut his costs on the annual picnic. He switched the location from Catalina to the Valley Park Country Club in the San Fernando Valley.)

Jeanette had originally turned down Nelson's invitation to the picnic. He had decided not to go himself, then Clark Gable persuaded him otherwise. Nelson drove to San Pedro, and was surprised to find Mayer giving his employees a pre-picnic lecture, reminding them of the expense of this outing, and warning them against "boozing and fooling around! This is a clean, family picnic!"

Nelson was angered by Mayer's words; after all, *he* wouldn't act like that. He was thinking about leaving when Gable came over and asked him how much booze he was bringing. Nelson protested, "But he just said no booze."

"Hell, nobody listens to him!" Gable laughed, and gave him directions to the liquor store. Nelson dutifully trotted off, and returned with his arms full of whiskey bottles. Most of the crowd had boarded the boat, and Nelson hurried over to the gangplank. He looked up, then stopped dead in his tracks. There she was, a vision, very quiet and demure in a long pale yellow dress with a matching picture hat that framed her flaming curls. She smiled down at him. The sunlight behind her surrounded her like a halo; according to Nelson's description, Jeanette's outfit must have been similar to the yellow dress she wore in the fashion sequence in *Sweethearts*.

Nelson stood mesmerized. "I had never seen such beauty," he said. "I knew that for all of my life, as long as I lived, I would always see her just as she was at that moment. For me, time had stopped."

They spent an idyllic day together, marred only by the other activity on the island. There was heavy drinking, and according to Nelson, even heavier breathing and giggling going on behind every available bush. He finally chuckled, "*Now* I understand why Louie B. made that speech. It certainly didn't do much good, did it?"

Marion Davies, quick to note that Nelson and Jeanette were an item, invited the two to sing at a benefit for her Marion Davies Foundation, which funded a children's clinic. They agreed to perform together at the Hollywood Bowl on June 25, and at the Biltmore Hotel the following night.

But Nelson's hopes that their relationship was making progress were quickly dashed. One morning he was visiting Jeanette on *The Merry Widow* set. A messenger arrived from Mr. Mayer's office with a personal note for Miss Mac-Donald. Nelson was oblivious to the snickers and gossip that quickly spread around the set.

He still knew surprisingly little about her. When it came to film making, Jeanette was a professional and commanded the respect of her co-workers, even if her perfectionism sometimes drove them crazy. With her personal life, it was another story. Maurice Chevalier strongly objected to Jeanette's relationship with Bob Ritchie. "I'm sure they [Jeanette and Bob Ritchie] were married, otherwise it's difficult to understand why she allowed him to mistreat her so," he said. "Ritchie would often come on the set, insult her, throw a jealous tantrum and leave after he had reduced her to tears. A moment later, when it was time to film a scene, she was ready to work, all smiles."

It was common knowledge that Jeanette was a "favorite" of Mayer's, and it was said that while Mayer slept with many of his female stars, he fell in love with only two of them, redheads Jeanette MacDonald and Greer Garson.

Sex with the studio head was considered almost a duty, a sort of initiation to the "family." It was solicited as a matter of routine. Even Shirley Temple, who went to MGM at the age of ten, was not spared. In her autobiography she states that she was chased around the office by producer Arthur Freed at the same time her mother was dodging Louis B. Mayer in his office.

MGM actress Luise Rainer won two Academy Awards in a row, then saw her film career sink because she would not give in to Mayer's demands. In 1991 Rainer told an interviewer, "We had a very bitter conversation. He told me: 'Jeanette MacDonald sits on my lap when I make a contract with her.' And I said: 'Well, Mr. Mayer, I never will do that.' "

In Jeanette's case, Mayer was infatuated. He tried for years to get her to his studio, and when he succeeded he promised to make her a bigger star than the queen of the lot, Norma Shearer. He also promised her Metro's first Technicolor feature. In time, he delivered on both promises. Jeanette was a star in her Paramount years; she hit the heights as a super-star only at MGM.

Many of her associates fell in love with her; most claimed she was more vibrant and beautiful off-screen than on. The majority of Hollywood books deny that she ever capitulated to Mayer's advances, arguing that she was "a prude," but this is fancy, not fact.

Jeanette ultimately had a confrontation with Nelson, in which she finally admitted to him that she was sleeping with Mayer. Nelson still refused to believe it. "What you did before I met you has nothing to do with us," he told her. "All that means anything is how we feel about each other now." But he finally lost his temper when he realized that her career meant more to her than he did. "If that's how you want it, fine! Kid yourself all you want to, but it's not over for us yet!" He warned her he'd haunt her thoughts whenever she was lonely or unhappy. "Play your game with Louie B., but when the chips are down and you want someone who really cares, just remember, I'm real." He kissed her hard, then stomped off.

Jeanette went to Mayer and insisted he find another co-star for her in *Naughty Marietta*. When Mayer refused, Jeanette asked to be taken off the film. It was then that an oft-told incident occurred, with Mayer reassuring Jeanette that *Marietta* would be a hit for her, and according to legend, he dropped to one knee and sang "Eli, Eli" in an effort to show her how to sing with real schmaltz in her voice. Jeanette continued to protest, but short of admitting her feelings for Nelson, she had to admit defeat. She was stuck working with Nelson, facing weeks of togetherness in which her resolve to forget him would be sorely tested.

June 1934 was an important date for Nelson; he became a father.

The previous fall he'd briefly met up with an old girlfriend, contralto Maybelle Marston. He'd known Maybelle since the mid 1920s, and they'd sung in the same opera company throughout the decade. Once engaged to be married, they'd been apart for some time, though on friendly terms (as was true of most of Nelson's ex-lovers). Some time in the fall of 1933 they met up again, and three months later Maybelle discovered she was pregnant. By that time abortion was out of the question, as was a shotgun marriage. It was unlikely that Nelson wanted to marry Maybelle, at any rate because Maybelle had several things against her—she was older than Nelson, divorced, and had a son from her marriage—though that child was living with her ex-husband. Maybelle's mother was German, her father Italian. Paulo Beretta might have been a clerk by profession, but he had connections with Amadeo Giannini, who founded the Bank of Italy—later the Bank of America. Years later, Maybelle's son by Nelson, Jon Eddy, wanted to meet his birth mother and make inquiries into his maternal heritage, but was warned not to "open a Pandora's box." Jon never quite understood the familial connection between the Gianninis and the Berettas, but was scared enough (perhaps needlessly) not to question any further.

Maybelle went into hiding for the balance of her pregnancy; it's unknown at what point Nelson was alerted to her condition. Maybelle delivered a slightly premature boy in June, 1934. Jon was told he was born in Toms River, New Jersey—not far from Philadelphia—but no birth certificate is on file there for him under any applicable name. The birth certificate he does have states he was born in Chicago, with his "adopted" parents' names listed.

Immediately after Jon's birth, he was given to a friend of Maybelle's to raise. The friend was married but childless. No legal adoption was ever done. Jon was raised by "foster" parents in the midwest, in a loving home. He was a teenager before he learned the real story of his birth.

Maybelle Marston returned to singing, then became a noted voice teacher and choral leader. She lived in Philadelphia the rest of her life; a gracious but personally unhappy woman. Not even her closest friends knew about her secret son by Nelson Eddy, though her romance with him was well known. But for the sake of Nelson's career and reputation, Maybelle remained silent.

The birth of his son was painful for Nelson. He had once again deprived himself of a normal lifestyle, all for the sake of his career. It was a heavy sacrifice to make. Nelson threw himself into his work that much harder, but the determination was there that some day he'd have a wife and children—a real family and a real home.

4

"That boy is going to sing some day!"

Nelson Ackerman Eddy was born in Providence, Rhode Island, on June 29, 1901. He was the only child of William ("Bill") Darius Eddy and Caroline Isabel Kendrick—or Isabel, as she preferred. Nelson was born in the family house at 26 Hartford Avenue. According to family legend, he let out such a lusty cry at birth that the attending doctor told them, "That young man ought to make a fine singer!"

Nelson was a seventh generation Eddy born in Providence. His family tree boasted the dubious distinction of two Eddy cousins who married each other. "My ancestors did not come over on the *Mayflower*," he reported in an interview. "They missed it by ten years. The original Eddy, so far as I can trace, was christened John Eddye. He came over from England and settled in Massachusetts. Awhile later, when Governor Winthrop paid the colony a tour of inspection with the object of listing the various trades and vocations of the colonists, he found bakers, farmers, fishermen, mechanics and dentists. But when he came to John Eddye, he was stumped. For John Eddye had no job. He wrote him down, finally, as 'John Eddye, Gentleman'!"

The Eddys were a musical clan. Nelson's grandfather, Isaac Nelson Eddy (for whom he was named), was bass drummer in the famous Reeves American Band for fifty-five years. When he retired in 1925, Isaac Eddy received a citation from the president of Brown University for having played in more than fifty commencement processions.

Nelson's father, Bill Eddy, was also a drummer. He performed in the First Regiment Coast Artillery Band and eventually became the drum major. He also sang in church choirs and in Gilbert & Sullivan and various other operettas performed at the old floating theater in Crescent Park.

On his mother's side, Nelson was of Dutch and Russian-Jewish descent. The Ackermans (his maternal grandmother's family) raised several generations in Pensacola, Florida, then moved north. On his maternal grandfather's side, the Kendrick family at one time owned plantations all over the South. Isabel was born in Atlanta, Georgia, and was raised a true Southern belle in spirit, even though her family had lost its wealth. Her parents eventually moved to Philadelphia and divorced at the turn of the century. Isabel remained there with her mother.

The Kendricks were also musical. Isabel performed as an oratorio singer, as did her mother, Caroline Ackerman Kendrick. A single phonograph recording exists, dated 1903, with Caroline Kendrick singing "The Last Rose of Summer." Nelson's aunt, Mrs. Edward Alvaez, was a pianist and a singer on the New York stage before her marriage. Isabel grew up hearing stories of her family's triumphs during the Civil War and of General Lee, who was a personal friend and who had dined often at the family plantation. On Nelson's family tree was American President Martin Van Buren. Nelson once laughingly explained, "When I first learned of it, I was all snobby. Then I found out he wasn't all that great a President and I came off my high horse in a hurry." When Nelson first arrived at MGM, Louie B. Mayer suggested Nelson change his name to something more prestigious. Nelson snickered, "How about Van Buren?"

Isabel incurred the wrath of her family by marrying the Yankee Bill Eddy in Philadelphia on December 23, 1899. Her only child Nelson was born eighteen months later when Isabel was twenty and Bill was twenty-five.

The Kendricks were concerned that Bill Eddy would never amount to much, and thought Isabel could have made a better choice. But Isabel, only eighteen when she met Bill Eddy, felt she's found the man of her dreams. Theirs was a wartime romance, brief but intense. Bill was stationed in Georgia during the Spanish-American War, but fell ill with typhoid and nearly died. Isabel nursed him back to health, her ardor no doubt aided by the fact that her own parents were going through a divorce. Marriage seemed a perfect solution. After tying the knot in Philadelphia, the young couple made their home on Bill's turf, in Providence, Rhode Island. Their only child, Nelson, was born eighteen months later when Isabel was twenty and Bill twenty-five.

Her parents' fears about Bill Eddy proved correct; though a hard worker, he was not financially successful. His profession, noted on Nelson's birth certificate, was "toolmaker," and he also worked as an inventor and machinist. Within a couple years of their marriage the romance fizzled and Isabel Eddy realized she'd made a mistake. But for Nelson she might have ended the marriage immediately.

Bill Eddy dragged his family with him from city to city, looking for work. He was a heavy drinker, and couldn't hold down a job. Additionally, Bill had a violent temper, he physically abused his wife and son, and he chased other women. Within a few years Isabel found her marriage intolerable, but for Nelson's sake she stuck it out.

Nelson's early childhood was full of adversity. He knew no established home and had no steady friends. He attended various schools, including the Edgewater Grammar and Rhode Island Normal Schools in Providence, the Grove Street Grammar School in Pawtucket, and then moved on to the Dartmouth Street Primary School in New Bedford, Massachusetts.

Nelson shared an unusually close relationship with his mother, no doubt due at least in part to the abuse that both suffered at the hands of Bill Eddy. Nelson was fussed and fawned over by Isabel, who tried to provide emotional constancy for her son. Despite their nomadic lifestyle the family always took a house in each city, even if this meant living with other people. Since she didn't have many close friends, Isabel devoted herself to cultivating her son's sensitive nature and instilling in him the gentlemanly manners of her southern heritage.

Nelson's earliest recollection was of wandering out of the house one day when just a toddler. "I'd been left alone for a little while, and the need for search and exploration possessed me suddenly. So I toddled delightedly out of the room, down the hall and stairs and through an open door. There was a garden around the place. I puttered there for a while, and then I found a gate.

"It seemed to me I went miles down the road. Probably I was fifty yards from the house when I realized the place that had sheltered me all my life was lost somewhere and that I didn't know how to get back to it. Something, an entirely horrible emotion, enclosed me. I sat down and howled. I was terrified. Then I heard a voice, arms caught me up, and mother made little astonished but reassuring noises at me. It was like being saved from drowning when you've given up hope!"

One of the few things Bill and Isabel had in common was their love of music. Isabel was a soloist at the Church of the Transfiguration in Providence, while Bill sang bass in the church chorus and worked as a stagehand and extra with the Providence Opera House. Nelson's parents also performed together in local Gilbert & Sullivan shows. At a young age Nelson learned *The Mikado* with his mother.

Not surprisingly, Nelson had a good singing voice. Even as a baby he attempted to warble, which prompted Grandpa Eddy to remark, "That boy is going to sing some day." When he was older, his boy soprano's voice was heard in various church choirs, including the Grace Church in Providence. Originally Methodist by family inheritance, Nelson attended churches of the Baptist, Congregational, Universalist, Episcopal and Presbyterian faiths. In adulthood he claimed he had no preference for any particular religion because he had sung in so many different houses of God. The sect wasn't important to him, but worship was.

"I was good enough to join a boys' choir in St. Stephen's Episcopal Church," Nelson remembered, "and later I went to Grace Church where they had an organist named Arthur Tracy-Baker. He developed my voice for two years, and made me into a soprano soloist." Nelson earned $1.50 a week singing at Grace

Nelson as a child.

Church for two services on Sunday, one on Thursday night, and the Saturday morning rehearsal. (His pay was later doubled.) As would most boys his age, he found the services tedious. When he squirmed too much, his mother jabbed his bottom with a pin. When Isabel wasn't around, Nelson used to play around in the choir stall and read the comics during the Sunday morning sermon. The choir mistress, Mrs. Alice Thorndyke, remembered Nelson as "a good boy, and one of the best singers the church ever had." She added that she always had trouble brushing Nelson's thick, unruly red hair.

Nelson next sang at the All Saints' Church, "and then one day my high C slipped madly into A-flat, cracked completely and became a thin squeak. Young Mr. Eddy's voice, it was apparent to a flustered congregation, had adolesced. Everyone said I'd better stop singing for a couple of years, and somehow it seemed like a good idea."

Although Nelson enjoyed singing, his first musical ambition was to play the drums, and at one time he actually entertained the idea of becoming a professional drummer. Years later, he "brought the house down" with a drum solo on his 1940s radio show. Isabel taught him to read music, and his grandmother Eddy gave him piano lessons, which he hated worse than sports. Contrary to rumor, Nelson, at the height of his career, could both read music and play piano, guitar and a few other instruments. In his Hollywood years, he denied that he could play well, otherwise he would have been expected to accompany himself and sing at any party he attended. He did play in public on a number of occasions, if he and Jeanette were giving an impromptu concert together.

Nonetheless, given the choice of practicing piano or sports, Nelson chose sports. "Like all other boys, he just wanted to play outdoors," his grandmother said.

Early photos of Nelson show a sturdy, plain-featured boy, with no traces of the sweet, dreamy quality that would in later years drive women wild. His childhood nickname was "Bricktop," and he had the temper to match his flaming red hair. He was always getting into some fight or another, and he usually lost. There was one boy named Penny who always beat Nelson up. Years later when Nelson was a star, Penny's wife wrote Nelson. It seemed Penny wanted an autographed photo but was too shy to write, remembering how badly he'd treated him. Nelson sent Penny the autographed picture. "Just for the joke of it, I had one of my photographs retouched so that both of my eyes looked as if they had just been blacked, my nose broken, my jaw askew and a couple of teeth knocked out. Then, after this retouched job was rephotographed, I sent [him] a copy."

While Isabel was appalled at young Nelson's display of hostility, Bill Eddy approved of anything that showed a macho side to Nelson. "I was a very dull child," Nelson said of himself. "My deportment in school was always and consistently 'D' because I always was minding other fellows' business, poking my nose in where it didn't belong. Meddling." He was, however, somewhat timid around his father, and much preferred vacationing at the farm of his paternal great-grandmother in Acushnet, Massachusetts, or at his paternal grandparents' home in Pawtucket. Nelson was sent there periodically as a respite from the never-ending fighting and instability at home. Of Mr. and Mrs. Isaac M. Eddy, his grandparents, Nelson said: "Their home was my real home. I spent most of my weekends there and it was there, with them, that I learned most of the lessons that have stood me in good stead all of my life. I learned the value of gentleness and kindliness, the beauty of simple living. My grandfather taught me to play the drum and the fife. My grandmother taught me a reverence for old things hallowed by long love and service.

"I spent dreamy hours among the old knick-knacks and daguerreotypes of that sweet-smelling, sweet-living house. I played with the toys my grandfather had played with. I ate the cookies my grandmother made for me and no food in all the world, neither on the Continent nor here, has ever tasted so good. Their sweetness and kindliness toward me was one of the joys of my childhood.

"My first acting was in a school show, 'The Merry Company,' at the Grove St. School, Pawtucket. I acted and sang. Then there were minstrel shows—I was in some of them." His grandmother commented that Nelson did excellent Charlie Chaplin imitations. "We thought he was very funny," she said.

In 1936, Nelson visited his grandparents' home and commented to a reporter, "I have been remembering these places as I saw them as a boy, and then it seemed like a terribly big world. The staircase in my grandmother's house used to seem to me the longest in the world. And now I find that you can get up them in four jumps.

"And I remember the time when we were living up in Smith Hill. My mother was hurt in an accident. My dad and I had to run down the hill to the station to get a cab, and it seemed like one of the longest trips I ever made on the run. It always has seemed so in recollection. Or did, until today I discovered that we didn't have to run more than two or three blocks."

Nelson often stayed with his grandparents during the summer months, though on two consecutive summers Bill took his son along with him for tours of duty with the Coast Artillery Band at Fort Grenable. Nelson said of the second summer, "I had to wash the mess dishes for the band—a taste of soldiering."

Nelson was the mascot for the band. He learned from his father how to play drums and cymbals. Nelson wanted desperately to play the cymbals in the parade. Bill asked the bandmaster for permission, but it was denied. "Nelson wouldn't take no for an answer," Bill remembered years later, "so I fixed up a little game with him. One night at evening parade I made out that I dropped the cymbals. Nelson dashed in, picked them up and played through the rest of the parade. Did pretty well, too."

Nelson recalled one Thanksgiving when the family was living in Pawtucket. He was singing at the Grace Church, in the holiday service. Isabel had given him ten cents for carfare to Providence and back. "After the service, I guess I was so excited about the prospects of a turkey dinner that I got on the wrong trolley car. Instead of taking the Pawtucket car, I got on the one that went out Camp Street to the Brown football field . . . Andrews Field. The line ended there.

"There I was, ten years old, hungry, without money and a grand turkey dinner several miles away. It wasn't a pleasant prospect and I did what any kid would have done, I suppose, I started to cry. The man on the car asked me what was the matter, but when I told him, he didn't seem inclined to do anything about it. I do think he might have taken me back downtown and put me on the right car. But he didn't. So I boo-hooed all the way home. It was a long hike and I was a couple of hours late for that turkey."

As the years passed, Bill and Isabel's marriage strained to the breaking point, and Bill repeatedly asked Isabel to leave. One of his upsets was his wife's complete devotion to and absorption in her son. He was angered to see Nelson become a mama's boy, and worried that his son might grow up to be "a sissy." So Bill took what he felt were appropriate measures to ensure his son's masculinity. Years later, Nelson angrily recalled how he was forced to dress up in a uniform and march back and forth with a rifle on his shoulder for hours—in the rain—outside their house. When he was afraid to learn how to swim, Bill took him out in a rowboat on Narragansett Bay and threw him overboard. A furious Nelson swam back to shore.

In one respect, at least, Bill needn't have worried. From early childhood Nelson had adored and chased after women. Isabel remembered an early birthday party Nelson attended. He found a little girl he liked, walked her out of the party, and brought her home. When the worried mother came to retrieve her daughter, Nelson refused to let go of her hand, kicking and screaming, "She's mine!" This incident, at first glance amusing, is less so when one realizes that Nelson never outgrew this attitude toward women.

"I liked little girls," Nelson recalled. "More especially little girls with *curls*.

And I manifested my liking by pulling their curls, teasing them, sneering loudly, 'Aw, an old *girl!*' "

His earliest recollection of puppy love was in the third grade. "That was my first love affair. Doubtless, the recipient of my rather murderous attentions didn't know then that it was love that was animating me. How should she? But it really was. I was seven, the young lady must have been all of six. Her name was Doris— you see, I *do* remember—and she had very pullable, golden curls, and sweet blue eyes. I teased her daily, hourly, all of the time. I threw spitballs at her. I dipped her curls in inkwells. I climaxed my attentions one day by chasing her home from school, throwing stones at her as she ran. Weird and wonderful are the ways of small boys, for all the time I was thinking how pretty she was, how much I loved her. At last, one particularly well-aimed stone cut her across the eye, a really bad gash. I followed her into her house and, above the din of her justifiable wails, asked her mother if I might be allowed to put butter on the bruise. My mother, I said angelically, had always told me that butter was very good. And her mother, touched by so much manly solicitude on my part, allowed me to minister to the hurt I had inflicted. She never knew, until later, that I was the culprit, the desperado of love."

Nelson described another romance at thirteen: "I was spending part of that summer at Sakonnet Point, Rhode Island. There was a little casino there where the summer folk danced two or three times a week. I got the job of ticket collector and had permission to dance when duty permitted. I always gravitated immediately to the acknowledged belle of the place, the daughter of the local constable. I had overcome considerably my third-grade shyness of girls, but I could never have asked her to dance with me, since I couldn't dance!

"She was very kind and patient with me, teaching me how to place my feet and go one-two, one-two, so that I could, at least, circle ineptly about the ballroom."

The two became an item. "We did all of the 'teenish' things. We carved our initials on the trunks of trees, heart-enclosed. We rode bicycles together. We took long walks, saying nothing and feeling all of the inexplicable keen agony of love at thirteen.

"It all came to what seemed to me a tragic and frustrated end when, seated cozily behind a rock one day—getting up courage to kiss her cool cheek—her father, the constable, looked up behind us and in the best movie constable blood-and-thunder voice bade me begone and his young daughter to run home to Maw and he'd tend to her later."

In 1914, when Nelson was thirteen, the family moved to Lyons Street in Pawtucket. Nelson attended Grove Street Grammar School, where his skill in woodworking was so much better than that of the manual training teacher that Nelson became the teacher's first assistant. He also showed an aptitude for making gadgets, for sketching and for poetry writing.

The following year found the Eddy family living in near-poverty at 103 Broadway, in Providence. Bill worked sporadically as a mechanic. "He did not get continually drunk but he drank all the time, and he played cards and that is where his money went, as far as I can see," Isabel later said. Bill swore at his wife, criticized her homemaking and was physically abusive to her. The few times visitors came into the house, Bill was intoxicated and so "discourteous" that these callers left. "He would not even permit us to have friends," Isabel said, and in her misery she turned more and more to her sympathetic son for comfort.

Despite the Eddy family's later claims that the marriage ended amicably, the truth was that Bill Eddy finally walked out on his family. He had come home drunk on the night of June 14, 1915. He was unemployed, fired from his most recent job at a meat market where he'd worked for two or three days. The next day he packed a suitcase and said he was going away. When Isabel asked what was to become of her and Nelson, Bill told her he didn't care, she could do what she liked. He left Isabel with about $100 in household bills outstanding. Isabel was ill at the time, suffering from "tubercular glands in the stomach." Distraught, she wired her mother in Philadelphia for help.

Caroline Kendrick later summed up her daughter's "unhappy" marriage: "I met my daughter after she was married, going there once or twice a year, and I always found her in very poor circumstances and poor health. Things seemed to get worse and finally on June 15th, 1915, she telegraphed me to come to her rescue, and I went there. I saw that her husband was poor and she needed the doctor's care." Caroline rented a cottage at West Barrington, where she stayed with her daughter and grandson. "[I] kept her down there with me a couple of months until some time in August, the 9th of August I guess it was, and then during that time Mr. Eddy came down one time. He was very discourteous and humiliating to her and I suggested to her then that she should come to Philadelphia and live with me and bring the boy, which she did. [Bill Eddy] was always discourteous and ungentlemanly. He was not a man at all in her strata of life."

Caroline took her daughter and grandson back to her home at 1409 Spruce Street, in Philadelphia. Isabel took a job at the plumbing supply business managed by her brother Clark Kendrick, the J. L. Mott Iron Works. After a year she changed jobs and continued working so that she could support herself and her son. They never received any financial support from Bill. Nelson wrote his father a single letter in 1916, asking what Bill could do to help him. He received a letter back, saying no help would be forthcoming. Bill had no further communication with his family, and Isabel filed for divorce in 1917, citing desertion. Testimony regarding Bill's physical and verbal abuse came up in the proceedings but wasn't pursued due to the fact that it was a clear-cut, uncontested case of desertion. Their divorce was finalized on April 24, 1918.

Despite his hatred of his father, the divorce was traumatic for Nelson. "My feelings about the subject of divorce amounts to a sort of madness," he later said. "I've watched the misery and agony that's come from the separation of man and wife. I know from private experience because of my parents." Indeed, divorce was a social stigma in those days, especially for the woman, and Nelson found himself subject to his school chums' ugly slurs against his mother. He retaliated by becoming even more pugnacious than before. In his teens he studied martial arts so he could fight without getting his face disfigured. He grew to hate prying into his personal life. In his adult years, he developed a fierce desire for privacy and often blatantly lied to the press in interviews, feeling that the real Nelson was none of their business.

He was supposed to start high school in Philadelphia, but it was soon apparent that Isabel needed financial help if they were to make ends meet. Nelson was only too glad to drop out "temporarily" to gallantly help out his mother, but he never thought that this was to be the end of his formal education. The next few years were difficult ones, with Nelson describing himself as "very poor" and "a rather shabby lad," but Nelson was the man of the family now, a role he relished. And he continued to study by taking correspondence courses and following an extensive program designed by his mother. He attacked his schoolbooks at night, sacrificing the normal teenage dating and socializing; still, he didn't mind the new lifestyle. "Mother helped me pick the best background books. I got Wells' *Outline of History* and a lot of general things on science and economics and mathematics—and it wasn't especially hard. You see, my attitude was different. Before, in school, reading these things would have been a task set for me by a kind of petty tyrant, a job that had to be done whether I liked it or not. But in my new estate no one insisted that I read history; I didn't have to re-check a lot of dates and names that bored me. I was able to spend an hour enjoying the fact that some Louis or other had put up a sign in a courtyard reading, 'God is hereby forbidden to work miracles in this spot, by order of the King,' instead of wasting that hour rehearsing meaningless names and statistics."

Nelson's first hope was to land a job in an orchestra as a drummer. Instead, he ended up with his mother at the Mott Iron Works as a switchboard operator for $8 a week, a generous salary for a boy in 1915. Nelson was soon promoted to the shipping department and his salary raised to $12 a week. *Shipping clerk*, according to Nelson, was just another way of saying *underdog*. "I was pretty young, and I hadn't the ghost of an idea as yet what my role in life was to be. But one thing I did know—that it was *not* to be that of underdog." Eventually he left the Iron Works simply because he hated the work. He had vague hopes of becoming a banker, but that idea took him nowhere. In desperation he pounded the streets, trying to find someone who would hire him. "I went into every show, cellar, loft, store and building from Sixteenth Street to Seventh. I didn't miss one. And finally landed at the corner of Seventh and Chestnut. It was the office of that famous daily, the Philadelphia *Press*. I got a job as night clerk, night cashier, night ad taker. I worked from five P.M. to midnight and eight dollars a week was my remuneration. And that four dollars deficit between the eight and the twelve irked my soul as nothing ever has done. I've never been able to endure the feeling of going back, of losing ground. There were some advantages, of course, in that I had more time for reading and also I was taking, at the time, a correspondence course in art."

As a sideline at the Philadelphia *Press*, Nelson wrote obituaries on a commission basis, but the paper wouldn't hire him as a reporter because he was only sixteen. Nelson, always a fast learner, now approached the *Evening Public Ledger* and told the city editor that he was eighteen. When asked what he knew about

The serious young newspaper reporter, who lied about his age to get hired.

reporting, Nelson replied: "Not a damn thing." He got the job, but his victory was short-lived when the *Ledger* cut back its staff. The persistent young man next tried the *Evening Bulletin*, again lied about his age, and was hired. At the *Bulletin* he covered police news, which included murders and trials, then he switched to sports news— Nelson convinced his boss he should cover baseball games, though he'd never attended one in his life. "It was a cinch," said Nelson. "I would just go out and interview Connie Mack and make disparaging remarks about his pitchers. The Mack bawling-out gave me enough copy for many columns." According to a fellow employee, Nelson was eventually fired for singing on the job.

During a couple of summers, Isabel took her son to her "real" home, to her roots in the South where she had relatives that didn't have to struggle for existence. It was like a breath of fresh air for Nelson; he could stuff himself endlessly with delicious food and didn't have to worry about money, at least for a short time. Nelson got along well with his Kendrick relatives, but it always amazed him that despite the half-century since the Civil War they were still Confederate sympathizers, as were many Southerners of their generation. The passage of time barely affected life on the plantation. It was like entering another, unreal world, where men treated women with the old Southern manners. In later years, whenever Nelson needed a retreat, he would head for a visit to his cousins, whose last known family holding was a plantation outside Richmond, Virginia. By the 1950s the owners were forced to grow and sell tobacco to cover expenses. Eventually the estate was sold and subdivided for a condominium project.

In an era when prejudice against blacks was high (the racist film *Birth of a*

Nation was released in 1915), Nelson had great respect for the butler and beloved "Mammy" on the plantation, who were treated as family. He would listen wide-eyed to them for hours, fascinated by their stories and historical knowledge. He learned to cook with their age-old family secrets, and was educated in home-made, natural remedies, thus prejudicing him against mainstream medicine for much of his adult life. And because of his childhood experience Nelson was a firm believer that a man should be judged by his accomplishments, not by his skin color.

In the summer of 1919, Isabel nearly lost her beloved son in a swimming accident. Nelson told the story:

"One day I started out by myself for a reef a quarter mile from shore. The ocean was turbulent. Swimming was difficult.

"Reaching the reef, I felt nearly spent. There was a huge rock which I clutched so that I might rest before returning. About this time a breaker hit me, dashing me against the rock. My arms and legs were ripped wide open. The fact that I was in salt water probably kept me from bleeding to death.

"Well, I began shouting at the top of my voice, 'Ship ahoy! Ship ahoy!' Why I ever shouted 'Ship ahoy!' I'll never know. It obviously was the wrong thing. It turned out that a boat was passing and the men in it heard my cries; but one man in the boat afterward related that he said, 'That's just that singer practicing again.'

"Then I doubled up in a knot. They saw me go under and came to my rescue. When we neared shore the man rowing the boat said, 'Eddy, I guess you'll have to jump out.' It was such a shock that I temporarily lost my voice."

Nelson managed to walk home. "I was so exhausted that on entering the front door I fainted. The next day I had a tonsil infection. It was eight months following the removal of my tonsils that I sang again."

A rumor once circulated that this accident rendered Nelson sterile. However, it is known that he impregnated at least two women: Jeanette, and Maybelle Marston. Another woman with whom he was intimate for a period of about two months claimed they never used birth control, and she never got pregnant (though later on she had two children by her husband).

The year 1920 found the nineteen-year-old Nelson working as an advertising copywriter for the N. W. Ayer advertising firm. After five months, he was fired. "My bosses didn't believe I could devote so much time to singing as an avocation and still do justice to my job," Nelson recalled in the mid-1930s. "On one of my recent concert tours, I met the man who dismissed me for this very reason. He's still with the same agency handling some of the programs for which I have been singing; when we were re-introduced he said, 'Nelson, I am certainly glad that I had foresight enough to fire you.'"

Nelson took another copywriting job with the George Edwards Agency, but didn't last there either. "I had been away on a vacation, and I remember very well that all of my work was cleared up 'way ahead. But on returning, I forgot that daylight savings time had come in. I arrived at the office at ten instead of nine o'clock and was promptly fired by an irate superior."

At nineteen, Nelson had been working for five years but was no closer to the real goal he had by then set for himself: to be a singer. Lacking a voice teacher, he set about to teach himself. "I bought records of Campanari and Scotti and Ruffo and Amato and sat listening until I had learned the aria and then I would bawl out the notes at the top of my lungs. Of course I recognized the difference in my handling of the song and the way Caruso would have done it. But then I tried very hard to learn from the masters who sang from the little wax discs. I was used to teaching myself things, after so many years of studying without any outside help.

"I had a good range and plenty of volume—and I would sing to the phonograph accompaniment when guests would visit. And when I'd get to a part of the aria where the difference between my technique and Campanari's was too obvious, I'd merely stick out my chest and take a long breath and drown Campanari out. It was very effective."

In 1920, Nelson auditioned for David Bispham, the ranking American baritone who'd retired from the Metropolitan Opera and who was now teaching in Philadelphia. "I'm pretty sure I can sing," Nelson told him, "so will you teach me?" The sixty-year-old Bispham heard him and was so impressed that he gave him an autographed photo inscribed "To Nelson Eddy, the coming baritone— or I miss my guess."

Nelson at first balked at the financial responsibility involved in training his voice. He told Bispham he couldn't give up his job. "I have a good game, advertising. It takes most of my time. Besides, lessons cost money and a copy-man makes very little."

"Singing is a good game, too," said Bispham. "It's been pretty good to me."

Nelson started voice lessons with Bispham. When Bispham died in October 1921, Nelson began the search for another teacher. In the meantime he landed his first paying singing job, at a meeting of the Colonial Dames of the Art Alliance, where a "lovely lady" asked him to entertain by singing a few songs and rewarded him with a check for $25. Delighted, Nelson was on his way!

By now Nelson had a steady girlfriend whom he had met while he was working for the Philadelphia *Evening Ledger*. "We were just friends, you understand, but we were in love. She was an assistant music reviewer on a rival paper. It was our mutual love of music that drew us together. [Mary] and I never missed a concert or an opera that came to Philadelphia. She got passes, otherwise we'd have spent every cent we made on tickets. Next to my mother and dad, she was the one who encouraged me most about my voice. We talked plenty about ourselves and our future; but, as is usual with an unselfish woman in love with a selfish man, we talked mostly about my future. I was going on to wonderful things, of course—I was going to conquer the world."

In a mid-1930s newspaper interview Nelson claimed that the affair ended because he was afraid of marriage. With added responsibilities of a wife and children (he mentioned wanting "a couple of kids"), he'd have to return to mundane jobs rather than pursue his singing career. The mysterious red-headed "Mary" was mentioned in several interviews, but each version of the breakup is different.

In actual fact, Nelson may have eloped with "Mary" in 1921. The precise date and location of the marriage is unknown, but a 1945 letter asserted that Nelson got married and Isabel Eddy had it annulled, citing the fact that her son was under age. Both Nelson and Mary were bitter over Isabel's intervention. Nelson was all for continuing the relationship until he was established financially. According to one source, at least one of the local newspapers mentioned the elopement. Opera singer Helen Jepson, who dated Nelson some years later, remembered that Nelson had been married, but he'd never told her the details. Another source claims the girl's name was Mary Smith, and that on the rebound she did a complete turnaround, marrying a doctor named Epstein. Nelson was heartsick and angry over this betrayal, and demanded to know why Mary had dumped him. "Because he can offer me financial security," Mary replied. "You're just a singer, you'll never be able to support me." Nelson grimly swore to her that he'd make millions with his voice. "I would have covered you with furs."

Despite their break-up, Nelson and Mary stayed in touch. She and her husband eventually had a son. When Nelson moved to Los Angeles in 1933, Mary considered leaving her husband and following him. Nelson told her not to bother; he refused to be the cause of a broken home.

In later years, Mary did move to Los Angeles, and lived out her days in a fashionable apartment on Los Feliz Boulevard. Among her treasured possessions were the early love letters Nelson had written her. She claimed they still corresponded sporadically throughout his Hollywood years. As for Nelson, in 1935 he said, "It isn't as though I ever really forgot Mary. There were other women, other temporary interests . . . The tough part of it is that there's no going back to the Marys in our lives."

By now he was more determined than ever to be a success with his voice. His first stage appearance was in January 1922, in *The Marriage Tax*, Mrs. George Dallas Dixon's society musical, which was elaborately produced at the Academy of Music in Philadelphia. "I played the King of Greece," Nelson said. "I had never been in print before and looked forward with more than ordinary eagerness to seeing my name on the program. I got hold of the program about a minute before I was scheduled to go on stage. Quickly my eyes went down the cast until they came to my character. Opposite it was a question mark! To say that I was upset would be putting it mildly. But somehow, I got through the songs." The next morning, he read his first press notice. "My anonymity had served me well, for it was all very flattering. There was a demand for the real name of the King of Greece."

In the next year, Nelson pursued his career aggressively, singing anywhere and everywhere he was asked, in some cases absolutely *gratis*. He performed at luncheons, weddings, funerals, bar mitzvahs, churches, musical groups and political rallies. "My pin money came from warbling to sewing circles, Rotary Clubs and for anyone else who desired a burst of melody between the cabinet pudding and 'Our Honored Speaker,' " Nelson quipped. "Gradually the rewards for warbling were greater than the stipends for 'shagging' proofs. I followed the job that paid the most."

On June 13, 1923, his father Bill Eddy married Marguerite Elliot and settled in Jamestown, Rhode Island. Nelson was invited to the ceremony but declined to attend because he had a singing engagement, which didn't exactly please his father. Nelson did attend a reception for the newlyweds, and over the years the two men gradually re-established a guarded relationship. Nelson liked his step-mother and his half-sister, Martha Virginia Eddy, born on February 21, 1925, and he was happy to see his dad finally find a seeming happiness. Nelson was cordial to his father's new family over the years, but he did not see them often; the dark-haired Virginia, as she was called (her hated childhood nickname was "Half Nelson"), once wrote that she'd seen Nelson about twenty times during his lifetime. Usually the three of them got together while Nelson was in New England on a concert tour.

From this time on, Nelson never lacked for benefactors. The best known was Gertrude Chesire Evans, who likened herself to Nelson's godmother. After the death of her husband, "Aunt" Gert busied herself by teaching bridge to more than three hundred students, culled mostly from Philadelphia's upper crust, and by tending to Nelson's budding career.

Aunt Gert took Nelson under her wing, inviting him to move into her apartment in the Lenox while his mother lived elsewhere. According to a good friend of Nelson's, Malcolm Poindexter, Nelson's and Aunt Gert's relationship was strictly platonic.

"Mrs. Evans had this apartment in the Lenox apartment house at the corner of Thirteenth and Spruce streets," recalled Poindexter. "Nelson lived there with her. She was his sponsor. The apartment house is still there. [Mrs. Evans] was very well-to-do because she owned a number of dry goods stores up and down the East Coast. I never saw or heard anything about [Nelson's mother] during the years I knew Nelson. However, I did meet Mrs. Evans one time when I was practicing with Nelson in his studio on the top floor of the apartment house. She came up there for some reason and he introduced me to her. Nelson was very poor at that time of his life. He had nothing really and I guess this wealthy lady recognized his potential and helped him. He used to tell me tales about how he used to stay around to get some free food and that sort of thing when he sang at special events." Malcolm described Nelson's living space: "He had a small room off the laundry facilities for the apartment house. This area was on the top floor of the building. He had a baby grand piano there and a cabinet for music."

It is said that Mrs. Evans impressed Nelson with the all-importance of his career, and she made him promise not to marry before he reached forty. To Nelson's credit, he worked hard to adjust to the stoic lifestyle that she demanded of him. On Sundays he sang at the Church of Our Savior, on Chestnut Street. Choirmaster Irving Hancock remembered that Aunt Gert dropped him off and picked him up after services. "He loved fun and used to like to stay around after the services and talk with the other members of the choir and with me," Hancock said. "He wasn't at all the serious-minded young man he's pictured now in stories. Of course, though, he didn't have much chance for fun. With a serious ambition to amount to something musically, no late hours, drinking or smoking are possible. But sometimes Nelson would beg me to let him get into the organ loft, then he'd pull out all the stops and make just as much noise as he could. Poor fellow, he was starved for fun!

"One night I invited him to my house after rehearsal. His eyes lit up like a kid's. 'Gee, I'd love to,' he said wistfully, 'but I'll have to ask Aunt Gertrude.' Apparently Mrs. Evans said no. Foolishly, I urged Nelson to come anyhow. He looked awfully uncomfortable, but he went home.

"Another time he did manage to have a free evening. He telephoned Mrs. Evans that he had to rehearse some special numbers with me. I got on the phone and corroborated it. She consented reluctantly. Nelson came to my house and we did rehearse some numbers. But my daughter had some young people in and they stayed afterward. Nelson remained until after midnight, laughing, dancing, having the time of his life.

"All the girls in the choir were simply starry-eyed about Nelson. One seventeen-year-old in particular had a violent crush on him. One day she made a pencil sketch of him and presented it to him. Nelson picked her right off her feet and kissed her in front of the whole choir."

Gertrude Evans had a summer home in Maine that Nelson used as a vacation home. She remained devoted to him over the years, even if she was sometimes critical of the way his life turned out. When she died in 1963 she left a gift of his choice from her estate to Nelson.

Mrs. Evans received a good deal of credit for aiding Nelson's career and was later written up in several fan magazine articles. However, there were others who helped. One of them was Sybil Thomas. Her money came from her late banker husband. It was at a singing audition that Sybil Thomas got her first glimpse of the red-haired, blue-eyed Nelson Eddy, whom she found extremely intriguing as he sat forlornly by himself. He was "tall, skinny, gorgeous, sad-looking, wearing gold wire-rimmed glasses." According to Sybil, Nelson was easily the best singer in the group of contestants and he knew it, but the judges were favoring a tenor whose family had some connection with the school hosting the event. Sybil spoke with Nelson at the audition; he was bitter about the inevitable outcome and seemed close to tears. At that point Sybil befriended him, "threw her weight around," and Nelson took first prize.

From that time on, Sybil was a family friend. She was determined to help Nelson in any way possible. Her interest was a bit more than godmotherly— decades later she still sighed, "If only I'd been twenty years younger!"—but the difference in age apparently didn't daunt her. In the early 1950s, Sybil helped another operatic singer (whose name will go unmentioned) launch his career by backing his first record album. They had an affair, and this singer later said, "She never told me one way or the other, but knowing Sybil Thomas as I did I would say it was highly likely that Nelson slept with her."

During the next several years, Nelson developed a reputation for having casual affairs with older women, often society matrons who sponsored musical events.

"Even without his fabulous voice he could easily have slept his way to the top," commented Marie Collick, a friend. Isabel Eddy was a bit more tactful. "He used to be quite wild and in his early career had a terrible reputation. For a time it was really a problem. He seemed to always attract married women."

Yet another benefactor was Sarah Tucker, a woman who remained a friend of Isabel's throughout Nelson's Hollywood years and who corresponded regularly until her death in 1950 at the age of ninety-four. Sarah Tucker first met the Eddys in Massachusetts while teaching piano and music, and much of her later correspondence with Isabel survived, in which intimate details were written of Nelson's daily life and his ongoing relationship with Jeanette.

There are many discrepancies in the stories about who raised money to fund Nelson's music studies, and some dispute over who had the most influence over his early development. Some blamed Jeanette for the sorrow he later suffered in his life, and some were disappointed that he gave up the opera for Hollywood. But in one area the benefactors were in perfect harmony: they had been right to help Nelson get started. Once he had made his public debut his career took off like a rocket.

5

A fish
out of water

Nelson's mother and mentors, though pleased with his career progress, were horrified when he fell in love once again. This time the object of his affections was the very married Maybelle Marston, whose husband was a prominent Philadelphia attorney. No one is exactly certain when they met, but in 1924 Marston endured a messy divorce, in which the custody of her four-year old son was awarded to her husband, a very uncommon practice in those days unless the wife was a known adulteress. It is likely that Nelson was the cause of Marston's divorce.

Nelson and Maybelle became engaged. His constituents objected to the union because Maybelle was seven years older than Nelson, and now divorced. Her associates and family felt Nelson was too young, too green, with no stable financial future. Money was forthcoming from Maybelle or her family to help subsidize some of Nelson's overseas vocal studies the next few years, even though eventually the engagement was called off. Nelson continued to sing with Maybelle in opera performances, and their personal relationship limped along for some time. In the end, Nelson once again bowed to pressure and broke up with her.

His attention back on his career, in 1924 he made his radio debut, giving a recital on local station WOO. He quickly became a regular on radio, with an avid following—mostly women!

Alexander Smallens, head of the now entitled Philadelphia Civic Opera Company, realized Nelson's potential and put him on the roster for the next season. On December 12, 1924, Nelson starred in the company's production of *I Pagliacci*. "I was still a beginner," he said, "but they thought I had promise so they cast me for the lead, much too heavy a role for a newcomer. I worried over it so much that my hair turned white in a single night—opening night—and I handed in my resignation—that letter saying I'd never sing again."

Of Nelson's performance as Tonio, the *Public Ledger* said: "Nelson Eddy fairly swept the audience off its feet with his rendition of the Prologue, and from that moment the high standard of performance never dropped. Mr. Eddy's characterization of the difficult role was so excellent throughout that it looks as though the Civic Opera Company might already have justified its existence by the discovery of a real operatic talent."

Nelson stayed on with the company, becoming its most popular singer and winning raves with both the audiences and the press. His red hair, which did in fact prematurely whiten, now looked blonde; by the time he got to Hollywood it was mistakenly assumed that he'd always had blonde hair.

In the 1925-26 opera season, Nelson sang in *Aida* ("Nelson Eddy, previously seen as Amonasro, was even better in the part last night," said a reviewer), *Cavalleria Rusticana, Gianni Schicchi, La Navarraise, Samson and Delilah* and *Tannhäuser*, where his debut as Wolfram earned him his greatest praise yet. The *Evening Bulletin* noted: "The biggest individual hit of the evening, judging by the

As Amonasro in *Aida*.

audience's applause, was scored by Nelson Eddy in his delivery of Wolfram's love song. His efforts stirred his hearers to continued hand-clapping which subsided only after he had stepped out of character in order to bow two or three times. Horrified Wagnerites trembled for fear that there might be an attempt to force an encore in violation of all tradition."

Nelson purchased a small black scrapbook in which to paste his clippings; he had added another seven scrapbooks to the collection before he turned the job over to a clipping service and a secretary when he moved to Hollywood. In these early scrapbooks he carefully dated and annotated his reviews and interviews, writing comments like "Liar!" or "Awful rot" or "Didn't say this!!" in the margin of a quote that had been attributed to him.

In 1925, Nelson also learned the role of Plunkett in the opera *Martha,* which he performed for the Matinee Musical Club. That year he sang in a variety of places—at Gimbel's department store, on radio station WIP, and at the Overbrook Presbyterian Church, in their choir of Negro spiritual singers. The following year, Nelson sang in several oratorios, and increased his repertoire of operatic roles to include the title role in *Rigoletto,* Sharpless in *Madama Butterfly,* Mercutio in *Romeo and Juliet,* Marcello in *La Bohème,* the Herald in *Lohengrin* and Dr. Malatesta in *Don Pasquale.* Christmas of 1926 found Nelson writing and directing a Christmas pageant entitled "Manifestation." It was performed on December 22, at the Overbrook Presbyterian Church before an audience of two hundred. That same year he wrote and recorded his first song, a cowboy ballad called "The Rainbow Trail." Piano arrangement and accompaniment on the record was provided by a young man named Theodore Paxson. The two had met in April while performing on the same bill for the Octave Club. They worked well together, and Paxson became Nelson's accompanist for the next forty years.

Then in 1927, Nelson landed his first radio series, the Newton Coal Hour. The hour-long program aired on Saturday nights from 9:00 P.M. to 10:00 P.M. Nelson built up such a following on this show that he sang on it as a regular, whenever possible, for the next three years.

Philadelphians were now touting him as the best young singer in the city. Not one single performance of his was panned by the usual bloodthirsty critics. In fact, their major complaint was that he didn't always get starring roles. An Eddy performance was an event to be written about in meticulous detail. For example, on April 26, 1927, Nelson gave a joint concert with soprano Elizabeth Harrison. At one point Miss Harrison lost her place in the music and stopped singing. Nelson put his arm around her, found her spot, and she finished her song with Nelson's arm still around her. "The byplay brought amusement to the audience, which responded with noisy applause," noted the *Evening Bulletin,* adding "Mr. Eddy's singing was very acceptable, with a noticeable improvement in the higher tones."

This improvement was due to the fact that Nelson had a new voice teacher. Since the death of Bispham, Nelson had studied with a total of eleven teachers, but he hadn't found the right one for him, and Nelson knew instinctively that his career wouldn't move forward without one. "I was pretty rotten for a long while and quite discouraged. One day Edouard Lippe, a well-known Philadelphia singer, told me right out I didn't know how to sing. That might have made me mad, but the truth was I knew it as well as he. So I just asked him what to do. He came over to my home every day and gave me lessons. Then he sent me to William W. Vilonat, who had been his teacher. Vilonat taught me how to sing."

Vilonat had a strict set of rules. "It means early hours and no girls and simple foods and no champagne. It means study. And it means a trip abroad, a year or two in Dresden and Paris."

"I don't have that much money," Nelson told Vilonat. But in the end, Nelson's loyal benefactors raised the money for him to study abroad. Nelson made three trips to Dresden and promised to pay back every cent before he married, even if it took him till the age of forty.

In July 1927, Nelson left for Dresden. There he found a German family willing to rent a room to him. The next few months were "an orgy of work." He learned the scores of several operas, mastered four more languages, studied larynx and breath control. He also learned to speak fluent German, which would enable him to work undercover for the government during World War II.

Vilonat was a much-loved teacher to his pupils, but he was a slave driver. "There is little time," he kept reminding Nelson. "You haven't much money. You've got no hours to spare, work is the thing." Nelson worked. After his third trip abroad, Vilonat finally proclaimed his pupil ready for a career. The night Nelson was to leave, Vilonat asked him to do a small favor. He had three female pupils auditioning that evening at the Dresden Opera. He wanted Nelson to audition as well, "Just to show those generals that I can teach *men* the art of singing."

"Sure," Nelson agreed. "Swell gag, too."

He hurried over to the Dresden Opera House and sang "Song to the Evening Star" from *Tannhäuser*. Fritz Busch, director of the opera, was startled at the audition. "A young, good-looking man [sang] without the usual stage fright, in such a fine voice, and with such beautiful expression that I at once offered him an engagement. It was Nelson Eddy who, to our regret, did not accept the contract —a case that did not happen every day at Dresden. It seems that Eddy, so I heard, later made a lot of money in Hollywood!"

Vilonat was furious that Nelson declined the contract, especially since Dresden wanted him as their leading baritone. But Nelson was determined to make his fame in his own country. "I've got reservations on tomorrow's boat for America," he told Vilonat, "and nothing on earth, not even the Dresden Opera, could keep me from catching it."

He left as scheduled. Vilonat never forgave him.

Nelson's return to Philadelphia found him appearing in several new operas. He learned thirty-three roles in all and sang in seven languages. He was also now in demand for solo concerts.

He resumed his voice study with Dr. Edouard Lippe. Lippe, who was hunchbacked and homosexual, had an interesting background. "You know, Dr. Lippe's name wasn't really Lippe," said Malcolm Poindexter, Nelson's protégé. "His name was really Edward Lipschultz and he had been a pharmacist in Philadelphia before turning to music as a career. That is also how he got the designation of doctor, it was from his pharmacist career and not through his musical training. He had a hobby of making very lovely fragrances for the people he knew and liked. He would analyze his friends' personalities and then prepare a fragrance with his knowledge of chemicals and preparations, just especially for them.

"Dr. Lippe was deformed from a youthful accident and could not hope for a major musical career, but he had an extraordinary ability to teach voice. Nelson had been quoted as saying that of all the fine and not so fine teachers he had since beginning his vocal training, Dr. Lippe did the most to shape his voice to what we know as the spectacular Nelson Eddy sound."

Other Philadelphia friends argue that Douglas Stanley, with whom Nelson studied in the early 1930s, had a greater effect on Nelson's technique than did Lippe. Nelson's son Jon agrees, based on what Nelson himself told Jon. In 1932 Nelson performed in a radio demonstration on the correct way to sing, with Stanley narrating.

At this point—once he began coaching with Dr. Lippe—Nelson's voice *did* seem better than ever; critics searched for new or better adjectives with which to describe him. After a concert version of *Boris Godunov* in December 1927, one paper noted: "His voice is a splendid resonant baritone, pure in quality, uniform throughout its ample register, and it was used with ease and freedom. Eddy put himself in immediate and hearty rapport with his audience by his magnificent delivery of the declamatory Monologue, called commonly the Czar's Song. It was absolutely faultless. Every tone was sung true to pitch and with a voice clear and resonant as a bell, and with a distinctness of verbal utterance that could be easily understood in every part of the large theatre."

And after a *La Bohème* in the same month: "Eddy, whose baritone voice has earned him so much praise during the past few years, continues to stand out as one of the most capable handlers of operatic comedy on any stage."

From a 1928 *Cavalleria*: "Nelson Eddy, the now-worshipped baritone, sang the ill-fated Silvio with feeling that is seldom equalled."

From the society column of the *Public Ledger*, April 15, 1928: "At 2:30 on Thursday we'll all be found, beyond a doubt, at the Charlotte Cushman club benefit in the Erlanger Theater. It is one of the things we look forward to every year, and the program for this one is extremely intriguing. Nelson Eddy is going to sing. If no one else were going to do anything at all, we'd go on just that account."

On November 11, 1928, Nelson sang in the American premiere of Strauss' *Ariadne auf Naxos,* at the Academy of Music. He portrayed both the wigmaker and Arlecchino. He followed this up with his debuts in operas *Die Meistersinger, Manon Lescaut, The Marriage of Figaro, Faust, The Magic Flute, L'Elisir d'Amore, Hansel and Gretel, The Secret of Suzanne, Das Rheingold* and *Gotterdämmerung.*

In 1929, Nelson had another first; he sang in vaudeville. Vaudeville in those days was a medium showcasing comics and song-and-dance men, not opera singers—the exception being opera great Rosa Ponselle and her sister Carmella, who were discovered singing in vaudeville. But Nelson was determined to accept any jobs offered him, so he sang in a pre-film vaudeville attraction entitled "Carmen Fantasy" at the Stanley Movie Theater. This extremely condensed version of *Carmen* had Nelson singing "The Toreador Song," Helen Jepson doing Micaela's aria, and Catherine Littlefield's ballet troupe dancing. The feature film that followed was *A Man's Man*, starring William Haines and Josephine Dunn.

By 1929, the *Daily News* reviewer, who had followed Nelson's career from the start, figuratively threw up his hands. "What more can be said about the ability of the favorite Nelson Eddy? It has not been a week since we said: 'He has but to open his mouth, warble a few notes, and the audience is his.' That goes again. His voice discloses improvement every time it is heard. He can hold any group enraptured with his personality.

"It is high time that Eddy starts off for broader fields."

■ In 1930, the Philadelphia Civic Opera Company went out of business. It had begun seven years earlier with $15 in the treasury and no subscriptions; it was ending its final season with a subscription of $50,000. The company, which only utilized American singers, had never been in debt, and it was the first American opera company to be subsidized. A single taxpayer's protest had launched a campaign to withdraw the subsidy, and the group was now unable to raise an additional $100,000 needed for the coming season.

Nelson was forced to look for work elsewhere, and on July 23, 1930, he made his New York debut before an audience of 18,000 singing in Beethoven's Ninth Symphony at Lewisohn Stadium. It was nerve-wracking, as it turned out. The performance, which was to be broadcast live on WOR, was originally scheduled for the twenty-second but rains were so heavy that the concert was postponed to the next day. The afternoon of the twenty-third Nelson took the train from Philadelphia with his evening clothes in a suitcase, but when he arrived in New York he learned that the soloists and orchestra were to appear in blue coats and white flannel trousers. A special messenger was immediately sent to retrieve the correct outfit, and Nelson scrambled into the correct clothes just minutes before going onstage.

For the first time in his nine-year career, Nelson received less than rave reviews. "Of the solo quartet (the other soloists were Jeanette Vreeland, Nevada Van der Veer, and Arthur Hackett), Nelson Eddy was the newcomer," explained the New York *Times*. "He sang with clarity of enunciation, good diction, excellent resonance and feeling for phrase. The extreme lower register was a bit weaker than the rest of his range, and the music from his throat would have gained had it been more vibrant and emotional. It was a more than promising debut under difficult circumstances." The *Herald-Tribune* added, "Mr. Eddy, after some nervousness in his opening measures, gave evidence of having a well-schooled voice of warm timbre, and of considerable power."

Nelson sang again with Vreeland, Hackett and Kathryn Meisle in Verdi's *Requiem*, again at Lewisohn. The New York *World* critic felt that Eddy was miscast. "The role is rather formidable for a purely lyric voice. And Mr. Eddy is a baritone, not a basso-profundo. In spite of these handicaps he acquitted himself with distinction."

Nelson returned to Philadelphia, where he apparently could do no wrong. He sang in another outdoor concert at Robin Hood Dell, had to repeat each number as an encore, and "scored the most emphatic success of any of the soloists of the season," bragged the *Public Ledger*.

Nelson was still living on the fifteenth floor of the Lenox apartments at Thirteenth and Spruce. One afternoon he was loudly rehearsing the death of Samson when a large crowd gathered outside the building, looking upward, wondering at the yelling and noise. The police squad had been summoned, and had surrounded the building when the sergeant, certain that a murder was in progress, stormed into Nelson's apartment. There he found Nelson at the piano, accompanying himself and a female singer. "Well, it didn't sound like singing to me!" said a regular patrolman who had called in for backup.

Nelson, now twenty-nine, was singing regularly on the Atwater Kent radio show, and he held two series of six concerts at the Warwick Hotel in which he performed with other guest artists. (In one corner he dueted with tenor Allan Jones.) That successful concert included numbers from *La Bohème* and *La Forza del Destino*.

Nelson granted his first newspaper interview in November 1930, consenting only to discuss his career. "I worked, worked and worked," he said. "And it's a constant grind even today. I don't believe anyone realizes how hard I work because I try to make it all look easy. It might detract from their enjoyment of the songs if they knew that I stayed awake nights, pulling at my hair and chewing my fingernails trying to learn them."

He described the secret of his success as "just being natural. A fellow's friends quickly detect artificial mannerisms and are the first to be annoyed by them.

"You've got to keep the people interested. You can't keep on singing the same old things time after time. I'm always hunting for new things to do for my home audiences. I try to make good use of the element of surprise. The people never quite know what I'm going to do next, and they stay interested."

His interviewer told him, "We're for you, kid, as long as you don't get a swelled head from all your big jobs. But the minute you do, we'll pan the ears off you!" To which Nelson replied:

"That's a bet! If you see my feet getting off the ground, give me the works, I know it will be good for me."

He was off to Milwaukee and Chicago on his first concert tour, where he sang to excellent reviews. Upon his return to Philadelphia he portrayed Robin Hood at the annual Charity Bowl, complete with costume and 200 maidens to whom he sang. "Needless to say, the affair was a tremendous success," noted the *Ledger*, "and a goodly sum was realized for the hospitals that will benefit by the affair." In January 1931, Nelson returned to New York to sing at Carnegie Hall with the

Schola Cantorum. He fell ill with the flu, but sang well anyway and received enthusiastic reviews from all the papers, which was a great relief to him. Then it was back on tour, introducing himself to audiences in Baltimore, Nashville, Camden, Detroit and Boston.

For the 1931–32 season, Nelson signed on with the Philadelphia Grand Opera Company. He was now running with a new crowd, a group of very talented young singers coming out of the Curtis Institute of Music. Some of them, such as Rose Bampton and Helen Jepson, went on to great fame.

"Nelson and I were with Columbia Concerts," Rose Bampton reminisced. "It was a wonderful thing. I started with them and I was so grateful to them, because I didn't know anything about concerts. But they put me on in all these little cities, who didn't know me from Adam. I was one of the three or five artists that they had during the season, with an audience that was already guaranteed to be there, because they bought for the season. So you went around the country.

"I did joint recitals [with Nelson]. Nelson was the handsomest young man, and doing some wonderful singing, you know. This is long before he went to Hollywood. I think we all felt he had star potential. I don't know that we were thinking about movies. We were certainly thinking about opera.

"Of course we were all madly in love with him. Everyone was. All of us would drool every time he came on. And he was so nice and so warm and no chi-chi about him. He was just a wonderful chap. He was with his mother then. I have wonderful memories of him.

"Helen Jepson and I—Helen was a soprano and I was a mezzo at that time— used to do quartets. Helen was closer to Nelson than I. Let's just say Nelson liked me, but he liked Helen better."

Helen Jepson denied that she and Nelson had a romance. "That story got started because he put his arm around me during a concert," she said. But according to Rose Bampton and others, they were going hot and heavy for some time. Nelson even got his own apartment for a short while, sharing a room with a piano student to cut expenses.

A major factor in his living arrangement was money. Although he was now starting to make a living off his voice, Nelson was very cautious with his funds, anxious as he was to repay the money he'd borrowed. He felt a financial responsibility to his mother Isabel as well as to his benefactors. He had always kept a bedroom at his mother's. "She's worked with me. She's had an understanding of me and the faith in me that nobody else bothered to have, until that understanding and faith became part of my own philosophy. I began to know myself, believe in myself . . . Now she's helping me enjoy the things her understanding has helped bring me. She helps run my household and is as popular with my guests as any young beauty. We get along marvelously together, we make allowances for each other and work together toward making a nice thing out of this business of living. And it's going to continue that way." Nelson was so close to his mother that he shared details of his private life with her, including his relationships with women, as evidenced by his letters to her over the years.

Meanwhile, Nelson's circle of friends widened, and grew to include tenors

Dimitri Onefrei and Reinhold Schmidt, soprano Grace Moore (with whom he
had an affair), and trumpet player Louis Armstrong. Nelson, a jazz lover, once
heard Armstrong play and the two of them had hit it off. Armstrong liked to tell
the story about how he fell on hard times and had to pawn his beloved trumpet.
He was so miserable that his pal Nelson "stole" it back for him from the
pawnshop, thus earning Satchmo's lifelong gratitude.

Another good friend was Malcolm Poindexter, a fellow singer who never had
the career he deserved because of the color of his skin. Poindexter, a light-
skinned black, was Nelson's protégé in the late 1920s.

"I heard [Nelson] sing and I wrote to him to ask if he knew a teacher who
would be willing to take me as a student," recalled Poindexter "He responded by
telling me to come sing with him, which I did. Then he and his own voice
teacher, Dr. Edouard Lippe, agreed to take me as a student.

"I had an afternoon teaching position which allowed me time in the morning
to practice with Nelson, and on some days Dr. Lippe would be there, too. He
had his own studio on Locust Street.

"What a kind, sensitive, and warm-hearted person [Nelson] was. At the time I
was studying with Nelson I was so poor that I had to carry the music I had
wrapped up in newspaper. Much of the music I did have was given to me by
Nelson. So one day Nelson called me on the phone to ask me to come meet him
at the corner of Thirteenth and Locust streets. He had just returned from a
singing engagement in Toronto, Canada, and he said that he had something for
me. When I arrived at the appointed place, there was Nelson waiting to present
me with a beautiful genuine leather case in which to carry my music. He had
bought it in Toronto with some of the money he had made singing there. As he
handed it to me he said, 'Now Malcolm, I don't want to see you with your music
wrapped up in newspaper anymore.' And it never was. I was so proud of that
leather case because it was Nelson's thoughtful gift to me. This was long before I
or anyone else could know he was to become a world celebrity. He was a
wonderful friend in so many ways."

Nelson attempted to establish a singing career for Malcolm, with little success
due to the prejudices of the time. "He did try," Malcolm said. "Occasionally
when he would get a call to sing at Conwell's church and other places too, he
would call them close to the time he was to perform and tell them he couldn't
make it, but he would send a replacement singer. He told them that they must
pay his substitute the same amount as they were to pay him. I was that substitute
vocalist. This was Nelson's way of trying to help me get a break."

Poindexter did land a concert in Ethical Hall. "This particular night the hall
was filled. Nelson also sang there and the people who came to hear my concert
also knew Nelson. When Nelson arrived to hear me sing, he didn't like the
placement of the piano on the stage. So he asked, 'Who's in charge here?' Since it
was the first time the place was let out to a Negro singer, everybody who had to
do with the management of the place was afraid to admit who was in charge. So
Nelson went over to a man who appeared to be in charge and said, 'I want that
piano moved. This man can't sing with it in that position.' The man said, 'We

don't have anybody to do that.' Nelson then asked, 'But is it all right to move it?' The man indicated that it was and with that Nelson jumped up on the stage and moved the piano around himself to where he wanted it to be. Well, the place came down. This is just one example of the kind of caring and unselfish person Nelson was."

As Nelson's successful concert tours and increasing repertoire would seem to indicate, things were looking up for him. As always, he was modest when discussing his early success. "The Depression enabled me to get good engagements. The giants of the old days were refusing to cut their fees. The public desired recitals but just couldn't pay the old prices. By being cheap, I became 'the popular young baritone.' There are plenty of young singers with better voices than mine, but I've worked harder than most of them and gotten further. If I heard that someone was going to give an opera I got the score and learned it and then when they wondered who to get, I would say, 'Why not me? I know it.' And I'd get the job. All the other singers who hadn't studied would say, 'Lucky dog! He gets all the breaks!' And I wasn't lucky at all. I'm not very quick at learning scores, either. Many's the time I've propped myself up with black coffee and gone over and over a score trying to get it through my head. It hasn't been easy for me, so consequently I've had to work harder.

"Art is not necessarily creative. There's too much bunk about opera. I recall an aspiring singer who refused to hear Scotti, explaining, 'It might destroy my originality.' He still has his originality. Enjoys it all by himself."

His frank, easygoing manner endeared him to reporters. One question frequently asked him was about his diet and any precautions he took with his voice.

"Yes, I started out by observing all that nonsense, and found out that when I was half through singing an operatic role, I was nearly starving to death! I've discovered that if I eat an ample dinner a reasonable time before singing, that it does not affect my voice in the least.

"A great many singers think that strenuous exercise is bad for their voices. Personally I've never found that to be so. I've never done anything or refrained from doing anything because of my voice. I eat what and when I like, smoke frequently, take a drink occasionally and in general do just about anything I like!

"Singers are the most childish, the most conceited people of any on earth. My prayer has been that I might remain normal and be myself."

■ By the end of 1932, Nelson was on his way to becoming a millionaire. His life had changed dramatically. He had paid back his singing debt in full, and now had two apartments, one in Philadelphia, the other in New York. Having lived frugally for so many years, it took some effort on his part to live more lavishly. Like many people who struggle against poverty in youth, Nelson was determined to save every possible dollar, thus ensuring that he would never be poor again. Aside from his WOR radio show on Friday nights, he spent a lot of time in New

York when he wasn't on tour. His idea of relaxing was haunting magic shops, buying little tricks to perform for the benefit of his friends.

During this period, Nelson had sung in two premieres in New York, the world premiere of Respighi's *Maria Egiziaca* with the New York Philharmonic at Carnegie Hall in 1932, and the New York premiere of *Wozzeck* with the Philadelphia Grand Opera Company at the Metropolitan Opera House in 1931. For *Maria Egiziaca (Mary in Egypt)*, Nelson had to audition for Arturo Toscanini, who was slated to conduct. The role Nelson wanted was that of an elderly man. After hearing him, Toscanini patted Nelson on the shoulder and said he'd do. When Toscanini fell ill, composer Respighi conducted the world premiere himself.

For *Wozzeck*, Nelson had to sing for Stokowski, who was also conducting the American premiere broadcast of *Parsifal*. Nelson utilized his fail-safe routine of learning both Wozzeck and Gurrelider (from *Parsifal*) beforehand. After hearing him, Stokowski asked if he knew the role of Gurrelider also, and Nelson was hired for both roles.

Along with his two apartments, Nelson had all the other trappings, including a full-time accompanist, a secretary and a maid/cook. He was pleased to see Isabel living a life of ease at last, but complained, "She spends most of her time trying to keep me out of trouble. She has lots of attention paid to her and lots of beaux— many more than I have girls. I am quite jealous of her."

There's an interesting story behind Nelson's sudden wealth. It wasn't all made from singing. In fact, Nelson claimed, "After my return from abroad, my singing netted me about three thousand dollars the first year, six thousand the second, and after that from fifteen thousand to thirty thousand a year."

Unknown to many, he had become friends with a very keen financial adviser. This man had some money, but unfortunately could not invest it as he wanted because he was black. Nelson at first had no money of his own to invest, but he trusted his friend's judgment, so they struck up a partnership whereby Nelson fronted with his friend's funds. Within a couple of years the two had bought stock in office buildings and apartments.

Nelson didn't let his financial success go to his head, either. Though he sometimes spent lavishly on friends, he tended to be cautious with money, thus earning himself a reputation for being "tight." But Nelson was far from miserly. In addition to repaying his major benefactors, he also refused to abandon those who had helped him along the way. Irving Hancock, the choirmaster from Church of Our Savior, recalled that Nelson continued to sing for him after he was successful. His contract with Columbia Concerts forbade him to sing anywhere for less than his base rate, but the church, which could only pay $50, couldn't afford it. Nelson decided to sing anyway. "I don't see why I can't sing for my own church if I want to, and this is my church." He joined the choir, which got him around the clause in his contract. "He was with us for four seasons," Hancock said, "then just before he left for Hollywood he came to me to say goodbye. He handed me an envelope. 'I'm in the money now, Irving. I don't really need this,' he said. When I opened the envelope, there was Nelson's check for every cent we'd paid him for the four seasons' work."

★ ★ ★

■ In January 1933, Nelson was once again on tour on the East Coast. But finally, on February 27, he made his first appearance on the West Coast, at the Savoy Theater in San Diego. For the audience and critics, it was love at first sight. The San Diego *Sun* wrote: "His concert was the sort of triumph young singers dream of. All of Eddy's advance notices said that he was tall, blonde and young, but no one mentioned that he looks like Adonis, Rupert Brooke, the poet, and the more attractive younger knights of King Arthur's court. And he has the most generous and friendly attitude to his audience, began singing encores after the first number and sang fourteen in all, besides a program of songs and arias in six languages that would have exhausted both the vocal organs and mentality of the average concert artist. He sings so that at the end of two hours singing, his voice was as fresh and rich as when he began." And the San Diego *Tribune* said: "There was no fuss or feathers about Nelson Eddy. He stood squarely on his feet, made no gestures. He has a fine voice and never spared it, although he never forced or strained it. He announced his songs in an informal, boyish manner, and always included his accompanist, saying: 'We shall give you—.' As he presented them, his songs were not merely a part of a well-chosen group of great or interesting airs. Each was an entity in itself. Each had a personality all its own, and each was thoroughly alive."

The consensus from the San Diego press was that Nelson was "better than his publicity."

The following morning Columbia Concerts in New York received a frantic call: Lotte Lehmann, scheduled to sing that night in Los Angeles, was ill. Could they find a last-minute replacement? Nelson was contacted and he agreed to drive up to Los Angeles.

Meanwhile, the phone wires were burning between San Diego and Los Angeles. The major film studios were alerted not to miss Nelson's Los Angeles debut. That night he sang to a capacity audience filled with everyone who was anyone in the film business. According to the write-ups, the concert was a "brilliant success." Nelson was described as "a youth of romantic presence and endowed with the golden gifts of a divine singer," who "delighted and amazed" his audience, and happily obliged them with fourteen encores and thirty-two curtain calls. The applause and cheering was so profuse that one critic wondered whether Nelson had hired a claque.

After the concert, Nelson was invited to do screen tests at RKO, Paramount and MGM. He agreed to RKO and Paramount, but hesitated about MGM. Nelson wasn't much of a moviegoer, but he'd seen what MGM had done to Lawrence Tibbett and Grace Moore, who had co-starred in the plodding 1930 version of *New Moon*, a dismal failure. "I regarded a motion picture contract as a serious gamble," he said. "I had worked like a slave to win my place in music. I had given up everything to build my voice. And Hollywood blandly requested me to chuck all that overboard. I couldn't do it. I remembered what had happened to Tibbett and to Grace Moore in Hollywood. If I signed with a studio, I would be jeopardizing a dependable career for something illusive and untried."

In the end he tested for Metro, ten days after his concert. His test was made with Maureen O'Sullivan, in a scene from *The Barretts of Wimpole Street*. Miss O'Sullivan was in costume and Nelson said his lines in his business suit. The footage was directed by Felix Feist, who was then directing shorts and tests at Metro (and later shot the famous *Every Sunday*, featuring Judy Garland and Deanna Durbin). Nelson's scene was shot fifty-eight times, but it was still terrible. Feist finally suggested that Nelson stop trying to act and just look into the camera and sing "On the Road to Mandalay."

Even after the fiasco at MGM, RKO wanted him and offered a contract with attractive terms. His first role was to be in a picture called *Melody Cruise*. Nelson signed his RKO contract on a Saturday night. Monday morning he reported to the studio, only to be told that he was now on half salary. All actors had been forced to take a pay cut. "I'm not an actor, I'm a singer," Nelson pointed out. "I went into the movies for the money. Nothing except the money will keep me in them." He was fired on the spot and was replaced by Phil Harris.

Having signed a movie contract, Nelson had already sent telegrams canceling the seventeen remaining concert dates on this tour. Now he sent wires advising that he would fulfill the dates, then booked passage on a train that was leaving Los Angeles in twenty minutes. He couldn't get out of town fast enough.

"I decided that now is not the logical time to go into the pictures," he said diplomatically while being interviewed in Boise, Idaho. "I've acquired an awful habit in Hollywood. I have a Hollywood haircut and overcoat and accent. By the time I get home the haircut will be grown out, the coat spotted and if the accent is not cleared up my mother will see to that."

While still on tour, Nelson received an unsettling telegram from MGM: they still wanted to sign him up. Nelson was tempted because they were offering $1,200 a week and were willing to work around his concert commitments. In fact, he wouldn't even have to report at the studio until June.

Nelson took his time thinking it over. He didn't want to be a movie star, but he knew that appearing in pictures would boost his concert appearances and the money he could command. "I didn't know whether to sign it [the MGM contract] or not, but while I was thinking about it, my agents practically did it for me."

In April 1933, it was announced that Nelson had joined the MGM roster. His first film, depending on which press release you read, would be either *I Married an Angel*, *The Prisoner of Zenda* or *The Duchess of Delmonaco*. In each case his proposed co-star was Jeanette MacDonald. Jeanette had just signed an MGM contract herself, in Europe, and was still there on an extended concert tour.

Nelson reported to the studio on June 1, 1933, ready to work. He took a suite at the Ambassador Hotel while searching for a house to rent. "For the first two weeks I was at the studio, everyone was most cordial to me. Then I began to observe that I was being left pretty much to myself. I learned that after seeing my screen tests some of the executives and directors had decided that I gave little promise. A casting director—now no longer with the studio—said that if I got a good part it would be over his dead body."

He requested to see Louis B. Mayer, the studio head, to find out what had happened to all those empty promises of starring roles. There he was subjected to a performance by Mayer that was deserving of an Oscar. His new boss told him in sweet tones that musicals were "out" right now, and that he could fill the empty time by taking acting lessons. In addition, he also insisted that Nelson be seen publicly escorting the many studio starlets, in order to ensure the appearance of his name in the press. When Nelson told him, "I want to sing, not run an escort service," Mayer suddenly launched into a sob sister act, weeping and wringing his hands, telling Nelson how he was his father now, and how important it was for him to do this little thing for him.

Nelson walked out of the office, ready to pack his bags and leave. "We'll see if I get fired," he said. "But if I do, I've got another ace in the hole; I'll sing in Wagnerian opera."

Instead of being fired he was put to work in three unbilled roles; he sang "Bicycle Built for Two" in a Pete Smith short, he had a fleeting moment on-screen as Jean Harlow's husband, and he sang for a Laurel and Hardy film called *Hollywood Party*, but his number was cut. The following month, he performed two numbers for *The March of Time*: "When Irish Eyes Are Smiling" and "In the Garden of My Dreams." He also tested for two roles—the Swedish and the Spanish lovers—in Greta Garbo's *Queen Christina*. While waiting between shots he sat on the sidelines of the set and sang at the top of his lungs.

"I'm drawing a monthly salary for doing nothing," he complained. "I hate to stand still." While marking time at the studio, he continued to perform in concerts, which were vital to him. "I would like to reach a state where the spirit of my country would breathe through me to my audience just as the spirit of Italy sprang from the throat of Caruso; the spirit of Russia from that of Chaliapin."

During the filming of *Hollywood Party*, Nelson experimented for the first time with doing four-part harmony in recording. He cut some records of himself singing bass, baritone, first and second tenor, and distributed the results to people in the cast. "I started by making a quartet number, which was comparatively simple," he said. "In fact, we thought of using it in the picture. Then, experimenting further, I found that a chorus was perfectly feasible. All it needs is a good recording apparatus and a range in voice."

Finally in August he was given a job in which he received billing. The picture was called *Dancing Lady* and the stars were Clark Gable and Joan Crawford. Both Nelson and another new MGM contractee, Fred Astaire, had small roles. Nelson sang a number called "Rhythm of the Day" in the film's finale, and was on-screen less than three minutes.

His second billed walk-on came that same summer when he sang "In the Garden of My Heart" in a picture called *Broadway to Hollywood*. It starred Alice Brady, Frank Morgan and a very young Mickey Rooney. Nelson, who had been put on a diet immediately upon joining the studio, looked thin and serious in his brief moment before the camera. He had cause to: except for one minute on-screen, the majority of his singing took place off-camera and was drowned out by an angry argument between the two main characters.

And that was that. No other films were forthcoming.

To pass the days Nelson took up sports such as tennis and swimming. In the mornings he reported to the studio and drank coffee in the commissary. He wasn't allowed to eat too much—Mayer had put him on his famous "chicken soup diet," which was just that. Nelson grumbled that he was a singer, not a movie star, and he needed his food. He tried several times to bribe the girl in the commissary to sneak him a sandwich or some sweets, but to no avail. Nelson's "warden" in the commissary always felt that Nelson disliked her because she wouldn't be bribed. However, when, years later, her husband fell ill, Nelson gave her $20,000 for the necessary operation. From then on she could never say enough about Nelson's kindness and generosity.

In any case, the diet was effective: in *Dancing Lady* he looked plump; by *Broadway to Hollywood* (which was released first, thereby his "official" film debut), he was his slimmest ever in Hollywood. Nelson liked to hang out in the commissary even if he couldn't eat because, if he was lucky, he'd run into his newest friend, Clark Gable, whom he had met while working on *Dancing Lady*. Through Gable, Nelson also became friends with Jean Harlow.

Of Hollywood, Nelson said, "The people are grand. Of course there are all kinds. But I managed to make many good friends. Clark Gable is the swellest guy." He added cynically, "Publicity is Hollywood's religion. Get your name in the paper—*no matter how* is the slogan."

Nelson and Gable had a lot in common. They were the same age, they liked nature, and they were both mavericks. Gable had heard how Nelson stood up to Mayer, and was pleased to see that Nelson was "a regular guy." He included Nelson in some hunting trips, went skeet shooting with him and introduced him to his friends, one of whom was actor Gene Raymond, who had played second lead in Gable's 1932 smash hit, *Red Dust*.

While Gable admired Nelson's integrity he was amused by his naivete. Nelson was so serious about everything. He made immature statements like "I'm not used to this type of life; I'm a serious singer." He wasn't a drinker, he seemed overwhelmed by the availability of young women, he was angered by the phoniness he observed in the business, and seemed in general "a fish out of water." Gable set about to loosen him up a bit and show him the ropes.

Despite Nelson's resolve, once he started hanging around Gable he began to pick up some of the Hollywood lingo, using words like "broads," "dames," "kiddo," and the four-letter variety that would have made his mother cringe. "Gable used slang twenty years before it was fashionable," Nelson remarked in the 1950s. "Words like 'fab,' 'hip' and 'groovy,' and sometimes it took some doing to figure out what he was saying. He was way before his time."

The two men discussed women and Nelson gave Gable his version of his sexual history: "For a while there it got too much. I was trying to study singing and getting laid every night, mostly by married women with their husbands gunning for me half the time. It seriously interfered with my goals. It got to the point where I had to stop and make a decision whether I was going to spend my life fooling around or singing."

"You sing pretty good," Gable quipped.

Nelson reassured him that he hadn't taken any vow of celibacy. There were many affairs, including his brief reunion with Maybelle Marston, his liaison with Lila Lee, Alice Brady and others but they were mostly short-lived. By November 1933, Nelson was tired of the "empty-heads."

"I don't want just dames," he told Gable. "I want one girl who's mine, all mine."

6

An unplanned child

Movie stars of the 1930s were subject to their early lives being fictionalized by the studio publicity department, and Jeanette MacDonald was no exception. Not only were four years cut off her birth date, she was immortalized as a virginal angel. "I am not the angelic creature I represent to a certain faction," she protested as late as 1962, but her denial fell on deaf ears; after decades of exposure to her studio image, her fans refused to accept any other version of Jeanette MacDonald.

Her tall, red-headed father Daniel McDonald was a building contractor by trade. Daniel struggled to find work because "the Irish weren't treated well in Philadelphia back then," according to Jeanette's first cousin Esther Shipp. Daniel's mother Jeanette Johnstone was from Scotland, and it was in deference to her that Daniel legally changed the family name to *Mac*Donald before he met his wife.

Daniel married Anna Mae Wright in February 1893. At year's end their first daughter Elsie Wallace was born. Edith Blossom, known as Blossom, followed shortly after in 1895. (Elsie and Blossom were less than honest about their age. Their correct birth dates, as recorded in the baptismal records, are [Elsie] December 17, 1893, and [Blossom] August 21, 1895.) The family lived at 3313 Wallace Street, in a middle-class neighborhood in Philadelphia. Later the MacDonalds moved into a home which Daniel himself built, a red brick house at 5123 Arch Street in West Philadelphia. Daniel's sister Marie lived with the family, as did his

Jeanette's parents, Anna Wright and Daniel McDonald (he later changed it to MacDonald).

invalid father Charles. The extent of Daniel's success in the construction business is unclear. Legend has it that Daniel contracted the entire housing development where they lived; more likely he only managed the wood framing company which built it. Anna MacDonald seemed to verify this by stating in an interview that her husband was "manager of a lumber company."

Though not affluent, the MacDonald household was a happy one. "They always had white poodle dogs," recalled Katherine Rice Pickens, Jeanette's cousin. "I remember going there for dinner and they had chicken pot pie. And as a little girl I thought this was a great place to visit because they gave you pie. The mother was a very good cook. Whatever you were going to have for dinner she put on a blackboard in the kitchen so you knew ahead of time what you were getting."

"Uncle Dan MacDonald was the only uncle who ever used 'bad words' in front of me when I was a small boy," recalled another of Jeanette's cousins, Charles Wright. "Aunt Annie would say, 'Now, Dan!' and he would promise to watch his language, but he never did. Actually, he had such a sense of fun that I liked him very much. He enjoyed practical jokes, such as allowing me to pick up and start to eat a camphor ball when I was very small, thinking it candy. I think it was this sense of humor which affected all three of the girls." A single photo has survived of Daniel MacDonald, posed with his wife. It shows a lanky man, mustached and balding, staring grimly at the camera. His heavyset wife is also unsmiling, a pince-nez perched on her nose. Neither is particularly handsome, nor does Jeanette resemble them much, though she did inherit her father's red hair and large eyes. Of the three daughters, she was by far the prettiest.

The young Jeanette.

Jeannette Anna McDonald (original spelling) was born at the Arch Street residence on June 18, 1903. No birth certificate survives, and the false 1907 birth date even appears on her crypt. However, her baptism record from the Olivet Presbyterian church verifies the 1903 date. Her school records, the 1910 census, and early reviews also gave her true age. Various sources over the years have incorrectly stated Jeanette's birth date as 1901, 1902, 1904 and 1906.

Her birth was unplanned, and over the years Anna MacDonald made no secret that her youngest daughter was 'the little mistake.' Jeanette always resented her mother's comments about her unwanted birth. As late as 1930, Anna MacDonald told an interviewer, 'My two oldest daughters, Elsie and Blossom, were no longer babies and I was just breathing a sigh of relief over my lessened responsibilities as a mother when I discovered that my family was not yet completed. But I simply applied the old adage 'Everything happens for the best,' and began making plans for the new baby.'' All three girls showed early musical inclination, but since Jeanette was so much younger than her sisters, she had to work double-time to grab any limelight. "There were no actors or actresses in our family," Jeanette later commented. "My father was a contract builder who later drifted into politics. Mother was just a wife and mother.

"Our entire family held to an unusually conventional and religious viewpoint," Jeanette recalled. She was raised as a Presbyterian and attended the Tennent Presbyterian Church at the corner of Fifty-first and Arch streets. It was there that Jeanette made her "debut" at the tender age of three by singing at the church social. Blossom remembered that Jeanette was so disappointed in the lack of applause for her song that she clapped for herself. At a very young age Jeanette was driven to prove herself, to be the best, and she demonstrated a powerful need to please and impress her mother.

It was in fact Elsie MacDonald who was considered something of a child prodigy; she learned to play the piano by ear while scarcely a toddler. And Blossom, who dreamed of being a dancer, was the prize-winning dance pupil in Philadelphia's largest school. Little Jeanette, who was always closest to Blossom, learned to dance and emulate her sister, but her goal was always to be a singer. "Jeanette was a darling baby—big-eyed and of sunny disposition," said Anna. "Oh, she wasn't too good to be true—she managed to get into enough mischief so that we were well aware of her existence." But, she added, "when most babies her age were crying, she was singing. She had a toy piano and she would sit on the porch and play it and sing by the hour to her grandfather—and to the neighbors."

From early childhood Jeanette was obsessed with the idea of going on the stage. "At the age of four," she remembered, "I gravely informed neighbors that I would someday be a 'great singer and take care of mama.' At six, I was talking about what I would do with my first earnings. It seemed, then, I would use the money to buy mother a gold bed and myself a pony. A few weeks later I was thrown by a pony and my desire to own one vanished. Mother has never had a gold bed either."

On days when Anna took her youngest daughter to the park to play, Jeanette loudly concertized from the sandbox. A park caretaker told Anna, "I've been here a long time and I've seen plenty of them sing but I never saw such a little one sing and never heard anyone sing so loud." He introduced Anna MacDonald to someone who arranged for Jeanette to make her first recording. "The record was made when she was about five or six years old," recalled Jeanette's aunt Henrietta Wright. "The superintendent of the Smith Memorial Playground, in Fairmont Park, recorded the voice of an old man and then Jeanette's, each singing 'Nearer My God to Thee.' Then he ran the records off, pointing out the contrast between the old and young voices." Anna MacDonald added, "Voice recording was not the art then that it is today but the reproduction wasn't bad. Years later we tried to locate that record but it had been broken."

"I can't remember as far back as when I first began to sing," Jeanette said, "nor is it known where I picked up the word 'opera.' I sang in all languages—at least, what I fondly imagined were many languages. The operas did not exist any more than did the words I invented. Yet wearing mama's apron to help with the dishes or sitting on the front porch banging away at a toy piano, I always sang at the top of my lungs.

"Some of my songs were taught me by my older sisters before I could read the words and music. Others I picked up from listening to a neighbor's gramophone while hanging on the fence. The majority, however, were of my own improvising.

"When we finally had a gramophone of our own, my joy knew no bounds. I played for hours old cylinder records of great stars of the day—Galli-Curci, Schumann-Heink, Tetrazzini—singing along with them. The records were worn out with playing long before I heard my first opera [*Tosca*] when I was almost seventeen."

Her sisters, in spite of their own ambitions, were helpful in initiating Jeanette's career. "Elsie taught me to sing little melodies while she played my accompaniments. Blossom taught me simple dance steps to the music of gramophone discs. I remember once when I went to dancing school with mother to call for Blossom, she insisted that I sing for the teacher. She wanted to 'show off' her little sister. I sang—and the teacher invited me to sing at the annual school recital. That was a big moment." After that performance, Jeanette had re-asserted that she was "going to sing songs on the stage all the time when she grew up."

Jeanette was rarely called by her first name in childhood. She had an assortment of nicknames, including "Jessie," "Jeanie," "Jimmie," "Jenny," "Jam" (her initials), and "Jim-Jam."

At six, Jeanette decided it was time for her to follow in her sisters' footsteps and go to dance school. "I thrived on their accomplishments," she said of Elsie and Blossom. "The whole family was so proud of them. I thought they were the most wonderful girls in the world. I was just young enough to be a hero worshipper." When her parents refused to send her to dance school, arguing that she was too young, Jeanette ran away from home. She was brought back home at four A.M. by Casey, the butter-and-egg man, but not before her frantic parents had notified both the police and fire departments. Shortly after this misadventure the independent child was allowed to join Blossom's dancing class, which apparently cured her wanderlust.

Each summer the dance director, James Littlefield, took a small group of his best pupils on a tour of Eastern resort towns to appear in the "Kiddie Revues." It was every girl's goal to be chosen for this tour, and Jeanette decided she wanted to go. During her second year at the school she was indeed chosen to join the troupe as a member of the dancing chorus, and she embarked on her first road tour at the tender age of seven. By the end of the season she was the star of the company.

The 1909 programs of the Kiddie Revues list their roster; along with six-year-old Jeanette, there was Ann Pennington (who went on to act on Broadway and in films) and the Littlefields' daughter, Catherine (who later became the premier danseuse of the Philadelphia Opera Company, where Nelson Eddy first sang). While Jeanette starred as Mother Hubbard, dressed in kilts, and singing a Scotch song, her older sisters were both relegated to bit parts in the show. It was a pattern the MacDonald sisters got used to.

Mrs. Minnie Barry, who costumed the children's show at the Philadelphia Academy of Music, remembered how Jeanette "brought down the house" with her Scotch ballad, but almost drove everyone out with the number called "Maybe It's a Bear." "Jeanette used to huddle in the corner at rehearsals during the bear number," Mrs. Barry said. "She knew the bear was only Mr. Littlefield in a bearskin, but as soon as he would put on the bear head, little Jeanette's imagination ran away with her. She never could seem to get herself to trust the animal. Thought maybe it might be a really-truly bear after all. Catherine Little-field, who was not quite three years old, danced while Jeanette sang to the bear, and both children had promised before they stepped out on the stage that they wouldn't be afraid. But when the bear growled, Catherine jumped clean across the footlights and Jeanette ran off the stage mid-song."

To make matters worse, Jeanette had been so excited about her performance that she'd somehow lost her gold bracelet at rehearsal. Blossom, even from childhood Jeanette's self-professed protector, was scolded for the loss of the bracelet. But Blossom made it up; that very night she earned a $2.50 prize by performing a song and dance at the Nixen Theater contest, and used the money to purchase a replacement.

Jeanette seemed, in general, plainly frustrated at being "just a child," and sometimes this led to complications within her family. It was on very rare occasions that Jeanette squabbled with Blossom, but when she did the fireworks really flew. And Jeanette also ran into trouble with Elsie on occasion. "I remember she was about seven," Elsie said. "As most kids do, she delighted in dressing up in my clothes and playing 'lady.' She always tried on my party dresses, my hats and shoes. Again and again I forbade her to touch my belongings. She'd pin things up and trip over the hems. One day when I got home from school she was hobbling around in my opera pumps. They didn't fit her little feet and they were all out of shape. I laid down the law with vehemence—she was so hurt and angry *she* slapped *my* face!"

Hardest for Jeanette was when her age interfered with her career as a "grand opera star." While appearing in several "pop" shows at the Pennsylvania Railroad YMCA, she sang a solo called "Take Me Up with You, Dearie." During the number a boy was lowered in a toy airplane, Jeanette climbed in, and the two of them joined in a duet as the plane "flew" away. After a successful run at the YMCA, the troupe acted in nickelodeon theaters in the area, which led to a theater tour—but Jeanette was forced to forego the tour because of her age. No one was more upset than she.

Though Jeanette's cousins recalled that the MacDonalds' marriage seemed a happy one, the dominant one in the relationship was without a doubt Anna. She criticized her husband's "fraternizing" with his construction crews, his eating lunch with them and discussing politics with them. Anna argued, "How can you maintain discipline? How can you make them feel your authority when you become so definitely one of them?" Clearly, she wanted bigger and better things for her husband, but Daniel MacDonald was not destined to be successful in the way Anna foresaw it. Herbert Ohmies, whose brother Jack dated Jeanette in 1923, recalled meeting the entire MacDonald family. "They all were at our home for an afternoon visit, followed by dinner," Ohmies recalled. He went on to describe Daniel MacDonald as "a pleasant enough man but rather on the mediocre side. I gathered he had a managerial position with a building supply company and sort of fit the image: not too self-possessing, and dominated by Mrs. MacDonald. When he and dad were alone, conversing, he did not lend much to the conversation, was somewhat ill-at-ease and appeared a bit out of his element. He loved his family, was proud of his daughters and was providing for them all to the best of his ability. But he was a plain man, and did not project a particularly successful image. Jeanette and he did not seem to be very close, for some reason."

Anna, not Daniel, was the disciplinarian in the household, often displaying the Victorian values under which she was raised. "She was very strict," said Katherine Pickens. Jeanette recalled many times when she was sent from the dinner table "for giggling." On one occasion when Anna caught her in a lie, Jeanette's mouth was washed out with castile soap. And Blossom recalled her mother's version of "the birds and the bees": according to Anna, sex was an unpleasant act desired only by men and never enjoyable for the woman. "Mother basically said you had to let the man have his way with you," Blossom said. "I was sixteen when I first did it. I tried to remember all that Mother had told me but, darn it, I couldn't help myself—I enjoyed it!"

▆▆▆Although not much is known about Daniel's attitude, one may suppose he did protest his youngest daughter's becoming an entertainer. But his opinions were overruled by Anna, who became the number-one driving force behind the girls' careers (and who in later years proved herself a formidable presence in Jeanette's life). "When we talked, as little girls, about going on the stage, Mother and Dad encouraged us," Jeanette remembered. "I shall always be grateful for that, because so many parents ruin promising careers because of their own other-generation ideas."

Whatever the case, Jeanette was a seasoned performer. "She had a magnificent voice even then," remembered Mrs. Barry. "She was a lovely child, always quite a little lady." Al White, who was her dancing instructor, said, "Jeanette and her sisters were taking lessons from me then and all three appeared in a children's carnival I staged at the old South Broad Street Theatre. Jeanette had a beautiful soprano voice and could reach high C without difficulty. Sometimes Jeanette would sing at recitals and concerts. I think the salary used to go as high as two dollars on those occasions."

Jeanette performed for anyone, anywhere: "I fully expected to entertain whenever visitors called. Knowing I would be asked, I was prepared. I faced my small audience in the parlor with greater assurance than I have been able to muster for any audience since."

While still a pre-teen, Jeanette attained her full height of five feet five inches. Tall and skinny, she earned some new nicknames at school: "Beanpole" and "Broomstick Legs."

"Growing up was torture," she said. "I shot up like a weed, all at once. It seemed I would never stop. Every day I measured my height. I was so afraid I would be too tall—I had heard somewhere that actresses must be small. [And] being teased about my size was no help to my feelings. I never let on that I was hurt. Then, when they began to point to my 'skinny' legs and tease me about being awkward, I nearly died of shame. Mother consoled me only indirectly for fear too much pampering would make me vain and conceited. She preached that everything would come out for the best."

Jeanette had little interest in formal studies, and her grades reflected it. "I enjoyed grammar school," she later said, "but I hated high school [because] when I entered I was working as a dancer, and school was thereafter only a nuisance. I was mildly conscious of English and French. I got a 52 in Algebra. When the teacher conferred with me about that I said I didn't even see why Algebra existed. She admitted she didn't know either, but didn't I want to pass? I replied, 'Only because I'll have to go through all this again if I don't!' She passed me on my promise not to tell anyone my low grade." Jeanette's cousin Esther Shipp also remembered that Jeanette failed French, a language in which she later sang and spoke well.

Jeanette's school experience was further muddied by an unpleasant teacher who brought charges to the Board of Education in an effort to have her career squelched. Jeanette and her parents were literally interrogated about their lifestyle. "As long as I live," Jeanette said, "I shall never forget the indignity of standing there before those people and answering the insinuating questions they put to me. I could hardly speak, I was trembling with such rage when they asked if Father beat me, if Mother beat me and if they took the money I earned away from me by force. I couldn't understand what it was all about. We had such fun with the act, Mother and I! And now we were almost all criminals. Answering those impudent questions put by total strangers while that woman sat on the sidelines and smirked. How I hated her! Yet I felt she hated me equally as much. Who painted my face? When did I go to bed? Did I ever see grown people smoking and drinking? Had I heard any 'bad language'?" To this last question, Jeanette hotly answered, "No, but I hear plenty from the boys in the schoolyard!"

Jeanette was understandably outraged by the questioning. "I suppose I answered the questions satisfactorily. At least, the report that came back stated that the board found me a very nice little girl and that my education had not suffered and that I had been exposed to no unmoral influences."

The same teacher made one last effort to ruin Jeanette's budding career. Al White remembered, "The kids were so good, some of them, that I organized a 'Kidland' act and took them to the Minor's Bronx Theatre in New York one Sunday night. Jeanette was only eleven and you had to be fifteen to play on a stage, so we borrowed a birth certificate for her. She was tall for her age and probably could have passed for fifteen."

But when Jeanette and her mother arrived in Manhattan they learned that Jeanette would not be allowed to perform. An unsigned telegram to the theater had revealed her true age. Al White said, "A cop came backstage and shook his finger at her and asked, 'Young lady, how old are you?'—stern, like that. Well, Jeanette just looked up, smiled, and answered, 'I'm eleven, sir.'"

Jeanette returned to Philadelphia, her career temporarily curtailed, "but it wasn't over, by any means," said White. "Two years later I put her out in a little act called 'Al White's Song Birds,' and we played most of the vaudeville houses in the city that season. It was a novelty act with three boys and three girls—it didn't take Jeanette long to become its star. She had a lot of talent, that kid, and created a sensation everywhere she went. Jeanette was with the act about a year while still going to the Dunlap Public School."

Jeanette next attended the West Philadelphia High School for Girls, where she began to demonstrate her dual nature—assured and eager while performing, emotionally insecure offstage. "As a child, I grew up much too fast," she said. "I was always several sizes larger than my classmates in school and, as a result, I had to play with older girls or seem mountainous among those of my own age. Naturally I chose the older ones.

"Being the youngest in a crowd of girls often helps to make advancement more rapid, but just as often it develops an inferiority complex and causes a child to become self-conscious. I was frightfully self-conscious, particularly about my physical appearance. I was gawky and no amount of dancing lessons seemed able to cure my awkwardness. My face was long and horrible freckled. There were wide spaces between my teeth and I thought my nose too large. But worst of all were my legs. They were veritable pipe stems, no shape, just length.

"Some of these defects I outgrew without effort . . . We all suffer more intensely in childhood than we do in maturity."

Jeanette was indisputably boy crazy throughout her childhood years, and very early on she found herself embroiled in romantic crises. Her first love, Raymond Scott, was a grammar school infatuation to whom Jeanette wrote passionate love letters which she threw at him in class. One day she wrote the ultimate love letter —one she had copied from the front page of a newspaper—and hurled it at Raymond, but it hit the teacher instead. Jeanette was sent home as punishment.

Another young fellow, Jack Graugh, fell for Jeanette. Unfortunately, Jack was also friends with Raymond, and the classical triangle erupted into violence. While the two boys were doing target practice with a .22 in the basement of Jack's house, Jack "accidentally" shot Raymond in the leg. Although the wound wasn't serious, Jeanette knew she'd been the source of the jealousy and thereafter vowed "to be good and not stick her tongue out at anybody." She also decided, briefly, to become a nun, which was typical of her "full speed ahead" temperament.

Her own first teenaged date was a fiasco. She was to attend a classmate's birthday party but had no one to escort her because she was too tall. Finally the birthday gal lined up a date for her, a boy named Freddy. Jeanette dressed for the big event. As the minutes passed and Freddy was becoming late, Jeanette went downstairs repeatedly to try to convince her mother to let her wear one of Blossom's beautiful lace dresses instead of the girlish one she had on. Each time Anna refused. At 10:30 P.M. Jeanette realized she'd been stood up, and ran upstairs to cry herself to sleep.

The next day she saw Freddy on the school grounds. When she demanded to know why he'd stood her up he told her to "go to hell." Years later, when she was on the stage, the very same Freddy called her to ask her out on a date.

"Do you remember what you yelled at me one day at school?" Jeanette asked.

"I told you to go to hell, didn't I?"

"That's right," Jeanette responded, "and now I'm telling *you* to go to hell!"

■■■Jeanette always claimed perfect family harmony, but when she was in her teens the older girls rebelled. They felt stifled by their mother's strict career guidelines for them, in which romance and marriage could play no part. Anna seemed determined to rise above her middle-class situation vicariously through her daughters.

First Blossom dropped out of high school. "I was too busy with weekend jobs singing and dancing. When I was ten, I was working in Scranton, Pennsylvania, on weekends in a little singing and dancing act. Elsie played the piano and I sang. I was crazy about show business, but Mother said I would have to prove I could hold a job and make a living . . . so I entered Bank's Business College to learn shorthand and got a job that paid eight dollars a week. I kept up with my singing and dancing engagements at night and on the weekends. One day I went with my kid sister Jeanette to investigate a show they were casting in Philadelphia. I did my act, they asked my name and said they might have a part for me. Next day a man came around the house and asked if this is where Blossom MacDonald lives? I had a week's vacation coming, so I took it, joined the show, intending to return to my job if things didn't work out. I never went back to the job, but I'm glad I learned shorthand!"

Elsie was sent to a finishing school called Beechwood. In 1910, when she was seventeen, she shocked her parents by getting pregnant and eloping with a sailor, Earl Krout. "My family was heartbroken," Jeanette remembered. "They tried to hide their anger from me. Elsie was in too big of a hurry to wait for a career . . . That night mother took Blossom and me upstairs, put her arms around us and asked us to promise that we wouldn't get married as long as she or Dad lived—without first asking their judgment in the matter, or without at least telling them about it. I made that promise very solemnly."

Anna finally made peace with Elsie, but not before warning her: "You can't have both marriage and a career. Since you've chosen marriage, the thing to do is to make it as great a success as possible." Elsie was unimpressed by Anna's preaching. This would be the first of three marriages for her, and she eventually had a rewarding career as well, running a school of dance in Upper Darby, Pennsylvania. Elsie had a son, Earl Krout, Jr., by her first husband. After they divorced, her son was given her middle name Wallace as his surname, and he has since been known as Earl Wallace. Elsie's second husband was Al Ward, who came into the marriage with a son. In 1939 Elsie wed Bernard Scheiter. They had no children, but the marriage was successful.

Anna soon saw the handwriting on the wall with Blossom as well. Though a talented dancer and comedienne, Blossom in womanhood did not have the looks to become a star. Herbert Ohmies remarked, "Blossom . . . was a very articulate, vivacious girl, not particularly good-looking but very personable and fun to be with . . . full of gaiety, witty." He described Elsie as a "rather stout, older-looking person, quite different from the other girls and a bit on the 'coarse' side . . . She did not appear to have the polish the others had."

Therefore, Anna trained her sights on Jeanette, reminding her over and over that marriage and a career didn't mix. Any feelings of desire were considered a weakness, any man unlucky enough to fall in love with Jeanette would find himself playing a poor second fiddle to her ambitions. Her career was to be her only passion. It's sad to note that at the end of her life Jeanette publicly admitted she'd made a mistake in her choice of sacrificing romance for her career.

In 1919, Blossom MacDonald struck out on her own. She moved by herself to New York, took a place in a theatrical rooming house and landed her first job dancing on Broadway in a flop called *Vogues and Frolics*. Her second show, *Dearie*, was also a failure. Undaunted, Blossom took work as a secretary while she continued to audition for her next dancing job, which came quickly. In July, she was hired for the dancing chorus for Ned Wayburn's *The Demi-Tasse Revue*. Wayburn at that time was one of the most important figures in the dancing world. He was under personal contract to Ziegfeld and staged many shows besides his own. He also ran what was probably the most successful dance studio on the East Coast.

Jeanette was thrilled at Blossom's success and she begged her parents to let her go to New York, too. Daniel finally agreed to a brief visit. His career was on the slide. He'd abandoned the construction business for a try at politics, which, according to Jeanette, "did not last long." Daniel hoped that, perhaps, he could make a new start in the Big Apple.

Daniel and Jeanette arrived in New York in September 1919, and Jeanette immediately went to work on Blossom, begging her to set up an audition for her with Ned Wayburn.

The *Revue*'s lead was Mae West (who performed a number called "Vampires" and sashayed around the stage singing "Oh, What a Moanin' Man"), and the dancers had all been hired. But Wayburn was still looking to cast a youngster for the part of an Indian girl. Blossom boldly informed Wayburn that she had a young sister who could play the part. She lied about Jeanette's age, knocking off four years, and Wayburn agreed to audition her.

Blossom dressed Jeanette up in her own clothes, and they went to the Capitol Theater. Jeanette watched her sister join the other dancers for a rehearsal. "The whole thing seemed like fairyland," she said, "something I had dreamed of in a vague sort of way, but never hoped to really see. Even the fact that my sister was among those other girls did not bring me back to reality.

"By the time Wayburn called for a rest, I had convinced myself that never again would I be completely happy without making the scene I had just witnessed a part of my life. I didn't like the role of bystander. I must either become a part of it or never again set foot inside a stage door."

Blossom reminded Wayburn that Jeanette was there, and she led her suddenly frightened little sister onto the stage. Wayburn, whom Jeanette later described as "my first skeptic," was "an enormously tall man. Dreadfully near-sighted. He wore very thick glasses. I later learned he was a taskmaster who terrified most of the company." Wayburn asked Jeanette to do a time-step. For a moment Jeanette went blank and couldn't remember what a time-step was. Then when she did start to dance she kicked too hard and fell into the orchestra pit.

Wayburn hired her because, Blossom said, "He thought she'd be a good comic." Her role consisted of sitting in the middle of the stage and getting hit over the head with a coffee can.

With her parents' blessings, Jeanette moved in with Blossom. Wayburn took her under his wing as well, and let her understudy a larger role. "Wayburn was nothing but kindness to me," Jeanette said, "and made everything quite possible for me to stay and achieve [my] ambition."

In November 1919, Jeanette was enrolled in morning classes at Washington Irving High School. At Blossom's suggestion she suffered through the commercial course, learning typing and shorthand. In February 1920, she transferred briefly to Julia Richman High School but soon dropped out. "It was obvious, since I knew so definitely what I wanted to do, that finishing school would have been a waste of time for me," Jeanette said, adding, "I do not regret missing college. I never wanted to go to one."

Nonetheless, Jeanette felt very much out of place among the other girls in the Wayburn revue. "I could have died when I started to share the big dressing room with the rest of the girls. I still wore cotton underwear. I wore the shirt and bloomers which were quite a contrast to what they were wearing! . . . As I began to undress the other girls would go into hysterics." When she received her first paycheck, she spent it all on lacy underwear. "It was with a great deal of pleasure that I went to the theater the next day and stripped before the girls!"

The Capitol Theater had its grand opening on October 24, 1919. Wayburn's *Demi-Tasse Revue* was the headliner before the premiere of a new Douglas Fairbanks picture, *His Majesty, the American*. Together, the two productions ran four hours long. Jeanette not only played the Indian maiden, she got to dance in the finale with Blossom and twenty-six other girls. Years later Jeanette confided that she'd felt guilty that her role was more showy than Blossom's. Jeanette always gave Blossom credit for launching her career, and the two sisters were so close that there was never any trace of resentment between them.

Five days into the run of the *Revue*, Wayburn started making cast changes. Mae West, who'd missed two days (supposedly due to tonsillitis) was dropped. Some weeks later the show was replaced by a slightly altered program entitled *Song Scenes*. Jeanette no longer played an Indian maiden, but she sang and danced in two new numbers. The show ran in its revised form until January 1920, when Wayburn had a falling out with the directors of the Capitol Theater. Suddenly Blossom and Jeanette were out of work, and they moved in with their parents, who had taken an apartment at 383 Central Park West.

"When I first went to New York I was all eyes and teeth," Jeanette said. "I didn't have beauty nor self-confidence nor glamour nor training nor pull. I did have ambition, I did have the physical energy to move the body from place to place. I did not sit and mope and pine and say, 'Oh, well, of course it was different for Jenny Lind!' "

Jeanette learned through Ned Wayburn that another Broadway producer named Charles Dillingham needed a replacement dancer for Jerome Kern's new show, *The Night Boat*, in Buffalo. For her audition Jeanette arrived late—on purpose. "Eight girls didn't make it," she recalled. "I went in even though his office was closed. A young janitor didn't want to let me in, so I played a little game with him. I told him how important I was, my name, my reputation, and with a smile he opened the door."

Jeanette asked to see Mr. Dillingham and was told that he wasn't seeing any more applicants. Then, tipped off by Ned Wayburn, she looked around for a door marked "Store Room." She marched over to it, opened it, and faced a startled, bald man seated behind a big desk.

"I'm looking for Mr. Dillingham," Jeanette demanded.

"You got your wish," he replied.

Jeanette later laughed, "He was so surprised at my audacity, he hired me." She understudied one of the leads, a young woman who had been ill, but when the actress recovered, Dillingham had to let Jeanette go. She refused to be fired, offering to understudy all *four* female leads for the price of one. Dillingham thought about it, and could only say yes. "The Buffalo run was without accident," Jeanette recalled, "but when the show moved into New York one of the leads fell downstairs and was so badly injured she was forced to leave the cast. I stepped into the role with only a few hours' notice."

The Night Boat was a successful Broadway show and ran for a total of 148 performances. The year 1920 was a good one for theater; there were 146 plays produced, and the average show ran about 98 performances. The most popular shows were the grand musicals.

Jeanette next landed the second female lead in the long-running *Irene*, which toured the cities of Pittsburgh, Cleveland, Cincinnati and Chicago until May 1921. Her mother accompanied Jeanette as chaperone all the while. Upon her return to New York, Jeanette immediately began searching for another play, demanding at least $100 a week. "I always tried to get a better job than the one I had before," she said. From other comments she made in interviews, it seemed she was now, at just nineteen, the major breadwinner for the family. And indeed she was.

Though no longer in school, Jeanette continued dance and voice lessons. She'd studied dance with Ned Wayburn until he recommended she work with Albertina Rasch, a noted Vienna-born teacher then married to a struggling young violinist named Dimitri Tiomkin. Rasch later choreographed many dance numbers for MGM.

Rasch was a tough teacher. "I well remember my sufferings under her sharp scolding and her whacks at my knee," said Jeanette, "but I had to learn what she had to give me, and in time my knees kept straight and I got no more whacks. Had it been necessary for me to study trapeze techniques, I would have done that, too!

"I attribute my own rise in the theater largely to the fact that I was an excellent dancer long before my voice was recognized. 'They' discouraged me about singing. 'They' said I was crazy. I became a featured dancer on Broadway; but I went ahead with dancing only because my singing was temporarily stalled. The only thing I have ever wanted to do in my life was to sing. But, as I look back over my career, I can see that it is the one thing on which I received absolutely no encouragement. I learned to dance, and worked hard and long and earnestly to become a good dancer, but it was only the means to an end."

Albertina Rasch said in retrospect about her most famous pupil, "Jeanette owes her success to the fact that she works twice as hard as any other star."

During the summer of 1921, Jeanette had no dancing jobs because she refused to work in the chorus. While times were lean she could always count on emotional support from her father. "I think, to be quite frank, my father was more proud of my childhood talents than my mother," said Jeanette. It was during this time that Jeanette began to use henna on her hair and paid more attention than ever to her appearance, so that soon she would be known as "The girl with the red-gold hair and sea-green eyes."

The 1921–22 Broadway season offered meager fare, and box office sales were slow. The biggest hit was *Tangerine*, which opened in August. In September, Jeanette answered an open call and landed the second lead in the show. She was later fired for refusing the advances of one of the show's producers. "I came to the theatre one night and there was my notice posted. I was frantic. I needed that sixty-a-week. I talked it over with the star who told me that the producer was putting in one of his own girls, but [told] me to keep on coming to the theatre, to wait. I waited. The girl was awful. He tried another of his girls and she was even worse. At the end of the week he sent for me again and offered me my job back. The star had advised me what to say. I demanded a raise in salary and a contract. He tried to argue with me but finally laughed and told me I was pretty smart . . . I got the contract and the raise. I remained with that show until it closed."

Tangerine played to full houses through its thirty-fourth week, then ticket sales began to drop. In May 1922, the production closed in New York and took to the road, but Jeanette was fired after trying unsuccessfully to get another raise, arguing that she refused to travel without her mother.

In September of that year Jeanette decided to approach one of the biggest agents in New York, Max Hart, who represented stars like Sophie Tucker, Fanny Brice and Eddie Cantor. Jeanette went to the Palace Theatre Building and took the elevator to Hart's office. On the ride up she noticed a small, middle-aged man staring intently at her. He got off at her floor and asked Jeanette to sing. He gave her his card and told her to come see him if things didn't work out. When Hart didn't take her on, Jeanette contacted her "Mr. J. Baldwin Sloan" who, as it turned out, was the producer of a Greenwich Village show called *The Fantastic Fricassee*. The production had opened to poor reviews and was little more than an amateur show, but Jeanette joined the company. She sang a solo, a torch song called "I've Got the Blues," and a duet, "Waiting for You." Her salary was $60 a week.

The Fantastic Fricassee looked headed for an early death. The New York *Times* referred to it as "an uncooked mess," while the *World* termed it "incredibly dull." Another critic called it the worst show ever in the Village. But in November 1922, a performance that had been scheduled to play for prisoners at Sing Sing prison was canceled by the Prison Reform Association, which announced that the show's "naked dancing girls" would not be allowed to appear before sex-denied prisoners. *The Fantastic Fricassee* subsequently ran for another six weeks, for a total of 112 performances.

As it turned out, Henry Savage, a major Broadway producer, was dragged to the show by one of his managers, Louis Wiswell, and his wife, former singing star and now playwright Zelda Sears. The Wiswells had previously seen the show and felt that Jeanette was right for the ingenue lead in Savage's next musical, *The Magic Ring*. However, Savage, who was later to play an important role in Jeanette's success, wasn't impressed.

The new year, 1923, found Jeanette out of work again. One afternoon she auditioned at the Knickerbocker Theater for another Savage production, the musical *The Left Over* by Vincent Youmans. Youmans later recalled two girls at the audition: "One had gleaming, rich gold hair, the other was a brunette with a cameo profile and an air of elegance." Youmans tried in vain to convince Savage to hire these two girls—Jeanette MacDonald and Irene Dunne.

Then in March, Savage opened auditions for *The Magic Ring*. It was Jeanette's worst audition ever. To begin with the pianist played her number in the wrong key. She asked him to transpose it lower. When he refused, she sang it anyway and cracked on the high note. Her dancing was equally disastrous; frozen with stage fright, she finally ran out of the theater. The next month she received a phone call from Henry Savage's office saying she'd won the role.

The Magic Ring began as a road show entitled *Minnie and Me*, opening in Binghamton, New York, in September. Its star was the popular Mitzie (who had starred in *The Merry Widow* in 1912), one of the male leads was Sydney Greenstreet (of *The Maltese Falcon* fame), and the costumes were designed by Adrian, who later did Jeanette's gowns at MGM. The show ran a lengthy three hours and twenty minutes; later it trimmed down to two hours and forty minutes. *Daily Variety* commented, "Mitzie keeps the audience in gales of laughter. But she doesn't detract from the other pleasing features. Jeanette MacDonald is a sweet singer and she can dance."

At last *The Magic Ring* moved to Broadway on October 1. The show had mixed reviews, but again Jeanette was noted. "Among the other merits of the evening must be listed the appearance and voice of Jeanette MacDonald," noted the *Times*, while the *Tribune* said, "The blonde beauty of Jeanette MacDonald is one of the glowing things to be commemorated." Other reviewers found her "refreshingly naive," "winsome," "strikingly pretty and clear-voiced."

By the second week, *The Magic Ring* was grossing top dollars and Jeanette's salary was raised to $250 a week. She had finally made it as a Broadway starlet.

Anna accompanied Jeanette when the show moved to Boston, but returned home when her husband fell ill. Jeanette stayed on with the show as it moved next to Cincinnati and in July returned to New York. Daniel MacDonald, who'd called Jeanette's voice "the sweetest voice I ever heard," died of heart problems on August 1, 1924, at the age of fifty-five. In his billfold was found a photo of only one of his children, Jeanette.

Anna and Jeanette returned to Philadelphia, where they were met by Elsie and Blossom for the funeral. Afterwards, Jeanette traveled to Chicago for the opening there of *The Magic Ring*. "My greatest regret is that my father did not live to see my success," she said.

Upon returning to New York, the twenty-one-year-old Jeanette took her own apartment at 1030 Cauldwell Avenue in the Bronx. She felt that she was finally breaking free from her mother's influence. She even indulged in her first fur coat. "I could flaunt myself anywhere after that," she remembered. "Every chorus girl in the production had come into my dressing room for a preview of that coat, though before I was through with it, it looked pretty shabby." Another "first" was attending the Beaux Arts Ball. One of the chorus girls had suggested that Jeanette be the "fourth" and she accepted going on a blind date.

"As it turned out he wasn't at all the sort of person I would have selected for myself," Jeanette remembered. "I think he found my lack of interest definitely dampening to his intention of having a very 'gay time,' indeed. Anyway, he decided I wasn't to interfere with his evening's enjoyment and, after our first dance, he muttered a vague excuse and wandered, not only away but out of my life.

"Clad in my 1880 costume, all be-ruffled and be-curled, I sat against the wall. Here I was, at the brilliant Beaux Arts Ball, to which I had looked forward so eagerly, a wallflower! In the midst of that gay throng of people intent upon the pursuit of pleasure, I sat soberly surveying the scene, an outsider. It never occurred to me to fortify myself with a visit to the punch bowl, even though everyone I saw rather obviously had done so. I felt more alone than I'd ever felt in my life.

"Just as I decided to go home a familiar face appeared; a charming man I had met casually, a doctor, came up and asked me to dance. Before we had got more than a few steps, however, a man tapped the doctor on the arm and said he was cutting in. The doctor introduced him to me and, as we danced away, called: 'Take care of her, Thorn!'

"My new partner was tall, blond and handsome, just about the handsomest man I'd ever seen. A divine dancer, too! My evening was saved. He was protective of me, not allowing any of the men to cut in. I liked him, liked the fact that he hadn't visited the punch bowl, either . . . He took me home, and I said 'yes' when he asked to call the following day. So started our romance, a romance that should have ended in marriage."

Jeanette later claimed that she and Thorn were engaged. He was an architectural student at New York University and came from a socially prominent family. On their second date Jeanette revealed that she was an actress, which might have been cause for some scorn in his mind. Happily, Thorn didn't seem to care, and the two of them began to spend their time together horseback riding in Central

Park, going to football games, dinner and dancing after performances. Thorn finally invited Jeanette to his Long Island home to meet his mother, who whole-heartedly approved of Jeanette.

With her family, though, it was another story.

"I was just beginning my career on the stage. It obviously would never have done at all. It wasn't just an infatuation; sincerely and with all my heart I loved that boy. One night he asked me to run away with him, to marry him. I wanted to do that—"

Yet Jeanette had promised her mother she would never marry without her permission. And Anna's response was predictable: "An emphatic refusal." Anna reminded her daughter that she was already married to her Career, and the degree to which Anna still held sway over her daughter was evidenced by Jeanette's quick breakup with Thorn, no matter how much she loved him.

Soon Jeanette was dating other men, though she didn't allow herself to be dragged into a serious relationship. While in Chicago with *The Magic Ring* tour, she was introduced to Irving Stone, nephew of the owner of The Boston Store, one of Chicago's and Milwaukee's most prestigious department stores. They hit it off, though the romance eventually evolved into a long-term, long-distance friendship. In the coming years, whenever Jeanette was in Chicago, Irving es-corted her to all the social events; when she was elsewhere, they wrote letters. The Boston Store employees always knew when Jeanette was in town; Stone would walk up and down every aisle in the store with Jeanette on his arm, bragging to everyone that he really was a friend of Jeanette MacDonald.

■■■ During 1925, Jeanette auditioned for European conductor Ferdinand Torri-ani, considered one of the finest voice teachers in New York. Torriani's father had himself been a noted teacher; he trained soprano Adelina Patti, the highest paid singer of the late nineteenth century. Ferdinand Torriani carried on his father's work and taught the Torriani technique to his co-teacher, Miss Grace Adele Newell. The technique emphasized the mind controlling the voice, rather than the singer putting attention on the diaphragm, throat, etc. Although Torri-ani never codified his work, a similar technique was written up in detail by E. Herbert Caesari in a series of five books, which were studied extensively by Nelson Eddy.

Jeanette studied with Torriani until his death in 1926, then continued daily vocal lessons with Miss Newell. Unlike Nelson Eddy, who constantly searched for new and better vocal techniques, Jeanette stayed with Newell all her life. Grace Newell later remarked of Jeanette: "She rarely plays. She has no girlfriend to call up and say, 'Let's go to lunch.' Years of extraordinary hard work left no room for the easygoing enjoyment of impromptu dates or meandering shopping trips.

"Jeanette never quits. She joined with me long ago to work out a principle of voice culture established by Ferdinand Torriani . . . . We both believed in his complex theories. In her first movies we'd get up at six in the morning for weeks at a stretch, going through this method of voice control. She had the voice—Torriani's principles carried her to perfection. He had taught me those theories in the twenty-six years we were associated, but he died before he could carry out the proof. That has been my life work, and in Jeanette MacDonald I have seen not only her great triumph, but Torriani's as well."

Miss Newell set rigid rules for Jeanette's lifestyle. "No smoking, no drinking, no gallivanting around." The last item Jeanette was forced to ignore because to make ends meet, she was forced to return to modeling. In those days, a model could make extra money by working at night as an escort. "Escort" had a nebulous definition; according to one contemporary it meant you were "one step away from a high-class hooker."

How far Jeanette went is unknown, but it is during this period of her life that the details become vague and murky. Some sources claim she had several abortions in New York. Others insist she worked as an escort even after she arrived at Paramount Studios in 1929. Starlets who agreed to be fixed up by the studio received additional pay of $100 per night, and Jeanette needed the money because she had several people to support. Still another source, PR person Sandy Reiss, remembers that in 1937, when Jeanette was at MGM, there was blackmail money being paid to someone, in cash, from the front office—and even Mayer couldn't stop it. Reiss insisted that the woman receiving the money was known as Emily West. He was unaware that West, (who also went under the name Wentz) had met Jeanette in New York, during the mid-1920s when they were both struggling actresses, later became Jeanette's secretary, a position she held until Jeanette's death. When Jeanette later told Nelson about her early days as an "escort," he said he couldn't understand how she could let men pay her $100 "to undress her."

"Jeanette did what she had to do to get to the top," said one friend diplomatically. Her mother Anna, who had once chaperoned her youngest daughter on her dates, "turned away and refused to see."

In November 1925, Jeanette landed the second lead in a Gershwin brothers show called *Tip Toes*. The star of the show was Queenie Smith, a ballerina who'd danced in *Aida*, in which Enrico Caruso was Radames. Miss Smith described Jeanette as a "sweet and lovely girl," adding, "The cast got a little tired of George Gershwin's irritating habit of showing up for principal song rehearsals [where he began] to play my or Jeanette's songs, then [lapsed] into some section of a piece called 'The Rhapsody in Blue.' He was more interested in polishing this piece of music for a premiere with Paul Whiteman than [he was] in polishing the *Tip Toes* score."

Tip Toes opened at the Liberty Theater on December 28, 1925. Jeanette danced six numbers and sang one song, "Nice Baby." She was paid $350 a week, which easily made up for the fact that she didn't have more to do in the show.

Despite good reviews, *Tip Toes* closed in New York on Valentine's Day, 1926, then went on the road, lasting only until July. During the run of the show Jeanette was spotted by a Warner Brothers talent scout, who arranged for her to make a screen test. The test was hastily shot and did not show Jeanette off to her best advantage. The studio passed on her.

In August, Jeanette got a call to go to Philadelphia to audition for *Bubbling Over*, a musical version of the stage farce *Brewster's Millions*. The show opened at the Garrick Theater, closed in two weeks, then moved away to Boston. While in Boston Jeanette was hired for the Chicago run of *Yes, Yes, Yvette*, the successor to the popular *No, No, Nanette*. She took time out in September 1926 to be maid of honor when Blossom married her vaudeville partner, Clarence "Rocky" Rock; but Jeanette quickly returned to the show and traveled with the company to Boston, where *Yes, Yes, Yvette* opened on April 14, 1927. The Boston *Evening Transcript* noted: "Miss Jeanette MacDonald, who makes a vivacious and charming Yvette, pleasant of voice, flexible of limb, facile in mimicry and well endowed with that elusive ability to bridge the footlights by nothing more spectacular than her smile . . . makes reminiscence exceedingly rewarding."

Blossom and Rocky remained married until his death in 1960. After vaudeville ended, Rocky became general manager of the Beverly Hills Hotel, then in 1945 managed the Knickerbocker Hotel in Hollywood. He returned to the Beverly Hills Hotel as promotion manager in 1947, where he was working at the time of his death. Blossom and Rocky were happy most of their married life, but separated in the mid-1950s, due to his "chasing women." They never divorced, and are buried together at Forest Lawn, Glendale.

From Boston, *Yes, Yes, Yvette* moved to Philadelphia in May 1927 for six weeks, then toured all summer while the score and book were "worked on." By all accounts, *Yes, Yes, Yvette* promised to be a great success, and on October 3, 1927, the show opened in New York at last. Jeanette received enthusiastic reviews—except from the *Herald Tribune* critic, who wrote: "As for Miss MacDonald, one finds some difficulty in understanding the furor she has created among the continental reviewers. She has, to be sure, a stunning figure, a pretty face and bright hair. She is graceful and pleasant, but her voice has been impaired by too-long exposure to the rigors of the two-a-day, and she gives full rein to an unfortunate tendency to act coy. If the horrid truth be told, she rolls her eyes. It isn't necessary, and someone really ought to tell her so."

Irving Caesar, the lyricist for *Yes, Yes, Yvette* and hundreds of popular songs including "Swanee," dated Jeanette during the run of the show. He recalled: "I would call her the All-American Girl—a beautiful girl. She sang very well, but the songs in *Yvette* were not the type that suited her particular voice. She was not a 'musical comedy' personality. She didn't have that nature. She wasn't outgoing enough. She was really out of her element in musical comedy—she was perfect for operetta. But audiences loved her—yet, she lacked warmth.

"Jeanette finally got her warmth out at MGM, with Eddy and those operettas. Before that, she seemed afraid to let go.

"I remember once after *Yvette* had opened in Atlantic City, I asked her for a date to go riding in one of those wheelchairs along the Boardwalk. So we rode in one chair, and her mother rode in one right next to us. Jeanette's mother never left her side. She was our chaperon, I guess. I had the feeling then that Jeanette's mother watched over her too much. So there in the moonlight in Atlantic City I held Jeanette MacDonald's hand. Oh, she let me do that much, naturally, because I was one of the show's authors. But she seemed a little afraid. She wouldn't let herself go. She struck me as a girl who never indulged in sex until she was married. Never. But she was very charming to be with."

Due to her overwhelming popularity in *Yvette*, Jeanette was able to afford a nicer apartment on West Fifty-fifth Street in Manhattan. "We had to ship up all our old furniture," she said. "I hated the upright piano that should have been a grand. I recall a rocking chair I loathed. I ducked out of taking anyone there. I was so glad to get rid of that old stuff when I was able to buy our furnishings brand new that I suspect I went overboard. Mother and I tramped through wholesale houses. I *had* to have an Oriental rug, damask draperies, and my bedroom *had* to be nothing less than the most elaborate Louis Quinze."

By the end of 1927, Jeanette had finally become a star. She later recalled, "When I arrived backstage for the Christmas Eve show, the entire cast was waiting to tell me the good news. The producer had decided to put my name in lights and star me, as a sort of Christmas present. I tried to be blasé in the face of their tingling emotion. I think I smiled and said, 'Isn't that nice?' As soon as possible, though, I slipped out the stage entrance, hired a taxi and began circling the block. Each time I passed the theater I looked back to see my name in lights. As I saw my name twinkling in the night, do you know my greatest thrill? A friend of the family's, Arnold Daly, had once advised me to shorten my name because it would never fit in the lights. But I had never been able to think of a shorter name. No other name seemed to suit me. And there it was! In lights—*all* of it. It wasn't too long. After about four trips around the block, I stopped at a drug store and called Mother about the good news and she and my sister came downtown to see the lights for themselves."

Broadway ingenue.

7

Married to her career

Inevitably for Jeanette, Hollywood beckoned.

Late in October 1927, Paramount Studios instructed one of its major stars, Richard Dix, to check out Jeanette's performance in *Yes, Yes, Yvette*, to see if she had any film potential. Paramount was planning to film *Yvette*'s parent story, *Nothing But the Truth*, as one of their first sound features starring Dix.

Dix was impressed with Jeanette and he arranged a screen test for her at Paramount's Astoria Studio on Long Island. "The red carpet was laid out for me," Jeanette remembered. "As for Dix himself, he couldn't have been kinder to me. He made the test with me which, of course, is a great advantage, and he had his own cameraman photograph me. When I ultimately saw the test I liked it. This sounds terribly conceited, but I thought I looked very well, and I must confess I was surprised that I did like it, because they tell me most people hate themselves the first time they see themselves on the screen. It was a sound test, with voice. I was surprised that my speaking voice was so low as it seemed to be. My singing voice was natural, no difference."

Paramount wanted to sign her immediately, but the Shuberts, with whom Jeanette had a contract, refused to let her go. She had two years remaining and they needed her for a new musical they were opening in Philadelphia. Jeanette pleaded for her freedom but was told that the pay-off was an outrageous $75,000; if she broke her contract she would be sued and would never work on Broadway again. Jeanette was summarily pulled out of *Yvette* and sent to Philadelphia to rehearse a show called *The Studio Girl*, an operetta version of Du Maurier's *Trilby*, boasting a cast of 125 people, a chorus of 60, and a ballet of 20. The show opened November 14, 1927. The Philadelphia *Inquirer* said of *The Studio Girl*: "The story of Svengali's dominance over the golden throated model . . . is effectively presented. A great job of casting has been done. Trilby herself in the person of Jeanette MacDonald has a voice of operatic degree."

Despite good reviews, *The Studio Girl* closed after twelve days. Jeanette returned to her role in *Yes, Yes, Yvette*, angry with the Shuberts for not letting her break her contract, and even angrier that they'd put her into a flop. By January 1928, *Yvette* had closed, and Jeanette was given the lead in *Sweet Daddy*. By the time the show opened on February 8, the name had been changed to *Sunny Days*, and Jeanette was once again the focus of critical praise. The New York *Times* noted "They have put the dainty Jeanette MacDonald in the part of the shopgirl to dance buoyantly and to sing with the best voice in the company." She stayed with the show until it closed after 101 performances.

Jesse Lasky of Paramount Studios saw Jeanette on Broadway and raved to director Ernst Lubitsch about her: "She must be at Paramount! We must have her, she's a perfect lady and a beautiful woman!" Universal Studios also wanted her for their first sound version of *Show Boat*, but again the Shuberts refused to release her. As consolation, her salary was raised to over $500 a week. After *Sunny Days* closed, Jeanette went immediately on to *The Right Girl*, a musical based on a former successful play called *The Royal Family*. *The Right Girl* previewed in Philadelphia on November 12, 1928, then opened in New York in early December. Jeanette's reviews were good in spite of the show's lackluster appeal. The New York *Times* wrote: "Miss MacDonald brought the only pleasing voice to the comedy and sang pleasantly whatever was set before her." *Variety* was more enthusiastic: "The lovely Jeanette MacDonald is a joy as Angela. Graceful, pretty, lithe, she is a stage thoroughbred."

Jeanette's co-stars were Eric Blore and Alison Skipworth (who later co-starred with Jeanette in *Oh, For a Man*), and Jeanette remembered them fondly: "My grandmother in the play was the famous Alison Skipworth. She was a character. She had violently dyed red hair. It was varying shades of red depending upon how recently she had dyed it, and she was most frank about it—she'd say, 'I did a bad job this week.' Sometimes it looked purple."

The Right Girl underwent two name changes, first to *The Queen's Taste* and finally to *Angela*. Under any name it was a disappointment, however, and lasted only forty performances.

In January 1929, Jeanette appeared in her final Broadway play, a musical farce called *Boom Boom*. "Jeanette hated the part," said Blossom. "She'd come home and cry and cry. She felt the flippant, loud role wasn't in keeping with her personality. The songs weren't suited to her voice. Though she pleaded and pleaded, the Shuberts refused to release her from her contract."

The critics agreed with Jeanette. The Brooklyn *Times* reviewer noted: "Miss

MacDonald, the auburn-haired prima donna, plays youthful Mrs. Smith, who is really in love with her stepson. This present part does not seem to quite fit her talents. Miss MacDonald is best in a calmer and more romantic role. She should not be called upon to act as a coy sophisticate, for she is not the type. This graceful girl is one of my favorite musical comedy heroines when she has a part that suits her, and while I enjoyed her performance last night, it was not up to her previous appearances . . . Archie Leach [Cary Grant] plays a dashing amateur actor with whom young Mrs. Smith plays around a bit."

Boom Boom finished its New York run after seventy-two performances, with cut-rate tickets sold to keep the show afloat. Jeanette and her mother then left New York with the road tour. Jeanette was miserable about having to remain in the show, and by the time it reached Chicago her weight had dropped from 125 pounds to an alarming 110, and she was frequently ill.

■■■On April 16, 1928, an announcement entitled "Lubitsch on Operetta" appeared in *Variety*. The announcement read: "First operetta to be written especially for talking pictures will be produced by Paramount here [Hollywood]. Ernst Lubitsch will direct it from libretto to be written by Guy Bolton."

Lubitsch was a German-born, silent-film director whom Mary Pickford had brought to Hollywood in 1923 to direct her in *Rosita*. Five years had passed and he was now one of the most respected directors in the business.

Lubitsch was planning his first sound film, an operetta to star Maurice Chevalier and an unknown actress. He remembered Jesse Lasky's recommendation about Jeanette, and while he was in New York in early 1929 he decided to see *Boom Boom*. However, by then the show had left town, and Jeanette with it. So Lubitsch sat down in the Astoria Studios projection room and screened all the female sound tests done since 1927. Among them was Jeanette's test that she did with Richard Dix. When Lubitsch saw her he jumped out of his chair and yelled, "That's her! That's her! Now if she can only sing!"

He followed Jeanette to Chicago, sat through *Boom Boom* (called by critics "the niftiest flop ever brought to Chicago"), and went backstage to meet her. "You're too thin!" he greeted her. "You were not this way in the test! You must gain fifteen pounds, at least!"

"I can reach any weight you say," Jeanette said excitedly.

She agreed to meet with Lubitsch the following morning at his hotel. Once she had ushered him out of her dressing room she ran to her friend Archie Leach's dressing room, gave him a hug, and said "Archie, I'm going to be in pictures!"

The next morning Jeanette had breakfast with Lubitsch in his suite. "I found him a very kindly, sweet little German with a great big cigar and snapping black eyes, and a wonderfully engaging smile and personality. Greasy hair—I don't know why he always greased it down, but it was always greasy. We chatted, and he told me the story of *The Love Parade*, and said, 'Do you think you could play it?' "

Jeanette told him she didn't know anything about motion pictures, but if it were a stage play she knew she could play it. "Well, don't worry then, because if you think you can play it on the stage, I know I can make you play it on the screen."

Lubitsch returned to Hollywood, and negotiations began with the Shuberts to release her from her contract. Jeanette was offered $2,500 a week on a one-picture contract with options for more films. At the same time Paramount was coming to a cash settlement with the Shuberts, Irving Thalberg of Metro-Goldwyn-Mayer contacted the studio's New York talent representative and instructed him to make a sound test of Jeanette MacDonald and Dennis King, who was currently starring in *The Vagabond King*. When MGM learned that Paramount was anxious to sign Jeanette, the idea of a screen test was abandoned, and her New York agent was immediately contacted instead with a proposed contract. On May 15, 1929, an MGM representative wired New York: "Dennis King not available at present. Have been discussing for three or four days with Harry Reichenbach [Jeanette's agent] the possibilities of Janet McDonald [*sic*]. She is playing Chicago. She made test which Famous [Paramount] has. Can you get it from them? Reichenbach told me they were anxious to get her and promised he would hold her for us if we want her."

Jeanette's final performance of *Boom Boom* was Saturday night, May 11, 1929. She left with her mother by train for New York to finalize her film contract and close up her apartment. She kept the lease in the event that Hollywood didn't turn out as she hoped.

When she arrived Reichenbach instructed her to wire MGM that she must have their final offer by four o'clock, Wednesday, May 15. A flurry of telegrams went back and forth from MGM to New York, and on the fifteenth MGM wired their New York representative: "Jack Bachman has test of Janet McDonald and Ernest [*sic*] Lubitsch has seen it. Either Bachman or Schulberg have it. She says she must have answer by four o'clock today as has promised Paramount to give them answer."

The MGM representative tried to obtain Jeanette's Paramount screen test from that studio, but finally wired back: "Famous refused point blank let us have test Janet McDonald [*sic*] claiming that they had signed her." A follow-up wire came three days later: "Have photographs of Archie Leach playing in show *Boom Boom* now in Chicago. Understand he is great bet. Can you have someone cover show and give us report on looks, personality and voice. This important. Famous claim they cannot locate Janet McDonald test." On May 20 the New York office, not realizing that Jeanette was now under contract to Paramount, wired MGM: "Did you see test of Janet McDonald? If not wire make test of her next week. She will be here."

Meanwhile, Lubitsch made a public statement announcing that he'd found

Jeanette and her sister Blossom—who under the stage name Marie Blake appeared in nearly one hundred films and shorts; her most notable role was of Sally, the telephone operator in the Lew Ayres-Lionel Barrymore *Dr. Kildare* films. Under her married name, Blossom Rock, she starred as "Grandmama" in the 1960s TV series, "The Addams Family."

his Queen for *The Love Parade*: "She has youth, beauty and ambition. She is a talented dancer and a distinguished singer; she has a radiant and wholesome charm."

On June 5, 1929, Jeanette and her mother left New York. Their first stop was at a milk farm outside of Trenton, New Jersey, where Jeanette was to be fattened up to the requisite 125 pounds. Instead, she apparently became ill from the forced feeding, developed symptoms of appendicitis, and was rushed to a hospital where she was placed in ice packs and prepared for an operation. Fortunately, the symptoms disappeared after three days and an operation was not necessary. Jeanette left the hospital and she and Anna boarded the Super Chief train for Hollywood.

Jeanette left behind her sister Blossom, who was still in vaudeville and dancing on Broadway, and Elsie, who had a dance school in the Philadelphia area—and a new boyfriend, a man named Robert George Ritchie. Jeanette had met him in April 1928, at a party. Ritchie was a tall, good-looking, red-head who somewhat resembled Jeanette's father. He was a self-made man, a high school and college athletic hero who had worked on the New York docks as a

Jeanette and Bob Ritchie.

stevedore, then ventured into acting and finally became a Wall Street broker. After taking up with Jeanette he abandoned his Wall Street career and became her personal business manager; Ritchie negotiated all her Hollywood contracts, invested her money for her and was generally indispensable—until Nelson Eddy came into her life.

Their first night of intimacy, according to a notation in Ritchie's "little black book," was April 7, 1928. Jeanette described some of their early dates, including one memorable evening when she decided to try smoking to impress him. They were out dancing at a club, and Jeanette smoked four cigarettes on an empty stomach between dancing the Black Bottom and the Charleston. When they returned to their table to eat Jeanette became violently ill and had to be carried from the room. Her career as a smoker was over.

The relationship progressed quickly, but Jeanette held firm to the promise she'd made to her mother. Ritchie asked Jeanette several times to marry him, but she continually turned him down. Jeanette was married to her career, and if Ritchie really loved her he would accept that. He did. For the next several years Jeanette and Ritchie shared an unusual relationship: while she was in Los Angeles he was mostly in New York or London. There was little intimacy between them for long stretches of time, except in letters, and they wrote sometimes as often as twice a week. Happily, many of the letters from Jeanette have survived; they were found among Ritchie's things after he died in New York in 1972.

★ ★ ★

████Jeanette arrived in Los Angeles "dripping with hay fever and most unhappy. Trains were not air conditioned in those days, and I was utterly miserable."

She and Anna were taken by limousine to a room at the Beverly Wilshire Hotel, Jeanette's home for the next several months. Then Jeanette was driven to Paramount Studios, where she was immediately assigned an extravagant dressing room. "I don't think I appreciated what I was walking into," she later said. "I was young and I guess I was spoiled. I didn't care too much. Even Ernst Lubitsch was not as important to me then as he became later because I didn't even appreciate his greatness, nor any of the greatness that I was bumbling into.

"I was the prima donna, and I got what I wanted. I'm sure lots of people called me odd names, other than 'MacDonald.' "

She *was* excited to meet her co-star Maurice Chevalier. Chevalier had made

Jeanette and her first film co-star, Maurice Chevalier. Chevalier was the greater celebrity and Jeanette merely a featured actress in their first film, *The Love Parade* (1929). Four films later, her star had surpassed his and she received equal billing in *The Merry Widow* (1934).

his talking film debut in Paramount's *Innocents of Paris*, in which he introduced the song "Louise." But Chevalier was forty-one and feeling his age, and was worried about playing opposite a co-star who was only twenty-six. He relaxed at Jeanette's response to him; she was star struck and adoring. Blossom remarked that her sister had a crush on Chevalier but that nothing came of it (although Jeanette called him the fastest derriere-pincher in Hollywood). The two had only a professional relationship during this, their first of four films. Chevalier was flattered by the respect she afforded him and they worked well together, their personal chemistry reflected on-screen.

Nat Finston, director of the musical department, commented: "Chevalier was a scene thief. Chevalier was very clever in front of the camera. When the camera would start he always said his lines facing the camera and not looking at Jeanette while he was speaking. He always managed to upstage everybody else. Jeanette learned a lot of tricks from him."

Photographer John Engstead added: "Chevalier's private personality was the exact opposite of his performance one. When not on the stage or standing before the camera, he looked as if the weight of the world was on his back. He would sit on the sidelines, morose and glum, waiting for his cue to step before the camera. He wouldn't talk to anybody. When Lubitsch gave the signal to start shooting, Chevalier's face would light up and all the Gallic charm that thrilled millions of men and women around the world came to life."

In *The Love Parade*, two stars-to-be played bit parts. Jean Harlow was an extra in the theater audience scene, seated on the left side of a box. And Virginia Bruce had a small role as one of Jeanette's ladies-in-waiting.

The film's second female lead was young, vivacious Lillian Roth, later of *I'll Cry Tomorrow* fame. She wrote:

Mr. Lubitsch greeted me with a smile when I arrived on the set. There before my awestruck gaze was Maurice Chevalier, the beautiful Jeanette MacDonald, and a little man with expressive, merry eyes, Lupino Lane, a British actor [related to Ida Lupino].

Mr. Lubitsch introduced me. "Do you remember me?" I ventured to ask Chevalier. "I worked with you in the *Frolics*."

He flashed his inimitable smile. "Of course I remember—how could I forget?" Lubitsch passed out copies of the script. "Now, will you please sit there, Mr. Chevalier." He pointed to a bench. "And Miss MacDonald—" He stopped. Script in hand, I was floating ecstatically toward Chevalier's bench.

"No, Miss Roth. I want you to sit on the other bench with Mr. Lane. You're playing opposite him."

I was crestfallen. How naive could I have been? Who else but lovely Jeanette MacDonald would play opposite Chevalier? And I—and Mr. Lane—what were we to do?

I soon found out.

"We have two identical sets here," Lubitsch explained. "Mr. Chevalier and Miss MacDonald will sit on that bench. You, Miss Roth, will sit with Mr. Lane on this bench. He is Mr. Chevalier's butler. You are playing maid to Miss Mac-Donald's [queen]. They are having a love affair, you and Mr. Lane are having one, too. You two are to parody everything your master and mistress do. When they kiss, you kiss. When Mr. Chevalier declares his love for Miss MacDonald, Mr. Lane will declare his love for you. Get it?"

I got it. As Chevalier pursued Jeanette, at a high point in the scene, Lupino was to pursue me, bringing his face so close to mine that I was to gaze cross-eyed with love at him.

I had to hold tears back as Lubitsch sketched the ridiculous role I was to play. But I went through my lines.

Lillian Roth made a second film with Jeanette, *The Vagabond King*. After a brief but promising movie career, her life went off the rails as she battled alcoholism. Many years later, when she was sober again, she made her nightclub debut at Hollywood's Coconut Grove. It was 1961, and many film celebrities were invited to attend. Very few did. But in the audience near the front was Jeanette MacDonald, who warmly greeted Lillian who was so thrilled that she publicly thanked Jeanette for her support and asked Jeanette to join her on the stage. They hugged and sang a song together. Roth made a successful comeback and later starred on Broadway. She died in 1980.

Lubitsch put Jeanette on his own version of a "milk-farm" diet. The studio commissary was instructed to send over, hourly, glasses of milk and milkshakes except on the days when Jeanette had to sing. This time she did gain the required weight (the style then was slightly plump), which worked to her benefit in her portrayal of the queen. In the early part of the story Jeanette is the unhappy, unloved queen; as the plot progresses—and Jeanette gains weight —she falls in love and marries, looking happy, healthy and content.

"Jeanette came to a wilderness when she came to the studio," said Finston. "The picture business was in turmoil because of the changeover to sound and the Depression.

"I did all of Lubitsch's pictures at Paramount. He used to listen to my remarks because I was the music man. All the planning for *The Love Parade* was done at the studio with conferences—a meeting, a meeting, a meeting, a rehearsal, then they'd shoot. Careful preparation. He was a great talent. I had a great respect for him."

Lubitsch, like Alfred Hitchcock, was a director who pre-planned every shot, every edit and camera angle before filming anything. He directed by acting out every role and demonstrating exactly what he wanted from his actors. He even dressed in his stars' costumes and dresses, showing them how he wanted them to walk. "A couple of times he ruined the scenes because he would jump up in the middle of a scene," recalled Jeanette. "Having been crouching in front of the camera he would jump up, and the cameraman would say, 'Cut! Mr. Lubitsch—you're right in front of the scene!' Lubitsch would stop all of a

With director Ernst Lubitsch, who rescued her from a mediocre stage career and made her a star in Hollywood.

sudden and say, rather sheepishly, 'Oh, what a fool I am.' " Though Lubitsch's forte was sophisticated comedy, all his films were known for "the Lubitsch touch." "He was a real boudoir diplomat," said Jeanette. "He could suggest more with a closed door than all the hay-rolling you see openly on the screen nowadays, yet he never offended."

As could be expected, the headstrong Jeanette had a couple of run-ins with her director. The first was over false eyelashes, which had just come into vogue. Lubitsch insisted that Jeanette wear them; she thought she didn't need them. After a few days of filming, she sneaked into the daily rushes and decided that she was right. The next day she showed up on the set without them. Lubitsch filmed for a while—then stopped, noticing something was different about her. "Maybe it's the eyelashes," she offered. Lubitsch shouted, "You've ruined my picture!" After arguing they both agreed to look at all the rushes, with and without the false eyelashes. In the end Lubitsch agreed that Jeanette was right and she went without them.

Another time they were filming a wedding scene. Jeanette's thirty-pound gown with its ten yards of train weighed heavy and hot in the July heat. No fans or coolers could be used on the sets because their noise would be picked up by the primitive sound cameras. Jeanette repeatedly told Lubitsch the dress was too heavy, and finally she told him it was impossible to do the scene in the dress.

She yelled, "You wear the damn thing!" and stomped to her dressing room, slamming the door behind her. Moments later the expensive dress was hurled onto the dirty studio floor.

After several minutes, Jeanette marched out of her dressing room, and stopped short: Lubitsch had the gown on. Cigar dangling from his mouth, he was walking through her paces with six ladies-in-waiting holding the train. Jeanette laughed and agreed to finish the scene.

One of the major problems with shooting films in 1929 was that cameras had to remain stationary and enclosed in a booth to keep any camera noise from being recorded by the microphones: stories are legendary of cameramen collapsing from heat and exhaustion after being cooped up in the airless box for too long. As a result, the motion picture had lost some of its artistic, sophisticated cinematography when sound came in, and the early talkies often came off looking like filmed stage plays. Microphones were placed in strategic spots to catch dialogue—overhead, in a flower pot, etc.—wherever the actors would be standing and speaking. If the actor turned away from the hidden mikes, his voice could quickly become inaudible. Meanwhile, any background music or vocal accompaniment was recorded live utilizing a full-piece orchestra.

"Most of Jeanette's songs were sung live while filming, recorded with hidden mikes," recalled Finston. "Sound film was still so new that pre-recording and lip-synching was unknown. We only pre-recorded one song in *The Love Parade*, the 'Grenadiers' March.' All the rest were recorded 'on camera' or 'direct recording.'

"I suggested that we do it separately, record the song, then photograph [Jeanette] singing it. Lubitsch looked at me and said, 'Man, you're crazy. You cannot record and then photograph!' I said to Lubitsch: 'How in hell are you going to do March of the Grenadiers? You haven't got any stages big enough!' My theory was that you could not handicap the sound for the camera, or the camera for the sound. Lubitsch said to me: 'We'll go to another studio.' So we went to Samuel Goldwyn on Santa Monica, and did the scene in an open square. But they could only do it with pre-recording. [Lubitsch] fought me, but [he] finally gave in to me. The pre-recording of the song was done on the Goldwyn lot, too, because they had the best sound stage . . . When Lubitsch saw the rushes, he said, 'It's great!'

"That was the beginning, but after a while everybody did it."

While recording the "Grenadiers" number, Finston noticed that Jeanette repeatedly blew the take, unable to hold the final long notes. When he asked her what the problem was she said, "I haven't got that much breath, Nat." Merrill Pye, the recording engineer working under Franklin Hansen, yelled over to Jeanette, "Never mind, just give me a little bit. I'll stretch it."

"We had this fellow named Merrill Pye," said Finston. "Oh, he was a genius. He could take a piece of sound or film and put it over here, and you'd never hear the cut. Whenever Jeanette would sound breathy I'd tell her: 'Don't worry, they can take it out.' He was so good. Sometimes they would make one take, and they would stretch it by repeating it and pasting it on."

Finston asserted that the only number in which this was done was the "Grenadiers." "There was no more patching. But when we developed Merrill Pye, we patched everybody at Paramount [later] when we began to pre-record.

"Jeanette was marvelous. She took direction like nobody did. I can't say enough about her. She was a very talented woman. A quick study. I remember if you told her something once—boom—she never forgot it. I used to call her 'the pink lady of the screen' because that was high praise in those days, to call a woman a 'pink lady,' and she liked to wear clothes in various shades of pink, not too loud, though.

"Jeanette's voice had a very pleasing quality to it. Beautiful tone production. There was a Miss Newell who worked with her. Whenever Jeanette had to learn something new, she'd go into her dressing room with Newell and stay there until she'd learn it, and then come out and do it perfectly." Then Jeanette took the record home and practiced singing her songs in front of a mirror so she would be synchronized perfectly—and look beautiful while doing it. "She was afraid of being ugly when she sang. So many singers open their mouths and they don't look beautiful when they sing. But I loved Jeanette; I used to think to myself: 'That's the most natural voice I've ever heard. She had a natural talent.' "

Jeanette had little social life outside of her work. On work days her policy was to be in bed by 9:30 P.M. When she was seen out on a date it was usually with Ernst Lubitsch. According to their co-worker the relationship was intimate. Lubitsch had been fascinated by her since he'd first seen her screen test; for Jeanette, Lubitsch was a mentor and a kind of father figure. Furthermore, she now had an ally at Paramount who was looking out for her interests, searching for new vehicles for her, someone to whom she could come with any problem, professional or personal.

"Lubitsch loved working with her," recalled Nat Finston. "He used to call her the 'queen of the screen.' Lubitsch would coach Jeanette and everyone else privately, he'd call her aside or go into her dressing room and tell her what he wanted in a particular scene."

Photographer John Engstead added diplomatically, "She was very playful on the set, kidding around a lot with everybody, and was *always* hanging around with Lubitsch. Lubitsch liked her a great deal."

Jeanette mentioned him frequently in letters to Bob Ritchie, though she described, for the most part, their professional collaboration. She and Ritchie had an "open" relationship, and over the years she wrote him of the men she was dating, but never in intimate detail. (As Chevalier and others have claimed, Ritchie was less tolerant of her lifestyle when he was in Hollywood with her, often appearing on the set and reducing Jeanette to tears with his verbal abuse.)

In her early letters Jeanette speaks of her love for Ritchie, saying she misses her "daddy" and wants to cuddle with him—she seemed in love with the idea of being in love, as opposed to craving physical intimacy. Then, in the balance of the letters, she discussed with equal or heightened intensity money or her career. These love letters are quite different from the ones she would later write to Nelson or about Nelson, in which she rarely mentions her career but dwells on their passion, their lovemaking sessions, her spiritual struggles, the minutest details of what they did or said. The Nelson letters reveal a far more sensuous and mature Jeanette than these early ones do.

It was in some degree her basic sexual naivete and frigidity—her apparent lack of experience—that drew so many men to her. "She lacked warmth," was a statement repeatedly made by the men who knew her best. "One might penetrate her physically but not emotionally," said another. "She was very, very pretty and she knew it," stated Ernst Lubitsch, "but she was underdeveloped within. She was still an ingenue at heart, within her soul. She did not make you 'feel.' "

Jeanette for her part was totally unaware of any emotional deficiencies. "My own Sweetheart," she wrote in a letter to Ritchie on July 21, 1929, "Darling, did you ever see such a glorious moon as tonight's? It made me think of you and how much I love you and wish you were here with me now. I'm so homesick for you—I wanna be loved by you, by you and nobody else but you . . . Gee! Gosh! I get almost sick thinking about you and how far away you are. Oh daddy darling of mine, I could weep for the love of you."

Two days later she wrote him again. "Ship ahoy! I'm off to the beach again—this time with Florence Leslie. Her and me's going to take a dip and flop on the beach and talk about our boyfriends—Bet I win! We're taking a picnic lunch and expect to munch sandwiches, with accents on the sand! . . . Florence talks even more than I do. And you know that's a lot!" She goes on to discuss her next film project, *The Vagabond King*: "Tomorrow I am to see Dennis King's tests and get a line on his way on the screen. He'll behave himself or else! . . .

"Well, Lubber of Jens—Remember Jen's your gal and she's just living for the time when she can be with you always 'cause she loves you more than anyone or anything in this here now whole wide world and there you have the gist of me heart's contents—open as a book. [Signed] Your own Mommy."

On July 26, 1929, Jeanette finished her work on *The Love Parade*. Paramount had filmed two pictures simultaneously, one in English, one in French, and had picked up her option, wanting her to sign the standard seven-year contract. Jeanette refused, remembering the problems she had had in getting released from the Shuberts. Instead, she had Bob Ritchie negotiate a different contract for four more films.

Though Jeanette denied that she and Ritchie were married at this time, in her letter to him of July 26, she writes on the back of the envelope: "JAR *that's me*!" and inside she closes with: "You're my boy—my own darling husband and I'm your all? I hope so—Your Jen."

Parade d'Amour was the French version of the film. The musical sequences were used, and some dialogue between Chevalier and Jeanette, spoken in French. Other parts of the film were silent, with written titles. *Variety* reviewed it: "French version of the Chevalier picture is nothing to write home about. Reproduction was thin and tinny in the musical numbers and the dialogue had

been cut in favor of titles in French, the half and half version being very unsatis-
factory. Song numbers came through well, however . . . Another detail
which worked against this exhibition were the awkward linguistic attempts of
Jeanette MacDonald's French."

The same day that she finished *The Love Parade*, she began working on her
next vehicle, *The Vagabond King*. "They made a sound track of my voice . . .
it was only about ¹/₂ hrs. work," Jeanette wrote Ritchie. "The [sound] track is
made in the recording room and then the photograph is done later—put together—and the effect is supposed to be the same as tho' it had been done
together. Well, here's the point altho' as yet no mention has been made—Does
my salary not start the very day the sound track is made? In other words, instead
of my rehearsing all this week for working—I get paid on acct [sic] of this
having made the sound track—Am I right? Also, have to make the 2 songs in
French on Saturday. So I'll draw my salary from V.K. and my retake money
from Love Parade, n'est-ce pas?" Jeanette was no fool when it came to money
matters, and she was as true as ever to her promise to put her career first. Her
long-term relationship with Ritchie, who was also her business manager, attests
to this.

The Vagabond King was a million-dollar production of the Rudolf Friml operetta starring Dennis King (reprising his Broadway role) and Jeanette MacDonald. It was filmed in two-strip Technicolor, which made filming expensive but
gave the scenes a painted, romantic look. Double-coated film stock was used,
one being orange-red, the other blue-green. Although no special makeup was
used to photograph the actors, the lights had to be twice as strong as normal
because of the special film. Complications were inevitable. "In the opening
scene, where [Dennis King] sings 'If I Were King,' all he does is blink," said
Miles Kruger, a film and stage historian. "I asked him about this, and he said
that the heat was so severe under the Technicolor lights that the makeup was
dripping off his eyelids right into his eyes during the filming. And it didn't
matter how many times they re-shot it. He said [the shot used in the final print]
was something like the nineteenth take."

Jeanette wasn't concerned with the lights as much as she was with her co-
star. She found him pompous and obnoxious, hogging every scene they were in
together and overacting to a ludicrous degree. Her big number, "Only a Rose,"
was supposed to be a solo overheard offscreen by the amorous Francois Villon
(King). But King kept leaning forward, creeping into the frame. After several
rehearsals, the director Ludwig Berger ordered a carpenter's horse to be put
on the set between Jeanette and Dennis King, but even then King refused to be
left out; the shot used in the final print has his nose sliding in and out of the
frame as Jeanette sings her solo, causing her to nickname the number "Only
a Nose."

Jeanette finished her work on *The Vagabond King* on October 1, 1929. She
had been working steadily since arriving at Paramount and was finally given
some time off. Immediately Louis B. Mayer's attorney was notified by cable
that Jeanette was available until April 1930, and was asking $3,000 a week.

MGM was ready to use Jeanette when Paramount had second thoughts about loaning her out. "Mayer never gave up on getting Jeanette over to Metro, and the 'inner circle' at Paramount always talked about that," remembered Nat Finston. "It was sexual. He [Mayer] was crazy for her." But Mayer would have to wait; Paramount asked him to "lay off Jeanette MacDonald."

■■■Jeanette returned to New York with her mother and Grace Newell on October 27, 1929, for the upcoming *Love Parade* world premiere. She and Chevalier were recalled to the Paramount Astoria Studio for one day of retakes, then on November 16, she sang her two solos from the film, "Dream Lover" and "March of the Grenadiers" on her first radio broadcast for the Paramount-Publix Radio Hour.

The Love Parade opened at the Criterion Theater on November 19. The lobby of the theater was roped off and microphones were set up for a radio interview with Lubitsch and his two stars. Jeanette stepped out of her car and was stunned by the huge crowd outside the theater, the bright lights, the police. She was so nervous she clung to the arm of her new friend, actress Colleen Moore, while being interviewed at the mike.

For the screening, she sat in a side box with her mother, sisters and Bob Ritchie. The place was sold out, even with $11 tickets, because it was promised that Maurice Chevalier would attend. However, a hastily shot film prologue starring Chevalier explained that he'd hurt his hand and couldn't be there. (Rumor had it that he didn't want to attend and find that Jeanette had stolen the picture from him.) Jeanette was called down to the stage to make a speech in his place and she spoke humbly, saying she was very lucky and excited and she hoped they liked the picture.

The film was an instant hit. The New York *Times* called the film "the first true screen musical," and the New York *Herald* noted: "There is the surprising work of Miss Jeanette MacDonald, late of Shubert musical comedies, as the Queen. On the stage Miss MacDonald was regarded as a competent player and singer, but nothing in her past career has given reason for anticipating the skillful and alluring performance she brings to *Love Parade*. Blessed with a fine voice, a sense of comedy and a definite screen personality, she registers an individual success that makes her future in the new medium an enviable one." *Variety* concurred: "Chevalier has an actress who all but steals the picture."

Only one review of Jeanette was negative, the one written by George Gerhard for the New York *Evening World*: "Despite her undoubted artistry, we cannot share Paramount's enthusiasm over her possibilities. As an artist, she is superb, but she photographs badly, this being caused by the peculiar contour of her face. Her face is abnormally long from her nose to her chin and her neck is long, too. Besides, her upper teeth are prominent. This may sound unkind, but we are merely appending it as a bit of reporting."

Jeanette cried hysterically over this review. The next day she went to the

Criterion Theater, watched the film again, and decided that Gerhard was right. She bought a variety of makeup and face powders and went back to her hotel to practice with each shade until she found the right combination. After Christmas when she returned to Hollywood she contacted Victor Milner, who had photographed *The Love Parade*, and read him the critical review. She vowed to Milner that she would prove Gerhard wrong if it was the last thing she ever did. Milner, who felt somewhat responsible, agreed to help her. The two worked together on their own time, experimenting with lighting, camera angles, and makeup for three full days until they had it perfect. In future films Jeanette was a pro; she knew how to do her own makeup, knew which was her best side (her left), and how she should be lit and photographed. In those days especially, such details could mean the difference between success and failure.

██Before returning to Los Angeles, Jeanette recorded her first records for RCA, her two solos from *The Love Parade*. Nathaniel Shilkret conducted the orchestra and later commented: "Victor was still in the experimental stages of using their new electrical recording equipment. They weren't sure of the electrical disk recording process, and they made each recording on two identical machines. They'd process them both and play them back. Whichever was the better of the two recordings, they kept. They'd throw the other away. They didn't know what they had on recordings until they came back. Once, I remember, we recorded somebody else, and when they came back there was nothing on them. But both of Jeanette's recordings were quite good.

"The microphones were very sensitive and they would rattle on the loud voices. Nowadays the microphone 'holds' the sound, but then it was different. It was better to have a soft voice like hers for recording. We tried to pick the recording that didn't have as many rattles on it. There was no piecing of Jeanette's voice on her Victor recordings. Those songs were always sung all the way through without any pickups."

The Love Parade had its West Coast premiere on January 19, 1930, and opened to critical raves, with the one exception of Louella Parsons. Parsons, who wrote for the Hearst syndicate, was the most powerful gossip columnist in Hollywood, and a bad review from her could potentially mean the end of a career.

One of the worst moves an actor could make was to antagonize Louella; she took her revenge in her column, which was read by millions of Americans very day. And Jeanette did get off on the wrong foot with Louella; her first mistake was being five minutes late for an interview with her. Even though Jeanette was known for always being late, Louella took this as a *personal* affront. Then Louella spotted Jeanette talking at a party while singer Carmel Meyers was performing. Louella berated Jeanette for her rudeness. "We started off at a great disadvantage," Jeanette later admitted. "Subsequently, we became very good friends but it wasn't until a great many years later, after she had slashed me from end to end in her column at every opportunity."

The Love Parade was a commercial success in spite of Parsons, garnering six Academy Award nominations, for Best Picture, Best Actor, Best Director, Best Cinematography, Best Interior Decoration, and Best Sound Recording—but this was the year of *All Quiet on the Western Front*, which ran away with most of the major awards. *The Love Parade* also launched a complete line of merchandise. Some of the items included "Chevalier Salades" and "Love Parade Sundaes" at restaurants, and "Chevalier Patties"—mints sold by the giant Loft Candy Company, which were advertised with movie stills of Jeanette holding a box. The Gimbel's department store featured the wedding gown worn by Jeanette in the film to advertise their spring wedding collection, and copies of the dress were sold in other shops. And cloned jewelry, hosiery and negligees worn by Jeanette in the film were sold, along with copies of Chevalier's pajamas.

Parade d'Amour was released in France on February 27, 1930, and was a hit there as well. *Le Figaro* predicted, "I can bet you that inside of fifteen days, the young American star Jeanette MacDonald, because of her voice, her spirits, her charm and her beauty, will be the Idol of Paris."

At a production conference after the film's release in Europe, Jesse Lasky told financial advisor Sam Katz: "We're keeping open the doors of Paramount because Jeanette is singing!"

■ Jeanette's second film, *The Vagabond King*, opened in double premieres at the Criterion in New York and at the Paramount Theater in Palm Beach, Florida, on February 19, 1930. The studio had gone to great expense to advertise the costly production, but to no avail—the reviews were almost uniformly bad. Despite the gorgeous color, the film was stagy, plodding and humorless. "Jeanette MacDonald's soprano is charming, but her screen presence lacks warmth," claimed the New York *Daily News*. From the *Daily Tribune*: "Mr. King's performance is as violent and overdone as ever . . . Miss MacDonald is hardly as successful as she was in *The Love Parade*." Noted the *American*: "She says 'I'll die for you' in a tone which might query: 'Will you take cream or lemon?'" Outlook magazine: "The only real trouble . . . is a completely blah performance by Jeanette MacDonald, the leading lady, who evidently thinks she is back on Broadway where you can run through musical comedy love scenes as though you were reciting Latin verbs. The movie public wants love scenes it can take seriously." And from the New York *Times*: "[Berger] has not succeeded in eliciting from Miss MacDonald much in the way of acting, and her enunciations never give the slightest suspicion of belonging to the period. Her lines, it is true, are very poorly penned. She, however, sings charmingly."

A silent version of the film was released overseas with titles and background music except for the songs, which were left in. In Germany, the film was dubbed by German actors.

Fortunately, Jeanette had predicted the failure of *The Vagabond King*, so when the reviews came in she was ready for them. On December 29, 1929, she wrote Bob Ritchie: "In view of the fact that my part is cut to nothing, I am going to Schulberg and tell him I wish to be taken off the billing— so I can sneak thru the picture . . . The picture is too long and Merle said when King sees how much of him has been cut he'll have pups and Berger will also have pups when he sees how much of his pet stuff has been cut and I must admit that my speeches were inconsequential . . . Vic Milner told me last nite at dinner time that he & Lubitsch had talked about me shortly after the first preview and Lu had told him that it was a shame that under no condition should I have been cast in that role and he wouldn't have done it if he'd never have found a singer for the part. He said "The girl has nothing to do—it's a waste of talent." It may be that as a result he wants to show people that his judgment is good by trying to find another vehicle for me. Let's concentrate on it, honey, for I can't afford any more Katherines [her character in the film]—no one can!" In spite of her wishes, Jeanette was not taken off the billing.

While Lubitsch searched for another showcase role for her, Jeanette was cast in a silly little comedy called *Let's Go Native*, co-starring Jack Oakie. Although it wasn't a story she would have chosen for herself, she had at this point little say in which films she made. Paramount, like most other studios of the day (except perhaps MGM) was interested in quantity, not quality. Films were cranked out on short shooting schedules, and contract players turned out one film after the next. Once in a while a great film was made, but in the Depression days high-budgeted classics were a rarity. "Last nite we worked on the shipwreck and had a lot of fun even tho' we were all pretty tired," Jeanette wrote Ritchie. "To-morrow we are to be in Balboa for the scenes on the catamarans and as the call was for 5 am to leave the studio, I decided I'd go to Balboa this afternoon and get several hours sleep in.

"Life once more holds a ray of sunshine, 'cause yesterday at lunch time I sat down with Schulberg & Lubitsch. He [Schulberg] said—We were just talking about you. How would you like to star in an operetta picture by (name I can't remember), music by Strauss, directed by Lubitsch. So I said—Does a duck like water. Also—Lubitsch asked me what I thought of the present vehicle and I said I thought it had possibilities but needed clever treatment—and he told me they want him to take it over 'cause they're not entirely satisfied with the way things are going. It would be quite a lucky development, wouldn't it?"

Lubitsch did not take over *Let's Go Native*. (Leo McCarey, who later directed some Marx Brothers' classics, rushed the film to completion in twenty-one days.) Nat Finston remembered that this was the beginning of the end for Jeanette at Paramount. Jeanette continuously complained to the front office about the need for script revisions. "That's when Paramount became disenchanted with her [too]," Finston claimed. "Bob [Ritchie] was always trying to influence her on how to play a scene or what to wear in a scene. She'd listen to him first, then used to stamp her tiny little foot—I can still see her like she was right in front of me—she'd stamp her little foot saying: 'No, no no! I want to do it my way!' Then she'd go off and do as Ritchie wanted."

Jeanette next filmed two songs for an all-star revue, *Paramount on Parade,* but her numbers were cut out of the American prints. (In the Spanish version, her songs remained and she was "Mistress of Ceremonies.") Then she was loaned to United Artists for another mediocre film, *The Lottery Bride.* Despite a story by Herbert Stothart—later the superb musical director at MGM—and original music by Rudolph Friml, the film was a laughable melodrama, and UA shelved the finished production for six months.

Jeanette made five films her first year in Hollywood. She worked at a killing pace because she needed the money. She didn't even rent or purchase a house, preferring to live at the Knickerbocker Hotel. "Am enclosing a check for $155.60 for Elsie to cover the expenses," she wrote Bob Ritchie. "Will you please see that she gets it O.K. I will send her personally a check for the other along with a note but I'm afraid it'll have to be after I get some money as my checking account here instead of being $2000 is down to $778."

Lubitsch finally found the right vehicle for her, *Monte Carlo*—complete with a hit tune in it called "Beyond the Blue Horizon"—and on April 1, 1930, they began shooting. Jeanette sparkled under Lubitsch, who had the skill to bring out her delightfully seductive child-woman qualities. "All women are sirens at heart," said Lubitsch, while describing Jeanette. "No matter how unemotional, how stolid a woman may be, she has moments when her greatest desire is to be —shall we call it—a courtesan, siren or seductress. If I manage to develop some quality in a player that the public has been unaware of, it is because I try to avoid the obvious in type. There is a thrill in seeing a lady of refined background and culture lose herself in the game of love."

People who knew and worked with Jeanette always claimed that her screen persona in her Lubitsch films was, in fact, the real Jeanette. Even Nelson Eddy, when he finally saw *Monte Carlo* in the mid-1930s, was inspired to say, "That's the Jeanette I know!"

■ Paramount had no bright ideas for Jeanette after she completed filming *Monte Carlo.* While it was being edited, Jeanette recorded "Beyond the Blue Horizon" and "Always in All Things" for RCA on August 1, 1930. *Let's Go Native,* the little comedy directed by McCarey, was finally released on August 16, 1930, and it did poorly, to no one's—least of all Jeanette's—surprise. "A ludicrous audible film hodge-podge," asserted the New York *Times,* adding, "Miss MacDonald gives as pleasing a performance as is possible in such a melange." The *American* said: "It is really something of a shock to find the heroine of *The Love Parade* . . . in such shoddy surroundings."

Jeanette was happy, however, to complete her contractual obligations at Paramount, and she at once instructed Bob Ritchie to negotiate a three-picture deal at Fox Films. It is unknown why MGM did not grab her up at this time.

However, Bob Ritchie was aware of Louis B. Mayer's personal interest in Jeanette, and no doubt predicted what would happen if Jeanette was at his studio. It was to his advantage to have Jeanette sign anywhere other than MGM.

The first project was *Oh, For a Man*, with co-stars Reginald Denny and Allison Skipworth. The charming script was adapted from a short story that ran in the *Saturday Evening Post* in June 1930, and filming began on September 6, with Jeanette playing temperamental opera singer Carlotta Manson, a character quite similar to the title role in *Rose Marie*, who has the misfortune of falling in love with a burglar. Jeanette was thrilled at the chance to sing opera in the picture. The opening number featured her performing Wagner's "Liebestod," but she had lost weight and looked a bit comical, dwarfed by the obligatory blonde braids that were almost as wide as she was. Bela Lugosi had a pre-*Dracula* role as her manager.

By the fall of 1930, the first wave of film musicals was over; audiences were growing tired of the same formula being used over and over. "Sol Wurzel, the producer [of *Oh, For a Man*] issued an edict," said Jeanette, while the film was in production: "'No more musicals'—and said I was to be limited to a minimum of song." Aside from her opening *Tristan and Isolde* number, Jeanette sang only one other song in the final cut, "On a Summer Night."

Monte Carlo was released in October and was a big hit. Paramount touted it as a novelty—a musical without dance numbers. "What an artist is Ernst Lubitsch!" wrote the San Francisco *Chronicle*. "If there had been more screen operettas like this one and fewer blatant, rubbishy things, the musical play would not have fallen under the ban in the picture houses. Lubitsch's subtle touches of humor, his skilful use of little things, his brilliance impress themselves on every foot of film and make *Monte Carlo* a continual joy." The New York *Sun* said that Jeanette "seems destined to play royalty in the movies," while the *Daily Mirror* called her "a gem." "She has lost the apparent self-consciousness—or whatever it may have been—that marred her earlier efforts," noted the *American*—and in *Monte Carlo* "shows magnificent promise." George Gerhard, the critic who had reduced Jeanette to tears, had finally capitulated to her indisputable charm: "Miss MacDonald is the best member of the cast, and she was never better, upon the stage or screen, than she is in a scene in which she tousles her hair and starts off for the opera in order to confound the man she loves. This scene is superbly done." Gerhard was surprised himself when Jeanette invited him to tea and thanked him for pointing out her deficiencies, giving her an opportunity to correct them.

Years later, Jeanette attended a screening of *Monte Carlo* at New York's Museum of Modern Art. She laughed at herself on the screen, at her clothes and her marcelled hairdo with lots of waves. An usher came down the aisle to quiet her, and she apologized, "I'm sorry. But one more wave and I'll drown."

United Artists released *The Lottery Bride* three weeks after *Monte Carlo*, hoping to cash in on Jeanette's success. But the critics found *The Lottery Bride* "boring," "weak," and "silly," and the film died at the box office.

Jeanette stayed in New York through the opening of *Oh, For a Man*, on

November 29, which met high praise from the press. "Jeanette and Denny work delightfully together," reported the *Daily News*. "Both have a keen comedy sense. The story is far-fetched, but it is funny." "Amusing and sexy in a manner which can prove offensive to nobody," praised Motion Picture magazine. "[Jeanette] exhibits a versatility that has not appeared in her earlier work. She gives an extremely good performance."

After months of denying a romantic relationship with Bob Ritchie, Jeanette suddenly announced her engagement to him. The press discovered that she was staying at the home of his parents in Newark, New Jersey, and it was rumored that they actually married in late November 1930. Jeanette later denied any marriage, offering $5,000 to anyone who could prove it by producing a marriage certificate.

On December 2, Jeanette left the East Coast and headed back to Fox Studios in Hollywood to begin work on *Don't Bet on Women*. It was a cheaply budgeted drawing room comedy co-starring silent heartthrob Edmund Lowe, comedian Roland Young and Una Merkel. Shot in a few weeks, it premiered with a lot of fanfare on February 15, 1931, at New York's Roxy Theater, but quickly disappeared from the scene.

Her final film for Fox was *Annabelle's Affairs*, a charming comedy featuring Victor McLaglen, Roland Young, Joyce Compton, Sally Blane and Louise Bea-

During her early film career Jeanette was usually scantily dressed, earning her the nickname "The Lingerie Queen."

vers. Jeanette sang only one number in the film, but she had her requisite bathtub and lingerie scenes which were so prevalent in her early films.

For many decades, all three of Jeanette's Fox films were thought to be lost. In the 1970s, nitrate prints were found of *Oh, For a Man* and *Don't Bet on Women*. One reel of *Oh, For a Man* had turned to dust, but it was just ten minutes of a subplot which did not involve Jeanette. In another part of the film, the sound track is gone and the picture flickers badly. *Don't Bet on Women* had deteriorated as well; the entire film is very softly focused. These two films were transferred to safety film and have been preserved. Unfortunately, only one reel (ten minutes) has survived from *Annabelle's Affairs*.

Annabelle's Affairs was released on June 14, 1931, to excellent reviews. "This picture gives every indication of winning for Miss MacDonald as many followers as her previous screen efforts combined," praised *Variety*. "She romps here and delightfully. A splendid farceur and, on this effort, the best among the femme contingent on the coast." Time magazine called the film a "hilariously funny farce of a sort rarely seen in the cinema."

After two years of working non-stop in films, Jeanette was mentally and physically exhausted. She had made nine pictures altogether, but her film career hadn't progressed as far as she felt it should have. She was somewhat cheered when her sister Blossom moved to Hollywood to be with her and to do some small supporting roles in movies (including a Three Stooges short), but Jeanette missed Bob Ritchie, and her letters—particularly those from February 1931—reveal her disappointment and a kind of growing desperation.

February 10: "I hope for the best [for *Oh, For a Man*]. Just shows how damned disappointing this lousy business can be. You've just got to save as much as possible—and be as cagey as possible. You never know from one moment to the next when you're in or when you're out."

February 11: "I'm anxious to have you make some money and get a fine job that will reassure your future in that we really should get married soon or else I'm liable to suffer you know; as it is people cannot understand why not and I can't say 'cause you have no money or job and there's no future—for you are simply taking care of my career. Besides there's not much dignity or prestige and what I want most is for Pop to make enough so the old lady can have a real papoos [sic] before old age creeps on and spoils it. Sometimes I get a little scared when I think that I'm really responsible for your going East to undertake a very ticklish job, for there's no telling what will happen if it goes wrong."

February 16: "I understand *Don't Bet on Women* opened Friday at Roxy's—I'm curious to learn how it goes—Wurtzel seemed to think it was a fine picture —if it makes money I suppose they'll like me and think I'm fine. If not I suppose they'll say I was lousy."

February 18: "Mother and I just had a sort of argument. She's decided that I'm not satisfied with anything she says or does whereas I do try, Pop, to make her happy— But, oh well, I just get a little tired."

February 21: "I worry a lot about you because I really don't think you have much sense of the value of money—'cause you always manage to get along without it but when we have our child—we gotta have it. I believe my French is improving, Pop. Besides, I'm taking my lessons nearly every day. It's really very hard when you get serious with it because you then realize how little you know. Am awfully tired again. I don't sleep well and it's all because I'm not content. My life seems all chopped up and so damned uncertain. I can't relax and my back aches."

February 24: "Don't be afraid of my vulgarity in jewelry—but remember that your own [financial] success may in some way be judged by any jewels that adorn me. And remember that now I can't afford to have meager or cheap looking stuff for people might think I'm not making so much money. It's unfortunate but true that people judge by what they see, especially the people we have to deal with."

■ Soon the feisty and determined little girl from Philadelphia would meet her match, quite literally, in Nelson Eddy, and so many of the questions and doubts that were growing inside her would fade away. But before that could happen, Jeanette had to face yet another, extremely bizarre twist of fate.

It seems a sports-car accident had occurred in Bruges, Belgium. The bodies of an unconscious man and woman were dragged from the wreck, and for some

Jeanette as *The Merry Widow*.

inexplicable reason were identified as Prince Umberto, heir to the Italian throne—and Jeanette MacDonald! Soon front-page headlines across Europe were announcing her death.

At this time Jeanette's films were playing all over Europe; she was extremely popular, especially in France.

"I first heard of the rumor that I was friendly with a royal prince and was shot at by a jealous princess from a newspaper clipping from a Belgian fan," Jeanette explained. "I didn't take notice until a newspaper woman in Hollywood came to see me to make sure that I still had two eyes. Then I began to take notice and asked a clipping agency to get me all the continental papers. After that I learned that I was in an automobile accident [and that] I had tried to commit suicide. Later I read I was shot at by a royal princess and still later, had vitriol thrown at me which disfigured my face."

While Jeanette was checking into the above fantastic story, another scandalous version broke out, this time in Monte Carlo:

"*Monte Carlo* had been released in Europe. The atmosphere was so beautifully done that most Europeans thought we had made the picture in Monte Carlo instead of Hollywood. So, when the story broke out in their newspapers concerning a certain crown prince and his clandestine love affair with a blond girl, the rumor started that the girl was Jeanette MacDonald. The story was that the prince's wife had caught her husband and his love together and shot the girl, who was taken to Italy. Whether she died or disappeared seems a mystery. At any rate, my pictures were immediately banned in certain sections of Europe.

"Meanwhile, musical pictures suffered a set-back in this country and I made three pictures for Fox in which I did no singing at all. This caused the further report in Europe that I was not only dead but that my sister who could not sing [Blossom] had taken my place on the screen! This concerned me a great deal; musical pictures made money in Europe and I couldn't afford to have mine lose the market by such nonsense."

One weekly magazine, Fantasio, went so far as to print an imaginary interview with Blossom, who "confirmed" that she was now making her sister's films.

"The only thing I could do was appear in Europe and prove my identity with my voice," Jeanette decided. But she was indecisive about such a tour. As she wrote to Bob Ritchie, "The more I think about the concert the less favorably I feel about it because it would involve preparing a program which concert and opera singers spend months learning—and as you know the main fault with me is that I have no repertoire and it would be silly to try to put one together in a week or two. You see, dear, I have spent my life learning how to use my voice but have had no time to learn anything except the songs I've had to sing in the show or picture I've been doing. Others have devoted their entire time to learning songs for their concerts. If it were with Chevalier it could include more popular songs and [be] less liable to criticism. So, I think it's better to forget it. Radio has more possibilities and involves less preparation."

Eventually Ritchie persuaded her to do the concert tour. Jeanette, he and Anna sailed for Europe in the summer of 1931. Arriving in France, Jeanette was barred for four hours from landing, she was hounded by reporters, and ultimately had to provide proof that she'd never set foot in Europe before. Finally she was allowed to appear in recital at the Empire Theatre in Paris on September 4, 1931. Despite sinister threats of violence she ventured out onstage. The sold-out audience was silent and suspicious. Jeanette simply smiled—and the audience responded with thunderous applause. She endeared herself forever to the French with her concert of English and French songs; by the close of the show, the scandal was a closed book as far as the French were concerned. Two nights later Maurice Chevalier attended the performance and came onstage to greet her, whereupon she greeted him with a kiss. The result was a new set of rumors—that Jeanette and Chevalier were lovers, and his marriage, which was known to be on the rocks, was over because of her.

Jeanette next conquered London, where she sang at the Dominion Theater on September 21. "Miss MacDonald herself was a little nervous about her ability to please," noted the London *Times*. "But the applause did not sag during her performance, and when, flushed with the appreciation of her most stirring film song, the 'March of the Grenadiers' from *The Love Parade*, and with glinting hair falling in waves to her shoulders, she took a succession of final curtains, there could be no question of her success."

Jeanette recorded four songs in London on September 25, 1931: "Dear, When I Met You," "Pardon, Madame," "Goodnight" and "Reviens."

Jeanette returned triumphantly home, having turned down offers to do films, stage and opera in Europe. Ritchie now easily negotiated for her a new contract to do two pictures at Paramount. The first was *One Hour With You*, produced by Ernst Lubitsch, directed by George Cukor and reuniting her with Maurice Chevalier. Lubitsch at first was scheduled to direct, but became intrigued with a project called *The Man I Killed*, a serious anti-war film.

One Hour With You was a remake of a silent Lubitsch classic *The Marriage Circle*. It was shot simultaneously in English and French (*Une Heure près de toi*) with a completely different French supporting cast, and director Cukor had his hands full. "With the best intentions in the world, I couldn't do a Lubitsch picture. Lubitsch was what they really wanted and what they should have had.

"I directed for about two weeks. I didn't like Chevalier, and he didn't like me, but Jeanette MacDonald and I subsequently became very good friends, and she wanted me to do a picture with her. We shot an English and French version simultaneously. Then B. P. Schulberg, head of the studio, saw a lot of rushes and didn't like them. Lubitsch had now finished shooting *The Man I Killed*, but they didn't officially 'remove' me. What happened was goddamn agony for me. I was under contract and had to stay on the picture, on the set, while Lubitsch took over.

"Lubitsch still couldn't give a hundred percent of his time to it because he was still cutting the other picture and so on. I still did a few things, I carried them out the way he wanted, but for most of the time I just sat there and really did less than when I was a dialogue director.

"I behaved very well, I think. I was very disciplined and acted as if I didn't mind. Officially, I finished the picture, but Lubitsch really directed it. I admire Lubitsch very much, but he shot things in a highly stylized way that is simply not my own.

"[Afterwards] Mr. Schulberg called me into his office. 'I'm going to ask you to do me a little favor,' he said. Mind you, he was all-powerful, and I was less than the dust beneath his chariot wheels. 'I'd like you to take your name off the picture,' he said. And I refused. If he didn't want my name on the picture, he should have taken me off after the first two weeks. 'Well,' Mr. Schulberg said, 'I'm taking your name off anyway.' I told him I'd sue, and I did. I wanted to leave the studio anyway."

One Hour With You was released on March 25, 1932. It did well with the critics and public, and was nominated for a Best Picture Academy Award. Reviewers praised Lubitsch and Chevalier for their work, and Jeanette was described as "charming," "beautiful" and "graceful."

Jeanette's last Paramount film was *Love Me Tonight*, now considered one of the greatest musicals of the early 1930s. Also co-starring Maurice Chevalier, the producer/director was Rouben Mamoulian, who was actually reluctant to take on the project. He was exhausted, having just finished *Dr. Jekyll and Mr. Hyde* with Fredric March, when he ran into Adolph Zukor, the head of the studio. Mamoulian related their conversation: "As you know, the executives of this era were often far more persuasive actors than the players under contract to them. Zukor, with tears in his eyes, implored me to produce and direct a film with Maurice Chevalier and Jeanette MacDonald. Both of them were under big salaried contracts to Paramount [$5,000 a week each] and, according to Zukor, the studio was on the brink of bankruptcy so it was imperative that stars like Chevalier and MacDonald be constantly used. I protested that I wasn't the man for the job, that Lubitsch had done very well with these two players in the past, and suggested [that] Mr. Zukor approach him. But Lubitsch was busy with other projects, Zukor said, and wouldn't I please give it a try.

"I said, 'Mr. Zukor, you make it impossible for me to say no.' I found a French playwright on the set, young [Leopold] Marchand, whose great-grand-father had been Napoleon's valet, and he came up with a fairy tale about a Parisian tailor who goes down south, falls in love with a princess and marries her. It was a charming fantasy.

"I then got Richard Rodgers and Lorenz Hart to develop songs for the film . . . When the screenwriters . . . came on the picture it was their job to construct the scenes and bridge the dialogue between the song numbers, so that the songs flowed from the action sequences and the actors didn't stop to sing a song. It worked perfectly.

"Only Chevalier was, in the beginning, disturbed. He approached me one day and said, 'I understand you're having story conferences on my next picture,' I told him yes, that was true, but I was first working with the songwriters. He wondered why he wasn't included in the discussions. Lubitsch, he said, always had him present at all pre-production meetings. I said that was all very well, that was the way Lubitsch worked, but Lubitsch wasn't doing *Love Me Tonight*—I was, and I worked my way, and I especially didn't want him on hand at my story conferences. He was hurt and said he would complain to the front office. I told him to please do so, that I didn't want to do this picture and was only doing it as a great personal favor to Mr. Zukor, and would consider it a very special favor if he could get me taken off of it.

"Maurice, of course, didn't go to the front office. He loved the script when it was shown to him and was enchanted by all the Rodgers and Hart songs. *Love Me Tonight* turned out to be one of my happiest film productions, and I was delighted that it met with such critical and public favor when it was released.

"On the first day of shooting, Jeanette MacDonald told me she did not like her costume for the first scene. In fact, she didn't like any of the wardrobe and preferred to pick her own. I said, 'Fine. We are shooting this scene tomorrow. Pick your wardrobe and if it is suitable and makes you happy, I will be happy.' The next morning I walked on the set and roared with laughter. I thought she was kidding. You never saw such a combination of irrelevant things in your life. Feathers!

" 'What are you laughing at?' she said, red in the face.

" 'You are putting me on!'

" 'This,' she said, 'is what I am wearing.'

"When I realized that she was serious, I told her I would go back to my office and would she be kind enough to let the studio know we were not shooting. Half an hour went by. One hour. Then my assistant called to say Miss MacDonald was on the set, ready, and hating my guts. By the end of the day, it was a love affair between us. She was a wonderful girl, Jeanette. I loved her but she never dressed well in life, either. She had talent and a sense of humor."

"I never thought she had much of a sense of humor," contradicted Chevalier, who resented Jeanette because she was receiving equal pay. "When we worked together she always objected to anyone telling a risqué story. I was not surprised when I later heard her referred to as 'The Iron Butterfly,' although I was surprised to hear she found that amusing."

It didn't help relations between Jeanette and Maurice when his jealous wife went off the deep end, barged into her dressing room and came at her with a knife, certain that Chevalier was in love with her. In fact, the purportedly bisexual Chevalier had relationships during this period with two bisexual women, Kay Francis and Marlene Dietrich. According to Dietrich, Chevalier was impotent but was intimate, however briefly, with Jeanette: "Chevalier says he can't stand her," Dietrich told her daughter. "He told me she smells of cheap talcum powder, and I said 'In what place did you smell it?' So, of course, he was stuck—and couldn't answer."

Myrna Loy, who had the second lead in the film, didn't get along with Jeanette either. Loy once related how jealous Jeanette became when she saw

Myrna wearing a beautiful white dress in a masquerade party scene. Jeanette pulled rank and insisted on wearing the dress herself. Myrna was forced to choose something else and she settled on a black gown that ultimately stole the limelight, leaving Jeanette more furious than ever. Vivienne Segal, who worked with Jeanette in *The Cat and the Fiddle*, also commented on her nastier side, recalling that on the first day of production, Jeanette said to her, "Viv, have you seen your part? It stinks."

Mamoulian continued to have problems with Jeanette—or rather, with Bob Ritchie. Time and again Ritchie came on the set and interrupted the filming, yelling at Jeanette and berating her for being untrue to him. "She was very much in love with Bob Ritchie," remembered Chevalier, "but he, of course, was not the man for her." Rouben Mamoulian made the remark: "Jeanette was the easiest lay in Hollywood," and while this comment is no doubt greatly exaggerated, it is a fact that Ritchie was having problems dealing with his real or imagined rivals.

The climactic scene of *Love Me Tonight* finally called for Jeanette's character to ride alongside a train, catch up to it, jump off her horse and stand on the track, arms akimbo, to stop the train. Jeanette insisted on doing her own stunt even though the train was very real and, if everything went as planned, stopped just inches from her on the tracks. Any miscalculation could result in injury or death. She did it, and earned the respect of her co-workers for proving she was more than just another prima donna.

Love Me Tonight was released on August 26, 1932, to good reviews, though many critics missed the Lubitsch touch. "What a picture," exclaimed Photoplay. "First, you have Chevalier and last, you have Chevalier, and all through this riot entertainment you have Chevalier. And adding her beauty and lovely voice, you have the delightful Jeanette MacDonald."

After recording for RCA several songs from her last two films, Jeanette headed back to Europe with her mother and Bob Ritchie for another concert tour. This time the itinerary was broadened to include Holland, Spain, Switzerland and Belgium in addition to France, and Jeanette was paid a reported $13,000 a week throughout most of the tour. She was now affluent enough to purchase a villa in the south of France. Truely McGee, Jeanette's coordinator in Paris and Brussels, recalled her as "the most startlingly beautiful person I'd ever seen," and the tour was a tremendous success from start to finish except for two minor points. "The management and the backstage personnel didn't much like Ritchie; and they dropped the piano legs off the piano during Jeanette's numbers, just to cause him trouble, also the King and Queen of Belgium gave her a puppy that peed on her costume and caused her some embarrassment."

While Jeanette toured Europe, increasing her freedom and generating worldwide reviews, Louis B. Mayer remained obsessed with Jeanette, and finally promised her anything and everything she wanted—she was to receive top money, star billing and the studio's first all-Technicolor film. Mayer told Jeanette he'd make her "bigger than Norma Shearer," who at that time was the reigning queen of the lot. For Jeanette, whose goal was to be the number one female movie star, this at last was an offer she could not refuse, and she signed with MGM in early 1933, with the stipulation that she be allowed to remain in Europe to complete her concert tour. Jeanette returned to New York on July 25, 1933, ready to begin her new career at Metro-Goldwyn-Mayer.

Naughty Marietta (1935).

8

Naughty Marietta

Nelson always remembered the first day of work on *Naughty Marietta* as a total nightmare. He shared a pre-dawn breakfast with his mother, then drove to the studio. Once he arrived in makeup, some people he didn't know argued and fussed over what to do with him, his makeup and his blonde hair. Once they finished with him, Nelson stared at himself in a mirror. His reflection was so unrecognizable and ghoulish that he jumped out of the chair, horrified, insisting that all the makeup be taken off. "What are you trying to do, make me look like a Gladys?" he yelled.

They finally managed to calm him down and convince him that blonde men were difficult to photograph, that all the makeup was necessary and that he'd look just fine.

Wardrobe wasn't much better. His outfit itched.

When he had a moment to himself, Nelson surveyed the "final product"—his hair had been rinsed a darker shade, and a ponytail hairpiece had been attached in the back. With that plus the makeup and the uncomfortable outfit, Nelson thought he looked terrible. It might have been better if he'd had his own dressing room in which to discuss all these indignities in private, but Nelson's status at MGM was still that of "featured player," and the studio treated him like an extra even though he was the male lead of the picture. Nelson was ready to walk out and call it quits. With some difficulty he suppressed the impulse, however, and he marched onto the set. He was familiar with sound stages but this one was a madhouse. People were running around everywhere. Somewhere from the midst of the chaos director Woody Van Dyke spotted Nelson and yelled: "Hey, kid! Over here!"

Nelson wasn't about to respond to anyone's calling him a kid, and so he ignored him. But Van Dyke kept yelling at Nelson until finally Nelson had to shuffle over to him. Nelson would later come to love Woody's affectionate nickname for him, but just now it was one more humiliation.

Woody tried to put Nelson at ease. He had a reputation in Hollywood as the fastest, most no-nonsense director on the lot, known as "One-Take Woody." (One MGM co-worker claimed, "Yeah, he shot his films fast, but then there were all the re-takes!") Van Dyke had begun in Hollywood as an extra working for D. W. Griffith, the great silent director, and his method of directing was, in fact, a holdover from the silent days: quietly, he talked and coached his actors through their scenes, and edited his voice off the sound track afterwards. Van Dyke was an action man, noted for classics like *Trader Horn* and *Tarzan, the Ape Man*, and his films were fast-paced and witty. He coaxed natural rather than heavy-handed performances out of his stars. For example, he was one of the few directors who allowed ad-libbing if the spontaneous action fit in with the intention of the scene. Although his latest hit was *The Thin Man* with William Powell and Myrna Loy, Van Dyke had worked with singers before, most notably Lawrence Tibbett in *Cuban Love Song*.

Nonetheless, Van Dyke had his hands full with Nelson Eddy. "I've had 'em green, but never this green!" he complained. He'd been told Nelson couldn't act; this was an understatement. Nelson's opera career had educated him in the Delsarte system of dramatics that hadn't changed in seventy-five years. In short, his acting consisted of three gestures: raise the right arm as you turn and look to the right, the left arm as you gaze to the left, or both arms either up or down, as the mood might be.

Nelson had received no preparatory script or coaching prior to day one, because Van Dyke felt that the less time Eddy had to prepare, the better off he'd be. Woody did count on getting some assistance from Jeanette since she had been so insistent that Nelson be her co-star in this film, and that he could handle the role with no problem.

But Woody was in for a rude awakening when his prima donna finally made her appearance on the set and brushed past Nelson, deliberately avoiding him. She waved a bejeweled arm under Woody's nose and said, "Are there any special instructions?" When Woody numbly shook his head, she responded icily, "Well, what's the delay? I'm ready."

From there it went downhill fast. Nelson spent most of the day standing stiffly around, or pacing in a corner. His face came off cold and lifeless. He assured Woody he knew his lines, but he couldn't get through a single take without going completely blank. At the end of the day Nelson returned home to his mother and fell exhausted into a chair. "They turn branding irons on in your eyes, make you sit through an agonizing paint job, then, to complete the torture, they make you have to be around people you don't want to be around, and make you say dialogue you used in kindergarten. I don't know how I got through it. The idea of going back tomorrow makes me sick."

"I know it's difficult, son," Isabel soothed, "but they'll soon find out how marvelous you are." He was asleep before she finished the sentence.

The next day was no better. Woody finally gave up on Nelson and decided to film a scene with Edouard Lippe, Nelson's voice teacher, who was on the set to give Nelson moral support. Woody felt Lippe was perfect for a small role as an innkeeper, and the crew prepared to shoot a closeup of Lippe standing on a balcony, looking surprised. Woody explained the shot to Lippe, who assured the director that he could register surprise. On the first take Lippe opened his eyes and stretched his mouth wide open, Delsarte gestures and all. "Cut!" yelled Woody, and tried to explain that he wanted a natural look, not an operatic one. "I'll show you how it's done in the movies," Woody said, and they prepared for another take. This time, Woody had someone poke Lippe on the back with a broomstick. Lippe jumped, with a perfect expression of surprise. Woody said casually, "That's how it's done in the movies, Doctor. Easy, isn't it?"

Lippe later said of Woody Van Dyke, "In all my experience as a vocal coach and opera singer, I have never seen anyone who could play with people's emotions, abilities and inabilities as Van Dyke could. He worked with them as a champion player moves his chess men."

Van Dyke continued to have his problems with Jeanette—so much so, he was moved to comment, "She sure ain't that sweet little thing I was introduced to in Louie's office." The same first day of filming she'd come out of her dressing room carrying two hats. "The producer told me I must wear this," she said, waving the small hat she held in her left hand. "You know it's not my type. Wardrobe designed *this* one," she said as she flashed from behind her back a big blue hat trimmed with ostrich feathers. "I want to wear this," she said ingratiatingly. "It's not temperament to know what's becoming to you, is it? Especially when you're being photographed?"

"No, it's not, honey," he replied. "Pity the star who doesn't know that."

"This is the opening shot in the picture and you know that the first impression is a most important one—isn't it?"

Woody sighed, "What do you want me to do about it?"

"I'll try both on for you, and *you* tell me which one I'm going to wear." She put on the small one with a total lack of enthusiasm. Then, switching hats, she instantly became all smiles.

"Fat chance I've got of telling you which one you're going to wear," Woody retorted. "Wear the big one!"

Jeanette returned to her dressing room, triumphant.

Their next run-in occurred soon afterwards while Jeanette was sitting in her dressing room waiting for her hairdo to dry. She was bored, and when her hairdresser said the dailies from the previous day were being screened in a projection room nearby, Jeanette took off to peek at them. She hadn't been gone five minutes when Woody finished the scene he was shooting and called for her. When there was no sign of her or her hairdresser, Van Dyke waited impatiently, until someone reluctantly informed him that his star was in projection room "A" looking at a picture. Woody blew his top. "That's just dandy! I'm holding up an entire company while my leading lady is enjoying a movie! That's all for today," he yelled. "Company dismissed!" He sent everyone home and left himself.

When Jeanette finally came to the set, it was deserted and the lights were out —all except the night work lamp which glowed eerily in the center of the sound stage. Jeanette found a watchman, learned from him what had happened, and went to the front office to speak with Eddie Mannix. By now the story was all over the lot. Mannix told her that this was simply how Woody was; you either worked when he was ready to work, or not at all. They attempted to call Woody to straighten things out but couldn't reach him. Finally Mannix advised Jeanette that the best thing she could do was to report to the set at her scheduled time tomorrow morning, 9 A.M. sharp.

At 8:45 the next morning the sound stage was crowded; rumor had it Woody was going to tell Jeanette off. The director had just finished a shot and was pacing back and forth rehearsing his lecture for Jeanette when six husky stagehands entered carrying a large doghouse. They set the doghouse down before him; a woman's arm shot out of the door of the doghouse and held a shiny red apple out to him. Woody grabbed it, and before he could say a word another arm popped out with another apple. Then Jeanette stuck her head out and said, "And now may I come out, please, Mr. Boss Man, may I please, hmmm?" Woody roared with laughter and pulled her out of the doghouse.

The director from that point had a rapport going with both his stars—separately. His main problem now was getting them to work together. Nelson was clumsy and introverted around Jeanette; she was smug and superior towards him. During one scene, Eddy and MacDonald had to walk across the set together. Nelson walked into a prop tree, knocking his hat sideways and over his eyes. He stopped, fixed his hat, and finished the scene. When Woody called "Cut!" Nelson was apologetic, thinking he'd wrecked yet another take, but Woody reassured him, "It was okay, kid. A nice shot. That tree stunt took your mind off yourself and it made a very natural scene."

Another day, they were trying to film one of Nelson's numbers. Even though he was lip synching, Nelson sang in full voice. He was so nervous he kept cracking on his high note and stopping mid-scene. Woody tried patiently to get Nelson through the shot, telling him they'd intercut closeups so it didn't matter if he missed a note, just keep going. It seemed a hopeless task, but Nelson kept at it. Finally, as he was about to let loose his high note, his voice and the music were drowned out by the sound of a steamship whistle, a deafening blast that fairly shook the building. Nelson was so startled he stood there, limp. Woody roared with laughter—proud of his prank—and put his arm around Nelson. "No one ever registered a better expression, kid! Nelson, you're a great actor!"

Still another time, Nelson was supposed to push Jeanette into a chair. He gave her such a shove that she fell into the chair, which started to topple over. He managed to steady her, keeping in character, but she stomped off in angry tears. (Woody kept an edited version of this shot in the picture.)

After a couple of weeks of filming, Nelson was ready to quit. The final straw was the scene where he had to assist Jeanette—who played a princess—onto land from a boat in which they had escaped. As they disembarked, they were accosted by royal soldiers ready to arrest her. When the soldiers informed Nelson that Jeanette was really a princess in disguise, he was supposed to register surprise and say, "A princess?!" He thought he'd done it fairly well, but obviously it had come out funnier than he had hoped. Everybody was doubled up with laughter, especially Jeanette. Even Woody collapsed weakly in his chair.

Nelson pulled Woody aside and told him he was through. "I've tried, but nothing I do is right. I itch from this damn shirt, I'm hurting in an unmentionable place from these stupid pants, and I'm broke out from nerves. I tell you, Woody, nothing's worth this agony. I'm going back to where I'm appreciated, where I don't have to dress in drafty rooms that kill my throat, and where if I do get upset, there's music to soothe me."

Woody urged Nelson to reconsider. "Whether you can act or not won't mean a hill of beans when the film comes out. Think of what it will mean to become so well known that your name becomes a household word—"

"So's garbage a household word," retorted Nelson.

Woody finally convinced Nelson to stay. Before the day was out, Nelson had his own dressing room and dresser. Woody had even arranged for music to be piped onto the set between scenes. He had gone to the front office and had a talk with Louis B. Mayer about treating Nelson better. Mayer agreed to a dressing room for Nelson, but Woody came away from that meeting convinced that Mayer had an ax to grind regarding "the baritone."

Nelson battled various ailments over the next few weeks, including the flu, laryngitis (he claimed he lost his voice for a week) and an attack of appendicitis. Generally healthy, his illnesses were no doubt psychological in origin; he was insecure and pessimistic about whether he could hold his own with the other, seasoned actors. "I looked at only a few of the rushes and thought they were terrible," he admitted. "I didn't know any tricks to pull in front of a camera. I just did what I was told. For the scene where we sing 'Ah, Sweet Mystery of Life' in the ballroom, an assistant director kept me waiting without anything to eat until I decided I was going to have food before I sang. When they yanked me onto the set, I started for the door to get something. Van Dyke ordered me back. I went on. I was halfway across the ballroom when I decided to see who was more important, Van Dyke the director, or Eddy the player. I decided Van Dyke was. I finished the scene and Van Dyke said, 'Now, go fill yourself.' "

Nelson finally made a few friends, including character actor Frank Morgan, of whom Nelson once said that one of the hardest things to do was to try and keep a straight face in scenes with him. "Morgan would go into the scene with only a general idea of his part and would then ad-lib as he saw fit. Afterwards he would apologize but they always kept his ad-libbing in the picture. Even when he really choked on a glass of punch, they kept that. I found myself breaking up all the time at the things he said. You knew what he was supposed to say but you could never be sure of what would come out."

Nelson also enjoyed working with Elsa Lanchester and established a strong friendship with her and her husband Charles Laughton. During their first Christmas in Hollywood, Nelson invited the Laughtons, who had recently emigrated from England, to eat turkey and plum pudding at his home.

Onscreen Nelson continued to have his problems, however, especially when it came to his scenes with Jeanette. Nelson tended to freeze up. "I've handled Indians, African natives, South Sea Islanders, rhinos, pygmies and Eskimos and made them act—but not Nelson Eddy!" Van Dyke said. In an effort to loosen him up, Woody called on actress Lina Basquette for help. "I've got to light a fire under this guy," he told Lina. "I don't know if he's queer or what, but I've got to get him together with you." Lina continued,

> So he arranges a date for Nelson Eddy and me. But Nelson had a mother that bossed him and guarded him and his virtue.
>
> We went to this very glamorous affair at the Ambassador, I think, and Nelson really fell for me like a ton of bricks. We came back to my house and were sitting in front of the fireplace. We were in the throes, the prelude to a seduction, and finally he picked me up and carried me to my bedroom, and we got into bed and were just on the verge . . . when the phone rang. It was his mother! She'd found out from Woody Van Dyke that he'd gone back home with me.
>
> I want to tell you, if that doesn't dampen things—Mother calling and saying 'Come home, darling, and don't have anything to do with that dreadful woman.' He fell apart at the seams. I got up, put my robe on, went into the kitchen and brought him a glass of milk, and sent him on his way.

Woody Van Dyke continued to get nowhere fast with Nelson. So it was when it came time to shoot the "love scene," which required the two stars to hug and kiss each other, Woody decided the best way to approach the scene was not to prepare them for it. He simply sprang it on them.

Nonchalantly Woody pulled out a list of what could and couldn't be included in a love scene, and read it off to his stars and crew as a kind of joke. Since the inception of the infamous censorship rules a year previously, there were endless arbitrary rules; they couldn't open their mouths while kissing, they had a certain time limit for the kiss, and in a bed scene the man had to always keep one foot on the floor.

Woody rattled off the censorable offenses, then said casually, "Hell, we might as well do it now while I still got all this fresh in my mind." As he'd predicted, both stars stammered and protested that they weren't ready, but Woody ushered them to their spots and talked them through the pre-kiss dialogue, commenting sarcastically, "I can throw this list away; there's no way you guys will break any of the rules—is there?" Meanwhile he secretly decided to have the rehearsal filmed, figuring he might not get another chance.

To Woody's amazement, when it came time for the clinch, Nelson grabbed

On the set of *Naughty Marietta*.

Jeanette and really kissed her. Finally she pushed him away, beet-red and near tears. Nelson stood smugly grinning at her. The shot was obviously unusable, so Woody had them do it again. This time Jeanette rattled off her dialogue; the kiss was quick and impersonal. Nelson listened to her excited chatter about their characters' glorious futures, beaming at her like a fool.

From that day forward, Nelson displayed a new certainty around Jeanette. Of the people interviewed who were involved with *Naughty Marietta*, all felt there was romance in the air, but none could agree on one point: who was in love with whom? Nelson's actions didn't seem to indicate any immediate change in his feelings for Jeanette. He continued to date many of the starlets portraying casquette girls in the film. Even makeup man Fred Phillips commented that Nelson came to him asking his advice as to which girls were "safe," and claiming that Nelson dated them one after the other in rapid succession. Yet despite this, it is clear that Nelson remained obsessed with Jeanette. Sybil Thomas remembered Nelson discussing the filming of *Naughty Marietta*, confining his explanation of the day's events to graphic descriptions of what gowns Jeanette was wearing and how she looked in them. He described her with a combination of reverence and lust, embarrassing Sybil with his "almost pornographic" details of Jeanette's lovely shoulders, her beautiful skin, her low-cut bodice, etc. When Sybil cynically asked whether Nelson did anything else on the set except stare at Jeanette, her point went totally over his head.

It was inevitable that things would come to a head, as they did during the filming of the final sequence. The crew had brought out a horse for Nelson to ride, with Jeanette on his lap, off into the sunset. Nelson was a good horseman and he decided to show off that he could do his own stunts with the horse. He attempted to make a running leap onto the animal, but just as he jumped, the horse moved and left Nelson sprawled out on his face. (This episode should not be confused with a similar occurrence during *Rose Marie*, when, according to a story Nelson repeatedly told on the Jack Paar TV show, he tried to mount his horse but slipped off.) Uncontrollable laughter filled the set as Nelson struggled to his feet, his face thunderous. He stared at Jeanette, who was screaming with laughter, then told Woody, "I've had it. I quit," and walked off the set.

Woody tried to stop him, but Nelson wouldn't listen. The set fell silent. Suddenly Jeanette ran over to him, blocking his path, begging him not to leave.

"You know you're glad I'm leaving," Nelson said angrily. "Congratulate yourself, you've won."

She continued to plead with him. "I know I've been horrible, but please—"

Despite himself, Nelson smiled. He allowed her to hug him, then he let her walk him back over to Woody, who threw his arms around both of them.

From that point on, Jeanette's attitude completely changed toward Nelson. She began to work with him on his lines. They rehearsed together, with her gently coaching him and teaching him how to act for the screen. Woody took a back seat as director, giving her full rein, and the result was dynamite. It soon became apparent to all involved that Jeanette and Nelson together had that indefinable spark that would make their film a hit. Jeanette went even further, insisting that Nelson be given more songs, including " 'Neath the Southern Moon," and more footage. She fought to ensure that he would have equal billing with her. Months later, Nelson told a reporter:

"I mean this professionally and personally. I was unknown to screen fame when *Naughty Marietta* was released, so it was to see Jeanette that people flocked to the theater. And I might still have been unknown . . . but for her kindness to me during the jittery months of filming. There are the hundred and one things Jeanette taught me about acting—how to relax before stepping in front of the camera, how to protect my eyes from the glaring lights, how to move and speak naturally with a hundred people staring at you from a dark void outside the circle of lamps. I'll never cease being grateful to her."

Studio executives now predicted that *Naughty Marietta* would make Nelson (thirty-three years old) a star, and Jeanette (thirty-one) a super-star. At the same time, Louis B. Mayer stopped seeing Jeanette. "The consensus of opinion is that the film will make you top box office," he told her. "And much as I hate to admit it, that moves you out of my range. Because, Lady, I love *all* my big stars."

Jeanette's response to her new status was to drag Nelson to his dressing room and inform him of the good news. "I'm a free woman," she told him. It took him a moment to comprehend, then he kissed her and said, "I don't think you'll be free very long."

★ ★ ★

▇▇▇▇They began their romance in earnest during the final days of filming *Naughty Marietta*. Nelson showered Jeanette with gifts, buying her jewelry, having flowers delivered to her dressing room on a daily basis, going completely overboard. On one occasion after an exhausting day on the set, Jeanette returned to her dressing room and was greeted with yards of red ribbon and a large arrow inviting her to follow it. She did, and the ribbon took her back onto the set, where she found a gigantic bouquet of flowers waiting for her. On top of the bouquet was a gold box. Jeanette tore it open and pulled out a tiny gold pin in the shape of a bee, with diamonds as eyes. The card, scrawled in Nelson's scribble, addressed her as "Honey Bee," one of his pet names for her. (At one point in the film, Nelson's dialogue had him calling actress Cecilia Parker "Honey Bee." Nelson protested, telling Woody it was his name for Jeanette. Woody wasn't impressed with the sentiment and insisted that he speak the line as written.)

Jeanette in turn plied him with gifts. She gave Nelson a sheepdog, which they named Sheba—the most memorable gift was a pair of shapeless socks she had painstakingly knitted for him. Nelson accepted the labor of love with a smile and hid the socks in the back of his dresser drawer, hoping she'd never ask him to wear them.

▇▇▇▇After knowing each other now for nearly a year, their relationship had yet to be consummated. For Jeanette, this state of affairs continued to be puzzling. Nelson was affectionate with her, liked to hold her on his lap and stroke her hair. As she continually told Blossom, "He's a great kisser." However, that was as far as he went. He made no attempt to sleep with her. Slowly Jeanette became aware that Nelson had placed her on a pedestal and saw her as a beautiful, angelic creature. In contrast to this was their strong physical attraction to each other, which Nelson for one reason or another refused to act on. Jeanette didn't push him because sex wasn't that important to her—though they did come close, as Jeanette reported to Blossom. They were walking along Santa Monica beach when Nelson suddenly became passionate, crushing Jeanette to him and pushing her down onto the sand. At the crucial moment he pulled away, his breathing ragged, and he buried his face in his hands, mumbling, "Forgive me, I got carried away. You're so beautiful." Jeanette made a move to touch him, but he pleaded, "Please stay over there or I won't be able to control myself. I want you so badly." None of this made any sense to Jeanette, but she dutifully trailed after him as he stomped back to his car, muttering angrily to himself. She couldn't fathom what all the fuss was about and complained to Blossom, "He's so strange."

In Nelson's mind, Jeanette was indeed a young, virginal girl, regardless of her past. Mayer, Ritchie and any others did not concern him, and as far as he was concerned, they never existed. Nelson adored Jeanette's child–woman quality, her femininity and fragility. Around him, when they were alone, she dropped her affected movie star manner and became herself. It was this side of Jeanette's nature that Nelson cultivated. In many ways Nelson was Victorian with old-fashioned ideals, and his intention was not to sleep with her until their wedding night.

Jeanette finally became accustomed to his platonic courtship and played along, which ingratiated her to Nelson's mother. Isabel was slowly coming around, seeing Jeanette through Nelson's eyes and sensing that she might be more than a mere dilettante. Perhaps Jeanette would be a suitable daughter-in-law after all.

Jeanette enjoyed watching Nelson's struggle with himself, figured he'd make the next move when he was ready. But when it finally happened, the circumstances were so unusual that she would never forget it.

It was a Sunday morning. Isabel and Nelson had invited Jeanette over for brunch. It was their custom to have a lavish, old-fashioned Southern spread on Sundays. Jeanette arrived at the door, dressed in a white lace blouse and blue skirt. Nelson stood staring at her for a moment, then said, "I never get used to how lovely you are." They sat down to eat at a table groaning with food. Jeanette, who ate like a bird, took one lone sausage on her plate. Nelson grinned, took her plate, heaped it with food, and told her to dig in. After they had finished eating, Nelson picked up the newspaper. He liked to read it at the table on Sundays, his only day of the week to relax. On this particular morning it seems there was a write-up that mentioned Jeanette being seen out with another man. Normally this wouldn't bother Nelson; since he refused most invitations to Hollywood parties, Jeanette often went alone or with another escort, sometimes Bob Ritchie if he was in town. But on this occasion Nelson blew up. He accused Jeanette of cheating on him and refused to believe any of her denials; the more she protested, the angrier he became.

At this point Isabel hastily excused herself from the table and announced that she was going to visit a friend. She knew Jeanette would have to learn to deal with Nelson's mood swings and rages sooner or later if their relationship was to survive.

Nelson also left the table and told Jeanette to stay away from him. As Jeanette later recalled, Nelson was like a complete stranger: his eyes were dark, almost black—even his features seemed cruel and different. Unwisely, she followed him to his room, where he grabbed her and angrily shook her: "I thought you understood about us. I *won't* share you with anyone. You're mine! I won't play this Hollywood game. I won't have you running around. All this time I've kept my hands off you, trying to be a gentleman. You push me too far!" She tried to break out of his grasp, but Nelson pinned her down, ignoring her frightened screams. "Get this through your head once and for all, and never forget it! You're mine!" He ripped off her blouse and described in graphic detail what he was going to do to her to make sure she never forgot she was his. Then he threw her down on the bed and raped her.

Jeanette was in shock. None of her romantic fantasies had prepared her for this. To her further amazement, no sooner did physical relief set in with him than shame replaced it. Highly repentant, he sat away from her, head in hands, almost in tears. He begged her forgiveness and verbally berated himself for being such an animal. Clearly, they were at a moment of crisis. And Jeanette sensed instinctively that how she reacted would certainly determine their future together—or lack of it. She decided to make light of the situation, saying, "It's all right. All I want to know is, what took you so long?"

Nelson embraced her and accepted her forgiveness. In the next breath he was asking her when they should announce the date.

"The date? What date?"

"Our marriage date, silly."

Jeanette turned him down. For all her forgiveness, Nelson's proposing to her was all too soon and unexpected, and there was too much she didn't know about this man who was capable of such violence.

Nelson didn't press his luck. He went to shower and dress, and told Jeanette to do the same in his mother's bathroom. Jeanette pointed out, "It'll be somewhat drafty," and showed him her blouse, which was torn beyond repair. Nelson embarrassed tossed her a light blue sweater to wear instead. Returning from the shower he found her struggling to button it correctly, and when he went over to help her, one thing led to the inevitable next. This time, however, the lovemaking was tender and loving, "everything I had ever dreamed of—and more," according to Jeanette.

Isabel returned later that night. She peeked timidly in the front door, not certain what she'd find. The house was dark and silent. She headed upstairs to her room and spotted the pair from the landing. They were asleep before the fireplace, Nelson's head on Jeanette's breast, her arm around him, covered only with a blanket. "They looked so innocent, so childlike," was Isabel's reaction, "and so beautiful together."

▰▰ "I'm a different person," Jeanette told a very interested Blossom, excitedly relating the details of her newfound intimacy with Nelson. Blossom was horrified at hearing how she had been treated, but Jeanette just grinned, embarrassed, and admitted that it wasn't entirely unexpected. In any case, it was worth it if that's what it took to bring then together—and afterwards, when Nelson made love to her, she admitted that she had sexually "lost control" for the first time in her life.

Nelson alluded to Jeanette's cured frigidity in a tenderly written diary entry: "My little shy sweet maiden, now a wife, but always a maiden. Since you first came to me, your hair a sheen of russet sunset—fields of ripe yellow grain—and now a pretty dishevelment in my arms, what meaning life has had for me. Our stars, our moon, our trees, how dear they have become, and how much more real are YOU than anything in nature. Last night your fear of yourself was just as great, and I hope that self fear will pass. You can't be anything but you in my arms, and I am going to always force you beyond the limits you have set for yourself, for that's the vanity in me, darling."

★ ★ ★

■■■ The change in both of them was immediately obvious to many. Isabel Eddy wrote, "I thought I had never seen her look so beautiful as now. She was radiant, with a glow of great happiness but [with] a new shyness which only made her seem more adorable to this understanding mother."

Returning to work at the studio, Jeanette and Nelson faced the curious and watchful eyes of their co-workers. "Every time he looked at her he blushed bright red," one person commented. "He was always touching her, always in some kind of physical contact with her." Another visitor to the set, Sandy Reiss, said: "His eyes gave him away. They were always on her. And everywhere she went, he followed. The funny thing was he didn't realize how obvious he was."

Sandy Reiss had worked in public relations for many years, specializing in motion picture fund-raising events for police charities. During the 1950s, he hosted a sports television show. An able athlete himself, he swam the English Channel in 1951 in seventeen and one-half hours. Two years later he crossed the Catalina Channel in eighteen hours. In 1968, he was the first U.S. journalist allowed into Red China to view athletic programs there.

"I met Jeanette during a luncheon at which the wonder boy Irving Thalberg of MGM was honored," Reiss recalled. "I had the good fortune to be seated next to Jeanette. At that stage in my life I was engaged as publicity director for a magazine that has since become defunct. It was a real pleasure to find how easily Jeanette broke the ice with talk of our mutual appreciation of hors d'oeuvres and crisp bacon. Finding yourself sitting next to such a great lady and talking animatedly about simple pleasures like baking and entertaining is a real thrill; and this was the beginning of a warm friendship. To this day I guard jealously the recipe she once revealed to me for her excellent Vienna strudel.

"Nelson I met during the filming of *Naughty Marietta*. He was talking to a representative from his publicity department, and said happily that all his life he had hoped to meet such a lady as Jeanette. To him it was love at first sight."

Sandy Reiss was to remain friends with the two of them, even after the studio years. Once, over drinks, Nelson confided to Reiss that aside from the sexual compatibility, he felt a spiritual completeness with Jeanette that was overwhelming and frightening in intensity.

Reiss remembered that by the end of production of *Naughty Marietta*, Jeanette and Nelson were openly dating. "They had lunch and dinner together in her dressing room, with orders not to be disturbed." Reiss said, "Van Dyke's crew nicknamed them 'the lovebirds.' " Between takes, the two often sat together, Jeanette's feet in his lap, as he vigorously rubbed them for her. As a preamble to her heart condition, she suffered in her thirties from poor circulation. Her hands and feet would go numb, and Nelson diligently took it upon himself to massage the life back into them. According to Jeanette, Nelson had a foot fetish, which she found disconcerting because she thought her feet were ugly. Other women with whom Nelson was intimate also mentioned his fascination with their feet.

Naughty Marietta gave the lovers plenty of time to know each other, professionally as well as personally. "The work was hard," Nelson commented. "Some of the scenes had to be shot twenty or thirty times. I think [Jeanette] and I sang the 'Sweet Mystery of Life' sequence forty or fifty times. It had to be taken from all angles, close up and at a distance, with overheard shots and shots of the audience reaction. It was a long, hard task, particularly when it had to be done in both French and English. We were up every morning at six A.M. We finished, with no time for visiting during the day, about eight P.M. each night. After that we would all go home, eat our dinners and begin studying lines for the next day's sequences."

Even in the first bloom of their affair, they weren't without vigorous disagreements. Each was stubborn, self-centered and temperamental. They could quarrel over something trivial, milking a fight for all it was worth. A number of people pointed out, however, that Jeanette was no physical match for Nelson. After crying and carrying on for a while, she tended to hyperventilate, turn blue and stop breathing. These friends were astonished to see Nelson calmly pick her up and slap her sharply across the face to bring her around.

"She was always flopping over," Sybil Thomas sniffed. "He'd have to sweep her off the pavement. He loved it; he could play the knight in shining armor."

Sybil herself became privy to the latest developments while over at the Eddy household one evening. She, Isabel and Nelson were off to some event, but Nelson was late getting ready. Sybil found him up in his bedroom, rifling through the disheveled bedsheets. He was missing a cufflink, a rare and valuable one that had been given to him by some notable person. When Sybil asked him why he was searching his bed for it he replied, with some embarrassment, "Jeanette lost it here somewhere."

Of all their friends, Sybil was the one skeptic. She was sure Nelson's infatuation for Jeanette would quickly run its course. She sensed trouble ahead with "the redhead," because the two were so headstrong and similar in their career drives.

From the first, Jeanette set about to change Nelson. It started with his hair. She got him to change the way he parted it, trying the other side, then the middle— before admitting it looked best the way he'd had it originally. Then came his clothes. Nelson liked loud-colored shorts; she disapproved of them. Then came his voice. Why, she protested, couldn't he be a tenor so they could do operas together? After listening to several of his voice lessons, she was sure it could be done. His range was versatile; he could sing bass, baritone and tenor, but the high C eluded him. She felt—correctly—that there was little difference between a lyric baritone and a dramatic tenor, and that if he found the right teacher he could successfully make the transition to tenor, as baritones Enrico Caruso and Lauritz Melchior had done before him.

Nelson promised to try, and indeed began to work on his upper range. But no matter what he tried, he couldn't get the high C. Sybil found him one day at the piano, running scales. She stopped him in disgust. "Would you jump off a cliff if she asked you to?"

Nelson finally had a confrontation with Jeanette about his voice. "I'm a baritone, and that's that." When she started to protest, he snapped, "Look, I can sing circles around you, so just shut up about it."

Even when Jeanette gave up on "improving" Nelson, Sybil Thomas wasn't too impressed with her. "Shallow-headed," she called her, pointing out that Jeanette seemed like the kind of girl Nelson had always avoided. One time Sybil was eating in Chasen's restaurant. A potted tree separated her from the next booth, but she could hear Jeanette's voice prattling on about her clothes, her costumes, what she should wear to this party or that. Sybil peeked around the tree to see Nelson, eating away, happily listening to Jeanette. She was waving her fork around and had barely touched her food, which seemed to concern Nelson, until finally he switched plates and dug into her meal, still patiently absorbed in her chatter.

Sybil had a talk with Nelson afterwards, and Nelson made sure to tell her in no uncertain terms that her opinion of Jeanette was way off. "If she was like that I'd never have spent five minutes with her. When we're alone she's a totally different person." His message was clear: Sybil's judgments were unwanted. So she kept her mouth shut—for the present.

With director Woody Van Dyke, who became one of their closest confidants. Woody's parties were famous in Hollywood; whenever Jeanette and Nelson attended, they instantly became the entertainmemt.

★ ★ ★

During the latter half of 1934, Nelson gave several local concerts, all attended by Jeanette. In August, he sang twice at the Hollywood Bowl: once in an all-Wagner concert, then a concertized *Carmen*. Gertrude Evans was visiting from Philadelphia, and she, Isabel, Jeanette, Doris Kenyon and her friend Ann Franklin all attended parties given in Nelson's honor. In November, Nelson sang several performances of *The Secret of Suzanne*, an opera in which he co-starred with Doris Kenyon and Edouard Lippe. Much ado was made by the critics of Jeanette's appearance in the audience, even to describing in detail what she was wearing. All the singers received excellent reviews, although the opera itself was considered "mediocre and banal." The Los Angeles *Examiner* commented, "Nelson Eddy is possessed of as beautiful a baritone voice as mere mortals have the right of expecting to hear . . . One wonders why he should be languishing in motion pictures when the opera stage needs him so."

His opera crowd, mentor Gertrude Evans and others, asked the same question. No one was certain of the impact *Naughty Marietta* would make on Nelson's life and career, nor were his friends thrilled with his close attachment to Jeanette. They worried that he might break free of his closely laid plans, that Hollywood and Jeanette could sidetrack him altogether from the purity of his goals.

In the 1930s, MGM previewed films in Westwood, then a quaint village (home of UCLA), surveying for public reaction, looking for indications that a film needed editing. Attending *Naughty Marietta*'s preview there were Jeanette and her family, Nelson, Woody Van Dyke and Isabel Eddy. Isabel was escorted by none other than Louis B. Mayer, who apparently made an unsuccessful play for her. He later told Nelson, "Such a nice lady. Where she got a son like you I'll never know."

Jeanette "tore the theater down" with her on-screen rendition of "The Italian Street Song" and "Chansonette," as did Nelson when he marched into the frame singing "Tramp, Tramp, Tramp." Nelson cringed at seeing himself, complaining he looked like "a fruitcake." Jeanette tried to calm him. When cheers broke out at the film's end, Mayer told Jeanette: "You are greater than you ever were." He then grudgingly admitted to Nelson: "I got to admit, you surprised me. You did pretty good up there."

Nelson laughed. "That's what everyone's been telling me. I'm starting to think that being in the movies isn't so bad after all." He put his arm around Mayer. "You know what? Tonight I love everybody, even you!"

In a typical operetta plot, Jeanette plays a princess forced to marry someone she doesn't love. She disguises herself as a casquette girl named Marietta, and leaves France with a shipload of girls bound for Louisiana. Captured by pirates, the girls are rescued by some mercenary soldiers, led by the handsome Captain Richard Warrington. Once in New Orleans, the princess and Warrington fall in love, but her family finds her, her identity is revealed and she is told she must return to France. Warrington manages to sneak her away from her guards; they elope and ride off together into the wilderness where the French government can never find them.

Jeanette was scheduled to travel to New Orleans for the film's 1935 opening, but she canceled out and went instead to Hawaii, where she was met some time later by Bob Ritchie. Presumably on vacation, there were rumors that she was annulling her marriage to him. Although no such records have surfaced, at least the Ritchie family was told that the marriage was dissolved in Hawaii at this time.

Whatever the legality of their relationship, it was now over for all practical purposes. Ritchie was made head of an MGM unit over in England; he moved to the Savoy Hotel in London, and was conveniently removed from Jeanette's personal life. He remained her business manager for another couple of years and corresponded frequently with her on business and personal matters. But instead of handling her career exclusively, he proceeded to sign up actors like Cary Grant, Judy Garland, Luise Rainer, Allan Jones and Robert Young. Later, after years of working for MGM in England and being a personal agent, Ritchie attempted to make a new career for himself producing plays. In his final years, he sold carpet to hotel chains.

Nelson hated to be separated from Jeanette, but he had to go to New York for a Town Hall recital and the *Naughty Marietta* premiere in Washington, D.C., hosted by Mrs. Mabel Willebrandt, former Assistant Attorney General of the United States. Mrs. Willebrandt, a friend of Woody Van Dyke's, had seen the film at a private screening at the studio. For the premiere she invited 350 members of official Washington to a formal dinner, then held a private showing of the film at midnight at Loew's Fox Theater.

Van Dyke was guest speaker at the dinner. In his speech, which was a hit, he stressed that Washington and Hollywood should work more closely together for the good of the nation. From dinner, the entire group went directly to the theater, where they received the film as enthusiastically as it had been at the Los Angeles preview. Afterwards, Mrs. Willebrandt hosted a late supper at her Georgetown home for some of the guests.

She and Woody left the theater early to set up. They headed for the kitchen, as Woody had convinced Mrs. Willebrandt that he would "take charge" of cooking omelets. He grabbed two skillets and said, "See? Both hands," and started to show her how they flipped eggs in Africa—but the handle came off one skillet and as he let go of the other one trying to catch the broken one, wet eggs sprayed all over the stove and the floor. By the time the guests arrived, Woody had everything "under control," wishing he'd been content to rest on his laurels.

Meanwhile, Nelson was organizing a quartet in the music room. He led his singing group in a performance for the other guests, then Woody recruited more senators and judges, and soon Nelson was directing a glee club. They drank and ate and sang until four in the morning. When the party finally broke up, all the official cars had returned to Washington, and the guests were suddenly left stranded. A foreign ambassador remarked, "You Americans have a genius for solving problems. How would you get around one like this?" Woody and Nelson, perhaps foolishly, accepted the challenge: they went outside to hail some taxis, but the streets were deserted of them. Finally, a milk wagon came into view, and Woody jumped at the chance—he ran after it, paid the driver for use of his wagon, then he and Nelson drove it straight up to the door. Nelson hopped off and held a hand out to the delighted guests. "Giddy-ap!" yelled Woody, and they drove off in triumph.

■ The reviews of *Naughty Marietta* were everything the studio could have hoped for. Critics raved about Jeanette, claiming this film was a rebirth of her career. She herself admitted to a reporter: "This is the first film in which I enjoyed my own performance." Both she and Nelson praised Woody Van Dyke for his help and his friendship. "I found Van Dyke so enigmatical and yet compatible," Jeanette said, "and then again absolutely pious at times—but always with the most delightful sense of humor."

"He is the greatest man in the world," added Nelson. "He has the knack of bringing out inexperienced people like myself. Other directors were fighting shy of me because of my lack of experience. He said he would take me, and I believe he did a good job.

"He did little with me. Everything was in a businesslike manner. He would simply say what he wanted done and I went ahead. I don't think that he gave me more than a couple hours of actual instruction, but he has the ability to show what he wants and to get the effect which he desires."

Nelson's feelings were echoed in the press, which praised Jeanette but gave special attention to him. "A new movie star emerged from the Capitol screen yesterday," announced the New York *Daily News*. "If his singing voice were all Mr. Eddy possessed, he would be a welcome addition to the screen, but he brings to it besides a canny sense of comedy and plenty of savoir faire."

The *Herald-Tribune* added: "The triumph of the Van Dyke version is registered by Nelson Eddy. Mr. Eddy has a brilliant baritone voice, he seems thoroughly masculine, he is engaging, and good looking and he gives the appearance of being unaffected."

"Mr. Eddy is very new, very handsome—and different," noted Screenland. "You've never seen a movie hero like him before. He has a really splendid voice, but he appeals first of all as a manly figure, romantic but believable . . . . Don't miss it."

Ed Sullivan raved: "It is terrific. MacDonald-Eddy are the new team sensation for the industry. Their duet of 'Sweet Mystery of Life' is the grandest thing ever recorded."

Naughty Marietta went on to become one of the New York film critics' Ten Best Pictures of 1935, and an Academy Award Best Picture nominee. It lost the Oscar to *Mutiny on the Bounty*, but in popularity polls such as the Photoplay Gold Medal Award, it consistently won Best Picture over *Mutiny*. *Naughty Marietta* did

The talent behind *Naughty Marietta*. From left to right: director Woody Van Dyke, actress Elsa Lanchester, Louie B. Mayer, Jeanette, executive Eddie Mannix, Nelson, producer Hunt Stromberg.

win an Oscar for Best Sound Recording; the award was accepted by Douglas Shearer, brother of actress Norma Shearer—who was reportedly tone-deaf!

Suddenly Nelson was an "overnight" success. He went on the road for his yearly concert tour, but this was like no tour he'd ever known. Everywhere he was besieged by reporters and mobbed by fans. "All this fuss," he complained. "What it is all about I don't quite know."

"I read about people becoming stars overnight but I didn't think such things actually happened," he told the New York *Telegram*. "I'm still flabbergasted. And naturally I'm tremendously happy."

In Richmond, Virginia, he admitted: "I always thought it was silly for these movie stars to have bodyguards and personal representatives and secretaries and what not. But now I've got to do all that. And I don't like it. When a thing like this happens to you the people you used to go to for counsel are no help, they all turn into 'yes men.' This business of the future is a one-man proposition. I've got to work it out myself. I don't know all of the answers yet but I know what I want to do, what I am determined to try to achieve. Two days ago nobody in Holly-wood knew or cared whether I lived or died. Today the place is literally swarming with people who seem to be vitally and personally concerned with my welfare. All because I sang some songs similar to others I have been singing over the radio for years—and incidentally, I didn't sing them any better than I had dozens of times before.

"Everybody from the newspapers and magazines offers me the same advice. It frightens me. They entreat me not to let my success go to my head; they ask me not to go Hollywood, whatever that is. It takes the fun out of the whole thing, almost. It seems too silly to think that doing something one has been doing for years should suddenly cause such a furor."

He answered endless questions about his lifestyle. "I have to get a fair amount of exercise in order to feel good. I can't swim anymore because last summer I got a rather bad infection in one eye. Since then that eye has become irritated every time I've gone into the water. So now I concentrate largely on tennis, golf and horseback riding.

"I never saw anyone quite so pleased as my mother was the night the picture was previewed. While we were making the picture she heard me singing snatches of songs and repeating bits of dialogue at home. But she couldn't connect them so as to make the least bit of sense. Not until she saw the picture did she realize how those fragments could be placed together."

He was still quite candid in interviews, a policy that would shortly change. "Movies are only secondary. I haven't changed my personal ambitions in the least. I have always known what I wanted to do and Hollywood isn't going to thwart me. But this success in *Naughty Marietta* has given me something I needed. It has given me the right to be authoritative. I've come to the place where I can be honest, I've won the right to dare." When told he'd always been a sincere artist, Nelson disagreed. "I've never been sincere. I used to copy my renditions of arias from phonograph records by famous baritones. Now I work out my own interpretations. They may be wrong, they may fail, but at all events they are mine, they are what I believe deep down inside of me. That's all any one can do.

"I would like to work in pictures two or three years more or as long as I am good for it—of course, my start came rather late in life for a motion picture star, but I don't want to give up music entirely. I want to continue in concert and radio work. I have no great desire to do opera, but if I can lay by sufficient money to permit it, I would like to try it sometime later. I also like radio work. It is the most remunerative. The other evening I sang two songs on a program and received twice what I get for a concert where I sing twenty-five songs. Of course the audience at the concert is limited, while the audience listening to the radio program may run into the millions."

For fun, Nelson delighted reporters with stories of the various bloopers he'd noticed in the final print. One occurred during the scene when Jeanette went upstairs, followed by a puppy. "The puppy changes color from white to black three or four times. In fact, we had a litter of five puppies and just reached in for one, regardless of color or spots, when we were shooting the scene.

"You see me shove MacDonald down into a chair and pick her up again. I threw her into the chair in December and helped her out in February. When I saw the preview, I saw that I had hair to here (he marked a point on his temples) at first and when I picked her up, a minute later on the screen, it was back over my ears.

"I noticed that marching down the street my uniform would be spic and span for a few seconds, then soiled, then bright and fresh again. In the scene where we are drifting on the bayou, which was made in a studio against a process background, the boat makes all sorts of turns around islands and I never once touch the tiller.

"I got a laugh out of one of the crowd scenes. I am supposed to be spiriting Marietta away from the city when I break into a loud song. No wonder the soldiers found us without difficulty!"

In San Francisco, Nelson saw the film in a theater and started explaining all the technical details again to a friend. An irate women finally turned to him and hissed, "Will you please stop talking and let me hear that man on the screen?"

Regarding acting, Nelson commented: "I don't know anything about it. I hope I can learn, but at present the best I can do is to try to be natural. A really emotional scene would floor me."

Nelson even encountered his first psychotic fan, a twenty-nine-year-old woman named Edith Ludwig who sent him endless letters and harassed him, until he was forced to take action. She was finally committed to the Patton State Hospital by Superior Court Judge Georgia Bullock in November 1935.

Nelson was constantly asked about Jeanette, and his comments were telling. The Lowell *Courier Citizen* noted that Nelson almost shouted when he said, "She's tops, marvelous, simply swell! There wasn't a harsh word from her during the making of the whole picture. Miss MacDonald is real and her acting and singing are legitimate."

In a Kalamazoo interview, Nelson revealed: "There was a great deal of care put on synchronizing the sound and the picture. You see, we sang the songs with orchestra off stage and a recording was made on the sound track. Then we went into the filming and during the action our songs were played back to us through loud speaker horns and we had to synchronize, and do it perfectly. No slip-shod synchronizing would do. We had to go through scenes time and time again, until they were perfect. But just mouthing the words was not good enough for Miss MacDonald. She sang right with the record, and in one place she closed with a high C, and took it every time, full voice, for I don't know how many retakes, until we had it right. We'd think it was perfect, but when they'd play it back, one of the assistant directors would say, 'Not quite right, the fourth word of the second verse,' or some other place, was just a little late. So we'd have to do it over. But the finished picture is perfect, so far as that part of it goes, and the audiences will have no feeling of faking or dubbing. Miss MacDonald is great, and I know the fans will love her."

Did he miss Jeanette while on tour? One sharp Dallas reporter was certain of the answer. Present with Nelson at a private screening of *Naughty Marietta* in the Interstate screening room, this reporter noted that when the song "I'm Falling in Love With Someone" came on the screen, Nelson signaled the projectionist to turn off the sound and he then sang to Jeanette himself. The following day, when Nelson gave his Dallas concert, a reviewer noted that he sang a number about a lad who loved a red-headed girl and didn't care who knew it.

Then toward the end of Nelson's two-month tour he grew tired of giving interviews. The reporter for the Houston *Post* found Mr. Eddy "very uncooperative." In a phone interview, the reporter asked Nelson:

"Have you ever been in Houston?"

"No," said Nelson.

"In Texas?"

"Yes, in Texas. But not Houston."

"Do you have friends here?"

"Yes, I do. Several of them."

"Will you name one?"

"No."

"Now, Mr. Eddy, since we cannot see you, perhaps you will forgive us for being a little skeptical as to who is on the other end of the line. How about singing a bar from the new picture to prove you are you?"

"No. It's too early in the morning. I've just got up. No." He hung up.

Nelson's concert reviews on this tour were excellent. The Utica *Daily Press* noted: "His tones are true, unforced; his diction is superb. His voice reveals every mood and thought, being resonant, yet sweet; vivacious or somber, capable of inflections that mere words can't express. Mr. Eddy is as much the actor as the vocalist. Occasionally he consulted his notebook. For the most part he sang spontaneously as though he himself had created the melodies to which he was giving expression."

If Nelson was surprised at his sudden fame, Jeanette was not. She wrote in a letter, "With his voice and charm I predict that Mr. Eddy will become one of the outstanding personalities in motion pictures." She elaborated elsewhere: "No other man on the screen gives such an impression of eagerness and sincerity as Nelson Eddy. He is unique in this respect. It is this boy-like quality which appeals most to women—the quality of unsophisticated eagerness in a mature and attractive man. He is exactly the same on the screen as off . . . anxious to please . . . the least theatrical artist I've ever known. There's not an ounce of affectation in him. He was destined for stardom from the beginning."

By May 1, 1935, Nelson had returned from his triumphant concert tour and was once again pressing Jeanette to marry him. Still she held back, the matter in question being once again her career. Nelson continued to insist that she would have to step aside and let him be the star of the family. He wanted a wife at home and a mother for his children, and felt that it would never do to have both of them competing for top billing, especially given the competitive, temperamental personalities.

Nelson made his feelings known publicly. "Generally speaking, I think an actor or actress shouldn't marry another in the profession, for in time one almost always overshadows the other, and that's bad. They try not to be jealous, but they just can't help it. Many times I have seen singers whose marriages were spoiled in this way. They would be in New York, looking for work, and one of them would get a job there, while the other would have to take a less important job in some state far away. And that would be the end of their marriage."

But Jeanette was not willing to give up all she had worked so hard for. She was just reaching her peak as a movie star. She tried to explain to Nelson that singing was her life, that she could no more give it up than Nelson could and that he was wrong to expect it of her; she might be willing to lighten her work load at some point in the future, but not now. Her vow that she loved Nelson regardless, and would work with him to create the marriage, fell on deaf ears. For Nelson, it was all or nothing.

They put the subject of marriage aside, hoping that time would resolve things for them. Over the next several weeks they were frequently seen in public together. Nelson even relented a bit and consented for them to be photographed together at the Trocadero and other movie star hangouts. They made the rounds of parties together and inevitably were asked to sing. One or the other would accompany at the piano, and they sang all the *Naughty Marietta* songs and other requests.

Friends who recalled seeing the two at parties together during this period always remarked that Nelson dogged Jeanette's movements "like a love-sick puppy dog." He was constantly at her heels, running to fetch her food and drink —once at a dinner party, he angrily pushed aside someone's hand so he could grab the salt for Jeanette. He even went so far as to follow her, on one occasion, into the bathroom. At first Jeanette enjoyed his earnest attentions, but in time the novelty wore off and she felt increasingly smothered by his possessiveness.

One Saturday morning Sandy Reiss received a phone call from Jeanette. She was staying at the El Encanto hotel in Santa Barbara, and there was a script at the studio she needed. Would Sandy be willing to pick it up and drive it to her? He agreed to come the next morning. When he arrived at the bungalow, the door was opened by Nelson, wearing nothing but shorts. Reiss got a glimpse of Jeanette as she waved to him on her way to the bathroom, naked and struggling into a robe. After she dressed, the three of them had breakfast (Nelson still in his shorts) before Sandy returned to Los Angeles.

Reiss didn't know the name of the script he delivered; it might have been *The Life of Johann Strauss*, scheduled as a follow-up for *Naughty Marietta*. Another possibility was *Let Freedom Ring*, which appeared in a photo ad by MGM as their next vehicle, to be released in the fall of 1935. Mayer had planned to co-star Nelson in *Rose Marie* with Grace Moore, but Nelson didn't want to work with Moore. He'd had an affair with her previously, and didn't "want it getting all involved again." He stalled around with various excuses and local singing engagements until Moore was no longer available for the film.

Jeanette, meanwhile, was intrigued with the story of *San Francisco* as her next vehicle: "Mrs. Koverman & I are trying to figure out a way to get Gable to read the script," she wrote to Bob Ritchie. "He simply won't read it and if we can (not too obviously) interest him in it he may be unwilling to give up some of his vacation to do it." She wanted to make another film with Nelson as well, but felt *San Francisco* was entirely wrong for him.

Although Nelson was good friends with Gable, he refused to encourage Gable on Jeanette's behalf. As far as Nelson was concerned, he didn't care if she made any more films, period. He needed her by his side, to help him deal with his newfound stardom. "All reports say the boy can't realize his own popularity," explained one reporter. "If he realizes it, he's just refusing to go Hollywood. Long may he waver."

In Beverly Hills one day, Nelson parked his car to buy Jeanette a bouquet of flowers. He was mobbed trying to get back to the car, while Jeanette cowered in the front seat, shrieking women pounding away on the windows and doors. And this wasn't an isolated experience. In the barber shop, women fought to pick up locks of his hair from the floor, on the street they'd pull buttons off his clothes and steal his handkerchiefs, after concerts they'd tear off pieces of his sheet music. By August 1935, Nelson reportedly received more fan mail than any other movie star, more even than Clark Gable. (Jeanette held the number-one position for female stars.) Nelson had risen to the number-four concert draw in the country, after Lawrence Tibbett, Grace Moore and Lily Pons, and by the following year, he was number one. He would hold the record as the highest paid singer in the world for several years, finally ousted from the top in the 1940s by a youngster named Frank Sinatra.

▮Jeanette had managed to put aside the unpleasant memory of Nelson's temper attack. However, with the passing weeks she found that this might not be an isolated incident. Nelson was frequently subject to mood swings, ranging from manic rages to deep anxiety attacks and depression. Though she attributed his instability to his childhood scars, it was still difficult to deal with it, and as she got to know him better, he proved to be a passionate but overbearing lover. He was extremely possessive, and grew to be more so. He watched her every move. In public he scowled if any man paid attention to her too long, and when he got tired of putting up with what he termed her "flirting," he'd grab her and rudely march her out. Occasionally he grew so angry that he forced her down, shouting that she was his and he'd make certain she never wanted to look at another man again. The novelty of his sexual aggressiveness quickly wore off, and Jeanette naturally resented being treated like a possession. She found his Jekyll-Hyde personality, as she termed it, unpredictable and hard to handle.

Then there was the looming disagreement over her career. Nelson was adamant about his plans for their future; they'd marry, Jeanette would retire and raise their children. He refused to have a career wife. Jeanette, for her part, was equally adamant. There was no way she'd consider giving up her film work, nor did her plans include children in the foreseeable future.

To Nelson, her refusal to listen meant that she didn't love him as much as he loved her. Jeanette tried repeatedly to convince him that she *did* love him, that she would be a good and supportive wife despite the career, and that she would be faithful to him. She had reason to have her own doubts that Nelson could remain monogamous, as demonstrated by her experience with him since they'd met. Every time they broke up or had a fight, he'd take up with other women so fast it "made her head swim."

Sandy Reiss told of an incident when Nelson called him from a bar, slightly drunk. Nelson was in Santa Barbara, he couldn't get hold of Jeanette at home in Los Angeles, and he was missing her terribly. "I'm sitting here in this bar with a floozie, and she's looking too good. If Jenny doesn't get here fast, I'm going to do something we'll both regret," he told Sandy. Sandy was able to locate Jeanette, who thanked him gratefully, and drove up to Santa Barbara to save Nelson from a fate worse than death.

As the weeks passed, Nelson grew irritated with Jeanette's refusal to drop everything and marry him. He became argumentative and refused to take her out socially and share her with "her public." Determined to overwhelm her with his passion and worth, the more he tightened the leash, the more Jeanette rebelled. By the middle of June 1935, they were at an impasse. For Jeanette, the final straw came one night at the Coconut Grove. She loved to dance. Nelson hated it, so on this particular evening when a fan asked Jeanette to dance, she accepted. Nelson watched this with his usual ill humor until, enraged, he grabbed Jeanette out of the fan's arms and literally carried her out of the place. She was furious and humiliated, but she was no match for Nelson when he was in this state. To Jeanette, he seemed near-insane; there was no reasoning with him, and she counted herself lucky to escape his wrath without being mentally and sexually abused.

Most fans would have considered Jeanette crazy not to marry Nelson anyway, but they never saw this side of him. "Living with Nelson is like living with World War II in your house," Isabel Eddy once remarked. Once even *she* moved out on him, after he hit her during an argument. Nelson told Jeanette, "The hell with her, I don't ever want to see her again." But the separation didn't last long, and the ever-forgiving Isabel soon returned.

Jeanette finally gave him an ultimatum. She would not consider marriage to Nelson until he cured his jealous Jekyll-Hyde temper. "You've made your last scene with me in public," Jeanette told him, assuring him that they were through.

Isabel Eddy was disgusted with her son. Clearly, after spending a considerable amount of time with Jeanette, she had completely reversed her opinion of her. In her unpublished memoirs, Isabel wrote of a weekend that Jeanette spent with the Eddys at their home. She described this "never-to-be-forgotten" weekend:

"I had never seen Nelson so happy. She shared my bedroom as we had only two, and this was the first time I ever saw that famous nightdress. I looked at her in amazement—not at the quaintness of it, but at the girl herself. I could think of nothing so much as that she was a white angel. It was more than a negligee, more a nightdress—long sleeved, a wide ruffle around the neck—as dainty as a flower with laces and ribbons—form fitting, yet it seemed to float around her as though she were an adorable little red-headed fairy. The golden curls hanging over her shoulders made her look no more than a child, and this night as I looked at her I thought how safe a man would be with her. Despite any career, with this girl a marriage vow would always come first. Alas, my son did not believe this and so the Gods forever ruled his peace away."

Rose Marie.

9

"The happiest summer of my life"

Personal problems or not, Jeanette and Nelson had to be professionally teamed again, thanks to the fantastic response to *Naughty Marietta*. Their next film vehicle was finally decided upon: *Rose Marie*. This was an operetta penned by Rudolf Friml and Herbert Stothart, now the musical director at MGM. Stothart, an extremely talented composer and arranger, rarely received credit for his genius. Although he shared royalties equally with Friml for *Rose Marie*, he did not share the fame, and most people are unaware that he co-authored it. Stothart later received an Academy Award for his musical direction on *The Wizard of Oz*, in 1939. Along with most of the MacDonald-Eddy films, he was responsible for memorable scores for films like *Queen Christina*, *Mrs. Miniver*, *Mutiny on the Bounty* and many other MGM classics.

While the script was being readied Jeanette and Nelson busied themselves with vocal appearances. Nelson sang his last oratorios in San Francisco; later in 1935 he gave his final operatic appearance in that same city, in *Aida*. His faithful following from the early days was heartsick that he seemed to be discarding opera for films. They didn't realize his obsession with Jeanette.

Meanwhile, feeling somewhat rejected, Nelson dived into a brief and unhappy romance with screenwriter Frances Marion, an older woman. The few photos taken of them together show a serious-looking Nelson, devoid of that radiant joy so evident when he was with Jeanette. He also dated Isabel Jewell and Alice Faye. Once, in mid-July, he escorted Mary Pickford to the Hollywood Bowl. In the candid photo captured of this date, Nelson is uncomfortable and looks downright miserable.

Jeanette, meanwhile, began attending parties unescorted, a further sign that, before *Rose Marie* began, things were falling apart. She went out once with a New York socialite, Guy Giroux. At one event, in mid-June, she arrived at the home of Rozika Dolly (one of the Dolly sisters) alone. Someone whistled at her. She turned and looked. The man introduced himself—actor Gene Raymond. Jeanette introduced herself, but of course Raymond knew who she was. Rozika Dolly had opened her front door and greeted the two as a couple, though of course they weren't. Gene was interested in someone else at the party, as Jeanette later confirmed.

Some nights later Jeanette and Gene met again under similar circumstances. After a third chance encounter at Grauman's Chinese Theater, Gene asked her out the following night to go dancing. "Since everyone has us in love," he said, "don't you think we should at least have one date so everyone won't be wrong?"

Jeanette dated Gene Raymond a handful of times during the summer of 1935. The first few dates seemed inconsequential; apparently, they couldn't find anything to talk about. But he was a good dancer and, more importantly, Anna MacDonald approved of him. What's more, Gene's features resembled Nelson's somewhat. As one observer put it, "Gene could have been Nelson's younger brother."

Jeanette was in no mood for heavy romance, and Raymond was smart enough not to overwhelm her. Though he seems to have been smitten, he moved slowly, first cultivating her friendship. It was a wise move. Raymond, a second-lead actor, never tried to position himself as Jeanette's professional equal. Instead, he showed interest and support in her career. Consequently, he was fun to be around.

Jeanette also kept up her correspondence with Bob Ritchie, who was staying at the Savoy in London. In a letter dated August 24, 1935, addressed from her home at 193 Carmelina Drive, in Brentwood, she wrote Ritchie of the latest *Rose Marie* developments: "Just done some more script on Rose Marie and it looks promising, of course I'm very thrilled about the music. I am going to sing the Romeo & Juliette aria in the first scene . . . You must not breathe it to a soul because someone else is liable to beat us to it and take the edge off it. Juliette is one of the few good lyric arias left and I'd hate G. M. [Grace Moore] to beat me to that one too. So hold your fingers crossed that I get this in first— I know you're wondering where grand opera comes in Rose Marie but this is a picture version of RM and nothing like the stage play—thank goodness."

The film version of *Rose Marie* told the story of haughty Canadian opera diva Marie de Flor (Jeanette), whose criminal brother John Flower (Jimmy Stewart) escapes from the penitentiary. She goes after him incognito, meeting up with Sergeant Bruce (Nelson) of the Mounted Police. Bruce catches on to her identity, and accompanies her in the wilderness, knowing that she will lead him to Flower. They fall in love in the meantime, but he arrests Flower anyway, to her dismay. She suffers a breakdown, which only can be cured by her beloved Mountie returning to her.

Nelson and Jeanette's hiatus from each other was short-lived, but good for both of them. By August the romance was once again in full swing. "I knew when I met Nelson that he was the love of my life, that I could never love another man," Jeanette told Isabel Eddy. Despite all the reasons she felt Nelson was wrong for her, she was unable to resist her attraction to him. And Nelson seemed to be making a supreme effort to control his jealousy and temper.

Blurbs about them began appearing again in the papers, items like: "Question of the Month—Can you name the beautiful, blonde star who has but to look across the room at a certain auburn-haired actress to make her cheeks match her hair?" And: "Nelson Eddy is sporting a dark gray Tux with black braid. Makes it easier to escape from pursuing females. The gray confuses 'em. With this he wears Jeanette MacDonald, on his arm."

In early September they went shopping together in Beverly Hills. While browsing through a jewelry store, Jeanette was attracted to a huge emerald ring surrounded by diamonds. Nelson made note of the ring and returned afterwards to the shop to purchase it for her. It set him back over $40,000, but Nelson paid it gladly, planning to present the ring when he asked for her hand in marriage. He sensed that this time, with things looking up for them, she would at last say yes.

On September 6, 1935, the cast and crew of *Rose Marie* traveled by car up to northern California to film on location at Lake Tahoe. Nelson and Jeanette traveled in separate automobiles. For Jeanette the drive was rough, as she was

Summer 1935.

plagued with motion sickness, but once at Tahoe, she recovered her good spirits.

The many automobiles making the trek to Tahoe were followed by a train of seventeen box cars with supplies and equipment for the shoot. Fifty canoes were used, as well as sleds needed for hauling equipment over the mountain trails that vehicles couldn't negotiate. Life preservers were necessary because few of the Indians knew how to swim (nearly 1,000 people were utilized for the filming, over 700 of them Indians gathered from Arizona, New Mexico, Oklahoma and Wyoming). The tribes were quartered in tents about five miles from the main camp, in large part because the Piute and Washoe tribes were hereditary enemies, and no one knew if serious fighting would break out. Nine marriages took place in the camp the first week, and director Woody Van Dyke eventually arranged for a group of "starlets" to come from Los Angeles to keep his regular crew happy.

Location filming had its drawbacks, as Jeanette soon learned. When they were filming in high country there were no bathrooms nearby. Jeanette insisted on bringing a portable potty, which had to be lugged each day by mule. The crew complained that she should go in the bushes like everybody else, but she stood her ground—then one day, several thousand feet up, the mule bucked and the potty went over the side. "Jeanette took it like a lady, which she apparently was," reported Fred Phillips, makeup man on *Rose Marie*.

The film was shot around the Lake Tahoe environs, in a fifty-mile radius. Forty-foot-high totem poles were erected at a state-owned park at Emerald Bay for the "Totem Tom Tom" number, shot in four grueling days of filming. (Some years later, the remaining totem poles used in *Rose Marie* were chopped up into pieces and sold to private collectors. One section of a totem pole can still be viewed today at the entrance of a shopping center in Lake Tahoe.) One of the main dancers for that sequence was Mary Anita Loos, niece of screenwriter Anita Loos, who had lied her way into the picture. She claimed that she was an Indian and an expert dancer; after she was signed she admitted that she didn't know how to dance, so choreographer Chester Hale worked with her for eight hours a day for two weeks to teach her. Another important actor was Iron Eyes Cody, an Indian who helped Van Dyke with translation between Woody, who certainly had his hands full, and the native Americans.

Because of the vagaries of the weather, the day began at 4:30 A.M., with filming at 6:00 A.M. sharp. If the sky was clear, they could shoot until 4:00 P.M. A single cloud in the sky could ruin the entire day; in one instance, they lost four days due to the weather. Because of the limited time each day, box lunches were utilized for a quick meal at noon. The first day on location, the prop department set up a small table for Woody outside his tent and presented him with a beautiful salad and hot beef stew. Woody asked, "Is this the same thing everybody else is getting for lunch?" When told it wasn't, he thanked the crew for their thoughtfulness and declined the meal. "I'm sorry, boys, I thought you knew there would be no discrimination in this unit," he said, and went to the end of the line to wait for his box lunch.

The dailies were screened in the local movie theater in nearby Truckee. One day Fred Phillips attended the rushes with Woody, the script girl, Jeanette's hairdresser and maid, and Jeanette. As they were waiting to see the footage, they heard some "godawful" piano music coming from behind the stage. Woody complained, and the playing stopped. Then the piano began again, this time played beautifully. They brought the player out: the young Jimmy Stewart, who was playing the small part of Jeanette's brother in the film. Woody was so impressed with Stewart that he kept him on the picture three weeks instead of three days.

In the original script for the film, Nelson was to break Stewart's wrist when he arrested him. "I was going to break into his cabin and pull my gun," Nelson explained. "He was going to struggle with me. I was going to crack him over the wrist, snap the cuffs on him, and then toss him a handkerchief to wipe the sweat from his brow. But as it turned out, things were different. They changed the script."

Against the beautiful lake setting, and with the erratic filming schedule, Jeanette and Nelson's romance flourished. Often they'd disappear together for hours, riding far from the studio base at Chambers Lodge. On Sunday mornings, they went to the banks of Emerald Bay and serenaded the locals with

On the set of *Rose Marie*.

"Indian Love Call," "Rose Marie" and religious hymns sung to each other. On one occasion, they sneaked into the Truckee movie theater playing *Naughty Marietta* in their honor, and giggled and carried on—with Nelson throwing popcorn at the screen—until they were asked to leave. Another time the film's cast had a party, and they were all a little drunk. Nelson and Jeanette took a canoe out onto the lake. One of the crew members had binoculars; he looked out and said, "All I can see is a plaid behind." (Jeanette had been wearing a plaid skirt.)

The few writers sent to cover the location filming for fan magazines were amazed at the change in Nelson. They used descriptions like "pleased with life," "enthusiastic" and "happy." Nelson told one reporter, "I truly believe I am in one of the most beautiful spots in the entire world—if not the most beautiful . . . I am sure Jeanette MacDonald is enjoying it every bit as much as I am. We both spend hours exploring and walking to interesting places. Huge trees, a gorgeous lake and the most picturesque scenery you have ever seen. Jeanette and I have had lots of fun practicing to see what echo effects we can get. This five-echo canyon we have found is the most amazing of all. It is the oddest feeling to sing and have your voice come back to you, not from one place but from five. I am pretty sure they are going to use this canyon in the picture."

Whenever possible, Woody held parties for his cast and crew to keep morale high. At one such party, Jeanette and Nelson stole the show dancing the rhumba, then singing the entire *Rose Marie* score.

The insecurities that had plagued Nelson during the filming of *Naughty Marietta* were nowhere in evidence at Tahoe. "At dinner, he is the life of the party," noted a visiting magazine writer. "After dinner he plays pool with all comers for an hour or so and frequently shakes the rafters with some extemporaneous song. And then, by nine o'clock he retires to his cabin." This writer watched the two stars together on the set, sitting side by side. Nelson was dozing, Jeanette was "just looking [at him], and her eyes are filled with dreams."

Another visiting reporter wrote:

> To many, Jeanette MacDonald seems to pull down a curtain which completely hides her real self. Even to those who know her rather closely, she has the knowledge of how to keep people at a distance. But to those whom she chooses to call "friend," Jeanette can be warm and loyal and loving. However, she weighs and balances her emotions . . . . It is not warmth or sex appeal that has built MacDonald into a big box-office draw. It is the elusive, unapproachable quality which people like, although they do not always understand it.
>
> Once I caught Jeanette off guard. It was at the Brown Derby a few years ago. She was lunching with Bill and Ella Wilkerson, the well-known Hollywood scribes. Ella is the lovely girl who has been confined to a wheelchair for many years, and Bill is her devoted and humorous brother. When they finished their

lunch, Jeanette insisted on wheeling Ella up and down the Boulevard while they both ate ice cream cones.

She wants to be a truly great singer. One of her fixed ambitions is to sing the role of Mignon in the opera of that name on the screen.

She likes Nelson Eddy, and is glad to have him showered with adulation and success.

Candid photos on the *Rose Marie* set demonstrate their newfound happiness. In one, they sit together, Jeanette with her daily fresh flowers, Nelson beaming at her, happily smoking a pipe. In another, he glares at the camera for catching them together in an intimate moment; she's sitting on his lap and their fingers are entwined. In yet another, he holds her makeup kit for her while she touches up her face. The makeup kit was a gift from him; inside it by the mirror he inscribed, "You're looking at my favorite person."

One of the stars' favorite scenes in the picture was the "beans and bacon" one. The script called for a famished Jeanette to gobble up Nelson's beans and bacon. The idea seemed amusing at first, and she and Nelson delightfully ad-libbed their way through it. However, five days later they were still filming the lengthy sequence. Nelson kidded Jeanette endlessly off-camera, and even Woody promised, "Don't worry, kid, I'll see that you get something good to eat in your next picture." Beans and bacon became a nostalgic meal for the two stars, and in later years, Nelson's idea of a romantic meal for them was the famous *Rose Marie* meal.

The song "Indian Love Call" was sung three times in the final film. The first version was Nelson's solo; he had to stand under a tree and serenade Jeanette. The shooting took a comic turn when he tangled with a pesky branch that kept whipping him in the face. During one take, he interrupted his own singing with a frustrated curse about the tree. Jeanette burst out laughing, as did Nelson and everyone else. Nelson was usually such a gentleman in public that few people had ever heard him swear.

The "Indian Love Call" outtake became the highlight of a reel of MacDonald-Eddy bloopers. Over the years, Jeanette frequently borrowed the reel from MGM and showed it at parties. Nelson cursing at the tree branch never failed to get a laugh.

Jeanette would ever after refer to their days at Tahoe as "the happiest summer of my life."

On September 12, 1936, Jeanette wrote Ritchie from her cottage, Number 36 at Chambers Lodge. "We will no doubt be here for 3 or 4 weeks (if we're lucky) . . . Saturday nite Nelson & I went shopping & caused a mild sensation —we saw "Anything Goes" which hadn't opened yet in NY . . . Enjoyed it, maybe because I hadn't seen a show for so long or because I enjoyed the music . . . Afterward to the Trocadero to dance where people started buzzing & pictures were taken."

Away from the pressures of the studio, they gained a new perspective of their future together. Jeanette conceded that she might lighten her work load, perhaps making only one film a year, so that she could be the wife Nelson wanted. They discussed the possibility of doing joint concert tours each spring, and even leaked to the press the exciting news that they were planning an opera together after the film was finished.

Jeanette had only one remaining fear about marriage. She was afraid that Nelson could not love her in the way she needed—she didn't want an open relationship. Jeanette had changed since first meeting Nelson—her promiscuous days were over forever. But Jeanette wasn't sure how Nelson would cope with long separations during concert tours, or temptation from future co-stars at the studio. In 1945, she reflected in a letter:

"You know, if I could live any of my life with Nelson over again I know when it would be. The time when I really began to believe in his love, far off in those glorious mountains. He kept asking me to be his wife . . . I loved him then far more than he loved me, and I was so afraid of being hurt. I thought he was the most wonderful thing I'd ever seen or known and it seemed too much to expect that he should really love me. And then one night as we stood watching the giant trees as they stretched their fingers skyward—his manner suddenly changed to one of great softness. And turning to take me in his arms, and burying his lips in my hair—as sweetly and tenderly as the night was coming to meet us, he said 'I will never love another woman. When will you believe that?'

Rowing on Lake Tahoe.

There was something in his voice then that went deep and I knew that I was being given a part of him that no other woman would ever be given. I never forgot that night, and have cherished those words as he will never know I have."

When Nelson proposed to Jeanette, she agreed to marry him. Against the setting of Tahoe's Emerald Bay, Nelson slipped the emerald engagement ring on her finger. They practiced their wedding vows, promising to love each other for all time.

Nelson's impulse was to elope to Reno, before Jeanette had time for second thoughts. She, however, had always wanted a big church wedding, and to be a June bride. Nelson grudgingly conceded. Jeanette's other stipulation was that the engagement be kept secret until they returned to Los Angeles. She wanted to break the news gently to her mother, and of course, she had to gain Mayer's consent as well.

One of the few people let in on the secret was Woody Van Dyke, who wished his "kids" the best, and was genuinely happy for them. Although no correspondence from that period has survived between Jeanette and Bob Ritchie, she also apparently notified him of the latest developments, since a letter from Steve Kroeger, a close friend of Ritchie's, has survived. Dated September 7, and addressed to Jeanette, it reads:

> I think I can understand the phase of life you are now passing through, seeking a youth and gaiety that you did not have in your normal time of life when younger. Of course it has come rather late in your life, and has whirled you off your feet. But if it is that you have been seeking and is really what you want in life most of all, it is your happiness only that matters and I wish you naught but well. Bob I know still loves you very much, and his love certainly has carried you in no small measure to that pinnacle of fame and success you now enjoy.

A carbon copy of this letter was found among Ritchie's possessions after his death in 1972. As far as is known, Jeanette never replied to Kroeger's letter.

▆▆▆ Then came the day when Jeanette discovered that she was pregnant.

Nelson was delighted with the news and insisted that they forget the church wedding and run off to Reno immediately. For Jeanette, the decision wasn't so simple. She made a call to MGM to discuss the entire matter with Louis B. Mayer. Per the morals clause in her contract, she had to obtain his permission to marry, divorce or have a child. She knew a shotgun wedding would never fly with Mayer, and she was right.

"She [Jeanette] and Nelson Eddy were sweethearts, and he got her pregnant," recalled June Thompson Swift, a dancer who worked on *Rose Marie*. "She was a kind person, sweet, it showed on her face. She was a lovely lady. Her affair with Nelson Eddy had to be broken up. She was told she had to have an abortion, because the studio wouldn't hear of her having a baby. They didn't want any scandal, they didn't want any hint that there was any relationship at all, so they tried to hush up everything connected with the two of them being romantically involved.

"He [Mayer] was a tyrant. He really was. He had everybody wanting to bump him off. He had no sensitivity at all, and was very callous in his feelings. Strictly money, money, money."

Jeanette was ordered to get rid of her "problem" and break up with "that chowderhead" immediately. Nelson was really on Mayer's "hit list" this time, and not only because he'd "knocked her up." Mayer was incensed because Nelson was threatening to take Louella Parsons to court.

Apparently gossip columnist Parsons was responsible for a blurb suggesting that Nelson and Jeanette were caught kissing in the parking lot of the Trocadero. Nelson felt that Parsons had overstepped her bounds, and he was determined to put an end to her snooping. Another source claims that he did in fact sue. As the story goes, he left the *Rose Marie* set for two days to consult with a judge—sources claim the location was either San Francisco or Sacramento. A settlement was reached, with Nelson stipulating that his private life never be mentioned again in Louella's column.

Jeanette intended to comply with Mayer's orders regarding the abortion, hoping that once the pressure was off she would still change Mayer's mind about her marrying Nelson. She communicated her intentions to Nelson, reminding him that they could always have a child at a future time. Her only problem now was finding a doctor up in Tahoe who could perform the abortion.

Nelson took the news worse than she had expected. He was furious that she seemed to love her career more than she loved him, and she was willing to kill their child. They had a series of violent arguments, then Nelson broke up with her in disgust.

As it turned out, nature handled the problem for her. One evening after work, she began to hemorrhage. Alone and frightened, she confided in Woody Van Dyke who nursed her through her miscarriage.

Jeanette missed a few days of filming due to "a cold" (the press version). She returned to work looking wan and weak. Dan Thomas, a writer for the New York *World-Telegram* admitted in print that "Jeanette became ill and was ordered on a special diet during her entire stay." However, she stuck it out and showed up for work.

Jeanette posted a letter to Bob Ritchie, telling him she had some news which she would share with him later. She added, "I'm warning you, you're in for a couple of shockers." Meanwhile, she attempted to patch things up with Nelson, to no avail. He refused to believe that she hadn't aborted his baby. "I'm finally wise to you," he told her. "You'd do anything for that lousy career of yours, even to getting yourself fixed. Anything not to have my name. Do me a favor, forget you ever met me. I've already forgotten it." Off the set, he refused to have anything further to do with her.

"One of the reasons Jeanette made such a mess of things was that she was frail physically," asserted a friend of Nelson's. "After she and Nelson fought she'd always be sick for a day or two. Even from the earliest days she was always leaning up against Nelson, and not from love. He was always grabbing chairs for her. On the set he'd yell at the grips to get her a chair fast. If they didn't move fast enough he'd get angry, and sometimes grabbed a chair out from someone else to give Jeanette. He'd take the chair away from God if Jeanette needed it."

This time, however, Nelson was frighteningly indifferent to Jeanette's physical sufferings. Upset, she called her sister Blossom, who was in New York with her mother. Blossom juggled her plans to come immediately to Tahoe to her sister's rescue. During her visit, Blossom snapped a single Kodak photo of her sister playing checkers with Jimmy Stewart.

Bob Ritchie, on his return to Los Angeles from London, came twice to visit Jeanette on location in the hopes of rekindling their relationship. He left with his hopes dashed. Gene Raymond, on the other hand, made progress. Jeanette was truly grateful for Gene's considerate attentions. Both Fred Phillips and dancer Mary Anita Loos admitted carrying messages and letters back and forth between Gene and Jeanette.

In the meantime, the indefatigable Van Dyke was saddled with trying to wrap up location shots with two co-stars who weren't on speaking terms. He attempted to reason with Nelson, assuring him that Jeanette hadn't aborted his child. After a while, Nelson seemed to believe him, but he still wasn't inclined to be any friendlier. That Jeanette's friendship with Gene Raymond seemed to be heating up didn't go unnoticed by him. "I couldn't care less what she does," he informed Woody. "She has what she wants, someone as phony as she is. Bless 'em both, they deserve each other."

"Yeah, kid," Woody replied. "Your acting hasn't improved a whole lot, has it?"

From the front office came strange news about changes to the *Rose Marie* production schedule. Certain scenes were to be deleted from the script, including the "Echo Duet" between the two stars, shot at the top of Cascade Falls. And the film, originally intended to be in color, was now expected to be released in black-and-white. Finally, orders were taken to change Nelson's makeup—for the worse. Makeup man Fred Phillips had no idea why, but he was ordered by makeup supervisor Jack Dawn to go heavy on the pancake. No one seemed to realize at the time that these changes were a deliberate effort to sabotage Nelson. Jeanette was the only one to query the makeup changes; faithful to Fred Phillips, she refused to have Jack Dawn take over. The one morning when Jack insisted on doing Jeanette's makeup himself, she wiped it all off after he had left and insisted that Fred do her over again.

Upon finishing the location shooting, the crew limped back to Los Angeles, where Mayer further unleased his wrath against Nelson: his scenes were chopped; some were re-shot. The most ludicrous example was Nelson's opening scene— which didn't occur until well into the film—in which he rides a horse with his "men" behind him, singing "The Mounties." Nelson was filmed on a badly disguised treadmill, with a grimace of a smile. His "men" are seen riding behind him, slightly out of focus, with a rear projection film. The contrast between the beautifully shot location footage and Nelson's cheap-looking studio shots is startling.

Mayer wanted Nelson *out*. As he had done with John Gilbert and Ramon Novarro, he hoped to showcase "troublemaker" Nelson to such bad effect that the fans "take one look at him and run the other way." Mayer told an unhappy Woody Van Dyke, "Any scene that bastard looks good in goes, scrapped, thrown in the garbage can! I'm going to destroy that bastard. I'm going to wipe him off the face of the earth. Wait'll you see what I do to that son of a bitch!"

Nelson was summoned to Mayer's office and severely lectured. He was warned never to step out of line again while at the studio, if he valued his life. Nelson snickered at the vague threats, which only infuriated Mayer further. "As long as I'm your boss, you listen to me!" Mayer screamed ominously. "When I roar, you listen!"

Yet Nelson was unimpressed. He didn't care about the outcome of *Rose Marie*. Woody did, however, and continued to work to make the picture the best possible product. In the end, except for bad makeup and a minimum of on-screen time, Nelson's performance was strong.

■■■ Woody's crew had returned from location for the studio shots in mid-October 1935, and production continued for two more months. The director attempted to lighten the mood by providing an abundance of pranks on the set. The first recipient was Dr. Edouard Lippe, who hung around to watch the goings-on when not coaching Nelson vocally.

Lippe had noticed that every time they were ready to shoot, the cameraman snapped a switch on a small box attached to the side of the camera. The box with its wires fascinated Lippe. He asked Van Dyke what the switch was for, and Woody lied magnificently. He told Lippe the box was hooked up to every sound stage in the studio, and by snapping the switch when they were making a take, all activity all over the lot was cut off.

"Practically shuts down the whole studio then, doesn't it?" asked Lippe.

"You bet it does," agreed Woody.

Cameraman Bill Daniels agreed to let Lippe snap the switch the next morning. It was a Saturday and Woody told the cast, "You know how I like football. If you all keep on your toes we can make this scene in one take." He reminded everyone that if they didn't blow the scene they could all go home early, get paid for a day, and he'd see his football game.

Lippe waited impatiently for his turn. When Bill Daniels finally gave him the signal, Lippe eagerly snapped the switch—whereupon a series of explosions rocked the stage. Daniels looked horrified as his camera blew up and film went flying all over the place. Four huge lights came crashing down and scenery toppled. Men with hand bellows pumped blue smoke around for added effect. Woody screamed at Lippe, "Do you know what you've done?" Lippe meekly offered to pay for the film if it would help. At that, Woody and Nelson revealed that it was all a gag. A crew of electricians and prop men had worked overtime to create the special effects.

Woody also pulled a stunt on Jeanette. In one scene, she was to fall off her horse in the river. To get the proper close-ups of her while flailing in the water, the studio water tank was utilized. This tank, located inside a special stage, had high sides, and the only way to get in or out was by climbing a ladder which was lowered inside. The water level was not high enough to drown anyone, but tank shots were uncomfortable nevertheless.

Woody scheduled the shoot just before the noon hour. Jeanette climbed into the tank and did the shot. At twelve a whistle blew, the lights were switched off, and everyone hurried off for lunch, leaving Jeanette alone in the tank. She figured it was a deliberate prank and decided against screaming for help. After ten minutes or so she heard footsteps, and Woody peered down, aiming a flashlight at her. "You little devil," Woody said, "I might have known you'd drown before you'd yell for help."

Despite Woody's attempts to ease tension on the set, his two stars still weren't talking to each other.

In November 1935, Jeanette filmed two operatic sequences for *Rose Marie*—arias from *Romeo and Juliet* and *Tosca*. A rehearsal recording of her Juliet number survived; she flubs the opening a couple of times, and finally is heard (almost intelligibly) cursing and berating herself. Musical director Herbert Stothart calms her down, and she finally sings the number to her liking.

With his footage completed on the film, Nelson gave some local concerts that month, and sang what turned out to be his final operatic role, in *Aida*. The reviews in the San Francisco papers were overwhelmingly laudatory. The *Examiner*: "Beautifully, nobly sung was the Amonasro of Nelson Eddy." The Oakland *Tribune*: "Just for the sake of the record, let it be noted that, according to the management of the opera house, the crowd last night was the largest ever to witness an opera performance there—surpassing even the throngs which attended the opening in 1932." The *Call-Bulletin*: "Eddy has lost some of the inhibition which last year gave his acting a savor of self-consciousness. As Amonasro he burned with hatred and plotted with malevolence. His voice was produced with ease and rang with tremendous vitality. Hollywood has done much histrionically for the young baritone." And the *Chronicle*: "He is one of the great voices of the century, suave, aristocratic, yet as forceful as the music demands. He is one of the major reasons for believing that, at least so far as baritones are concerned, America need not import its future opera stars from abroad."

Nelson also gave concerts in Los Angeles and Pasadena. Jeanette attended both. The Los Angeles *Times* commented on one concert, "To most of the auditors, Eddy's musical peak was attained with his rendition of 'Ah, Sweet Mystery of Life.' When he declared, 'I don't sing it without Jeanette MacDonald,' the audience applauded vociferously, in the obvious hope that she would emerge from the audience in approved vaudeville style and make it a duo. But she went only so far as to bow, and exchange salutations."

The other concert was attended by Lee Temple, a writer for Screenplay magazine. Temple noted that an almost identical occurrence happened: "In Hollywood these days the name Jeanette MacDonald is the best romantic copy. Every day one sees her name coupled with either that of her manager, Bob Ritchie, or Gene Raymond. Each one has had it said about him that he will be the lucky one to lead Miss MacDonald to the altar, and maybe one of them will, but some can't help but discount it. There seems to be something stronger behind all this. Many can't help but feel that in *Naughty Marietta* and in Jeanette MacDonald, Nelson Eddy found the antidote for loneliness. They can't help but feel that if it wasn't for Eddy's sanely and sensibly looking at the situation, long before this the newspapers and magazines would have been running stories of their romance. Just recently something happened to confirm these feelings.

"Eddy was appearing in a concert in Los Angeles. Jeanette MacDonald was in the audience; Eddy didn't know this. It came time for him to sing. He did. The applause demanded an encore. Nelson began, and the aria was 'Love's Old Sweet Song.' Suddenly he stopped, waved to his accompanist to stop. He took a step toward his audience and in a voice that seemed to quake a little, he said, "This piece—this 'Love's Old Sweet Song,' without Jeanette MacDonald at my side, I doubt my ability to give it its proper interpretation. So please bear with me as I try to sing this lovely old favorite.

"Out in the audience a woman rose from her seat—it was Miss MacDonald. For a few hurried moments they looked at one another Then the song, and Nelson Eddy gave it a deep, soft interpretation that will last in the memory of every one who heard."

Jeanette was seeing little of Gene Raymond at this time; whenever out in public she was usually with Bob Ritchie. Her relationship with Ritchie remained platonic. (No dates were noted in Ritchie's little black book of his sleeping with Jeanette during this period; however, he did name six other women.) Jeanette was still pining over Nelson, angry that he was dating both silent star Lila Lee and Mamo Clark, a Polynesian actress who'd appeared in *Mutiny on the Bounty*. In desperation, Jeanette finally arranged to see Nelson alone and tried to resolve things with him. They talked things over and over— between periods of lovemaking—trying to find a way a union between them could work. This marathon lasted for over twenty-seven hours, with endless discussions and arguments and lots of tears—mostly Jeanette's. Finally they had to agree that it would never work. They loved each other, they needed each other, but they were too similar; neither one was willing to give an inch, or sacrifice their career goals. "I used to think that Love was the most powerful emotion," Nelson said bitterly, years later. "But I found out it wasn't. Pride is the greater emotion." In the end, they decided to part friends, knowing they would love each other always, but determined to break both the spiritual and sexual bond.

Nelson later related the story of this breakup to illustrate a point; he claimed that the final shot of *Rose Marie*, in which his and Jeanette's characters are reunited, was filmed after their talk. Their emotions in that scene were real, and the tenderness with which Jeanette caresses and kisses him was real.

The romance, as far as either believed, was over forever.

Rose Marie.

10

The breakup

Rose Marie previewed in Westwood, Los Angeles, on January 9, 1936. The Hollywood *Reporter* called the film "a smash hit" and a "triumph for MacDonald and Eddy." Nelson, who'd already begun his spring tour, had just arrived in Seattle for a concert the following night. Isabel Eddy was at the theater in Westwood. Just before the picture's final fadeout, she went to a telephone in the lobby and called Nelson, keeping the door of the booth open so he could hear the audience response. Isabel held the phone for five minutes of applause, then said, "You see, son, it's a hit. I'm proud of you. Congratulations." (She reversed the phone charges; the call ended up costing Nelson $65.)

The next morning at 10:20 A.M. the press started banging on Nelson's hotel door. Nelson yelled, "You said 10:30, I'm not quite ready! Wait a minute!" Soon the doorknob was turned from within. Then it was shaken hard, again and again. Finally he got the door open. "The darn thing was open all the time," he said. "Come in, sit down, make yourself at home, and excuse the room. I just got up." In answer to how he prepared for a concert: "I hadn't any particular schedule planned for today. I don't want anybody to get the idea I'm one of these long-haired guys. About fifteen minutes before I'm to start my concert I go into the bathroom and 'yap' a few tones—that's about all the bother of it." The phone rang. Nelson answered it. "No, I don't know any young ladies here. I said I didn't know anybody here. Tell her to run along. Tell her I said so. Goodbye." He sat on a desk, his legs on a chair, and offered gum and cigarettes. "It's the same everywhere I go. They come flocking in—cousins, sisters, uncles, aunts, even my mother. Well, I haven't many relatives and I know where they are. Nobody gets by with anything like that, but it's rather embarrassing." The phone kept ringing, "Let it ring. It can ring all day." A knock at the door, "Let them knock." Finally he took one phone call, and listened a moment. "No," he chuckled. "No thanks, we don't go in for things like that." He hung up and addressed the reporters. "Say, let's go downstairs and let that ring in peace."

Rose Marie opened around the country to rave reviews and big box office. Even in its botched form it was a bigger hit than *Naughty Marietta*. This fact amazed Louis B. Mayer, who had been certain the film would end Nelson's movie career. Nelson's fans were quick to note the shabby treatment he received in the film, and their response was to deluge the studio with letters protesting such treatment, demanding that Nelson be given more screen time and better songs and scenes in the next MacDonald-Eddy film.

What next MacDonald-Eddy film? Mayer had not planned one. But by the end of the month, he'd purchased a Rudolf Friml operetta, *The Firefly*, for their next film. He'd give the public what they wanted, even though he and other top execs at Metro claimed then—and throughout all the years Nelson was at the studio—that they could not understand Nelson's appeal to audiences. Plans to dump Nelson were put on hold; he'd become too valuable a star.

One postcard postmarked May 6, 1936, was sent to MGM and later found its way into Nelson's personal scrapbook. It had a photo of him on it, and was addressed simply: To *THE* star of Metro-Goldwyn-Mayer, Culver City, California.

The New York *Journal* stated, "Nelson Eddy has become a serious threat to Clark Gable for the honor of being the movies' #1 matinee idol."

Jeanette too found her popularity reaching new heights because of *Rose Marie*. The *American* commented, "Miss MacDonald eclipses all previous brilliance in her present scintillance . . . Ecstatic is the word for Jeanette."

The film was summed up as "One of the outstanding screen musicals of this or any season." It went on to become the most popular of all the MacDonald-Eddy movies, the one most associated with them.

▄▄▄ Nelson dutifully threw himself into his work. He recorded thirty-nine songs in a few hours for RCA before launching his yearly concert tour on January 3, 1936, in San Diego. From there he traveled up the Pacific coast, then east to the Midwest, East Coast, Toronto, and then down to the South.

On January 9, an interview he'd granted with columnist Sheilah Graham hit the papers. It caused a furor in Hollywood and around the country, and was a painful reminder to Louis B. Mayer that Nelson was not to be trusted when it came to the press. In the interview, Nelson bitterly described movie actresses as "Egotistical, insincere, self-centered, and look[ing] like animated paintboxes. The whole place [Hollywood] is like a madhouse. Most film actresses are incredibly boring. I haven't met one that I'd even vaguely like to marry. But it isn't entirely their fault. Movie actresses are forced to lead an unnatural life. When they come to Hollywood their personalities are changed. They must be selfish and ruthless, or they won't get beyond their first featured role.

"I have to change my phone number at least once a week—to avoid film people inviting me to their parties. Hollywood parties are very boring. Nearly all follow the same dull pattern. When eight or more people are present, a horde of photographers are invited to crash the gates and take pictures of everyone in every conceivable place and position—not omitting the shower.

"A few film people, like Jeanette MacDonald and Basil Rathbone, give parties because they want to see friends, not because they have a mad desire to see their names and pictures in the papers."

When asked about marriage in another interview that same week, Nelson retorted, "I don't intend marrying for a long, long time; I'm just not in the marrying mood." He added bitterly, "I work all the time. I'm surrounded by people, and yet I'm lonely. Now that I've reached my goals, I have no one to share my life."

In Denver, a riot broke out among two thousand shrieking women. Nelson had a concert scheduled for Tulsa on January 23, but on the twentieth he received word that his uncle Clark Kendrick, who'd resettled in Tulsa and gotten into the oil business, had died. Isabel took the train and met up with Nelson in time for the funeral.

As the tour continued Nelson moved toward the East Coast. He received a bad review in the Chicago *Daily Times*. The review was clipped for his scrapbook, and Nelson scrawled "Bastard" in the margin of the article.

A topic of major publicity and scandal on this tour was a South Bend, Indiana, heiress named Barbara Clark. She was a groupie who followed Nelson on his tour, claiming that she simply liked his voice. Her photo appeared in papers all over the nation, and she was warned not to harass Nelson and to leave him alone.

Despite his grueling schedule, Nelson gave several interviews a day, tirelessly answering questions. "My fan mail is up to five thousand a week. Fan mail is most interesting to me and I give it a great deal of attention. Between radio, pictures and concert work, I have a wide coverage and I get letters from China, Brazil, Australia, South America—all over the world. It costs one hundred fifty dollars a week to handle all my mail.

"In most towns, we register at the principal hotel and then sneak out and stay at some other hotel. We have to do it, just to protect ourselves, and I hope that doesn't sound stuck up. But protection really is necessary. In two southern cities people hammered on our hotel door all night, and in one place, three women brought along a picnic lunch and camped outside our hotel rooms until we came out.

"When we were leaving Grand Rapids, I just managed to catch the train. There was quite a crowd of autograph hunters in the station and one girl ran alongside the train and grabbed onto the railing of the car steps. She said she wouldn't let go until I gave her an autograph. I told her she had better get off while she could. Finally, when the train was moving pretty fast, she jumped off and took an awful header. I was really scared. By that time, I'd signed her book, and threw it off to her, wondering whether she was badly hurt or not. But she picked herself up, got the book and yelled 'Thank you!' The crowd gathered around her and she was quite a heroine, even though her dress was ruined."

In Spokane, Nelson was asked if he would ever give up films and return to the opera. "I have requests from the Metropolitan every year for auditions," he responded, "but I don't want to be just one more baritone and they pay so little. After I have saved some money—say in about ten years—and can build up a repertoire, I would like to sign at the Metropolitan."

Regarding *Rose Marie*, Nelson commented, "I am by nature antipathetic to the character I'm playing. Consequently, it is easier to study and understand the man, and thus easier to portray him . . . I read his character in the script with awe. His motives, his reactions, I took pains to study well."

In Nashville, he woke up in his hotel room one morning to find a woman staring down at him. "I was so mad I was speechless. Finally I sputtered, 'What are you doing here and what do you want?' She wanted my autograph. Can you imagine that? She had broken into the room. I yelled for her to get out of my room. I could shoot you for this, I told her. She got out."

"People are always asking me what my favorite song is. My favorite is the one I'm singing at the time . . . I don't mind singing about love, for instance. But most of the love I sing about isn't love. It's just necking . . . It's so darned phony to sing your love-making—it's just an artificial situation, that's all.

"I never was an actor and may never be. If you don't believe it, ask Van Dyke. He'll tell you I'm not. I just walk through it and try to be natural. No acting to it . . . I shudder when I see myself on the screen, because I notice all the mistakes. In *Rose Marie*, for instance, I had to lift Miss MacDonald onto a tree limb, and I did it so clumsily that my hat scratched her nose and it had to be fixed up. I thought everyone else would notice my hammish acting, but apparently no one did.

"Smoking isn't bad for my voice, just for my morals. Can't let my public see me."

In all the chaos of the tour, Nelson's anger toward Jeanette began to evaporate. In Memphis, he admitted that she was "one of his best friends." In Spokane, he called her "a peach." In Evansville he told a reporter: "Jeanette MacDonald is one of the swellest girls I've ever met in my life. One of the prettiest and smartest." In Birmingham: "Jeanette has everything. Jeanette is a gorgeous creature with a glorious voice . . . not only lovely to look upon, she is one of the finest characters I've ever known. She has a brilliant mind, is sparkling and full of fun, but she doesn't smoke or drink or go to wild parties. My only criticism is that when a fellow takes her out at night he has to have her home by eleven." A New Orleans interviewer noted: "He prefers to talk about Jeanette MacDonald."

In New York, Nelson made an April radio broadcast for WOR, but seemed exhausted and on the verge of a breakdown. He admitted, "I am so worn out that

I'm just about able to get through this program and that's all." Observers noted that he stooped over the music rack that held his songs. His hands twitched nervously, and according to one critic, his voice "lacked the fire and drama of the WOR broadcasts of four years ago."

The tour ended in El Paso, Texas, and none too soon. "I'm tired of answering the same questions," Nelson quipped. "It's always Who's your favorite composer, star, book or play." When he was met by his mother at the train station in Pasadena, he kissed her on the lips and announced, "I want to sleep for a week."

■ Jeanette, meanwhile, plunged into work on *San Francisco*, with Clark Gable and Spencer Tracy as co-stars. This was a project very dear to her heart, one she had struggled to see made. As early as March 20, 1935, she'd sent Felix Feist of MGM management in New York the following letter:

> The situation is something like this: Some months ago I was approached about a story (based on an original idea) by one Hopkins out here, momentarily called "San Francisco" to be done with Clark Gable. The idea is a swell one with great dramatic background, punch, but happily not a musical comedy or operetta, but with music opportunities and scope so great that unless I am entirely crazy, it is a natural. In its present embryonic state it fits Gable and me like a pair of gloves, he being the King of the Barbary Coast and I being the girl who comes to sing in one of his joints.
>
> Just last week I turned down "The Life of Johann Strauss" for various reasons, one being that it is not the kind of part I like playing, and secondly that I am not convinced of its popular appeal. It is definitely not the type of thing that the shop girls will go for, although in all possibilities would be an artistic success.
>
> On the strength of "Marietta" (I am keeping my fingers crossed) which I think has such strong romantic appeal that it will definitely intrigue the shop girl type of trade, as well as the high-brows, I am more than ever determined that I want to continue making my appeal to this former type of trade who comprise the majority of audiences.
>
> Having turned down the Strauss story brought on further negotiations resulting in my granting the studio ten weeks' extension on my contract (dam' decent of me I say) so that they can concentrate on San Fran. to replace "Johann Strauss" as the next vehicle for me. Now I am told Gable will not be available for San Francisco and a list of assignments will prevent his being teamed with me . . . I am heartbroken at the same time furious that such an opportunity is going to be missed.
>
> Isn't there anything the Sales department can do in having one of Gable's other assignments postponed so that this picture can be made as great as it should be with him in it?

In the end, not only was Gable freed-up to work with her, but she handpicked Spencer Tracy for the second male lead as well.

The screenwriter on *San Francisco* was Anita Loos, who disliked both Nelson and Jeanette. She wanted Grace Moore to star, but Jeanette wanted the role.

"They get more out of a look than I get out of the whole sex act," said Spencer Tracy of Jeanette and Nelson.

Mayer, who was interested in keeping Jeanette happy, told Loos that if she wanted Clark Gable she had to take Jeanette as well.

Gable's reluctance to work with Jeanette was multifaceted. He wasn't interested in appearing in a "musical," but his main problem with her was how she'd treated Nelson. Gable had remained buddies with Nelson, and was only too aware of the recent broken engagement. He felt Jeanette was a phony and not worthy of Nelson's devotion. Later he claimed that Jeanette was the only co-star he didn't even try to bed.

At the time, Jeanette wasn't fully aware of Gable's reasons for not wanting to work with her. His decision hinged, in part, on the fact that he'd recently gotten some girl pregnant, and the studio had to pay $2,000 in hush money to avoid a scandal. Louis B. Mayer reminded Gable that he "owed him one."

San Francisco began production on Valentine's Day, 1936, with Woody Van Dyke once more at the helm. He had his hands full again with two stars who didn't get along. Furthermore, Jeanette had become so high-strung that she couldn't eat, and she dropped a dramatic amount of weight. She was thinner in this film than she was in any other before or since. Desperate to put aside memories of Nelson, she played the field; the press had her in love with Gene Raymond, but she dated Jimmy Stewart and Henry Fonda, among others. Her letters to Ritchie continued after he returned to London. Although their ro-

With Clark Gable on the set of *San Francisco*.

mance was still off, she poured out to him intimate details of her personal life, as though he were her father confessor as well as her business manager. In a letter dated February 28, 1936, she wrote to him:

I'm afraid you're taking too many jobs at one time to succeed in any. But enough preaching, I've done too much already, I guess, but I am naturally concerned.

There are so many things I think should be done and it's hard to know how to go about doing them— First of all, Bob I've just *got* to *be* and *feel* entirely free and cut loose from you before I'll ever know if I can care for you (that way) again—Do you know what I mean—Men (most of them) are a bit diffident about seeing me because they feel you're still head man— and so unless I'm free and clear—I'll never feel I've had a chance to interest others and so will never know by comparison if you are or was *the best*! You've really left me in a pretty bad position. And you are the only one to relieve it, you know! There was another article in Read Kenasall's column last wk saying before you left you'd assured everyone everything was just the same between us but they were still wondering as I'd been seen out with Henry Fonda who seems to be cutting in on Gene Raymond's time. You see, Bob, it isn't quite fair to me 'cause a girl can never be the aggressor—whereas you can do all the dating & chasing you want to. And so I wish you'd make it clear from your end. The easiest way is to establish it as sometime ago—then there is no possibility of anyone's thinking you were cut out while away. That's why I said in one of my letters to you—that I bet you wouldn't say it was really established on a different basis 2 years ago—that it's about the time you first went to Europe alone. Also that takes the curse off your having stayed at 912 Rexford—when you returned—Oh hell! It's all very confusing and as you can guess it's had me terribly worried and upset and I now weigh *110 lbs*! So thin that everyone is commenting on it and I am rather unhappy over the entire situation as I feel whenever I go out people are speculating as to whether or not I'm cheating on you etc.

Rose Marie is breaking records everywhere and so I am being well treated at the studio—*Frisco* is going along—Gable seems lots of fun and we all have lots of laughs.

I am OK except for dreadful nervousness and sleeplessness . . . I just thot [*sic*] of someone for you to run around with—Mary Brian she's lots of laughs I'm told. Ever—the old lady.

The next day, Jeanette was ill in bed with a cold. She wrote Ritchie again. They were shooting the earthquake scene, but Jeanette was flying to Palm Springs the following day in Amelia Earhart's plane for a week's rest. She discussed establishing life insurance for her mother—a trust fund of $50,000—because Anna MacDonald didn't pass her medical exam for regular life insurance.

I am thinking seriously of having the trust fund made irrevocable because I'm allowed 50 grand free of inheritance tax anyway and the tax on the remainder would be less than what I pay every year. Anyway it's another means of bringing down my income at present and I can always make provisions in the trust that I am sole inheritor or something like that.

About the $10,000 you have—I should like you to make out a draft in my favor in the Natl Promisal then it's there for me whenever I may want it and there is no record of the transaction in this country. About other money being sent over—I'd like you to investigate the Scandinavian countries & their financial possibilities: they are after all the *least* likely to get involved in any warfare and I think England *should*, and the pound wouldn't be any better off than the dollar. There must be some good solid bonds in Norway & Sweden that could yield a neat income to be held in those respective countries—to accumulate so that my income here wouldn't be affected at all.

I am going to buy Elsie's [her sister's] house in Philly—she pays 75 a month rent and it's for sale about around $11,000. So I've decided it will be a fair investment & she can pay me the rent—and I'll own the property which is increasing all the time . . . She's got over 200 pupils now—isn't that remarkable?

I may go to Honolulu again after the picture or run around to New York via Canal. Certainly, gotta get out of here or go nutz.

Gable is a *mess*! I've never been more disappointed in anyone in my life—It seems (according to Mayer) he's terribly jealous of me and acts very sulky if I get more attention on the set than he. The third day on production he & I had quite a blow up and it all came out in Mayer's office that evening. I like Tracy very much there's as much difference between the 2 as day from nite. Gable acts as tho he were really too bored to play the scenes with me. Typical *ham* result—I'm not terribly interested in *San Francisco*.

If Gable wasn't impressed with his co-star, another co-worker had only fond memories of his experience with Jeanette. "A lump comes to my throat as I remember back to MGM, 1936, and that beautiful, gracious red-haired beauty Jeanette MacDonald," wrote Noble "Kid" Chissell. "I was privileged to work as a stuntman and extra in *San Francisco*, directed by another wonderful person, U. S. Marine Major Woody Van Dyke. I worked on the picture for twelve weeks, mainly the earthquake scenes, including the collapse of the huge supper club, where I rescued Jeanette's double, Mary Arden (whom I later married).

"In addition to the regular cast, *San Francisco* boasted the services of a stock roster of at least a hundred players. Van Dyke always made certain to utilize as many of the old-time stars as possible, the great names from the silent era who had fallen onto hard times. A partial list of names included King Baggott, Elmo Lincoln (the first Tarzan), Charles Ray, Gertrude Astor and Minta Durfee Arbuckle, Fatty's widow. Minta told me much about the unselfish Jeanette and director Van Dyke, how they were both feeding and paying the rent for at least thirty families of film players during the Depression years. What impressed me most about the lovely Miss MacDonald was her deep concern about these old-timers. When she first arrived on the set in the morning, she would go amongst them, inquiring about them and family. There was something highly spiritual about Jeanette. Her eyes sparkled like two bright stars in Heaven, and when she walked on the set, it seemed to light up with a wondrous glow."

Woody also allowed another silent film great, director D. W. Griffith, the chance to work again. Woody had started in the motion picture business as an extra in Griffith's 1916 masterpiece *Intolerance*. He worked hard and stuck his neck out to be noticed by the great director. Woody's ploy worked; Griffith recognized his talent and gave him several bit parts, and hired him as a first assistant director. Van Dyke always credited Griffith for teaching him filmmaking.

Woody gave Griffith, who was now a drunk and forgotten by the industry, a new lease on life by calling him in to help direct the earthquake sequence. Anita Loos, who was on the set for the filming, described Woody's direction, as he yelled to all the extras: "Believe it's a real earthquake! Run for your lives! Try to help your friends!" One extra was so excited that he grabbed up Anita—who was in street clothes—and ran off with her. "As I wasn't wearing a costume, I was cut out of the final footage," said Loos, "which was unfortunate since nobody shrieked as realistically as I did."

Jeanette performed several numbers in *San Francisco*, including scenes from *La Traviata* and *Faust*. "The title song was to be a torch number, but Jeanette felt uncomfortable with it, and argued endlessly with Woody about singing it that way. Finally, she agreed to bow to Woody's wishes, after betting him five hundred dollars that he was wrong. When Woody proved correct—the song became the hit of the film—Jeanette presented Woody with a check, and he cashed it."

Jeanette finished work on *San Francisco* around the time Nelson returned from his tour. To her great joy, he came to see her and wordlessly embraced her. The devastation of being separated from her had proved worse than having to play second fiddle to her career. He wanted her back, even if only on her terms. Nelson also had it out with Gable, chiding him for his behavior toward Jeanette during the filming. It was Spencer Tracy who, observing Jeanette and Nelson together at this time, commented, "They get more out of a look than I get out of the whole sex act."

The next few weeks Nelson was seen escorting Jeanette to premieres. They danced together at the Trocadero. They were happily preparing to start their next film together, *Maytime* instead of *The Firefly*, scheduled for an August start.

Then Jeanette came up with the brilliant idea of trying to get Nelson back into the good graces of Louella Parsons. Since his concert tour, his vitriolic comments

Jeanette immortalizing the song "San Francisco."

to the press had made him unpopular and given him a reputation for being difficult. Fully appreciating the power Louella wielded in Hollywood, Jeanette hoped that a reconciliation with Nelson would turn the tide. Jeanette set up a luncheon date with Nelson at one of their favorite restaurants, giving him no other details. She arrived early with Louella in tow. As they waited for Nelson to arrive, Jeanette reassured Louella that Nelson was a perfect gentleman and was willing to apologize and be friends again.

But she hadn't reckoned with Nelson's stubborn streak. When he entered the restaurant, he sailed right past them and sat down at a table at the other end of the room. Jeanette tried to calm Louella. "He probably didn't see us, he's not wearing his glasses." She rushed over to Nelson and attempted to talk sense to him. He angrily refused to speak to Louella, disgusted that Jeanette would trick him like this. Jeanette finally walked out of the restaurant in tears.

Louella, still miffed, called Louis B. Mayer and demanded satisfaction. She would have preferred to trash Nelson in her column, but that was out of the question. She irritated Mayer until he was pressured into issuing an ultimatum to Nelson: Nelson was hauled into Mayer's office, where he received a severe lecture. A shouting match ensued, with both men calling each other names. Nelson was one of the few stars who could get away with telling Mayer off—on a few occasions he even physically attacked Mayer when enraged; under normal

. . . Jeanette's birthday, June 18, 1936. Her new beau, Gene Raymond, irritated Nelson by donning a Mountie costume. Though he was now dating Jeanette's ex-best friend, Anita Louise, Nelson was unsmiling at the party. Behind Jeanette stands Jimmy Stewart, who had one of his first film roles as her younger brother in *Rose Marie*.

circumstances, this would have spelled the end of his film career, but Mayer wasn't stupid enough to let such a gold mine slip through his fingers.

Through all the years Nelson was at Metro, he and Mayer constantly battled. Nelson later said that Mayer brought out all the evil in him, and no matter how hard he tried, he just never could behave with him around. In retrospect, Nelson said, "After it was all over, he and I found out we really missed our little run-ins. They kept us both young."

Finding themselves under extreme pressure from the studio, Nelson and Jeanette briefly resumed their "pact of friendship." At Jeanette's thirty-third birthday party, on June 18, 1936, her date was Gene Raymond, who wore a Mountie uniform in a subtle dig to Nelson. Nelson, who looked miserable in some of the candid shots taken at the party, brought along his latest rage, actress Anita Louise, who had been a friend of Jeanette's; once she took up with Nelson she attained the status of "ex-friend." Years later, in 1952, Anita Louise did the live commercials when Jeanette was feted on the TV show "This Is Your Life." Ralph Edwards pointed out Anita to Jeanette, saying excitedly, "Remember your old friend Anita Louise?" Jeanette looked over at her, managed a grimace and said with forced cheerfulness, "Hi, Anita."

On June 23, *San Francisco* premiered in Los Angeles and was an immediate smash hit. "*San Francisco* is due for outstanding business everywhere," noted the Hollywood *Reporter*. "There is no denying the excellence of its lavish production nor the amazing effects achieved by its technical crew. Nothing nearer perfection in staged effects has ever been attained on the screen than these scenes of the destruction of a city by earthquake and burning.

"The performance of Jeanette MacDonald establishes her unchallenged right to the title of first lady in the ranks of singing actresses. Formerly regarded almost entirely as a sophisticate of films, Jeanette now plays a simple miss from the country forced by circumstances to invade the dives of the old Barbary Coast at its heyday. And her playing is flawless. It is a job of real acting, starting in a low key, and graduating, episode by episode, in splendid characterization . . . Her singing is equally notable, although this we have learned to expect.

"Clark Gable has an assignment here that returns him to the type of role in which he scored his first terrific success . . . It is a dominant part, made more memorable by Gable's vigorous portrayal.

"Spencer Tracy plays the priest for a solid personal hit. He handles his part with a quiet, forceful dignity and highlights it with a humorous strength, a delightful piece of work.

"You have never seen anything that approaches the power of the scenes of buildings toppling and catching fire. The MGM technical effects department eclipses by a wide margin all previous efforts of the sort."

The New York *World-Telegram* noted: "There comes a time in every motion picture reviewer's life when he is afflicted by a sense of remorse for having squandered his stock of adjectives, for having abused such words as 'great,' 'magnificent,' 'superb,' because when a truly notable film comes along, he really has nothing left with which to describe it . . . Jeanette MacDonald is superb. Looking more attractive and appearing in better voice than ever before, she plays the part with uncommon charm, forbearance and emotional depth. Not only does she give the finest performance of her screen career, but she has never sung more thrillingly than she does here."

In its first week of release, *San Francisco* broke all attendance records. By the end of June, Mayor Rossi of the city of San Francisco had proclaimed the title song the city song. In mid-July, the top-grossing films for the first half of 1936 were named as follows: *Mutiny on the Bounty* (which had been released in 1935), *Follow the Fleet*, *Rose Marie* and *San Francisco*.

Jeanette had achieved her professional goal to be the outstanding female personality on the screen. Her two films released in 1936 were among the top money-makers, both in America and abroad. *San Francisco* won Photoplay's Gold Medal Award as the best film of the year, and was nominated for six Academy Awards, including Best Picture, Best Supporting Actor (Spencer Tracy), Best Writing, Best Original Story, Best Assistant Director and Best Sound Recording (the only Academy Award it won). Bob Ritchie spoke from London of the power Jeanette now wielded in the business: "I have to invest for Jeanette MacDonald one million dollars every two years. Under her new contract, if a picture takes more than five minutes over the eight months she works out of every twelve, it will cost the producing firm five thousand pounds for a week's work."

Jeanette's personal life was a shambles. She was seeing Gene Raymond again, and was polite and professional in her letters to Bob Ritchie. She and Nelson managed to spend some much-needed time together at a hideaway house in Lake Arrowhead, a mountain resort two hours away from Los Angeles. Their Arrowhead trysts were noted in actor Robert Stack's autobiography, *Straight Shooting*, and he was in a position to know. The house they stayed in was owned by his mother.

Jeanette and Nelson were in a deadlock. Nelson desperately wanted to marry her, with no delay, and she was willing, but only if he allowed her to continue her career full-time. Again, he refused. His own possessiveness, combined with his acute awareness of the ridiculousness of Mayer's ultimatums and the lengths to which he had affected their relationship, kept him from his love. Very soon, his own stubbornness and the rage he had struggled so long to control would cost him dearly. The day finally came when Jeanette felt she could no longer tolerate his irrational sexual attacks.

On August 20, 1936, Anna MacDonald announced publicly that her daughter Jeanette was engaged to marry Gene Raymond.

Maytime

11

Maytime

Maytime began production, ironically, the same week that Jeanette's engagement to Gene Raymond was announced.

Nelson and Jeanette had a new crew to get used to, without the fatherly understanding of Woody Van Dyke. Irving Thalberg was producer, Edmund Goulding director. The supporting cast included Paul Lukas and Frank Morgan. The picture was to be shot in Technicolor, and the musical highlight was Nelson playing Scarpia and Jeanette Tosca in the Act II duet from the Puccini opera.

Also recorded for the film was the song "Farewell to Dreams," a poignant Romberg number that was later dropped from the final cut. Nelson later said that this song, the lyrics of which so closely paralleled their own lives, was his all-time favorite recording ever with Jeanette.

Recording sessions were long, with Herbert Stothart and the orchestra working as long as eighteen hours at a stretch. Nelson was indefatigable but Jeanette, always frail, tired easily. Stubborn and willful, she refused to let anyone see that she couldn't keep up, and she literally worked until she dropped. Despite their personal differences, Nelson admired her professionalism, and he kept a careful eye on her. On more than one occasion he had to catch her before she hit the floor in a faint. Finally he bought her a wicker rocking chair, which was kept in the recording studio. When he saw that she was tiring, he ordered her to rest in her chair. In this manner, she was able to take catnaps and to tolerate the heavy schedule.

Recording the music for *Maytime*. Despite their differences, Nelson was extremely protective of Jeanette's health.
The wicker rocker behind them was his
idea, to force her to rest during the grueling hours of recording.

Once the actual filming began, director Goulding found his two stars temperamental and difficult to work with. Several candid shots from the early days of
filming show them glaring at each other with obvious dislike. Gene Raymond
was seen on the set and around the studio, holding hands and keeping company
with his new fiancée—protecting his investment. Nelson, meanwhile, paraded an
astonishing number of "dates" onto the set, including Elissa Landi, Julie Haydon
and others. He spent his free time in his dressing room with a relative of ever-
changing women.

On September 14, 1936, Irving Thalberg unexpectedly died of pneumonia at
the age of thirty-seven. Production of all of his films was halted until each one
could be reassigned to new producers. While *Maytime* was on hiatus Jeanette,
who had recently moved to a new house at 401 June Street in Hancock Park,
went back East with her mother for a two-week vacation while Gene remained
in Hollywood.

Jeanette sent Bob Ritchie a letter, reassuring him that she still wanted him to
represent her. She alluded to the fact that she might be having second thoughts
about her engagement by writing: "I'm having a pretty bad time to pull myself
together these days. Someday I'll tell you about it but not now."

While in New York, Jeanette met with Ritchie's friend Steve Kroeger. Kroeger later related the outcome of their visit in a letter to Bob Ritchie. Dated
October 7, 1936, it read:

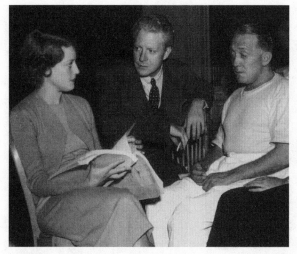

With director Edmund Goulding on the set of the first *Maytime*.

Have some news for you Bob. Jeanette and her mother are here stopping at the Ambassador under the name of Helen Ferguson [her publicity agent]. She dropped me a note saying she wanted to see me, so I went down last Friday night, had dinner at the hotel and then the three of us went to see Helen Hayes in "Victoria Regina." Then back to the hotel, and after a drink Anna went to bed and Jeanette and I had a talk until 2:30 . . . After she had finished telling me about Gene Raymond, there was a sort of lull and I put my hand over Jeanette's which was on the arm of the sofa, and happened to ask, "Well, Jeanette, are you happy now?" The poor kid just couldn't answer me, and the tears just welled up in her eyes and rolled down her cheeks. I was damn near bawling myself.

Kroeger was so amazed at Jeanette's unhappiness over her engagement that he suggested to Bob that he might still have a chance to win her back. Ritchie appears to have taken Kroeger's advice to heart. He continued to remind Jeanette that he still loved her and would be there for her if Gene Raymond didn't work out. Ritchie continued to hope for the best until a week before Jeanette's marriage, but his family maintains that he never got over her.

Jeanette returned to Los Angeles to learn that all the color footage shot for *Maytime*—nearly three-fourths of the film, costing the studio $800,000—had been scrapped. Hunt Stromberg was now producer and Robert "Pop" Z. Leonard director, and they were set to shoot a new story from scratch. The supporting cast was changed: Paul Lukas and Frank Morgan were replaced by John Barrymore and Herman Bing. In view of the money wasted, the new *Maytime* was in black-and-white, and corners were cut in the musical department to avoid having to pay royalties. Except for *Maytime*'s theme song "Will You Remember," all the Sigmund Romberg tunes from the original operetta were tossed out. Musical director Herbert Stothart had to choose from songs in the public domain.

Even the script was rewritten. Mayer had never liked the plot of the first *Maytime*—the two stars were married to other people and having an affair. He

A scene from the first *Maytime*.

ordered many of the staff screenwriters to take a stab at writing a revised story that would meet with his approval. Screenwriter Noel Langley, who was twenty-six years old and had only been at Metro four months, won out. Langley later said,

> Alice Duer Miller was ahead of me on *Maytime*, but everybody had taken a whack at it. Ogden Nash had, Dorothy Parker had, Albert Hackett and Frances Goodrich had, and, I believe, Vicki Baum had. I completed the whole script in three and a half days flat, and Pop Leonard was directing it by the end of the same week; no changes, no alterations, no midnight conferences. Leonard and producer Hunt Stromberg were happy, but MGM's eighty-eight contract screenwriters weren't. They were sore as hell that I got a script done in three and a half days. They wanted a year of fooling around. When the picture turned out to be a commercial hit, they wanted me out of town on a rail. I suffered from some nasty infighting. Mayer was told I was a Communist, as cross-eyed as Ben Turpin, and totally untalented.

Langley had a successful career nonetheless. Among his screenwriting credits were *The Wizard of Oz* (1939), *A Christmas Carol* (1951) and *The Vagabond King* (1956).

As with *Rose Marie*, the revised *Maytime* script favored Jeanette, giving her far more on-screen time than Nelson. The plot was told in flashback. Jeanette, an old lady, tells how in her youth she married her voice teacher (John Barrymore) out of loyalty rather than the young singer (Nelson) she loved. Years later the two meet up again and proclaim their love, but her jealous husband shoots her lover, forcing her to grow old alone, waiting to be reunited with her lover in death.

She had her hands full working with John Barrymore. The great actor was by now past his prime and drinking heavily. Cue cards were used so that he could recite his dialogue, since he was beyond memorizing lines. In one of their scenes together he visibly breathed garlic breath in her face, causing her to instinctively move back. Her singing irritated him until he finally announced, "If I have to hear her warble one more time I'll cram my fist down her throat!" Despite his disliking her, on other occasions she had to keep pushing his hand away from her private parts. And while they were filming on the fairgrounds set, Barrymore casually relieved himself against a prop tree. But the favorite Barrymore anecdote occurred when he wandered into the ladies' room to use the facilities. A woman walked in and gasped, "But Mr. Barrymore, this is for the ladies!" Barrymore turned to her, organ in hand, and replied, "So, my dear, is this!"

In late November, the May Day scenes were begun. Thus far Jeanette and Nelson had been professional and civil to each other during production. Publicist Sandy Reiss, who visited the set, noted that Nelson needed only one take to do a shot with Jeanette. In his own scenes, it took many takes to get it right.

One evening Nelson was driving aimlessly through West Los Angeles. He did this many evenings when he left the studio, driving around for hours. This

John Barrymore with Nelson on the set.

particular night he decided to stop back at the studio. His pal Clark Gable had begun work on *Parnell*, and he suggested that Nelson might stop by and visit while they were doing some night shooting. Nelson checked in at Gable's dressing room, only to find that his pal was busy with a "pal" of the opposite sex.

Smiling, Nelson left. But he didn't want to go home, so he decided to catch up on some letters left in his portable dressing room. To get there, he had to walk through the fairgrounds set. A single light nearby added an eerie glow to the scene. The stillness and beauty of the set charmed him, and he sat down under a tree and closed his eyes. Suddenly, a sound startled him. He jumped up to see who was there, and smelled her perfume before he ever saw her. Jeanette called out fearfully, "Is anyone there?" Nelson was silent. He waited until she recognized him, then wordlessly started to walk away.

In later years, many commented to Nelson about the beautiful "Will You Remember?" love scene filmed under that tree. Once, after Nelson's tongue had been loosened with a few drinks, he told a close friend, "Yeah? Well, you should hear what *really* happened under that tree!"

According to Nelson's own account, Jeanette stopped him and tried to convince him that they still could be friends. "It's not friendship I want from you," he retorted. "You've made your choice." He again started to walk away, but she threw herself at him.

"This time *she* seduced *me!*" Nelson concluded proudly.

Maytime

They spent the night under the tree, returning at last to her dressing room before dawn, and discovery. They arrived on the set for the day's shooting reportedly looking exhilarated. It was obvious to the crew that their relationship had suddenly and drastically changed. Jeanette approached Sandy Reiss, a friend she felt could be trusted, and asked if he could arrange a discreet trysting place for her and Nelson. He arranged for a trailer to be parked behind the *Maytime* sets. "They were back to having lunch and dinner in their trailer, leaving orders not to be disturbed," Reiss claimed.

How this all fit in with Jeanette's marriage plans is a mystery. Jeanette apparently wasn't thinking about the future, she just impulsively threw caution to the winds. Her mother and Gene were summarily banned from the set, while she and Nelson became inseparable and the crew began calling them "the lovebirds" again. Nelson termed these final days of 1936 the time "when we were in lust with each other." He alluded to the fact that previously he had always felt he had to hold back a little in their lovemaking for fear of overwhelming her with his passion, and because she was physically frail. Now, suddenly, things had changed. Nelson delighted in her new aggressiveness. "No woman has ever satisfied me as she does," Nelson told Sandy Reiss. "It goes beyond sex."

Nelson, always a prankster at heart, decided to pull a fast one on Louis B. Mayer. It was his way of getting back at his boss for trying to cause trouble between him and Jeanette. He arranged with some of the crew to film some extra footage after hours, which was then spliced into the dailies. Mayer was then

An intimate moment together on the *Maytime* set.

urged to view the footage. Nelson had briefed Clark Gable on the gag, and the two men joined Jeanette outside the screening room as Mayer watched Nelson "seducing" Jeanette on a couch, lecherously kissing her arm and mugging in his best Valentino fashion. As Nelson had hoped, Mayer burst out of the screening room cursing "that goddamned baritone!" and shouting his wrath for everyone to hear. Gable apparently was so impressed with the film clip that Nelson gave it to him to keep.

It didn't take Mayer too long to figure out what was really happening on the *Maytime* set, and he hit the roof. Another scandal was in the works, and all because of "that baritone." Jeanette was summoned to Mayer's office, where she was informed that it was all over between her and Nelson. If she wanted her career as a big star, she was to go back to Gene Raymond where she belonged.

One would think that Mayer would be delighted that his two "singing sweethearts" were in love. But Mayer didn't see things that way. "Anticipation is greater than consummation," was Mayer's philosophy, explained Sandy Reiss. "On the screen the dynamics became more powerful. By keeping them apart, Mayer kept the passion high." Mayer also feared that if the two married they would soon after land in the divorce courts and he would have no team left.

Mayer elicited the help of a powerful ally in convincing Jeanette to break off with Nelson: Anna MacDonald. "Jeanette listened to mother; she couldn't make her own decisions," claimed Blossom. "If Anna had approved, Jeanette might have married Nelson," agreed Katherine Pickens.

"The marriage was Mayer's doing," Sandy Reiss said. "Nelson later told me himself that Jeanette's mother also had a lot to do with it. She wouldn't sanction Jeanette marrying Nelson. Nelson called her a witch, and blamed her for a lot of Jeanette's hangups. In fact, Nelson thought very little of Jeanette's family at all, with one exception. He said, 'They're all worthless, every one, except Blossom. She's the only one worth two cents.' "

Nelson had tried to reason with Anna. He arranged for Isabel and Anna to get together, hoping that they could become friends. Anna refused to be friendly, to which Blossom reassured Isabel, "We don't like our mother. We have to love her, but we don't like her."

Jeanette's cousins observed while visiting Anna that their aunt clearly did not like Nelson; it wasn't anything she said, just the look on her face when he was mentioned. Nelson tried to get around this with her, reassuring her that he would be a good husband for Jeanette. "We won't cut you off; you can see your daughter whenever you want. I won't stop her supporting you." According to Nelson's friend Marie Collick, "Not till just before Anna died did she admit Nelson was a good man. She was sorry she had interfered. She and Louis screwed up Jeanette's life."

In an attempt to force Jeanette's hand, Mayer resorted to posting security police by her dressing room so she couldn't meet intimately with Nelson. Her mother, meantime, monitored her movements away from the studio. When Jeanette still refused to break up with Nelson, Mayer began threatening more than simply her career. "Mayer told Jeanette they'd put Nelson in a cement overcoat," said Marie Collick. "And they would blind him. He'd be a blind baritone, and would never see again."

Some people have scoffed that Mayer couldn't force Jeanette to marry anyone, even claiming that Mayer was "misunderstood" and a really nice guy, not a villain. Nonetheless, in 1987, actress Lillian Gish said, "D. W. [Griffith] made me famous. By the '20s I was getting 5,000 letters a week. I also got offers to work with other directors for huge sums, $8,000 a week, and he forced me to accept. When sound came in, I was at MGM. L. B. Mayer told me he wanted to stir up the public by inventing a scandal involving me and an actor. When I refused, he said: 'I can ruin you!' And he did. He had me blackballed at every other studio in town. So I left Hollywood. I've made only a few movies since 1930."

Actor Kirk Douglas recalled working with silent star Francis X. Bushman in *The Bad and the Beautiful*. Bushman told Douglas that this was his first film at MGM in twenty-five years. When Douglas asked why, Bushman replied, "I was doing a play once, and Louis B. Mayer came backstage to see me. I was taking off my makeup, and he had to wait a couple of minutes. He ran off in a huff and said, 'That man will never work in my studio again.' And I never did."

Two-time Oscar winner Luise Rainer recalled that after crossing Mayer and refusing to become sexually involved with him, her film career was over. She'd talked back to him; when he roared that he was the one who'd made her, she replied that God had made her, not Louis B. Mayer.

There were others: Ramon Novarro, John Gilbert, etc. And there are still more who relate how the studio forced them to break up a relationship. It was on Mayer's direct orders that Clark Gable and Joan Crawford had to part. Betty Jaynes, a young opera singer who appeared with her husband Douglas McPhail in *Sweethearts*, was later ordered by the studio to divorce her husband, who was abusive and had a drinking problem. "Left to my own devices, I might not have done that [divorced him]," Jaynes claimed. McPhail later took his own life.

Their contemporaries argued that Jeanette was wrong, she should have dropped everything to marry Nelson. "Yes, but let's face it; he blew it," Marie Collick argued. "He always had to open his big mouth. She'd probably have married him right off, but he told her, 'Finish the picture and say goodbye, because that's it for you. You're quitting.' He wanted her home. And Jeanette responded, 'You'll get brighter every day. I get duller, more stupid. And you're going to keep me home every day, locked up in the house, like a cage?' He finally came around and thought maybe she could make a movie once in awhile but it was too late, she didn't trust him."

Jeanette couldn't muster the courage to break the news to Nelson, that she couldn't call off her wedding. In the end, Nelson finally figured it out for himself. He had it out with her in her dressing room and walked out in disgust.

Nelson went from being blissfully happy to irritable and drunk. He started hanging out with Clark Gable, and became his drinking buddy. "Nelson would go to lunch and never come back," said a studio co-worker. "They'd eventually find Nelson off with Gable somewhere, but he couldn't hold his liquor the way

Gable could. In one instance, the two got smashed in the commissary. Nelson was later told (but had no recollection of) that Gable whipped out a pile of bills to buy off Gene [Raymond]. They dipped them in their drinks and Nelson wallpapered the table with them. Another time Nelson and Gable were missing for two days before Isabel and a studio guard broke into his dressing room and found the two of them passed out. Each time Nelson disappeared, Mayer ordered security guards to follow Jeanette, as she often could lead them to him sooner or later."

When Nelson was on the set, he was a challenge to direct. More than once he broke down crying, accusing Jeanette of ruining his life. She too would burst into tears and run off to her dressing room.

Their antics became increasingly childish. One time Jeanette came onto the set and was greeted by Nelson playing his guitar singing his latest composition for her:

You've had three or four
I've had a dozen more.
Let it rain,
Let it snow,
I don't care,
Oh, no, no, no.

Jeanette's response was to throw a glass of lemonade at him.

Isabel Eddy tried unsuccessfully to get her son under control. She did convince Leonard to film him when he was rehearsing—he still stiffened up when he knew the cameras were rolling. She also had a talk with Mayer, warning him, "This is not the time to get smart with Nelson."

Recording "Will You Remember" under the famous tree.

The "Will You Remember?" number was a nightmare to film. Nelson, resigned at last to losing Jeanette forever, could not sing and look at her without crying. Leonard finally instructed Nelson to look at the tree beyond Jeanette and to sing to the tree. Nelson did so, the "rehearsals" were used in the final print, edited to cut away each time Nelson's eyes misted up. Jeanette, too, was teary-eyed in this scene, but the crew's sympathies seemed to be with Nelson.

The film's climactic number was entitled "Czaritza," an "opera" written for the film by Herbert Stothart, who was nominated for an Academy Award for the score, utilizing the melodies of Tchaikovsky's Fifth Symphony. Stunningly written, filmed and sung, the two stars portrayed lovers who were forced to part. According to Jeanette, they cried so much they couldn't get through the duet. Again, careful editing hid this, although in one long shot Jeanette is seen slumping against Nelson just before the camera cuts. An order finally came down from the front office for them to cut the waterworks and get the scene in the can or they'd all be put on pay suspension.

As the year 1936 drew to a close, Nelson made one last attempt to get Jeanette back. He'd never forgotten Clark Gable's brilliant idea about "buying Gene off." So one Sunday, he impulsively called his banker, and insisted on meeting him to pick up a suitcase of cash—all the money he could get his hands on immediately. Nelson went to see Raymond and offered him $250,000 not to go through with the wedding. To his amazement, Gene agreed. Some funds exchanged hands, with the condition that the rest would be paid after an official announcement came from the studio that the marriage was off.

Nelson never realized the extent of Mayer's power and influence. Only when Gene returned the money, saying the deal was off because of Mayer, did Nelson finally admit defeat.

██ Nelson began his yearly concert tour on January 2, 1937, singing in Santa Ana, California. By mid-month, he had left the state. The tour began well, with rave reviews from the critics as well as his fans. On the rebound from Jeanette, he impulsively plunged into a new romance with Mae Mann, a young, blonde Hollywood newspaper writer from Salt Lake City. Nelson sang at the Salt Lake Tabernacle on January 15, and Mae covered it for the press. Salt Lake was a huge success; the audience consisted of 99 percent women, who "fought like Amazons afterward for the blond star's autograph." Nelson spent some time with Mae Mann, was smitten, and only days later asked her to marry him. "Look, I'm starting on my second million dollars. I can afford a wife. What do you think?" But it was the same old story; she was eighteen and just starting out on a career. "I don't want to marry this young, before I can see what I can do." She turned him down and later, when articles were published under her byline about their "dates," Nelson dropped her. In an interview Nelson once commented, "It's surprising how near I have come to marrying a number of girls."

The emotional strain of this most recent rejection caught up with him, and

Nelson fell ill. In mid-February he had throat surgery in Kansas City. He managed to joke with the doctor that he was worried about ending up a soprano,
then after the operation broke into "Ol' Man River." A week later he was
hospitalized in Chicago with complications, forced to cancel several concerts and
take a two-week rest.

Nelson managed to pull himself together and sing most of his remaining
scheduled concerts. But a Philadelphia reporter noted: "Nelson has changed
quite a bit since he left Philadelphia for points west. He has acquired a sureness, a
got-to-get-along attitude, a can't-miss insistence, since those early '30s days. He
has a swagger and a heartiness that smacks too much of Hollywood. And he has a
voice that has taken on much more beauty and depth. His tones are surer and
firmer. His range is wider, his diction is one of the clearest that any artist can
claim. Nelson still has that charming mannerism of making every listener feel
that he is singing expressly for that individual . . . Hollywood must have put its
finger on him, though. The freshness and vitality, one of his grandest assets,
appear to have disintegrated."

This tour Nelson was less candid in interviews. He made one comment about
Maytime: "I got the greatest kick out of dying than out of anything I ever did.
Right up to the finish, they don't believe he's going to kill me. And when he
does, you can hear the whole audience groan. It's simply great!"

He seemed very much on the defensive. "I'm not blind, I'm not going to
Phoenix because I have tuberculosis and I am on speaking terms with Jeanette
MacDonald. And as for Jeanette's forthcoming wedding being a publicity stunt—
well, if it is I've lost a lot of money on linen showers.

"I'll try to go along for a couple more years in the movies, and quit before the
public kicks me out. I ought to have enough by then to spend the rest of my life
as I please. I want to sing some more opera when I don't have to depend on it for
a living."

He refused to discuss his private life except to say, "I would marry anyone if I
fell in love with her and she was in love with me. I have met one whom I thought
to be my ideal but there was no feeling . . . I have no feeling for Miss Mac-
Donald. She is a very lovely girl. She has been engaged to one person or another
ever since I have known her . . . You can't help it if you have an ideal, but I
shall probably marry some softy, a dumpy little girl perhaps." He added, "I
believe in matrimony as a permanent solution."

■ *Maytime* was released in mid-March 1937, following its predecessors as yet
another box office smash. The critics' adjectives were more enthusiastic than ever
for this, Jeanette's own personal favorite of all her films. "It is a temptation to hail
a new Jeanette MacDonald, for this is unquestionably her greatest performance,"
praised the Hollywood *Reporter*. "She portrays an old lady and a breathtakingly
beautiful young woman with unprecedented skill. And her singing surpasses
everything she has done before."

From the *American*: "Second only to Jeanette is Nelson Eddy, who sings perfectly and carries off his romantic role in high triumph. Not only is his voice more thrilling than ever before, but his acting is that of a true trooper."

The New York *Times* summed up the film as "the most entrancing operetta the screen has given us. It establishes Jeanette MacDonald as the possessor of the cinema's loveliest voice—this with all deference to the probably superior off-screen voices of Lily Pons, Grace Moore and Gladys Swarthout—and it affirms Nelson Eddy's pre-eminence among the baritones of filmdom. The screen can do no wrong while these two are singing. *Maytime* is the most joyous operetta of the season, a picture to treasure."

Jeanette and Gene Raymond's wedding party, which consisted of bridesmaids Helen Ferguson, Blossom, Fay Wray, Ginger Rogers, and Mrs. Johnny Mack Brown. Ushers included Allan Jones, Gene's brother Robert Marlowe, Blossom's husband Clarence "Rocky" Rock, and Basil Rathbone. Nelson is on the left.

12

"Something about Gene"

Jeanette's next film, *The Firefly*, went into production on April 12, 1937. As compensation for not marrying Nelson, Mayer had promised to give Jeanette the star vehicle of a lifetime, and he delivered. No expense was spared in bringing this lavish historical drama to the screen. In plot and dramatics, *The Firefly* was a prima donna's delight.

Jeanette played a Spanish spy in Madrid, in 1808. Her assignment is to discover Napoleon's plan of invasion, which she accomplishes by cozying up to various French officers. Her plan is thwarted by Allan Jones, a French spy pretending to be Spanish. Of course they fall in love, are separated by their politics, but then are reunited in a happy ending.

Allan Jones, Jeanette's co-star, had played a small role in *Rose Marie*, singing with her in two operatic scenes. Jones was a good friend of Nelson's, having known him and sung with him back in Philadelphia. In December 1936, Jones, Jeanette and Nelson had made a recording on Nelson's equipment of the trio from *Faust* which they had given out as Christmas gifts. In the last two years Jones had been featured in two very successful Marx Brothers' films, *A Night at the Opera* and *A Day at the Races*. But *The Firefly* was thought to be his first real break.

A self-proclaimed Don Juan, Jones apparently tried his old powers on Jeanette, who was later quoted as saying, "Six weeks before the fatal day I was still being propositioned. I vowed to myself that my marriage would not go the route of all the others." There was apparently some friction between the two stars due to

Jeanette's attempts to shake Jones off. Finally, he settled on being friends with her. "I loved her dearly," Jones said years later, but, evidenced from the numerous photos taken on the set, Jeanette spent more time sitting with the second male lead, Warren Williams. In one candid photo she is seated with Jones at a table. He is smoking a cigar and Jeanette has her elbow resting on the tabletop, leaning her head on her hand. She's ignoring him and looks extremely bored.

A poignant incident occurred during the filming of *The Firefly*, related by Noble "Kid" Chissell:

> About a year [after *San Francisco*], I was sitting in the old Lucky Spot nightclub on Western Avenue, listening to my screen star pal Frankie Darro entertain. I was approached by Chicago boxer Mickey Gregory, who handed me a "kite"—a letter smuggled out of prison. It was from an old school mate. We hadn't seen each other in years; but had parted friends back in 1931 when he became involved with bootlegging, and I joined the Navy. His letter explained that he was confined on Death Row at the Ohio State Prison in Columbus. He had gotten involved with John Dillinger's mob, and during a laundry payroll holdup in Cincinnati, the owner went for a pistol and was killed by one of the gang. My friend swore to me he was not a killer, but would die before squealing on the rest. He felt he was just as guilty, and deeply regretted the disgrace he had brought his wife and mother. Although he had never once pulled the trigger, he expressed repentance for his life of crime.
>
> His letter moved me, and I showed it to Frankie Darro, who asked if it would be all right to write my friend. Instructions in the letter urged me to correspond and clearly mark on the envelope that I was an old friend. I suggested to Frankie that he do the same.
>
> In time, I heard back from my friend. He had received both our letters. He was surprised to learn that screen stars were so friendly, and had a request for me. Would it be possible for me to arrange for Jeanette MacDonald to sing on the radio "Ah, Sweet Mystery of Life"? He and three others on Death Row shared one radio, and he wrote, "No song ever affected me like her singing that one, and I can go and meet my Maker in peace after that."
>
> I immediately phoned her secretary and related the letter's content. She very indignantly stated, "Miss MacDonald cannot have her name involved with criminals." I pleaded with her to bring it to Jeanette's attention. She was adamant and retorted, "I told you she won't have anything to do with killers."
>
> Time passed, and I found myself portraying a soldier in the new Robert Z. Leonard production of *The Firefly*. Early into the filming, the gypsy dance sequence was shot on MGM's Lot 2. I waited for an opportune time, and when Jeanette was casually seated with no one around her, I walked over and related the story of my friend. To my shock, she replied, "I'll be glad to comply with his request."
>
> When I told her he'd already gone to the electric chair, she said angrily, "Why didn't you tell me this sooner?" I explained my futile attempt with her secretary. She exclaimed, "My God, how could she judge for me what I would do or wouldn't?" With tears streaming down her lovely face, she continued, "I'll have to go into the dressing room and regain my composure." She returned awhile later and asked if I still had the letter. "Will you bring it tomorrow?" she begged.

The next day she sat and read it and started crying again. "My God, to think I had the opportunity to bring some solace to those boys before they died, and my callous secretary denied me that right. I don't want a person like her in my employ." Sobbing, she again went into her dressing room. When the assistant director called, she had somehow regained her composure. She sought me out and said, "I suppose you would like to keep this letter?"

"Would you like it, Miss MacDonald?" I asked.

"May I?" she replied with a grateful look. "It will be among my most cherished memories."

There were a few lighthearted moments during the filming. In one instance, Jeanette did not come through a doorway just as director Robert Z. Leonard wanted her to. He suggested they re-do the take, and this time she should come sweeping through. Dressed in her evening gown, Jeanette did as she was told— she came through the doorway with a broom.

Meanwhile, Jeanette seemed to have come to terms with her impending marriage. Just as she threw herself wholeheartedly into her film roles, so she took on this new challenge. "She really tried to convince herself she was in love with Gene Raymond," commented a friend. "And Gene seemed the ideal husband for her; he was charming and likeable, he respected her career, made no domestic demands on her, did not try to compete with her success—all the things she'd had problems with in the past with Nelson."

Still, none of the above fully answers the question of *why* she married Gene Raymond. Jeanette herself once attempted an explanation to Isabel Eddy: "He's just like Nelson but without the rough edges." Not so many months later, though, she gave what was no doubt the most accurate reason: "I must have had rocks in my head."

Nelson returned from his spring concert tour and wasted no time in inquiring around, trying to learn the latest about Jeanette. He had heard rumors about her and Allan Jones, which drove him into a rage. Although Nelson had worked overtime to convince himself he was over Jeanette, he knew that in his heart Jeanette was his, would always be his. No so-called friend could steal her from him under his own eyes. He proceeded to crash a party attended by *The Firefly* co-stars. Before anyone could even greet him, he collared Allan and beat him senseless. (He later graciously picked up the hospital tab.)

Not many people were aware of Nelson's skills in fighting. While very young he had learned karate because he could not afford to have his face marked up. But unfortunately he fought dirty, first decking his victim with a few choice hits, then pounding him with his fists long after the poor fellow was down.

If his physical thrashing of Allan Jones was not enough, Nelson now informed Louis B. Mayer that he would not work at the same studio as "that white-faced tenor." Either Allan went, or he would. Mayer knew Nelson meant business, and much as he despised him personally, all the millions Nelson earned for him made the decision easy.

After *The Firefly* was completed, Allan Jones departed MGM, and his film career—which had once seemed so promising—never quite took off at any other studio. In later years Jones denied that Nelson ever beat him up. He claimed that he and Nelson were lifelong friends, that they had business dealings together and that he continued to see Nelson socially over the years, both of which were true. However, he also stated publicly on several occasions that Nelson had ruined his career and had had him thrown out of MGM. As late as 1987 Jones was defaming Nelson, making outrageous claims. In an interview that year, Jones made no attempt to hide his animosity toward Nelson. "Jeanette wanted to do more pictures with me, but Nelson was very insecure. He was after them to cut all my arias. There wasn't a place for two of us in the same studio . . . One thing: When they see my pictures today, they applaud. When they see Nelson, they laugh." In 1988 Jones got a little more personal in an interview with a MacDonald-Eddy fan. He claimed that *he* was virile and slept with everyone in sight, but that Nelson was gay and never slept with any woman until the mid-1940s. Jones also gave contradictory opinions about Jeanette, sometimes claiming she was a great lady and a good singer, other times stating that her voice was "manufactured."

Nelson was informed by MGM that he would be singing at Jeanette's wedding. His reaction was to laugh. He still refused to believe that the wedding was actually going to take place. He attempted to phone Jeanette, but was thwarted each time by Mayer or Jeanette's mother. He finally managed to slip by Mayer's spies and sneak into Jeanette's portable dressing room on *The Firefly* set. He sat and waited for her to arrive. When she finally opened the door and saw him, she stared at him in shock, then sank into a chair, crying. Nelson took this as a hopeful sign. He spent several minutes trying to comfort her. Yes, she admitted, she still loved him but what was she to do? It was too late to change things, too late to get out of the marriage. She had pleaded with Mayer, to no avail. Now her mother was constantly around and watched her like a hawk.

Nelson reminded her that no one could force her to do something she didn't agree to do. He told her he would handle everything—he would confront Mayer, even if it meant their having to leave MGM. Yet the conversation did not end there. Somehow it got around to the subject of Allan Jones, and Jeanette reprimanded Nelson for his barbaric treatment of him. She hated his fighting, and the way he kept hitting even after his victim was down. Nelson reminded her that Allan had deserved it; one thing led to another, and suddenly the two were fighting again, yelling so loud that everyone in the near vicinity was privy to it. Nelson finally stomped out of her dressing room, yanking the thin door open and finding nearly a dozen unhappy-looking people standing quietly, listening, dismayed at the shouting.

Later, Nelson mentally kicked himself for letting himself blow up the way he had. "It's just so much harder for us," he said. "We don't live normal lives and we don't have time to quietly work out our problems like other people. There's so many pressures and obligations that always come first." Nelson wondered seriously whether all the fame and fortune was worth the sacrifice he was making. But for the time being, he discarded any plans to coerce Jeanette out of her wedding plans.

Douglas Dumbrille, a character actor in *The Firefly*, also worked with Jeanette and Nelson in *Naughty Marietta* and *I Married an Angel*. He said he didn't like working with them because "they weren't professional, they were always crying about something." He much preferred working with the Marx Brothers!

On June 7, 1937, all Hollywood was stunned to learn that Jean Harlow had died. Nelson had spoken with Clark Gable days earlier, and Gable looked worried as he discussed his current project, *Saratoga*, with Jean "Baby" Harlow. "Baby" hadn't been well lately. She was haggard and pale, and just the previous day she'd fainted in Gable's arms and was sent home. Nelson was unaware of the subsequent events, that Harlow's mother had refused medical treatment for her daughter, that Gable and Frank Morgan had gone to the Harlow residence and finally convinced the mother to have her daughter hospitalized. But it was too late; the twenty-six-year-old girl had died.

Nelson was notified that he and Jeanette were to sing at the funeral, and that he was to be an honorary pallbearer. The funeral was a solemn, heartbreaking affair, for Harlow had been loved in the industry. Jeanette and Nelson were called upon to sing Harlow's favorite songs, "Indian Love Call" and "Ah, Sweet Mystery of Life." Many times at parties Harlow had demanded that her favorite singers perform her favorite songs, and she'd sentimentally wipe away tears at hearing them. Now Jeanette was in tears, so distraught that she started to collapse during her number, but Nelson managed to keep her on her feet and held her close, grimly finishing the song himself.

Nelson remained depressed after the funeral. The loss was no doubt intensified by the knowledge that he was about to lose something even more precious to him.

■■■ Both Anna MacDonald and Gene Raymond, who had been barred from visiting the *Maytime* set, were allowed onto *The Firefly* set to help celebrate Jeanette's birthday week. She looked happy, if somewhat detached. On June 14, two days before her marriage, she wrote a letter to Bob Ritchie at the Savoy Hotel in London. The tone of her letter is curious for a woman supposedly madly in love and about to go to the altar.

> Dear Bob, your letter came as a pleasant surprise as I was beginning to think I was off your list and you were not going to write . . . It made me very happy and yet a little sad—for I believe wholeheartedly that you meant everything you wrote and it was sweet. I have had fears and qualms but lately none at all and as the date approaches I feel more relaxed and certain I am not making a mistake—I am going to try and make this go as I have always with everything else. Wish me luck as you have in everything else! I wish you a great deal of happiness and success and feel that

at last you are well on the way to achieving something really splendid—Heaven knows you deserve it. This is Goodbye—but with it goes much love and all the fine thoughts any girl could have for a fine fellow. Let's always think of each other kindly. Ever, Jen.

The next day, June 15, Jeanette was still in a pensive mood. Her thoughts turning to Nelson, she wrote another letter, this time to his mother. Jeanette tried to rationalize to Isabel why their relationship hadn't worked out. She reiterated that Nelson had refused to marry her under her terms, and her words were sad and resigned.

My beautiful ring, that sweet symbol of the love I thought was mine—that I have put away with the other dear ring. They will go with me to my grave—dearly remembered—and I shall visit them often and see them always through a shining glory.

I must be a happy bride tomorrow—I must—I must go to Gene not with my heart's love, for that is impossible, but with purity of spirit—and a calm mind—a prayer in my heart. These two men are so strangely alike—I must try to find enough of Nelson in Gene to make me contented. Gene understands and he thinks he can help me.

The night of June 15 should have been a quiet one for Jeanette. She was alone with her mother and her sister Blossom, trying to get some rest before the big day. Unable to sleep, she paced her bedroom. Suddenly she heard a commotion downstairs. She went to see what it was, and was startled to see a red-faced Nelson pushing her mother aside and heading directly for her. She tried to run back into her bedroom, but he was too fast for her. He grabbed her up in his arms, went back down the stairs, and headed for his car. When she tried to protest, he clapped a hand over her mouth to shut her up.

Getting Jeanette into the car was another story. She fought and kicked so hard that Nelson finally set her on her feet, forcing her to look at him. "Jenny, tell me you don't love me! Look me in the eye and tell me. If you can do that, I'll believe you and I'll never bother you again."

Jeanette was unable to meet his gaze. But as she verbally protested being kidnapped like this, and gave him her usual arguments about her career, Nelson suddenly realized he was beating a dead horse. He said in desperation, "Angel, Angel, what is there in you that only destroys us? People search all their lives for what we have, and you're willing to throw it all away with your wanton greediness." Defeated, he drove away, leaving her standing in the street alone.

Wednesday, June 16, was a warm, sunny day in Los Angeles. The wedding was scheduled for 9:00 P.M., to take place at the Wilshire Methodist Church. Several hours earlier, crowds began to from along Wilshire Boulevard in front of the church. Traffic was diverted to side streets as fans choked the sidewalks, waiting for the film celebrities to arrive. By the time the bride and groom arrived, the line of "cursing, sweating and struggling" spectators was estimated at between

10,000 and 15,000, and the crowd spread out over twelve city blocks. It took a herculean effort on the part of the police department to bring a thin stream of cars through, and even then, the bridesmaids were forty minutes late getting inside the church. Two hundred policemen attempted to hold the crowd at bay, but they did not entirely succeed. Several of the 1,000 Hollywood "names" were mobbed. Due to the mass hysteria, the ceremony began a half hour late.

Nelson arrived with his mother. Isabel usually sported a friendly smile for the camera, but on this evening her eyes were lowered and her head was bowed. Nelson, ignoring the camera altogether, stared straight ahead. He was biting his lip and looked close to tears. Why a photo of the two unsmiling Eddys was published among all the other happy ones is a mystery. They looked as though they were attending a funeral. In fact, if one were to compare the photos of Nelson taken at Jeanette's wedding with those taken the previous week at Harlow's funeral, one would find that Nelson has the same expression on his face.

The press had tried in vain to get specifics in advance about the wedding, as cameras were barred from the proceedings. Jeanette refused to grant any interviews herself, saying it was bad luck. Gene also begged off: "I'm so nervous I can't even talk to myself."

The MacRaymond wedding was covered by papers all over the world. "The big premiere of the week was the wedding of Jeanette MacDonald and Gene Raymond," wrote Sidney Skolsky. "It was a usual Metro production—lavish, with red lanterns hanging outside, while inside the church was decorated with pink roses and pink ribbons . . . The Metro publicity men stood at the door to see that the right guests entered and distributed the credit sheets, which told about principals and supporting cast."

The "supporting cast" included Blossom as the maid of honor and Gene's brother Robert Marlow as best man. The bridal attendants included Ginger Rogers, Fay Wray, Helen Ferguson and Mrs. Johnny Mack Brown. The ushers were Richard Hargraves (Helen Ferguson's husband), Johnny Mack Brown, Harold Lloyd, Basil Rathbone and Allan Jones. The clergyman was Reverend Willsie Martin. In true MGM style, no expense was spared. The event was called the biggest Hollywood wedding since that of Rod La Rocque and Vilma Banky a decade earlier. Costs were estimated at $25,000, and the money was spent where everyone could see it. The inside of the church was decorated with "nearly a million roses." Six candelabra, each bearing seven slender tapers, burned in the chancel. The middle aisle, bounded by pink silk ribbon along the whole length, was also lined with seven candles on a side.

Jeanette refuted the extravagant estimates in a letter to Life magazine. She stated that the entire event came in under $5,000. Maybe her end of it did, but it was known that MGM had footed much, if not all, of the bill.

The ceremony began with Nelson singing "I Love You Truly." One critic couldn't help but notice the "look of resignation" on his face. Then Anna MacDonald came down the aisle. (True to her word, Gene Raymond's mother refused to attend the wedding publicly accusing Jeanette of being a "cradle snatcher." The march from *Lohengrin* announced the arrival of the ushers. It was noted that Basil Rathbone had difficulty keeping step, and that Allan Jones' shoes squeaked, to his evident embarrassment. After the bridesmaids came Jeanette, looking pale but exquisite. Her gown was made of flesh pink mousseline, designed by Adrian, with long full sleeves, a high neck, lace collar and a lace cap to match. She held a tiny bouquet of flowers and a gold embroidered pink satin prayer book. Gene greeted her, happy and handsome. One reporter wrote, "It was difficult to tell which of the two was more beautiful."

"It didn't seem real," the same reviewer continued. "It looked as if it were happening on a movie set." As the service began, a woman in the audience gasped and fainted. It was a single-ring ceremony, and one of the guests later noted that Jeanette hesitated slightly before accepting the ring on her finger. As Reverend Martin intoned the Lord's Prayer near the end of the ceremony a roar rose up from the thousands outside, echoing in the church. Then Nelson sang again: "Oh Perfect Love." A couple of reports revealed that Nelson's voice shook and he had to read the words of the song off sheet music, very unusual for Nelson. Additionally, his hands were trembling so badly he could hardly hold the pages still. During the exchange of vows, in which the word "obey" was omitted, the sound of Nelson Eddy's choked sobs were heard. One writer explained this away by claiming that Nelson was exhausted from overwork. The bride and groom kissed, "a medium-long kiss." Then they ran up the aisle. They were stopped at the door, which was slightly opened, and Jeanette gasped at the size of the crowd. Gene rubbed Jeanette's lipstick off his mouth with his gloved hand. "You'll have to run for it," the newlyweds were told. "The police can hold them just long enough for you to get out." Jeanette was worried that she couldn't run with her train, but it was wrapped around her arm and the doors were flung open. An explosion of light came from the photographers' flashbulbs. Police fought the crowd back, and with six motorcycle officers in screaming escort, the couple raced away in Jeanette's limousine.

The attendants and the guests were less fortunate. It took more than an hour for them to exit the church and make their way over to Jeanette's house, where the reception was being held.

One of the guests was Herbert Stothart. His son Herb Jr., was just seven years old, but he recalls the day of Jeanette's wedding. For some reason Mrs. Stothart refused to attend, so Stothart went alone. When he returned, Mrs. Stothart asked how it had gone. Herb Jr. remembers his father shaking his head incredulously, saying nothing, and pouring a couple of stiff drinks.

The self-appointed "father of the bride," Louis B. Mayer, concluded that the expense of the wedding was justified. "Just the look on the face of the baritone was worth every penny," Mayer gloated. "If I live to be a hundred I couldn't ask for a better revenge than to see him singing with tears in his eyes. But you have to hand it to him, it took a lot of guts to do it."

One reporter summed up: "It was a grand premiere, a great nite, and there was only one touch missing. The publicity men did not give out the usual preview cards to ask the audience what they thought of the show. One wit, very much concerned, wondered whether Jeanette and Gene would sit up all night and wait for the reviews." In the confusion, no one seemed to notice that Nelson was missing from the reception. He later made a brief appearance, obediently posing for a group shot. In this photo he is standing at the end of the line and looks miserable while everyone else is smiling. Surprisingly, when the photo was widely published, both the press and the fans seemed to overlook Nelson's distress. In a few of the other poses with her bridesmaids, Jeanette is also unsmiling.

Louella Parsons wrote: "Jeanette had been very firm that there was to be nothing 'commercial' about her wedding. No flash bulbs popping inside the church, no reporters scrambling for vantage points. 'You are the only newspaper guest at the church and the reception,' she told me pointedly . . . But a story as glamorous as this was not to be 'lost' by this gal. I tucked a typewriter under my silver fox cape (very chic then) and when we returned for the reception at Jeanette's home, I headed straight for the powder room. Locked the door and started writing my bird's-eye scoop for my paper.

"Suddenly there was a knock at the door. And the bride called, 'Louella, you and that typewriter come right out here.' And when I came out, sheepishly, I found a table set up.

" 'You might as well work in comfort,' laughed the lovely Jeanette. 'You're going to do it anyway!' "

Photographers felt slighted by not being allowed to cover the nuptials. After the wedding, a press report claimed that Jeanette would soothe their wounded feelings by seeing that they all received handsome gifts.

Nelson had left the church alone, telling Isabel to go on to the reception because he couldn't. "I got home as soon as I could," Isabel later noted in her diary.

I found him with his head on his desk and I knew instantly that he had been drinking. I had the maid bring me some black coffee and after he had had several cups he felt a little better . . . As he realized it was me he held up his arms to me and was my little boy again and his words were terrible. "Mommie," he said, just as he did when he was a tiny hurt little boy, "Mommie—my heart and soul are dead. I can't ever sing another note—what will I ever do? I learned too late how terribly I love her." . . . I said, "You must find courage, dear. Only God can help us now." And in that awful moment the phone rang and as I answered I heard Blossom's voice. I tried not to let Nelson know, but suddenly Jeanette came on . . . "Isabel, where is he? Tell him to please come to see me—I can't go if he doesn't." And then I knew that another heart was breaking. Nelson took the phone and spoke to her in a voice shaken with emotion, saying, "I'll come to see you, sure I will, you look for me." And we left for Jeanette's house. Nelson kept holding my hand all during the ride and as we entered the flower-decked living room the butler met us and took us directly upstairs to a small room where we found Jeanette, Gene, Blossom, and her mother and Gene's brother. Nelson shook hands with them all, leaving Jeanette for last. As he took her hand her arms were around his neck and he kissed her and I am sure Anna didn't like it one little bit by the look on her face. Jeanette looked drawn and tired and even Gene looked sad and weary—and then Jeanette said, "Darling, go up to the dining room and I'll join you in ten minutes. Now, I want Nelson alone for that time. I have something to say to him, it's important." And Gene very graciously took us all from the room. Ten minutes later they appeared and joined us . . . An hour later Jeanette and Gene had gone. Never to this day has anyone of us known what Nelson and Jeanette said to each other in that room. When I mentioned it to Nelson on the way home he said, "It will always remain our secret alone and will die with us." So none of us know. I can only say Nelson was a little more peaceful, but both their hearts were aching and well I knew it.

Jeanette had a good week left to shoot on *The Firefly*; then she and Gene joined another newlywed couple, Mary Pickford and Buddy Rogers, on a honeymoon cruise to Hawaii. They sailed on the *Lurline* and the press was informed that they would vacation for two months. Before the *Lurline* docked, however, the Hollywood press was abuzz with a scandal so hot they couldn't print it. Everyone from Mae Mann to Walter Winchell knew the scoop and was itching so spill it, but at a cost of their jobs, their eager lips were sealed.

Jeanette and Gene had taken two cabins on the *Lurline,* while Mary Pickford and Buddy Rogers shared a double room. Mary, already an alcoholic, spent much of the voyage in her cups, and it was widely known that she still held a flame for her ex-husband Douglas Fairbanks. Jeanette, on the other hand, who'd apparently married for love, rarely left her room and was said to be "crying her eyes out. " And for good reason too: there *was* a honeymoon going on—but the ones sleeping together were Gene Raymond and Buddy Rogers.

■ In early July, Sybil Thomas visited the Eddy household. She wanted to see for herself how Nelson was adjusting to Jeanette's marriage. She found Nelson at the bar, drowning his sorrows in drink. Isabel explained that he wasn't up to socializing, so the two women sat and talked together, ignoring him.

During the visit, the telephone rang. Isabel answered, listened for a moment, then handed the phone to Nelson. It was the overseas operator, she announced, from Hawaii. There was no doubt who could be placing the call. The two women watched and listened as Nelson finally heard Jeanette's voice. He greeted her by saying, "It's nighttime there. Isn't there something you should be doing just about now?" Jeanette didn't answer, she was crying too hard. Nelson looked confused as he tried to make out what she was saying. He kept telling her to calm down and speak clearly. Finally he gave up. "You made your bed, now lie in it," he said, and hung up on her. He turned to the two women. "I don't know what she wanted. She kept trying to tell me something about Gene."

13

A marriage
made in heaven?

Gene Raymond's childhood was similar to Nelson Eddy's in several key ways. He was forced to go to work at a young age, he was highly ambitious, and he was raised by a domineering mother who apparently lived vicariously through her son's success. Born Raymond Guion in New York City on August 13, 1908, there never seemed any doubt that Raymond would become an actor. (An article in the New York *Times* from June 11, 1933, lists his birth date as 1903, while a 1932 Motion Picture magazine article claims the year is 1905. However, Gene looked several years younger than Jeanette, so it is likely that the 1908 figure is accurate.) He left public school after fourth grade and attended the Professional Children's School, where his classmates included Helen Chandler and Marguerite Churchill. At age fourteen he was cast as an extra in a Broadway play called *The Potters*. Serious about his career, Raymond carefully attended all the rehearsals.

> In those days you had seven days to prove yourself in a part. And if you didn't measure up, that was it. And you didn't get any money. There was a man named Russell Metcalf who was playing the part of the older boy, Bill Potter. And on the seventh day, when I happened to be standing in the wings, he said to me, "Well, I got it—I won't be seeing you again!"

Apparently Metcalf looked too young for the part. Raymond took over the role, and stayed with *The Potters* for its two seasons on Broadway and the road show.

At age seventeen, Raymond was signed to play Oscar, the big Swede, in the smash hit play *Cradle Snatchers*. One of the play's co-authors was Russell Metcalf, who recommended Raymond for the role. Other cast members included Edna May Oliver, Humphrey Bogart and Mary Boland. Raymond looked so young with his blonde hair standing straight up that when he first made an entrance the audience burst into laughter. Nonetheless, *Cradle Snatchers* enjoyed more than a two-year run. After it closed, Raymond found himself cast in a series of flops and near-flops until he finally landed another hit, starring as Gene Bigson in *Young Sinners*. The play and its star packed them in for a year in New York and another year on tour. Based on the success of *Young Sinners*, Raymond was tested by Paramount studios and signed to a contract. As part of the deal, his name was changed to Gene Raymond.

The Paramount contract lasted two years, then he signed long-term with RKO. He seemed star material, and it appeared that, given a few more years, he might really "make it." He played second lead in "A" films like *Red Dust* with Gable and Harlow, and leads in forgettable "B" pictures. The finest films of his career came during this period, notably *Flying Down to Rio*, in which he co-starred with Dolores Del Rio, and the whimsical *Zoo in Budapest*, as Loretta Young's co-star.

Unfortunately, Gene's personal life intervened. According to a friend, he became involved with a teenaged boy whose parents decided to press charges. The studio managed to arrange a cash settlement and stave off any scandal, but an announcement hit the trades that Gene was gone from RKO and now free-lancing. He continued to appear in several films a year, but it was again as second lead in "A" films, or as star in "B" films. Gene at this point was smart enough to realize that his film career might never reach the heights: "An actor's peak of popularity is short-lived and when mine is past I want to step into another branch of the industry. As I act in the movies I make it a point to learn all I can about direction and production. Some day, perhaps, I may realize my ambition to write, direct and produce my own picture for a major studio."

He started working as a composer, and one of his songs, "Will You," was published and used in the film *The Smartest Girl in Town* (1936). He was realistic about his film career, and rated it "so-so. Naturally I'm impressed with the medium, but so far it hasn't—for me—lived up to expectations. They've been sort of like that California scenery you hear so much about in the East and can't find when you get out here . . . The nearest I've come to doing what I really want to do was in *Zoo in Budapest* . . . I like to ride and swim, but I seldom have a chance to do either in pictures. I'd like parts which would give me a chance to do that sort of thing. Quite frankly, I think a big gap has been left by Douglas Fairbanks Senior and my ambition is to try to fill that gap."

Not much was known about his family life. He had a younger brother, known as Robert Marlow. His parents divorced and his mother remarried a Mr. Kip-pling. He lived for a long time with his mother, who was thought to have "a stranglehold" on him. In January 1934, he went on a three-month vacation to Europe with her as companion. "There's no romance, light or heavy, in the life of Gene Raymond," claimed a 1932 article entitled "Indifferent to Girls." "Staying single is the easiest thing I do," Gene was quoted as saying. Still another article made it clear to readers that Gene was "only a pal" to the infrequent women he escorted. As late as two months before his engagement to Jeanette, Gene said that he was not seriously involved with anyone, though he was seen occasionally with Jeanette or Janet Gaynor (who was known to be a lesbian).

In Jeanette's case, Gene finally seemed to find a woman he could love. "He really was in love with Jeanette," claimed one of his friends. "He wanted to make the marriage work. But he couldn't get past the ghost between them— Nelson. Maybe she loved Gene, but she was 'in love' with Nelson. Once [years later] we were sitting out at the pool at Twin Gables [the MacRaymond home]. Gene had been drinking and he was feeling sorry for himself. 'I love her, but I'm not man enough for her,' he said tearfully. 'For her, happiness is spelled N-E-L-S-O-N.' "

Jeanette learned of Gene's bisexuality, as it turned out, on their honeymoon. She was shocked. A woman who had prided herself on being so careful—doing the right thing, finding the perfect husband for herself—now found that she had been deceived in the most ludicrous way. Her marriage, in any case, was not be the "happily ever after" scenario she had imagined for herself. The irony of her situation was that, in the eyes of the world, she was considered the epitome of innocent love. Jeanette's initial impulse was to run home to Nelson, but she also realized how impossible this would be, given the massive publicity at her wedding. The adverse press would badly damage her career. She and Gene had a confrontation. "Let's face it, you're no angel either," Gene pointed out to Jeanette. "You married me, loving him. Would you call that honesty?" They decided to stay married, at least for the time being, and the truth is that there were many marriages in Hollywood, so-called "working relationships," where both parties concentrated on their careers, living separate private lives. Many such marriages were lasting. Now Jeanette and Gene joined the ranks.

"She did not know about Gene before the marriage," Blossom insisted. "I found out later that our mother knew—but she said nothing." According to Blossom, Anna MacDonald learned about Gene from gossiping with her Hollywood mothers' group, of which Mary Kippling (Gene's mother) was also a member. Anna chose not to tell Jeanette, believing Gene to be a good man anyway. "And she didn't care who Jeanette married," Blossom said wryly, "as long as it wasn't Nelson."

The photos taken on their honeymoon show a smiling, radiant Gene, and a strained, pasty-faced Jeanette. In various candids her eyes are puffy, with black circles under them. She either forces a smile or looks down, embarrassed. But her eyes are not smiling; in one shot she looks close to tears. They stayed at a home owned by the Robert Z. Leonards. One photo was snapped of the newlyweds in front of the house. It is a long shot, which shows Gene, tanned and handsome in swim shorts, and Jeanette in the background, fully dressed. A puzzling development was the announcement that the Leonards had later followed the Raymonds

Jeanette and Gene arrive in Hawaii on their honeymoon.

to Hawaii, and it appeared that they were all staying together. Most likely Leonard rushed to Jeanette's side to help her get through the "honeymoon."

According to the press, Jeanette and Gene were to remain in Hawaii through August. However, according to more than one report, Jeanette quietly returned to Los Angeles sometime in July, where she was seen at a picnic. Nelson was there as well. According to the source, during the dancing, the MC announced that for the next number, each man should dance with his sweetheart. Nelson grabbed Jeanette and defiantly danced her across the lawn, to the amazement of everyone there.

If Jeanette was in fact back in Los Angeles, she remained otherwise hidden for the next few weeks. Varied versions were published detailing when she and Gene were scheduled to return to the mainland; in one, they would be traveling with the Bob Leonards. But on August 5 it was reported that the Raymonds had returned to California, where they settled into their new home, Twin Gables, located at 783 Bel Air Road. They had separate bedrooms.

Although the fan magazines reported that Gene had purchased the house as a surprise wedding gift for Jeanette, Twin Gables was, in fact, leased. A record filed at the Los Angeles County Court indicates the house was finally purchased by Jeanette and Gene in 1938. But tax records give conflicting data, suggesting that the house was purchased twice, once in 1937, and once in 1938. The sellers were listed alternately as Security National Bank, and Helen Ferguson (Jeanette's press agent). Employees at the courthouse are at a loss to explain the contradictory facts. What has been confirmed by friends of the Raymonds is that the studio helped Gene financially with the purchase.

One who was almost daily on the scene during these first weeks of their marriage was Richard Halverson. Today, he's Reverend Richard Halverson, the United States Senate Chaplain. In 1937, he worked as Jeanette's chauffeur/butler.

Halverson had been on the vaudeville stage since the age of ten. He came to

Hollywood at nineteen for a Paramount screen test, then decided his true calling was the ministry. Prior to Jeanette's marriage, he accepted what was to be a two-week stint as her chauffeur, and he found himself helping Jeanette move her possessions from 401 June Street to Twin Gables. "One of the most vivid memories I have is moving her clothing, especially her shoes. She owned a twelve-cylinder Packard town car, which I was driving. I filled the back of it with shoes and clothes. As a boy who was always poor, I was overwhelmed by all those clothes."

When Jeanette's regular chauffeur quit to work for Norma Shearer, Halverson replaced him. While the Raymonds were in Hawaii, he chauffeured Anna Mac-Donald to her various social events, including a weekly mah-jongg game. He liked Mrs. MacDonald. He also had occasion to drive Blossom and her husband Rocky. "I liked them too. They were real people. I remember laughing a lot with Blossom, at things she would say and do. She was a character and so much fun."

When the Raymonds returned from Hawaii, Halverson found he liked his job less once Gene made his presence known. "Jeanette was absolutely a tremendous person. She was very good to me. She was interested in my faith, my life plans, my conversion to Christ, why I was going into the ministry and so forth. Often, as I would be driving her some place, maybe just to MGM Studios, she would ask me a lot of questions. At the end of the day, she just let me take the car home, and I'd pick her up the next day, whenever she needed me. She treated me like a brother or a member of the family. Which all changed, incidently, when her husband came into the picture. He believed chauffeurs should be spoken to, not heard from. He treated me like a servant. And I was a servant. But she had been so nice to me, and so family-like. For example, once in awhile we'd go to a drive-in to eat. She'd get something in the back seat and I'd get something in the front. But when Gene got there, he wanted me to go out of the car and go into the restaurant, not to eat with them . . . I didn't like her husband at all. Gene was a stuffed shirt. He was kind of effeminate. I felt he bossed her around. She took it, as though she was one of his servants or subjects. It was like he needed to control her somehow. He seemed to resent the fact that he hadn't really made it, like Nelson Eddy, for example. So he could control her and that was sort of a substitute.

"I felt Gene Raymond dominated her life. I think I resented him. Don't ask me why, I didn't have any right to."

Later on, Halverson had occasion to wonder about just how happy a couple Gene and Jeanette were. In the fall, he left Jeanette's employ to go to school, returning to work for her the following summer while Jeanette and Nelson were filming Sweethearts. Halverson visited the set a number of times. "I didn't know about any kind of relationship between them except the professional relationship," he claimed. "But they got along very well. He was a trickster, of course, and did a lot of funny things on the set. He made her laugh a lot." After seeing the difference in Jeanette when she was around Nelson, Richard Halverson pondered the inevitable question: "I wonder why she didn't marry Nelson Eddy?"

Despite her personal problems, the summer of 1937 was professionally a high point for Jeanette. *Maytime*, noted as one of the top domestic money-makers of the year, continued to break box office records all over the world. In Manila it topped the gross of every other MGM picture to ever play the house by 35 percent. In Santiago, *Maytime* was called the best musical ever made, and the Chilean president, Alessandri, had three private screenings. In Trinidad, the film broke house box office records by 50 percent. The overseas critics and audience raved; Stockholm reported a MacDonald-Eddy mania and a rush to re-release the earlier films; Bogotá, Colombia, had to extend its run due to the demand; Durban, South Africa, had a three-week run with every performance a complete sell-out. In the Orient, Jeanette was named the number-one movie star, and she would remain a favorite for years.

MGM capitalized on *Maytime*'s success and the recent world-wide publicity of Jeanette's marriage by going all-out with the release of *The Firefly*, which Jeanette had finished filming just before she and Gene left for Hawaii. A press release revealed that the studio was planning to use the new "tint-tone color" for the first time in an entire film. "The studio has purchased three machines to add to the one it has," stated the Hollywood *Reporter*, "for printing film in the sepia-platinum and various combinations with the process."

The preview process to *The Firefly* was encouraging. It was called "a big money picture," and "a box office attraction of smash calibre." And for Jeanette: "Jeanette MacDonald is exquisite in the title role, probably the peak performance of her career. She is at her best in voice and appearance, breathtakingly beautiful in every scene." Yet the film, at two hours and seventeen minutes, was thought to be too long, and it was indicated that after the preview the film would be trimmed. However, when *The Firefly* went into general release in early September, the film was at its full original length.

Amid much fanfare, *The Firefly* was viewed and dissected by the critics. Irving Hoffman wrote of the New York opening:

> The sound apparatus for a time was stepped too high, causing the actors to talk and sing louder than the roar of the MGM lion. Jeanette MacDonald's first number received surprisingly meager applause, which may have been due to the sound projection flaw. It was apparent that, because of the picture's over-long running time, the spectators became a bit impatient, shifting uncomfortably in their pews. A few fans couldn't reconcile the mixture of light musical treatment with the heavy interpolation of war montage, and one critical comedian was heard to crack at the finish, "It's beginning to look like *San Francisco!*" Jeanette MacDonald's singing, while bombs were bursting in such profusion, also was ridiculed. Allan Jones copped the largest salvo of applause for the evening, after the "Donkey Serenade" sequence. With the exception of "Giannina Mia," most of the other renditions met with only half-hearted applause. There were oh's and ah's at the opulence of *The*

Firefly, but ho's and hum's at the petrified plot. Critical reviews averaged sixty-nine percent.

Most critics agreed that the film should have been trimmed. *Variety* was unimpressed with the sepia tone, complaining it was "monotonous and not nearly so effective as the conventional natural tone." The New York *World-Telegram* called the production "beautifully photographed dullness," and mourned that Jeanette didn't sing enough. The New York *Post*, on the other hand, argued that Jeanette sang too much, but had to admit: "The scientific aspect of Miss MacDonald's larynx is not wholly clear . . . but surely something is there, perhaps high frequency if there is such a thing, that records better than other soprano voices. It is clear, rounded and effortlessly melodious."

Leonard's heavy-handed directing was attacked as well. "Done in the manner of old-fashioned operettas, it throws right out the window all the crusading work done by directors such as W. S. Van Dyke, Rouben Mamoulian and others in trying to convert the screen operetta into a realistic, pungent, believable medium," said the *World-Telegram*. "Miss MacDonald needs a Van Dyke or a Mamoulian to direct her and it may be too that she needs rescuing from the kind of picture in which people write with feathers."

Despite the critics, *The Firefly* did well with the public, owing to Jeanette's loyal following. The film was also clearly the high point of Allan Jones' film career. He would forever be associated with the song "Donkey Serenade. However, the viewers' reaction was "thumbs down" to him as a screen lover for Jeanette, and the studio was inundated with a barrage of mail during the summer of 1937, demanding a re-teaming of Jeanette and Nelson. Metro obliged by quickly announcing that they would star together in The *Girl of the Golden West*.

In July, Jeanette took over the hosting of the Vicks Open House radio show. Her time slot was opposite Jack Benny, and through her ratings were high, Benny was one of the most popular radio stars and was stiff competition. This single season of Vicks was the only radio series Jeanette ever hosted. In truth, live radio made her nervous; during one broadcast she actually fainted while on the air. The press, jumping onto the fainting story, explained it away by claiming that Jeanette had been wearing an orchid during the broadcast, and her "allergy" to the flower had caused her collapse. This is a ludicrous explanation in light of the fact that she was photographed many times over the years wearing orchids— without fainting.

After this embarrassing experience, she continued to make guest appearances on dozens of other radio shows, but refused to ever host a series again. During the war years, Jeanette burst into tears and walked off a radio show broadcast live from WOR in New York. The stress of live radio, when added to her personal problems at that time, proved too much for her, despite her usual professionalism.

Nelson, meanwhile, signed up with The Chase & Sanborn Hour starring Edgar Bergen and Charlie McCarthy, and his presence had an immediate, positive effect on the show. Nelson loved radio and appeared as a regular in several series for fourteen years.

Putting on a happy face by day, Jeanette was anything but happy at night. She was plagued with insomnia, the press reported. She attempted all sorts of cures, even appealing to her fans for successful methods. But none of the Band-Aid cures could compensate for the real cause of her sleepless nights. Apparently, her withdrawal symptoms from Nelson were more agonizing that she had anticipated. Once she told Isabel, "We had so much to share—our great love of music, our complete understanding, our love of nature." As she would do for the rest of her life, Jeanette reflected back to the days of Lake Tahoe as the happiest in her life. "Always I will remember the night . . . he took my hand and then my other one and then his arms held me closely, and there beneath the pines he spoke words of such tender beauty that I could never repeat them—not now— they would make me too sad, too unhappy. I must bury all this and try never to let it be remembered."

Naturally, divorce was out of the question—not only for publicity reasons, but for personal ones as well. "It was in character for her to stay with Gene," Richard Halverson says. "She was totally into her career and her music. That was her life. She was a very hard worker and she took her work very seriously." Halverson also concludes that a strong factor in her decision to make the marriage work was her mother. "Jeanette loved her mother. And she wasn't a divorcing kind of person; she had tremendous integrity."

Nelson riding alone through the hills of Griffith Park.

Jeanette confided to her sister Blossom that she picked up the phone "a hundred times" over the summer to call Nelson, just to talk or to invite him to one of her parties, but she always lost her courage and hung up. Frustrated with herself, she paced her bedroom floor night after night.

Things weren't much better at the Eddy household. Isabel wrote of her son: "Oh, the nights I have seen him pace the floor when his bed was never slept in—when long hours dragged by and only the comfort of her picture could make him even sit down—when he drank cups of black coffee to the extreme—and nothing mattered." A snapshot of Nelson taken a few weeks after Jeanette's wedding shows him thinner than usual, his tired face etched with sadness. But as time progressed, he made an effort to put the past behind him. "The number of females that drifted in and out of my son's life was amazing," Isabel remarked of that summer. "I never met any of them—he never asked me to, so I know from this that in none of them had he been able to feel the necessary spark that would create a lasting interest."

One woman did manage to capture Nelson's attention for a little while, at least. She was twenty-seven-year-old Eleanor Powell, his *Rosalie* co-star, a religious, down-to-earth girl. They hit it off during the film's rehearsals in July, and by the time the picture started shooting on August 30, they were dating. Both mothers encouraged the union. In time, the relationship cooled, at least on Nelson's part. He told Isabel, "She's a nice girl, but [if I married her] I'd have to spend half my life in church." They remained friends, as did many of the women

Nelson, who once wanted to be a professional drummer, impresses his *Rosalie* co-star and current flame, dancer Eleanor Powell.

with whom Nelson was involved. Decades later, when Eleanor Powell was asked about Nelson in an interview, she grew misty-eyed.

Rosalie was a hodgepodge extravaganza. The plot had to do with a West Point cadet (Nelson) falling in love with a mythical kingdom princess (Powell). But the picture had so many subplots going on with top-notch character actors like Frank Morgan, Edna May Oliver, Ray Bolger, Billy Gilbert and Ilona Massey that Nelson nearly got lost in the shuffle. (*Rosalie* was Ilona Massey's film debut. Mayer had discovered her, along with Hedy Lamarr and Greer Garson, while on a European talent hunt in 1936.) Fortunately for Nelson, the film featured some memorable songs for her by Cole Porter, most notably the title song, "Rosalie," and "In the Still of the Night." Nelson purportedly disliked the latter song, claiming it wasn't right for his voice and that he sounded "like a zombie" singing it. But his fans loved it and the number became a popular standard for him.

The filming, with Woody Van Dyke at the helm, began the week of Jeanette's wedding. The mood of the set was deliberately lighthearted, and Nelson responded to it. Eleanor Powell spoke of his sense of humor and love of practical jokes, telling of the birthday party thrown for her by Nelson and Ray Bolger. They blindfolded her and marched her around in circles until she was utterly confused. When the blindfold was removed, she found her birthday party was being hosted in the men's room. Another comic incident occurred when she was filming her famous drum dance number. The set, which was outdoors, was wet and slick from an unexpected rain. Nelson and Ray Bolger drove up in an ambulance, stepped out gowned in white uniforms, and set up a stretcher, ready to haul her away should the need arise.

After the first day of filming, the studio added twenty-five days to the shooting schedule. Even with the speedy Van Dyke directing, *Rosalie* went way over schedule, taking up the entire summer, and finally wrapping in late November. This presented a problem for Nelson, who was scheduled to start work on *The Girl of the Golden West* with Jeanette at the beginning of October. Accordingly, Woody completed Nelson's scenes as quickly as possible.

Rosalie was released Christmas week of 1937 with record-breaking returns. At the San Francisco premiere (which Eleanor Powell attended), the opening day take surpassed that of *Maytime*. In Los Angeles, the film opened both at Grauman's Chinese and Loew's State, and both theaters reported the best Christmas week business in five years. In New York it was "SROsalie indeed at the Capitol." Reporter Irving Hoffman wrote:

> Matinee crowds . . . flooded the opening shows, and evening throngs filled the playhouse until the last performance. There was a definite dissension of opinion as to the merit of the gargantuan musical. Less discriminating fans—in fact, those making up the bulk of the audience—found it a good show and were awed by its spectacle and abundance of talent.
>
> But on the other hand, those who were inclined to be critical were bitter in their condemnation. To them, even the excellent musical sequences were deemed too numerous. They felt that no amount of singing and dancing could compensate for

the lack of an acceptable story. In singling out those who met with unanimous approval, first to head the list was Billy Gilbert. Customers were held in convulsions during his sneezing routine, and were of the opinion that this scene offered more entertainment than the mammoth numbers in the picture . . . Ray Bolger could be classed as an outstanding click, although New Yorkers familiar with his talent were surprised that he was not permitted to go into his dance. The ventriloquist routine as delivered by Frank Morgan was another highly appreciated contribution.

Nelson Eddy pleases everybody. At the matinee shows, thronged with school-girls, they ooh'd and aah'd over him in a manner that hasn't been displayed since the days of Valentino. Decided disapproval was directed towards Eleanor Powell—not for any specific reason that we could gather—but merely because she lacked appeal.

Another who came in for Capitol punishment was MGM's Magyar import, Ilona Massey. We approached several exiting patrons with direct questions on Miss Massey, being curious as to their reaction towards this new personality. They agreed unanimously that she found no favor with them.

Of the production numbers, Miss Powell's cadet drill, the wedding finale and the festival sequence received most acclaim, although spectators couldn't figure out why the camera work was so shaky towards the end of the latter number.

Rosalie went into general release New Year's week, to mixed reviews. While one paper called *Rosalie* "big, handsome, melodious, youthfully romantic," another condemned it as "a mythical kingdom bore, and toward the end it seemed as if the film had perpetual motion and would never stop." A third wrote it off as "a 250 lb. elf."

"Eddy . . . looks adorable in his cadet uniform," reported *Variety*. "If Nelson Eddy is not an example of perfect casting as a graduating cadet," commented the New York *Post*, "at least he plays the role with a boyish sincerity and ease." Most other critics disagreed. The New York *Times* sniped that Nelson "sings as well and inopportunely as can be imagined," while the *World-Telegram* said, "Nelson Eddy sings well, of course, but for the most part his performance must be as embarrassing to him as it is to the spectator."

Even Woody did not escape unscathed. "If the film had not been directed by W. S. Van Dyke 2nd," said *Variety*, "its defects might be easier to understand."

As usual, the studio laughed all the way to the bank. *Rosalie* did excellent business. Nelson's recording of the title song was noted as the most-played song on radio, and his popularity by the end of 1937 was at a new high.

■ Meantime, Nelson was growing increasingly agitated at the prospect of working with Jeanette again in *The Girl of the Golden West*. He dated others, trying to push her from his thoughts. One of his escorts during this time was a girl named Belle. She went out with him a few times, remembering him as "a gentleman, very polite, but preoccupied." He seemed to desire little from her but companionship, and told her, "I like you because you don't bother me with questions I can't answer." He spoke often of wanting a home and children. One night they were driving back from a date, and Nelson pulled over to enjoy the moonlight. Belle, delighted that her relationship with this handsome and passionate man had progressed beyond the platonic, was startled as Nelson suddenly pulled away from her. Gripping the steering wheel, he said in despair, "Forget it, just forget it. Who am I kidding? It's no use, damn it." Belle apologized, wondering what she'd done to upset him. He grimly drove her home, saying, "It's not you, you're a very nice girl. But I'm in love with another woman, and I can't get away from that. I don't know what I'm going to do, but it's my problem, not yours." At her doorstep he kissed her hand, then left. She never saw him again.

He was similarly candid with another date. "Look, if you want a fling, fine," he told a prospective girlfriend. "Come on, we'll go right now. Nobody'll know about it. I'm being very honest with you; I wouldn't remember it tomorrow, what we did tonight."

In spite of these distractions, the day came when Jeanette and Nelson were forced to meet face to face. When Nelson first arrived at the studio, he got predictably cold feet. "You know I don't want to see certain people," he told his agent, and refused to enter the room where Jeanette and others were waiting. His agent's response was to shove Nelson into the room so hard that he nearly fell.

This humiliation was only the first Nelson suffered during the production of

Filming *Girl of the Golden West* (1938).

Girl. He had vowed to get through the filming as fast and as gracefully as possible, but after the first day he found he couldn't tolerate being near Jeanette without a few drinks to relax him. Indeed, during much of the filming, Nelson was more than "relaxed." Candid photos taken on the set show his expression alternating between a glassy-eyed stare and a silly grin. During the shooting of the musical number "Soldiers of Fortune," when he and his group of bandits were riding down a hill, Nelson was so drunk he slipped off his horse and would have been trampled had it not been for the quick thinking of co-star Leo Carillo, who rescued him.

The Girl of the Golden West had looked like a sure-fire hit for MacDonald and Eddy. It had been a famous 1905 stage play by David Belasco, running 224 performances at the Belasco Theater. Composer Giacomo Puccini had seen the show while in New York to premiere his new opera, *Madama Butterfly* (also based on a Belasco play), and decided to set the tale to opera. It premiered in the United States in 1910 with Enrico Caruso starring, Belasco as stage manager, and Arturo Toscanini conducting. The opera was a success, and two silent film versions of the play were filmed, one in 1914 by Cecil B. DeMille, and a second in 1923. In 1930, an early sound rendition was released, starring Ann Harding and James Rennie.

The melodramatic plot concerns Mary (Minnie in the original story), a virginal saloon owner in the gold rush days of California, who falls in love with Lieutenant Dick Johnson, not knowing he is also Ramerez, a Robin Hood–type bandit. She learns the truth from Sheriff Jack Rance (Walter Pidgeon), who is also in love with her. When Ramerez is badly wounded, Mary and the Sheriff play a game of poker, with Ramerez as the stakes. The film ends with Mary and Johnson (Ramerez) riding off into the sunset together.

The MacDonald-Eddy version used none of the music from the opera, but did have some lovely Sigmund Romberg originals like "Obey Your Heart," "Senorita," "Shadows on the Moon," and Nelson's obligatory marching song, "Soldiers of Fortune."

Originally, *Girl* was going to be shot in Technicolor—and a few color frames still exist from some early footage—but there were so many problems with the two stars that Mayer ultimately refused to waste his money on the picture. It had now become a studio joke; this was the third MacDonald-Eddy film to be started in color. The other major studios had all released important Technicolor productions. MGM was the last one to hold out; and still Mayer promised Jeanette that the first Technicolor production would be hers. It just would not be *The Girl of the Golden West*.

The studio skimped in other ways on the production costs. No location filming was done. The mountains and forests of Monterey, California, were created on sound stages with plaster and papier-mâché. Process shots of the gleaming Pacific looked crude. The one extravagant scene of the entire film was the "Mariachi" number, which employed 725 extras, according to a press release. Mayer defended his extravagant use of extras by claiming, "The great circuses of the world measure the size of their shows by how many elephants they have. I measure mine by how many extras I have. So sue me." The only other added expense Mayer agreed to was to release the final product in sepia rather than black-and-white. (MGM later discontinued use of the sepia tinting, as audience response to it ranged from indifference to dislike. It was an unnecessary expense that didn't add to the profits. By the early 1940s, MGM broke down and admitted Technicolor was the wave of the future. Increasingly, more of their lavish musicals were thereafter released in color.)

While *The Girl of the Golden West* suffered from lack of outdoor location shooting (which had so enhanced *Rose Marie*), Robert Z. Leonard's slow-paced direction further hindered the ponderous story. Miles of footage had to be cut to bring the film in at two hours. Originally the cast list read Jeanette MacDonald, Nelson Eddy, Walter Pidgeon, Ray Bolger and Buddy Ebsen. Ray Bolger, who did a song and dance with Carol Tevis, had his scenes completely cut from the film. Buddy Ebsen, also a song and dance man, moved up to fourth billing, making a memorable comic contribution with his "The West Ain't Wild Anymore" number. Bolger, who'd got along well with Nelson during *Rosalie*, was very bitter about being cut out of *Girl*, and apparently blamed Nelson in some way. Bolger did a televised interview for Canadian TV some time before his death; wearing a sly smile, Bolger told host Elwy Yost what a "dull" person Nelson was, and how he was known as "The Blond Capon." He had nothing complimentary to say, even while discussing the next film they both appeared in, *Sweethearts*. According to Bolger, his role in *Sweethearts* was butchered as well, and he was ready to pack up and return to New York—until *The Wizard of Oz* beckoned.

The main failing of *The Girl of the Golden West* was the strained relations between the two stars. "I have to get used to working with her [Jeanette] all over again," Nelson complained. Because he'd cut his hair too short, they slapped an unattractive wig on him and overdid the makeup with two sets of eyebrows, making his pallor look pasty. And his dialogue made him retch. "Hell, no self-respecting Mexican would behave the way they ask me to." Regarding his attire for the film: "They must have a bunch of faggots dreaming up these costumes." He was in a rather surly mood.

While director Leonard tried to humor Nelson, Mayer was disgusted with Nelson's drinking and his "uncooperative" attitude, and decided that a stern father-and-son lecture might do the trick. Since Nelson wouldn't listen to Mayer, the studio head had Nelson's father, Bill Eddy, flown out from New England to visit his son. Nelson's reaction to his dad's appearance was to snarl at Mayer, "What are you going to do next, spank me?" The reunion was less than successful, but Mayer decided it shouldn't be a total loss. A publicity sitting for father and son was arranged on the *Girl* set, and Nelson managed to bare his teeth for the camera.

Mayer had less trouble with Jeanette. She dutifully threw herself into the role of Movie Star, happily granting interviews about her blissful marriage. But she spent frequent nights in her studio dressing room answering fan mail and prepar-

Mayer summoned Nelson's father Bill Eddy to visit the set. Nelson managed to smile for the camera, but snarled, "What's he going to do next, spank me?"

ing her lines into the wee hours, far from her house at Twin Gables. One morning she was found asleep at her desk, where she had sat working throughout the night. "As if she didn't have anywhere to go home to," one MGM employee commented. Her insomnia couldn't be tolerated by the studio, so she was dutifully supplied with an assortment of pills to keep her on a normal sleeping schedule. Today it is Hollywood folklore that the studio kept its overworked and overwrought stars (most notoriously Judy Garland) on a vicious cycle of "uppers" and "downers." Jeanette, to a lesser degree, was a victim of the vicious cycle.

On the set, Jeanette eyed Nelson's drinking with disgust, and told him flat out she wouldn't talk to him until he sobered up. To the surprise of many, he listened to her. The result was that their tension eased into a cautious friendship. Isabel Eddy described one time when Nelson returned from the studio, excited and very talkative. He told his mother, "She may be Gene's wife but she certainly hasn't forgotten me. Today as usual we went over our lines in her dressing room, and we did some tough studying too. When it was over we had some tea and sandwiches and I couldn't help it. I just had to ask her if she was happy. Well, Mother, she started to say something and then seemed to change her mind, and finally she said, 'Of course, do you doubt it?' But she couldn't look me in the eyes when she said it."

Jeanette was also anxious to know how Nelson's love life was faring. When she asked Nelson if he'd "been a good boy," he replied. "Oh, I've had about a dozen girls all summer, but I don't think they have made me a bad boy."

One afternoon, Nelson was preparing to leave the studio when he spotted Jeanette returning to her dressing room. She had locked her keys in her car, she said, and searched in vain for a spare set. Nelson didn't bother to query where the chauffeur was, nor did he fully believe her story. Nevertheless, he gallantly

Girl of the Golden West.

offered to drive her home. Only small talk passed between them. After he dropped her off, he drove straight to Sybil's in an agitated state.

"I can't trust myself to be alone with her," he told her. "It was all I could do not to jump her." Nelson said that his infatuation with Jeanette was driving him crazy, and that he had lost interest in singing. He was even toying with the idea of canceling his upcoming concert tour. Sybil suggested that Nelson should at last give up films and return to opera, where his voice belonged. "You've accomplished what you wanted here," she said. "How many times have you said you hate film making and Hollywood? So chuck it before it destroys you, before it's too late."

Nelson sat silent, his eyes lowered. Finally he said, "I can't. At least this way I get to see her. At least I have that. I can't help myself, I'll go to my grave loving her."

The sexual tension between them grew more intense as the filming progressed. "My baby's arms were softly tender in our love scene today," Nelson noted in his diary. "I feel very badly tonight." Another day they filmed the scene in which Nelson's character, having been shot, falls from his hiding place and lies near death while Jeanette and Walter Pidgeon debate his fate. Nelson made a lively corpse, as a photograph from that scene demonstrates. Eyes closed, with Jeanette hovering over him, he wears a half-smile and sports an obvious erection.

After shooting one of their scenes together Nelson told Isabel: "When I kissed her, believe me, it was no make believe, my heart was torn with despair. When it was over, she turned her head quickly away from the camera and I saw tears on her face. Somehow they maddened me. I wanted the *right* to gather her close and make her say she loved me." Instead, he sniped, "Weep not, my dear. It was only acting." Jeanette looked at him for a moment, then ran off to her dressing room and refused to open the door for over two hours.

Woody Van Dyke heard of the histrionics on the *Girl* set, and took a spare moment to visit Nelson and give him a pep talk. He found his friend sitting on the set, slouched in a chair with a huge sombrero half-covering his face. Woody's suggestions for improving Nelson's performance and attitude fell on deaf ears. "Who cares?" Nelson said. "Louie is lucky I'm here at all."

"Okay, kid, however you want it," Woody said agreeably. He knew Nelson well enough to realize how hardheaded he could get if pushed too hard. Nelson hated being maneuvered, and if he suspected it, was completely immovable. Woody had a rough idea about Jeanette's so-called ideal marriage, and tried to suggest to Nelson that maybe she was suffering too, but Nelson belligerently replied, "So what? She chose what she wanted."

"God, you're stubborn," Woody sighed. "Believe me, kid, I never interfere. I never have, and the only reason I'm taking a chance on getting clobbered now is that I think too much of you to stand calmly by when maybe I can help."

Nelson nervously asked Woody what his point was. When the director suggested that maybe the two of them should get back together anyway, despite her marriage, Nelson angrily jumped up and nearly hit him. Woody managed to

Robert "Pop" Leonard directs the "Obey Your Heart" duet, which was later scrapped from the picture.

calm him, but not before he was subjected to Nelson's enraged dissertation on the horrors and bigotry of divorce. "Besides," he told Woody when he'd finally calmed down, "I don't like sharing. I want someone who's all mine."

■ The main love scene in *The Girl of the Golden West* was the duet "Obey Your Heart," sung under a tree. As in the similar love scene in *Maytime*, Nelson was to sing one verse, then they were to join together. The plaintive duet was already recorded. Jeanette, who'd managed to keep up her professional facade thus far, suddenly fell to pieces. She started to cry each time Nelson sang his solo. Finally, after many takes, she was so drained she could sit expressionless through his number. But in the final cut, the strain and unhappiness on her face are evident, a mood quite out of character for the scene.

"She tries so hard to hide it," Nelson said. "But I have a feeling she still loves me. But she will fight till the death of it, I know that."

In the end, the duet simply could not be done. Leonard told Mayer the number would have to be cut—otherwise, he feared that Jeanette might be headed for a breakdown. Mayer agreed that it was better to have Jeanette in one piece and forego the duet, although he couldn't understand what all the fuss was about. To Mayer, they were just being melodramatic children, overreacting to everything. Still, if the kindly, patient Leonard couldn't coax a performance out of Jeanette, no one could, and, Mayer figured—incorrectly—that the public wouldn't notice the film's obvious flaws: no duet, and very few scenes with Jeanette and Nelson together.

■ December 1937, produced the inevitable popularity polls, and both Nelson and Jeanette scored in the top ten in virtually all of them. In the *Daily News* reader poll, for example, Jeanette rated third for the women, behind Myrna Loy and Loretta Young. Nelson rated sixth after Clark Gable, Robert Taylor, Tyrone Power, William Powell and Spencer Tracy. Since Nelson had joined the Chase & Sanborn show, it had jumped to the top of the ratings. It was now voted the best show on radio, and the Hollywood *Reporter* directly credited Nelson for the show's ascent. It was noted that one year before, Edgar Bergen and Charlie McCarthy had been drawing $260 for a week's stint at the Orpheum Theater downtown. But by December 1937, they were opening at the Paramount at $5,000 per week plus percentages—with a $6,500 weekly guarantee.

Despite the year-end plaudits, Christmas week found Nelson and Jeanette still hard at work at the studio. Photos from the *Girl* set party showed the two stars mingling with everyone but each other, and Nelson with a drink in hand. At last Nelson decided to confront Jeanette about her marriage. At an opportune moment, he sat down and said, "I have a suspicion you are making a fool of your husband, and I am going to get some things straight in my head before you make one of me too. You are going to answer some questions. Do you love your husband or are you just fond of him?"

"You have no right to ask me that," Jeanette hedged.

"Oh yes, I have the right, the right of the man who loves you and whose wife you once promised to be. Answer me, do you love your husband?"

Jeanette, unable to lie to him, said nothing.

"Very well," said Nelson. "You don't need to answer. If you loved him you'd be glad enough to tell me so. Now—another question. Has your love for *me* died?" She still said nothing, but he saw she was fighting back tears. "I *have* been answered," he said. "I was so damned jealous of Gene. If you could have told me you had learned to love him I would have stepped out of your life forever and remained just a friend. But now I never will. I want my wife and my home, so when are you going to end this foolish marriage and come to me?"

Jeanette burst out crying and ran off.

That week Jeanette and Gene made the rounds of Christmas parties together, while Nelson spent New Year's Eve alone at the Trocadero. He delighted the overfilled house by taking over the microphone and giving an impromptu performance, singing most of the *Rosalie* score. Happily toasting the new year, Nelson had no idea of the dramatic events that would, in a matter of days, completely change the course of his life.

Nelson shortly after Jeanette's marriage. "I learned too late how terribly I loved her," he told his mother.

14

"I've never
stopped loving you"

January 1938 began as a normal, busy month for Nelson. *The Girl of the Golden West* was scheduled to finish shooting before the end of the month, and his last Chase & Sanborn appearance would be on the thirtieth. He would soon be preparing his annual concert tour, scheduled to preview in Redlands, California, on January 12, followed by a second preview in Long Beach before its official launch in Los Angeles on February 2.

One night that January, Isabel Eddy found herself unable to sleep. Wandering through the house, she discovered that Nelson was also sleepless. Behind his closed bedroom door she heard him pacing. She sighed. Lately this was how Nelson seemed to spend most of his nights. His old habit upon returning from the studio had been to practice his singing and make recordings of himself, or invite a few friends over—usually singers—and record them. But now all that expensive equipment sat gathering dust. Isabel retired to her own room and sat in front of the window, letting the soft night air calm her nerves. As she watched the street below, she saw a car race up the street past their house. In a few minutes it came by again. By the third run she was certain it was Jeanette's. She ran downstairs, calling for Nelson. The car finally stopped in front of their house and Isabel ran out, leaving the front door wide open.

She found a hysterical Jeanette slumped over the wheel, sobbing uncontrollably and gasping, apparently having difficulty breathing.

Isabel called again for Nelson and turned to see him running to her, a frightened look on his face. When he saw his mother was all right he visibly relaxed, but when he spotted Jeanette he stopped dead in his tracks. Isabel called urgently for him to get Jeanette inside; her lips were blue and she didn't appear to be breathing.

Nelson grabbed Jeanette, carried her into the house and laid her gently on the couch. While Isabel ran for brandy, Nelson slapped Jeanette's wrists and her face, calling her name. She didn't respond. Finally Nelson slapped her hard and shook her, and this time she managed a breath. She lay limp in Nelson's arms, her color slowly returning, while Nelson smoothed her hair and forced brandy between her lips. Isabel sat across from her, watching her son play doctor.

Jeanette finally opened her eyes. Seeing Nelson, she looked confused and pulled out of his arms. Nelson stiffened and moved away from her.

"My dear, whatever happened?" queried Isabel. "You really gave us a turn."

Jeanette mumbled a response. Nelson wandered nonchalantly around the room, while Jeanette seemed to have recovered and was back to her charming self, making inane conversation about the drapes. After listening to her prattle, Nelson finally told her to shut up. "Just what are you doing here?"

Jeanette rose indignantly to her feet and headed for the door. She thanked Isabel for her hospitality and promised not to bother them again. At the door she stopped and stood hesitantly, then turned back to them. "I can't go back there, I can't—"

Nelson sat her down again, demanding that she tell the truth. Jeanette first addressed herself to Isabel, she was worried that what she had to say would shock and offend her. Isabel reassured her: "Don't worry about me, my dear. I do know a little something of life, and I stopped being shocked at the behavior of people a long time ago."

Finally, with difficulty, Jeanette spilled what she had learned about Gene's sexual preferences and told of the traumatic events that had culminated in her collapse.

Earlier that same evening, Gene had been arrested—the polite term in those days was "on a morals charge." Specifically, he had been at a homosexual club that was raided by the police. Jeanette was subjected to the humiliation of having to bail him out, after first having gone to the club to try to rescue him with as little publicity as possible. According to Sandy Reiss, a friend of his at the Los Angeles Police Department had said that Jeanette paid $1,000 in hush money to keep the arrest off the records. Unfortunately, in her shock and confusion, she didn't think of calling the one person who could have taken command of the situation—Howard Strickling at MGM. No one at MGM phoned their own attorneys first if arrested or involved in a drunk driving accident or any other embarrassing or potentially damaging incident. Strickling, MGM's master of cover-ups, was responsible for getting many big stars, including Gable and Crawford, out of some pretty serious scrapes. Today it is common knowledge that

L. B. Mayer was friends with the chief of police, and that certain charges could be—and were—dropped, never entered, or completely changed to some minor offense. But one had to have the presence of mind to contact Strickling immediately.

Nelson and Isabel listened to Jeanette, speechless. When she finished her story, Nelson asked Isabel to leave them alone. Isabel reluctantly left the room. Nelson could not believe that Jeanette had stayed in the marriage for six months, pretending that all was well. "You're still the same," he told her. "Anything for your career."

"There's nothing you can say to me that I haven't said a thousand times to myself," she replied. "I'm not content just to ruin my life, I have to be sure I drag everyone else down with me. You're right not to trust me; I can't seem to help what I am. Something seems to drive me to do things that only destroy me, and anyone who loves me." She headed for the door. "I'm going now. I know I've killed your love, but if it's any consolation for the hell I've caused you, I've never stopped loving you, never stopped wanting you."

Jumping to his feet, Nelson ran after her. "Jenny, Jenny, wait!"

When Nelson finally came to fetch Isabel, she was told that Jeanette's marriage was over and that she would be seeing her lawyer to start divorce proceedings. Meanwhile, Jeanette would spend the rest of the night with them. Isabel couldn't help but notice the sudden change in her son. He lovingly tucked Jeanette into bed in his room, and sat stroking her hair and singing softly to her until she fell into a troubled sleep. He sat in a chair next to the bed, his eyes never leaving her face, flinching when she occasionally sobbed in her sleep. Isabel observed a new excitement in him. He had come alive again.

Ultimately, Gene's arrest was hushed up and was never leaked to the press. But it *was* logged in the book in the Los Angeles Municipal Court. In a column of names for January 1938, "Gene Raymond" is listed. It must be noted that female arrests are specified by entries such as "Miss Aileen Ray" and "Mrs. Vertis Ratten." Furthermore, the women's case numbers in nearly every instance have five digits, beginning with "8." Male arrests have six-digit numbers beginning with "0." In Gene Raymond's entry, the file number has been incompletely erased and a new number written over it. Two Los Angeles detectives studied the original document and verified the tampering. The faintly seen first digit of the original case number was without a doubt "0." That number was removed and a five-digit number replaced it, starting with an "8." In tracing what the altered file represented, the records indicated that a "Miss Gene Raymond" had been arrested for prostitution and released for a nominal fee.

"By 1938 I knew about Gene," recalled Sandy Reiss. "I've done a lot of work for police charities, and my friend at the LAPD knew I was a friend of Jeanette's and thought I would be interested. He kept me informed as to Gene's latest escapades. The studio arranged for a lot of it to be removed from the books.

Jeanette filed for divorce the first time, shortly after he was arrested in early 1938." Sandy was unable to pin down the exact day this occurred, but also indicated that there were later arrests that were handled more discreetly. "I don't know how many times Jeanette had to shell out money to keep this type of thing out of the papers, but it caused her no end of grief."

It is said that Gene, confronted with the news that Jeanette was leaving him, decided to sit still and bide his time. Anyone with any understanding of Louis B. Mayer could predict what his reaction would be to the idea of Jeanette, his angel of the screen, getting a divorce—and only six months after the wedding of the century! What's more, if she went against Mayer's wishes and obtained a divorce anyway, it would be a direct violation of the morals clause in her contract. No one close to Jeanette could accept that she'd be willing to put her career at risk in such a manner. Gene also naturally concluded that, divorce or no divorce, his own career might be at risk were things to get too noisy. Homophobic Mayer had the power to blacklist Gene at every studio, ruining his career as he'd done Ramon Novarro's. (It was common knowledge that in Hollywood you could do as you liked—as long as you weren't caught. Being found out was the ultimate no-no.) In an effort to counteract possible repercussions, the MacDonald-Raymond publicist, Helen Ferguson, spent the next few months planting various tidbits in the papers and trades implying that the marriage was still solid and that Gene's career was on the rise. For example, a blurb in the Hollywood *Reporter* of February 5 imparted this bit of domestic news: "The Gene Raymonds have 1,200 lily bulbs planted around their Bel Air grounds."

In December 1937, Gene had replaced Fred MacMurray in a Paramount feature called *Stolen Heaven*, with Olympe Bradna as co-star. Though a "B" feature, it would open in May 1938, to good reviews. As a boost to himself and the picture, Gene agreed to travel cross-country to promote the picture. By now it was evident to him that his marriage to Jeanette had not benefited his career; neither MGM nor any other studios were clamoring for him. He said in an interview: "You know my parts this past year haven't been interesting. I made a good many pictures, but I didn't have any parts I could get excited about. Mostly they were comedy. Well, I don't mind comedy, if it's good comedy. I rather like it. But three of my parts were exactly alike—the same character, the same jokes, even the same lines sometimes." Under the circumstances, *Stolen Heaven*, a drama, seemed his best, indeed his only, shot at stardom. Yet as it turned out, Gene's ill-fortune of "getting caught" in January overshadowed his efforts with *Stolen Heaven*. Since his start in films, Gene Raymond had averaged five films a year and was a popular, if not top-name, star. After *Stolen Heaven* he did not work in Hollywood for almost two years.

■ During the last week of January 1938, Jeanette and Nelson were finishing up their work on *The Girl of the Golden West*. Still ahead of them was the recording and filming of the final scene. Their attitude on the set these last days

Together again, 1938.

was a complete turnabout. They were all smiles, and inseparable. It didn't take a lot of guessing for the crew to figure out what was going on. "You could always tell when they'd been together," said one crew member. "He had a grin on his face you couldn't kill, and he followed her around like a puppy dog. With those two, either they weren't speaking or they couldn't keep their hands off each other. There was no in-between."

Before leaving on his February concert tour, Nelson made a surprise visit to Sybil's. She heard banging on the sliding glass door and hurried to let him in. His excited grin and the lack of interest in having a drink told Sybil that something indeed had changed in his life. "Don't tell me you're back with the redhead again," she said half-seriously.

He grinned. "Yup! And I'm falling in love with her all over again!" According to Sybil, he practically danced around the room, gushing in nauseating detail how beautiful and wonderful Jeanette was. Sybil had known Nelson all these years, and the effect Jeanette had on him still never ceased to amaze her. Always a cynic, she thought that the latest developments were literally too good to be true. It was a long time till Jeanette's divorce would be final, and, furthermore, Louis B. Mayer had not yet been informed of Jeanette's plans. Weren't Jeanette and Nelson being extremely naive in thinking there would be no hitches? Sybil hoped for Nelson's sake that events would go as planned, but she wasn't holding her breath.

In February, Nelson left town on his concert tour. *Girl* would be shooting a couple of more weeks—a lengthy prologue in which child actors Bill Cody, Jr., and Jeanne Ellis portrayed the youthful Nelson and Jeanette. Jeanette, meanwhile, kept herself busy in Los Angeles, continuing her Sunday Vicks broadcasts through March 20.

Nelson commented about the film to a reporter: "It's all finished now but the prologue . . . I was awfully sorry for that Salem boy they brought down to try out to play the prologue. He's a nice kid. He hadn't been there long enough to know what it was all about—he hadn't taken it in at all. He was dazed by the whole business. Many of the other boys had been around motion pictures lots of years—they knew how to turn it on and off when the director told them to. I hear Bill Cody, Jr., got the part—he's a nice kid, too, and he can act." About the film in general Nelson said diplomatically, "It's taken from the Belasco play—a bit romanticized, as they do in Hollywood."

In every city he visited, Nelson was a sensation. He was given police protection and added bodyguards. A San Francisco paper described the typical concert:

In a double sense of the word, Nelson Eddy is the fair-haired boy of the present-day concert world. The blond baritone sang at the Memorial Opera House last night. The scene that surrounded him was typical of his national success.

Every seat in the theater was sold. Standees fringed the back of the hall. Extra chairs roosted in the orchestra pit. Behind him sat the vast array of 1,000 stage listeners . . . and there were girls, girls, girls . . . Out he dashed from the wings, like a man walking at once for health and pleasure. He did look suitably romantic. He is handsome, stalwart and pleasant. No humbug about him.

As for his voice, it is extraordinary, both as a native instrument and in the smoothness of his singing . . . One of his masterful achievements is the common sense clarity with which he utters his words.

The reviewer noted that Nelson was still singing his many encores late into the evening, namely songs from his films, when the morning reviewers had to leave to run to their typewriters.

In February, news reports showed the MacDonald-Eddy team's popularity to be at a steady high. From Sweden: "MGM has every reason to be proud of its Jeanette MacDonald and Nelson Eddy, for *Rose Marie* . . . is going its merry way in Stockholm after 36 weeks of excellent business, and there seems to be no end in sight." From MGM: "Domestic gross [for 1937] was $43,500,000." *Maytime* was listed as one of the top money-makers.

The Girl of the Golden West opened in Los Angeles at two theaters on March 16, and the following week it premiered in several other cities around the country. It did strong business at the beginning, and according to studio prediction, would top the other three Mac-Eddy pictures. In the end, although the film was successful, it was not a mega-hit. Reviewers such as Irving Hoffman seemed to accurately pinpoint the problems:

> In the pretty-well-filled Capitol [in New York] on Thursday evening, there were scores sleeping. Whether they found the film more of a sedative than an entertainment, or whether it was just Spring, we could not testify. But it is no exaggeration that our personal survey, conducted among those in the orchestra section during the second half of the feature, revealed sleeping, snoring seat-holders. Many who remained awake through the Metopera, however, definitely stated that they were satisfied and had spent a pleasurable two hours.
>
> Of course, the most effective moments were supplied via the vocalesthenics of Nelson Eddy and Jeanette MacDonald. Much of the dialogue and action was scorned as ludicrous, especially the villantics of Walter Pidgeon and MacDonald's attempt at western lingo. One lobby bystander remarked 'It took me back thirty years,' another said, 'This is old stuff.' A group of schoolgirls were delighting with the warbling of their favorite, Nelson Eddy.
>
> In the middle of the big production number, at the fiesta as a hundred or more dancers and a herd of horses appeared on the screen, we overheard a girl turn to her companion and say, 'Gee, this is a terrible picture!' Whatever favorable mention was made, was directed to the singing of stars MacDonald and Eddy, the former getting the edge, by comparison. 'Any picture in which Jeanette MacDonald appears,' one of the feminine followers stated, 'is a sufficient recompense for the price of admission I paid.' The Metro nightingale's 'Ave Maria' rendition was unquestionably her high spot.

Other reviewers agreed the film was too long, but couldn't decide whether twenty or thirty minutes should be cut. The New York *World-Telegram* simply stated that few other films had *seemed* so long. The overall consensus was well-put by the *World-Telegram*: "If you are one of those fans who simply cannot get enough of Jeanette MacDonald and Nelson Eddy, then this film will be right up your alley." Liberty magazine added, "For Jeanette MacDonald-Nelson Eddy enthusiasts we give this three stars. For others, we warn you that the production has about as much zip as a turtle who's had a busy day."

With the release of *The Girl of the Golden West* came a new problem, one that had been simmering under the surface. The so-called "MacDonald-Eddy Feud" was erupting all over the papers. One magazine wrote:

> How do these Hollywood "feuds" originate? There are several possibilities. In Hollywood now there are thirty-eight people who broadcast Hollywood gossip one or more times a week. There just isn't that much gossip. These thirty-eight air chatterers have any number of stooges or operators or legmen working for them. There are also over three hundred and sixteen *bona fide* writers and columnists who have pages, but endless pages to fill every day, every week, every month. Everybody

The MacDonald-Eddy
"feud."

wants a scoop. The town has just gone mad with gossipers. They'll grab at anything. "Just give me a lead," they'll mourn in the publicity offices. "I'll make it into a story." A little thing like accuracy, in this race for news, has simply collapsed and died by the wayside. So all that is necessary for a good first-class feud is the following: "Hello, what goes on with your little dream children today? Did the new MacDonald-Eddy picture start? She didn't smile when he came on the set? Thank you, my lad, we've got something here." It's on the air in another hour that Jeanette and Nelson aren't speaking. All the columnists pick it up and so do all the other air chatterers. In less than twenty-four hours it is all over the world that Jeanette MacDonald and Nelson Eddy are having a feud. As casual as that.

The real basis for this trumped-up MacDonald-Eddy "feud" seems not their personal ups and downs on the set as much as the animosity between their fans, who argued endlessly as to which team member had been more responsible for their success.

By 1938, Jeanette and Nelson were receiving more letters than any other Metro stars, including Clark Gable, and theirs were the most vocal fans of the lot. To the studio, the number of letters received about the duo was an important measure of their popularity, and to keep the "feud" alive, the studio craftily ensured that in the next Mac-Eddy film, *Sweethearts*, Nelson would again make his screen entrance well after Jeanette did, much to the chagrin of the Nelson camp. He continued to command less overall screen time than she. Fans had no reason to believe in their deepening relationship offscreen.

■■■ At the end of March 1938, a press release informed those who were interested that Jeanette and Gene were on a "two-month motoring vacation." However, Gene arrived in Kansas City in mid-April (no mention of Jeanette) on a train that was sixteen hours late; according to a published report, he shouted at the approaching photographers: "I'll poke the first one of you in the nose who tries to snap my picture!" Late in the month, Gene spent a couple of weeks in New York awaiting the opening of *Stolen Heaven* and Jeanette was there briefly with him. She was honored at a luncheon given by film critic Regina Crewe, and she and Gene both attended, giving the appearance of a happy couple. One reporter quoted Jeanette as praising *Stolen Heaven*, saying it was "really grand." (A friend commented: "Of course she wanted his film to do well. If he was finally successful it meant she'd have to pay less alimony.")

Variety reviewed Gene's ten-minute pre-screening program of "song, patter, and band setting" at the Paramount theater, noting that this was his first time on Broadway since he quit the stage for films. "While he's no great shakes as a crooner, Raymond carries a tune easily enough . . . But they didn't care to hear him sing and didn't hesitate to say so, loudly if good naturedly.

"An unfortunate choice was 'Ti-Pi-Tin,' which has a lot of verses. Not content with that, he added some extra ones, in spite of his audience indicating by loud applause in the middle of the number, that they had had enough." Gene also introduced one of his own numbers, "Alligator Swing," which didn't go over well. "Mr. Raymond's 'getting hot' is barely lukewarm," reported the same paper. Coincidentally, Gene's film opened at a theater across the street from the Capitol, where *The Girl of the Golden West* was still doing solid business.

The press reported that after being seen with Gene in New York, Jeanette had to return to Los Angeles to start work on *Sweethearts* with Nelson. Gene, still on his "personal appearance tour," was not scheduled to return home till the end of May. Except for a few public appearances with Gene in New York, Jeanette was elsewhere in April 1938—more specifically, she was with Nelson on the Eastern leg of his tour.

"Nelson did love Jeanette," said Eva Justice, whose grandfather John Francis Boyles (known as "Red" Boyles) was Nelson's bodyguard for the East Coast concert dates. "The first tour my grandfather went on was the spring 1936 one. Most people don't know that Jeanette traveled with Nelson on the 1938 tour, but she was there."

Sometimes Jeanette remained backstage during Nelson's concerts; less frequently she sat in the audience. On very rare occasions, Nelson would motion for her to come up and sing a duet with him. The audience went wild at such times, and those sitting close enough to the stage commented on how emotional Nelson was when Jeanette stood at his side—he'd get tears in his eyes. Jeanette later commented that it sometimes embarrassed her to sing live with Nelson because he put all his attention on her, and seemed to draw the audience's toward her also, as if to silently say, "See? Isn't she incredible?" The rush of admiration was overwhelming to her. Off-stage, Nelson usually hated giving interviews and was forever criticized by reporters as being uncooperative. But on this tour he was different. He was demonstrably happy, for the first time in a long time. "Nelson Eddy, blond baritone star, tilted back his chair at the Roosevelt Wednesday night and smiled his good humor at New Orleans," noted the *Times*

Picayune. "Completely relaxed, he led his interviewers a merry conversational race." The Oregon Daily Journal described Nelson as "fit and friendly." The Atlanta *Georgian* noted that Nelson "doesn't like to talk about love and hasn't found time to read 'Gone With the Wind.' "

The trades announced that Jeanette and Nelson were returning to Los Angeles at the beginning of May, "at the same time." It would be nearly six weeks before *Sweethearts* started shooting. MGM announced that it was contemplating yet another film for the duo, a musical remake of *The Guardsman*, to be produced and directed by Bob Leonard. Meanwhile, the two stars had some time to themselves. Nelson was so pleased at Jeanette's apparent willingness to put him first before her career—at least temporarily—that he rapidly made plans for their future together. He surprised her by handing her the key to a small, newly built house in Burbank at 812 Mariposa. Set way back from the street, it was on a dirt road overlooking the Los Angeles River, next door to the stables where their horses were kept. In time, Nelson planted rose bushes around the white picket fence surrounding the house; his pride and joy were the orange flowers that reminded him of Jeanette's hair. The rose bushes remained at that residence until shortly before the house was torn down in January 1990.

Nelson also took over a hunting lodge in the Angeles Forest. Located at 2118 Stonyvale, the place was built originally by MGM for use in "rustic" candid photo shoots. Clark Gable was photographed there often, and later on Errol Flynn used it. It was a perfect setting—a forty-five-minute drive from Burbank, but like entering another world: mountains, pine trees, huge rocks, water and sometimes even a bit of snow in the winter. Their privacy was assured by a gated entry, and a ranger station was just across the dirt road.

Yet a third hideaway was located closest to home, in Beverly Hills off Benedict Canyon. Standing on the old Fred Niblo estate, at 1330 Angelo Drive, was a house Nelson nicknamed "Mists." Alternately, he called it "Misty Mountain" because of the morning fogs that backed up against the mountain range. The house couldn't be seen from the street, and was protected by both guard and gate. Nelson had leased "Mists" in 1937, using it as a second home for himself and Isabel.

The three homes had different functions. The Mariposa house was a romantic hideaway when the lovers wanted to be alone, often while working, as it was only a short drive back into the city. At Mariposa they could ride their horses and lose themselves in the mountains surrounding Griffith Park. The Stonyvale house was more rustic, up in the mountains, and used less frequently. "Mists" was their family home. They often stayed on weekends, or during vacation times. Isabel usually accompanied them; occasionally Blossom visited and at various times other guests were invited as well. Nelson covered his tracks carefully and rarely bought anything in his own name. Locating his property and differentiating between what he leased and what he purchased, and under what name or company, has always presented a puzzle.

That June, Nelson surprisingly agreed to be photographed on the Santa Monica beach with his horse and dog. This series of candid shots of him riding along the water's edge shows him happier and more relaxed than at any other photo sitting in his career. And his renewed relationship with Jeanette did not go unnoticed in Hollywood. "That MGM star, who is supposed to be an arch-enemy of one of the studio's featured femmes, is really madly in love with her," blabbed a gossip column. Isabel chided her son for being so blatant about the affair before Jeanette was divorced, and for in effect shacking up with her. "Yes, mother, I know," she quoted Nelson as saying, "but would you keep such joy from me?" And Jeanette reassured Isabel that the divorce would be handled "when Gene returns." Isabel wrote, in her flowery fashion: "And so it was that they went into the making of the picture [*Sweethearts*], with their love shining once more supreme in their hearts. No wonder it broke box office records the country over. It was warm and real and beautiful. I was on the set a great deal of the time, although [Woody] kept the sets closed to visitors—especially for the love scenes. He knew so very much and was so very wise. Once he said to me, 'Isabel, how can you ever bear not having that girl at your fireside?' "

Isabel was not the only person to observe Jeanette and Nelson's radiance. After two days of filming in black-and-white, the studio announced that *Sweethearts* would be MGM's first all-Technicolor feature. (Nelson snickered, "Hopefully this will be the first film started—and completed—in color!")

The script of *Sweethearts* was comic and lighthearted. The story was suppos-

Nelson with the excellent character actors of *Sweethearts*: Frank Morgan, Ray Bolger, Herman Bing and Mischa Auer.

edly adapted from the 1913 Victor Herbert operetta, but in usual MGM style, the final script was so completely rewritten as to be unrecognizable from the original. Victor Herbert's music was used, but new lyrics were written by the outstanding team of Chet Forrest and Bob Wright. Jeanette and Nelson played a happily married Broadway couple who've appeared for six years in an operetta entitled *Sweethearts*. Hollywood beckons and the couple, tired of the grind, decides to go west. The show's producer (Frank Morgan) and his motley cohorts (including the hilarious Herman Bing and Mischa Auer) plot to keep the team from defecting, and devise an elaborate scheme to break them up. It works, temporarily. In the end MacDonald and Eddy realize they were tricked, reunite, and return home to Broadway. The witty, satirical Dorothy Parker-Alan Campbell script is one of the best ever written for a MacDonald-Eddy film. *Sweethearts* boasted Technicolor, a fine script, an outstanding supporting cast and extravagant production values. The two stars were in top form as well, enjoying themselves tremendously.

Richard Halverson, Jeanette's chauffeur, remembered visiting the set one day when Nelson pulled one of his pranks. He and Jeanette were supposed to be at the top of a runway, and to the chorus of "Sweethearts," glide down to the stage below. Jeanette, in an immense hoop skirt, was on her mark. They yelled "Lights! Camera! Action" but Nelson was nowhere to be found. Director Van Dyke kept calling for Nelson, perplexed; he'd simply vanished. Finally he came out from his hiding place, under Jeanette's skirt.

Everyone was looking forward to an enjoyable, smooth-running production. Then an unexpected complication arose—Jeanette was pregnant again.

Sweethearts.

15

"They're doing it again"

Jeanette's child was conceived during the first days of reconciliation with Nelson in late January 1938. During the spring she was on the road a lot and no doubt attributed any symptoms to the fact that she had a poor stomach for any type of travel. It wasn't until she returned to Los Angeles in early May that she was sure. She told no one, not even Nelson, while she tried to decide the best way to handle the situation. Jeanette had been well taught that her present condition was one to avoid at all costs, but this time she made up her own mind about it. She did not want an abortion, but the timing was terrible with she and Nelson about to go into *Sweethearts*. Also, she was beginning to realize that at some point a confrontation with Mayer would have to occur, both over the divorce and the baby.

Nelson finally figured things out for himself. One night they stayed over at the Mariposa house, and he was awakened pre-dawn by the sound of her retching. He settled her back into bed and said, "How long has this been going on?" When she admitted she was three months pregnant, he turned bitter. "How long did you intend keeping it from me? Or weren't you *ever* going to enlighten me?" Jeanette reassured him that she wanted this baby. Over the next days, Nelson was like a man reborn; he viewed life with a new light. He made time to pop in on Sybil with the latest; when she pointed out to him that Jeanette's divorce would not be final when this love child made its appearance, Nelson seemed unconcerned. He already had that worked out, he claimed; he had no intention of having his child born with another man's name. He had found some doctor in Arizona who would deliver the baby and then falsify the birth certificate. They would finish *Sweethearts*, then drop out of sight until the baby's arrival. Nelson was already planning their honeymoon in the Mediterranean. Once again, Sybil doubted the rationality of Nelson's plans, but Nelson would have none of it. His life was going fine, thank you. He was not interested in hearing anyone's negative opinions.

Woody Van Dyke was taken into confidence out of necessity. The director agreed to get Jeanette's scenes over as quickly as possible, before her condition became too visible. Others, particularly in the wardrobe department, also had to be informed, so Jeanette's gowns could be altered throughout the filming. It is a credit to the respect and love both Jeanette and Nelson had earned with their studio co-workers that no one gave their secret away.

Of course Isabel knew, as did Blossom, but Jeanette did not want her own mother informed, fearing she would go straight to Mayer. The idea was to give Mayer a wonderful color smash hit with *Sweethearts*; then perhaps he would be more lenient with his stars' personal wishes after the production wrapped. If not, there was another alternative. Nelson had put feelers out and had learned that both RKO and Paramount were "willing to pay through the nose" to get the

Nelson painted the portrait of Jeanette used in *Sweethearts*. Its fate after the film is unknown, as is that of the various other paintings Nelson did of Jeanette over the years.

MacDonald-Eddy team. If Mayer pushed them too far, they could buy out their contracts and go elsewhere.

When Jeanette told her sister she was expecting, Blossom asked why they hadn't been more careful. Jeanette replied wryly, "With Nelson, there's never time to think about things like that." On another occasion, she quipped, "We spent too much time in the rumble seat."

A Nelson fan spotted Jeanette at Santa Monica beach that summer and "was disappointed to see how plump Jeanette was off the screen. Her hips were wide and she had a bulging stomach." Photos taken at Stonyvale—some of Jeanette alone, others of her and Nelson—show them standing near the fireplace, Jeanette with a bandanna on her head, her pregnancy very evident. On the *Sweethearts* set, some candid photos of Jeanette show heavy touching-up around her middle. In the "Pretty as a Picture" number, the change in her bust size is striking, and at certain angles while she is dancing with Nelson, the viewer can easily observe her condition. Later in the filming, an outfit was designed for her with an accompanying muff, which she held in front of her stomach while singing "Badinage."

Not everyone involved with *Sweethearts* knew what was going on. Betty Jaynes, a seventeen-year-old soprano featured in the film, had her attention

Jeanette's mother, Anna MacDonald, visits the *Sweethearts* set with Jeanette's oldest sister Elsie, who was still living in the Philadelphia area.

elsewhere. Jaynes had made a sensation in Chicago a year earlier by debuting as Mimi in *La Bohème*. She soon wound up in Hollywood. "I was interviewed and my picture was in the paper; they asked me who my favorite singer was, Rosa Ponselle or Jeanette MacDonald. I said Jeanette MacDonald . . . We were offered a contract at MGM. My mother was a widow and that's what she chose to do, pack up our little family and come to California." Early into the filming she married her on-screen sweetheart, baritone Douglas McPhail. If any intrigues were going on elsewhere on the set, "it was all over my head." But she remembered eating lunch in the commissary with Jeanette and Nelson, and seeing them together at some of Mayer's famous Sunday brunches. "Judy [Garland] and I would walk through his house," she says. "It was unbelievable. We'd never seen a marble bathroom or a marble bathtub. We'd walk around giggling like two little kids."

"Jeanette was my idol," Jaynes continued. "She was a very lovely lady, and she was always very nice to me." Jaynes and her new husband sang in a montage sequence with Jeanette and Nelson. "As I recall, Jeanette and Doug—it took them a while to really warm up [vocally] to make the recordings. And for myself and Nelson Eddy, we were at our best in the beginning."

Jeanette was directly responsible for Jayne's and McPhail's casting in *Sweethearts*. She also publicly announced them as her protégés.

> It's easy enough to obtain a test in this business if you have any sort of influence behind you, but the trick is to find the opportunities to show your talent after you've been tested. I decided long ago that if I were ever going to aid anyone's career I'd have to follow up and see that roles were provided to give my "find" an opportunity to develop.
>
> When I heard Douglas McPhail sing in *Maytime* I was convinced that here was a boy who, with proper training, had a potentially great voice. I took him to Mr. Mayer and he sang two numbers for him, which I applauded.
>
> "Do you really think he's as good as that?" Mr. Mayer asked me. I assured him that I did. Without further ado the boy was given a test and a contract and has been singing in bits and short subjects ever since. Now, in *Sweethearts* there's a chance for him to win some attention.

After *Sweethearts* was completed, Betty Jaynes and Douglas McPhail were touted as "the next MacDonald and Eddy." They appeared together in *Babes in Arms*, and separately in a handful of other musicals. But their film careers never reached the heights. According to Jaynes, she was not driven to be a star, and preferred retirement and raising a family. McPhail, upset at the way his career was going, became an alcoholic and finally took his life at age thirty-four. Jaynes says McPhail was violent when he drank, but she eventually divorced him only because of studio pressure.

Doug McPhail was not the only one, however, whose personality changed while drinking: Gene Raymond, who had returned to Los Angeles from his publicity tour to find everything in an uproar, "was thoroughly sick and discouraged about his career," said Isabel Eddy. If, as many had suggested, he'd married Jeanette in hopes of furthering his career, his hopes were now dashed. He was being referred to in the press as "Mr. MacDonald." On top of that, he had to deal with all of Jeanette's personal problems and the fact that he was being eased out of the picture.

One day Nelson stopped by Twin Gables to pick up Jeanette. He found her cowering in fear behind a sofa while an intoxicated Gene smashed picture frames holding his and Jeanette's photos. Gene had hit her, but apparently hadn't hurt her. Nonetheless, Nelson threatened to kill Gene if he ever laid a hand on her again. Nelson's opportunity came more quickly than he'd thought it would. In early July, a second incident occurred, more serious this time.

As the story goes, Woody Van Dyke was hosting a small dinner party. Nelson had planned to take Jeanette. He phoned her before leaving his house, but there was no answer. Finally calling Woody's, he learned she was already there. Puzzled, he drove directly to Woody's. When the butler opened the door, Nelson knew immediately that something was wrong. He went into the living room where a small combo was playing and guests were milling around talking. Nelson looked for Jeanette and finally spotted her in the corner, talking to Woody. She was wearing a plain cotton dress and had a scarf half-covering her face. As Nelson headed over to them, the party stopped. Even the combo fell silent, such was the intensity of Nelson's silent anger. Reaching Jeanette, he pulled at the scarf. It floated off to uncover the inevitable black and blue marks. Nelson said nothing, just turned and left the house. Jeanette grew hysterical, begging Woody to stop Nelson before he killed Gene as he'd threatened to do.

When Woody arrived at Twin Gables he found Nelson, blind with rage, pounding and cursing at a bloodied, senseless Gene. It was all Woody could do to stop Nelson from killing him. Gene was taken to the hospital. Two gossip blurbs later came out, one stating that he'd fallen down a flight of stairs, another claiming that he was mobbed by hysterical fans.

Nelson left Isabel to look after Jeanette till her face healed. She was unable to go before the *Sweethearts* cameras for a week. The trades learned the set had been closed down, but as usual gave an inaccurate reason. (In studying the trade papers of Hollywood's Golden Years, one is amused by the frequency of reported ailments like "ptomaine poisoning"—often attributed to John Barrymore—"bad colds" and "appendicitis." In Jeanette's case, she supposedly suffered from appendicitis several times over the years—the first attack being in 1929, on her way to Hollywood!) With hindsight, history has proven that the many hospitalizations and collapses occurred as noted in the trades, but the real reasons rarely resembled the ludicrous explanations released to the press. This is a practice continued in Hollywood even today, the only difference being that reporters in those days were heavily censored by the studios and subject to losing their jobs if they spilled Hollywood secrets.

With those few days of time off the set, Jeanette decided to put some personal touches into the Mariposa house. Later, she recalled:

I remember this one day when I wasn't working at the studio. I was pregnant then and trying to take things easy. Anyway, we'd just moved some things into this tiny little house, and I got this brilliant idea of decorating it and surprising Nelson with this gourmet meal.

I'd brought over a lot of little knickknacks to decorate. I told Nelson I would rest, but you know me, can't ever sit still. So I started putting things away. The living room was easy enough, but there was this fairly long hallway up to the bedroom and I started hanging pictures on the wall. I don't know what was wrong with it, but I couldn't get those damn pictures to hang straight. Finally I gave up, but you should have seen that wall. It was a real disaster, like an earthquake had hit it.

Then I started working on the dinner. It was some fancy dish with spaghetti. Nelson's a spaghetti nut, so I figured even if it didn't come out just right, he'd still love it. I don't know how it happened—now, don't laugh—but I burned the spaghetti. I must have left it on the stove too long, or something. Anyway, it was this single glob of paste, black on one side. While I'm standing here, contemplating this mess, Nelson walks in. Here I am in this old robe about this pregnant—and my hair is a fright. Now Nelson's a hopeless romantic, but that's stretching it just a bit, don't you think?

So I go to show him all the work I've done all day, and the living room's okay, but when he sees the hall his mouth starts to twitch and he's being very polite and you can see him racking his brain trying to find something good to say about it. Then he goes into the bedroom and all the clothes are all over the floor and chairs. I guess I'd started unpacking but never got around to finishing. It was too much for him, he fell on the bed and just howled! He was crying, he was laughing so hard, he's just rolling around on the bed, kicking his legs—and getting tangled up in clothes, I might add! Every so often he'd manage to say, "Goddamn, you're just too much!" and then laugh some more. Then he says, "I can just see Photoplay sending over some guys to do a four-page layout!" Finally I started to get upset; it wasn't *that* funny. I mean, I'd worked hard all day and was very tired. So he sobered up and said, "Honey, you're great, I wouldn't change a thing about you," and he hauls me off to the kitchen to salvage dinner. The spaghetti sauce was okay, so he made some omelets and threw everything in them—he makes great omelets, you know—and poured the sauce over it and we had quite a feast.

He's quite a chef. He's always teasing me that he had to learn to cook because if he depended on me, he'd starve. It's a slight exaggeration; I mean, I *can* boil water without burning it. And you know I can prepare a mean eggplant parmesan.

Oh—anyway, the next day I woke up and all the pictures were off the wall, and he'd redone everything, even in the living room. It did look a lot better, I had to admit. He didn't say a word, though, and neither did I. Guess he didn't think much of my talents as an interior decorator, hmm?

Nelson threw himself into his impending fatherhood role with gusto. "He bought out half of Beverly Hills," reported Sybil Thomas. Blossom remarked how amusing it was to watch Woody Van Dyke, an experienced father, showing Nelson what to do with all the infant items he'd purchased, and teaching him how to diaper by practicing on a doll. Jeanette teased Nelson over his "symptoms," which seemed worse at times than her own.

Early in the filming, Nelson painted a portrait of Jeanette, to be used in the film. The original was splashed with bright colors so that it was almost blinding. After seeing the finished product, Woody asked Nelson, "Isn't it a little too much color?" Nelson grinned and said, "Yup, but that's how I see her, full of color." The painting's fate after the filming is unknown.

For Jeanette's birthday on June 18, a party was held on the set. A photographer snapped away as Nelson helped her cut the cake, fed her and embraced her. Later a grinning Nelson grabbed Jeanette and playfully kissed her, then *really* kissed her, holding her in a passionate embrace. The photographer caught all of this on film. That Nelson allowed such an obvious expression of their intimacy to be photographed is nothing short of incredible.

For Nelson's birthday, June 29, another studio party was thrown. This round of photos showed less physical intimacy, but it was all there in the looks. One photo shows Nelson playing one of his presents from Jeanette, a miniature saxophone. Sitting in full camera view is yet another gift, a champagne bottle capped with a baby bottle nipple.

As Jeanette and Nelson openly flaunted their affair, Gene, too, came out of the closet. Marshall Wright, a Hollywood promoter who later founded the Hollywood Appreciation Society, and who knew Jeanette early on, said that in 1938 he learned that Gene Raymond had taken a house with a nineteen-year-old male under contract to Universal. (The actor in question made his successful film debut the following year.) "I was disappointed because this was commonly known around town, and I didn't think he [Gene] should be so obvious about it. It wasn't fair to Jeanette." Isabel Eddy alluded to Gene's activities at this time in her memoirs: "Much of the time Gene was not at home, since his interest in sports frequently kept him away over the weekend."

Jeanette didn't seem worried about Gene's activities at this time. Her happiness with Nelson was spilling over into the film characterizations. (Blossom commented that these roles were most like their off-screen personalities, though in real life they were even more high-strung.) Since their characters started off the picture married, Jeanette and Nelson could get away with a lot more than in other films. Whether consciously or not, they were often touching or caressing. There's plenty of that fingerplay going on that fans had come to look for. In the "Pretty as a Picture" number, the camera is focused on some dancing girls, with the two stars off to the side and slightly out of focus. Nelson is seated at a piano with Jeanette standing behind him, her hands on his shoulders. Impulsively, she leans over and kisses him. At another point in that same scene, they're both at the piano, with Jeanette singing. Nelson gazes at her adoringly, then playfully blows on her neck. For 1938—and a MacDonald-Eddy picture—this was heavy stuff!

While all this sexual intrigue was going on, rumors started to spread once again that Jeanette and Nelson were on the outs. In a 1965 interview, Nelson explained how this story started.

"*Sweethearts* was very mushy and very sweetheartish. And the boys in the pressroom were wondering what angle they could use. They said: 'Wouldn't it be funny if MacDonald and Eddy were such sickeningly sweet partners? Wouldn't it be funny if they hated each other? This is a great angle.' They started putting this out, actually put it out, and people believed it and now there's a MacDonald-Eddy feud which we don't know anything about. It kind of got out of hand, and finally the same director, W. S. Van Dyke—he posed us in some pictures where she had some boxing gloves and she was knocking me out and he was counting me out on the floor; anything to refute this silly thing. There never was anything to it. One time an important writer from the East came out to visit the set, and he said, 'I want to see about the MacDonald-Eddy feud.' We were doing a scene in *Sweethearts* where in the picture we were very bitter to each other, we were all but divorced at the moment and we were stepping on each other's toes and we were digging at each other's ribs, and we were being very nasty to each other while apparently appearing in public, you see, in a show. And the fellow said, 'You see? Look how they're acting. They're cross!' And he wrote a big story about this thing and they said, 'No! This is not so! You'll see when the picture comes out that this is part of the picture. They're acting this.' He says, 'Okay, when the picture comes out, I'll see this scene and I'll print a retraction.' You know something? They cut that scene."

The rumors were rampant. A few major columnists knew the truth—for example Hedda Hopper, who was aware of Jeanette's pregnancy and was itching to spill the beans—but others gleefully reported tidbits like "They say things are not so palsy-walsy between Jeanette MacDonald and Nelson Eddy on the *Sweethearts* set." And another: "They don't even like each other." Nonetheless, Louis B. Mayer inevitably got wind of what was really going on. Among a group of photos tossed on his desk was the one of Jeanette and Nelson kissing at Jeanette's birthday party. Mayer looked at it and said in dismay, "They're 'doing it' again." He immediately sent some spies over to the set to snoop around for details, and used other means to get the particulars he wanted.

Jackie Cooper, in his autobiography, *Please Don't Shoot My Dog*, explained how Mayer's intellignece system worked. He wrote: "What I doubt more than a handful of MGM employees knew was that Mayer had almost every sound stage bugged. There was a little room somewhere in the administration building (now called the Thalberg building) where Mayer's brother, Jerry, was stationed with earphones on his head. The open mikes in all the studios were fed into this secret room, and Mayer tuned around, hoping to catch somebody saying something terrible."

Jeanette, Nelson and Gene were hauled into Mayer's office, and Mayer made his point frighteningly clear. Jeanette was to have an abortion immediately and call off any divorce plans. End of discussion. The meeting turned into a screaming match between Mayer and Nelson. For them, this was the culmination of three years of mutual hatred and resentment. In his more civil moments, Mayer tried to explain that a scandal could ruin their careers, but Nelson would have none of it. "When our fans find out the truth, they'll stand up and cheer! And if they can't accept it, then I'll find some other way to make a living." He finally dragged a weeping Jeanette out, and while walking back to the set, got into an argument with her which was overheard by enough people to start a new group of "feud" rumors.

Jeanette angered Nelson by still refusing to make a public statement about her divorce. She argued that she would do so as soon as the picture was finished and they could drop out of public view. Nelson retaliated by getting away from it all for a few days; he and Clark Gable went on a fishing trip together in Corpus Christi, Texas. Jeanette also upset Mayer by her refusal to bow to his wishes. He was shocked that she had not confided in him; furthermore, he realized that for the first time in her life she was putting Nelson even before her career. Mayer was forced to admit that he'd lost his hold over Jeanette. He was placated a bit when, in the coming days, Jeanette continued to look happily married. She was seen with a mustached Gene at the premiere of *Marie Antoinette* on July 8. Jeanette seemed to hold no grudges against Gene and, according to one source, felt responsible and sorry for the mess she had dragged him into.

Despite her socializing with Gene, a new siege of gossip erupted in mid-month, this time telling the truth, that her marriage was over. "What two people whom everyone thinks are very apart are still very close?" one paper asked. "Who is the gallant star who is taking the blame in a recent marital crack-up rather than allow the truth to come out and damage her soon-to-be ex-husband?" The Hollywood *Reporter* tattled, "There will be another divorce suit filed in the star bracket at Metro within a couple of weeks." Also: "Hunt Stromberg laughs at the reports that Jeanette MacDonald and Nelson Eddy are phiffing on the *Sweethearts* set and says it's the happiest spirit he has ever seen on a picture." Even Woody Van Dyke made a statement for the press, unusual for him: "Believe me, there are no finer friends in all Hollywood than Nelson and Jeanette—and I know."

Yet with the latest turn of events, the filming of *Sweethearts* became a little less jovial. A couple of accidents on the set dampened their spirits further. The first one was Nelson's. They were working on the "Every Lover Must Meet His Fate" number, and he and Jeanette were standing atop a two-sided staircase, waiting. Nelson was telling an off-color joke for the benefit of the crew below. Jeanette laughingly shoved him, and to her horror, he lost his footing and toppled off the high platform. Jeanette ran down the stairs to him, screaming, "I've killed him!" Both she and Woody tried in vain to revive him, but he was thoroughly knocked out. Woody finally called an ambulance, and Jeanette accompanied Nelson to the emergency room. Still in her Dutch girl costume and heavy Technicolor makeup, she sat nervously in the waiting room attracting curious glances until someone finally showed her into a private waiting area. When Nelson finally regained consciousness, he had a terrific headache but otherwise no broken bones. The doctor, after checking him thoroughly, proclaimed he could go home the next day, as they wanted to keep him overnight for observation. He added that there was a very worried young lady awaiting news. Nelson was hit with a sudden idea. He made the doctor promise not to tell Jeanette he was awake.

When Jeanette timidly entered the room, she found Nelson apparently asleep. As Nelson later told it, he dramatically began to talk as though delirious, calling out various women's names. Carefully opening one eye, he saw Jeanette biting her finger, saying, "Oh, poor Nelson, your poor head." The more he talked the more upset she got. Finally he sat up, laughing, and grabbed her. Jeanette couldn't decide whether to be angry or relieved, retorting, "That's the best job of acting you ever did!"

"Yeah, I know," he said proudly. "But thank God I have a hard head. I sure need one with you around." Although he had a lingering headache for days, Nelson otherwise made a speedy recovery from what was termed a slight concussion.

Meanwhile Woody, not willing to hold up production while Nelson was in sick bay, shot the balance of the "Every Lover Must Meet His Fate" scene in long shots, using Nelson's stand-in.

Nelson was thereafter much more careful on the various high-winding *Sweethearts* sets. In his scenes with Jeanette, his eyes are always on her, and in some of the production numbers his expression often looks grim. In a couple of instances in the final print, she's spotted taking a misstep, and he quickly steadies her. But for all Nelson's protective measures, Jeanette did have an accident. He was not on the set when it occurred.

The shot called for Jeanette to run angrily up a flight of steps. As she plowed ahead, in a floor-length dress, she tripped and fell heavily, sliding down the stairs some distance on her stomach. One of the cast members called out for her to be careful. Her face beet red through the makeup, and still apparently in character, she whirled around and yelled, "Why? Am I going to fall again?" Picking herself up, she ran to the top of the staircase (where the shot ended), certain she had ruined the take and too angry to know if she was hurt or not. Woody raced up to her, worried because she'd fallen so hard. Word of the mishap spread through the set, and within minutes Nelson, who was recording, heard the news. Before Woody knew what hit him, Nelson angrily collared him and all but threatened his life for allowing any harm to come to Jeanette. Both Woody and Jeanette were able to convince him she was all right. Woody left Jeanette's fall and the ensuing dialogue in the film.

Nelson insisted that she be checked by her doctor immediately. All seemed to be well, or so he thought. But for Jeanette, the coming days were a nightmare. She had a lingering nagging pain in her back and middle that refused to subside. "I loved making *Sweethearts*," she once said, "and I hated it too. I was in such pain all the time, I could hardly stand it." Knowing Nelson would immediately pull her off the film if she complained, and certain that a few more weeks of work couldn't hurt her, she kept to herself, taking occasional medication when it became too aggravating. However, she began to look haggard and show the pain. Nelson arranged to have her day shortened so she could rest more (and a blurb hit the papers mentioning how "tired" she was every day). In an unretouched photo from one of her musical solos, "Angelus," she looked very ill. That number was ultimately cut from the picture after the premiere, the only footage to be trimmed.

The pregnancy was doomed. On July 26 it was announced that she was in Good Samaritan Hospital and had been operated on the previous night for "an abscess in her right ear." In fact, she had collapsed in Nelson's arms while filming. He had quickly carried her to her dressing room, but what he hoped at first was a faint became much more ominous when she started hemorrhaging. "I never saw so much blood in my life," he said later. He wrapped her in blankets while Woody called for the nearest studio car. Jeanette, in terrible pain, lapsed back into unconsciousness. During the drive to the hospital, Nelson held her on his lap, begging her not to leave him. She was so cold, so pale, he thought she was already dead. When they arrived at Good Samaritan, Nelson stumbled out of the car, clutching Jeanette to him. He was in such a daze that he refused to let the attendants take her away. They actually had to pry open his hands. He was so agitated that the admitting nurses could not calm him. To their surprise, he suddenly crumbled at their feet and had to be carried away by two attendants. Nelson awoke to the pungent odor of smelling salts. Regaining his senses, he was still so distraught that the doctor realized he had a second patient. Nelson was administered a strong sedative and slept through the next few hours. (The studio obligingly sent over a change of clothes to replace his bloodsoaked ones.) When he awoke he learned that Jeanette had lost the baby.

Though Gene was on the scene as Jeanette's legal husband, it was Nelson who sat by her bedside the next day, holding her hand, trying to comfort her. To his dismay, she sank into a deep depression, feeling an utter failure. Her despondency frightened Nelson, and he refused to leave her side.

Eddie Mannix came over from the studio to check up on Jeanette and find out how "the baritone" was holding up. When Nelson learned who the visitor was, he refused to let him enter the room. Mayer himself finally made a personal appearance to try and reason with "that madman." Nelson would not open the door even to speak with Mayer, and yelled through it that Mayer had murdered his child. His wrath was so damning that Mayer, stunned, quickly left.

News of this latest tragedy spread quickly through the Hollywood community. Makeup artist William Tuttle, who had worked on earlier MacDonald-Eddy pictures, was not at Metro during the summer of 1938, but he heard about the pregnancy and its outcome, and commented that "Nelson hadn't done right by her."

Sybil Thomas recalled:

> The happiest I ever saw him [Nelson] was when he was awaiting the birth of that baby. You never saw a more expectant father. The years seemed to drop away from him, even the sadness in his eyes had vanished. Jeanette, too, seemed different. I would say she was more caring about him and herself, less about her career. I remember Nelson came to my house one day and as was his usual habit, banged on

the sliding glass door instead of the doorbell. When I let him in he nearly snowed me under with his armful of packages. Throwing them down excitedly, he tore open box after box, explaining he was on his way home and had to show me all the baby goodies he'd bought. The ecstasy, the delight on his face was unmatched by any happiness I remember before or after. He wanted that baby more than anything in the world; he was so proud of Jeanette—and himself.

The worst I ever saw him was weeks later, when the baby died. I'd known about it beforehand because he called me briefly from the hospital to tell me what had happened. No emotion, just a brief statement. I didn't see or hear from him . . . Then came the urgent knock on the sliding glass door. I hurried to answer it and nearly fell over at what greeted me. His face was deathly gray and drawn, his hands trembling. He looked as though he hadn't slept in weeks. His eyes were clouded, unbelieving, shocked. I tried to offer him some food, but he could not eat. He said nothing, but sat down on the couch. I sat opposite him and waited, sensing I shouldn't press him. We sat in silence.

In his own good time he finally spoke. He voice shook and he spoke in that spasmodic way when he was trying desperately to keep in control. Yes, Jeanette was all right, she'd pull through. She was out of danger.

Nelson explained to Sybil that the doctor had spoken to Jeanette. There could never be any more babies; she wasn't built for it nor did she have the stamina to sustain a pregnancy. Sybil asked how Jeanette was taking it. Nelson's face crumbled—Jeanette hadn't fully grasped things; she couldn't accept it. She'd told him she wanted to die.

Suddenly the dam burst. He buried his face in his hands and cried like I'd never seen him before. I knew he didn't want sympathy or comfort so I sat quietly, occasionally handing him a dry handkerchief. If you don't think it was difficult to sit there and watch this—it was all I could do not to cry myself.

After an hour or so he fell into an exhausted sleep on the couch . . . I covered him with a blanket. Even in his sleep he was restless. When he woke up, he managed to choke down a cup of coffee and some food. He seemed slightly more in control, but said nothing further, just a brief "thank you" when he left out through the sliding glass door again.

After her initial depression, Jeanette's recovery was swift. Friends and family attributed this rapid improvement to Nelson's presence. Over the years Blossom, Isabel and others would marvel at how Jeanette could be close to death's door, but with Nelson at her side, amazingly bounce back. This time was no exception.

When she was feeling better, Nelson returned to work. On August 7, he rejoined the Chase & Sanborn team. On the ninth, one of his fan club presidents, who had traveled all the way from Montreal, was allowed to have lunch at the studio and to visit the *Sweethearts* set. She wrote to her members:

No big scenes were being filmed that day as Miss MacDonald was indisposed. However, Nelson was recording "On Parade" for the film on another stage so we went over there to hear him. The orchestra was under the direction of Herbert Stothart. During the actual recording we could not hear Nelson's voice, as he sang right into a mike and the orchestra played unusually loud. The sound enters the "sound track" through four channels, two for the orchestra, one for the chorus and one for the singer. The sound engineer controls the volume of each as he sees fit— we heard two playbacks which I believe were not good enough to be included in the film. More rehearsals!

Nelson came over several times for a brief chat . . . We were introduced to Dr. Lippe, who has been Nelson's singing teacher for the past fourteen years. Nelson told us briefly the story of *Sweethearts*, and showed us a few of the settings . . . We then went over to the . . . set where W. S. Van Dyke was directing the "switch-board" scenes to be used in the film. We were introduced to Florence Thomas, Mr. Van Dyke's "Girl Friday," who is very confident that *Sweethearts* will be great.

On August 12, 1938, this same woman had lunch with Jeanette's secretary, then hurried back to her hotel to change for dinner at Nelson's.

Mr. Eddy's driver picked us up at the hotel at 4:30 and we drove out to Beverly Hills, arriving there about 5:15 P.M. Mrs. Eddy (his mother) is the same gracious and lovely lady you all know her to be. At her suggestion Miss Nordstrom (Nelson's secretary), Win (the club vice-president) and I decided in favor of a swim before dinner, so we changed and had a perfectly delightful time. Mrs. Eddy took some snaps of us in the water. We met "Ogy," Nelson's roguish little Welsh terrier. At 6:15 we dressed, and were sitting in the bar when Nelson came home from the studio about 6:40.

Mr. Eddy—the comedian—was present during dinner, and kept us all very amused. As Mrs. Eddy, a friend, Miss Nordstrom, Win and I were going to the theater, we left the house shortly after dinner. We went to the Biltmore Theater to see *Pins and Needles*—after which we went to Melody Lane for a soda. Then back to our hotel where we had to say goodbye to Miss Nordstrom and Mrs. Eddy. Before Mrs. Eddy left us, she gave Win and me a box, containing a cut-glass bottle of her favorite cologne and to me, a very lovely 11x14 of herself.

The "On Parade" number was wrapped up by Friday, August 12. According to Woody's scheduling, the entire picture should have been completed by then, and would have been, but for the days lost due to Jeanette's illness. He had to begin work the following week on another feature, *Northwest Passage*, yet there were still two *Sweethearts* sequences left to shoot—the montage (with Betty Jaynes and Doug McPhail) and the finale. By Monday morning, Robert Z. Leonard had been assigned to finish *Sweethearts*. Woody was later pulled off *Northwest Passage* and assigned *Stand Up and Fight* with Robert Taylor. *Northwest Passage* was in and out of production for two years, and was finally released in 1940.

With Woody directing, it might have taken an additional week or two to put

Sweethearts into the can, but it took Leonard nearly a month. Jeanette returned to work for the montage sequence. Onscreen she looked a bit weary, and her face had a new mature look to it. Then she and Nelson took a week's trip together, back to Lake Tahoe, to have some peace and quiet and try to sort out their lives.

When in Tahoe they stayed, as they always did, at Chambers Lodge, where they'd filmed *Rose Marie*. This was a sentimental place for them, and the owners never pried or went public about their trysts.

The press, however, got wind that Nelson, at least, was on an automobile trip to northern California. With Jeanette, the focus of attention was still her impending divorce, which continued to be alluded to throughout the fall season. *Look* magazine didn't bother beating around the bush; in its pages an astrologer predicted: "Jeanette MacDonald and Gene Raymond will separate because she will continue to be more famous than her husband, thus creating friction to a person of his type. She was born in the air sign of Gemini and he in the fire sign of Leo. Jeanette will marry again." This same man said in another publication, "Jeanette's will be the first Hollywood divorce of 1939."

Hedda Hopper, meanwhile, counted herself lucky to get a photograph of herself with Jeanette, while Jeanette was in bed recuperating from the miscarriage. Jeanette, in a white nightgown, with a food platter on her lap, actually covered her face with the back of her hand when the photographer shot. Hedda gleefully published the photo, with this daring caption: "Jeanette MacDonald was going to have a baby, Hedda heard, but Jeanette just laughs and says she wishes it were true, but it's not."

When Jeanette and Nelson returned from their trip in mid-September 1938, they were called in to see Mayer. Louie, who was thrilled that the pregnancy issue had been resolved to his satisfaction, did not bring up the subject of divorce, knowing that he would get nowhere arguing with Nelson. Mayer had his own idea of how to bring Jeanette around on the subject of her marriage. Mayer sweet-talked the two stars, telling them how he was looking out for their interests. He had purchased two new vehicles for them, *Rio Rita* from RKO, and *The Desert Song* from Warners. But meanwhile, since they'd been "bad boys and girls," their next films would be with other co-stars. Jeanette was to film *Remember Tomorrow* (later retitled *Broadway Serenade*) with Lew Ayres and Walter Pidgeon; Nelson's project was *Song of the West* (released as *Let Freedom Ring*) with Virginia Bruce, Victor McLaglen and Lionel Barrymore.

Meanwhile, Jeanette had, according to some sources, filed for a California divorce that would become final in 1939. Unfortunately, no documentation exists to prove or disprove this claim.

In another version that has more recently come to light, Jeanette and Nelson went to Mexico, where she obtained a proxy divorce, and she and Nelson married there. Herbert Gahagan, cousin of actress Helen Gahagan Douglas and a well-known set designer, reported, "I had friends in publicity at some of the studios. The one from Metro used to tell me this kind of stuff, because he knew I worked with some of the people. He thought I'd be interested, so he told me about Jeanette and Nelson. They had married . . . They eloped, in Mexico . . . He said Mayer was furious and had the marriage annulled." Gahagan also knew there had been a child and that it had died. And Frank Laric, who appeared in Nelson's last film, and who studied with Nelson's voice teacher of the late 1940s, Major Herbert Wall, heard about the Mexican marriage in 1946. It was being discussed on the set of *Northwest Outpost*. Frank recalled that one of the other cast members on the set that day was Johnny Pickard (who later made a name for himself as a television actor). When Pickard was asked about the possibility of a Mexican marriage, he couldn't shed much light. He verified their relationship, and admitted: "I don't remember very much about it. I know they were very close . . . She filed for divorce. I remember that. I don't know if they went through with it. But I definitely remember that, and the studio PR people were in on it, trying to calm it down and hush it up a bit."

Milo Speriglio, famed investigator and author, is an expert in this area, having uncovered the fact that Marilyn Monroe once had a secret Mexican marriage. In his book, *The Marilyn Conspiracy*, Speriglio quoted Bob Slatzer: "[Marilyn and I] got married for five days in Mexico in August of 1952. We spent our wedding night at the Rosarita Beach Hotel. We had a witness by the name of Noble Chissell. After we got back, we quietly destroyed the marriage license because at that time marriage just didn't fit into her plans. Marilyn wasn't looking for an ideal husband. Her career was just taking off, and she wasn't interested in a house with a white fence and kids romping in the backyard."

When Speriglio was asked in a telephone interview how one would go about proving or disproving a Mexican marriage for MacDonald and Eddy, he replied, "There would likely be no records to prove it, as the bookkeeping in Mexico was much worse then than in the fifties, when Marilyn got married. Even if the marriage was recorded, when the news got back to Mayer—and it would—he would have paid to get it off the books. He was known for doing this.

"The only proof of such a marriage would be the actual marriage license. You could prove it if you could get hold of that piece of paper. Or find the witness—there had to be a witness—maybe someone who drove with them down to Mexico. If this marriage existed, it was never legally dissolved. Mayer just had it wiped off the books, as though it never happened."

To date, no witnesses have come forward. If the Mexican marriage actually occurred and was removed from the records, it meant Jeanette and Nelson couldn't have claimed they were married without a lot of negative publicity. For example, during the same time period, Charlie Chaplin and Paulette Goddard were rumored to be married—and they actually were. But because it was done secretly, mystery clouded the issue. It was later claimed that Paulette lost the role of Scarlett O'Hara in *Gone With the Wind* because of the ambiguity surrounding her marital status. Not until the Chaplins obtained a conventional divorce was it known for certain that they'd been legally married (though Chaplin introduced Goddard as "my wife" at *The Great Dictator* premiere in October 1940). Therefore, a more conventional divorce for Jeanette and Gene seemed to be prescribed, with no loose ends.

Jeanette was hospitalized again in late September 1938. The reason is unknown; the newspaper versions report a secondary ear infection. The ailment was probably gynecological in nature, perhaps a complication from the pregnancy. The clues that support this theory are a comment by Nelson that Jeanette could never have any more children (a statement which later proved false), and some mention in later letters that one of her ovaries had gone bad. Interesting enough, by late November, it was suddenly okay for reporters to leak out that she had been seriously ill, although no mention was made of what the illness actually was. Several papers mentioned it. "Mrs. MacRaymond says she feels much better after her recent illness," wrote critic Regina Crewe in December, after speaking with Jeanette, "and is going ahead with concert tour plans for the Spring. Nelson Eddy, too, will make a tour. They'll have something to talk about between shots of their next picture."

They were talking about more than simply "concert tours for the spring." Nelson was now saying that Jeanette should go to Reno to establish residency— and file for divorce—upon completion of her film.

But Louis B. Mayer continued to interfere. Mayer, who had kept quiet all this time (assuming that Jeanette would call off her divorce plans once she had lost her baby), now decided to squelch her relationship with Nelson once and for all and get Jeanette's priorities back to where they belonged—her movie career.

16

A foolish marriage

Those in the know were surprised to see that in the final months of 1938, Jeanette and Gene were making the social rounds together, looking happily married, despite Nelson's insistence that Jeanette's divorce was in the works.

The reason for this newfound closeness was an early morning visit to Twin Gables by Louis B. Mayer. Jeanette had been awakened by a pre-dawn phone call announcing his arrival—no reason given. She watched him pull up in a big black limousine like "a messenger of doom." While she numbly served him coffee and sweet rolls, he plied her with questions as to where Gene was staying and why he wasn't home where he belonged. She was forced to phone Gene and have him come to Twin Gables immediately. Mayer sat the two of them down and explained the new scenario for their lives. One: Jeanette was not getting a divorce. Two: Gene was moving home. Three: The Raymonds were to be smiling and happy for the press who would be doing feature articles on their blissful union. "You are going to make this marriage look like everybody's missing something great," Mayer ordered. "You are going to constantly let the world know how happy you are." He further warned Gene not to "step out of line."

Jeanette tried to protest, to no avail. "It'll all be for the best," Mayer told her. "I always treated you right. I've always given you the best. Now I'll give you better." His parting shot as he left: "Oh, by the way, you better straighten the baritone out. I don't want any backtalk from him."

Nelson's response to Mayer's ultimatums was an angry retort, "Don't listen to anything he says." He insisted that Jeanette stay at his house, with Isabel to look after her. But she had now hesitated so long about going to Reno to establish residency that doing so was now out of the question; both she and Nelson were starting new films in mid-November. Divorce plans would have to be pushed back to the spring, which angered Nelson. Already he was anticipating that Jeanette would back out altogether and he'd be left in the lurch.

The tug of war continued. Mayer next showed up at Nelson's house, after first making certain Nelson wasn't home. He knew that the only way to weaken Jeanette's resolve was to get her alone. He made vague threats against Nelson, correctly concluding that this was the only inroad that would hit home. Shortly afterwards, Nelson made the mistake of mentioning to Jeanette that he'd been involved in a minor car accident. It seemed that another car tried to push him off the road. He wasn't hurt, but for Jeanette, that wasn't the point. She was certain Mayer was behind it, that this was a warning to her.

Jeanette dutifully returned to Twin Gables; she had no fight left in her. Nelson was so disgusted that he impulsively considered marrying Ann Franklin, his friend from his opera crowd whom he'd escorted occasionally. Ann seemed like a nice person, could provide a home for him that he had always wanted, and he wouldn't have to worry about where he stood in *her* feelings. Nelson actually informed a few close friends that he was thinking of marrying her. Nowhere, however, did he mention loving Ann, and in fact wrote to Mae Mann that he was through with love forever and was devoting his life to music.

Mayer, happy with his latest victory, had decided to split the team professionally as an added guarantee that they would remain apart personally. During

The cast of *Let Freedom Ring* (1939): Edward Arnold, Nelson, Virginia Bruce, Lionel Barrymore, and Victor McLaglen, whom Nelson got to beat up in his first real "he-man" role.

the week of November 21, they reported to the studio to pre-record their numbers. Meanwhile, last minute cast changes occurred. Jeanette's film, *Broadway Serenade*, started out with George Murphy and Walter Pidgeon in the leads. The following week, her co-stars were named as Ian Hunter and Lew Ayres, who had made several films with Jeanette's sister Blossom. (Under her stage name, Marie Blake, Blossom played Sally, the telephone operator in the popular Dr. Kildare series starring Ayres and Lionel Barrymore.) Ayres was doing double duty, appearing simultaneously in *Ice Follies of 1939*. Nelson, meanwhile, was joined by Virginia Bruce and Lionel Barrymore for *Let Freedom Ring*, a film that had once been scheduled for him and Jeanette.

Jeanette's performance in *Broadway Serenade* was subdued; her exuberant radiance from *Sweethearts* had clearly vanished. Emotionally drained, her heart just wasn't in her work. Physically she looked tired, and still seemed a bit paunchy around the middle. The candid shots on the set show her pensive and sometimes sad, with tears in her eyes. There was no on-screen charisma with Ayres, but they were professional and courteous to each other. "I cannot ever remember working with anyone who so lived up to their position in life according to the ideal conception," Lew Ayres later said. "She was a star as a star should be in the finest sense of the word. She had more dignity with warmth, exuberance tempered with a sweet, calm control, graciousness unsullied by affectation than any other person I've ever known."

Jeanette was invited back to Vicks Open House, but she declined, no doubt due to her health. The press wondered why she was "conspicuously absent" from the radio during the 1938–39 season.

Nelson, for his part, enjoyed working on *Let Freedom Ring*. Jack Conway, one of Gable's favorite directors, worked well with Nelson, eliciting a relaxed, confident performance. It was a man's picture; Nelson got to duke it out with Victor McLaglen, and best of all, he wore no makeup. "He was a real tough character in real life," said Nelson of McLaglen. "And brother, he was really a good boxer. I had to fight Vic for three long days while they shot that fight scene. He kept knocking me down on to rocks—rubber 'rocks,' fortunately. It was rough going for me."

At year's end, the inevitable motion picture polls were tabulated. The Brisbane *Courier-Mail* announced that in a film star popularity contest covering all of Australia, Jeanette had placed first for women (with Shirley Temple second), and Nelson was second for men (after Robert Taylor). In the United States, Nelson polled first in many fan magazines as top radio star, top classical singer and top male movie star. Furthermore, he was acclaimed as the highest-paid singer in the world, and the top wage-earner in motion pictures, thanks to his radio and concert activity. He was now commanding $15,000 per concert and $5,000 a week for singing a few songs on the Chase & Sanborn show. Jeanette also won fanzine contests and more important, in a poll of fifty major newspapers across the country culled by the New York *Daily News*, Jeanette won as most popular actress with 59,608 votes. (The male winner was Tyrone Power with 89,647 votes.)

To add to the plaudits, *Sweethearts* was previewed in Westwood, California, in mid–December. It was a smash hit, and the critics raved. "By far the best of the MacDonald and Eddy series," said the Hollywood *Reporter*. "This has a freshness and humor which will win a new audience for them besides sending their vast and loyal followers into new transports of delight . . . Neither of them has ever been better, nor as good, and Technicolor is more than kind; it works some kind of magic." *Sweethearts* was released Christmas week, and topped all previous MacDonald-Eddy pictures, with grosses in excess of $1,500,000 in its first two weeks, an all-time high for MGM.

Nelson was invited to place his handprints and footprints at Grauman's Chinese Theater. He did so, in a spot adjoining Jeanette's (she'd placed hers there with Maurice Chevalier during the filming of *The Merry Widow*). That same week, he paid for a Christmas party for the children at the Orthopedic Hospital. His spirits were high, and not just with holiday cheer. Jeanette suddenly agreed to discuss divorce again, and agreed to go to Reno as soon as her film wrapped. Nelson cheerfully renewed his Metro contract for more films: *Balalaika*, which had previously been thought to be his next picture, was set aside; the trades announced that he and Jeanette would team again, probably in *Katinka*, an Otto Harbach-Rudolf Friml operetta that had been purchased for them two years earlier.

Jeanette granted a year–end newspaper interview, in which the attentive reporter listened to all she had to say, then came away with this perceptive comment:

"Jeanette may be married to Gene Raymond, but there's nothing she doesn't know about Nelson Eddy."

On the evening of January 1, 1939, Nelson attended a party at the Trocadero, where he, Don Ameche and Chico Marx put on an impromptu show that "had the crowd in stitches." His mood continued to be jovial as he did his final work on *Let Freedom Ring*. He was looking forward to his concert tour, as he was making his debut in Cuba.

But Jeanette's film wasn't faring so well. Due in part to her listless performance, Busby Berkeley was called in to spice things up by adding an elaborate finale number. Retakes for *Broadway Serenade* dragged on till the end of January.

One morning Nelson showed up unexpectedly at Twin Gables to see Jeanette. He was agitated and insisted she set a definite date to leave for Reno, where a "quickie" divorce could be obtained after establishing a residency for six weeks. He pressured her to leave immediately, then he could meet up with her while on his tour and they would marry as soon as she had her final papers. When she protested that she would finish her film first and then go, and that a few weeks wouldn't matter one way or another, they quarreled. Jeanette couldn't understand his urgency, especially since there was no longer any baby to think of. Finally Nelson left in a rage, yelling, "You'll do anything not to have my name! Let me tell you something, I'll never ask you again! Since you don't want to be Mrs. Nelson Eddy, that's okay. I'll never marry you!"

Something in Nelson had snapped. This latest, unexpected rejection, was the final straw for him. He made an uninvited visit to Mayer's office, where his boss was forced to listen to Nelson's enraged accusations. Nelson may have been ignorant of all the details but he knew the bottom line; Mayer had once again influenced Jeanette against him. Mayer won this round, Nelson conceded, but at a dear price. "I'll never make another film with that redhead as long as I live," he yelled in Mayer's face. "I'll sing in the streets for nothing rather than to ever have to see her face or hear her name again!"

Jeanette reported early to the studio on the morning of January 20, 1939. She had two numbers to finish, then her work on the film was done. She had not seen a morning paper by the time she arrived at the set, nor had anyone volunteered the startling news that was now circulating at the studio like wildfire. A studio messenger came on to the set to end the speculation. Yes, it was true, Nelson Eddy had eloped with Ann Franklin in Las Vegas yesterday. The news had come as a surprise to everyone, including Mayer, who was furious. Jeanette screamed in horror and ran off the set, sobbing. The entire crew was silent, in shock. Until now, sympathies among the crew had tended to be with Nelson. Studio workers, who perceived what they thought were Jeanette's roller-coaster emotions toward Nelson, felt that he'd had it pretty tough. But now—suddenly the roles were reversed.

Jeanette locked herself in her dressing room and refused to see anyone. Woody Van Dyke was on another set, filming *It's a Wonderful World* with Jimmy Stewart and Claudette Colbert. When he had a free moment, he came over to the *Broadway Serenade* set to see how Jeanette was taking the news. He was worried when he learned she was still in her dressing room. He knocked on the door, waiting in vain for her to answer. Finally he kicked the door in and found her sprawled out semi-conscious on her bed. The empty bottle of sleeping pills was all he had to see. The quick-thinking director phoned for the studio doctor and tried in vain to get her on her feet. Woody listened helplessly as she wept and called for Nelson. Suddenly Mayer appeared at the door. He rushed to Jeanette and tenderly took her hand. Crying real tears, Mayer sobbed, "Jeanette, baby, I never meant to hurt you! Like your own father I wanted what was good for you. Speak to me! Be a good girl and speak to me!" When there was no response, he turned to Woody. "It's that baritone's fault. It's him, he's doing this to my beautiful star." To Woody's surprise, Mayer picked Jeanette up and carried her to a waiting car.

Her stomach was pumped, and Jeanette was sent home to recuperate. Gene was ordered to keep a suicide watch. When Isabel Eddy later called to speak with Jeanette, she took the phone, listened to Isabel's words, then dropped the receiver. Gene pushed her into a chair, afraid she was going to faint, then got on the line with Isabel, who insisted on coming over immediately to see Jean-

ette. After her husband hung up Jeanette said, "Oh, Gene, don't ever leave me
—be patient—" Gene later told Isabel, "She clung to me for the very first time
in her life and for long minutes she wept in bitter anguish."

When Isabel arrived, the two women hugged each other and cried. Finally
Isabel related the details. Nelson, who'd been ill with a cold and temperamen-
tally out of sorts, informed his mother he was eloping with Ann. If Isabel
wanted to accompany them, she was invited. Then he locked himself in his
bedroom and Isabel banged on his door for hours, trying to reason with him.
When he finally came out he'd been drinking, but they left for Vegas anyway.

Isabel noted in her diary: "I could not believe it was my son who faced me,
his face set in deep lines—tragic and terrible. I said, 'Nelson, you have lost all
your balance and common sense—you will be breaking a sacred promise to the
girl who loves you.' He answered, 'I HAVE to marry Ann, mother, it is a duty.'

"I was bitter and I said so. 'There is much more to this than you are telling
me—now my only prayer is that Jeanette may be able to give her heart to the
man who deserves it much more than you do—you will be a sorry man if her
life is ruined and her heart broken. I shall witness your marriage but do not ask
me to linger. My place will be with the girl whom I shall always consider my
own—I have a feeling she will need me.' "

Isabel joined Nelson, Ann, Doris Kenyon (Ann's close friend) and Nelson's
business manager E. J. Osborne as they drove to Las Vegas and found a justice of
the peace. Isabel attempted several times to change her son's mind, to no avail.

Nelson with Ann Franklin—just married, January 19, 1939.

Nelson, on medication for his cold, was still drinking. He was so drunk, in fact, that the wedding ceremony was half over before he realized Doris Kenyon was standing at his side instead of Ann. A candid photo taken after the wedding ceremony shows a bewildered and miserable-looking Nelson with Ann, who lied on the wedding license, giving her age as forty. She was actually forty-four.

The wedding party returned to Los Angeles by train. Nelson fell into an exhausted sleep, and awoke to ask his mother what they were doing on a train! Isabel was hysterical when she realized her son had no recollection of what he'd done. By the time the train arrived in Los Angeles, Nelson had pulled himself together. Reporters greeted the newlyweds at the train station, and Nelson said, "Well, I'm happier than I ever have been, but I wish we had had more time. Our honeymoon was a twenty-minute look at Hoover Dam."

Isabel later went into more detail about the wedding in her memoirs, in a section entitled "My Son's Wedding."

> I shall mention this as briefly as possible—even now I feel sick when I think of that day. The ceremony was about two minutes long and I am sure that Nelson didn't hear a single word that was said. The judge had to repeat the response twice and when he finally did answer, it was so low I never even heard it, for which I am thankful. It was a rough, bare room without one item of beauty around— appropriate—but terrible when I think of my son who loves his trees and flowers —whose roots have always had to sink down and grow—who cherishes only those things that have grown with him. How well I know this woman now—if only I had known her a few months before—but even on this terrible day I knew with sick certainty that she would never even be able to be a companion to him. When it was over she turned and kissed me and I took Nelson's hand in mine and held it for a long moment as I looked deep into his eyes—and a spasm of deep pain crossed his face as I said, "Now I am going to Jeanette, dear." I want my little girl to know that moment as I knew it—for I am sure that it was not until then that he really realized the terrible thing he had done.

Jeanette had little time to grieve. *Broadway Serenade* had to be wrapped. She was photographed in bed, recovering from her "cold," looking dazed and miserable. A radio hookup was established so she could continue working on the film, even from her sick-bed. By January 23, she was back at the studio, looking as radiant as ever, to accept her award along with Tyrone Power as the King and Queen of the Screen for 1939. With *Broadway Serenade* finally finished at the end of the month, Mayer decided she needed a break. Her mental state was such that he agreed with her request to get away for a while, and go on a concert tour.

Nelson, meanwhile, was crushed when he learned of Jeanette's suicide attempt. His eyes filled with tears and he said defeatedly, "What can I do, mother? I'm helpless to do anything." The studio tried to make the best of his marriage, arranging a publicity sitting for Nelson and Ann. After his initial anger, Mayer ordered a meeting with Nelson. He greeted him by gloating,

Jeanette and Tyrone Power accepting their awards (from Ed Sullivan) as the King and Queen of Hollywood. Jeanette was now the top female star in the world.

"Well! You look as though you personally pushed the train all the way from Las Vegas." Mayer's main concern was how the marriage would go over with the fans at the box office. "To hell with my box office," was Nelson's retort. "Of course, you've got your concerts coming up, so we'll see," said Mayer, dismissing him from the office with a parting shot: "At least I won't have to worry about you and the redhead anymore."

One newspaper relayed the curious fact that Nelson and his new wife had decided to live in their respective houses until a new home was found. On February 1, 1939, Nelson previewed his spring concert tour at Redlands. On the sixth he did his first scheduled appearance in Redlands. Ann accompanied him as he traveled an itinerary that took him through Texas, Oklahoma, the Midwest, to Toronto, Philadelphia, and then down South. Ann Eddy immediately assumed a proprietary attitude toward Nelson and made it clear that, public figure though he was, she considered him her personal property. Short, plump and nondescript in appearance, her only claim to fame appeared to be an ability to play the piano and run a smooth household. It was clear she believed she had reached the pinnacle of her "career" when she became "Mrs. Nelson Eddy," and that nothing short of death would loose her hold on that title.

Ann had so completely misrepresented herself during the "courtship" period, that Nelson was surprised to see her display a vicious, vengeful streak—generally to his fans, and particularly to Jeanette. Shilo Hatfield, a man whose job was making train connections, reported that Ann Eddy left Nelson mid-tour and returned home from the Huntington, West Virginia, station. Her excuse was "an illness in her family." But in reality, Nelson could no longer stand having Ann around. They fought constantly, and Nelson finally ordered her to leave. He admitted to Red Boyles, again his bodyguard on the Eastern leg of his tour, that he was still in love with Jeanette.

On March 16, Nelson gave a concert in Philadelphia, at the Academy of Music. The fans filled the place to the rafters. Five hundred women sat behind Nelson on the stage, and occasionally he turned to sing to them. One newspaper noticed that this was the first Eddy concert in Philadelphia that Gertrude Evans had not attended.

Nelson's 1939 tour ended on April 27 in Wichita, Kansas. He returned home to find his new wife and his mother barely speaking to each other. Nelson bluntly asked Ann for a divorce, admitting he'd made a mistake, and offering her a handsome settlement To his amazement, she refused his offer. Feeling he had no other choice, Nelson left his mother at his residence, 805 North Alpine Drive, and moved in with Ann, at 720 Maple Drive, to try to make a go of the marriage.

From Isabel: "The brief period which followed his tour is like a nightmare to me—I cannot even try to write of it—I knew my son was confused and bewildered but he confided nothing to me. I knew only that where he once was a carefree happy boy he now—despite a brave effort at keeping up appearances—was facing life with a heart that was cold and hard."

■■■Some time after Nelson's marriage, both the Eddys and the Raymonds were invited to the same party. Jeanette had declined the invitation, pleading illness, but at the last minute phoned to say she was well enough to attend. A friend remembered, "She arrived late, as usual. She looked delicate. She rarely wore makeup when among friends, but tonight she wore it, no doubt in an effort to hide her pallor and those circles under her eyes. A few people came over with the usual lies about how great she looked, and then one catty woman couldn't resist. She told Jeanette Nelson was there. Jeanette whispered, 'Nelson, here?' and for a moment we thought she would faint, but she regained her composure and very calmly explained she'd have to go home as she still wasn't feeling well. She pulled it off like the actress she was, and escaped out of there before Nelson even got wind she'd arrived. We heard her crying even before she got out the front door. It was a cruel joke, and I think Nelson would have left in disgust had he known what had happened."

Jeanette left on a concert tour shortly after Nelson and returned home in May 1939. Her tour, too, was a triumphant success. She'd had time to distance herself from her problems, and decided to try for a divorce again, even if she could not return to Nelson. She was in a position to negotiate with Mayer, as it was time to renew her contract, and she thought she might get away with it. Once again, she thought wrong.

Rumors started once again that she and Gene were breaking up. The Philadelphia *Evening Bulletin* ran a very catty blurb: "No one will ever be able to accuse Jeanette MacDonald of marrying Gene Raymond for his money. Gene was doing all right for himself at the time (he is now minus a movie job), but Jeanette's income, even then, was at least five times as large as Gene's." Surprisingly, Jeanette demonstrated a new intolerance of the press and their prying, highly unusual for her. On one occasion, a snide reporter asked her how she felt about Nelson marrying. Jeanette's answer was to slap him across the face. A second reporter posing the same question received a kick in the leg and was told where to go. When Jeanette and Gene spent a few days in the mountains with a group of Hollywood celebrity couples, Jeanette walked out in disgust and returned home before the first night was up. How this fight was prettied up for the fan magazines she never knew, but she left it up to the publicity department to handle. At this point she couldn't care less what people thought.

During the summer, she saw Nelson again—once. He attended a cocktail party at her home, in an attempt to at least be friends with her. Isabel remarked, "He returned bitter and sick with the sure knowledge that he had wounded her past all hope of forgiveness."

Jeanette, realizing she was still obsessed with Nelson, nonetheless found the time away from him rejuvenating. She wrote Margaret Ritchie, Bob's mother: "This summer I'm relaxing for a change. I think I should take a real rest while I can; doing a lot of gardening, horseback riding and in general getting free and healthy." But her mind always turned toward him. Jeanette continued to remain friends with Isabel, meeting her often for lunch, and pumping her for information about Nelson.

One day, Nelson handed his mother a special diary. He told her it was for Jeanette. Isabel was to read it first, then show it to her, as it would explain her unanswered questions about his marriage. Isabel read the lengthy entry, then phoned Jeanette. They arranged to meet for a weekend in Palm Springs.

Isabel also copied the diary entry verbatim, and sent it to her friend Sarah Tucker. Isabel periodically copied diary entries to send to her friend, also letters, love letters, her in-progress memoirs, and transcripts of various conversations between Nelson, Jeanette, Blossom and others. One person commented, "If Nelson had known his mother was doing this, he would have killed her."

In Palm Springs, Isabel handed Nelson's diary to Jeanette and waited as she read the shocking account.

> Darling, the hardest thing I ever faced is to tell you this. Your pure sweet mind should not have to hear it, but I can't bear the slightest secret between us—so come close to me now—I'll need your hand in mind.
>
> Of course you know for several years Ann had been mother's friend, and I accepted her as such. She was always present and appeared to be a lady in every respect. A time or two I took her out when it was impossible for mother to go with me—but I never had a date with her until after we finished *Sweethearts*. They were not really dates at that—but rather, I fell into the habit of staying to talk to her after taking her home from mother's house. I was so depressed over Gene and

you not being able to ask for the divorce, and though I never talked about you at first she was wise enough to know what was wrong with me. At last one night she saw I was very much in the dumps and became very kind and understanding and insisted on talking about you. I told her that I was miserable because I could never get over you—that there was something eternal about it and I would rather go on the rest of my life alone than ever to give my name to another woman. Then she said, "But she is happy with Gene—so what hope have you?" And because I thought she was a family friend and could be trusted I told her that your marriage was based on friendship only and that we were trying to make adjustments as soon as possible. How very foolish that was of me because I know that from that time on she made her plans. A few days later—with another woman friend of hers I had dinner at her home. The three of us sat around the fire and cocktails were served. I didn't know this "witness" (because I know now that is just what she was) very well at the time—but suddenly there was something very distasteful about the whole thing to me. I kept seeing your face—it was the strangest thing— and if only I'd heeded that warning and left. But she insisted I must have just ONE more cocktail before I left. And darling—I know now that that cocktail contained more than the ordinary ingredients—I was doped—knocked out with one blow—but this didn't dawn on me for many weeks. I was too horrified at the later developments to think clearly. I just took her word for it that I had had many drinks and did not remember. I only know that that night not even your prayers could follow me. Darling, believe me when I tell you that I have absolutely no memory of anything that happened—I cannot possibly believe that anything did —yet when I came out of it, there I was on the divan in her living room and it was morning. Before I had time to think clearly, she appeared weeping violently and told me a nightmare of a story about my becoming violent in my lovemaking while her friend was out of the room and that she had returned just in time to find us in a very compromising condition. And now she was half crazy because this woman was not to be trusted and her reputation would be ruined. I must say she did look in a terribly disheveled condition, and oh darling—worst of all—I discovered to my horror that most of my own clothing had been removed. You see, at that time I never knew there could be that kind of woman—and so I never dreamed this was just an act she was staging—I had always thought she was a sincere person and just took it for granted that something terrible must have happened—though even then I had a hard time picturing myself in any such light as this. I asked her if she thought she should marry me and she said "no" and wept all the harder—and of course I know now that was only a trick to get me back. But by the time I saw her the next day I had decided. I told her that I was very sure she was in no way personally harmed and I was not prepared to go through with any foolish marriage—since I must wait for the woman I loved. And then, darling, is when she played her trump card. She started weeping all over again and said then there was only one thing to do—she must go to you and plead with you to give me up so her reputation could be saved. Well, that did it—I would have shot myself on the spot rather than let her go to you and tell you some sort of terrible story that would let you think I had fallen so low. And dearest— she put the whole thing in such nice words that I was just too stupid to see that it was only a threat—for of course she would have done no such thing—she would have been compromising herself—and if only I had thought of this at the time I would have called her bluff. So this is why I came to you that night and asked you to come to me at once—if you had promised to end your marriage I would have gone to her and told her it was all settled between us and I would have thrown over every other obligation regardless of the consequences. Even with her witness she could not have done anything if I had publicly announced my intention of marrying you. When you wouldn't say you would ask for the divorce—I was bitter and desperate—I thought surely you didn't love me after all—not enough to face a divorce—so I thought I might as well try to make Ann happy and relieve her fears—remember, I did not yet know the type of woman she was and I hadn't yet doubted her sincerity. I thought that perhaps she would be a companion and that together we could try.

And the marriage—my dear—I knew even on the wedding night that I had sadly overestimated that woman. I thought she understood that there could never be much of any kind of physical emotion between us—I never thought she would expect that. Dearest, it is very terrible to realize that you have lost the only thing you ever loved and that you have not even understanding from the person who should share your life—for a little while I went to pieces. I could never tell you what happened to me—I lost my balance. By keeping me half-drunk most of the time she managed to arouse all the worst that was in me—but she surely aroused nothing else. And my darling, right here I want to tell you this—never was she able to erase your face before me—and also, she knew I still loved you—I never kept it from her. In fact I never let her forget it. She had me trying to sink to her level but never quite doing it. And darling, those nights were awful—not even drunk could I make myself go through with it. There was not enough beast in me to view her wild emotion with anything but disgust. I assure you I think she would gladly have killed me during that awful time when I kept seeing your face and leaving the room in disgust—usually to walk all night and hate myself with a bitter hatred. And there was no excuse for my conduct—even drunk I did not have to TRY to sink so low. But those days were brief and not clear in my mind, thank God.

Darling, I don't think you know half I am trying to say—you are the other kind of woman. But I want you to know this—all my life unless you some day come to me and prove that physical love is only beautiful and wonderful to those who love I will have a terrible fear of my own emotions—I will even be afraid of loving you. Now I promise you that I shall never touch her or any woman in any such fashion again. Even if you never find it possible to forget—still it will be only you. I truly hope she does not want to go on with this foolish marriage—for my part it was over and done with long ago.

Oh darling, when I think of you as I used to see you—I just can't stand it.

My still beloved baby—God keep you happy, for I must forever live in a world of lost dreams. I didn't believe my angel baby when she told me her love was greater than her career. Now, my darling, I shall live in the past with you. There is no present—now I have no future—but there is no one to say I can't have you in the past. It will be a shadow world wherein my spirit dwells—but you will be there. You MUST be there, my darling—as I write this tears are dimming my eyes and my heart is dead.

Mother will give you this when she sees fit.

After her first American concert tour, Jeanette was grateful to relax at home and re-evaluate her life. MGM still photographer Clarence Bull was driving past Twin Gables one day and spotted Jeanette playing with her dogs on the lawn. He quickly shot a roll of film, claiming the candids were among his best shots of Jeanette. Bull commented that his two favorite stars to photograph were Greta Garbo and Jeanette MacDonald.

17

"Wanting You"

The news of Nelson's marriage in January 1939, was a shock to fans and the industry bigwigs alike. In particular, MGM was concerned about the possible adverse effect on Nelson's box office potential.

His current film, *Let Freedom Ring*, was sneak-previewed in Pomona, a Los Angeles suburb, in mid-January. The audience response was so positive that MGM shoved its release date ahead one month. The plot concerns Harvard lawyer Nelson leading his father (Lionel Barrymore) and a group of ranchers against the suave villainy of Edward Arnold, who tries to drive everyone off their land while building the new railroad through town.

On February 14, the film officially previewed in Westwood to critical raves, such as the following review from the Hollywood *Reporter*:

> Gutty. It gives MGM the opportunity to take advantage of a lot of things that Nelson Eddy has, that have always been buried under a bushel of light opera, comic opera and other ideas too artificial for successful, down-to-earth, lusty entertainment. And does Mr. Eddy stand out. He is perfect in his role . . . He sings eight or more songs . . . and each one was given merited applause by a very excited preview audience.
>
> It's a swell story, given excellent production and acted by a well nigh perfect cast. It has punch from beginning to end, and should be one of MGM's top grossers, in addition to teaching movie fans a lot of patriotism.

The picture deserves heavy exploitation, because it's a swell show and one that will return almost a hundred dollars for every single dollar spent in telling an audience about it before its arrival.

Let Freedom Ring opened in general release on February 24, 1939. It did solid business, aided by the political climate of the times. *Variety* called the film "Momentous. It's the first in the cycle of film offerings to stress the American type of democracy and freedom for the classes and masses."

Jeanette's *Broadway Serenade* fared less well. It was sneak-previewed in mid-February, previewed in late March and finally released on April 7. In the film, Jeanette and Lew Ayres are a struggling young couple—she a singer, he a composer. She makes it big, which breaks them up. Later he sells one of his works that she is slated to star in, and they are reunited even though she was supposed to marry someone else (Ian Hunter).

The Hollywood *Reporter* praised Lew Ayres for turning in "a sterling performance," but complained:

> *Broadway Serenade* is a lavish musical, and as such falls quite snugly into formula patter . . . It is doubtful that the familiar format will endear it to its audience, however, or that it may hope for more than average patronage in the top budget class.
>
> The picture impressed as being overlong in preview. This impression was intensified by its trite book, which is all too familiar to film audiences. It will therefore lean heavily on the box office pull of its star.
>
> Jeanette MacDonald is in excellent voice and is required to make frequent and diverting use of her familiar talents in this medium. Likewise she is elaborately gowned and given every other opportunity to appear visually glamorous. The net effect, however, is a suspicion of overacting in at least one scene.

Even Jeanette's big number, "Un Bel Di" from *Madama Butterfly*, was criticized:

> The "Madame Butterfly" number loses vitally in expected poignant effect through its over-spectacular "production."

The New York *Times* summed up the general consensus, calling *Broadway Serenade* "The biggest bad show of the year."

The public still wanted Jeanette and Nelson together, as the studio soon learned. MGM put a teaser ad in four national magazines, asking anyone who wanted an autographed photo of MacDonald and Eddy to write to the studio. The studio was immediately flooded with 120,000 requests, and continued to receive additional letters at the rate of 1,000 per day. But Nelson still refused to work with her. His next picture was slated to be *Balalaika*. Miliza Korjus, who'd become an overnight star in *The Great Waltz*, was offered the lead. According to Miliza, she laughed when asked if she wanted *Balalaika*, because she knew Nelson was supposed to film it with "his girlfriend." "I thought it was a joke," she said, and passed on the project. To her dismay, the role was next offered to Ilona Massey, who accepted. For years, Miliza bemoaned losing out on working with "that gorgeous hunk of baritone."

Jeanette signed a new contract with Metro in the summer of 1939. Similar to Nelson's, she agreed to make two films a year and was allowed time off each spring for a concert tour. Her first vehicle was announced as a remake of *Smilin' Through*, with Jimmy Stewart and Robert Taylor co-starring. Production was not expected to begin till the fall.

Nelson began work on *Balalaika* in June. He and Ilona Massey got along well, and some friends claim they had an affair. A curious blurb hit the trades: "A singing actor is absorbing an awful blow to his ego these days because the young thing he has been courting sub rosa (he's already hitched) won't accept any of his offers to help her get a contract. The lassie's momma is all for this aid, but the gal won't touch his assistance—or his advances." Less than two weeks after this clipping appeared, it was announced that Ilona had signed a new and better contract with MGM. The reason given was "the basis of her work in *Balalaika*."

Balalaika was in production until the end of August. On August 13, Nelson returned for the third season of the Chase & Sanborn show. To his surprise, a

Nelson on concert tour after his marriage. Behind him are Gertrude Evans, Sarah Tucker and his mother.

congratulatory telegram awaited him at the station, wishing him good luck with the series. It was from Jeanette.

Jeanette had read his words to her at her meeting with Isabel; on the one hand, she felt she could never forgive him for marrying Ann, but, despite herself, she was still in love with him, and the knowledge that he was suffering disturbed her.

The following week there was a second telegram awaiting Nelson at the station. Gossip ran rife among the radio staff. One person recalled,

Yeah, those telegrams! It was really something. I remember when the first one came; it was right before the show aired. No one knew whether it was bad news or not, but you certainly didn't want him hearing about a death or illness just before going on the air. So we read it, to make sure. Well, it was from her, wishing him good luck on the show, and telling him he was great. It looked very innocent, but who knew how he'd react to it? So we held it till afterwards. Nelson read it wordlessly, unaware we were all watching for his reaction. The following week, same thing, another telegram from her. This went on and on. Sometimes she asked, even pleaded, to see him. Obviously, he was refusing, because she'd continue to make the request.

After awhile it started getting to him. He'd be nervous and even worried if the telegram was late getting to him. He finally got wise that everyone knew about it and got more aloof than before, making sure, of course, that the telegrams were no longer sidetracked. He was frustrated, you could see it. During conferences he'd drift off, jumping and saying "Huh?" when he suddenly realized someone was talking to him. Sometimes he was needlessly curt and lost his temper over some minor thing.

It was no secret his marriage was a mess. He could have easily compensated for it with dozens of girls. But he didn't; he just threw himself into his work that much harder. But I think it was hopeless. Face it, he was silly over her, he couldn't help himself. He worshipped the ground she walked on.

In early September, Jeanette and Nelson were told they'd be co-starring in *Bittersweet*. Nelson didn't argue. Woody Van Dyke was to direct, and the film would be in Technicolor.

Nine months of married life had changed Nelson. He socialized less; his eyes were sadder. Though polite and considerate to his wife in public, in private they rarely did anything but fight. Ann insisted on calling him "Nelsie," a name he *despised*. They had separate bedrooms and according to Nelson, little or no sex life. This infuriated Ann, who continually tried to find out if her husband was unfaithful to her. She accused him, rightly, of being in love with Jeanette. "If *she* were here, you'd be all over her," she said once, to which Nelson replied, "You're right, and I wouldn't even wait to get her into the bed."

Despite some pre-production work, the filming of *Bittersweet* never got off the ground. There were numerous script problems because the original Noel

Coward play was nearly identical to the plot of *Maytime*. The story opens with a prologue: Jeanette's character, Sarah Millick, is an old lady, retelling her sad story to a young singer, in hopes of preventing the girl from making a mistake in choosing a career over love. Then a flashback tells the story of Sarah's ill-fated romance with her voice teacher, Carl Linden.

Bittersweet was finally scrapped, and the studio looked around for another vehicle, finally settling on *New Moon*. But Nelson, agonized at being around Jeanette again, flatly refused the project. Mayer laid pressure on, to no avail, then decided to try a new tactic, appealing to Ann Eddy to convince Nelson. In the meantime, Woody Van Dyke was busy filming *Another Thin Man*. Van Dyke considered himself a good friend of Nelson and Jeanette; he was one of the few who recognized that their love was more than just a passing physical attraction. Jeanette recalled: "I once asked him [Woody] why he kept helping us, why he cared for us. He did love us so. And he said, 'I have a feeling I'm watching the story of *Tristan and Isolde*. I don't want to get to the last act and find that I turned out be one of the villains.' That was one of his corny lines, but he really meant it."

Woody made the time to sit Nelson down for a heart-to-heart talk. Nelson was not unappreciative. "That man's honesty is a rare virtue," he said of Woody. "The thing that impressed me from the time I first him was his absolute frankness." Nevertheless, he told Woody he couldn't work with Jeanette.

Woody next asked Clark Gable to speak with him. Gable obliged him by going to see Nelson at Isabel's beach house in Santa Monica, which Nelson had purchased: 17720 Porto Marina Way, across the street from the infamous cafe where actress Thelma Todd was murdered. The house was small by movie star standards, but a staircase behind it led right down to the beach. Isabel lived there after the sale of 805 Alpine Drive. Nelson was there frequently, happy to get away from his wife. Isabel reported that her son favored taking long, solitary walks on the beach.

Nelson was annoyed when he learned the reason for Gable's visit. While the two men were speaking, a knock at the door announced the unexpected arrival of Ann Eddy. "Do forgive me," she said, "but I've come to see my husband."

"What are you doing here?" Nelson asked. "How did you find me?"

"Of course you're going to ask me to sit down," Ann said pointedly to Isabel, who went into the kitchen to make some coffee. When she returned with the coffee, Ann refused it. "I'll come to the reason for my visit without delay," she said. "Of course, if *you* don't care if your friends know about your business, *I* certainly don't."

Gable got up to leave, but Nelson pushed him back down. "All right, cut the preliminaries. What's on that mind of yours, and what's it going to cost me?" Ann launched into a tirade about how Mayer had called her regarding *New Moon*. "*I'm* your wife now and just because that egomaniac threatens me if you don't do that asinine picture, doesn't mean I'm going to listen to him. I'm your boss now, and I'm not going to let you work with *that woman*." Nelson angrily grabbed her. "Get this straight and never forget it! Keep your nose out of my business!

Nobody tells me what to do! I wasn't going to do the film, but now you've talked me into it. That should make you happy." He shoved her out the front door. "Don't ever come to my mother's house again!"

New Moon began production on Monday, November 6, 1939. Woody Van Dyke was director, Robert Z. Leonard produced. On the first day of production, Leonard sent his two stars an enormous bouquet, with the following message: "May your *New Moon* be a full one."

Everyone was, of course, extremely curious to see how the two stars would interact. "I am keeping my fingers crossed because I know him too well," wrote Isabel Eddy. "He doesn't forget anything that ever touches his heart deeply—and Jeanette gave him the greatest happiness he has ever known. I am afraid for him."

Once Nelson had agreed to work with Jeanette, the roles suddenly reversed. He seemed eager to plunge back into a relationship with her. He had flowers sent daily to her dressing room. "I guess she is just a sort of religion with me," he admitted. "I don't care what the world is going to think."

Jeanette, once insistent on rekindling their friendship, now found herself torn. She remained coolly professional toward him—nor would she socialize with him off the set. Nelson ignored her attitude, saying, "I don't give a damn; I'm determined to break down that wall of icy pride." When she was about to film the "One Kiss" number, he sent her the following note:

> Sing even if you don't mean it—sing it just for me.
> You can take all the time you want, but you are coming back to me, you have to. Meanwhile, remember this, my love for you is indestructible. No matter what happens, nothing and no one in all the universe can change or hurt it. Remember that.

Jeanette's response to this was to demonstrate even more restraint. She had changed in the years since Nelson entered her life. Carefree and promiscuous when she met him, she'd swung to the other extreme, where no other man interested her. Then, when he married, she desperately tried to put him out of her thoughts, to turn herself off emotionally. She was prepared to remain that way for the rest of her life, if necessary. But she told her sister Blossom, "Not a day goes by that I don't think of him, and a sick longing grips me." She didn't allow herself to be alone with him outside of work, but once, he pulled her aside and humbled himself, asking her forgiveness for marrying Ann. "I have forgiven you, Nelson," she replied, "but I'm afraid I have not forgotten. I can't give you my heart as it once was."

Several days into the filming, Woody approached Nelson, concerned that his on-screen chemistry with Jeanette seemed "lacking in warmth." Nelson told the director: "One does not hurt a woman as deeply as I have hurt Jeanette, then expect her to forgive him—even for the sake of a picture." He did agree to speak with Jeanette about it. To his amazement, she finally admitted to him, "I still love you, you know that. I always will. I tried so hard to kill it but nothing could make

One of the few candid shots of Nelson and Jeanette together during the filming of *Bittersweet*.

it die." On one other occasion she revealed her suffering to him: In the midst of studying their lines, she suddenly burst into tears and blurted out, "Oh, Nelson, it hurts so, this love of mine. Can't you take the hurt away?" His reply: "Darling, until you stop fighting it so, it will always hurt."

The strain of Jeanette's emotional turmoil was apparent onscreen. In certain shots, even careful lighting was unable to hide a tired and stressed appearance about her eyes. She'd visibly aged and her features looked more mature. Her performance seemed slightly self-conscious. Offscreen, her self-esteem was at an all-time low. Nelson, on the other hand, thrived on working with her. He noticeably gained weight during the filming, and his acting was assured and aggressive. "Even if things weren't the way they had been, she was still around," he commented. "I got to see her. That was some sort of comfort. Still, I didn't kid myself, my feelings for her had never changed. I got to where I could almost read her thoughts. I knew exactly what she was thinking. Even if she wasn't near me, I knew instinctively where she was and what was in her mind. It was uncanny. That was the first time I noticed I could do that. Sometimes she'd look up at me, startled, as if she knew too."

One day on the set, he got into an argument with Jeanette, and she stormed out in a huff. On the way home another vehicle side-swiped her; she was shook up but unharmed. Nelson was still at the studio rehearsing when someone came onto the sound stage and reported that the news had been phoned in about

Jeanette's car accident. "Nelson just threw the music in all directions and tore out of there like a bullet out of a gun," said an eyewitness. When he finally learned she was all right, Nelson told Isabel, "That taught me a lesson, never leave quarrels in mid-air."

New Moon was fraught with problems. Nelson nicknamed it *Son of Naughty Marietta* because the plot was so similar to their first hit. The script had constant rewrites, and the film was shot "ass-backwards," according to Nelson. Herbert Stothart, the musical director, also found his work cut out for him on *New Moon*. Music rehearsals and recording sessions were lengthy on a Mac-Eddy film, sometimes running as much as eighteen hours without a break, but his two glamorous movie stars were a sight in these rehearsals; Jeanette was often decked out in an oversized sweatshirt and skirt, while Nelson sported a flannel shirt and jeans. Many nights Stothart and his crew came home from the studio at two in the morning, or even later.

Jeanette finally had trouble keeping up with the rest of the group. She fatigued easily, causing delays. She had trouble remembering lyrics, and blew many takes. In other takes, her voice seemed weak. Nelson noted that she seemed "more fragile than usual, and more lovely." On more than one occasion he "bodily pushed her into a chair to prevent her from keeling over with exhaustion and nerves." Nelson hauled out the old wicker chair and forced her to rest in it whenever possible. She refused to leave rehearsals when he was singing solo, but quietly listened, or grabbed a quick nap.

Poppy Delvando was Jeanette's vocal stand-in; she'd cover for Jeanette in music rehearsals. "Jeanette had a voice that tired easily," recalled Poppy. "It was not a strong voice. Jeanette was a nice person, sweet but reserved. She was an introvert, didn't like people. She rehearsed alone and recorded in the booth. Nelson was charming, eager and anxious to please. He would socialize and make friends with everybody on the set. Not Jeanette; she would be by herself or in the dressing room. She was aloof, and they rarely spoke to each other [at that time]."

Stothart pre-recorded some of Jeanette's numbers, then decided it might be easier on Jeanette to record the songs while filming, a practice rarely done anymore at that time. This was later attempted, but was not very successful. In the end, some of her numbers were recorded and dubbed in after they were filmed.

In the original cast list, Dick Purcell had third billing (after Nelson), and Buster Keaton had fifth billing. Woody had handpicked Keaton, who was considered washed up in Hollywood. But Woody, known for his compassion for film pioneers, gave him a break. Keaton played one of Nelson's stout-hearted men, and there were many candid photos of the comedian snapped on the set. Van Dyke also gave Maurice Costello, another silent film star, a role in *New Moon*.

Along with production problems, Woody had his attention on other matters. An extremely patriotic major in the Marines reserve, he'd long been concerned about the war in Europe and his country's apparent isolationist attitude toward it. On December 1, 1939, the press announced that Woody Van Dyke had turned

New Moon. Nelson with director Woody Van Dyke. An enlargement of the bust Nelson sculpted here went on display in the Director's Guild.

his studio office into headquarters for a Marines recruiting staff. The following day, December 2, Woody's wife delivered their second son. On the third, the studio decided to take Woody off *New Moon,* and assigned him to *I Take This Woman* with Spencer Tracy and Hedy Lamarr. "Pop" Leonard took over both producing and directing chores on *New Moon.*

Woody's light-handed, intimate direction was lost once Leonard took over the film. Suddenly, the tone of the production was grandiose. One hundred and seventy-five extras were used in the "Stout-Hearted Men" number. During a

Silent star Buster Keaton had a major role in *New Moon,* but all his scenes were scrapped when Robert "Pop" Leonard took over the director's chores.

shot in the early part of the story, which took place in the hold of a ship loaded with livestock, real chaos erupted when one of the goats gave birth to a kid.

During the week of December 4, all the MGM companies started work an hour earlier and stayed an hour later in order to leave Saturday, December 9, free for an important UCLA game. (The *New Moon* crew had a partial day on that Saturday because Arturo Toscanini visited the set and was serenaded by the two stars. The minute the last note was sung, everyone left for the game.) The following day, Leonard flew to Catalina Island to scout a location for the film's second unit. On the twelfth, 225 extras were sent to Catalina.

As the holidays approached, Jeanette busied herself with the various parties, making the rounds with her husband. She also donated a "bought-out" house at the Hollywood Playhouse, for orphans to attend the opening of *Hansel and Gretel*.

Nelson was busy with radio, though the Chase & Sanborn program had been cut to a half-hour slot due to the refusal of its stars to take a substantial salary cut. His social life was nearly nonexistent, though he did attend a party at Woody's (Jeanette wasn't there). According to Van Dyke's wife Ruth, Nelson had too much to drink, hit on Hedy Lamarr and went home with her. Yet if Nelson turned to others for sex, his heart still belonged to Jeanette. "Any truth to the yarn that a top singing actor and his wife may soon talk divorce with their attorneys?" asked the Hollywood *Reporter*.

Jeanette put on a happy face when out on the town with her husband.

Nelson with wife Ann.

"We knew what we wanted, but it seemed impossible," Nelson commented. "Not a word about it passed our lips, but I knew she [Jeanette] was trying to think of a way out, as I was.

"Every time I brought it [divorce] up, Ann came across with the same story, how she'd drag out all the dirt and smear Jeanette's name in court. She had this little black book with everyone's name in it, Louella, Hedda, and the rest. And she'd wave it at me and start rattling off the order in which she would call them. She meant it, too. I could never subject Jeanette to that, never.

"The alternative was only a little less frightening. It wasn't the kind of lifestyle I wanted—for her or for me. Sure, everyone in Hollywood had a few lovers on the side, if you didn't, you were the exception. But that's not how it was with me. This wasn't some hot and heavy fling that would soon burn out, then you move on to the next one. This was something that would last a lifetime. My God, look at all we'd been through till then and we still didn't give up. I tried to convince myself I could just grit my teeth and get along the way things were. I'm not always particularly realistic, though."

One of their co-workers reflected, "It was not unusual for film stars to have a romance while making a picture together. Doing one or more love scenes together did make an effect on you, and sometimes the stars would leave the set after a screen clinch to continue the love scene in their dressing room. In more and more show biz biographies today, you're reading that this was a fairly common occurrence.

"But this was different. They were extremely cautious. They were torn, you could see them hashing it out in their minds, what to do about it. It became almost an obsession. But you had to hand it to them, they fought it with all the strength they had.

"Finally it got around to shooting the 'Wanting You' number. By this time everyone was behind them, hoping they'd find some kind of happiness for themselves. The rehearsals were pretty stiff, and the old man [Mayer] would have been mighty pleased with that nothing of a kiss Nelson woodenly gave her after the song. It was killing them, though. Nelson looked grim and Jeanette close to tears. Their nerves were shot. 'Pop' didn't push it; he knew when the cameras started rolling, they'd give it all they could.

"And he wasn't wrong. They sang their hearts out. You know, I worked on many sets, but very few where the actors could emotionally move the crew the way these two did. It was chilling and exciting. And then came the clinch. I don't think they realized what was going on. Finally Jeanette pushed him away, crying, and ran off. Nelson looked dazed and went after her.

"The next day they walked in together, arm in arm, with smiles you couldn't kill. It was great to see them that way again. A few days later there were rumors that she was filing for divorce again. It fell through, but for awhile they had that naive freshness we remembered from the early days. They were kids again."

18

"I don't care if the whole world sees us"

"I have loved Nelson from the beginning of time—I will love him as long as time endures," declared Jeanette. To which Nelson responded in kind, noting in his diary: "Our love could not be stopped. That was written in the cosmos before the stars were born."

Thus justifying their renewed intimacy, they shared a few happy moments together in late 1939. Jeanette later spoke of two evenings of passion, in which they made love "five or six times a night," and endlessly had to remind each other that this was not a dream. Ecstasy was mingled with bitter tears, while each one took turns berating himself for their present circumstances. Finally they resolved to discard all past recriminations and upsets. "We're together now," Nelson vowed, "and nothing or no one will ever separate us again."

By day, they worked nonstop on *New Moon*, snatching whatever moments together they could. Outside of the studio they kept up appearances with their respective spouses. Divorces were briefly discussed, but both of them realized the futility of pressing for them at this time. For now they had to be content with the knowledge that their love was an unbreakable spiritual bond between them.

Balalaika opened on December 14 at the Music Hall to rave reviews. Nelson plays a Russian prince in the days before the Revolution, who poses as a proletarian in order to woo Ilona Massey. The war breaks them up but years later, after much suffering, they're reunited. In the finale of the picture, Ilona wears Jean-ette's "Czaritza" gown from *Maytime*. It's slightly altered but Nelson claimed it made him "physically ill" to see Ilona wearing it.

Nelson didn't bother to attend the premiere, although co-star Ilona Massey made an appearance. The Hollywood *Reporter* summed up the general critical consensus by terming *Balalaika* a "sensation."

> Chalk up another hit for MGM. *Balalaika* is absolutely the tops of any picture this industry has ever had . . . it has one of the most beautiful productions that has ever been photographed; magnificent direction, an astounding musical score that was excellently sung and played, a cast such as only MGM could gather . . . It creates a new star in Ilona Massey and brings the fans a Nelson Eddy such as they have never had before.
>
> If you have liked Nelson Eddy, you will go into raves because of his performance, his singing, which have been made possible by the best part he has ever had in pictures. It is a he-man role, and how Mr. Eddy gives out with everything it takes. If you have been indifferent to this star on past occasions, you will now rate him as one of your favorites as a result of this picture.
>
> It's a top show and headed for top business. There is one scene, done in the Russian trenches on a Christmas night, with the Austrian army in an adjoining trench serenading the Russians with "Holy Night" and Nelson Eddy returning the compliment, that will be talked about for many years to come.

In its first week of release at one theater, *Balalaika* made $92,000. The second week, earnings jumped to $102,000. (*Gone With the Wind*, released the day after *Balalaika*, grossed only $82,500 its second week.) The opening of Charles Laughton's *Hunchback of Notre Dame* was pushed back a few days to accommodate the Nelson Eddy fans. When *Balalaika* opened in Philadelphia, the critics there termed it a "box office stampede."

Balalaika, released at the end of a stellar year for motion pictures, started off with a bang in its general release. It was slightly overshadowed by the hoopla surrounding the premiere of *Gone With the Wind*—though within a couple of weeks, reports started coming in from around the country that *Balalaika* was "flopping." The reason given was a vicious rumor circulating nationwide that Nelson was blind and had to be led around the sets by other actors. A barrage of letters from concerned and upset fans poured into MGM, which could do little to offset the whispering campaign except to push the current production, *New Moon*, to completion. On November 27, Nelson signed a new contract, his next film to be *I Married An Angel*, with Jeanette.

Nelson and Jeanette spent Christmas apart. Jeanette and her husband were off to the trendy B-Bar-H Ranch in Palm Springs with friends, while Nelson stayed in Los Angeles. On Christmas Eve, he appeared on the Screen Guild Theater radio production of *The Blue Bird*. This radio show was notable for two reasons. It marked Shirley Temple's radio debut in which she and Nelson dueted in "Silent

Nelson with Shirley Temple during her radio debut, December, 1939.

Night." It was also the night that eleven-year-old Shirley was nearly murdered by a crazed fan.

Shirley Temple recalled the event: "Earlier, I had looked out of the dressing rooms at CBS Radio and seen a woman with a very mean look on her face. I told Mother, who called the police and FBI because the woman looked so angry and was shaking her fist at me. A little later, I'm on stage singing 'Someday You'll Find Your Bluebird.' She was about twelve feet away in the front row, and she pulled out a rather big gun and started to point it at me. The police and a lot of people in trench coats and hats on are coming down the aisle. I'm trying to sing. The men came in from the side, picked her up by the elbows and carried her out. I later learned that she wanted to destroy me because her baby had been born dead and she thought I had taken the child's place. The studio had taken one year off my age. The woman with the gun thought I was born in 1929. I was born in 1928."

Jeanette's first national concert tour in 1939 had been so successful she decided to make it a yearly event. The 1940 tour topped her first effort, as noted by a Birmingham reporter:

> It you weren't at the station or at the Tutwiler Hotel last night to see that red-haired girl from Philadelphia via Hollywood, then you must have broken a leg on your way, for everyone else was on hand.
>
> Jeanette MacDonald is learning "what price glory" on her barnstorming tour . . . Despite a police escort worthy of a President, the singing star of cinematic operettas was almost swept off her tiny, size three and a half feet by the autograph-seeking, celebrity-hungry mob.

But she apparently likes it for she held court for two hours with the press, the embryonic press from local and nearby schools and a "reception committee." Only once when a raucous guffaw drowned her attempts to answer questions did she show signs of strain. She posed for innumerable pictures.

Her reviews were almost uniformly raves as, in some cities, she pulled even better crowds than Nelson:

> Musical history was made in Birmingham last night when an audience of 5,200 —the greatest crowd ever to attend a concert here—jammed the Municipal Auditorium to the eaves, standing-room-only signs were hung out for the first time, and music lovers from four states gave tumultuous ovations to Jeanette MacDonald, lovely lyric soprano with the joy of all music in her voice.
>
> One would, indeed, have been immune to beauty, charm and infectious feeling not to have responded to the little singer's radiant smile, engaging courtesy and disarming naivete and appeal. She immediately established that intimate contact between herself and her hearers which made each individual in the audience feel that she was singing directly to him or to her.
>
> But added to her vivid personality is a voice of entrancing loveliness, fresh, free, clear and warm, with unusual volume for a lyric soprano, and a carrying quality that reached to the furthermost corners of the auditorium; a voice that is round and full and rich in the middle and lower registers, and, in the higher vocal altitudes, of penetrating sweetness. Her tonal coloring is exquisite. She has a sense of the humorous and dramatic and sings with a fine musical intelligence. But more important, she sings from the heart and her singing unfailingly reaches the heart.

As his first wedding anniversary approached, Nelson again requested a divorce from his wife. Her refusal bewildered him; he was at a loss to understand why she would want to remain married to a man who didn't love her.

Ann Eddy has always presented something of an enigma. She was born Ann Denitz in 1894, a full seven years older than Nelson. Her father made his money in Texas oil, and Ann, originally of Jewish faith, was raised as a proper young lady, with all the social graces. Later her family had homes in both Denver and Beverly Hills. Her first husband was director Sidney Franklin, from which union a son was produced, Sidney Franklin, Jr. Ann's marriage broke up in 1933, and a divorce was obtained the following year. The reason given was "Incompatibility," but the real story was far more interesting.

The Sidney Franklins had become good friends with actor Conrad Nagel and his wife. The two couples indulged in spouse-swapping, and both ultimately divorced. Sidney Franklin married Nagel's wife, and Ann was to marry Nagel. It didn't work out, though, and Ann spent the next four years alone, raising her son. There is a mention of one serious interim relationship with a man known only as "Mr. Post," and a suggestion that Ann Franklin might even have been briefly married to this mystery man.

Financially, Ann Franklin had few worries. She busied herself with a typical Hollywood ex-wife routine, making the social rounds. She had one close friend, silent star turned opera singer Doris Kenyon. Kenyon sang with Nelson, and it was through her that Ann and Nelson first met. When Ann set her sights on Nelson, as early as 1933, it was Doris Kenyon who plotted and schemed with her how to snare her man.

Her acquaintances described Ann as polite, quiet, mousy and socially correct. Because she was in Nelson's opera crowd, they saw each other frequently. Ann seemed to pop up every once in a while, even visiting the *Rose Marie* crew up at Lake Tahoe. Her interest in Nelson started early on, and she ingratiated herself to Isabel in order to get closer to him. By 1938, Isabel Eddy considered Ann a friend. At the wrap party for *Sweethearts*, Isabel attended with Ann Franklin. Nelson drove them home afterwards, first dropping Isabel off, then driving on to Ann's home. This was a typical "date" for them. Ann presented herself as an extremely sympathetic person, and according to Isabel, "She gave him her sympathy too much, and at that time he desperately needed sympathy. Soon he had told her everything about the relationship with Jeanette, believing she was a sincere person and one he could talk to."

After their marriage, Nelson's opinion of Ann changed drastically. He accused her of tricking him into marriage, and claimed the judge who married them must have been paid off, "because no one could have ethically performed the ceremony seeing the shape I was in." In fact, a relative of the judge made a statement in 1993 asserting that Nelson's case was not an isolated incident. This man admitted that one of his own relatives was married by Judge Orr while drunk, and there were other cases as well, including one that had gotten the judge into legal trouble. He was about to elaborate when his wife quieted him, admonishing, "I think you've said enough." Whatever the case, the fact is that Ann's meek, pleasant demeanor vanished once she had snared her man. Nelson was surprised to see her display, in private, a vicious, vengeful streak, which soon drove him to wonder why she had married him in the first place. His early attempts to end the marriage brought more surprises. It turned out that Ann had had a series of photos taken of her and Nelson in compromising positions, presumably while he was passed out after being drugged. Ann made it clear that she was ready and willing to make use of the photos if Nelson pushed her too far. "I've never seen them but Nelson has, and he says they'll do the trick in spades," Jeanette later told a friend.

The full impact of his predicament hit Nelson hard during his 1940 concert tour, which began on February 3, in Ventura, California. One month later, after a Chicago concert, he collapsed. His Cleveland, Ohio, performance, scheduled for March 5, was canceled. He managed to pull himself together to get through eight more concerts, traveling a grueling route from Flint, Michigan, up to Toronto, back down to Rochester, New York, into North Carolina, Washington, D.C., then back up north to Boston and his hometown, Providence. He had to cancel Baltimore, managed to get through Philadelphia, then bowed out for an

entire week, canceling two other dates. The last week of April he gave four final
concerts, then, according to his mother, suffered "a final crackup." Knowing he
was too ill to take the train back to Los Angeles, he summoned his mother, who
immediately flew to Milwaukee to bring him home. "I went to him as quickly as
possible," Isabel wrote, "and I shall never forget the shock of the condition I
found him in. The doctor told me I must get him back to the coast at once, and
we took a plane for home almost immediately with a nurse in attendance. He was
running a high temperature and was very restless most of the night. How thankful I was as we flew through the dark hours that we were homeward bound, for I
knew it would make him happier to be there. Our own doctor was waiting at the
airport and we headed straight for the hospital. He was there two weeks. His wife
came to see him once and upset him so completely that the doctor would not let
her in again."

According to the press, Nelson was hospitalized for an adenoid operation.
Clearly, he had suffered an emotional breakdown as well. "After the operation he
failed to gain strength and his nervous system was so completely shot to pieces
that he could neither sleep nor eat," Isabel explained. "The doctor was puzzled
for days that he did not react to any kind of treatment. But I knew what was
wrong, his heart was broken so that mentally he cared for nothing."

Taking matters into her own hands, Isabel contacted Jeanette who'd just
returned from her own tour. Her plan was to sneak Jeanette into the hospital to
visit Nelson. Her son was so desperate, she told Jeanette, that "It will be enough
just to hold your hand again." The idea of smuggling Jeanette in was ultimately
dropped for fear of discovery and scandal, but Jeanette told Isabel she was scheduled to guest on the Chase & Sanborn program the following night, May 18.
"Tell him to listen and I'll try to talk to him."

Isabel continued, "I took him home from the hospital the same day as the
broadcast, and it was then I told him firmly that I would not see Ann again nor
would I have her in my house. Just why the newspapers missed so many clues at
this time is a mystery—but they did. Here I would like to say for the record that
my son never did leave me—not one personal item or one sheet of music was
ever moved to the new house. His bedroom and study remained intact, and
though he maintained separate quarters at the Brentwood house for a time for
appearance's sake, he really spent very little time there.

"About an hour after the broadcast she [Jeanette] called and asked if she might
see Nelson, saying, 'Don't tell him, I'll surprise him.' Surprise him she did. I
took her to his room and she went in softly alone. About two hours later I took
some refreshments up to them and found Jeanette sitting on the bed, holding
Nelson's hand, and saying words of encouragement as she urged him to get well
quickly because of the picture [New Moon], which was being held for retakes. She
looked at him with her beautiful smile and then said, 'This time we'll show
Woody what his kids can do for a picture.' And Nelson laughed. I silently
thanked God for a prayer answered. As she left, Nelson drew her down for a
kiss."

★ ★ ★

While Nelson recuperated, Jeanette was back at the studio, filming retakes so that *New Moon* could be released. Nelson finally reported to the studio as well, so pale and drawn that he refused to let photographers shoot him.

During the latter part of May 1940, *I Married An Angel* was announced as their next feature, and they began recording their numbers with music director Herbert Stothart. In mid-June, *Angel* was scrapped due to various problems—mainly with the script—and *Bittersweet* was substituted instead. Woody Van Dyke signed on as director, and they began recording again, this time the tunes from *Bittersweet*.

New Moon was previewed on June 12 and was released to reviews that were generally antagonistic. "Made to order," commented the Hollywood *Reporter*. "It seems just what their public has requested of them, which should leave no doubt of box office success . . . The picture is patterned upon a strictly light operetta formula inasmuch as it deliberately ignores realities. In the music of Sigmund Romberg, they find a score worthy of their voices . . . Like many recent MGM musicals, the overlength show would profit by recutting." The New York *Telegram* added, "Not even Nelson Eddy's robust baritone and Jeanette MacDonald's dulcet soprano can overcome the handicaps of a stilted, ponderous, ofttimes silly narrative." Other reviewers made nasty comments about Nelson's weight gain (he was up to 200 pounds) and Jeanette's "coyness." Bosley Crowther of the New York *Times* was snide but prophetically accurate: "With tears welling in our eyes (sniff, sniff) we rather sadly suspect that this sort of sugar-coated musical fiction has seen its better days."

Jeanette spent a quiet birthday on June 18. In the evening, she and Gene dined alone at Ciro's, sitting at a small table in the back. On her thirty-seventh birthday, Jeanette wanted only one gift: a divorce. She decided that in all fairness to herself, Gene and Nelson, she must stop living a lie. Nelson's recent breakdown was the catalyst for this decision; she felt that his future sanity and their careers hinged on their personal happiness. She harbored no animosity toward Gene at this time, and she wanted to part friends. Crucial at this time was the fact that Gene's two-year professional blacklist had inexplicitly been lifted. He was given top billing in an RKO film called *Cross Country Romance*. Co-starring Wendy Barrie and Hedda Hopper, the picture was a blatant remake of Frank Capra's *It Happened One Night*, and opened to good notices. "*New Moon* came into the Capitol like an MGM lion, with Nelson Eddy roaring to his lady love, Jeanette MacDonald," noted reviewer Irving Hoffman. "While Nelson was making vocal love to Jeanette for MGM, Jeanette's husband Gene Raymond was wooing Wendy Barrie for RKO at the Palace a few blocks away." Hoffman agreed that *Cross Country Romance* was "a breezy little lark," adding, "The cast was cute, particularly Gene Raymond in a comedy comeback after two years out of pictures." So it seemed that Gene's professional future was more secure, and Jeanette felt that she would not be leaving him worse off than when they first got together. The fact that she approached her lawyer to start divorce proceedings did not escape the press. On June 21, the Hollywood *Reporter* tattled: "A male singer may be named in the suit for divorce soon to be filed in a film couple's bust-up."

Jeanette had not yet notified Louis B. Mayer of her decision—and once again, she didn't have to. The studio head had two new spies working for him, eager to report that the erring singers were "that way" again. The traitors were none other than Ann Eddy and Anna MacDonald. Ann had been harassing Mayer with angry phone calls about her husband's philandering, and when Jeanette at first refused to believe that her mother was working for Mayer, Nelson verified that he had run into Anna as he was summoned to Mayer's office. She was just leaving, and seemed uncomfortable, refusing to meet his gaze. Nelson had barely entered Mayer's office when the verbal accusations began; Mayer rattled off with frightening accuracy times and places Nelson had been with Jeanette. "I don't know where you're staying now," Mayer roared, "but you go home to your loving wife and behave like a husband!"

Jeanette was also summoned for a lecture by Mayer, who made his usual threats about ruining their careers and hurting Nelson. Jeanette sat pale and scared, and Nelson reached over to comfort her. "Get back to your seat and be quick about it," Mayer warned Nelson. "You start getting smart, baritone, and I'll make life tougher for you and *yours* than you ever believed possible." When Nelson was seated again, Mayer continued, "I'll paint you a little picture so there's no mistaking my meaning. The only time I want to see you two together is in front of the camera, no place else. That means no place else. If I do, or hear anything to make me feel you're not obeying me, I'll make you both regret the day you were born. Is that understood?"

They understood.

■■■ During early July 1940, Jeanette and Nelson recorded, and color tests were done, as *Bittersweet* was being filmed in Technicolor. Filming began in mid-July, and director Woody Van Dyke found his two stars in a frankly pitiful state. They were following Mayer's orders, but at great sacrifice. Nelson had lost weight, and he looked miserable and tired. He seemed uncaring that his hairdo in this film was slicked back and unflattering and his on-screen clothes ill-fitting and crumpled. Jeanette wasn't much better, the period wigs and costumes were unflattering and she looked pudgy in them. Her puffiness may have been partially attributable to her heavy reliance on pills to calm her nerves. Additionally, her speech patterns were rapid and jerky; she played a young heroine with almost frantic gaiety.

The film had other problems as well. The studio insisted on chopping out the prologue of the story because it was so similar to *Maytime*. Noel Coward, author of *Bittersweet*, was incensed with the butchered film script, and ultimately "disowned" the film and, as it turned out, Hollywood. Woody's reaction to the various upsets regarding the production was to ignore everyone, race through the filming and slap together the best product possible under the circumstances. The two stars avoided each other as much as possible during the filming; very few candid shots of them together exist off-camera, and even in those a third person usually sits between them. Nelson's face broke out "from nerves." He grumbled, "I get within a mile of her and I've got a hard-on." Finally, one day he burst into her dressing room, slammed her against the wall and informed her, "I can't take it anymore, I'll die if I don't have you." Despite her weak protests that someone would find out, and that she would wrinkle her costume, Nelson wrinkled her costume anyway, and they were back on the set in ten quick minutes.

Nelson ventured into her dressing room only one other time, but any amorous ideas were quickly forgotten. Jeanette was so nervous and high-strung she reached for a bottle of her pills, realized it was empty, and threw it down in disgust. "Damn, I forgot to get this filled," she told him. Nelson later related:

"She told me to get her pocketbook; there was a prescription inside. I didn't know what she was taking; I mean, all those pretty colored pills, I thought they were candy or something, the way she was popping them. So I fish through her purse for the prescription, and then she tells me to take out $200 and asks me if I could fill it for her on the way home? She won't have any time. I totally hit the roof. 'Two hundred dollars for that garbage?' I yell at her. She looks at me, wide-eyed. 'But Nelson, I'm using my own money, I'm not making you pay for it.' So I start lecturing her about depending on dope like that. Everyone thought it was great in those days; they'd just come out with 'pep pills' and the like, but I never bought all the pretty stories. I figured it could become addicting and besides, it only covers up a deeper problem. I never believed in the junk and I didn't want her using it. So here I am, laying into her pretty hard, and finally she starts crying and I feel like an ogre. 'But Nelson,' she says, 'I'm so nervous and I can't sleep at night. They don't hurt me, honest.' And I realize that Mayer or no Mayer, this craziness has to stop. The pressures are just too much for us."

The decision was made to ignore Mayer's threats, even though it meant having to be extremely careful, and trusting virtually no one. If nothing else, they gained peace of mind and were finally able to relax for the latter part of the filming. The set was even opened to visitors, which included magazine writers, Gene Raymond and the officials of both stars' fan clubs. One Jeanette club visitor wrote:

Our party went direct to Jeanette's portable dressing room, where we were received most cordially by Jeanette . . . . She was waiting then to be called to the set, but she appeared to have nothing on her mind except to make us comfortable. In response to an inquiry about her wedding ring, which we could see was covered in some manner, Jeanette explained to us that her own platinum wedding ring naturally was not the kind of ring worn at the time in which the story of *Bittersweet* took place and, since she was sentimental about removing her wedding ring, Gene, on their recent wedding anniversary, gave her a plain gold band which fit perfectly over her wedding ring, covering it completely; in fact, as she commented with a laugh, it was such a perfect fit that, when she did want to remove it, it took Gene about fifteen minutes to loosen it with a bobby pin.

There were one or two interruptions, one or two persons to confer with Jeanette about something or other and, finally, a call to the set. As we left her dressing room, we immediately came face to face with Nelson Eddy. Again we were warmly greeted and we joined his visitors as spectators for the scene about to be shot. It was a love scene, and very realistically done, too.

Between takes, both Jeanette and Nelson joined us and became a part of our friendly group. On one such occasion, Nelson asked my husband for a coin. Upon receiving it, he looked at it, and without a comment to anyone, called out, "Concentrate now, and tell me the date on this coin." We looked around, not knowing to whom he was addressing his remark. Jeanette, who had been sitting a little distance away, apparently indifferent to what was taking place, looked up, smiled, and called the correct date. Then he asked me for a coin. I handed him a five dollar bill; however, the fact that it was paper made no difference to Jeanette for, as a result of Nelson's "questioning," she read the correct serial number, after which Nelson returned the five dollar bill—not to me, but to my husband. To say that we were amazed at the performance is putting it mildly and both Jeanette and Nelson derived a great deal of enjoyment from our puzzled expressions. They told us, very confidentially, of course, that just a day or two previous to our visit, each one had discovered the other one was psychic. Mr. Van Dyke, the director, who had been sitting on the set while the fun was going on, came out and held up a large book— the script—some little distance form Jeanette, with the remark, "All right, young lady, let's see just how good you are. Tell me your lines for tomorrow." Jeanette laughed heartily and said, "Well, really, I'm not *that* good!"

In mid-August, after four weeks of production on *Bittersweet*, Woody had the picture completely shot except for the finale. As in *Maytime*, Nelson was killed in this story, stabbed in the briefest duel ever in film history—villain George Sanders simply pulled out his sword and stuck it in him. Nelson's role was finished, and production was halted for two weeks for construction of the huge set for the finale number, "Ziguener," to be sung by Jeanette. After shooting the ending, the picture wrapped on September 7. Nelson returned to the studio for one last unofficial task. In celebration of Herbert Stothart's fifty-fifth birthday on September 11, Nelson and Jeanette made a special recorded tribute to their friend. They called many of their MGM friends to the mike to say hello and happy birthday, including Clark Gable and W. C. Fields. Nelson sang "Give me some men who are stout-hearted men—duh duh duh" (crashing discords on the piano accompany him, followed by his laughter), while Jeanette giggled at Nelson's antics, and added a few silly comments of her own. In short, they behaved like a couple of adolescents, pleased with their unique birthday gift.

No new project was planned for them, so they had some time together, out of the limelight. Louis B. Mayer was in New York; Gene was busy filming Alfred Hitchcock's RKO comedy, *Mr. and Mrs. Smith*, with co-stars Carole Lombard and Robert Montgomery; and Ann Eddy, thankfully, seemed to have simmered down, at least for the time being. It was Nelson's latest tactic with his wife to be extra courteous and attentive, to convince her that he was no longer seeing Jeanette. He had hoped that, given time, she would agree to a divorce. In October 1940, he took a short vacation with his wife.

Jeanette, meanwhile, had scheduled a new concert tour from November 1940, through the following February. After Gene finished his film, he came East to be with Jeanette through much of her travels.

Strangely, the gossip columns were quiet at this time regarding the singing sweethearts, their marital squabbles and their future films. One of the likely reasons was that Hollywood had more serious worries, namely the war raging away in Europe. The film industry in particular could no longer adopt an isolationist attitude, as it was fast losing its overseas market; already eleven countries had stopped distributing American pictures. In the United States, public anger and consciousness was being aroused by films such as *The Great Dictator*, *Escape* and *The Mortal Storm*. Woody Van Dyke, in the Marines reserve, was himself called to active duty in October 1940, and MGM and the Screen Directors' Guild threw a huge farewell party for him at the studio. Louis B. Mayer spoke at the event, insisting that all Americans should pray that war shall not come. "But if those who would stamp Democracy from the earth seek to invade our rights to life, liberty and the pursuit of happiness, we shall face them without fear." Jeanette opened the program by singing the national anthem, while Nelson sang the dedication of the Twenty-second Battalion March, composed for Woody's unit by Herbert Stothart.

In early October 1940 *Bittersweet* was previewed in the Los Angeles area; a month later it opened in that city, followed by a Thanksgiving release in New York. The film opened with promise, initially breaking records, then quickly fizzled. "Metro's massive and magnificent remake of Noel Coward's *Bittersweet* was dripping its Technicolor all over the Music Hall to the delight of the Nelson Eddy-Jeanette MacDonald lovers and the polite operetta customers," wrote columnist Irving Hoffman. "The critics, however, were of the opinion that *Bittersweet* was a little too sweet for their taste . . . They thought the picture better suited to Valentine's Day than Thanksgiving and as gushing as a school-girl's poem. But the reviewers still liked the music, particularly 'I'll See You Again' and other Coward numbers." The Nelson fans were furious again that their star had so little screen time, a sentiment echoed by the New York *Post*: "Miss MacDonald is a red-haired, blue-eyed perfect Technicolor subject. Her wardrobe is stunningly picturesque (ladies will adore it), her voice lovely. Mr. Eddy, who gives over the bulk of camera footage and song to his pretty partner, doesn't get much of a break even when he's under lens focus." Bosley Crowther termed *Bittersweet* "Metro's battered screen version, patched together out of Mr. Coward's fragile and tender work. Miss MacDonald and Mr. Eddy play it all with such an embarrassing lack of ease—she with self-conscious high spirits and he with painful pomposity." Nonetheless, the film was nominated for two Academy Awards, Color Cinematography and Color Interior Decoration.

Bittersweet was the first MacDonald-Eddy film to lose money. Had the European market not been cut off, it surely would have turned a profit. But the signs were there, if only slightly. Jeanette and Nelson had hit their peak in films. If they couldn't change with the times, they would soon find themselves outdated.

"I've never yet refused to play a part they've asked me to play, even when it's not much of a part, as in *Bittersweet*," Nelson told a reporter. "I still take on the job. I'd rather work than not, and that's the truth." While the studio was mulling over what to do with them next, Nelson had a meeting with Mayer, in which he attempted to explain that he and Jeanette needed a new kind of picture. "We've grown up a bit," he explained, "and the public wouldn't mind us in a more sophisticated film with a little more story. Really, those same corny scripts, dated material—hell, fifty years ago they were old. I think—"

"You think?" Mayer retorted. "Who gives a damn what you think? I run this show. I know what the public wants. They want you two the same way as your first film together. They want you in that formula, sequel after sequel! That's what made the money, and that's what will continue to make money! So don't tell me how to run my business. What do you know? You're just an actor!"

Mayer wasn't giving in on any fronts.

■ Meanwhile, Jeanette's concert tour, spanning four months, was a phenomenal success. In city after city she was treated like royalty: she sang for the first time in Havana, Cuba; in Georgia, the state legislature passed a special resolution inviting her to visit the House; mayors of Columbus, Ohio and Selma, Alabama, declared her concert days city holidays and merchants closed their shops; in a number of cities she broke tenor John McCormack's twenty-two-year standing records; she also topped the personal appearance attendance of FDR, Wendell Wilkie and Will Rogers; in Stillwater, Kansas, the highways and main thoroughfares became so congested with people traveling to her concert that state troopers were called out; in Columbia, South Carolina, special busses were granted franchises to transport the thousands from outlying towns to the concert; in many areas trailer camps sprang up along her itinerary route to house the crowds swarming in from a radius of two hundred miles; in Peoria, her concert was sold out three months in advance of her appearance—within four hours after the time of her recital date appeared in the local paper; in Providence, Nelson's father Bill Eddy came backstage to see her—they embraced and spent a few private minutes together, to the amazement and curiosity of her fans; in Beaumont, Texas, the reviewer summed up the general consensus of the tour, saying, "Such beauty is in her that she could have just stood there and recited the alphabet."

Nelson spent the last weeks of 1940 in Los Angeles, with his wife. He recorded several selections for Columbia Records, including Christmas songs, arias and

Gilbert & Sullivan selections. On December 22, he co-starred with Ronald Colman in a Gulf Screen Guild version of *The Juggler of Notre Dame*. The half-hour Christmas story was so popular that the same cast would do a repeat broadcast the following year. On Christmas Day, Nelson sang on a benefit program called "Good Cheer to Britain." On New Year's Eve, he was at Ciro's with Ann.

Jeanette was home only briefly for the holidays, returning to her normal social schedule, looking happily married as usual. (During her concert tour, she even sang a composition written for her by Gene titled "Let Me Always Sing." Whenever he was in the audience and she sang this number, she motioned to him to take a bow.) A fan visiting her home wrote: "The music room is actually a guest house about a hundred yards from the main dwelling. There they have two pianos. Gene has two Irish setters and Jeanette has a Bedlington and a Skye terrier, both of rare pedigree. Their favorite manner of entertaining is the informal Sunday morning breakfast party, at which Jeanette excels as hostess and chef. She bakes the waffles personally, from her own recipe, on the latest in modern electric equipment. Breakfast is served on the terrace, overlooking the gardens. Outside of family, her small circle of friends include Irene Dunne and hubby, the Johnny Mack Browns, Fay Wray, Lily Pons and the Nelson Eddys, who are entertained often in their home." The only hint that all wasn't domestic bliss during this time was a magazine blurb that reported that Jeanette and Gene had gone to spend a weekend in the mountains with friends; Jeanette returned home —alone—the first night, in a huff.

In January 1941, Nelson began his own yearly concert tour, the highlight of which was his singing at FDR's Inaugural Ball on January 19. Ann accompanied Nelson on the tour, yet even with his wife present he was asked repeatedly about Jeanette. "Our relations are exceedingly friendly," he told a Mobile reporter. "Of course, we get angry every now and then like anybody does. Maybe we are a couple of dopes. Maybe Jeanette and I should get mad at each other off the set in order to get page one space in every newspaper." A Beaumont reporter noted, "He speaks with great fondness of Jeanette MacDonald."

In Newark, New Jersey, Nelson was taking a bow when a girl climbed on stage and moved forward toward him, staring fixedly at him. Nelson slowly backed off stage, frightened. The girl was taken to the police where she said she'd heard Nelson was going blind, and she merely wished to pin a religious medal on him. She showed the medal to the police, who held her for mental observation. Nelson was extremely shaken, but after a few minutes in the wings continued the concert.

A Cincinnati reviewer noted, "Nelson Eddy evidently finds himself torn between the antagonistic desires of preserving his integrity as an artist and of maintaining his position as the idol of an adoring public." The Chicago writer added, "Mr. Eddy is as handsome as ever, and his voice still has that smooth, maple cream quality, but both his singing and his acting (there is always a lot of acting at an Eddy recital) are more restrained than in the great days of the late 1930s."

★ ★ ★

███ MGM had finally decided on the pair's next films. The team was to be split: Jeanette would make a remake of *Smilin' Through* with James Stewart and Robert Taylor, while Nelson handpicked Met opera star Risë Stevens for *The Chocolate Soldier*.

Jeanette completed her concert tour in late February and returned home to start her picture in mid-March. Her plans were changed when Jimmy Stewart joined the army—"I had looked forward to working with him," she said—and a new co-star was needed. In early April Brian Aherne was signed to replace Stewart. (Aherne was married to Joan Fontaine, who'd just scored big in *Rebecca* and the following year won the Best Actress Oscar for *Suspicion*.) Then Robert Taylor bowed out also, having been promised a two-month vacation with his wife Barbara Stanwyck. *Smilin' Through* finally began production the beginning of May, minus the second lead actor. After a week of filming, Gene Raymond took over the role. He received third billing under Jeanette and Brian Aherne, a curious fact since Jeanette could have easily insisted otherwise.

Smilin' Through seemed a perfect choice for Jeanette, with Technicolor and the opportunity to play dual roles. A famous stage play, the story had been filmed both as a silent, with Norma Talmadge, and a sound film, with Norma Shearer. Nine songs were added for Jeanette, and the studio spared no expense on the lavish production. Jeanette's wedding gown in the picture was made from the last seventy-five yards of a priceless French lace of crown pattern dating before the French Revolution. Designer Adrian had brought it back from Paris years earlier

Smilin' Through (1941): Gene and Jeanette did not click with movie audiences or critics as a romantic duo.

while he was buying material for gowns used in *Marie Antoinette*. The film took place in England, and despite wartime conditions, six hundred shrubs were imported to create a set of an English garden and flowing brook. Additionally, three huge willow trees were used, some 1,450 feet of grass were woven into the floor, and the "brook" required 2,000 gallons of water a day. Many of the props, including furniture, clocks and tapestries, were expensive antiques.

The sentimental story of *Smilin' Through* takes place in England during World War I. Jeanette, as Kathleen, falls in love with Kenneth Wayne (Gene Raymond) but is forbidden to marry by her guardian, Sir John Carteret (Brian Aherne). Carteret explains in flashback that years ago he was to marry his beloved Moonyean (Jeanette again, in a black wig), but her jealous former suitor Jeremy Wayne (Kenneth's father, played also by Gene Raymond) shot and killed Moonyean during the wedding. In the end, Carteret puts aside his hatred, agrees to Kathleen marrying, dies and is reunited with Moonyean.

The only problem with *Smilin' Through* was the unfortunate lack of chemistry between Jeanette and her two co-stars. During a love scene with Jeanette and Gene, director Frank Borzage impatiently told Gene: "Don't kiss her as though you are already married, kiss her as though you're in love!"

Nelson visits Jeanette on the set of *Smilin' Through*. In spite of Mayer's wishes, they threw all caution to the wind.

Nelson returned from his spring tour. His film, *The Chocolate Soldier*, didn't start production until early June, so he busied himself visiting Jeanette on her set. Several candid shots were taken of them together; in one, his arms are around her and he grins at her with that special look of lust and adoration reserved solely for her. Even more unusual, he borrowed an extra's costume and sneaked onto the set with the countless other extras, watching Jeanette film two songs. He loved her as Moonyean; for her birthday he gave her a large cameo pin that had belonged to his great-grandmother, to which he'd added a circle of diamonds. Jeanette wore the cameo on her wedding dress, in the scene in which she is murdered by Gene Raymond's character.

In the final cut of *Smilin' Through* one can catch a quick glimpse of Nelson, standing way in the back of group of soldiers while Jeanette sings. He's badly out of focus but there's no mistaking his towering height and that head of hair.

Mezzo-soprano Risë Stevens explained how she came to co-star with Nelson in *The Chocolate Soldier*.

> We had the same concert manager, Arthur Judson. The reason I got *Chocolate Soldier* was because of a photograph. It showed me on a ship going to South America with Bidu Sayao, who was a singer at the Met for many years. The two of us were together in the photo.
>
> Now, Jeanette had decided she did not want to make *Chocolate Soldier* or, I don't know, there was a split between her and Nelson. They were looking for someone else to co-star. I did question it at the time, that's how I found out there was something wrong. He wanted very much to make the film with her. The same thing happened with *Balalaika*, if you recall. That was Ilona Massey.
>
> Then Nelson spied this photo and said, "That's the girl I'd like to have try out for the film." I was in San Francisco singing *Der Rosenkavalier* and Louis B. Mayer came back afterwards, and asked me to come for a screen test.
>
> I heard [they had a romance] and when I met Jeanette, there was a slight friction there, like "hands off, he's mine." I was unaware of what it was at the time, just that she was nervous about Nelson working with me.
>
> My feeling was that he [Nelson] was extremely happy at that studio, and the only problem he had at that time was with Jeanette. He would never speak about her when we were there, or only fleetingly. I always wondered what was going on; I sensed there was something. But he wouldn't talk about it.

Both *Smilin' Through* and *The Chocolate Soldier* shared the same producer, Victor Saville, but *Chocolate Soldier*'s director was Roy Del Ruth, whom Risë Stevens rated as "so-so." She didn't feel he was very effective, and that Nelson, who played a dual role, had to work out his direction for himself. Stevens also did not consider Nelson a good actor, but his voice was another story. Her comment notwithstanding, many critics felt that Nelson had delivered his best acting performance in *The Chocolate Soldier*, portraying a whining, nail-biting jealous husband who tempts his wife's faithfulness by disguising himself as a hot-blooded Russian on the make.

Stevens recalls:

> Nelson was an exceptional man. He was a big man, very tall, very impressive looking. I really thought he could have made a fantastic opera career. When I heard him [sing], even then, I said to him, "What a damned shame, what a loss to the opera world." In a way I don't blame him, you get much better known in films, and there's more money—but he could have, because there was a magnificent organ.
>
> He was a jokester. I don't recall what he did exactly, but he was. Most people don't know that; he had a reputation for being stodgy. In life he was just the opposite. He was a fun person to be around; he liked to play tricks on people, but never when you were shooting. That I recall. He was a real disciplinarian while you were shooting.
>
> He was a very even-tempered person, I thought. Even in the film I was surprised that he kept such an even keel all the time.
>
> He was friends with Clark Gable. He asked me to lunch one afternoon and took me to the commissary. There was Gable and Judy Garland, and he took me over to Gable to introduce me to him. That was the first time I met Gable. At MGM, they were all like brothers and sisters, everyone ate at the commissary.

Irving Jones was Nelson's dance double in the film, and he recalled Nelson's sense of humor. "Nelson and Rise were sitting at a table decorated with a bowl of grapes. Eddy was to lean over and kiss Rise. A moment before the 'role 'em' cue Nelson—the practical joker—surreptitiously slipped a grape in his mouth . . . and proceeded with the kiss." Jones doubled for Nelson in the scene in a cafe where Nelson—disguised as a Russian—dances on top of a table. "An oddity was that Mr. Eddy stood some 6'2" with the build of a football player and I was 5'10" with the average build of a person of my one hundred sixty-five pounds. Needless to say, the makeup department had quite a time padding my shoulders, fitting boots with 4" lifts, then encasing my entire body in a heavy Cossack coat. Then I, as Nelson's character, danced as him on the table top. In the final cutting the whole scene lasted a mere five to ten seconds. And in the final moment of the dance instead of jumping off the table, I fell flat on my seat."

The production values of *The Chocolate Soldier* were far inferior to those of *Smilin' Through*; the studio had purchased rights to the operetta *The Chocolate Soldier* by Oscar Straus, but couldn't obtain rights to the story, so the two stars portrayed singers in that operetta (thus justifying the songs) and for a plot, director Del Ruth shot a scene-by-scene remake of the famous Lunt-Fontanne 1931 film, *The Guardsman*, filmed in black-and-white, utilizing standard sets, with a small cast. Had Nelson cared, he might have complained to Mayer that he deserved star treatment like Jeanette. But he didn't care, nor did Mayer feel Nelson was worth backing up with a "Class A production."

Jeanette surprised Nelson on his birthday with a party on his set. Candid photos show them radiantly happy, but Jeanette had an ulterior motive as well for visiting his set—namely to keep an eye on her man. Rumors persisted that Nelson and Risë were having an affair, which Risë denied.

> We were just wonderful friends. I was married then, just off my honeymoon, and I wasn't ready to have an affair with anyone except my husband!
>
> As a matter of fact, Nelson had a dog which we called "Lambie," that I fell in love with. He had invited us for dinner. His home had nothing but white rugs; it was newly built for Ann and him. And all of a sudden this cute little poodle comes running up and he was so darling, I fell in love with that poodle. Ann started complaining, she didn't want the poodle because of all the white rugs; it was staining all the rugs, and she was furious, just furious. I said, "Fine, I'll take it!" And with that, Nelson handed me the poodle and I went home with the first dog that I ever had!

Despite Risë Stevens' disclaimer, correspondence between Isabel Eddy and her friend Sarah Tucker mention a fight between Jeanette and Nelson concerning Risë Stevens. Sketchily described in the correspondence was Jeanette's extreme jealousy over some mysterious letters from Risë, and the fact that Risë had once come to his dressing room. Jeanette asked Nelson, "How would you feel if I let other men come to my dressing room?" He replied, "I'd kill them and you too." Nelson denied everything—"Nothing happened, but it wasn't her fault that it didn't"—but Jeanette refused to believe him, citing his past affairs. In the end he managed to convince her of his innocence. The clincher was his forcing her to sing "My Hero" for him, his duet in *The Chocolate Soldier* with Risë Stevens. Nelson told Jeanette that anytime he had to sing that song in the future, it was Jeanette he would see and remember; it was now "their" song. He added, "From now on if anyone sings songs to me, you have to sing them too." This apparently appeased Jeanette's hurt feelings and all was forgiven. This is yet another example that their on-screen image as romantics who made love through their songs was paralleled by their lives off-screen. There are several mentions in Isabel's correspondence of fights or arguments being settled by one or the other singing a special song, or making a home recording, as a way of making up.

Jeanette was increasingly depressed as her film neared completion the first week of July 1941. She feared *Smilin' Through* would cement her happy marriage in the public eye, thus making divorce an impossibility at any time in the near future. It had been easier to carry on with her career and life when she and Nelson were avoiding each other, but now, when they wanted to be together and rarely could be, it was nearly impossible to tolerate. One evening after the day's shooting was completed, a weary Jeanette waited impatiently for Gene so they could go home. Gene finally rushed up to her, excitedly waving a note, and informed her that something had come up so she should go home alone. Jeanette got into her car, barely nodding at her studio chauffeur, and quickly fell asleep. After a short nap she awoke, looked out the window, and saw that they were out in the country. She rolled back the divider to tell her driver that they were going the wrong way; to her horror, he stopped the car, got out, and headed toward her. Realizing it was not her assigned chauffeur, and fearful she was being kidnapped, she started to run. Then she took another look at her "chauffeur," and recognized him through the disguise. She flung herself into Nelson's waiting arms.

They had a good laugh when Nelson explained that he'd bribed her driver and had found an ingenious way of getting rid of Gene. "I sent him a mash note," Nelson explained. "Right now he's waiting for his boyfriend. I sure hope he doesn't catch cold—the note said to meet him at the end of the Santa Monica pier!"

They made love under a nearby tree despite Jeanette's nervous protest that someone might see them. "I don't care," Nelson told her, "I don't care if the whole world sees us."

On the set of *I Married An Angel*, 1942.

19

Leaving MGM

Jeanette completed *Smilin' Through* in early July 1941, and Nelson wrapped *The Chocolate Soldier* a month later. During August, the studio made the decision to team them again for *I Married An Angel*, a play that had been purchased for Jeanette in 1933, presumably for her first MGM feature. The plot concerned a playboy who dreams he marries an angel from heaven (who loses her wings after they consummate the marriage). Hunt Stromberg produced, Anita Loos wrote the script, and on September 3, the studio announced that George Cukor would direct. But according to Anita Loos, Cukor begged off the project, saying he lacked the skills required by a musical. According to Loos this excuse was nonsense and his way out of getting out of working with Jeanette and Nelson.

Roy Del Ruth was named as replacement director, and *Angel* was officially off the ground the second week of October. But after twenty days of filming, Del Ruth was pulled off the film. He thought the script too provocative. When producer Stromberg argued that it had been cleared by the censors, Del Ruth replied, "They're too liberal." Anita Loos told Stromberg, "Get rid of him." Stromberg warned her that Woody Van Dyke would have to take over, to which Loos retorted, "Anything's better than Del Ruth."

While many of their studio co-workers had nothing but fond memories of working with MacDonald and Eddy, there were others who couldn't tolerate them. Anita Loos was one who hated them (and vehemently denied any romance between them). She felt Nelson's acting was "impossible," and she depended on Jeanette to carry the picture. Jeanette portrayed dual roles, playing a shy secretary whom playboy Nelson finally marries, and the angel in his dream. Her wings weighed forty pounds; she was physically uncomfortable during much of the filming. In addition, they were filming two versions of the film, one for the United States and a slightly different one for English release. Laws in England prohibited an angel being shown on screen, even in a fantasy. "All of Jeanette's scenes have to be done twice," noted *Variety*. "Most of the scenes for the non-angelic treatment are being directed off the cuff, since necessity for changes for the English market were not anticipated. They're taking the wings off her shoulders during the dream sequences, and changing some dialogue." These problems didn't concern Loos, but when she saw Jeanette "simpering," she said she knew the film was doomed. Jeanette had a myriad of disagreements with Loos over the script. In a subplot that was ultimately axed, Jeanette wore an apron and baked sugar cakes. Her protest: "My fans wouldn't like me to be banal." A scene which remained in had Jeanette playing a seductress, but it was filmed over her protest that her fans "would disapprove if I were tawdry."

Even in the music department there were problems. Rodgers and Hart, who wrote the original score, were "unavailable" to help on the film. Bob Wright and Chet Forrest, called upon to rewrite many of the songs' lyrics, had so many disagreements with the film that they finally left MGM. Producer Hunt Stromberg also had a falling out and left the studio following the picture's completion.

"In our films together, [we] always depicted pure love and we had a lot of trouble with this script because religious groups disapproved of an angel going to bed with a man," Nelson stated. "Everyone on the lot told us it was either going to be the best picture we ever did, or the worst. It was the worst. It took the studio years to figure out how to present it without offending anybody and then they slashed it to pieces. When we finally finished it, it was a horrible mess."

Nelson and Jeanette felt they had increasingly fewer people looking out for their interests at MGM. Early into the filming, Jeanette alienated Mayer by refusing his advances. Since *Naughty Marietta*, he'd made only one other attempt, chasing her around his office during the filming of *Sweethearts*. Jeanette had complained about this to Miliza Korjus, but warned Miliza not to mention anything to Nelson about it, because "Nelson will kill him."

Now, during the filming of *Angel*, Jeanette came back from Mayer's office looking distressed, but told Nelson it was nothing. Not believing her, he interrogated her as to what Mayer had said or done to upset her. Finally figuring it out for himself, he stormed over to Mayer's office, grabbed him by the neck and started choking him. Then he dragged him over to the window and threatened to throw him out. He was in such a blind rage that he didn't notice when Frank Morgan came into the office and tried to intervene. Only after he'd knocked the

Years of animosity between Nelson and his boss, Louis B. Mayer, fianlly came to a head during the filming of *I Married An Angel*.

elderly Morgan to the floor did Nelson realize what he was doing. He let go of Mayer, helped Morgan to his feet and walked out.

Smilin' Through was released in October 1941, to generally poor reviews. Critics were unimpressed with the unabashed tearjerker, although no one could fault Jeanette's singing.

The Chocolate Soldier, released in November, fared better with critics. The film was nominated for three Academy Awards, including Best Black-and-White Cinematography, Best Sound Recording and Best Score. "Both Eddy and Miss Stevens are in fine fettle," noted *Variety*. "Eddy does a remarkable impersonation as the Russian singer, perhaps his finest endeavor as an actor. The characterization is alive with humor." Columnist Jimmy Fidler added, "A great singer proves he's become a fine actor." Hollywood *Reporter*. "Eddy surpasses anything he has done previously. As the prima donna wife, Miss Stevens makes a noteworthy debut. She shows bright promise, and is attractive in face and figure, and her rich mezzo-soprano is magnificent." Risë Stevens left Hollywood after her first film. In 1944 she co-starred with Bing Crosby in the Oscar-winning *Going My Way*, then she returned to the Metropolitan Opera.

★   ★   ★

With all the craziness surrounding the filming of *I Married An Angel*, the two stars were grateful to have Woody Van Dyke take over the directing chores. But even he seemed on edge and disinterested in the film.

Major W. S. Van Dyke had quietly returned to MGM in June 1941, honorably discharged from the Marines. He'd collapsed from heart trouble, but the reason for his "retirement" was an ominous throat problem that was eventually diagnosed as cancer. "I've had a cough for twenty-five years, and will probably have it for another twenty-five years," he publicly joked, adding, "The medical examiners didn't like it." In private, though, Woody was crushed by his diagnosis. He wanted nothing more than to be able to fight for his country and democracy. Instead he spent the next months directing films like *The Feminine Touch* (with Rosalind Russell and Don Ameche), *Shadow of the Thin Man* (William Powell and Myrna Loy) and *Dr. Kildare's Victory* (Lew Ayres, Lionel Barrymore and Jeanette's sister Blossom). He refused medical treatment due to his Christian Science beliefs, certain he would recover. In fact, he lived an active life for nearly two more years, working almost up to the end.

Mayer was frantic over Woody's refusal of medical aid. He and Eddie Mannix tried to convince Woody to go the medical route, to no avail. In desperation, Mayer finally summoned Nelson and Jeanette to his office, appealing to them to talk some sense into their friend. Nelson ultimately had a talk with the director, but came away from it convinced that no one had the right to interfere with Woody's decision. Instead, he and Jeanette offered their love and support, and a vow of silence, since Woody wanted his condition kept a secret.

It's no wonder that most of the principals involved in making *I Married An Angel* simply gave up on the film, considering it a lost cause. Still, there were lighthearted moments on the set. Sharp-eyed viewers will note in an early shot, when Nelson hurries into the bank, he walks by two busts which he had sculpted, one of his grandfather, one of his great-grandfather. And in an early sequence in the story, a shy, anxious Jeanette has to brave kissing playboy Nelson at his birthday party. She stands next to him, leans forward tentatively, but she can't do it. She tries again, and as she moves forward, Nelson crosses his eyes at her. Her eyes cross in response and she bursts out laughing, completely breaking character. Woody left this shot in the picture.

Harry Crocker, a columnist for the Los Angeles *Examiner*, visited the *Angel* set. "Nelson Eddy raised havoc with my nerves," he wrote. "While chatting with Jeanette MacDonald I noticed sculptor Nelson toiling across the stage with a huge stone bust. 'One of his own works,' I thought idly as I watched him. As he neared me he tripped and the heavy bust hurtled at my feet. I went right straight up in the air, while Jeanette and Nelson roared as the prop bust BOUNCED!"

One of the hairdressers on the film was newly employed, joining MGM as a novice just days before a job freeze due to war being declared. On her first day, she walked onto the set to find herself amidst hundreds of extras rehearsing a production number. She looked all around for the two stars and finally spotted them off in a corner. Jeanette sat with her feet in Nelson's lap. He was rubbing them and they were giggling. She was waving a script at Nelson and trying to get him to study their lines. "Nelson, this is serious," she scolded. Nelson tickled her feet and replied, "*This* is serious." They were in their own little world. The hairdresser was amazed. "I thought they hated each other!" she said to the person escorting her around the set. She was told, "If you want to work for Van Dyke, you'll never let on otherwise."

On December 7, 1941, war was declared and the next day, Monday, all the film studios were in an uproar. Most male stars were ready to run off and join the Army, Navy or Air Force. By Thursday, December 11, Jeanette, Clark Gable and other stars had formed the Hollywood Victory Committee, gearing up to perform for the soldiers. In the coming weeks, Louis B. Mayer made his personal sacrifice to the war effort, losing stars like Clark Gable and James Stewart to the Air Force, while many other actors and actresses left for USO Camp Show tours, both at home and overseas.

One morning, Nelson asked Woody if he and Jeanette could take the afternoon off, as they weren't needed in the upcoming shots. Woody agreed. Nelson went to the commissary, put together a picnic lunch, got a thermos of coffee, then took Jeanette for a drive, telling her he had to talk to her about something. They drove out of the city; Nelson looked miserable and didn't say anything. Finally he parked and Jeanette said, "All right, Nelse, get it over with. What have you gotten yourself into now?"

Nelson blurted out, "Have you heard the rumor that Ann is going to have a baby?"

Her reaction was worse than he'd feared. She fell over in a faint. "When I came to, he had the car robe around me and his sweater around my feet, and was making me drink hot coffee from the thermos jar," Jeanette later recalled. "Then I had a little case of hysterics and as soon as I was quieter he took me in his arms and I just forgot everything except how strong and tender he was and how terribly I loved him. I didn't even care if Ann was having ten babies as long as he kept holding me in his arms like that and saying 'Darling! Darling!'"

Nelson finally explained to Jeanette that Ann was asserting she was pregnant (at age forty-seven), he didn't know for sure whether she was or not, and that if indeed she was, he wasn't the father. He wasn't looking forward to having to raise another child that was not his; he'd had enough problems with her son from her first marriage, Sidney Franklin, Jr.

Nelson had never adopted his stepson, and their relationship was never as close as Sid, Jr., maintained in public statements. Sid, Jr., had been put in boarding school after the elopement. Their first Christmas as a family Nelson had taken Sid out and bought him lots of gifts. Afterwards Ann got angry at Nelson, and when Sid sided with his mother, that was it for Nelson. He never tried to win the boy's affection, nor did he consider adopting him. In August 1940, Sid angered his stepfather further by crashing Nelson's car at the corner of Carmelita and Maple drives. Nelson, Ann and Sid were sued by actress Helen Lynd Melnick, who claimed the accident was negligence on Sid's part. The jury denied damages but the plaintiff appealed the case, which dragged on in court until 1941 when it was finally settled out of court. Nelson was bitter about having to pay; for years to come he complained about the accident and the ensuing lawsuit with all its negative publicity.

Jeanette was still so unnerved by Ann's announcement that Nelson drove her to Blossom's, insisting that she spend the night with her sister. The next day Blossom reported that Jeanette was terribly nervous and cried a lot, and kept saying she didn't want to wait to have Nelson's baby until it was too late. Nelson, meanwhile, went home and tried to reason with Ann; after a nasty argument he spent the night with his mother. Still anguished over Jeanette's collapse, Nelson berated himself. "Oh, God, never again do I want to see the light go out of her eyes," he told Isabel. "It almost killed me. There never will be time enough for me to make up for all the hurt I've caused her."

Ann's pregnancy, predictably, turned out to be a false alarm. Nelson demonstrated his relief and love for Jeanette by showering her with early Christmas gifts, mostly jewelry. Isabel estimated that by this time, her son had spent over $1,000,000 on jewelry for Jeanette—his way of contributing to her financial support. And Jeanette's Christmas gift to him was an English riding saddle, which he discovered hidden in a closet at the Mariposa house. Over the years, Jeanette gave Nelson a variety of gifts. His favorite was a trick gold cigarette lighter that shot a stream of water. Nelson was reportedly so delighted with it that he went immediately to Mayer's office and offered him a light.

I Married An Angel was completed Christmas week, but not without on last major upset. Louis B. Mayer had prided himself that Jeanette and Nelson were following his orders, that they were "good boys and girls," and that Nelson was "staying out of her pants." Then he learned otherwise from his spies, and made an unannounced visit to the set to see for himself if they were disobeying him. He found the two culprits sitting together, radiant in their happiness. In front of the crew, Mayer called Jeanette a whore. Nelson leaped at him and had to be restrained from hitting Mayer. Nelson finally walked off the set, telling Jeanette he was through at MGM. After he calmed down, Nelson agreed to finish *Angel* but still insisted that he was leaving the studio. Both he and Jeanette had one film left under their present contract, but Nelson didn't care, and he was ready to buy his freedom. Jeanette finally pacified him, convincing him to think about it while on his concert tour; he could make a final decision when he returned to Los Angeles in May 1942. Nelson agreed, but the damage was done. As early as January 1942, trade blurbs noted that five MGM stars were being dropped, and Nelson's name was noted as one of them. Elsewhere it was rumored that Jeanette was leaving also, even though she was willing to finish the existing contract. Mayer's way of punishing her for her recent transgressions was *not* to team her with Nelson for her next film; instead he put her into a cheap little "programmer" that would show everyone how fast and far she had plunged in the Metro hierarchy.

★ ★ ★

One month after Pearl Harbor, Gene Raymond made the rounds in Washington military circles trying to get into the Air Force. He went to Bolling Air Force Base and was interviewed by a recruiter. Because he already had a pilot's license he was made a first lieutenant, went into training and by June he was off to England. With Gene out of the picture Jeanette naturally had more free time to spend with Nelson, who pushed back his concert tour to February. From January 18 through February 2, Nelson recorded twenty-two songs for Columbia. Recording sessions went from 8:00 P.M. until 1:00 A.M.—very odd hours, but desirable ones for Nelson because he had some time afterwards in the middle of the night to meet with Jeanette without Ann's becoming suspicious.

Nelson drove down to San Diego during the afternoon of February 2 to prepare for his first concert the following evening. The February 3 concert was attended by Frank Laric, a singer who later sang with Nelson in his last film. Laric, who sat in the third row, described the concert.

Unknown to anyone, and unexpected even to Nelson himself, Jeanette showed up at the concert. Nelson had just gotten through singing "Rose Marie," I think it was, and started singing "Will You Remember?" And he got through the intro, and to "Sweetheart, sweetheart, sweetheart," And lo and behold, Jeanette's voice came into the theater singing "Sweetheart," and everyone stopped and looked around. She started walking down the aisle; she'd been seated up at the back. Halfway down she started to sing. The look on Nelson's face was unbelievable, he was so touched. But he was a trouper and kept on singing. You could see how pleased he was. And of course everybody was looking around at Jeanette and Nelson, everyone was excited, it was so dramatic.

She walked right up, and by the time they got to the last chorus they were both on the stage. They were practically touching, you know, looking into each other's eyes and singing. And then they finished the song and everybody was standing up and cheering.

I heard him—I was so close—I heard him say to her, "Where'd you come from?" She said, "I got in last night." And he said, "Are you alone?" She said no, some girl was with her, I didn't know who she was. "Where are you staying?" She named the hotel. And he says, "Well, let's have dinner tonight," or something about dinner. There was so much going on I couldn't hear it all. But they were like two little kids, they seemed so thrilled, so happy. She seemed so happy. Then they turned around and the audience cheered, and they sang "Indian Love Call" together. Then she graciously left the stage and went back up the aisle to her seat. Nelson kept on and sang a few more songs, and you could tell he was just really excited.

After the performance, everybody turned around to see Jeanette, but she'd already got up and left. She had gone out the back; she went around to the dressing room.

Nelson left for Reno and the rest of his tour on February 7. He kept in constant touch with Jeanette, and managed to keep up the grueling pace of the tour until mid-March, canceling only his Chicago concert. When the announcement came that Nelson had laryngitis and was canceling Chicago, one girl at the theater yelled, "I don't believe it! They can't do this to me!" (Of all the cities Nelson sang in, he fell ill in Chicago the most frequently. He blamed the weather, but his illnesses often seemed psychosomatic in origin. It's interesting to consider that his son by Maybelle Marston was being brought up in the Chicago area.)

Then, in Philadelphia, Ann suddenly showed up for the last leg of the tour. She and Nelson quarreled and Nelson canceled his concert, supposedly due to laryngitis. He phoned Jeanette, telling her he was too upset to sing anymore. She managed to calm him down, but the strain was evident. The next couple of weeks it was touch and go for Nelson; on April 4 he called Jeanette again, telling her he was canceling a Washington, D.C., date on Tuesday, the seventh. Again she calmed him, telling him to listen to her Chase & Sanborn broadcast the following day. She was scheduled to sing an Air Corps song but instead sang "Will You Remember?" for him. This cheered him up and he found the strength to sing his rescheduled D.C. concert the following week, as well as his other scheduled dates.

During his illness, Nelson was in the middle of negotiations for a new radio show sponsored by Old Gold cigarettes. His salary was $3,500 a week, and a letter dated April 1 said:

> Nelson Eddy will donate his proceeds from April 29–July 28, 1942, that P. Lorillard & Co. (the sponsor) will deliver to the Red Cross a quantity of Old Gold cigarettes which would cost, including all excise and/or sales tax, approximately $3,500, it being understood that the Red Cross in turn will distribute these cigarettes to the men in the armed forces. The option can be extended, if notified no later than June 28. On each of said programs on which Mr. Eddy appears, there will be an announcement in appropriate language, that Nelson receives no compensation for his appearance. He consented to appear if P. Lorillard & Co. would give the Red Cross half a million (or other appropriate figure) Old Gold cigarettes for each of his appearances on the program.
>
> Per his Metro contract, he is restricted in rendering his services in radio broadcasting to no more than sixteen broadcasts not more frequently than once in any week and that Nelson Eddy has obtained from Louis B. Mayer an oral agreement to waive said restriction, but it is agreed that in the event that Metro-Goldwyn-Mayer shall insist upon compliance with the aforesaid restriction, Nelson Eddy shall be obligated hereunder to perform in and have his name and/or likeness used in the advertising of only sixteen of the programs provided for herein.

Nelson wanted his income from Old Gold to be tax-free, but as the various lawyers involved didn't know what to make of a salary paid in cigarettes, Nelson finally sent a telegram deciding to drop that idea. He ultimately signed the Old

Gold contract in Los Angeles, on April 28, the day before The Nelson Eddy Show had its very successful debut. After the first week, soprano Nadine Conner joined the program. Producers had shown interest in pairing Nelson and Jeanette on radio, but their combined salaries were too high on a steady basis.

On April 30, Nelson received a congratulatory telegram from D. W. Griffith, sent from the Drake Hotel in Philadelphia.

Dear Nelson, tonight as usual we got the same old thrill from hearing you sing but have serious complaint when you sing "I'm a ruler of the Queen's Navy" there should be at least ten more verses. I was delighted to hear my dear friend Neil Hamilton as announcer on your program. I thought he was grand and worked beautifully with you. It all sounded so friendly and very pleasant to the ears. Long life to you and that golden voice. Always D. W. Griffith.

I Married An Angel was previewed in March, was re-edited, previewed again in May, but the prognosis was still negative. Reviews were scathing. Photoplay magazine rated it "Much below the standard . . . is this piece of trivia taken from the paper-thin stage play of several seasons ago. Neither star is given songs that come even near meeting his vocal ability. Because this pair is your favorite and you approve them in anything, we give this our one-check blessing and hope for better things next time. Your reviewer says: Two artists in search of a good

Jeanette's all-time favorite photo of herself, on the set of *I Married An Angel*.

story." The New York *Times* was more sarcastic: "Mr. Eddy and Miss MacDonald are just not geared to toss a gossamer fable like this one about in the air.
Granted they can sing—and they do so in voices loud enough to wake the dead.
Their heavy and unesthetic mooning is just too much for the sensibilities to
take." The fans didn't know what to make of *Angel*. Most of them saw it at least
once, as opposed to the earlier MacDonald-Eddy films, which many of the true
enthusiasts had seen ten, twenty or even a hundred times.

■■■Jeanette skipped a spring concert tour, but sang frequently in and around
Los Angeles. She also traveled to San Francisco at the request of Ronald Reagan,
who recalled:

> It was early in World War II. Our men were still fighting on Bataan. I was a
> lieutenant at Fort Mason in San Francisco. There was no USO, nor any program for
> entertainment in those early days. The commanding general had asked if I could get
> someone to sing the National Anthem at ceremonies for I Am an American Day.
> Jeanette said yes without hesitation, but then said if she was coming all that way,
> couldn't she do something more to help. So on a Sunday afternoon she stood in
> one of the boxes at the old Dog Racing Track while 20,000 boys headed for the
> South Pacific sat in the infield. She sang until there weren't any more songs left and
> still they wanted more. Finally she told them she only knew one more song that was
> a great favorite of hers, and she started singing the Battle Hymn of the Republic. I
> will never forget her, nor forget how she sang—these 20,000 boys came to their feet
> and finished singing the hymn with her.

On April 1, Jeanette began work on *Cairo*, with Robert Young as co-star.
Lena Horne was chosen to play the role of Jeanette's maid. "My first screen test
was a farce," remembered Horne. "They were planning a picture co-starring
Jeanette MacDonald and Robert Young and were thinking of Eddie Anderson
(Rochester) and me to play their servants and, I guess, to have a romance in the
film too. It was a good role—the maid was to be just as flippant and fresh as
anyone. She was a human being, not a stereotype. They asked Rochester and me
to do a test together. They wanted me to match Rochester's color so they kept
smearing dark makeup on me. And then they had a problem in lighting and
photographing me because they said my features were too small. Meantime, poor
Rochester had to stand around and wait while they fussed over me. It was
embarrassing to me, though he was very pleasant about it. In the end, the test was
a disaster. I looked as if I were some white person trying to do a part in blackface.
I did not do the picture: Ethel Waters got the part."

The film was started in Technicolor and a color reel apparently still exists in the
MGM files, but in the end the picture was completed and released in black-and-
white, with shoddy production values. Even so, the script had some funny lines.
Jeanette played a movie star, Young a war correspondent; both are searching for a
Nazi spy heading the "Big Six," and each suspects the other. In one scene,

Jeanette and Robert Young are arguing about which is better, northern or southern California. Young asks, "Have you ever *been* to northern California?" "Yes," replies Jeanette, "Once with Gable and Tracy and the joint fell apart."

In candid shots taken on the set, director Woody Van Dyke looked strained and aged, his hair whitened. Always a heavy drinker, he was able to continue working even though he was undoubtedly in great pain. He never lost his comic touch; in one scene, Jeanette and Ethel Waters confront Robert Young in a movie theater. Hanging on the wall in the theater lobby is a large framed photo of Nelson.

Cairo finished shooting four days under schedule, in late May. About this time, Nelson had been scheduled to start work on *Lucky Star* with Kathryn Grayson. (In this story he played a dual role, himself and an actor who resembled Nelson Eddy, called "Duke." The plot had Duke posing as the real Eddy, and getting entertained in a small town by Kathryn Grayson, who draws a number for the privilege of being his hostess.) On June 1, Jeanette and Nelson did a Screen Guild Theater adaptation of *I Married An Angel*, clearly an attempt to boost interest in the film. It didn't help.

In early June 1942, Busby Berkeley was named as *Lucky Star*'s director. Nelson received a final script on July 3 and read through his lines, marking his dialogue, and making some notes. For example, when he played himself his singing voice would be relaxed, low, and his hair blonde. For the role of Duke, he'd use his natural voice with a cheap accent, hair "wash-dark." The starting date for *Lucky Star* kept being pushed back. Meanwhile, the trades alternately stated that Jeanette had been dropped by MGM, and that she had signed a picture-by-picture contract. Nelson finally decided he had had it with Mayer, and followed through on his original intention of six months ago: he bought out his contract, and *Lucky Star* was never made. One report claimed that the studio ordered him to return all the salary he'd been paid in 1942; Nelson later reported that he'd paid $250,000 for his freedom and that it was worth every penny.

Both Jeanette and Nelson harbored bitterness over their treatment at the studio in the last year. But they had made an enemy of Mayer and that sealed their fate. Had Jeanette bowed to Mayer's sexual desires and severed her relationship with Nelson, she might have continued at the studio a few more years. But it just wasn't worth it to her anymore. Nor did they care that MGM was receiving a barrage of hate mail for allowing the team to leave.

They were unceremoniously ushered out of the studio, without any sentiment or thanks for their years of loyalty. "When Nelson drove back to get his stuff, they wouldn't let him in the gate," said Harper McKay, who worked with Nelson as arranger during his nightclub years. "I heard it from him. The guard, whom he'd done something for, the guard's kid was in the hospital, something like that had happened—and the guard had to refuse." Once they left the studio, Nelson and Jeanette lost touch with many of their fair weather friends. There's no mention of Nelson ever socializing with Clark Gable in later years, for example. Many studio co-workers only remembered their temperament, their professional quarrels, Nelson's "bad" acting, Jeanette's pre-menstrual irritability, her extreme perfectionism.

In July 1942, Nelson and Jeanette were finally free of Mayer and the studio system that had ruled and ruined their lives for nine years. On July 22, they attended a benefit premiere of *Mrs. Miniver* together, then for the rest of the summer they forced themselves to relax and re-evaluate their lives and future. Aside from Nelson's weekly radio show, they had few commitments outside of pitching in for the war effort. Nelson's most industrious projects that summer were to move his mother into a new house in Beverly Hills at 608 North Walden, and to plant a hill of orange roses in the back yard of Twin Gables, which he faithfully tended. He sculpted a bust of Jeanette (which he later said didn't do her justice), and brought his oil paints over and set up his easel in the guest house/music room. When he wasn't staying with Jeanette, he visited Isabel. He had the perfect excuse for staying away from Ann; her son Sid had the measles.

Ann did attend several of Nelson's Old Gold radio shows, though it was noted by a regular in the studio audience that she seemed "bored most of the time." Nelson complained frequently of the heat that summer, and generally suffered through his radio shows. He was described as "terribly tired, awfully nervous, very hot."

Nelson found that he was now able to walk the streets like a normal person, without being mobbed. On one occasion he even took the bus from Hollywood to his house. He explained to an incredulous fan that someone had driven fourteen screws into the tires of his two cars. Jeanette also seemed weary of her movie star status; spotted one night at the Hollywood Bowl with Blossom, she reluctantly signed autographs. An observer described her as "tired, very pretty, hair a trifle too red. Pins on a smile for autographers which disappears instantaneously." For the first time since they'd known each other, Nelson and Jeanette were able to create their relationship in a non-antagonistic atmosphere of love, serenity and peace.

20

The War Years

Cairo opened in the fall of 1942 to disastrous reviews. The New York *Post* carped, "Today's problem is what to do with Jeanette MacDonald. She does not crack, wither or blow away. She stays pretty much the same, the same limpid soprano voice, the same archly wooden O-how surprising operetta technique of acting. Only the popularity is different." From *Variety:* "*Cairo* is about the third straight weaky for Miss MacDonald." The New York *Times:* "Major W. S. Van Dyke II has directed as though he were laying bricks. In the musical line, however, Miss MacDonald does much better . . . in a medley of old time favorites she leans rather heavily on sentiment and manages not to fall."

While Jeanette may have been distressed by these notices, Woody Van Dyke was uncaring, having a more important project on his mind. The director, sensing he didn't have much time to live, longed to make one last film that would show the world how much he loved his country and his freedom, and to remind the Allies what they were fighting for.

On June 15, 1942, production began on a picture entitled *Journey for Margaret.* A low-budget film, it rated a secondary director from the documentary department, Herbert Kline. But bombing raids in England were in the news, and made the film's plot about the London blitz and its effect on homeless, orphaned children suddenly topical. Woody was asked to take over the production and to capture the emotional importance of this story. The adult stars were Robert Young and Laraine Day; Woody handpicked his child star, a young girl named

Maxine O'Brien. Before the film wrapped in mid-September, Maxine had become Margaret (her screen name) O'Brien and Woody knew the talented child
would be an "overnight" star.

Journey for Margaret previewed in Los Angeles in late October 1942, and went
into general release at Christmastime. The Hollywood *Reporter* raved:

> We saw the most astonishing screen performance last night that these old eyes
> ever viewed . . . It was thrilling because it was performed by a six-year-old child,
> Margaret O'Brien.
>
> Little Miss O'Brien's opening scene in the picture picks her up in a war found-
> ling nursery for children right at the height of the London blitz. She affects a
> nervous rubbing of her eyes, an action the script later explains as due to her desire
> to cry but, through chastising on the part of her guardians, is forced to repress any
> weeping. Finally, when it is explained to her that she may cry if she feels like it, she
> affects weeping and sobbing that really wring tears from your heart . . . It will go
> down in the picture books as one of the all-time acting triumphs.

The New York *Times* added: "W. S. Van Dyke II directed a drama to stand
alongside the few unballyhooed classics of the screen . . . a picture of tormented childhood that will not soon be forgotten by anyone who has ever loved
a child. Not in recent experience has Broadway seen a film so fervent, so tender
or so perceptive and true."

Woody had put his heart into his final film. He was assigned another project,
Gentle Annie, starring Robert Taylor and Susan Peters, but quit after two weeks
because he was too ill to work. He was confined to his home but he refused to
stay in bed, unable to tolerate the idea of being bedridden. He slept in his Marine
fatigues on the couch in his den and lived virtually alone; his wife had taken their
three children to their upstate ranch. Woody continued to read scripts and make
plans for future projects, still refusing Mayer's pleas to seek medical help before it
was too late. Aside from his secretary and a few studio personnel, there were few
people he wanted to see, but Nelson and Jeanette were always welcome. Woody
had separate talks with each of his "kids" about the future, and made them
promise that when the time came, they would officiate at his funeral. "Everything is all right with you two, little Jenny?" he asked Jeanette affectionately.
"You're both young, Mayer isn't the beginning and the end of the world. As long
as you have each other, that's all that matters when the chips are down."

"You're so right," she reassured him. "We're fine and things are going good,
Nelson says."

"That's my girl. In some ways you've changed, and for the better."

Woody discussed the war with Nelson, and his frustration that he was failing
his country when it needed him most. When Nelson complained, "I'm too old
for this war and I was too young for the last," Woody chuckled. "Don't worry
about it, kid, some people would call that luck." He made Nelson promise to do
something significant for the war effort, adding: "When you do, you'll be
putting in a lick for me."

★ ★ ★

Jeanette expressed hopes that by the end of 1942, Ann would finally agree to give Nelson a divorce. But during the summer her hopes dwindled. Ann started insisting that she was pregnant again, and planted this newsworthy tidbit in the columns, hoping to force Nelson to pay attention to her. When it didn't work she had a confrontation with Jeanette, telling her, "No doubt you can be his mistress whenever you like, but you will never be his wife." Nelson next told his mother that Ann had a detective following him, trying to catch him with Jeanette. Apparently Ann gathered the evidence she had wanted, for suddenly she informed Nelson she was agreeable to a divorce, though it wouldn't come cheaply.

That night Nelson had dinner at his mother's, with Jeanette and Isabel, to celebrate his good fortune. As he was driving Jeanette home afterwards, she suddenly said, "Nelson, something is wrong. I'm going to call mother [Isabel] when I get home and see if everything is all right there." Nelson laughed at her fear. When they arrived at Twin Gables, she phoned and found out everything was fine. Then she said, "I know what's wrong, it's Ann. You have to call there right away." Nelson didn't want to do it, but she kept persisting until he finally did. He got no answer. Jeanette made him drive back to his home immediately. When he pulled up he saw all the lights were on, and the doors open, and no servants. He switched on the light in the backyard and saw Ann lying face up, a white foam around her mouth. He didn't know what to do nor did he want any publicity. So he called Jeanette; she told him to sit tight and she'd bring a doctor. When the doctor examined Ann he announced, "It's poison. I'll have to have a nurse quickly."

"There's no time for that," Jeanette said. "I'll do it, just tell me what to do and I'll follow you." Nelson had to leave the room—he was a nervous wreck and no help. After about two hours they managed to bring Ann around. It turned out she'd gotten drunk and then took some pills Nelson had used several years before as a gargle for strep throat. The pills were deadly poison when swallowed. When Ann was safe a nurse was called in and was told that it had been an accident.

Finally around dawn Nelson insisted on driving Jeanette back to Twin Gables. She was so exhausted and nervous she collapsed in his arms. He carried her to his car, drove her home, undressed her and put her to bed. Then he brought her warm milk to make her sleep, and refused to leave her side. When he thought she had finally drifted off, he took her hand, held it against her cheek and whispered, "You're mine and I am going to take care of you always. Nothing will keep me from you, and no woman will ever be given a greater love."

The subject of divorce was dropped for the time being, and it is unlikely that Ann Eddy ever learned that Jeanette was at least partly responsible for saving her life.

Jeanette meanwhile put her personal problems aside and decided to do an extensive concert tour to raise money for the Army Emergency Relief Fund.

She'd come up with the bright idea of auctioning off encores, as well as donating her services and paying all her expenses. It's unclear whether her heart condition had been diagnosed this early, but she failed a medical exam that would have allowed her to go overseas as many other entertainers were doing. Instead, she became the only singer licensed by the USO Camp Shows to do solo programs in the United States. The tour was a smashing success, and Jeanette gave tirelessly of herself. "I never realized how much movie stars mean to people," she said. "Not what you do or what you say, but just your presence, your being there. It makes you feel embarrassed and rather humble and happy all at once. To be able to bring that much pleasure to people makes me a very lucky woman. Very lucky."

As she traveled by train through "the heat belt," she made a point of meeting as many servicemen as she could. When she arrived in Arkansas it was payday for the soldiers as well, but every soldier elected to stay at the post to hear her concert. Thousands of men were there, and the commanding general personally stepped up on the stage to congratulate her. She gave several concerts in hospitals, and toured the wards of men recuperating from action at Pearl Harbor and Bataan. She traveled through blistering temperatures, by train, bus or jeep, often going directly from the train to the concert stage, with no time to rest. "If the men can train in these temperatures, I can sing and travel in them," she asserted. She sang from thirty to thirty-five songs a night, answered endless requests, sang every song she knew. Most asked for were "Ave Maria" and "Nearer My God to Thee." She said proudly, "When boys want religious songs, you don't have to worry about them. Americans have always prayed as they fought for their ideals. The fighting men of this war are proving no exception."

In Oklahoma City, her first stop, Jeanette raised $600 in encores. The *Daily Oklahoman* noted: "One of the surprises of the program was the vocal arrangement of Victor Herbert's 'Badinage.' In the middle part the singer suddenly jumped a whole tenth, instead of the third as in the instrumental version, and she hit it cleanly and with that extraordinarily beautiful half voice quality, as satisfying as it was unexpected." The Chicago *Sun*: "Her manner on the stage was more as though she was before a camera rather than a large audience, so self-assured was she. Some of her encores she sang with her back to the audience for the benefit of the group of Army nurses who were seated on the stage as her guests." She raised $800 in Chicago.

In Indianapolis she sang outdoors, with the sun beating down on her. "When she began, the audience with one accord leaned forward to listen to that glorious voice," noted one viewer. The donations at this concert were over $1,000. One girl had offered one dollar; Jeanette had told her to pool it, and later the girl returned with $29. Jeanette asked the audience for one additional dollar to make $30, and when she got it, she shook hands and kissed the girl on the cheek. When a man offered $100 for a song called "One Dozen Roses," Jeanette replied that she wasn't familiar with the song, but she would comply with his request. She brought forward a beautiful bouquet of roses, saying, "Here are two dozen roses, will you give $200?" While she was in Indianapolis, Gene Raymond appeared on a radio show from England, and he greeted his wife on the air.

In Birmingham, Jeanette drew over 5,000 people despite a torrential downpour. She collected over $1,400 or, as she told the audience, "More than Atlanta by $200." She opened the concert with "The Star Spangled Banner," with the audience singing with her. They whistled the accompaniment for "Donkey Serenade," and she sang "Keep the Light Burning Bright in the Harbor" from *Cairo*, which became a standard on this tour. A reviewer noted: "Miss MacDonald's personality extended far beyond the footlights and every person in the audience felt that intimate association as though she were singing to him or her alone." In Chattanooga, a lady sent up a check for $100, requesting Jeanette to sing "Chattanooga Choo-Choo." Jeanette told the lady this song wasn't in her repertoire, but if she desired, she would be glad to oblige with "San Francisco," which caused an uproar.

From the Atlanta *Constitution*: "She has a voice of exquisite quality. Her high notes in pianissimo carry amazingly throughout the auditorium. Her middle register is fine and smooth. And her voice is quite flexible. Her diction is superb." The Boston *Post*: "She did the work of a dozen singers and managed to look and seem fresh throughout." A Springfield critic described her with adjectives that would have pleased Nelson: "One could not imagine a more beautiful picture than that of the artist as she stood with poise, self-assurance, looking like an exquisite bit of Dresden china, dressed in snowy, flimsy, white, with touches of heavenly blue on bodice and skirt."

At the final concert, Jeanette asked the soldiers to bring out the "loot" in giant money bags, on which was printed the name of the city in which the money was raised, and the amount. In total, she presented the Army Emergency Relief Fund with $94,682.87, the largest war contribution due to an individual effort. She was awarded a medal by President Roosevelt for her efforts.

Jeanette was the first movie star to open her home to soldiers visiting the Los Angeles area. Throughout the war, she sang wherever and whenever asked.

★   ★   ★

■■■ Jeanette was back in Los Angeles in December 1942. Nelson was urging her to sign a new film contract with him at Universal; they were willing to "pay through the nose" to get the team. Jeanette refused to sign. She was exhausted and needed time to recuperate from her tour. Also, she was afraid to work with Nelson because she felt there was no way they could hide their feelings for each other at a new studio; they'd slip up somehow. She told Nelson: "Every time you took me in your arms in the love scenes our fans would be sure to read through it all." He didn't buy her excuses, but advised her that if that's how she felt, her film career was over because "There aren't going to be any other leading men." Jeanette voiced one last objection to which Nelson had no argument; their working together would antagonize Ann and thus perhaps delay his chances for a divorce. They quarreled, but Jeanette remained firm. She finally agreed to make a film with him at Universal later on, but not now. Based on her verbal promise, Nelson signed a short-term contract with Universal; his solo film was to be a high-budget (over $1,500,000) Technicolor remake of *The Phantom of the Opera*. (The opera house set used in the original 1925 Lon Chaney classic was used in this 1943 version.)

Before the year's end, Nelson managed to steal a couple of days' vacation with Jeanette. If anything, they seemed more infatuated than they'd ever been, if Nelson's writings were any measure. He penned a lengthy description of the trip to his mother, defending their right to be together despite the fact it was technically adultery.

> Perhaps some day we will see and understand why we had to go through years of cruel agony—and in the end obey the law of God while we break the law of man. But I know that we break no law. Jeanette has never been a wife and I have never had one—we owe no affection or vows to anyone. But we do owe them to each other, we took them long ago and have never broken them. Now they are made secure and forever.

The letter took a more graphic turn:

> She had on a heavy robe over that dear little nightie, and after I combed her hair and got it ready for the night, she cuddled up in my arms by the fire and looked exactly sixteen. How I loved her! It was an aching, desperate longing. And as I held her close I asked her to sing "Song to an Evening Star" and she did—so tenderly—so beautifully—it was then I held her tightly to me and whispered, "The roses and violets have hinted things to me about you—they have told me I would find my lost dream. May I try to find it in your arms tonight? Will you help me find it, my baby?" And without a word—but all starry-eyed tenderness, she slipped her arms tightly around my neck, and it was there I discovered her little hands were icy cold. It frightened me so—and I picked her up in my arms and tucked her snugly into bed—where I had first to warm those cold little hands with kisses. Well, mother!

How beautifully, how tenderly, how naturally she gave herself to me—a quick joyous catch of her breath, and she was my darling wife—And here I am telling you priceless secrets such as I never dreamed of telling my mother.

Isabel was dismayed at her son's all-consuming obsession. She told Sarah Tucker, who was visiting Los Angeles, that she feared she had made some grave errors in raising Nelson, forcing him to live an unnatural life for so many years. Now he seemed to have swung to the opposite extreme, to where his career was all but meaningless. Isabel felt that only a divorce could guarantee her son's continued sanity. Mrs. Tucker agreed to speak with Nelson about Ann to see just where matters stood. Nelson did open up with Tucker about Ann, he went on and on about what a blot she was on his life, how Jeanette had "held his hand" through everything and made it possible for him to face the world with some kind of self-respect. Mrs. Tucker came away from that conversation with no solutions, but this observation: "Nelson just lives and breathes and dreams of Jeanette and nothing else."

Christmas season found Jeanette singing at the Hollywood Canteen; Nelson and Ronald Colman performed "The Juggler of Notre Dame" on radio for a third year. Eighteen-year-old Susanna Foster was signed as Nelson's singing co-star for *The Phantom of the Opera*, someone Jeanette considered "safe." She'd met Susanna back at MGM when the young girl was signed as a possible replacement for Deanna Durbin, who'd just gone over to Universal. Recalled Susanna:

I met Jeanette on the set of *The Firefly* in February 1937. I adored her, but what a shock! She treated me like I was two. She meant to be nice, but I was a brainy little girl. I had a very high IQ.

I was so excited about meeting my idol, but I was also seeing her in the worst scene in the movie, where she had those bangs and that hair hanging down, and she didn't look the way I wanted to see her look. Although her face was lovely, I wanted to see her as she was in *Naughty Marietta*.

And then she sat in the chair and I talked to her, and Robert Leonard was standing behind her. Then she started saying, "Now, imitate me: (cleared throat) Johnny, Johnny, Johnny, whoops, Johnny." I mean, here I was, looking at her—I could read the Bible when I was four, all the newspapers, and was doing mathematical problems.

So—then I go, "Johnny, Johnny . . ." and Jeanette says "No! That's not it!" She just didn't know who she was talking to—she should have talked about music, that would have been the logical thing.

So, finally, I'm doing it over and over and she says no, that's not right. Leonard looked at me and motioned and I got it, she was clearing her throat first. I can't stand dirty tricks, I was really teed off. But I forgave her because I loved her, I didn't care. I walked away, laughing to myself, "Oh brother, I'm gonna watch *Naughty Marietta*, I don't want to meet anyone!"

Susanna eventually left MGM and went to Paramount for two years. She was featured in two films prior to *The Phantom of the Opera*. The best known was *The Great Victor Herbert* (1939). She met Nelson at one of Woody Van Dyke's parties in 1942. "He came over and sat and talked with me. I wondered why; I wasn't anybody. I wondered if he was interested in me as a person, or what he had in his mind." Nothing came of their meeting, but some months later a man at Paramount suggested that Susanna audition for *Phantom*, and she easily landed the role of Christine. The second week of January 1943, Nelson and Susanna began recording the operatic sequences of the film. The sound director, Bernard Brown ("Brownie"), was intrigued with Nelson's voice. He felt it had never been accurately duplicated on a film sound track, always being toned down or muffled. He had a special booth built for Nelson to record in. When Nelson heard the playbacks, he was astonished. "I sound like that?" Most people feel that Brownie did capture the power and glitter of Nelson's voice; seeing *Phantom* in a theater with a good sound system was like hearing him in concert. Along with performing his own arias and songs in the film, Nelson also sang the minor tenor and bass solos in the operatic scene (*Le Prince de Caucasie*) in which the Phantom cuts the chandelier.

Nelson wore a black wig and mustache in the film, supposedly to make him look French, which met with violent disapproval from his fans. His description of his character was amusing: "I'm the guy who's in love with the girl, and there's another guy in love with her [played by Edgar Barrier] and we spend our time glaring at one another." He added, "One of the scenes called for a Polonaise, and one of the casting men was asked to get thirty-two dancers for it. The day the scene was to be shot he came dashing in full of enthusiasm, saying, 'Wait til you see what I've got. I've located thirty-two real Polynesian girls to do your Polonaise dance and they're all outside now.' They were too, dark hair, dark eyes and sarongs, but we did finally get the dancers we needed. I've told that story a lot of times, but I can't get very many people to believe me. They think it sounds too much like a Hollywood story."

Claude Rains joined the cast as the Phantom. Susanna Foster remembered:

> The scar on Claude Rains was a big issue. Jack Pierce did the makeup. It was during the war, and a lot of boys were returning with these problems. They didn't want to offend anybody, or hurt anybody. So there was a great amount of talk on how they were going to handle that scar. Maybe [the audiences] expected something more grotesque or horrible. But I think actually that what they finally decided on, irrespective of the war, was classically the best.
>
> Rains was the only really great actor I ever worked with. Now, Karloff [with whom Susanna starred in *The Climax* the following year] was just plain cold. I know people adored him. Pierce adored him. He said, "No one could play [the Frankenstein monster] as he did." It's true, no one had the sadness and all in the face. But for me, I felt nothing. It was like working with a stick. Maybe being English, he was reserved. Rains was reserved too, but there was a little twinkle about Rains.
>
> I think I mentioned to Rains that I was a little shy in this, my first big film, you

know, with Nelson Eddy. My God—I didn't dare even tell Nelson how much I'd loved him—I never did that. What a shame, I wish now I had. But I was young and I didn't want to say, "I've always liked you—" I felt like every idiot. I didn't even ask him for an autographed picture or anything.

They could never decide whether there was doing to be a love interest. Besides, I was scared stiff that I'd have to kiss Nelson Eddy. Of course, to kiss anybody, I was scared stiff. [The love scene] was never done. And I think Nelson got it cut because he felt that I'd be embarrassed as hell.

Susanna, even at eighteen, was extremely perceptive in her summation of Nelson.

He was a great gentleman, with a lot of humor. He had very dark blue eyes, almost black-blue. And they were very burning, you know. Typically the opposite of his mouth, which turned up at the corners and smiled and was sweet. His eyes had a lot of feeling. You didn't see any meanness in Nelson's face, but he had a fiery streak in him. Spiteful. I realized he wasn't all harmony and sweetness; if he ever lost his temper, I wouldn't want to be around. He kept everything calm, quiet, so when he burst, he burst like crazy.

There was a certain shyness in Nelson. I think he was more sensitive, in a different way than Jeanette. She was a fragile woman, small boned, even though she was 5'5"—slender little feet, little hands, and all that. She had hay fever all her life, suffered from a lot of minor illnesses. Nelson was a strong man. Big, husky man. Very durable.

[At the end of the filming] he gave everyone a book, beautifully bound, the most expensive leather. He gave Hal Mohr [cameraman]—a big, rough, tough son of a gun with lots of intellect—a book of Aristophanes. Mohr had married a beautiful lady, a vegetarian, Evelyn Venable. Nelson didn't know, because we didn't talk much, that I read T. S. Eliot, and he gave me "Indian Love Lyrics." Well, I read that when I was about ten. I don't remember what he gave to everyone else, just Hal.

On February 4, 1943, Louis B. Mayer and Howard Strickling visited Woody Van Dyke. They found him dressed in his Marine casuals, quite cheerful and happy. The topic of discussion was several new possible projects for Woody to direct. After they left, Woody called some of his friends from his early days of film making, invited them over, and they talked over old times. When they departed he called his wife to inquire how their children were, then his mother, assuring her that he was fine. He painstakingly changed into a suit of khaki and then took enough pills to end his suffering. He fell asleep on the divan in his den and was found dead the next morning.

Van Dyke was deeply mourned by the industry; in a show of respect the newspapers were convinced not to mention the cause of his death. His memorial service was as he had wanted, with Jeanette and Nelson officiating. Nelson sent a wreath of white roses to the funeral, Jeanette white lilies. Her card read, "From the kid," and Nelson's "From the other kid." Two songs were performed: a Christian Science hymn called "Oh, Gentle Presence," and "Ah, Sweet Mystery of Life." Nelson broke down during the "Sweet Mystery" duet and Jeanette had to finish it alone. Nelson was so distraught over Woody's passing that he had to miss a few days of filming, calling in sick.

During the two months he was filming *Phantom*, Nelson had little time for Jeanette, except during the week of Woody's death. He was upset at having to be away from her, and he tried repeatedly to convince her to do a film with him. She finally consented to a project called *Reunion in Vienna*, then she changed her mind. Working daily with Nelson would only make it that much easier for him to endure his existence—without getting his divorce. Jeanette was anxious to force his hand; in letters of the period she starts talking about having his baby before it's too late; she was approaching her fortieth birthday.

In the last year, Ann Eddy had seen no less than seven doctors and was termed mentally unstable and "on the borderline." She'd become increasingly vicious toward Jeanette, threatening to harm or disfigure her. Ann's doctors and even her mother tried to convince her to divorce Nelson for the sake of her health but she refused, claiming, "He ruined my life, now his must be ruined as well." Nelson felt that his hands were tied. Due to Ann's emotional problems he felt that he could not in good conscience initiate the divorce, she would have to take the first step. He just didn't know how to go about convincing her to do that without pushing her over the brink, or having her call the press in and making a scandal. He even had his attorney talk with the various columnists, alerting them to her precarious condition, and gaining their cooperation in not gossiping about them and Jeanette, or the state of his marriage. It is a credit to Nelson and Jeanette that gossips like Hedda Hopper and Louella Parsons were willing to keep mum on a scoop like this, year after year.

Nelson lived in constant fear of what Ann would say or do regarding Jeanette. He warned her regularly that if she opened her mouth he would tell the world what he knew about her and ruin her with all her friends. She kept quiet, but according to Sarah Tucker, "Ann hates Jeanette with a terrible hatred, also Nelson, and especially Gene, because he protects them."

Blossom worried about her sister's mental health as well. "She seems happy but a desperate sort of happiness, to my mind." Blossom was encouraged when Jeanette finally made a decision about her career; she would fulfill her original goal as a singer and make her grand opera debut. "Life is fluid and keeps moving and motion means change," Jeanette reflected. "I know that everything I have now can pass away . . . Youth passes and the lustre of fame dies. There are inevitabilities. You say that I have my voice, too. Yes, but that also can go. It has happened to others. It could happen to me . . . I want to be big enough to take the downgrades if they come; to be able to hold the memory of this happiness, when, inevitably, some of it must go."

In February 1943, a newspaper blurb announced that Jeanette was making her debut at the Metropolitan Opera in the fall in Gounod's *Roméo et Juliette*. This seems to have been a press plant, since the Met's manager, Edward Johnson, denied signing her or knowing anything about her plans. One of Jeanette's friends claimed that the Met wouldn't even consider Jeanette without an audition, that her friend Lily Pons arranged one, but Jeanette declined, realizing the Met didn't want her. The Metropolitan's archives do not indicate that an audition was ever held. Still, she was determined to sing *Juliette*, and at last she landed a Canadian engagement in May 1943, with a stellar cast: Ezio Pinza as Friar Lawrence and Armand Tokatyan as Romeo. Wilfred Pelletier, Rose Bampton's husband, conducted. Jeanette would be singing in several Canadian cities, and for her debut Jeanette coached with Pelletier and the Met's French bass Leon Rothier. She'd asked Nelson to help her as well; but he had little time to give her. Also, he was upset that she was branching off into a new career, when he preferred her to be by his side, working with him if she felt she had to work at all.

Nelson had pushed back his spring concert tour a month, but even so, it was doubtful that his scenes in *Phantom* could be finished in time for the start of the tour. Starting on February 24, he worked at Universal from early morning till eleven at night. On his last day, March 4, he left the studio at midnight. Eight hours later he boarded a train for Phoenix, Arizona, where he sang a concert that evening.

His last meeting with Jeanette had ended in bitterness. He'd purchased a ring for her, a token to mark her upcoming debut (which he would miss, due to his own tour). Jeanette had seen the ring, but Nelson was waiting for a special moment to give it to her. "I asked him to let me see my ring again tonight," a weeping Jeanette told Isabel later on the phone. "He went over and unlocked the safe and took out a box, then he came over and started to hand it to me and it seemed he just couldn't. With a supreme effort at self-control, he just dropped the whole thing in my lap, he wouldn't even unlock it for me. He sometimes gives me a feeling that he is making me climb a rocky hill up to him, and that he won't even hold out a hand to help me. He's still hurt because I once turned his love away, something he will never quite forgive."

"What else happened?" Isabel asked eagerly.

"After I had the box unlocked," Jeanette continued, "he took out the ring and laid it in my hand and said, 'You can see it, but you can't keep it.' "

As Nelson was rushing to grab his train to Phoenix, Jeanette was at the Academy Awards dinner, giving "a thrilling rendition of the national anthem," said the Hollywood *Reporter*. This was her first active participation in the Oscars since *Naughty Marietta* lost Best Picture to *Mutiny on the Bounty*. Jeanette firmly believed that vote was fixed, stating that MGM employees were encouraged to choose the more costly *Mutiny*, the strategy being that the vital factor was to have *any* Metro picture win. (Other oldtimers at MGM admitted that Jeanette was correct on this point.) She boycotted the Oscars after that. Another upset she had was being told by Mayer that she would never be nominated for an acting award, even if she deserved one, because she was considered merely a singer.

In mid-March, Jeanette traveled to New York to prepare for her operatic debut. She managed to meet up briefly with Nelson, who was singing at both New York's Town Hall and Philadelphia's Academy of Music. Together, they visited her sister Elsie, who was still living in the Philadelphia area, and Nelson was introduced to some of Jeanette's cousins as well. They had a single night of privacy together; according to the story Nelson told, he checked her into his hotel under the name Miss L. (for Lucie) Glutzenheimer. Someone had tipped off his fans to where he was staying, so Jeanette donned a disguise and even fooled the desk clerk, though she complained to Nelson, "I don't know why you had me register under such an atrocious name. I spent five minutes at the front desk figuring out how to spell it. I know that clerk thought I was a basket case."

Nelson had a faithful following in each city he visited. A group of fans checked into his hotel, staked out the lobby to note his comings and goings, ate in the hotel coffee shop or restaurant when he did, and even lurked on his floor, eager to catch a glimpse of him. It was virtually impossible for him to have a private life all the months he was on tour, especially since he traveled with his accompanist Theodore Paxson and his manager, Art Rush. But at times like this, when he needed privacy, he resorted to disguises and service entrances.

Jeanette had worked so hard preparing for her opera debut that she fell ill and had to delay final rehearsals in Montreal, where her debut was scheduled. She claimed she had pneumonia and was still unwell on opening night, although the cast and audience was unaware of her discomfort. Rose Bampton recalled that her husband, Wilfred Pelletier ("Pelle"), was surprised and impressed with Jeanette. After all the years of unkind rumors that Jeanette's voice was manufactured for films, was inaudible, thin and not suited for opera, Pelletier didn't know quite what to expect. "Pelle said she came so well prepared that she knew that role perfectly when she got here for rehearsals," said Bampton. "Pelle had never worked with anyone like that before. He said she was absolutely marvelous, he never worked with an artist so eager to get things right. And he said she would stop and say, 'Oh, maestro, that wasn't quite right, could we try it again?' I never heard her performances because I was busy at the time, but if Pelle said she was great, she was great. I would believe him over the critics. He was very honest."

"She was a beautiful and sensitive Juliet, poetic in the balcony scene and passionate in the last two scenes," Pelletier wrote. "Her success as an operatic singer was genuine, and as a colleague she was admired and beloved by her companions, the orchestra and the chorus."

Jeanette's May 8, 1943, debut was "a triumph for Miss MacDonald and an honor to Montreal," praised the Montreal *Gazette*. "The voice is sweet in quality, it has in person that sureness and cleanness which has always been noted in the soprano's screen work and has made her one of the most accomplished singers Hollywood ever had . . . Her personal beauty, softer and more fragile than when seen through the eye of the camera, was admirably suited to the part."

"She telephoned me from Montreal on Mother's Day, the morning after the opera," wrote Anna MacDonald. "I had been worried because of her illness and wondered if she would be able to stand the ordeal of opening in a brand-new role in a new field with a bad cold. The succeeding performances at Quebec and Ottawa have been just as sensational and much easier for her, I am very thankful to say."

Jeanette also received raves in Toronto. "Not a quiver spoiled the limpid steadiness of her light floating voice," noted the Toronto *Telegram*. "Her tones were sweet, serene and comforting to the very last." "Most of Juliet's music is for the middle voice and the sincerity of her phrasing and tender beauty of her production carried conviction at all times," added the *Globe and Mail*. "Her middle and lower tones are singularly warm and beautiful." At the end of the performance when Jeanette took a solo bow, the audience rose to their feet, stamped, cheered and whistled. One reviewer noted, "It was, in fact, the most deafening demonstration of approval I have ever heard in my life."

▄▄▄ Gene Raymond returned from England in April 1943 as a captain in the Army Air Corps Bomber Command. While overseas he was arrested in a homosexual scandal, a fact verified by detective Joe Sampson, formerly of Scotland Yard, but it didn't warrant much attention in wartime England and never made the papers in the States. Gene joined his wife in Toronto, and when her operatic tour was finished, they spent some time in New York, where she sang at the Stage Door Canteen, finally returning to Los Angeles together at the end of June. Nelson, meanwhile, had completed his concert tour, and returned to New York for an appearance on the Bell Telephone Hour. Ann insisted on coming with him; with both spouses in tow, whatever rendezvous plans Jeanette and Nelson had were thwarted. Nelson had the inevitable fight with Ann and then ordered the hotel desk to hold all phone calls. "I don't care if it's my mother, I don't care if it's Jesus Christ, I'm going to bed." The next morning Nelson was devastated when he learned that Jeanette had called several times; unable to get through, she'd left for the West Coast.

The lovers were back in Los Angeles in July. Jeanette had decided to surprise Nelson and began considering their film offers, which included *Reunion in Vienna*, with Rudolf Friml at work on the score, and *Knickerbocker Holiday*, in which Nelson was investing on the strength of its number, "September Song." Then she learned that in her absence, Nelson had sung at the Hollywood Canteen with Risë Stevens, and there was heavy talk among the canteen personnel and their friends that Nelson and Risë were having an affair.

Jeanette was furious. She refused to work with Nelson, nor did she believe anymore in his fidelity to her. The summer was a rocky period for them; Nelson was committed to *Knickerbocker Holiday* with or without Jeanette. Now he was forced to have another co-star and make a film he no longer had any interest in. Their relationship hit rock bottom as all the old bitterness resurfaced. For Jeanette, the sore points were Nelson's refusal to get a divorce, no matter the cost, and his seeming inability to resist having sex with others, despite his supposed all-encompassing love for her. In Nelson's eyes, the blame belonged to Jeanette for marrying Gene in the first place, and her refusal to be constantly at his side.

The relationships with their spouses were also strained to the breaking point. Gene was home for only sporadic short visits, sometimes only a day, for the rest of the war, spending much of his time stationed in Yuma, Arizona. The only amicable time with his wife at home was when they opened Twin Gables to the servicemen, for "Date Leaves." They received lots of press for having the soldiers as their guests, swimming in their pool, eating their barbecue, etc. But when not on show, their basic incompatibility resulted in verbal and physical fights. Sybil Thomas related one incident:

> We had gone to visit a friend who lived up Bel Air road. When we were coming back down the hill, we of course had to go past *her* house. Suddenly the car screeched to a halt. Before I knew what was happening Nelson jumped out, leaped across the hood, and raced up the driveway. I looked to see Jeanette and Gene getting out of *their* car. They were fighting, or at least, Gene was. Jeanette had already hit the pavement. How Nelson saw all this in a flash was a mystery to me. He grabbed Gene and kept beating on his face, yelling and cursing, while Jeanette screamed, trying to pull him away. He suddenly saw she was crying and bleeding, and he took her inside.
>
> I must have sat there in the car for about twenty minutes. Gene was still lying out in the driveway. Suddenly Nelson burst back out the front door, his face grim. He stepped over Gene, stopping long enough to kick him in disgust, hurried back to the car, and without comment, pulled away. I couldn't resist. "What happened?" I asked.
>
> Nelson shook his head. "I can't believe it. That bastard nearly killed her, and all she's upset about is that I beat him up so badly. He's lucky I didn't finish him off."
>
> I said nothing, for this was one subject that refused to be resolved all the years I knew these two. Jeanette abhorred fighting; she couldn't tolerate violence of any kind. She could never stand even seeing an animal mistreated. She was never able to accept that Jekyll and Hyde mean streak in him when it came to fighting.
>
> I asked, "Is she all right?"
>
> Nelson nodded, "Pretty battered up, but if she can yell at me, I'm sure she'll be fine." End of conversation. I have to admit, though, I did wonder how long Gene laid out in the driveway!
>
> I think Gene enjoyed tangling with him, either that or he was a glutton for punishment. I never did figure why Jeanette put up with it, though. Maybe she felt she deserved it.

One of Nelson's neighbors made the following statement:

> Whenever people say Nelson Eddy was happily married, I have to laugh. The man was rarely home. When he was there, he never stayed long. Usually after a few hours I'd hear yelling and shouting, and without fail, he'd come stomping back out the front door, get in his car and drive away. That was the last you'd see of him for days. Usually he looked furious, but sometimes he seemed very tired and beaten. One time I heard screaming. I ran over to see what was wrong. He was standing in the doorway, his hands around her neck, choking her. He was blind with rage. He finally saw me and ran to his car.

The Phantom of the Opera previewed in mid-August 1943. It was well received although the emphasis was less on the horror and more on the music. The

Hollywood *Reporter* agreed: "You can call it a rare musical treat, an arrestingly beautiful spectacle in the magnificence of its Technicolor photography, or a handsomely performed psychological melodrama. And on each account you would be correct. [Eddy and Foster] both give performances under [Arthur] Lubin's direction that surpass anything they have ever done . . . Eddy appears to his best advantage. He is in splendid voice, as is Miss Foster, the faultless recording certain to win an Academy nomination for Bernard B. Brown." (Brown did win an Oscar. The film took home four awards in all: Best Color Cinematography, Best Color Interior Design, Best Sound Recording and Best Scoring for a Musical Picture.)

Phantom was a hit with the public and most of the critics. Many in the opera world felt they'd won a victory with this film, and that audiences might be ready for the next logical step: filming an entire opera. But the New York *Times* disagreed: "The fact that the name of Nelson Eddy appears at the head of the cast . . . is not to be taken as evidence that Mr. Eddy has finally found his role. He is no phantom in this one; he is very much in solid evidence, and his lungs are working as strongly and as loudly as they have ever worked before. Indeed, you might also think the picture was made just so he might sing . . . A lengthy scene from the third act of the opera *Martha* is at the opening of the film, and then Mr. Eddy and Miss Foster sing a fictitious opera based on themes of Chopin . . . and then, for that memorable sequence in which the Phantom drops the huge chandelier . . . Mr. Eddy is roaring another 'opera.'

"The role of the Phantom has been very much watered down, and Claude Rains has been made to play it in a sort of Lone Ranger style . . . Meanwhile, the windy Mr. Eddy is up there on the stage, singing songs, usually in company with Susanna Foster, who plays—and sings—the daughter role quite pleasingly. And when he isn't singing or preparing, he is usually making ponderous love, which is oddly supposed to be funny, to Miss Foster, along with Edgar Barrier. Mr. Barrier is the high-hat detective who tries to solve the mysteries of the opera house. Together they make about as boring a pair of rival suitors as we dread to see."

By September 1943, Nelson and Jeanette had put aside their disagreements once again. Nelson described the reconciliation, which took place at "Mists," in a long letter to his mother, relating how at first Jeanette had broken down, crying uncontrollably over his unfaithfulness to her.

I kissed her and tried to tell her her words were untrue. My beautiful darling— had I hurt so terribly the tender love of this girl for whom, week after week, day after day, I had been eating my heart out? The beautiful story I had repeated to her so many times, did she think I had not believed my own words? Had I once more wounded the heart of this girl who was the joy of my life? My eyes were blinded with tears as I looked at her there in my arms and thought what hardships I had made for her. All I could was say 'forgive me.' How well I know I am not worthy of this golden beauty, and of all the doors that love can enter perhaps pity is the widest. All I could do was hold her close, while a wisp of her hair caressed my cheek—the past was forgotten in that minute. I only knew that my baby's face was buried in my neck—that she was lying very still and quiet. When she moved again I picked her up and carried her to the couch bed, where I tucked a pillow under her head and covered her with a robe . . . A wave of sadness engulfed me, and looking at Jeanette I lost all control of myself and wept. And then suddenly I found my head pillowed on her firm little bosom, her arms enclosed me, and her whispering mother love held me close. Blessed moments of our own, when her healing hands, her tender kiss, told me of her great understanding for a very mixed-up little boy.

Later, when he was calmer, Nelson asked Jeanette: 'You love me and trust me, don't you?' She replied, 'To the grave, and beyond that.' Nelson told her: 'My darling, I need you in public as well as private. I am not happy or satisfied that I must hide you. I longed so for you last night . . . I wanted you in my arms, in my own bedroom, secure. Almost two months have passed since I have known that joy . . . Whether I could have had the strength to remain away from you I don't know.' "

There was no doubt that they'd spend the night together, though Jeanette first insisted on preparing a supper of "coffee and salad." Nelson continued his narrative:

> She knew I was in a very emotional state this night, and when she joined me after dinner, I was so amused. She had put on an extremely tailored robe over her new nightie, which her sister had given her, and there was just the tiniest edge of lace peeking from the neckline . . . I wonder if she knew how much more desirable she was than she had ever been in her frilly chiffon and lace? All I can say is she looked a goddess now. I had seen that little nightie before but now I had to see it on its lovely figure. So when she came to me I took her in my arms and said,
>
> "May I see the new nightdress?"
>
> "You have seen it."
>
> "Not on its model," I said.
>
> "I'm sorry, but it's not for little boys to see."
>
> "Indeed not," said I, "Only one little boy."
>
> "I'm afraid you can't," she said grinning.
>
> "You won't make me loosen that robe myself?" I said.
>
> "Oh, you won't be able to this time." And right then and there I knew I would see that little nightie or else—my baby was offering me a dare. I caught her hand, but before I had a chance to grasp it firmly, she stood poised for a minute and then calmly undid it herself and let the robe fall to the floor at her feet. For a moment I looked at that angel, and then I lost my head.

For once Nelson left something to his mother's imagination, without filling in the rest of the details.

◼ In mid-September 1943, Nelson began work on *Knickerbocker Holiday*, which was shot on the back lot of the Samuel Goldwyn Studios. His co-stars were Constance Dowling, Charles Coburn and a young Shelley Winters. From the first Nelson sensed the film was a disaster but he tried to get through it as quickly and professionally as possible. A local reporter visited the set and reported on the goings-on:

> Eddy, with his hair natural blond again . . . said he had spent so much time in the cobble-stoned streets arguing with Peter Stuyvesant that the part in his hair was sore and sunburned. Between shots he . . . leaned on a stool while the makeup department mopped the sweat from his brow and Director [Harry Joe] Brown worried about airplanes. Every time he'd get his actors set, the Army'd send a P-38 across the sky and blooie went the scene. "Not like it used to be," said Eddy. "Before the war the studios would send up yellow balloons on long cables to keep the airplanes away. And I remember at Metro that if a plane came close enough to mess the soundtrack, the studio would call up the Army and tell it to keep its planes away from there, and the Army'd say 'Yes, sir!' "

Jeanette felt unthreatened by Nelson's "love interest" Constance Dowling, and she agreed to join Nelson at Universal for a film with him when *Knickerbocker* was completed. On September 21, she filmed two numbers for a Universal picture called *Follow the Boys*, an all-star revue featuring many of the studio's leading performers. In *Follow the Boys*, Jeanette played herself and sang "Beyond the Blue Horizon" and "I'll See You in My Dreams." The latter number was memorable because while she sang she unconsciously twisted a ring on her wedding finger— the emerald engagement ring Nelson had given her in 1935. Other highlight acts were Orson Welles sawing Marlene Dietrich in half and W. C. Fields doing his

Jeanette proudly wears Nelson's engagement ring, evident in many portraits and candids taken over the years.

classic pool table routine. Dinah Shore, the Andrews Sisters, Sophie Tucker, Nigel Bruce, and Donald O'Connor were also in the cast.

Jeanette had scheduled a concert tour beginning in mid-October, but the coming months of separation had suddenly become unbearable to her. Nelson asserted that they must go to Lake Tahoe and perform their own marriage ceremony. To him it made a difference, in his eyes and hopefully in God's eyes. Jeanette had a week off between her Portland, Oregon, and Seattle, Washington, concerts. Nelson called in sick at the studio, and he met Jeanette at Tahoe.

Once they returned from the "honeymoon," Jeanette went on the road, and Nelson privately crashed emotionally. The reality of his sporadic love life with her, marriage or no marriage, was more than he could take. Being "married" to Jeanette didn't seem to be making things any easier. Nelson didn't report back to work at the Samuel Goldwyn Studios until Monday morning, November 1, 1943, where he continued filming *Knickerbocker Holiday*. It had now been in production for six weeks, and everyone involved knew it was a bomb.

Several of Nelson's fans were allowed to visit the set the week after Nelson returned from his "illness." They watched while Nelson and the other featured players sang "Make Tomorrow a Happy Day." One fan wrote:

> Over and over they sang it, and each time it wasn't quite perfect. When things went wrong the director would get mad. Nelson said between his teeth, "Let's not get so goddamned technical." At the end of one take the director said, "Okay, print it." But Nelson retorted, "Go ahead and print that if you want to, but it's not perfect, so if you want it perfect, don't print it." He was never satisfied with his performance, and made them do it over and over . . . We got all worn out just watching them work so hard. And they had been going since early morning.

Filming continued six days a week, and late into the evenings. Shelley Winters, who played the second female lead, reported that Nelson was a perfect, even-tempered gentleman, even though visibly depressed over the film, which he knew would do his career no good. She chronicled Nelson's depth of despair over his life at this time:

> One evening I was napping in my dressing room when a key turned in the lock and the dignified Nelson Eddy stumbled into my dressing room, quite drunk, still in costume and weeping. He made it straight for the bathroom and didn't seem to notice me as I sat up. It occurred to me that he thought it was his dressing room since they all looked alike.
>
> Suddenly he came out of the bathroom wearing long red underwear, just like my father's, and muttered, "The rushes were lousier today. I think I'd better go back to the Mounties. Hey, move over." I was stunned. Up to that point in the filming he had been the very proper New England gentleman whom I had never heard even say "darn". . . . I jumped out of bed . . . "Mr. Eddy," I yelled, "Think of your image! What would Jeanette MacDonald say?"
>
> "Who cares? She slides off her Cs."

I made for the door as he sort of lunged for me and fell on the sofa. I slammed the door behind me and ran down the hall and out of the dressing room building to the front gate . . . [The next day] Nelson Eddy was his usual reserved, polite self and seemed not to remember the embarrassing dressing room incident.

Knickerbocker Holiday wrapped just before Thanksgiving, 1943.

Jeanette, equally depressed, was ready to cancel the rest of her tour and come home to salvage their lives together. To her amazement, Nelson suddenly swung to the opposite extreme, swearing his undying devotion to her; he even insisted on trying to telepathically communicate with her before each concert. As she was on the East Coast, Nelson kept track of the time difference, and at the appropriate hour, before she went on stage, he made sure he was alone and was thinking of her.

On one occasion he had to work late at the studio and became extremely agitated because it was nearing her performance time. The director saw how nervous he was and, assuming he was overtired, finally let him quit for the day. Nelson rushed to his dressing room and locked the door. Glancing at the clock, he realized she was now several numbers into the concert, but he tried to contact her telepathically anyway. Later that night Jeanette phoned him, and he asked how the concert had gone. "It was terrible at first," she told him. "Where were you? But it turned out fine."

The two stars by now seemed to be teetering on the edge of disaster. In December 1943, both Jeanette and Nelson had unraveled emotionally to where they were both bordering on breakdowns. Within weeks, Jeanette would indeed succumb to a nervous collapse. Nelson was spared a similar fate by being asked to go overseas on a mission for his country. Suddenly he had a new purpose in life, a challenge that would divert his attention from the personal problems that were threatening to rob him of his sanity. On December 15, Nelson quietly left Los Angeles and headed to Washington, D.C. He was recruited by the CIC (the Counter-Intelligence Corps, a division of the Army) and was sent overseas on a concert tour, which encompassed Brazil, Central Africa, Arabia, Egypt and Persia. According to an English researcher, this was not Nelson's first trip over-seas during the war. She was able to verify from audience members that Nelson sang at Hullavington Camp, near Chippenham, in 1942.

The story of Nelson's undercover work was documented by Frank Laric, John Pickard and others, and rumors of it were even discussed on the set of *Northwest Outpost*. Lawrence Tibbett, Jr., said that his father did similar work for the CIC.

Opera singers who spoke or understood German were assets. Nelson's job was apparently to check up on someone whom they suspected of being a double agent, but it is unclear what exactly his mission was—all U.S. government documents relating to his wartime mission remain classified.

Newspaper reports of the time place him in one city when in fact he was in another; Nelson moved around constantly and quickly; he showed up suddenly in England and then disappeared, and an English newspaper even accused him of being a Nazi spy. In a few short weeks he was in Africa, South America and

Europe, seemingly without any plan and certainly outside any normal USO tour schedule. When Nelson returned stateside, he repeated in writing that he was not at liberty to discuss details of his tour.

As the story goes, Nelson was on a leg of his tour in Cairo when it was discovered, either by the double agent or by an associate, that Nelson was working for the U.S. government. Problems arose immediately, and a desperate effort was made to keep Nelson from leaving Egypt. At some point in his attempts to flee the country, Nelson had to make the choice to kill an Axis sympathizer who himself had designs on Nelson's life.

Any records of Nelson as informant would be filed under a code name and, unfortunately, Nelson's code name is unknown. After the war, a friend of Jeanette's noted that there was a number in Washington that she was able to call during the war, and that she was always put in touch with Nelson (while he was stateside). Jeanette commented that while Gene Raymond's work in the Air Force was acknowledged, Nelson would never receive the medal he deserved for serving his country.

A rare shot of Nelson overseas, December, 1943.

21

The Princess of Opera

Jeanette continued her concert tour into December, 1943. She returned home before Christmas, underweight, exhausted, agitated over Nelson being overseas and the futility of their lives. On Christmas Day Jeanette had her whole family together; Elsie had come from Philadelphia to visit her husband, who was stationed at Camp Haan. On New Year's Eve Jeanette sang at the Hollywood Canteen, then went home and quietly suffered a breakdown.

"It was right in the middle of the war," remembered Sybil Thomas. "Nelson was overseas, and I received a frantic telegram from him. He'd stopped getting letters from Jeanette, and was very worried. Something must be wrong. Would I check into it for him?"

Sybil continued:

> I was furious with her, she should at least have had the decency to write a line or two. I called over to that house [Twin Gables] a few times to give her a piece of my mind. Either her mother or that secretary answered, saying she wouldn't come to the phone, or wasn't home. This went on for days. Finally I got suspicious, something funny going on. I went over there, unannounced. Her mother opened the door but refused to let me in—can you believe it? I finally told her I suspected Jeanette was being held in there against her will, and that I would go straight to the police if I wasn't allowed to see her immediately.
>
> She told me Jeanette was in her bedroom. I found her lying on a divan near the

window, asleep. At least I thought she was asleep. The first thing I noticed was how frail she looked; her wrists and hands were very thin.

I shook her a few times. She was awake but appeared dazed, and didn't seem to know who I was, which surprised me. After all, I'd known her for ten years, even if we weren't the best of friends. I didn't care if she was sick or not, I shoved Nelson's telegram under her nose and berated her for treating him so badly. It was hard to get through to her. She shook the telegram and stared at it as if she couldn't read. Finally she said, "But I wrote him, I'm sure I did. Didn't I?"

"Obviously you didn't," I snapped. "I've come here to make certain you write him now. Otherwise, knowing him, he'll be on the next plane home, and he's needed much more there."

Jeanette nodded. I helped her up. She almost fell, she was so weak. Somehow I got her over to the writing desk. It was a minute or two before she could even hold the pen. "I'm sure I wrote him," she kept mumbling. "I'm sure I did." She stared at the blank stationery before her and said, "What do I write?"

I couldn't believe it—I had to dictate a love letter for her! "You know the kind of stuff he'll want to hear, you love him, you miss him." She slowly wrote what I said. I made her address it and lick the stamp. When I had the letter safely in my pocketbook I felt a little more kindly toward her. She almost fainted getting back to the divan, and I got a damp washcloth for her forehead to bring her around. I kept asking what was wrong, but she either looked puzzled or sad, and shook her head. Finally she said she was all right, just a little tired. I asked if a doctor had seen her and she said yes.

She was exhausted, so I left. I tried to get out of her mother what had happened; by now I'd figured out she'd had a collapse. I asked if there were anything I could do to help, not for myself, but because I knew Nelson would expect it of me—but she said no, and warned me not to come back or tell anyone what I'd seen here today. They didn't want the press getting wind of Jeanette's "cold" because it could jeopardize her career. She assured me Jeanette was doing much better and would be up on her feet in a matter of days. Well, she didn't look better to me but I realized I'd done what I could, and left.

Awhile later I got another telegram from Nelson, telling me how relieved he was, he'd heard from Jeanette and she was fine. Boy, I choked on that one!

On January 19, 1944, a press release from Cairo reported that Nelson had completed his tour of Central Africa and Brazil, having given twenty-nine concerts in twenty-six days. He next surfaced in Edinburgh, Scotland, where he was spotted in a church. He joined in the last verse of the hymn "Crown Him with Many Thorns" and led the singing without a hymn book. Then he sang a solo, "The Lord's Prayer," slipped out of the church, and was not seen again in that country. There were reports of his plane nearly crashing, and problems with the ship that finally deposited him in West Palm Beach on Valentine's Day, several days later than scheduled. Jeanette, meanwhile, had managed to pull herself together; she did a radio show on February 7, then headed for Florida to meet Nelson. They had a brief reunion when his ship finally pulled in, then he headed north to Washington, D.C., and New York.

Ann Eddy bought a box at the Metropolitan Opera and arranged a big party in Nelson's name. But he never showed up; he was still with Jeanette. "It was obvious to their friends that Nelson hadn't even bothered to contact Ann, and they were all laughing their heads off," said an insider. "Ann was furious; she went to the box office and made a terrible scene demanding her money back. Then she went back to Hollywood and gave a welcome home party but Nelson wasn't there either."

Nelson ultimately settled back into married life with Ann while Jeanette attempted another concert tour. But she collapsed again in El Paso. When Nelson saw her he was devastated. She was so weak she couldn't feed herself, and "so thin there's hardly anything left of her." Fearful she would die, Nelson took her away "to the mountains" and nursed her back to health.

"They were gone only a short time, a few days maybe," said Sybil Thomas. "I saw them together at a party a few weeks later. You wouldn't have believed it was the same woman. She had gained back some weight and was back to her chattering self. Talked a lot, very social. The only thing I noticed was a vacant look to her, a tight, suffering look in her eyes. And I think it got worse from that point on, not better. Nelson, on the other hand, looked great. He'd lost some weight and had a great tan."

"Upon my return to California a few weeks ago, I was put to bed immediately with a very bad cold and am just now feeling myself again," wrote Jeanette to her fans on March 31. Two weeks later Anna MacDonald penned a similar message: "Of course you know that Jeanette was ill and had to cancel or postpone the concert at El Paso. She is better now."

With Nelson around Jeanette *was* better. They spent the month of April on their separate tours, but before leaving Los Angeles they had their usual pre-concert practice sessions together. One of Nelson's numbers this season was Schubert's "An Silvia" ("Who is Sylvia?"). He insisted that Jeanette sing it for him and was so moved by her rendition of it that when he finally took her home he said, "Goodnight, little Sylvia." (Months later, Jeanette made a private re-cording of "Who is Sylvia?" as a Christmas gift for Nelson.)

On April 14, Jeanette arrived back in El Paso ready to sing, but she fell ill again, this time with an attack of food poisoning. It was serious enough for her to be hospitalized. That night and the next day Nelson was a wreck, waiting for word of her recovery. He was in New York for a Carnegie Hall concert the night of the fifteenth, and wasn't certain he could perform. He did finally go on as scheduled, but in his second set of songs he had difficulties getting through "Who is Sylvia?" The critic from the New York *Herald-Tribune* noted this in his review, writing that Nelson was "vocally uneven . . . characterized by senti-mentality of style which reached its nadir in a treacly, dragged version of Schu-bert's 'Who is Sylvia?'" At intermission, Nelson received a wire that had been sent to his hotel, stating that Jeanette's condition was much improved. He was elated at the news and sang better during the second half of the evening. When it was time for encores, he stepped up to the front of the stage, held up his hand to quiet the audience, and said, "If you don't mind I am going to sing a song that is very dear to me," and he sang "Indian Love Call."

Jeanette was able to fulfill her next two performances, in Houston and Beaumont, Texas, on April 18 and 19. Then she had five days before her Montgomery, Alabama, concert. Nelson canceled his April 21 appearance in Rochester, New York, pleading laryngitis (he did have a cold), and took off to meet Jeanette. He drove to Kansas City where Jeanette met him via train. They ate at a "darling little roadhouse" according to Jeanette, and were not recognized. Throughout the meal Nelson kept calling her Mrs. Eddy. "Well, darling, I know you love to hear it," Jeanette told him, "but after all, somebody around here might think Mrs. Eddy has changed considerably and somewhat suddenly." They "spent the whole day riding around Kansas." After one night together, Nelson drove to Cleveland for his next concert (Rochester was rescheduled for May 2) and Jeanette hopped the train for Alabama. She finally sang her El Paso concert on May 20, at the end of her tour.

■■■ *Knickerbocker Holiday* opened in mid-March to disastrous reviews. One of the chief complaints was that Charles Coburn, not Nelson, sang the famous "September Song." Nelson himself admitted that the film was "all chopped up." The New York *Times* commented, "The picture no sooner is underway in a cheerful mood than long-faced Dutch councilmen go ardently into a discussion of life, liberty and the pursuit of somebody to hang. From then on the story of old New York, under Dutch colony rule, unwinds to the accompaniment of generally good music and generally bad comedy . . . Nelson Eddy carries his musical chores as he always does, but his attempted acting of the role of the harum-scarum young firebrand, Brom Broeck, is too much of a drain on his vitality."

Knickerbocker died a quick death in theaters. *The Phantom of the Opera*, which had done excellent business in major cities, had also quickly petered out. Nelson knew he needed a hit if he was to retain his film popularity. During the concert tour, his manager informed his fans that a MacDonald-Eddy film was definitely in the works, and that they were also going to do a radio series together. So June, 1944, found Nelson and Jeanette once again in Los Angeles, surging ahead with their plans for a professional comeback. Their first teaming was on the Lux Radio Theater in a production of *Naughty Marietta*. During the summer they entertained at the Hollywood Canteen and other war-related benefits.

Gene was still stationed in Yuma, Arizona, and Jeanette saw him infrequently. Eventually promoted to major, Gene was unpopular with some of the men there because of his apparently anti-Semitic views. Leonard Knazik, also stationed at Yuma, termed Gene Raymond "a glorified office boy," saying, "The only reason he got as far as he did was because of who he was married to." Knazik described an ugly incident in which Gene called one of the men, who happened to be Jewish, some derogatory names and picked a fight with him. Then, when they were caught fighting, Gene insisted the other man had initiated it, and allowed the innocent man to be thrown in the brig. Knazik and many others were incensed by this and "had no use" for Gene Raymond after that.

How much of her husband's war activities Jeanette was aware of is unknown, but by June 1944, she had advised Nelson and her lawyer that she was going ahead with her plan to divorce Gene. According to one source, this was her second divorce filing in two years. The Hollywood *Reporter* alluded to the split in a gossip column from June 14: "The long-brewing, long-expected divorce of a big femme star and her husband can be expected to pop as soon as he is out of the army—which will be soon. Heaven knows, she's tried hard to make a go of things."

Jeanette's attorney at this time was Louis Schwartz. Susanna Foster, who had the same lawyer, recalled:

[Schwartz] was invited to dinner at Jeanette's and said, "Would you like to come too? Jeanette's invited you." So I went to their home, and Gene wasn't there. We had ham for dinner. I'll never forget, because we had ham and her maid was named Virginia. And she was so old, she could hardly walk.

I remember Jeanette telling me at dinner something about a tonsillectomy she'd had. She said, "We often wondered what my voice could have been if it hadn't been for that tonsillectomy." And we started talking about opera, and she said, "Oh, Susanna, don't get mixed up in that bunch. That's the worse intrigue in the world. You think you've seen intrigue in Hollywood, wait till you see it in the opera."

She told me, and she was so right.

Belying Jeanette's divorce plans, which were ultimately dropped, she wrote her fans about the goings-on at her birthday weekend (June 18). "The Captain was able to come home for the weekend, and we had two parties—one Saturday evening to celebrate our anniversary and on Sunday, my birthday, we had the family and a few friends. The Saturday party turned out to be quite a musical affair with José Iturbi playing for us, Nelson Eddy singing and Lauritz Melchior singing. José Iturbi accompanied Lauritz to sing 'Ich Liebe Dich,' then Nelson and Lauritz sang the duet from the last act of *La Bohème*. I sang one of Gene's compositions and then sang 'Sweethearts' with Nelson. It ended with everyone singing together."

During the summer months, Jeanette took a characteristically aggressive stand regarding her career. She made three radio appearances with Nelson, consulted with Ernst Lubitsch about directing them in a film, and purchased the rights to Frances Parkinson Keyes's *Crescent Carnival*. She also began coaching with Lotte Lehmann, determined to make her American opera debut, and added a second opera to her repertoire, Gounod's *Faust*.

The reason for her sudden enthusiasm toward her career was Nelson's abruptly abandoning his. He'd begun planning a new concert tour, then called it off. He invited Jeanette to dinner, then dropped his bombshell, informing her he was through singing. "I know I'm a disappointment to you," he told her, "but what can I do? I can't sing. I love you so much that I could die for that love." Jeanette argued with him, pointing out that their careers were important, if only to bolster their morales until their divorces came through. She had an uphill battle with him, but finally convinced him. "You must pull yourself together and work. A true man lives and lives nobly for the woman he loves. Only a coward dies for her."

"All right, I'll work," he told her, but he still refused to do a tour. (It was 1948 before Nelson finally resumed his regular concert tours again.) Jeanette worked with him on radio and developed some film projects with him. She was pleased when he rekindled his old interest in their movie careers, even though his choice for the script was a remake of *Mayerling*, a depressing star-crossed true story of an unhappily married prince and his lover who chose death over separation. Nelson went so far as to approach composer Rudolf Friml about writing a musical score for this proposed film. Additionally, Nelson toyed with writing an original script for them; in October, he penned a treatment called *Timothy Waits for Love*.

This was not Nelson's first attempt at screenwriting. In 1942 he wrote a complete script of the life of singer Feodor Chaliapin entitled *Song of the Giant*. He registered it with the Writer's Guild under the pseudonym Issac Ackerman, giving credit to Feodor Chaliapin, Jr., for the original treatment. (Chaliapin, Jr., is best known to today's film audiences as the grandfather in *Moonstruck*.) In Nelson's screenplay, he portrayed himself, telling the great basso's story in flashback, and he also played Chaliapin. The plot told Chaliapin's story through his arrival in Hollywood in the early 1930s, when he met an eager young baritone at a party—the young Nelson Eddy. Certain moments in the script give insight into Nelson's character, and his attempt at writing a love scene are reminiscent of his own early relationship with Jeanette. Shot 129 reads: "He grabs Iole roughly and kisses her like an animal. She is a sensitive creature and this impulsive treatment frightens her. She struggles a minute in his embrace, then angrily gives him a good smack in the face." Later, another character warns Chaliapin: "She [Iole] is a flower, she doesn't want to be crushed. Please control yourself."

Nelson had difficulties controlling himself during his first professional venture with Jeanette since *I Married An Angel*. He was so excited about working with her in the Lux radio version of *Naughty Marietta* on June 12 that the fans in the studio audience instinctively knew something was up between them—even the Nelson fans who hated Jeanette and vice versa. They observed how he was always touching her or trying to kiss her—and how when he was singing solo, she sat back and closed her eyes, listening rapturously. During one of Nelson's songs Jeanette choked on a drink of water, which prompted the Jeanette-haters in the audience to claim she was trying to steal Nelson's limelight by coughing. Their respective fans, especially the Nelson contingent, began a furious correspondence regarding "the situation." Over the next few years, thousands of pages of letters were written discussing (and often disavowing) the possibility of a MacDonald-Eddy romance, Nelson's other philanderings, his comings and goings as noted by fans who literally parked in front of his house and followed him almost daily by car.

On August 23, Nelson and Jeanette taped another radio show, Mail Call, for broadcast the following week. They co-starred with George Burns and Gracie Allen, in an amusing skit that had Gracie trying to break them up personally so George could team professionally with Jeanette. Gracie unintentionally was the hit of the show; while praising Jeanette to George, she said, "You know, if you had a woman behind you like that YOU could be the greatest romantic *sinner* in the world." She was supposed to say *singer*. Nelson turned bright red with embarrassment, then walked around, slapping his knee, doubled up with laughter. On September 4, Nelson and Jeanette teamed again for Lux in *Maytime*. Fans in the audience noted that Jeanette seemed less nervous and sang better than she had in *Naughty Marietta*.

Fans hoping for a joint radio series were disappointed when Nelson accepted his own series, The Electric Hour. He had different guest stars for each week, though during the early months his most frequent teaming was with a young singer named Gloria Scott. Nelson viewed The Electric Hour as a showcase for upcoming singers, and during the three seasons he hosted the show he featured a

Nelson also was a guest on many other radio shows during the war, even appearing with a young Frank Sinatra, who finally ousted Nelson out of the position as the highest paid singer in the world.

variety of young talent, including Kathryn Grayson, Jane Powell and twelve-year-old Lois Butler. Even if he'd wanted to work steadily with Jeanette, no sponsor could afford their combined fees on a regular basis. Fans were excited when an announcement was made that they were to co-host "The Ford Sunday Hour" series, but the plans fell through. Besides, Jeanette had been preparing for her American opera debut. She'd been studying for months with Lotte Lehmann at the recommendation of her opera agent, Constance Hope. Lehmann lived in Santa Barbara, and Jeanette drove there frequently for coaching sessions. Hope recalled, "[Jeanette] called me up that day [after her first session with Lehmann]. She wasn't a quick caller-upper . . . [she] was a writer, she didn't spend money. She was not extravagant, she was not small, but she was *not* extravagant. She called me up and said 'Constance, I wondered what it was that made you say that I should go to Lehmann. But I went to Lehmann, and I can only tell you than an hour with her on a role is as if the room is dark, and you open the windows and sunshine flies in.'"

Lehmann herself commented, "When Jeanette MacDonald approached me for some coaching lessons I was really curious how a glamorous movie star, certainly spoiled by the adoration of a limitless world, would be able to devote herself to another, a higher, level of art. I had the surprise of my life: there couldn't have been a more diligent, a more serious, a more pliable person than Jeanette. The lessons, which I started with a kind of suspicious curiosity, turned out to be sheer delight for me. She studied Marguerite with me—and Lieder. These were the ones which astounded me the most. I am quite sure that Jeanette would have developed into a serious and successful Lieder singer if time would have allowed it."

After her lessons, Jeanette often stayed the night at the El Encanto Hotel in Santa Barbara. The evening of July 14, 1944, she'd just climbed into bed when a bellboy broke into her cottage and attempted to wrap a blanket around her head. Jeanette fought back and screamed; her assailant punched her in the eye and scratched her face, then fled. Jeanette later dropped assault charges, but was badly shaken by the experience and suffered from shock for several days. "I think Jeanette has fully recovered from the black eye," Anna MacDonald wrote on August 28, "but her nerves are still shaky and she hasn't slept well since that time. It was a horrible experience, but we're all so thankful it was no worse."

Nelson had a remedy for Jeanette's sleeping problems; he insisted that Jeanette stay with him for several nights. When Isabel asked whether Jeanette had a good rest, Nelson replied, "She should have, there is no place where she gets it better than in my arms. Jeanette has insomnia for only one reason: She needs happiness and peace of mind. There wasn't a night that she didn't sleep like a baby. And I know she slept all right because I didn't very much. I was too afraid she would get cold in the night, and I put an extra blanket over her toward morning."

Jeanette left on her concert-opera tour on October 24, 1944. Nelson was desolate at her going, but he gave her a string of pearls to wear during her operas. Their last night together was memorable enough for Nelson to record in his diary; the subject of his dissertation was her new nightie, which he found intriguing because of its "silky soft entanglements." Jeanette teased him: "Mr. Eddy, there are going to be more and better yards and yards of nightie than you ever dreamed of. After all, I have to protect myself."

Nelson replied, "Well, it will be much wasted effort. You will only suffer more than I do while you are protecting yourself." She blushed, prompting him to add, "Oh, you precious darling, if I lived with you a hundred years, you would still be shy, and I love you so much that I shall probably die before I get you back from your tour." Then he grew serious. "Don't ever change. I don't want you modern *ever*."

Jeanette sang with the Chicago Symphony on October 28 and 29, then rehearsed for her Chicago debuts as Juliette and Marguerite. In the November 4 *Roméo*, her co-stars were Captain Michael Bartlett, USMC, as Roméo, and Nicola Moscona as Friar Lawrence. Life magazine did a photo feature on the production. After all the months of preparation for the roles, which Jeanette termed "the grimmest time of my life," the reviews were gratifying. "Jeanette MacDonald set her Juliet cap at opera and to judge by the uproar, opera capitulated," wrote Chicago *Tribune* critic Claudia Cassidy. "Her Juliet is breathtakingly beautiful to the eye and dulcet to the ear." "A personal triumph," agreed the *Herald-Tribune*, nicknaming her the "Princess of Opera."

The November 15 debut in *Faust* (co-stars were Ezio Pinza and Raoul Jobin) was no less momentous. Claudia Cassidy, usually hard to please, again raved. "*Faust* is superbly sung. From where I sit at the opera, Jeanette MacDonald has turned out to be one of the welcome surprises of the season . . . and her Marguerite was better than her Juliet . . . beautifully sung with purity of line and tone, a good trill, and a Gallic inflection that understood Gounod's phrasing." The *Daily News* added, "Jeanette . . . deserved the gale of applause she got last night at the Civic Opera House for the Jewel Song. In the scene in the church, however, between Mephistopheles and Marguerite, Miss MacDonald acquitted herself vocally and dramatically with the highest operatic power she has shown in her whole 'career' in her new medium . . . The emotion she and Pinza together stirred here was as authentic as it was gripping." (Jeanette sang *Faust* again in Chicago the following year, with co-stars Nino Martini and Nicola Moscona, and at that time Claudia Cassidy described Jeanette as "a singing actress of such beauty you felt if Faust must sell his soul to the devil, at least this time he got his money's worth.")

Jeanette was thrilled at her reception, and a newspaper interview reported that she planned to debut one new operatic role a year. "Last year it was *Roméo et Juliette*. This year is the *Faust* year. *La Bohème* is set for next year. And from overhearing a conversation with Oscar Hild [the Opera Association manager], there's a bet on about *Traviata*."

Meanwhile, though, she continued concertizing. In Pittsburgh on November 21, the highlight of the show was her stopping in the middle of "Annie Laurie" and informing the stunned audience, "I've forgotten the words! And to a song I know so well. I'm ashamed of myself." The audience laughed, waiting patiently while she looked up the lyrics in her little notebook, then cheered as she found them and finished the number. She had made it a practice to sing one of Gene's compositions in each of her tours, but this time she didn't, and one fan asked her about this. Jeanette answered tellingly, "I've sung his songs so much lately, I thought I'd confine myself to songs that everyone likes." She quickly added, "I love his songs, though."

While on the East Coast, Jeanette was approached by producer Mike Todd about starring in an unpublished Victor Herbert operetta. Louella Parsons stated in her column that Jeanette was reporting for rehearsals in New York on January 1, with the show opening in Boston in early February, then on to Broadway. What wasn't revealed in the press release was that Jeanette (and Todd) wanted Nelson to co-star with her; but when he backed out, she bowed out as well. Nelson was just as happy to stay in Los Angeles and do his weekly radio show. He refused to let her do the show anyway with another co-star, reminding her, "You should know by now who you are taking orders from." He was even angrier when he learned she'd attended a party given by Mike Todd, where she danced with "married men." He insisted she return home, telling her he wouldn't put up with her dancing with other men, married or not. When Gene Raymond learned about this incident, he was incredulous. "Is this going on the rest of Jeanette's life? Won't dance with anybody else? Just to please that nut, who didn't have sense enough to keep her when he had her."

The week all this was occurring, Nelson showed up at his radio show in a surprisingly bad mood. One fan, who attended every broadcast, noted that Nelson "sat down and surveyed the audience and, boy, from the look on his face, he sure didn't think much of us. His expression was so different from the smiling boyish one he wears when entertaining. It wasn't a put-on-for-the-public look but, rather, a personal what-I-think-about-all-this-foolishness look, and it wasn't complimentary. It wasn't particularly pleasing to see Nelson thus."

Isabel was also amazed that Nelson had taken a stance on Jeanette's career. "Did you tell her she couldn't work anymore this spring?" she asked her son. Nelson answered, "Yes, I told her she couldn't, but she doesn't want to anyway."

Jeanette returned home in time for Christmas. This year it was a family affair; for the first time both mothers were invited for the holiday meal. Anna MacDonald and Isabel Eddy sat at the table like two new mothers-in-law trying to like each other. It was a big step for Anna. For years she had touted Gene Raymond and had refused to be sympathetic with her daughter's marital problems. She had never warmed up to Nelson and had little to do with Isabel, resenting the fact that Jeanette called her "mother" and turned to her for advice.

For Christmas that year Nelson gave Jeanette an evening dress, fur wrap and jewel-studded slippers. He bought them all without Isabel's help and reportedly they all "fit like a glove." Jeanette gave him twelve private "records of memories and then spoken memories." The titles of her recordings were "Beautiful Dreamer," "Come, Where My Love Lies Dreaming," "Brown Bird Singing,"

"Dream Dance," "One Kiss," "My Hero," "Speak to Me of Love," "Love's Old Sweet Song," "Mother's Prayer," "Smilin' Through," "Annie Laurie," and "Who is Sylvia?" The fate of these priceless recordings, with her personalized introductions preceding the songs, is unknown.

Jeanette returned briefly to New York in late January 1945, to record two albums for RCA Victor: one of religious songs, and *Up in Central Park* with a young Robert Merrill. She returned to Los Angeles, where she remained until the summer, when she gave a short concert tour. Nelson also recorded for Columbia. A war-caused ban on recordings had recently been lifted.

Blossom was hospitalized with a serious case of pneumonia in February, and there is mention in a letter from Isabel that Nelson was concerned about Jeanette's heart. Eventually the health crises ended, and attention was directed to revitalizing Jeanette and Nelson's careers. Various film projects were announced for them, including *Song of Norway* and Sigmund Romberg's *East Wind*, which was purchased by RKO for the team. But nothing materialized. Isabel wrote to Sarah Tucker: "I have just received the most beautiful letter from my little Jeanette that I believe I have ever read. How she poured out her heart to me, poor little thing. I will keep the letter so you may read it later. Meanwhile this will give you some idea.

"She began by talking about the little things, dating from the first, such as his look, his smile, his courteous attentions. The way he always took her arm even when there was only a wire to cross. How he remembered the deserts she liked—sent flowers on every occasion, and hundreds of dear little things. And then, when she had completely lost her heart to him, how she loved the anxiety he always had for her sleepless nights. His protective instinct, the kiss he gave her . . .

"Then she went on to the more intimate things, using the sweetest language and thoughts I ever heard from any girl. How I love her for this confession to me. She said this year, of course, had been the dearest of all. How she loved his possessive feeling for her. His demands of what to do and not to do. She said she loved him most of all in this mood—when he could be so very firm at times, yet always so tender and kind. And then the times when he was so lonely . . . And then came the loveliest part of her letter, and from here on I will quote.

> All my life I have thought that to be truly and sincerely loved by one man would be the greatest happiness that could come to me . . . That I am truly the love of all his life is something I am even now almost afraid to believe. It seems too much to expect. But it is surely true that it is greater to give than to receive. During this past heartbreaking year I have been able to give him courage when he most needed it—hope when it seemed there was none. He has brought me a love beyond my sweetest dreams, but it has meant even more to me to be able to give him love. To subordinate all my own life and habits to his wishes. . . .
>
> During these past weeks he has learned the value of prayer. He knows that my love will surround him always, that his name will be in my daily prayers. He knows that no matter what happens, he can always come to me when he needs me. And he

knows one other thing about me that I think will always help when he is lonely.
But as for myself, mother, without him now I am not sure I won't go to pieces. I
shall try to pick up the threads of my career—but I am not sure I care enough. I
know I have to have some other interest in life. My voice should supply it—I am
hoping so. But this much you must promise me. He must never know that I am
suffering, for he would never for one moment permit it, and then all I have tried to
inspire in him would be for naught. We are both paying now for our past mistakes.
Paying a bitter price in heartaches and tears. But one thing sure, no matter if I am
dying for his love and the joy of his arms around me, he must never know how
much I want it. He has built an altar around me, and all my life I must remain the
shining ideal he has made of me.

I badly need the power to understand why a divine providence has made me love
him so, if it has been ordained that I can never have that love. Just now we can only
place our lives in God's hands. May he have mercy on us both.

The fans were oblivious to the tormented sufferings of their idols. They
couldn't understand why the two weren't working more, even as they claimed to
be very busy when there was little to show for their efforts. Many sensed it was a
deliberate sabotage of their careers, but for what reason? This lack of understanding infuriated fans who had been fiercely loyal for a decade now. The bickering
among the fans and the rival clubs finally reached is zenith in 1945. For the
Nelson clubs, the catalyst was a project to establish a scholarship in Nelson's
name at Juilliard. The scholarship fund was headed by a "team" fan, Dorothy
Dillard, who appealed to fans of all Nelson's clubs to raise $1,000. Through her
diligence the money was collected, but now the presidents of the Nelson clubs
fought over who had more status, and they each plagued Nelson with petty and
nasty letters. The scholarship, which should have brought pleasure and pride all
around, only served to sour the relationship between Nelson and his clubs.
Furthermore, one of them was run by two sisters who quite vocally hated
Jeanette. They went so far as to have their feelings verbalized on a radio show,
then they lied and denied they'd ever said it. Nelson was enraged. He tried to
remain neutral, but was ready to wash his hands of the clubs altogether.

Among Jeanette's clubs, the New York chapter of one had an insider who also
knew Sarah Tucker and received periodic updates. Additionally, her brother
worked at Columbia Records and had contacts of his own. A few select fans
gathered each month at this woman's Staten Island home for briefings, and soon
selected details of the romance were leaked around the East Coast. Some fans
were at first willing to believe it, then changed their minds as they waited in vain
for Nelson and Jeanette to leave their spouses.

One of the presidents of Jeanette's other club was Marie Waddy (later Gerdes).
Marie was also a friend of Blossom's, and learned some of the truth, mostly from
ever-talkative Blossom, who, under the name Marie Blake, briefly had her own
fan club as well. When faced with the dilemma of perpetuating the happy Gene-
Jeanette marriage, Marie Waddy felt that her loyalties lay with Jeanette, whatever

the truth. She resigned her presidency, preferring to cultivate a lifetime friendship with the two sisters.

As far as the fans were concerned, 1945 was a rock bottom year for MacDonald and Eddy, and they lost hundreds of faithful devotees who had finally given up on them in disgust.

Radio studio audiences were always amazed at their blatant intimacy, Nelson's constant teasing and touching, and Jeanette's determined efforts to concentrate on the task at hand.

22

"My lover's arms were tender"

The year 1945 marked the tenth anniversary of *Naughty Marietta*. But there hadn't been a film with Jeanette and Nelson together in three years, and Jeanette had been absent from movies altogether during this time, with the exception of her brief appearance in *Follow the Boys*. Even the columnists wondered in print what had happened to "America's Singing Sweethearts." Jeanette and Nelson considered many projects carefully, but the truth was that they were too preoccupied with their personal situation to take on any new film commitments. They didn't want the close scrutiny of co-workers, nor that of Ann Eddy, nor did they look forward to the months of long work hours that would deny them the private moments they so craved.

Their only joint appearances during this period were on radio. On April 15, Jeanette was scheduled to guest on the Electric Hour with Nelson. His radio shows were broadcast live. As his time slot was 9:00 P.M., he broadcast two complete shows, one at 6:00 P.M. for the East Coast, and again at 9:00 P.M. for the West Coast. The Lux shows he did with Jeanette were also broadcast twice. The April 15 Electric Hour was a tribute to their films, but due to the sudden death of President Roosevelt, they sang a solemn tribute to him instead, with no studio audience. She then returned the following week, and performed with Nelson all of their film hits. Once again, fans carefully scrutinized Nelson's reaction to working with Jeanette. Some of them attended every weekly broadcast and rehearsals of the Electric Hour, plus his other regular guest appearances on shows such as Bell Telephone Hour, Command Performance and Mail Call. So they were familiar with Nelson's moods and behaviors, some of them seeing him at work two or even three times a week.

The April 22 show found Nelson in unusually high spirits. Before air time he told the audience that he and Jeanette were going to do a scene from one of their movies. Then he said to Jeanette, "Hiya, Princess, gimme a little smack!" Jeanette responded by slapping him on the cheek. One eyewitness wrote that Jeanette laughed frequently and was "positively blushing," while Nelson radiated "personality plus—plus ham!" The eyewitness, through normally a "Jeanette-hater," had to admit, "There is an ease and naturalness to their performance together that neither is able to achieve alone. The easy familiarity that exists between them allows each to give expression to his or her slightest desire with the full assurance that the other will understand and cooperate. Jeanette seems to get quite a kick out of Nelson's antics and under her admiring gaze he expands himself almost to the point of bursting. There is a maturity about her that emphasizes the boyish nature of Nelson's personality in contrast, and it is this boyishness that is Nelson's greatest asset, especially at the box office." Without a doubt their relationship during this period was stronger than it ever had been. But since they weren't at a studio, there were few witnesses to their intimacy. Nor did they have many confidants with whom the details could be shared. The following list was compiled by one insider in November 1945, of the only people who could be trusted:

Frank Lloyds—Helen and Johnny Mack Brown—Paxson—Lippe—Lily Pons and husband—Woody Van Dyke's mother—Nelson's lawyer—Bobby Armbruster—Kenny Baker—Jimmy Wallington—John Charles Thomas—John Brownlee—Nadine Conner—Lauritz Melchior—Dr. John Wyman—Irene Dunne—Jimmie Fidler— Mary Pickford—Edgar Bergen—Louis B. Mayer—Cecil B. DeMille—Allan Jones and wife—Adrian and wife—Emily Wentz [and] Sylvia Grogg [Jeanette's secretaries]—and Helen Ferguson (doesn't like it)—also Gene's brother (doesn't like it)—Anna MacDonald (doesn't like it).

Meantime, Gene was home again, now a major, and Jeanette had to keep up appearances. Her relationship with Gene had mellowed; she was truly grateful for his understanding and patience over the years. Their correspondence during the stretches of time he'd been away was affectionate, reminiscent of her correspondence with Bob Ritchie after their intimacy had ended. Once again, as she'd done with Ritchie, she simply avoided discussing the Nelson part of her life with Gene. Those in the know described their relationship as "like brother and sister." Of course, there was an understanding that the marriage was over once Nelson obtained his freedom.

Nelson also played the dutiful husband, but he told Ann that he needed to spend time with his mother, and he frequently stayed with Isabel. He had his own bedroom in her home, as well as a study, and added a second bathroom upstairs so that each would have privacy. Isabel had moved to 526 North Palm Drive, in

Beverly Hills, in December 1944. Before that she lived briefly at 1347 North Doheny Drive, and on Roxbury Drive. Ann was not allowed over to Isabel's. Privately they were not on speaking terms but were socially polite when in public together at Nelson's concert or radio appearances. Had Ann visited Isabel's home she would have been enraged, for her husband's study was a virtual shrine to Jeanette. A large oil painting of her as Naughty Marietta hung on the wall (a Christmas gift from Jeanette), the bookshelves displayed their records, stills and picture albums; all the letters and cards she'd ever sent him he kept. Nelson had a movie projector in the room; his film collection included *San Francisco*, which he loved for Jeanette's opera scenes, and *Smilin' Through*.

Nelson had his mother as guest on a special Mother's Day edition of the Electric Hour on May 13. They sang a duet of "Love's Old Sweet Song," and the show was so popular that Nelson had her on the following year as well.

The current scene was summed up by an insider: "Jeanette halfway makes a pretense of going around with her friends as she once did, but Nelson makes no pretense of any kind, and in fact he has all but told everybody he knows that he can't work because of his private life. But he is very careful not to say anything about *her* [Jeanette's] side of it. It is quite well known all over Hollywood now that his marriage is nothing at all. But most people think he is such an old fogy he will never do anything about it. And of course they haven't figured out that his love for Jeanette is why they don't work together, but they don't connect her side of it because of the Gene business."

Jeanette's main goal for the year was to force Nelson to get a divorce. She'd been talked out of filing first, since this would raise Ann's suspicions that they were still seeing each other. And Nelson had worked very hard to convince Ann otherwise. He went overboard being a devoted and wonderful husband to her, and they even socialized at the Raymonds' parties, so Ann could see how happy Jeanette and Gene were as well. It was all very civilized. Ann soon rewrote history, claiming her marriage was blissful; she fabricated a scenario about how she and Nelson were in love from 1933 on, how he was faithful to her all those years before they married, and how devoted they were now to each other. This tale was passed down to her son and her relatives and became their gospel version of the marriage. But when Nelson seemed increasingly unable to extricate himself from his marriage, Jeanette gave him an ultimatum. Blossom commented: "Jeanette will give him all the time he needs to straighten out his life, but she will expect him to do it in a reasonable length of time. If he doesn't she will give him up, even though I am not sure she would be able to go on living."

Everyone had an opinion on this latest move of Jeanette's. Sarah Tucker wrote: "You'll see, Jeanette will stick to him through everything, and long after the rest of us have lost all patience. That girl understands him as no one else on earth does, and she loves him with such a love as you never heard of." Gertrude Evans pronounced herself angry and ready to "wash her hands" of Nelson and his entire scene, but she never did. Isabel wrote: "I have had the joy of raising him and taking care of him but he isn't really mine, he belongs to Jeanette. If I was a normal mother I suppose I would be very jealous of that girl, but I am too grateful that he has her to turn to. She is the only person in the world who will ever be able to penetrate the deepest recesses of his heart and share his entire life and all its secrets. I knew that long ago."

The lovers had been negotiating with RKO to do a color version of *East Wind*. Writer Dewitt Bodeen was present at Twin Gables one evening while Jeanette accompanied herself and Nelson singing the score of *East Wind*. A producer named Kerner was funding the film, but according to Bodeen, when Kerner died the project was abandoned. Meanwhile, Jeanette decided to do a July concert tour on the East Coast instead. Making herself less accessible to Nelson finally did have the desired effect: Nelson and Ann separated. During the summer of 1945, a Santa Monica newspaper broke the news that they were divorcing.

Unfortunately, the separation was short-lived. No documentation exists to explain what went wrong, but Nelson was soon back with Ann and they were photographed at parties together. A letter from Jeanette during this period sheds possible insight. In it, she expresses fear that their relationship would always have a wedge between it, should their freedom come at the expense of Ann's suicide.

Jeanette coached with Lotte Lehmann in Santa Barbara, came home to spend a few days with Nelson and Isabel at "Mists," then hopped the train for her first concert in Detroit, on July 4. Isabel wrote Sarah Tucker: "They have been singing their throats out these many evenings. Nelson is so interested in her operas, and likes to think that he has a hand in their success. It is really a sight to watch him decide when it is time for her to rest, put her on the sofa with pillows all around her—and then go and make hot tea to soothe her throat. Even with my eyes shut I would know then exactly what will happen. Jeanette talks to him in that quiet, gentle voice—different from any voice I have ever heard, and then he will be beside her, holding her hand. Everything is so beautiful for them because in the sight of heaven they are so entirely one and so tenderly conscious that this is true. Nelson is *her* possession now and she is no longer timid as she once was. And soon with a reverent look and through a close embrace he will be kissing those lips he adores. They have completely forgotten my presence—if I am here—and I usually am because *she* will not have it otherwise. Her manner to me is so wonderful. God keep them both safe for me." Isabel gave Jeanette as a parting gift a hand-knitted white silk and wool scarf, large enough to wrap around her head and shoulders. Once on the train, Jeanette discovered a huge roll of bills in her purse, with a note from Nelson attached:

My baby—

Unimportant as it may seem in comparison to other things—even this belongs to you. Please take it and do with it what you like—just one more thing I do not intend that creature shall get her hands on. I am sorry darling—but I can no longer even mention her name in your presence.

Jeanette thanked Nelson with the following letter:

My dear—

My first note to you since I arrived last evening—and I have a confession to make. I love you —did you know I loved you? I miss you too. I still feel the kiss you gave me one day ago. I now have a new little picture in the back of my locket—and darling, when I opened my purse on the train last night I was astonished to find such a token there. What am I to do with you? You are so generous—but I accept this with thanks, my dear—and it shall be taken care of for US. Thank you for that beautiful loyalty—your constant care.

I am lonely—would like to find myself in your arms tonight. Keep well until I return. I am yours so gladly—so proudly—my prayers for you until I see you.

> Goodnight my sweet—
> Baby Jam

P.S. Give our mommy a big kiss and hug for me and tell her to take very good care of our big little boy—and I'll write her tomorrow evening.

> Jam

Jeanette had barely arrived in Detroit when Nelson, equally lonely, impulsively took a plane to meet her. After a short reunion, he flew home to sing on the Bell Telephone Hour (which was switched from July 16 to the ninth). Before the Detroit concert began, a guard confided to one of her friends that Jeanette was "rather upset" because "her husband had been with her that day but had to leave a few hours before and was flying home. And her secretary says she's always nervous when he's flying." Several nights later Jeanette was asked by someone else if Gene had been able to meet her at all on this tour and she answered, "No, he can't get away." The guard had mistaken Nelson for the husband.

Back in Los Angeles, Nelson agreed to do the voices for a short animated

Make Mine Music was a 1946 Disney feature that had indifferent box office receipts. A series of short segments, similar in format to *Fantasia,* the best-received episode was Nelson in his portrayal of "Willie the Operatic Whale." Walt Disney is pictured here with Nelson.

segment in a new Walt Disney feature, *Make Mine Music.* Then he flew to Cincinnati to catch up with Jeanette once again on tour (she was singing *Roméo et Juliette* and *Faust*), and continued on to Philadelphia for her July 19 outdoor concert there. Philadelphia was canceled due to rain; Jeanette spent the evening instead with her sister Elsie while Nelson, Elsie's husband, and Jeanette's accompanist Collins Smith went to a nightclub. A group of fans who'd come from New York for the concert were at the same nightclub by chance and were amazed when Nelson recognized them, smiled, and even spoke to them. The next day Jeanette went to Elsie's dance studio and signed autographs and served home-made ice cream to her fans. One of the girls asked Jeanette when Nelson was making another film. She replied, "Well! When he does it will be with *me*!" The Philadelphia concert was rescheduled for the next evening. Nelson was nowhere in sight at the performance, and the fans were puzzled to learn that no one was allowed backstage. A few of them got back anyway, and discovered Jeanette's dressing room filled with relatives, including her aunts Margaret and Sally. Jeanette seemed very anxious to leave and her secretary finally explained, "She's going to New York at 11:00 tomorrow morning for a few days." Jeanette was radiant; she happily kissed all her relations, then dashed out. One of the relatives remarked that they'd never seen Jeanette such "an affectionate little soul" before.

Nelson and Jeanette spent two days at Lily Pons's home in Connecticut, then Nelson had to return to Los Angeles to begin recording his "Willie the Operatic Whale" sequence for Disney. Jeanette continued alone through the beginning of August, and carried on with heavy heart.

She and Nelson were good friends with Met opera star John Brownlee and his wife. Brownlee, who had sung with her in *Faust* in Chicago, was in her Cincinnati production of *Roméo et Juliette* as well. Jeanette returned to Cincinnati for one last Juliette on July 25. Brownlee's secretary, who wasn't in on all the intrigue, was puzzled at Jeanette's behavior. The woman noted that Jeanette kept herself together for the rehearsals, but was devastated afterwards. After the performance she took only three curtain calls, without a smile on her face, and didn't return to the stage even though the applause continued for several minutes. The secretary hurried backstage to see if anything was wrong; Brownlee told her Jeanette had collapsed and the doctor thought it might be the heat. He added, "But of course I know better. She has everything in the world that any woman could want, except happiness. She's the most unhappy person I have ever known—" Brownlee's wife cut him off, warning him he'd said enough.

Before her collapse, Jeanette had sent off a poignant letter to Blossom:

> . . . If I get sick on any tour, come to me quickly—but never let my darling know that he is the cause of it entirely—he is so sweet and kind. Of course, few people think that it is possible to die of a heartbreak—but I know that it is.

Once back in Los Angeles, Jeanette quickly recovered. Nelson forced her to eat and regain her strength. Observers at a restaurant were amused to see him pile her plate with two helpings of mashed potatoes and pork chops. He cut up the meat like she was a baby, and said, "Now, I don't want to see any of that left. You're staying right here till you eat every bite of it." Nelson further helped Jeanette regain her peace of mind by assigning her the task of redecorating "Mists." The outcome was described in detail by Isabel.

The living room walls were paneled in knotty pine—very attractive—but they wanted a softer shade—so had the wall painted a turquoise and then quickly rubbed off. It now has a pinkish blue effect—very lovely. The curtains are plaid cotton in Delft blue-grey and soft yellow. The divan is covered in yellow with quilted blue cushions. The hooked rugs combine blue-grey-rose-cedar and black—a perfectly stunning color note. Pictures are all in grayish pine frames—one of Jeanette in N. M. [*Naughty Marietta*] costume over the desk. One of Jeanette and Nelson in R. M. [*Rose Marie*] over the radio. On either side of the large windows where the divan is are twelve painted stills from N. M.—six on either side. Jeanette had a lovely one of me made which she has over the fireplace. The Victorian arm chairs by the fireplace are covered in rose and cedar plaid. Blossom gave them the radio and one easy chair and I gave them the low stool and covered it with needle point and how Jeanette loves that. She herself got the coffee table that sits before the fireplace—and on it she has a brass smoking tray—beautiful old-fashioned pink and blue tea set and pink vase for flowers. The lamps have pottery and copper bases with plain light-colored shades. Jeanette has copper candle sticks on the fireplace. The bunks Nelson had taken out and comfortable couch beds installed—table and lamp by each and all very lovely. The breakfast corner is truly a picture in soft yellow drapes and chair cushions of beautiful pastel print-flower design. On the Dutch sideboard Jeanette has lovely silver pieces and old china. She has brought practically everything from [Twin] Gables that Nelson ever specially noted or admired—and as for HIM—well—he has such a glow of possessive pride these days that I can scarcely hold him. Jeanette's room which he furnished himself is really in excellent taste—settee and bedspreads of cream-colored homespun with sprays of evergreen worked through it—green and white hooked rugs and ruffled curtains—or drapes of cream-colored background with sprays of evergreen and white roses scattered through them. The bathroom is a dream with mirrors all over and a huge dressing table complete to the last detail. On the wall of the bedroom Jeanette has a picture of her whole family in one frame—and on the dresser is a picture of Gene—but that Nelson put there himself—with the stern reminder to Jeanette that Gene was a dearly loved friend and that she was no more to forget that than was he. I have to laugh at his devotion to Gene—without him at this time he would indeed be in a bad fix.

As for Nelson's room, it is a man's dream—Jeanette is such a creative artist and it has everything he could possibly need—and all so perfectly suited to his moody taste, which she knows so well. Drapes and bedspread are of dark green homespun —furniture of cedar and pine in a natural finish—two oil lamps which she had electrified and which he loves because he is such a dreamer and they remind him of his grandparents' home (he says). The vivid color notes are in the chairs which she had upholstered in a beautiful print with sprays of pine and huge pine cones.

When Nelson bought the cabin the former owners had a handyman that cleaned and cooked for them and attended to the grounds as well. He has stayed on with Nelson but now Nelson has had the grounds so improved that it keeps the man busy just doing that. The entire wooded hill on the front side has been cleaned out until it looks like a big, lovely park. He was able to get a gas mower so George can cut the grass quickly. As for the house—none of us want a curious woman about—so for the time being we are doing it ourselves. Blossom and I together manage to keep it in good condition and occasionally I take Mary [Isabel's housekeeper and cook] up and she gives it a thorough going over, even to washing the windows. Of course I don't dare let Jeanette do much of anything—for if Nelson ever saw her with more than a dust rag in her hand we would all be murdered in cold blood. However, she insists these duties relax her and she loves them. On the day she fixed Nelson's room she wouldn't let a one of us go near her, but did it all herself—but she was tired and I persuaded her to rest before he got there. In fact, she was in dreamland when he came and I had to wake her because of course I couldn't let him see his room until she could show it to him. Well—he was speechless with surprise—he is always so touched by her every devotion to him. And in just a little while he went off for a walk all by himself—and we both knew that he was saying "thank you" for whenever he is deeply touched he does just that.

I wish it were possible for Jeanette's public to see her in her little gingham dress—white sox and low heeled shoes—and a dust rag in her hand. I know they would love her even more than they do—for this dazzling and glamorous girl (as they know her) has such an adorable little girl quality—and she is just as lovely—just as beautiful—whether doing down to earth housework or singing on an opera stage. Of course I know that I see through the eyes of gratitude and love because of Nelson, but I truly believe the angels threw away the pattern when she was made. I have never met her equal before and I don't expect to in the future. I wonder what my son has done to have this girl for his own.

On August 9, 1945, Jeanette made her much anticipated Hollywood Bowl debut. She broke the house attendance record, singing for 20,000 people, among them Governor and Mrs. Earl Warren, Louis B. Mayer, Isabel Eddy, and Ann Eddy with escort Doris Kenyon. Nelson was conspicuously absent; according to several reports he was in the hospital (reason unknown). Reviewer Florabel Muir wrote, "[Jeanette] looked every bit as young and as lovely as the first time I ever laid eyes on her in person, which must have been all of 16 years ago. Her voice doesn't grow old and neither does she. Yet it has a ripe richness, a strength and authority, qualities that seem to take on emphasis with the years." Afterwards, Gene hosted a reception in his wife's honor at the Beverly Hills Hotel for 400 people.

In the coming days Jeanette and Nelson pondered their future together. He was delighted when she finally agreed to make a film with him at RKO. Jack J. Gross was assigned as executive producer for *East Wind*, an operetta with music by Sigmund Romberg and words by Oscar Hammerstein. Jeanette informed her fans that she and Nelson were going to work together; Nelson was more cautious, saying he would have to approve the script before the project became a reality.

Their plans were daunted by a new crisis. One of Ann's doctors, Dr. John Wyman, consulted with Nelson and informed him that Ann's mental health was shaky and that she could easily be "pushed over the brink." It was recommended that she see a psychiatrist, and Nelson was encouraged to attend some of the sessions. After several consultations with both doctors and his lawyer, Nelson was informed that his hands were tied in regard to a divorce. If he filed, Ann would produce enough medical evidence of her own problems to stop him. Nor would she agree to give him his freedom without a major scandal, in which she'd trash Jeanette's reputation forever, as well as clean Nelson out financially. Nelson was finally forced to realize that he might be bound forever to his wife, that he would never be free to marry Jeanette. Devastated, he informed Jeanette he would end their relationship if she wished; he didn't want to string her along endlessly. She turned him down, certain there was still hope that Ann would come around. Nelson was happy to continue seeing her, but decided to end their intimacy, feeling he didn't deserve it.

His celibacy was short-lived. They'd finally decided to spend a "spiritual" overnight at "Mists," which meant sleeping in separate bedrooms. "I had never felt so lonely as I did that morning," Nelson later wrote. "It was the realization that Jeanette was here alone with me—she was my wife, yet I had no right to her love. All week I had been so miserable. I longed for her intensely. I wanted her in my arms, wanted my wife, wanted her body as well as her spirit. My darling knew I was determined not to again kindle that flame to the burning point, and yet the desire was so great I was faint with it."

He was unable to sleep that night; he tucked her in, then returned to his own room. Jeanette continued the narrative in a letter to Blossom: "Some time during the night I woke up and instantly knew that Nelson was not sleeping, so without bothering to slip on my robe I went across to his door, and there he was sitting up in bed reading a mystery story—can you imagine? And there it was three o'clock in the morning. I realized then that I had no robe on and reached for his big one, but he said, 'No, don't put it on. You look so beautiful standing there, come in with me before you get chilled.' So I slid into bed with him." Jeanette decided to read the book out loud to him to help him fall asleep, but after a few minutes of this the ludicrousness of the situation became apparent. "I would like to tell you just *how* my little boy went to sleep last night," Jeanette wrote Blossom, "but it is a secret. Oh me, my lover—even when I am an old, old lady I shall look over at this date in my diary and say, 'Yes, my lover's arms were tender.' I will remember how we waited so long for passions to be fulfilled—but how glorious was the fulfillment."

John Wyman soon became an important person in Jeanette's and Nelson's life. No longer treating Ann, he became a family doctor/confidant for Nelson. At Nelson's insistence, Jeanette was given a complete physical because she'd been suffering for months with debilitating headaches. "Dr. John" was unable to find a physical cause for her distress, but he elaborated on his findings in a very unorthodox letter to her.

My dear—I have known you for a very long time and I know much of your life's history. Now as your *friend* I could not say these things—but as your Dr. I can. You have life but your are not living it. You are loving a man with all your heart and mind, and keeping your love bottled up in an invisible tunnel until your nervous system is being wrecked. And do you realize that *his* health is being affected as well? If you had fallen in love with a different type of man this would be a different story, but he is the strangest man I ever saw. He has not only become my dear friend, but has done me the honor of becoming my patient as well, and it is hard to keep these things from one's doctor. I know that for the past three years he has fought his love for you night and day, because his one thought has been to protect you. But a "spiritual" marriage such as you two have been experiencing is impossible forever. I know what a good little girl you are and God will bless you for your goodness, but end this masquerade and see that Nelson ends it too. I am on your side and God is with you. Obey his law and you will find a great happiness and your souls will be at peace.

Jeanette was so amazed by this letter that she loaned it to Blossom to read and analyze. Blossom took the letter straight to Isabel, who then gave it to Nelson. Nelson read and reread it until his mother snapped, "For heaven's sakes, don't wear it out, I have to give it back to Blossom!"

With all the emotional highs and lows, Jeanette felt she was cracking up again. Nelson had wanted her to co-star with him on September 16 for the opening show of his new season of the Electric Hour, but she felt "too self-conscious" and couldn't go through with it. Nelson sang alone on that program, with no guest star. Jeanette escaped to Santa Barbara to coach with Lotte Lehmann again, after scheduling another concert tour for October and November. She had asked Nelson not to make an unexpected visit or even phone her because she would not be able to get through the tour. If they stayed in touch by letter she felt she could keep her attention on her work. Nelson was dismayed at her decision, but grudgingly went along with her. Jeanette informed her family she was leaving directly from Santa Barbara for the tour, but in fact she met Nelson at "Mists" and they had two days together before her departure.

"His concert gift to Jeanette was a hostess gown of pale lavender chiffon over pink," wrote Isabel to Sarah Tucker. "I haven't seen Jeanette wearing it, but he told me that he was sure proud of his purchase. When she walked out of her room wearing it he said 'She took my breath away and was so beautiful—with her own coloring and the coloring of that gown it was a magnificent picture. For a minute I couldn't believe this glorious person was real and belonged to me. And then she came to my arms and kissed me, expressing her thanks for the gift. And then I knew—there was the breath of wild roses among those golden curls, and smiles and stars in her eyes.' " Nelson was plunged into his usual depression after she left. He was able to pull himself out of it by turning to religion. Over the past year he'd begun to query standard dogma, and was leaning toward New Age philosophies. He was a firm believer in past lives and karma, and had come to feel that he and Jeanette were twin souls who had loved before and must, somehow, straighten things out in this lifetime. Some of his fans were shocked to see Nelson walking out of a Hindu center while in New York. On September 24 he showed up in Los Angeles for a Bell Telephone Hour limping badly, and walking with a cane. The fans whispered furiously among themselves when it was learned that Nelson had torn some ligaments in his leg trying to stretch into a yoga position. He was unable to drive for over a month, and was still limping six weeks later.

Jeanette meanwhile had time to collect herself while on tour. She sent off a letter to Blossom voicing a newfound optimism and strategy: "Some day soon, I hope, I am going to try to visit Ann at her home. I feel somehow that if she could forget who I am, I could get through her clouded mind. I believe I could help her mentally. I don't think she has a real true woman friend in the world, and she needs one badly just now. I am sure I will be snubbed the first time, and perhaps for many times. But I shall try over and over again. Somehow I will find a way. I feel so sorry for her for so many things. She has lost her self-respect for one thing, and I want to help her find honor and pride. You must not breathe a word of this either to Nelson or Gene, for they have both forbidden me to go near her and would no doubt put a stop to it at once, but I am not afraid of Ann. She isn't going to hurt me. I want to help her, and besides, I feel it is our one last chance. Even if she were well I would never let Nelson sue for the divorce, I would never let him humiliate her so. I think I should lose some respect for him if he did such a thing. The most awful thing I can imagine for a woman is for a man to take her to the divorce courts. A woman must do that. No, it is bad enough that her life is ruined by her inability to cope with a situation in which she realizes her own inferiority. When Nelson is set free she must do it willingly—I would never allow him to humiliate her any farther."

Blossom answered her letter by writing that she'd run into Nelson and Ann

Jeanette returns to MGM, hoping to make another film with Nelson, but ultimately making two solo films. Here she greets Louis B. Mayer, who never lost his affection for her.

shopping in a Beverly Hills department store together. She received an angry rebuttal back from Jeanette: "Don't ever again insult Nelson by writing such stuff to me. I knew all about that the day after it happened—and I don't need any help to keep track of Nelson. It seems that even *you* can't understand what he is going through. Now you just worry about Blossom and leave him to me!"

Jeanette surprised Nelson by informing him that she'd had yet another change of heart and was willing to make a film. She'd set the stage by staying in touch with Louis B. Mayer since the summer, and had brought about a cautious truce between Nelson and his old boss. In late October 1945, with Jeanette's word that she'd sign up for any script Nelson wanted to make, Nelson returned to MGM to discuss possible projects. He decided on *Reunion in Vienna*—as long as he was shown an acceptable script. MGM insisted on two films, so Nelson agreed if the studio could get *Song of Norway* for them.

Jeanette was quick to inform her fans that she and Nelson were definitely working together; Nelson celebrated in a less obvious manner. After singing his November 11 Electric Hour and November 12 Telephone Hour broadcasts, he set off for New York on some unspecified business. Suffering from a cold, he called in sick for the November 18 Electric Hour (Kenny Baker replaced him), but was well enough to buy Jeanette five gowns from a shop on Fifty-seventh Street, presenting them to her between concerts in Kansas City (their old rendez-vous spot), before returning to Los Angeles. Then, knowing his mother would want complete details, he started a letter to her.

"I am alone here today [at "Mists"] writing this on Baby's little desk in her bedroom, where I can see all her dainty things about me. When I see you I know you will ask me a million questions—and I shall try to answer them. Today Baby sings her concert and how I wish I could hear it. I am very happy just now, but before this reaches you I may be needing you badly, for worry over her health may cloud my joy."

Upon Jeanette's return home, she was true to her word and began cultivating a friendship of sorts with Ann. She found the one thing they could agree about was recipes; she shared some of her favorites with Ann, and vice versa. As the year's end approached, Jeanette felt she was making real progress. She also reported to MGM for conferences, and it looked as if *Reunion in Vienna* was a go. Jeanette was put on a diet in preparation for filming.

She was at last Nelson's guest on his December 16 Electric Hour. Jeanette reported that after their first rehearsal ended at noon on Saturday, the fifteenth, they walked over to the nearby Columbia commissary for lunch. Jeanette invited the show's producer to join them. "I really could have spanked Nelson," Jeanette said. "He pouted all through the lunch. Of course I knew exactly what was wrong. He was so disappointed simply because he wanted to take me in all alone (pride of course). All the stars eat there, and today he had a good excuse, we were in rehearsal—and he wanted to march me in there with him and show me off. So to make it up to him without knowing it, I pretended I wanted some tea when we were through with the rehearsal [on December 16, which ended at 1:30], and my very little boy went with me alone to have tea. The room was even more crowded than it had been at lunch time, and the broad grin on Nelson's face showed me his satisfaction.''

Just before Christmas, Jeanette invited her PR gal, Helen Ferguson, to dinner at "Mists." Also present were Nelson and Gene. Helen, who represented other top stars such as Barbara Stanwyck, was famous for personally retouching photos and catching every flaw before approving her clients' stills for broad release. Ferguson had been extremely disapproving of the MacDonald-Eddy affair, and it's likely that Jeanette arranged this dinner to soften Ferguson's attitude towards them. The night of the dinner Jeanette was nervous and upset about something, and was, for whatever reason, too high-strung to share in the meal. Nelson insisted that she eat, and when she still wouldn't, he cut up her food and spoon-fed her like a child. Helen Ferguson watched this in silent amazement. After dinner she told Gene, "I'll never get over that sight," to which Gene replied, "Think nothing of it, that's been going on for years."

Christmas Eve and day was spent at "Mists." Jeanette and Gene generally held a party at Christmastime, but begged off this year since Twin Gables was being renovated. Gertrude Evans was in Los Angeles visiting, so she was included in the intimate group comprised that evening of Jeanette, Nelson, Blossom, Isabel and Isabel's cook Mary Ann Sorenson. Isabel described their holiday festivities in her memoirs, in an entry entitled "Xmas at Misty—1945."

Upon arriving, Blossom and I left the packages and took a long mountain ride, leaving the children to trim the tree and Mary to busy herself in the kitchen with tomorrow's dinner. When we returned, the tree was finished and Mary had a light supper ready for them. In the evening Nelson lighted the fireplace, and with the glitter from the tree the room took on an appearance of magical moonlight, with no other light anywhere and the scene of Xmas greens adding a real spirit to the holiday season.

Jeanette was busy arranging gifts about the tree, and Nelson was sitting in his big chair beside the fire talking of other Xmas's, when he had been so lonely. No one noticed that Jeanette had slipped from the room. It was now about a half hour before midnight, and suddenly Blossom took her seat at the organ, and they knew that they were in for some sort of a surprise. And suddenly an angel had slipped into the room and now took her place beside the organ. She was more beautiful than humble words could describe, a shining presence dressed in a gown of pale pink chiffon, her hair bound back with tiny rosebuds. I glanced at my son and saw that he had leaned forward in his chair. A wave of color passed over his face as she smiled at him. His eyes filled with tears, and then he smiled. She began to sing, and the songs were chosen for only one listener, but the others loved them too. When her voice took up their "love call," he arose and joined in the singing, his arm encircling her, and their voices became one. It was now Xmas morning, and he turned and took his darling in his arms and kissed her, wishing her a glorious Xmas. And we heard him whisper, "You are beautiful." Then he kissed us all and laughingly called Mary to come get her Xmas kiss. She brought us hot cups of cocoa, and small cookies she had just made. Then Nelson told the others they should get a good night's rest, and he and Jeanette went for a walk, coming in about a half hour later.

The next morning they had breakfast about ten o'clock, and a few hours later Gene arrived with Rocky [Blossom's husband]. Then the gifts were opened and a happy time enjoyed by all. Nelson had a long talk with Gene in his own room. Since his military service Gene had a new dignity that became him well.

Nelson and Jeanette then went for a long walk and returned only in time to dress for dinner, which was to be a very special occasion. Blossom wore a blue gown, Jeanette one of the new dinner gowns Nelson had given her, a flowing affair with loose sleeves in a deep golden color that set off her hair to perfection. She was breathtaking. In her face this day there was nobility, great courage and hope, and she must now give it to this man, who seldom could take his eyes from her face. At the end of the day she asked me to leave her alone with her boy for the next two days. He had been depressed for days, and his work was not up to standard. She must take him in her arms, must bring to him the promise of life, must give him the refuge he needed.

Jeanette apparently worked her magic with Nelson; over the next few days his depression lifted. His newfound enthusiasm was demonstrated by his decision to sing, on the air, a song he'd written for her some time earlier. "My Wonder One" (alternate title, "My Magic You") had been set to music by Ted Paxson, but the lyrics were deeply personal:

> My wonder one
> My shining sun
> I feel your thrilling vibration.
> Your witching face,
> Enchanting grace,
> Have cast a spell of elation.
>
> My magic you
> My dream come true
> My world's divinest creation.
> My search is done
> My prize is won
> The wonder is, you're mine!
>
> I see in your smile
> Something mesmerizing.
> You have a winning guile
> Your touch is magnetizing.
> I stand before you in surrender,
> How I adore you.
> With a tender yearning
> I am burning.

Fans who heard Nelson sing the number on January 13, 1946 were struck by the lyrics, wondering who the subject was of such lovesick lyrics. Many of them knew or suspected the answer, and once again letters were exchanged between Eddyites around the country as they waited to see if now, in the new year, Nelson and Jeanette would finally make their moves.

23

"I shall suffer far more than he does"

The new year started on a sour note. Jeanette and Nelson had a serious falling out just after Christmas. On January 7, 1946, she took off to Palm Springs with Gene, supposedly recovering from "the flu." There were several causes for this latest conflict: Nelson was furious at discovering that Jeanette had disobeyed him and was visiting Ann; they had a disagreement over the new film—for which the plans appeared to be dropped. The main upset, however, seemed to be Jeanette's discovery that Nelson had been unfaithful to her some months earlier. However, as usual, she forgave him, and told a fan on January 20 that they still hoped to work together; after the first January 21 Bell Telephone Hour broadcast, the same fan repeated to Nelson what Jeanette had said and he answered sarcastically, "Well, she's kind of anxious, isn't she?" He was obviously agitated, and during the second broadcast, he cracked on a high note. Both he and the studio audience were horrified. More bad luck followed. On Tuesday, February 12, he was doing some repairs in his garage when the weights on the garage doors fell, struck him on the foot and broke two toes. The next day he was battling a cold, by Thursday he had pneumonia and over the weekend he had to be rushed by ambulance to the hospital. With little notice, Jeanette agreed to cover his radio show, and on Sunday, February 17, she hosted the Electric Hour. At the end of the program, she said while on the air, "And Nelson, hurry up and get well." The next day, Nelson's secretary Louise visited him at the hospital; he was unconscious and pumped full of drugs to battle pneumonia. By Friday, when she visited again,

Nelson was awake and joking. He was finally released and sent home to Isabel's to recuperate.

The first day home he tried to sing and start rehearsing for that week's radio show; the next day he had a relapse and the doctor proclaimed him too ill to be moved. He was hooked up to an oxygen tank, and three nurses rotated shifts, monitoring him at all times. His condition worsened drastically. Isabel wired Aunt Gert in Philadelphia to fly out immediately, which she did. "Dr. John" was one of the attending physicians; he finally instructed Isabel to phone Jeanette and have her come at once, as Nelson was in a semi-coma and was not expected to survive the night. Jeanette went in to see Nelson, them came out and collapsed into a chair and cried. One of the on-duty nurses, Ellen, was surprised when Jeanette blurted out that she and Nelson had been in love for many years, and "I can't face the thought of a future without him." Isabel, Aunt Gert, and Jeanette sat vigil long into the night, until Dr. John once again summoned Jeanette. Aunt Gert later described "Nelson's crisis" in a letter to a friend penned on her flight back to Philadelphia.

on plane bound for home

Have little to tell you at this time—we have been in such turmoil and under such a strain I have hardly known what went on. I had to get back home as soon as possible —but hope to have more details soon.

Jeanette has us at our wits ends trying to figure out what has happened. Something went wrong or has upset her. It happened on the night he was very low and John called her into the room just before he passed into a semi-coma. He had asked for her while she was with us in the study. It was four o'clock in the morning. At six she came back into the study, and Isabel gave a cry when she saw her face—it was like one that had lost all hope and she looked like death itself. She came over and took Isabel's hand and said, "No, darling, he is better and Dr. has told me not to worry." And then she went out and home. We tried to analyze her look but we couldn't—she looked like she had seen a thousand ghosts and was faint with a deadly whiteness. The next day and the next Nelson knew nothing and nobody and she *didn't* come to the house. She called every three hours on the dot—and then the morning of the third day Nelson began to come back quickly. The first thing he did was to ask for Jeanette—so John called her and she came immediately, but as she walked into the room and spoke to us gently we both nearly collapsed at the way she looked—so changed—don't ask how. I can't explain it—but her smile was forced and she paused at his door and seemed to brace herself as for an ordeal of some sort and then she went in. What on earth happened in that two hours she watched Nelson's fight for life? Could it be he spoke of someone or said something out of his feverish mind that hurt or upset her? Isabel is nearly crazy trying to get her to talk —she just looks mysterious and changes the subject. Isabel asked John what went on that night and he just turned away and pretended not to know anything. But from the minute Nelson was out of the fog he howled for Jeanette and she has been there most of the time and to him she is her same old self. Only when she comes away from him does she get that strange look. Isabel says she reminds her of a poor little wounded bird that can't understand what has happened to it. But to me she just seems like a completely bewildered child who needs her sweetheart to do some explaining, or some such thing. Whatever it is, I know he will sense it as quickly as he is well enough, and no doubt he will be able to set it right again. But she lost weight noticeably during his illness and after that night we never saw her when her eyes were free from tears, except when she forced them back to go into his room.

Ann Eddy had not been allowed to see Nelson during his illness. Aunt Gert, who'd nicknamed Ann "Nutty," added almost as an afterthought,

Nutty knows better than to even try to step her foot in Isabel's house without an invitation (which she never gets) so we had no trouble about her. But she called up quite often to see how Nelson was and Isabel informed her each time that no one was allowed to see him—so that ended that.

Nelson made a quick recovery, missed only two more radio shows, which Kenny Baker and Dinah Shore hosted in his absence, and by March 10 he was able to return to work. The aftermath of his illness was that Jeanette announced she was quitting her career. She'd decided to devote her energies to keeping Nelson well and singing. Furthermore, she wanted to get pregnant immediately, even if the child had to be born with Gene's name.

Nelson was at first thrilled at her decision regarding her career; for over a decade he'd played second fiddle and had waited for the day that she'd drop everything for him. Then, to his surprise, he realized that this was no longer important to him. Jeanette had managed to balance both her career and her relationship with him—as she had always told him she would. He wanted her working with him by his side. And he felt that until his own personal situation changed she was much better off doing occasional concert tours. By being outside of Los Angeles they could rendezvous more easily than while under the close scrutiny of Ann Eddy and their local fans.

And the fans did indeed still faithfully trail them. One woman followed Nelson as he drove to Twin Gables and picked up Jeanette, who was in a disguise of sorts, with a scarf on her head that half-covered her face. Then they drove into Westwood village, and got into line at a movie theater playing a new Van Johnson film. The fan, who was still tailing them, watched as other people in the line started to notice Nelson and his date. He suddenly grabbed Jeanette's hand and pulled her out of line and across the street, where they ducked into a theater with no line that was playing *The Bells of St. Mary's*.

During the third week of March, Nelson spent a couple of nights with Jeanette at "Mists," explaining to his mother that they needed time alone since "there hasn't been any physical love between us since December." They were scheduled to do *Sweethearts* on the Lux Radio Theater the following week, but Jeanette had threatened to back out. After spending two nights with Nelson, she'd changed her mind and agreed to sing. Nelson triumphantly briefed his mother:

Jeanette has listened to my pleas and will work with me. What I demanded she give up ten years ago I now begged her to hold onto for my sake. Such a sweet little girl. If you could have seen her stubborn little face! Curled up on my lap, she kept saying: "But I don't want any more career!" I said, "But darling, I can't have you before the world unless you will let me have you in my career and I *need* you before the world, it would make me so happy." Here she replied (still stubbornly) "I only want a few things—and they are all things that only you can give me. I want a home, your home, provided for me, and I want to live in it." Here I held her close, and she whispered, "And most of all, Nelson dear, I want my baby. I want the experience of bearing your child. You are my entire world now, and *I don't want any more career!*"

So, of course I adore her for this and soon I hope it may be so. But now I want her to share all glory with me—to stand beside me whether it be radio, movies, or concert stage. I want to look over the crowds and hear the audience thunder out their applause for my lovely darling—call it pride if you will.

The March 25 *Sweethearts* broadcast was a hit with the studio audience, who once again carefully scrutinized the two stars' behavior. Nelson was more playful than usual, but Jeanette's private fears about working with him were realized; he blatantly showed off their intimacy every chance he got, and teased her so much that she could barely concentrate on her work. This started even before the broadcast, while Jeanette was moving her stool back and forth on the stage, trying to position it correctly. As one observer noted:

Nelson, noticing all the attention she was getting, admonished, "Now don't hog it all!" Jeanette just laughed that infectious, bell-like laugh of hers and began adjusting her music stand. Nelson quickly stepped up and raised it to the height she wanted, muttering critically, "Always so fussy!"

Shortly after the program started, Jeanette decided her perky little bonnet was a bother so she pulled it off and laid it over on her chair. Nelson, not having any lines to read at the moment, was sitting down. With exaggerated interest he scrutinized the hat, turned it over, examined it carefully, and then discovering to his amazement that it had an open crown, he ran his hand and arm through the hat and held it up like a monstrosity for all to see. The studio audience enjoyed a hearty laugh at his apparent amazement at the latest thing in ladies' millinery. Jeanette was laughing too, in fact she had a hard time trying to read her lines and watch Nelson cut up at the same time.

As the show drew to a close Jeanette and Nelson, having finished their part of the show, sat down and Jeanette began putting her hat on. Nelson watched her intently, and then decided he should lend a helping hand. He insisted upon poking her hair in the back up under the hat and as fast as she'd arrange it to her satisfaction, he'd take another poke at it. He finally let her fix it to suit herself, and then as a gesture of mock disgust at all that primping, Nelson drew his hand through his own hair, all the way from the back of his neck, over the top of his head, and down over his face. Every hair in his head stood up on end and since he had it cut rather short, the general effect produced was that of a butch haircut. The audience howled with glee and Jeanette was convulsed with laughter at the way he looked. Then with great ceremony she took a rat-tail comb out of her purse and handed it to him. First he combed the right side of his hair neatly into place and then as he drew the comb through the left side he tried to use the rat-tail to make himself a curl, but despite all his hard work he could produce no sign of a curl, so he finally gave up and returned the comb to Jeanette. With elaborate gestures she pretended to clean the hair out of the comb before replacing it in her purse.

As the announcer launched into his closing commercial Nelson drew a bunch of keys out of his pocket and dropped them on the floor by Jeanette's feet. As he leaned back to pick up the keys, he gave a quick yank at one of Jeanette's pumps, pulling it off and tossing it out onto the stage. He laughed heartily as she scrambled wildly to retrieve her shoe.

[After the broadcast] Nelson wanted to kiss Jeanette, he just grabbed her in his arms and tried to kiss her but she kept pulling back and pushing on his "manly chest" for all she was worth. He kept trying to drag her out in front of the rapidly closing curtains and I heard him say something about wanting to kiss her out in front of the curtains, but she just kept wrestling with him until he finally had to let go.

The following day, March 26, Nelson wrote a lengthy entry in the diary he kept for Jeanette.

As you read this sometime you will remember so well these last sweet days at the Mists. How often have I needed your tender mother love, and received it in full measure—but Friday, darling, it was you who needed me. Curled up in my arms you were only about six years old as I held you in my arms and stilled your childlike emotions. It touched me deeply, darling, deeper than anything I have known, your asking me to hold you and sing to you as I might my own little daughter—and yet in that hour you were a woman so completely—hurt over something I knew nothing of—and yet there was such faith in me—faith that I could heal the hurt. I am sure you knew that when I had my little sweetheart tucked in my arms and a long beautiful night—a sweet night of close affinity—to figure all this out that things would all come right. Never, my darling, have you been so completely my own as you were this night, before the morning mists had rolled away the stars of night, with utmost tenderness—with childlike simplicity—you told me again of those hours of sickness—never have you been so completely my wife—your arms, your lips—their magical effect on me—your whispered words—things you have never before said to me—how much I have missed you at night—how I want you always in my arms as I sleep, just as you were this night—to know that so great an understanding can be yours, that you know you and you alone are my existence— dearer than ever this day.

Yes, dearest, I know that your prayers and mother's brought me back from the very edge of eternity—they were taken to the feet of our Lord, and I was aware of those prayers, even when I was all but lost—aware of your gentle voice speaking. I would lose sight of you for a moment and find myself wandering into strange winds —but always to come back finally hearing your voice. I had so much time to think of you while I was ill, our glad times—our sad ones—all the things we have gone through together. More vivid than anything to me were the times when I felt I couldn't stand it another minute—when I would rush to your side—much as a small boy when he has tried so hard to straighten things out and still has a bad report card to show for his work. It was at these bad moments that I always found your arms held out to me—my head pillowed on your warm little breast—while you whispered words of peace and comfort to soothe me. Now, this night, it was you who needed this spiritual strength which I have so often taken from you. Up there in our own little nest, I know my darling, that you will always show me the depths of your heart and soul. Our perfect relationship has deep roots and we can face any problem because between us there is such a lovely thing. Shall I tell you about our bond, darling?

It is built of deep spiritual love mixed with tempered desire—mellowed by sorrow—tears—our love is very different from other couples—partly because it is a holy thing, and then it has been made perfect on an altar of suffering. I want to write this for you to keep always, my beloved little wife. Our marriage to me is a thing of such dignity and beauty that its lovely nights of sweet passion are a glorious string of pearls sent by the angels to bless us, and I shall love you through all eternity.

And now I will tell YOU a little more about the first day of my recovery—so that you may always have this memory. I awoke that morning restless. John and Ellen were there—my head ached terribly and Mommie was sitting on the bed with my hot hand held in her cool one. My aching eyes wandered around the room but found no Jeanette. I asked for her at once and John said, "She will be here soon." I must have drifted off in a kind of coma then, and at last I saw you faintly as though you came to me from afar, and great joy filled my heart when I sensed that you were leaning over me—kissing my damp forehead. I saw you smile—I knew you sat beside me—and then I drifted off. But darling, last night I made you—really made you—tell me what happened that morning, and these were your sweet words.

"My darling little boy—I came to you that morning very sad, but not letting you see it. They left me alone with you—saying I must not talk too much or be upsetting in any way—and as I leaned over you it was all I could do to keep from bursting into tears, you were so white, so weak—and I loved you so very much. Your dear hand, so weak it could hardly bear its own weight, tried to touch my cheek as I laid my face close to yours. I didn't want to excite you emotionally—so I took your hand and looked deep into your eyes—and there I saw my little boy—not my lover—needing mother love—and your dear soul was in your eyes as you said 'please' in a faintly whispered voice. I knew then that you wanted me to hold your head on my breast as you always do when the 'bad times' come, and my dear, I was very near the breaking point myself. It was very hard to humor you just then—but I tried to hold you close and hide from you my own very nervous state. I forced myself to relax and give in to the sweet boy love you were giving me."

Yes, darling, you did give me the strength I needed that day. I remember you singing Schubert's "Serenade" to me as you held me close—just before I went to sleep—as I write this I know that I shall always rush to you at times for just this little boy comfort. Thank you, my baby—that there can be such a beautiful understanding between us about this. I suppose it is some sort of mother complex—but darling, there is plenty of the sweetheart lover's love in store for you than you will be able to handle. And last of all, remember this—our beautiful last night —I went over to the organ where you were playing and raised your fingers to my lips, and asked you this, "Dearest one, have I set your world to rights?" And you answered, with your lips on mine, "Oh yes, my dear, no matter what happens I shall always have utter faith in your love. I trust you with an adoration that is beyond my words to tell." And I held you so close to me then.

Oh darling—to have you in my arms—so warm and sweet—the scent of your hair on my shoulder— knowing that your soul seeks and has found an exquisite dream—to me you are the flower sweet crown of rapturous love and I call you both wife and mother and crown you with the lilies and roses that grow on lovely hillsides.

Jeanette sang again with Nelson on the April 7 Electric Hour. There was no studio audience. Then she went off to New York briefly to record for RCA. They parted somewhat at odds over Jeanette's insistence that she have his baby. Nelson tried to explain to her the potential folly of such a move, but she refused to listen. She was determined, and in fact was already pregnant, though she hadn't yet realized it. While in New York, she received a letter from Nelson clearly establishing his viewpoint regarding a child: "Oh no, darling, that can't be. We decided that a long time ago. I am willing to give you all my love—and a baby—yes, my little wife—it should end that way, dearest one, but this I must deny you. I will give you any earthly gift—but this I will not do. And can you imagine how I would feel? A baby—yours and mine—a darling rose bud like its mother. Sweet little trembling feet to patter around this room perhaps? It would be the greatest joy I could imagine to look forward to—but darling, it can't be— and this dream you must not ask me to share with you. You don't want a crazy husband, do you? How do you think I would ever live through such a thing—not being able to be by your side every minute of the time? And then too—even if you were legally my wife, I doubt I would agree to such a thing—it would be dangerous at your age." Jeanette was almost forty-three at this time.

Over the next month, Nelson and Jeanette considered several film projects. In May, the Hollywood *Reporter* leaked the news that "Seton I. Miller, one of Paramount's top writer-producers who resigned a few days ago, is getting ready to produce *Crescent Carnival* as an independent—starring Jeanette MacDonald and Nelson Eddy. George Schaefer is financing." At the same time, another blurb noted that Nelson was considering a script for them called *Russian River* at Republic. Still another offer came from producer Harold Fielding in England, this one directed at Jeanette. She could "name her price" for doing a concert tour throughout the British Isles, solo or with Nelson. They bandied about the pros and cons of each project, but as Gertrude Evans noted, "If only they could get that 'honeymoon' over with, there is no doubt that we would get plenty of work from them. But about the time they get all set to decide on something, they go off on another 'weekend' and end up forgetting everything else in the world except each other."

After one of their "weekends," Jeanette dropped Nelson off at the Vine Street Playhouse, where the Electric Hour was broadcast, and was heading home in Nelson's new car when she saw Hedda Hopper. "Well," said Hedda, "so you have a new car too?"

"No," Jeanette replied.

"I wish you would ask that Eddy guy where he gets his pull. I need a new car too," said Hedda.

Jeanette grinned at her. "Why don't you come up to Gables for dinner? Blossom and I are all alone." Hedda agreed. During the meal she asked, "When are you going to give me a scoop on yourself, young lady?"

"Oh, Hedda, Nelson and I are so grateful to all of you for being so kind to us."

"Well, Jeanette, I've been tempted to talk plenty of times, but you two are too well loved, and if I did, every other reporter in Hollywood would murder me."

In May, Jeanette confirmed she was pregnant. Without telling Nelson the reason, she informed him she flat-out refused to make *Russian River*. They'd been on the verge of signing, and Nelson was so angry with her for once again backing out that he signed the contract anyway. Now Jeanette was furious, since they had a long-standing agreement that neither one would make a film without the other. She still refused to sign her contract, and when she learned that Ilona Massey would co-star with Nelson, she was further enraged. Nelson argued that he hadn't hand-chosen Ilona, that he was just as surprised as she was, but Jeanette was not convinced. She anticipated his working for months with Ilona would end up in his having an affair with her.

Jeanette had long struggled to deal with Nelson's occasional infidelities. She tried to explain them away, blaming the combination of his extreme attraction to the opposite sex and his general vulnerability that was the product of their unnatural lifestyles. During the run of the Electric Hour Nelson picked up a few young women, mostly blonde. How far he went with some of these women is unknown, though two women who met him in 1946 and were later intimate claimed the friendship was platonic—at this time. There was even a minor scandal over Nelson and his script girl, Norma Nelson. Norma was a cute blonde with a good soprano voice. She auditioned for Nelson, and he arranged for her radio debut on Art Linkletter's House Party. In addition, he arranged for her to study with Dr. Lippe. Their relationship warmed up, with Nelson showing up for her coaching lessons. Before the lesson, Lippe left them alone to "talk." Norma admitted that they kissed and there was some "petting," but it didn't progress beyond that. Lippe told her that Nelson and Jeanette were lovers, but when she asked Nelson about it, he denied it, saying that they were just friends. Lippe also told Norma that Nelson's marriage was a mess, and that he should have married someone like Norma.

Norma had a front row seat in the audience for each broadcast, and soon the trades were commenting on the "romance." Later on, their relationship waned. Nelson became furious when Lippe tried to tell Norma she was a mezzo, and he found another teacher for her, Major Herbert Wall, with whom Nelson had just begun studying.

Nelson had also been taking weekly art classes at the home of Delmer Daves. At least one of the women who modeled for Nelson admitted having an affair with him. Jeanette tried to deal with these infidelities by seducing the seducer. "I've been kissed for the first time in my life," she said triumphantly to Blossom, after spending a passionate weekend with Nelson.

"At your age? I'd be ashamed to admit it," Blossom laughed.

Jeanette went on to explain how she'd given Nelson "a weekend he'd never forget," and had successfully cured his wandering eye, at least for the present. She later wrote the details about the seduction, which had something to do about a new brassiere:

"Nelson was broiling a steak and after I set a card table before the fireplace, I went to fix my hair and put on a fresh dress for dinner. I helped him with the last minute preparations and we were very happy kidding, laughing and teasing each other. It had been a hard day for us, very tiring, so as soon as dinner was over Nelson carried the dishes to the sink and said they would have to stay there until morning.

Coming back he found me on a cushion by the fire, and I said, "Come dear, sit beside me. I need you to lean on tonight, and I need to be loved a little bit."

As he sat beside me I noticed his eyes straying over me, and there was a cute smile on that obstinate mouth. I knew exactly what was coming. I had waited for it all day, but Nelson has a way of waiting for just the right moment. So now he said, 'Well, darling, suppose I attend to this first before I give you any lovings.' And Blossom, he simply snapped open my dress, undid the offending article, had it off before I could say boo, threw it on a chair, snapped up my dress again, and gathered me in his arms, where I lay for a motionless minute—too surprised to say anything. He kissed me then, and across his broad forehead a delightful frown appeared. 'All day,' he said, 'I have had to watch my very own little darlings being tortured with that nasty old thing. Didn't you know I wouldn't permit that? My dear little snowdrifts—what are you trying to do, make them lifeless? My two finely chiseled dear little breasts are a fetish of mine, and I want them constantly expressed in my presence in relaxed attitudes.'

Well, I looked at him and burst out laughing. He had the most adorable impish look on his face. And I said, 'Mr. Eddy, I should be very angry with you. It is your fault that I must wear the thing.'

'Well, you can wear high-necked dresses—or if you must wear the thing, don't do it in my presence. I am an appreciator of rare beauty in nature, my darling, and besides, I don't want to have to rebuild you all over again.' And he bent to kiss me. I couldn't help it—a little devil in me made me say, 'I shouldn't mind too much.'

His impish look grew deeper. And he said, 'Why Mrs. Eddy, you surprise me. I am indeed looking into the shimmering pools of your eyes this evening and seeing a woman still breathlessly being born. I assure you I shall always find supreme contentment in contributing to that process.'

Oh me, my lover, these delightfully familiar hours.

Soon I was almost asleep. It was growing late, and my husband suggested that I get ready for bed as we had to leave early the next morning. He said, 'Sleep well, little baby.' And I kissed him in return. I had the blessed feeling this night of knowing that I was home, the only home I shall ever need. I was peaceful and so very happy. I drifted off to sleep on clouds of beauty, and saw the heavenly blue of his eyes keep watch over me.

In spite of these romantic moments, Jeanette still felt unable to trust him. Eventually, fed up, she agreed to do the English concert tour. She would be far away from Nelson and could enjoy her pregnancy in peace. She intended to remain in Britain after the tour ended, to visit her relatives and perhaps even have her child there. Their relationship again tenuous, Nelson and Jeanette spent a last night together before she left for New York and ultimately England. Nelson was still unaware that she was pregnant, however. He noted in his diary:

I tried so hard to make my darling break her plans for England—but my dear was so very firm—and I know I deserve this.

My little diary and I keep all the lovely things for our baby to remember when she reads them on some future day—and so I know she will remember this last night with happiness and a little sadness too as she recalls how she choose to punish me.

Now she is sweetly tender in my arms—the fire deepening the color in her face —her starry eyes betraying her thoughts and her emotions. In her burst of passion this evening she was more beautiful than ever. I knew that she meant I was not to forget for one moment the beginning joy of this night—she meant to be sure I would remember this hour for all the weeks she was away. As I bent to those lips pressed close to mine I felt her fingers like tiny butterflies hover over my hair and softly touch my cheek, making me tell her that I love her—I love her so much. And then at this moment and without warning, my darling whirled away, her lovely hair disheveled—dainty negligee flowing about her graceful little figure. She stopped at the bedroom door, turned around, and with a mischievous little smile said "Goodnight," and the door was closed.

I didn't enter it until very late—found her fast asleep. Should I have left you, dear, like this? I longed so for you then, to feel the sweet fragility of your body—the breathless joy of the way you respond to my touch like a delicate musical instrument —but then and always I need your deepest respect—even though I know I can so easily break down these little barriers you choose to put between us. So on this night I decided to sleep on the couch. Even though I ached for her, on this, our last night together, I love my wife so dearly that when she closes a door it must always remain closed.

They quarreled yet again the day she left. Nelson tried in vain to get her to cancel the tour; finally, in disgust he told her was sorry he'd ever met her or fallen in love with her.

If Nelson expected sympathy from their small circle of confidants, he had a rude awakening when they unanimously sided with Jeanette. "Nelson's friends are all turning against him because the scene with Ann goes on and on and he won't make a move," said an insider. "They see Jeanette going to pieces before their very eyes, and they resent it terribly." En route to England, Jeanette wrote Isabel, "A woman wants security with her husband—she wants to feel she can lean on him in times of trouble and doubt—and she must feel that he can be at all times on his own two feet. Oh yes, she wants him as her baby too—in her own boudoir and these moments of tenderness are perhaps the dearest of all when she holds him close to her heart. But in his work he should be complete unto himself. I must feel that he can settle matters promptly and act quickly but intelligently—on all points—that make up his professional life. He must not let his moments of anger give way to senseless emotions. Once before this same uncontrolled anger put him in the mess he is in. Now he has done another foolish thing—he signed for the one picture that I asked him specially not to do. Now he must learn that I won't be here this time when the man becomes a little boy and needs someone to kiss his tears away. Now he must go through this alone and only on his own strength. Mother, don't let me be weak with him this time —I must stay in England for awhile and teach him a lesson. This darling precious little boy of mine—I shall suffer far more than he does—and my prayers will be with him every hour of every day. But I must leave him to fight this out alone."

Jeanette arrived in England just before her birthday, June 18. She looked unwell and felt worse, suffering both from air sickness and morning sickness. During the ride from the airport to the Savoy Hotel in London, her car had to pull over twice for her to be sick. Once at the hotel she was unable to sleep; after being up all night she was spotted walking at 6 am, and even gave early morning interviews to reporters. When the nausea refused to subside she wired Dr. Wyman to come to her rescue, fearing for her baby. He had little time to act; she suffered a miscarriage and had to be hospitalized. She was three months pregnant.

Her first concert was scheduled in Blackpool but had to be rescheduled at the end of her tour. News of her hospitalization reached the press, with the usual fabricated reason. Not even her closest associates were aware of the personal anguish she was suffering during her trip through the British Isles. Nelson, meanwhile, agonized through his usual depression at her departure and had made a reservation at the Savoy; he was determined to fly out to meet her. When he finally spoke with Jeanette she talked him out of his plans. The last thing she needed was for him to show up in England and learn what had happened. She did send him a letter and a special birthday gift—she had signed her contract to make *Crescent Carnival* and enclosed a carbon copy for him.

Nelson never canceled his reservation at the Savoy. The London gossip column of the *Hollywood Reporter* finally blabbed: "Calling Nelson Eddy. Say, Nelson, there's a big fan mail waiting for you at the London Savoy Hotel. You've been expected there for some time and a room was booked for you, all ready. Someone telephoned and reserved it for you on behalf of Harold Fielding, the concert impresario. What's happened to that concert tour anyway? Those fans are still waiting to welcome you, autograph book and pencil in hand."

Jeanette sent off another letter. This one was to Gene; in it she expressed how miserable she was, and how she wasn't well but couldn't tell anyone. But she intended to stick it out and not return until September. Somehow Nelson learned about Gene's letter and insisted on reading it. Isabel said, "He was fit to be tied, and I almost had to sit on him to keep him from leaving for England that night. The thing that upset him the most was that she turned to Gene with the truth instead of him." Isabel told her son in disgust, "As long as you keep on making her miserable with your temper, she will probably never feel that she can turn to you completely. I'm sure she discovered years ago that Gene is more reliable than you." Isabel left the next day for an East Coast vacation and told Nelson not to come to her with any of his troubles, as she was having nothing to do with him until the fall.

Nelson and Jeanette "burned up the phone wires" while she was overseas. Later she wrote her fans that she created a staggering bill keeping in touch with her "husband." Mostly they quarreled, with Jeanette finally deciding that if Nelson was intent upon making *Russian River* she would outdo him by returning to MGM, where they wanted her for a remake of the 1936 Deanna Durbin hit, *Three Smart Girls*. Entitled *The Birds and the Bees* (later *Three Daring Daughters*), Jeanette would co-star with José Iturbi and Jane Powell, and report to work as soon as she returned to the States. Nelson was furious at Jeanette's latest career move, and told her so. She retaliated by telling him she hoped *Russian River* would be the biggest flop he ever made.

"You will get your wish all right," he replied. "But how would you feel if I said that to you?"

"*My* picture won't be a flop. I'm wise enough not to try to carry a picture alone after five years' absence from the screen. I have established stars with me, but I'm afraid Massey won't be any asset to you."

"*You* broke the first promise by refusing to work with me."

"You ruined my life and the only wise thing I ever did since I met you was to try to put Gene in your place. At least Gene is a comfort, not a torture."

"Well, if I'm so inferior, maybe you'd like to call it all off and go back to Gene."

"No, I would have to love the wrong man all my life and anyway, Gene wouldn't be interested."

Their attempts at a quick reconciliation got nowhere—until Nelson heard the truth about the pregnancy. How exactly he found out is unclear; it's possible that Jeanette in a low moment finally blurted it out. As she had feared, he was devastated, not only because of the child but because she had been diagnosed as having a bad ovary, and Nelson felt somehow responsible. Appalled that she had not confided in him, and that their relationship had disintegrated to this point, Nelson withdrew into himself. He had been staying with Ann, but now he went to the Mariposa house and took to riding his horse daily from the nearby Dineen stables into the Griffith Park mountains. Another contributing factor to Nelson's

breakdown was the discovery at Mists of more home recordings Jeanette had left
for him. She'd recorded seven songs with introductions, "Jeanie With the Light
Brown Hair," "Believe Me If All Those Endearing Young Charms," "Porgi
Amor" [from *Marriage of Figaro*], "Non Mi Dir" and "Batti, Batti", both from
Don Giovanni, "Ich Liebe Dich" ["I Love Thee"] by Grieg, "Komm Hoffnung."
Then there were four sides of organ solos: "Moonlight Sonata," Brahms' "Cra-
dle Song," "Rejoice Greatly" from Handel's Messiah, and "The Hills of
Home."

Transcripts of Jeanette's introductions have not survived, but Isabel Eddy
described her son's emotional pain at listening to them: " 'Porgi Amor' upset
him so that he was nervous all the rest of the day because he said she had such
tears in her voice and he couldn't stand it. 'Komm Hoffnung' had long been a
favorite of his but he could never get her to sing it for him because one time he
raved about some other woman's singing of it and from then on she was too
jealous to sing it herself. But on the record she told him that now she just wanted
him to know that she could sing it. He said the record of 'Ich Leibe Dich' was a
joy to his soul, and the Don Giovanni records kept him in silent prayer and
worship, while the 'Jeannie' and 'Endearing Charms' brought a darling smile to
his lips and he said Jeanette meant him to remember Tahoe. 'Porgi amor' was the
old hurt because he broke his promise about never working without her in a
picture. 'Komm Hoffnung' is from *Fidelio*."

Nelson's reaction to Jeanette's recordings was to drop all his projects and start
recording selections for her. Isabel felt her son had gone off the deep end,
writing, "He is so completely nutty that I don't know what is going on." It was
several months before Nelson confided in his mother about Jeanette's pregnancy,
which angered Isabel as she didn't like being left out of important matters.

From the end of July through mid-August, Nelson was beside himself. He had
an office in Beverly Hills, but his new secretary Sally reported that he hadn't
shown up or called. On August 15, Sally informed a visitor to the office that for
sure Nelson had to make an appearance the next day to sign checks and to answer
the many phone messages that had piled up. The next day, Friday, Sally was
mystified when, once again, Nelson didn't show. Sally was at a loss to understand
Nelson's peculiar behavior, noting that the few times she had seen him (she
worked for him less than a month) he seemed very "jumpy."

To the amazement of many, Nelson finally shut down his office, got a new
secretary and sold his Brentwood home on Halvern (it fell out of escrow and
remained unsold for a long time; originally assessed at $7,500 when built, it was
now valued at $40,000 and by the time Fred MacMurray bought it the price had
escalated to $135,000). Nelson moved with Ann to a house at 155 South Hudson
in Hancock Park near Hollywood. He settled his Electric Hour contract, the first
time he'd been without a regular radio series in years, and signed a new Columbia Concerts contract, though he hadn't yet decided on doing a tour. Jeanette
returned to Los Angeles to find Nelson in a highly agitated state. Dr. Wyman
warned her, "We have to pull him out of this very carefully or we may have him
in a sanatorium for a year."

With Jeanette home assuring him that she still loved him, Nelson was able to pick up his professional life again. Within a week of her return they worked together as judges for the Atwater Kent opera auditions. One observer wrote about the men's finals, which took place and was broadcast live the evening of September 14.

Judges for this big event consisted of Nelson, Jeanette, Lauritz Melchior, Helen Traubel and John Charles Thomas, all of whom were of course present in the studio. Paxson was the accompanist and played a couple of solos.

Nelson's complete absorption in Jeanette was most shocking! He whispered to her, constantly gazed at her soulfully, and in general conducted himself like a hopelessly lovestruck young man. Jeanette, for her part, had eyes and ears only for him, actually turning her back to Melchior who sat on the other side of her!

When all the judges had to take a bow at the end, Nelson was quite the young gallant, pulling out Jeanette's chair and helping her get seated again.

Gene was there, sitting in the first row of the audience. And Ann was also present. She appeared at the stage exit afterwards. She glared coldly at Nelson's fans who waited to greet him. He finally emerged with Jeanette and Gene and a group of other people and Ann was definitely on the outside looking in.

When a fan asked if Jeanette and Nelson were going to make another picture together, Nelson beamed fondly on Jeanette and said, "We'd certainly like to!"

Finally Ann came up and took Nelson's arm and said with finality, "I think it's time we were going home!" And off they went.

Jeanette began recording for *Three Daring Daughters* in late September; *Russian River*, which was eventually retitled *Northwest Outpost*, was to have begun shooting on September 15 on location at Fort Ross, eighty-five miles north of San Francisco, but filming was delayed a month. Nelson grumbled, "They don't know what they're doing out at Republic!" He'd already lost interest in his new film, even complaining about the musical score. "[Rudolf] Friml could either be brilliant or write garbage. His songs for *Northwest Outpost* were lousy."

On September 25, Jeanette and Nelson returned for another round of Atwater Kent judging, for the women's category. One fan sitting in the parking lot saw Jeanette and Gene walking toward the building; Nelson was sitting in his car waiting for them. He jumped out and escorted them in. The first four rows were roped off for special guests; Ann Eddy was spotted already sitting in the third row. The fan observed that when she took off her hat, her hair was very thin and in places she was bald. Ann remained in her seat the entire time, while Gene was allowed backstage until just before airtime, when he took his seat in the first row. Nelson seemed bored by the auditions, noted the fan.

He sprawled out in his chair, hooked his thumbs in his vest pockets, and concentrated on only two things, the studio audience and the clock on the wall. Jeanette took copious notes as did most of the other judges, but Nelson couldn't be bothered. He fooled with a scrap of paper and contented himself reading over Jeanette's shoulder what she wrote. He looked oh so intently at Jeanette and at one point he even rested his chin in the crook of his elbow and just stared up at her.

Finally all the judges had finished except Jeanette. So Nelson decided it was time to hurry her along. He began telling her to hurry and went on to put action into words by bouncing up and down in his seat in imitation of a jockey urging his mount across the finish line. Jeanette laughingly ignored his advice and went on writing, concentrating as best she could with his cutting up beside her. At last she finished and handed in her ballots, and Nelson, with feigned exhaustion, collapsed onto the table.

While the ballots were being tabulated, Nelson was keenly aware of the state of nervous expectancy in which the girls found themselves. He grinned down at them understandingly and then, putting his right hand inside the left side of his coat, he tapped his chest rapidly, making his coat flutter in imitation of their palpitating hearts. The girls laughed and the tension was broken.

The judges couldn't talk among themselves during the actual competition, but after the ballots were cast they began to chatter away. Nelson and Jeanette talked and argued back and forth over the relative merits of the singers. At one point Nelson even reached the table-pounding stage in trying to persuade Jeanette to his point of view. They had their heads together and were really going around and around in argument and at that point Ann, who had evidently been watching them intently, dropped Nelson's hat on the floor and there was a mad scramble while she and the other woman retrieved it.

Jeanette finally turned to Melchior and began talking to him, leaving Nelson off by himself on the other side, and so help me he looked like he was pouting at this neglect. The woman in back of me remarked that "they should have given poor Nelson someone to talk to," so he must have looked a little lonely.

Traubel really upstaged Jeanette; she never cast so much as a glance in Jeanette's direction. When the judges stood up to take a bow at the beginning of the broadcast, Jeanette peeked around Melchior at Traubel and, noticing the way Traubel had settled her furs back on her shoulders, Jeanette did the same thing. It was the cutest little gesture you ever saw.

Traubel and Thomas were very palsy walsy and Melchior sort of joined in, but Nelson and Jeanette seemed quite content to be together on a little island of their own.

After the broadcast Jeanette and Gene came out together and hurried down the street while Nelson and Ann came out together. For a moment Nelson and Jeanette were together in the crowd of fans that milled about for autographs, but then Jeanette and Gene hurried on. Ann stuck close to Nelson's coat tails this time, and when one fan handed him a picture to autograph she said in affected tones, "Oh, Nelson, deah, are you going to sign another picture?" Nelson just glared at her and then went on and signed the picture.

During the fall of 1946, Nelson filmed *Northwest Outpost* and Jeanette sporadically worked on *Three Daring Daughters*. Production was halted after she fell seriously ill with near-pneumonia, and for a while it seemed the film would be shelved altogether.

Make Mine Music had gone into general release during the fall, but it had little impact on Nelson's career. Nor did it perform well at the box office.. Nelson's segment, which comprised the finale of the film, was highly touted.

Nelson and Jeanette had little time together during this period. When Nelson wasn't filming he stayed home with Ann, as chronicled by certain fans who almost daily drove by his house. Jeanette visited Republic Studios one day, but refused to come onto the set. Instead, she met Nelson in the commissary and they had lunch together.

Nelson had a generally miserable time filming *Northwest Outpost*. The film's director, Allan Dwan, came away from the production with only snide and derogatory comments regarding Nelson's acting ability. Nelson garnered considerably more respect at Herbert Wall's voice school, where he was asked to lecture the students who made up the American G. I. Chorus, which sang and acted in *Northwest Outpost* as well. One of the students, Frank Laric, recalled that after Nelson addressed the students, they were sitting around, talking. Nelson was asked about his movies and his career. He was asked why he was studying with Major Wall. Nelson replied he was having some trouble with his high notes, and Major Wall had helped. "How many teachers have you had?" he was asked. Nelson replied, "I don't know, I stopped counting when I got past twenty-five." He was friendly until someone asked him if he was in love with Jeanette. Nelson was upset by the question. "Why, of course," he answered. "Well, I gotta go now."

By December, Jeanette was in despair over their situation, which never seemed to be moving any closer to the ideal. Her hopes that their lives could ever be straightened out had all but died. For Nelson, however, there was one solution left that would ultimately put an end to their misery and entrapment. On Christmas night, he did what he felt was the only honorable thing he could do: he broke up with Jeanette.

24

The Parting

In a letter dated December 26, 1946, Nelson somewhat incoherently tried to express why he felt this parting was necessary:

My own—

Last night—our dearest tenderest memory—hug it close to your heart. I have held you in my arms on many of these nights, my wife—my entire reason for living is love. I have found the true fountain of life, and when we are together we are equal and serene—asking no more than each can give with joy—and so willingly, because we never can give less than our all to each other. We are whole—in two parts—someday these two halves will come together in either an earthly or heavenly union—this I know and this you must believe. . . .

Now, my heart's love, it is a parting time. My darling, I must say this once more, "I love you." The sweet little girl—the vital passionate woman—the beautiful nights—the dear familiarity of the sweet long nights. A glorious love story. Always I shall remember last night . . . Our marriage has been so perfect, but it cannot be —because, you see, darling, without a day by day close companionship and a mutual binding of interests a love marriage becomes a tortured thing. When the time is right God will let us have our love complete—for we are touched by the timeless ages and there can be no parting. That is why our expressions have always been found in singing . . . this is why, my darling, you must now try to follow me as we walk the straight path to good fortune.

This home is yours always—I promise not to come here when you are here. You have just told me this room of mine will be a heaven of memories and a quiet prayer for you. I want you to use it when you are here, for your sleeping hours and thinking of the boy who became the love of your life and then could not keep that love. And remember that love is not love until it has paid the price—which you must now try to help me do.

Not for a moment shall I try to forget you—every one of your gifts will be with me wherever I go, and in my heart I wear always the image of the golden girl whom the angels let me have for a brief time, that I might be brought back to prayer and the true meaning of God. I will never go astray, believe me, rather your soul can find me kneeling somewhere in simple prayer before Him who I now know can alone give us the peace we want.

Jeanette was devastated by their breakup. "My work will be my salvation," she asserted, but couldn't bring herself to sing just yet. She turned to Gene for comfort, and over the next weeks, she devoted her time and attention to being with him, taking a new interest in his work. Gene's film career had also stagnated and he was returning to the stage for the first time in fifteen years.

Nelson did attempt to establish a closer relationship with Ann. Feeling totally responsible for her condition, he felt he must finally show her some kindness if she was ever to regain her mental health. Behind this strategy Nelson harbored the vague hope that perhaps at some later date Ann would be agreeable to a divorce, since she knew Jeanette would be out of the picture. And maybe if that day ever arrived, he would be free to return to her forever.

After the breakup, Nelson took Ann on vacation to the Camelback Inn, near Phoenix. When they returned, he played the happy husband; he and Ann frequently socialized with their neighbors, composer Eleanor Remmick Warren and her husband Z. Wayne Griffin. He tried to involve himself in Ann's life, even went shopping with her. A woman noticing Ann and Nelson standing next to her in Farmer's Market, was amazed when Ann turned to her and said, "Have you ever gotten pastry here, my deah?" The woman said yes. Ann continued, "My husband won't eat them unless they're *gooey.*"

Nelson's new lifestyle wasn't achieved easily. He'd sung on a local Christmas broadcast; to the shock of the observant fans, he was drunk. On January 19, he sang again on the Chase & Sanborn ten-year reunion. Once again he was drunk, and he arrived so late that his manager was "almost tearing his hair out."

One observer at the Christmas show was at a loss to understand what was wrong with Nelson, but sensed that there had been a dramatic change.

It was the way Nelson acted . . . a strange exuberance . . . You know how reserved and dignified he usually is—and even when he clowns around and indulges in a bit of horseplay he somehow manages to maintain a certain dignity. But this night there was none of that. In fact, I don't know quite how to describe it. There was none of the sensitive artistic side of his nature in evidence. Somehow he reminded me of John Barrymore—he was every inch the actor and there was something rather hard and cheap about it all—all of the sensitive, boyish Nelson we know so well was gone and in its place was a total stranger who mugged oh so willingly for the cameras and was a little too much the "hail-fellow-well-met" among his fellow actors. He was just a little too sure of himself— yet, when he actually stepped up on the stage he seemed unusually nervous and ill-at-ease. Of course, it was not really an Eddy audience—most of the people had brought their kids to see [Gene] Autry, but considering his supreme self-confidence when sitting down in the audience, it was surprising he didn't carry the appearance off with a little more bravado.

Ann and Nelson were very friendly—they whispered in one another's ear every now and then. After he sang his first number, he hurried back to his seat and lit a cigarette for himself and Ann. And she solicitously helped him on with his coat.

In accordance with his new life without Jeanette, Nelson signed up to make four more appearances on Chase & Sanborn, and he began negotiations to host a new series of his own in the fall. He even made plans to do a spring concert tour, but ultimately changed his mind, saying, "I have nothing left to offer the world."

In early February, Jeanette attended a concert given by Maggie Teyte, sitting with Blossom and Rocky. Nelson was also there; he sat at the opposite side of the audience. They didn't speak or even acknowledge each other's presence. Later in February she went to Detroit with Gene, for the opening of his play, *The Greatest of These*, on the eighteenth. She told fans she was "just doing nothing," would stay with Gene for the two-week run, then go to Chicago, finally returning to Los Angeles for retakes on *Three Daring Daughters*. But Gene's play folded, and he left for New York while Jeanette returned to Los Angeles.

███Nelson threw himself into religion with a fanaticism that worried everyone. Not only was he studying Scriptures with a fine-toothed comb, he was also into some "crazy Eastern stuff" (Aunt Gert) and the latest New Age doctrine making the rounds in Hollywood, headed by a man named Doreal. Isabel couldn't make any sense of any of it and only worried that Nelson was involving himself in a cult. Gradually, during 1947, Nelson confided less and less in his mother and they never returned to the unique closeness they had always shared before. Nelson's religious goal was to somehow purge himself of all the errors he had made, to make amends for the hurts he'd caused, and to set his future straight— future meaning a future lifetime, if not this one—so that he and Jeanette could be reunited with no suffering and no self-imposed mistakes. He was certain that he and Jeanette had loved each other before, had "messed up" somehow and were now paying in this life for those mistakes. Only by leading an ethical life now could they find happiness in their next life together, for he was also certain that they would love each other again. And again. One of the ways he hoped to achieve a straightening out of their fate was by putting aside the "desires of the flesh." He intended to remain celibate, and asserted that he was not having a sexual relationship with either his wife or any other woman. The fact that he knew he could not resist Jeanette sexually was the main reason he'd broken up with her.

Religion became the guiding force in Nelson's life; he decided against a spring concert tour because he wanted to devote his time to religious study. He further confounded everyone by sharing his studies with Jeanette. Nelson's idea of breaking up was unusual by any standards. He wrote her voluminous letters discussing his beliefs and spiritual growth, just as if nothing had changed for them. He even wrote her of a sexual fantasy he'd had:

> I was utterly adrift without you until your letter came—then peace returned. I have been lonely during your absence—lonely but never lost. Your lovely self is here. I can see your physically beautiful body, wondrous eyes, tender eyes, but most of all your soul—your mind and soul are before me. When you think of your boy, think of lonely walks, solitary meals—the inadequacy of people's company.
>
> Darling, I was able to be with you for about two hours last night, it was a glorious, lightly spiritual experience—a dream—but not a dream. I found you asleep—my eyes swept over your tired face—how I yearned to comfort you. You awoke—so like a child—stretching the lines of your body—not conscious of me at first—your eyes held the absent look of one who has been in distant pastures—wanting me to come to you. Desire gripped me intolerably—how I needed your recognition! How I wanted your love—your kiss! I know my kiss surprised you because it was the one that demanded. I drew you to me—the delicate subtle you—who knew I must once more claim your beauty. No, darling, I know for you there will not be a memory—just always for me I will see your beautiful smile as you returned my kiss, whispering, "My dear—this was why I was born."

For Easter, Nelson sent Jeanette a white satin prayer book of Psalms with passages marked for her to study; and a custom-made hair clasp, a single purple violet on a green leaf with a large diamond center and a tiny diamond stem. The attached note read: "Darling, marriage is not always being together—it is this love—tenderness—sympathy and pity—through which we learn to accept this journey through the years—smiling through our tears—this is marriage. My Angel Wife you will always be."

To his great joy, and everyone's amazement, Jeanette delved into religious studies as well. Though she embraced the dogma, the one disagreement she had was that they had to be separated now. In all their years together they'd never had a normal sex life. It was sporadic at best, but being denied it altogether was torture to her. It wasn't just the sex, but the absence of intimacy that left in her an emotional vacuum. Through their letters (because Nelson refused to see her, as he might waver in his resolve) Nelson gently chided her that she had to put thoughts of all that aside and concentrate on her spiritual growth. They were a regular modern-day Abelard and Heloise—with, of course, one notable exception.

An example of Jeanette's writings during this period demonstrates her own spiritual torment and her bowing to his wishes, no matter how agonizing for her, as she finally was able to discuss with him her feelings during their last night together.

My dearest—

My mind is wandering today as I sit here in my own lovely room. Outside the wind is talking to the birds and the old pine here by my window is warm and friendly. I am alone—save for memories. Sometimes I think they are your memories instead of mine—they are such beautiful ones—as old as these trees—as tireless as the clouds floating in the heavens—*your* lovely soul—so much a part of my own. My darling —no woman has ever known such beauty in the delicate tenderness of a man's love given complete.

I know you did not want that night to be the night of magic and wonder it became for us. I can never forget you as you sat at my feet before the fire with your head in my lap like the darling little boy you sometimes are, and then with your hand kind but firm holding mine, how you told me you must bring about a parting. But with what glorious beauty you talked to me—your eyes looking into mine were deep wells of mystery—bathed in heaven's own blue and filled with such goodness. The windows of your soul—how I love them—and from them I can draw strange strength.

That hour was the most beautiful of my life—except the one that came later— kissing me goodbye for the last time you were nervous and anxious about me — knowing you must let me go to my room alone—yet worried about my reaction to all this.

When I reached my room I quickly closed the door. I sat on the window seat and looked at the dark heavens—no more light this late Xmas night—long ago it had gone and with it a girl's dreams. At last, safe in my bed, I gave up to the grief that I would not let you see. It had been so long since I had been held in your arms in the sweet night—now I knew I was giving this up forever. How could I ever go on? For what seemed several hours I tried to stifle the ache in my tortured heart and was only half asleep when I heard you come softly into the room, tenderly touch my cheek to see if there were tears. Yes, there were tears still freely flowing. Then I felt myself being gently lifted and held close to you, and dimly I realized that I was being carried upstairs. I was trembling in every nerve, icy cold, almost hysterical as you sat down with me in the big chair by the window and drew a white blanket about me. To the last day of my life I will remember your tender care this night. Not a word passed between us because there was no need of any. With your kiss then the floodgates were opened and I was sobbing wildly in your arms, while you held me close to you—so close I could scarcely breathe. When the storm was over —still silently—you washed my face—combed my hair—forced me to drink hot cocoa and eat the food I had refused earlier in the day—all so dearly, so sweetly, that it was all the more priceless than all the jewels in the world to a weary, sick girl. And at last how sweet your comforting hands as they held my face. How dear your whispered words, "Now, my poor little sweetheart, you will stay here with me for the rest of this night, it was cruel of me to let you go in the first place." And all the warm joy of heaven flooded my being—and I hope you will always remember the girl of this night—no longer afraid to sleep once more in your arms—lost in the wonder of the reverence you give her at these times—thrilled at your touch—and yet making of the whole world a heaven of beauty and security. And now I will tell you a secret—the most priceless part of your love for me is the beautiful tender wooing that last night as never before—came only from the soul—a spiritual bond truly linked with the divine. You said true love never dies . . . it becomes a miracle that can conquer death and love again in continual rebirth. Yes! My darling, it is ever true and I know it well—we are heirs to the grace of God. You explained so many things to me and I know that they are true—for your love awakened my sleeping soul and now life will forever be deathless and exalted. I know too that we have a love that is strong enough to go unspoken—it should need no physical touch. So when I long for your arms around me—need your kisses—I should try to remember that we must suffer the great loneliness of time and that now I must specially dedicate myself to this mission. But please, darling, try not to bury yourself so completely in this task that you no longer need me or love me.

As the weeks passed, their new sterile lifestyle took its toll on Jeanette. She spent a weekend with Isabel at "Mists," but become so distraught that she collapsed. She fainted again at home some days later, and an irritable Gene phoned Nelson, complaining that she hadn't eaten in three days. Nelson came over and spoon-fed her, reprimanding her for her behavior. Jeanette was so grateful to see him she didn't care what he said to her. Once he left, she was again unable to eat or sleep. A few days later Nelson received another irate phone call. Gene had awakened in the middle of the night and heard Jeanette crying hysterically; now she was incoherent and didn't even know who he was. Nelson rushed over, grabbed her out of bed, and sat her in his lap, rocking her like a child. When she finally fell asleep, he gently settled her back in bed and sat staring out the window the rest of the night. Jeanette seemed to rally after this incident, but it wasn't many days before Nelson received yet another call. This time Gene was also sick and needed help; Jeanette had become hysterical and collapsed again after listening to some of Nelson's records. Nelson did his usual ministering to her, and once she was safely tucked in bed and fed, they talked. He tried to get her to see that she had to pull herself together; she begged him to give her a child; she could bear the separation better if she had their child to raise. Nelson was astounded that the baby issue had resurfaced; despite his religious bent he was stirred by her anguished words. In one of the few letters he wrote his mother that year, he described the conversation, in which she fantasized about what their son would be like and his own resolve was weakened.

"What a child he would grow up to be! His father would teach him as he did me the language of the winds. Through you he would learn to feel the beauty of the blue skies—to understand the little woodland creatures—in the garden to study the bird calls and learn to talk to them. And most of all you would teach him to know and understand the God that made all these things and who loves us all."

I was overcome—for years I have wrought such havoc in this girl's life—she gave me her love so long ago—has given her whole life to me, while I have not been able even to give her peace, and now she wants to give me more. I could only hold her tighter as she went on.

"And you would teach him to know and feel music as only you can feel it—great masterpieces of wonder—and one day he would be a great singer with a beautiful soul that would be a joy and inspiration to the whole world. But darling, I know that your dreams now are for the spirit only and that spiritual beauty means more to you than symbolism."

Though it killed me to say it, I answered, "Yes, my darling, it does. And once I mouthed those dreams as much as you do—but now there must not be any more physical love between us. For though it is a great material comfort it is a spiritual hurt. I know it is hard for you to accept the deeper spiritual truths about us, but I am more determined than ever to make you see them. No mortal has a right to love like ours until he has earned that right."

To Nelson's amazement, Jeanette agreed, saying she thought she could find some sort of peace with Gene, and that he even kissed her goodnight when he was home. Nelson continued his narrative:

I was downright jealous. I clasped her to me and said, "Well, tonight you kiss *me*." And the softness of her lips—the sweet freshness of her—the first thing I knew I was kissing her passionately—until I came to my senses and said, "Forgive me" as I put her back on the pillow. She said, "Of course, darling," with a cute smile. "But don't do it again."

Had Nelson been able to find any kind of fulfillment in his life with Ann, he might have endured his circumstances better. As it was, they had little in common except music and the social circles they moved in. Otherwise there was little substance. He was always very considerate to Ann when in public, he called her "Mama" and they spoke baby talk together, to the amazement of many—but their day-to-day life painted a different picture. Fans who drove by his house daily and watched him through the windows noted the following occurrences: Nelson at the dinner table with Ann, holding a spoon in the air and gazing sadly out the window for several minutes; Nelson and Ann retiring at night to their separate bedrooms on different sides of the house; the frequency of violent arguments. One observer wrote: "On one occasion Ann seemed to be doing all the talking and Nelson, looking very sad, was sort of all squashed down in a corner. Another time, Nelson was standing in the middle of the floor, firing away at Ann who was sitting on the sofa. His jaw was stuck out determinedly, he had his coat open and his left hand on his hip, and his mouth was just going a mile a minute."

Nelson continued to drink heavily when out with Ann, and although he may have been denying himself carnal pleasures, he still had an eye for a good-looking woman. One of Nelson's groupies attended a concert given by John Charles Thomas. She'd learned that Nelson had purchased tickets in the ninth row, so she made certain she was just behind him, in the tenth row. The fan was amazed not so much at the fact that Nelson was tipsy (which she was used to seeing recently) but at the highjinks that followed.

The concert started and Nelson's seats were still empty. I'd about given up hope. Thomas strode on stage and sang his first number and still no Nelson! But during the applause for the opening song, I caught a glimpse of Nelson's head appearing among the crowd of latecomers waiting at the back of the aisle to be seated. Thomas was into his second number before it was Nelson's turn, so of course he had to wait until the end of the number. Finally Nelson and his party came down the aisle and there was quite a flurry of awed whispering as everyone recognized Nelson. "Oh, look, there's Nelson Eddy! My, isn't he handsome," could be heard all around.

Eleanor Warren went into the row first and right after her went Nelson and then in climbed [Z. Wayne] Griffin, leaving poor Ann to bring up the rear. And when it came to passing the four or five people already seated in the row, Nelson, for some inexplicable reason, tried to walk straight in instead of sliding in sideways as everyone else in the party did. Consequently he tramped all over everybody's toes, lost his balance several times and sort of fell, dropped his hat, blushed furiously, and in general caused the maximum amount of commotion. At one point he even almost fell plop into a cute little blonde girl's lap—that I'm not sure was entirely an accident. Anyhow, when he finally reached his seat, he was beet red with embarrassment.

Nelson hadn't been in his seat for more than two numbers when, between songs, Ann leaned way over across Griffin and tugged on Nelson's coat sleeve. He dutifully leaned over and she whispered something to him. Then to everybody's amazement, most of the Eddy party got up and started changing seats. Eleanor Warren remained seated, but Nelson stepped forward and Griffin slipped over into the seat Nelson had occupied and Ann moved over into Griffin's seat. Nelson, meanwhile, was slipping along in front of the others, working his way toward the seat now vacant at the extreme left. As Nelson passed in front of Ann, who had her seat folded up and was standing in front of it letting him by, he suddenly lunged back against her and almost knocked her backwards into the row of seats behind them! He just flattened her against the back of the seat, so help me! Ann, when she finally managed to recover her balance, started shoving Nelson off and an angrier woman I never hope to see! For a second there we all thought she was going to haul off and slap Nelson. Nelson, by this time blushing furiously and grinning devilishly like a small boy, moved on over into the vacant seat to the left of Ann and the two of them sat down. Ann's hat had been knocked on the side of her head and Nelson, still grinning from ear to ear, helpfully put his hand up to help her adjust it, but she brusquely pushed his hand away. Then, to our complete amazement, Nelson just looked back at us and grinned.

During the intermission Nelson was very talkative, but the others in his party kept trying to hush him up. He seemed to talk awfully loud. Ann would turn her back to him, Griffin would pay little attention, and only Eleanor Warren seemed inclined to humor him. Once he got to talking about an experience he'd had on tour, when he and his manager were on the way from Boston to New York before they realized they didn't even have a booking in New York! One time Eleanor Warren even leaned over and said something to him and kind of quieted him down —she seemed to have more influence over him than Ann did. Ann and Nelson certainly didn't have much to say to one another.

We got a big kick out of the sly little glances Nelson stole at the luscious blonde who was sitting on his left. Ann must have overlooked her when she insisted upon all that seat changing. It was the same blonde into whose lap Nelson stumbled when he first came in. His head would cautiously turn in her direction every now and then, and I know I wasn't just imagining this because as we left the auditorium we were right behind the blonde and we heard her remarking to her escort how "Nelson Eddy kept looking at me."

In May 1947, *Northwest Outpost* was previewed and from all appearances looked to be a solid imitation of Nelson's earlier films. Production values were cheaper than at MGM, since Republic had built its reputation cranking out inexpensive westerns. Audience reaction was positive but Nelson snidely nick-named the film "Northwest Outcast."

Jeanette was singing again; in May, Gene accompanied her on a tour of hospitals. The night of May 16, Anna MacDonald played mah-jongg with her friends, then went to bed, suffered a heart attack and died before Blossom and Rocky could get her to the hospital. Jeanette and Gene, still out of town, couldn't get home until the next morning. Nelson was there to comfort Jeanette and Blossom but in the late afternoon he returned home to Ann. That evening and the next he was judging again at the Atwater Kent auditions. On Monday, May 19, a private memorial service was held for Anna before her body was sent back to Philadelphia to be buried. At Jeanette's request, Nelson sang Schubert's "Serenade." For Jeanette, the loss of her mother was just one more blow during this unsettling year. The next few weeks she was wrapped up with her family, and Elsie, the oldest sister, came back to Los Angeles after the funeral for an extended visit.

Nelson, meanwhile, seemed to be fast losing his spiritual battle. An eyewitness at the Atwater Kent women's auditions (Jeanette was not judging this time) noted that he seemed to be back to his own self:

The girls were allowed to sing two numbers in their rehearsal—the one they were going to do on the show and another. Nelson gave the gals his undivided attention —at least the pretty ones he did. The other judges seemed to be able to remember it was their voices they were supposed to be primarily interested in, but not Nelson. After each girl sang, she would cross the stage, pick up her music from the pianist, and then come down from the stage and cross back in front of the judges to a row of seats on the opposite side of the auditorium. After each contestant finished singing, the other judges would all concentrate on marking their ballots, but not Nelson— his eyes quite obviously looked the girls up and down, never missing a trick, and he followed them with his eyes across the stage and then back across the auditorium. Then at long last he'd get interested in his ballot.

His ogling was not lost on the contestants either—I heard them in the restroom talking about Nelson. One said he made her so nervous the way he looked at her, but another cute little blonde gal piped up that he could sit in her lap any old day!

When the auditions went on the air, Nelson, always a stickler for accuracy, got all hot and bothered when they announced Melchior as one of the judges. He had been replaced this evening because he had done the Charlie McCarthy show that afternoon. Nelson had to write a little note on the back of his program to the producer pointing out the error and then when the producer took the program and didn't read the note, Nelson got more upset than ever. He gestured and gestured and finally in a loud, disgusted whisper said something about reading the note. Then he finally gave up in disgust, but at last the producer read the note and instructed the announcer to make a correcting announcement and Nelson was once again happy.

One of the girl contestants was a slightly built, rather shy Negro girl who had worked as a seamstress to pay for all her voice lessons. During her turn at the rehearsal, she was kept waiting an endless time on the stage before she was allowed to sing and she grew terribly nervous—she obviously had a bad case of stage fright. But in spite of her nerves it was plainly evident she had a magnificent voice. Nelson began to realize that his presence perhaps more than that of any other judge was making her nervous so after her first number, he quietly slipped out of his seat and went to the rear of the auditorium where she would be less conscious of him. Immediately she did much better. When she finished he returned to his seat. But he was very much concerned over her. She didn't sit with her family during the rest of the rehearsal as the others did, but rather sat alone on the first row to the side. Nelson kept leaning forward and looking at her. In the actual competition she did beautifully and I think she should have had first prize and I believe Nelson gave her his first vote too. But unfortunately she came in second.

The winner in the girls' division was a snappy Costa Rican trick who obviously won the first prize for sex and second for voice. It's a good thing Ann was in the back row and couldn't see how Nelson gaped at the gal! When the announcer said she was the mother of three children, Nelson's mouth dropped open and he almost fell out of his seat. And during the picture-taking he really cornered her and whipped out his little notebook and evidently got such necessary data as her phone number.

When the contestants gathered on the stage for pictures afterwards, the judges all gathered round and offered congratulations, but the poor little Negro girl was beautifully ignored. Suddenly Nelson discovered her plight and immediately he went over, shook hands with her, and talked and posed for pictures with her. The rest of the crowd finally took notice of her, but it was Nelson who was the real hero of the situation.

After all the picture-taking was over and the auditorium was clearing, Nelson walked up the aisle talking to friends. The colored girl was with her family just a little ahead of him. Her poor old mother was crying for joy, her sisters were hugging and kissing her, and her boyfriend was shyly beaming upon her. Up came Nelson, and smilingly inquired if that was her family and proceeded to have himself introduced to each and every member of her clan. The family was beside itself with

joy. The girl was carrying a huge box of gorgeous red roses which she proudly
showed to Nelson. He admired them so much she asked if he wouldn't like to have
one and he said, "Oh, may I?" and proceeded to pull off a bud. First he tried to put
it in his hat band, but that wasn't very secure, so he tried his suit coat lapel button
hole, but he found that sewed up and remarked, "The button holes aren't cut in
these new suits." The girl's mother then began rummaging in her purse for a pin
and finally came up with one so Nelson leaned over so the lady could pin it on his
overcoat lapel. Then he bade them all goodnight and joined his own party.

A number of people and fans gathered around Nelson when he rejoined Ann and
Paxson, and his party waited while all clamored for his attention. Finally she
petulantly said, "Come on, Nelson, let's go home," and taking him by the hand
pulled him off. He held her hand till they got out of the auditorium and up the
main steps leading to the main corridor and then he abruptly dropped her hand like
a hot potato. And they walked on out to their car.

In June, Jeanette visited Isabel at her home to catch her up on the latest in her
life. Isabel learned that "Jeanette recently settled a lot of money on Gene so he
doesn't have to work ever again if he doesn't want to." (An insider remarked,
"This puts Gene in the class of a well-paid gigolo.") Isabel was at a loss all these
months to understand the new developments. When she'd asked her son why he
didn't just divorce Ann and get it over with, Nelson answered: "We are so
grateful to you for not trying to tell us what to do. You are the only one of our
family or friends who hasn't, and believe me, we must fight it out alone. If there
had been a thing we could have done we would have done it long ago. We will
work out our lives if only people will leave us alone. But try to get Jeanette to talk
to you—she has no one to talk to—she has not even been able to talk to Blossom
for months now." Now Isabel pressed Jeanette for data and was told: "I could
break down that armor of Nelson's in five minutes if I wanted to—I know all his
weak spots—but I would be a foolish woman to do that. It would be a dreadful
thing to make my darling break a vow to himself—and besides, I love him so
terribly for his sweet spirit that can put aside all physical things. I want the
spiritual first as much as he does—but some day he will come back, with his
hands held out to me—because *he* wants it so. And that is why I am contented to
let things go first as they are for the present. I was ill when I thought of losing him
and even now I can't stay well. My mind simply does a tumble at the thought that
I might not see him." Jeanette grew distraught confiding all this to Isabel; despite
her desire to cope, the rejection was devastating. She worked herself into such a
fit of hysterics that Isabel finally had to put her to bed to recover, and then went
to the kitchen to make some food for her. Nelson unexpectedly arrived; he
hadn't been visiting much lately, but when he saw the food tray he demanded to
know who it was for. Before Isabel could say a word, he suddenly looked
frightened, called Jeanette's name and ran up the stairs. Isabel didn't know what
to do so she just finished preparing the food, and finally went up to see them.
"When I took the tray up a few minutes later, there the big thing was stretched
out on the bed and Jeanette had him in her arms and *she* was trying to comfort

him. It ended up with the three of us having dinner together. I must say, this is one occasion when it didn't take him long to forget how 'spiritual' he is." Despite himself, Nelson began spending more time with Jeanette. "He doesn't make love to me," Jeanette told Blossom, "but just sits holding my hand for long minutes, saying scarcely a word, but his blue eyes are saying 'I am home again—it is enough.' "

The next gradient of reconciliation, naturally, was their working together. On June 23 they did another Screen Guild Theater production of *Rose Marie*. The studio audience was quick to note something was very wrong between them, or rather, with Jeanette. She was extremely nervous and aloof in her manner toward Nelson.

Jeanette wanted an empty chair between herself and Nelson to lay her purse and script on, but every time she'd move down a chair, Nelson would quickly move after her before she could lay her things down. Jeanette had almost worked her way to the end of the row of chairs before Nelson finally stopped teasing her and moved back to the chair he had originally taken and indicated for her to put her things down beside him as she wanted to do.

By this time the orchestra was playing the "overture" and Truman Bradley was reading the introduction to the play. The orchestra leader began signalling frantically in the direction of Nelson and Jeanette. Jeanette was so busy arranging her things she didn't even notice him, and Nelson, though he saw him, couldn't imagine what he wanted. Nelson looked off into the wings and then all over the stage to try to see what on earth was disturbing the conductor so. Finally, the conductor made Nelson understand he was trying to give Jeanette her cue. Nelson quickly told Jeanette and she hurriedly snatched up her script and rushed to the mike just in time to sing her opening aria. At the end of the number, Truman Bradley signalled the audience for applause, since the scene was supposed to be an opera house with a large audience present. Nelson not only joined the audience in rousing applause for Jeanette, but he added a few lusty "Bravos" for good measure.

Nelson was his usual playful self—you know how cute and boyish he gets when Jeanette is around. Well sir, this time she appeared to want none of him . . . Not only was there very little of the usual cutting-up between them, but during the between-acts commercial, Jeanette politely walked off stage and left Nelson all alone—and believe me, he looked alone!

Whether it was singing the nostalgic *Rose Marie* numbers or Nelson's fear over Jeanette's professional frigidity, he abruptly decided to end their separation by asking her to take a short vacation with him. Some details were related in his diary.

I wish I could put down every precious moment of this trip for you to remember always, my darling. Do you recall how you felt when I asked you to come with me? I saw first surprise, then doubt—fear of the wisdom of this trip—and then a lovely smile crossed your face as I held you close and begged you not to refuse—no, darling! I was not being weak—and I have grown strong again. I know the pain will come again—but it will be beautiful, glorious pain. God does not intend us to shut ourselves up in a cloister as I planned a few months ago. We had a bad time of it for awhile, didn't we, darling? All due to my stubbornness. But I thought I was right. Ever since I was a little boy and used to sit in Grandma's dear old kitchen and dream my boyhood dreams, I have been trying to find myself. Now I know that all the years of sorrow and suffering have been only as God intended so that we might come to understand fully the grace and beauty of his given love. We two were intended for each other, and now I can put aside the rebellion of the spirit against the needs of the flesh—for I know that there is no rebellion—that is for those whose love is of the flesh—all our love was born through a spirit and then made mortal and I know now that if I live at all it must be in you and through you—the object of my world.

My darling—how shall I explain the pure and holy spirit that possesses me when I hold your body—more precious than any priceless jewel? There is only one way to explain this rapture, this ecstasy, this joyous mystery that surrounds our physical love. We are mates and this love will live forever in the misty ages from whence it came. This is why it is oh so deeply spiritual and why only you and I can give to each other this love, this religion.

25

> ## "I can never have my baby"

Everyone concerned was pleased to see that things seemed back to normal during the summer of 1947. Of course, the definition of "normal" was a little sticky. Nelson continued to live with Ann; Jeanette was still with Gene. Nelson tried to juggle his lifestyle so he'd have some time with Jeanette; this usually meant leaving his house late at night while Ann slept and returning before dawn; or telling a lie during the daytime hours and rushing off to "appointments." Nelson was now taking voice lessons exclusively with Herbert Wall, but as far as Ann knew he was also still coaching with Lippe. Since Lippe was trustworthy, he always covered for Nelson. Still another acceptable excuse to Ann was Nelson's renewed interest in visiting his mother. More often than not, Jeanette was included on this "visit."

Jeanette's career was still on the back burner. Her film *Three Daring Daughters* previewed on July 15. Jeanette attended with Gene and her two sisters, but fans noted that she looked very tired. She then took off with Gene for Mexico for two weeks, singing on a radio show there. When she returned, she posed for a new painting, which was to be a surprise Christmas present for Nelson.

Somehow Nelson managed to keep Ann and Jeanette relatively happy. But before long Jeanette began talking again of having a child. "She seems to have it in her head that she and Nelson are supposed to give a body to some very rare soul," remarked an insider. Nelson admitted to his mother that they weren't using birth control, figuring that since Jeanette was now forty-four, she wouldn't get pregnant.

Nelson stopped drinking, a fact happily noted by the fans who attended his weekly radio broadcasts. He was hosting Kraft Music Hall with Nadine Conner as co-star, and the fans were glad to see his mind was back on the music. During the summer, Nelson also recorded an album with Risë Stevens, as well as over thirty Stephen Foster numbers.

Jeanette's only complaint was that Nelson soon returned to his old ways, striking up friendships with other women. Sarah Tucker commented diplomatically, "It's surprising to know what a wild history Nelson has at this point, and what a terribly difficult time Jeanette is having with him." Jeanette resented Nelson's ways, but once again felt helpless to intervene. For Nelson, these encounters were a brief respite from the no-win situation in his life. Around Ann and even Jeanette, he was constantly reminded of the failures and mistakes in his life. With other women there were no responsibilities, and no doubt he felt less weighed down by the burdens of his everyday existence. He had women readily available, and often he picked them up at his radio show. One fan noted that only when Nelson's manager was absent did Nelson "begin to operate." One week it was a dark-haired "Spanish girl" whom Nelson had met at a restaurant. She showed up at Kraft and Nelson said "Come on and get in" as he drove out of the parking lot. Then there was a Mexican girl who "always went backstage, and he displayed quite a fondness for her, talking long and earnestly to her, hugging her, holding her hand, and even taking her home in his car on several occasions," said a fan. "She used to sit in the first row and she gurgled worse than any bobbysoxer at him and he'd give her 'radar' glances in return. Then, as with all his other girlfriends, he began to cool off and give her a fast brush when she came round and I guess she finally got disgusted for we haven't seen her recently." The same fan noted that Nelson spoke repeatedly of Jeanette during his summer radio series, which was unusual, and added, "Nelson definitely does not 'ogle' the blondes or the brunettes either when Jeanette is around—he appears to be unaware that another woman exists."

By mid–August, 1947, Nelson's lifestyle was as disturbing to him as it was to Jeanette. He was in agony at not being able to go public about Jeanette, and angry that they were so restricted as to where they could be seen together. One day they took a rare stroll on the Santa Monica Beach; even though it was an off-hour someone with a camera saw them. Nelson tore the camera out of the man's hand, opened it, removed the film and tossed the camera on the sand in disgust. On his August 21 Kraft show, he was scheduled to sing "The Lost Chord" and he informed Jeanette of his intention to publicly dedicate the song to her, saying on the air: "For the little redhead who gave music its meaning for me." Jeanette talked him out of this latest idea, but the following week he sang "Smilin' Through," another special song for them, and nearly broke down. "I've never seen his face portray such anguish as while he sang that song," noted one observer. "And when it was over, he looked like he was going to burst into tears for almost a minute. He just didn't seem to be able to regain his composure and to bring himself back from wherever the memory of the song had taken him. Hours seemed to pass before the audience's applause recalled Nelson to the present and he smiled and bowed in acknowledgement."

Nelson and Jeanette's "anniversary" was in October and they'd planned to return to Tahoe to renew their marriage vows. But, feeling they were close to cracking up, they pushed the trip forward to late September, when Nelson had finished the Kraft season and his Stephen Foster recordings. Nelson, who supposedly was on a ten-day vacation with Ann in Santa Barbara, wrote Isabel from Tahoe: "I have no pity for Ann as Jeanette has. I feel nothing whatever except that it is all a terrible mistake which must be borne. And I am only grateful that I have found my God. I find much comfort in the Psalms. At times things are so bad it is almost beyond endurance—for instance, tonight I was annoyed almost to the point of desperation. And then I picked up my Psalms and turned to the words 'Stand in awe and sin not, commune with your own heart upon your bed —and be still—' All worry seemed to pass after this one line. Oh, yes! My spirit needs to 'be still' and I have learned to turn to the God within me and pray—in this way truth arises within us and we know when we are right—we pray and we bring things to right."

Once they returned to Los Angeles it was back to unhappy reality. Nelson now had to take that vacation with Ann; they were spotted in a movie theater watching a double feature of *The Red House* and *It's a Wonderful Life*. He was decked out like a cowboy, blue checkered shirt, grey cowboy dress trousers, black boots and the leather jacket from *Northwest Outpost*. An observer in the row behind them noted, "He and Ann hardly spoke a word all evening, but when Ann noticed him biting his nails, a very bad habit that he has, she tapped him on the shoulder with her glasses." Nelson showed little reaction to either film, except when in *It's a Wonderful Life* Donna Reed tells Jimmy Stewart that she's going to have a baby, and Jimmy incredulously replies, "You mean you're on the nest!" At that point, Nelson roared with laughter. He wasn't laughing when in October, Jeanette announced that she was pregnant again. He was frantic. He'd already arranged a spring concert tour, but he quickly instructed his agent to get him a new radio series instead, and cancel the tour. This way he could remain in Los Angeles with Jeanette. He suffered new frustration over his inability to *do* anything about their situation. He didn't want his child being born with Gene Raymond's name, but nothing had changed; Ann still threatened to ruin Jeanette if Nelson insisted on a divorce. Nelson was beaten and he knew it.

Several incidents during this time demonstrate the impotent anger and hopelessness he felt about his life. A man hired to clean furniture at the Eddy home came away with this impression: "Nelson seemed like quite a nice fellow, but that wife of his certainly keeps him under her thumb, the old battle axe!" Another night a fan drove by Nelson's home late at night and saw him standing at his upstairs bedroom window, hands on the window sill, staring blankly out.

A publicist from J. Walter Thompson was lecturing a group of students in a radio advertising class and commented: "Nelson can be the soul of cooperation and on the other hand he can be terribly difficult. Nelson will always go for a publicity idea if you can sell him on a comedy or gag angle. But if in any way he suspects the publicity is going to touch on his private life he flatly refuses to go through with it. I've never seen a star who kept his personal life so private."

Jeanette had a talk with Nelson about his sadly neglected concert career, to little avail. "She is worried about me and I am afraid I am not living up to all her hopes for me," Nelson said. "I'm not fit to work just now. I am blind to the world, blind to my career, they are of no importance. I look at a sea of faces but I see only one face. I linger on the notes of a song, but I hear another voice in soft refrain. Tonight I looked at the ceiling and saw the vision that now constantly haunts my dreams through soft clouds of mists—an angel! In her hand she holds the wand of time, and stardust falls on her feet." Sarah Tucker responded to this latest revelation by telling Isabel, "Now he's completely crazy!"

On October 26, Nelson attended Atwater Kent's annual opera party in honor of the stars from the San Francisco Opera. He arrived alone; Jeanette came with Gene. One of the guests noted that Nelson "couldn't keep his hands off Jeanette" and he "followed her around like a puppy." (This description is very similar to previous ones given by publicist Sandy Reiss and others while observing the two at parties as early as 1935.) Nelson tried to be careful; he danced with other women and left long after the Raymonds did. He got through the evening by downing five old-fashioneds. One of the guests at this party was baritone Theodor Uppman, who'd recently won the Atwater Kent auditions at which Nelson judged. Uppman became friendly with Nelson during this period, and heard bits and pieces of the story from Nelson's friends and associates. Despite Nelson and Jeanette thinking their romance was a secret, Uppman learned much of the story, even that Jeanette was pregnant. "I know that he was unhappy with his marriage, and she [Ann] was a difficult person about things for him," Uppman recalled. "He was terribly frustrated and knew that he was not going to be able to get away from his marriage that easily. And I knew Jeanette had been involved. I understood it was a very intense love affair."

One of Nelson's fears at this time was that Ann would learn of Jeanette's pregnancy and go off the deep end, or carry through with her most vicious threats to make a scandal. A blurb appeared in Dorothy Kilgallen's column which summed up the current scene: "The wife of a movie idol, who for many years refused to divorce him, has finally consented to go to Reno—but the star turned her down because of the terms she specified. They were: a $1,000,000 settlement and the income on another $1,000,000 he has invested, annually—plus which she wanted to name the cause of it all as correspondent. Her husband was willing to give her the money requested, but drew the line at dragging a fair lady's name through the mire."

No documentation exists to explain how Nelson intended to deal with Jeanette's pregnancy, but in early December he quite suddenly began tests and pre-production on a new film at Republic called *Hollywood Story*. It was a murder mystery, and would *not* co-star Jeanette. Screenwriter Richard Sale recalled that he wrote about half the script, and that "the story was about an actor and his look-alike. The look-alike is killed and he becomes the look-alike instead of himself." During the filming Jeanette planned to be out of town on a concert tour. As a "consolation" for their upcoming separation, they sang a hastily arranged Screen Guild *Sweethearts* broadcast on December 15. Jeanette looked "wonderful," according to eyewitnesses, but Nelson was very pale, which surprised the fans since he hadn't been sick lately. Nelson relaxed once the show began, but it was quickly apparent to the fans that this production had been sloppily slapped together. "Jeanette fluffed her lines right and left and Nelson just didn't seem to be particularly interested in the whole thing," noted an observer. "They gave the impression that they hadn't been very well rehearsed." A new duet was added to the show, "Cricket on the Hearth," which they bungled. Jeanette was mortified and the same observer noted:

After the number they both had a breathing spell so they went over and sat down. Jeanette held her script up in front of her face and whispered something to Nelson —we just knew she was commenting on how they loused up that song—you could see by her eyes she was embarrassed. But Nelson, "the perfectionist"— what did he do? He just sprawled confidently in his chair and with an airy wave of his hand to Jeanette whispered so all could read his lips, "Nobody will ever notice."

On Friday, December 19, Nelson and Jeanette went together to a local Episcopalian church. Lately they had done this a few times, entering the sanctuary in an off-hour when there were few witnesses, or when the place was deserted. The denomination of the church was unimportant to them; prior to this they'd prayed at a Catholic church, and a "Scotch" one. They were just happy to be able to worship together. While in church Jeanette was stricken with abdominal pain, but it passed and she said nothing to Nelson. That night she, Nelson and Isabel met at "Mists" for a pre-Christmas weekend. After a late supper, Jeanette sat down at the organ, but instead of playing, suddenly buried her face in her hands and started to cry. Nelson rushed to her side; when she told him the pain had returned he bundled her off to bed, and ordered Isabel to call Dr. Wyman. They didn't need the doctor's diagnosis to realize that Jeanette was losing her baby. Dr. Wyman attempted to locate the same nurse, Ellen, who had helped Nelson during his bout with pneumonia, since she could be trusted, but owing to the late hour, she could not be reached. Isabel and her cook Mary ended up assisting the doctor. "Jeanette suffered terribly for three hours," Isabel wrote later, "but she was so heartbroken that she was even worse off mentally than she was physically. Nelson wouldn't leave her for a single instant, he had every pain she had, only worse. He couldn't stand to see her suffer."

The next morning Ellen was reached; she and the doctor attended Jeanette while Isabel and Mary slept. Nelson refused to sleep; he sat holding Jeanette's hand. Isabel continued, "She was too far in the shadows to recognize him. This alone nearly killed him. He dropped to his knees and clasping her hand firmly, began to talk to God. Never have I heard anything like it. It was the most terrible, the most beautiful, the most awful thing—but beautiful beyond any power of mine to describe.

"As I looked at her I thought what greatness there is in this woman—trying so hard to give this man a child, because she remembers how dearly he once wanted that. I had a terrible vision of her great determination—if this goes on she may easily lose her life."

Nelson had "neither eaten anything nor slept a wink," added Isabel, "and poor Mary (who loves Nelson so) was practically in hysterics and going around saying 'If only Mr. Nelson would eat something! If I could only get Mr. Nelson to eat something!' The doctor finally gave both Nelson and Jeanette 'sleeping tablets' " and left them in Isabel's care. By the next day Jeanette was well rested but very bitter and "didn't know if life was worth living."

"For awhile there I thought she wouldn't snap out of it," Nelson said. "I had to talk very fast and let her know what would happen to me. I had to give her enough love and fidelity to bring her out of this, and I guess I did it. It was one of those hours when love can conquer every other emotion. What a joy when she put her weak little hand up to my face and just said 'I love you.' And now I have my little girl safe again."

Christmas Eve was spent quietly. Nelson and Ann had scheduled a party at their home; Ann was left to host the eight or nine guests by herself and somehow account for her husband's absence. Jeanette and Gene, who normally held a Christmas party, pushed back their festivities until December 27.

The night of December 30 the Eddys and the Raymonds attended a performance given by Maurice Chevalier; observers were surprised to see Jeanette and Ann speaking to each other. On New Year's Eve, a sad-looking Nelson was photographed dancing with his wife at Atwater Kent's party.

And to everyone's amazement, Jeanette decided to go on her January concert tour as scheduled. She was "heartbroken" over the miscarriage and felt it was better for her to be away for a while; if the tour was unbearable she would cancel part of it. Nelson was furious but was unable to talk her out of it. "Just always love me and want me," she told me. "My whole life is yours. I know there are women who prefer secrecy to honesty, but between you and me there just can't be anything but honesty. And so I just say—want me always."

From the road Jeanette wrote Isabel: "These have been days of pain for me—yes, but the close companionship, the lovely inarticulate hours when his sweet silence alone is a song of love—sweeter than all else. No girl was ever so tenderly loved. I thought I knew every phase of his love—but never has he been like this. Now I know the gentle healing power of that love, know what it is to have him sing me to sleep—know what it is to have my tears kissed away. Oh, he has done that before, yes, but never as now—like a mother he has tried to smooth the sorrow away. Did you ever read Longfellow's poem 'Footsteps of the Angels'? He recited every verse to me, and it was indeed the footsteps of the angels to my soul.

"I didn't know my baby would leave me so soon and I was happy . . . I was going on a tour, which I planned would be my last—my songs had all been planned by Nelson—all rehearsed with him. Now my dream is over—over for all time—I know now that I can never have my baby—but I will have my darling boy, and a wise woman doesn't sit and wail about her woes, she finds means of preventing the wail. Soon he will have his tour, and I must be happy again for him. And my darling is going to sing this year, he is going to be a concert artist again—and a great one—I know it and I shall make him do it. We might even make a tour together soon—we talked about it last night."

Nelson abruptly canceled his film project, *Hollywood Story*, though, as Jeanette had promised, he did his first concert tour in four years. Aside from spending one night with Jeanette in February in Plattsburgh, New York, they stayed in touch mostly via letters: "How shall I tell you what these terrible yet beautiful days have meant to me, my darling?" Nelson wrote Jeanette. "Except to remind you once again that marriage—as the shining and perfect thing we know it to be—is the greatest of all God's sacraments. Perhaps the most wonderful thing of all is its secret and mysterious promise of birth. I have so long been afraid that you could never be content unless a child could come from this great rapture—but my darling, now you must face the fact that this, for us, is not to be. I have not really wanted this for many years. I am content with you alone. And this carries from the knowledge that I am surrounded by my wife's love. Can't your husband's love do as much for you? I have only to look in my mind's eye and remember my wife—she is so femininely lovely—so utterly desirable with her sweet shyness— yet uncontrollable passion in my arms—oh, my darling, have you not counted this enough in the past? Can you not do so now when you must? I am very sure you can if you try. Believe me, now there will be a strange, sweet poignancy of a newly awakened love—take my word for it—we shall be closer than ever and without a beautiful baby. Oh yes, darling! I know how deep the disappointment is for you and only a great woman could feel as you do. But I love you so much. Let my love heal the hurt and when you come to me again, be ready for it. I shall always be able to fill your whole being with rapture as we go forward in our life and love."

In Plattsburgh they stayed at an old colonial inn, in a room with a canopy bed, a fireplace and a table centerpiece of white and purple violets and lilacs. Jeanette described their romantic dinner, their favorite *Rose Marie* meal served with a green salad and ice cream for dessert. "The nostalgic old beauty of it all brought tears to my eyes," Jeanette wrote, "and I couldn't tell him why. When he put his arm around me and said 'I give you two pennies for those thoughts,' somehow a great sadness came over me and I didn't know myself just what it was. It wasn't until I was tucked softly in his arms in that beautiful old bed that complete peace returned and I began to realize how very lucky I am. He had gone to so much trouble to arrange this meeting just to give me beautiful memories. I could hardly bear to leave the next day—I took all the violets, a sprig of lilacs, and a dozen kisses from a man's eternal love."

Nelson had also given Jeanette a book entitled "The Rosary" to read. Written in 1909, the main character was called Jane, but was briefly nicknamed Jeanette. From Chicago Jeanette sent Nelson a letter discussing it.

I have been so happy to have "The Rosary" with me. These are lonely days. What I can't understand is why you haven't read it to me before! It is such a beautiful story—and how can I pity poor foolish Jeanette when she was afraid to believe in her lover's love. I have had to weep such bitter tears over Garth too—he is so like my own darling was in that pride and deep hurt—I too wanted desperately to make things up to you before it was too late, but you wouldn't give me a chance. The story is so like the course of our own lives it was amazing. But I want it all read over to me again in your own voice, as soon as we are home alone.

Please don't worry anymore. I know how hard this has all been for you and I promise never to be so much trouble again. You really didn't think, my darling, that I might lose faith in God? Why, I would have to lose our love if I did that. You have taught me too well that it was the divine father who gave us that love and who has made it so perfect. Oh! No! I only lost my peace of mind for a little while when I had to face the fact that I can never have a child of your blood and body. It is the hardest thing I will ever have to go through, but I shall learn to kiss that cross. And darling, I have the most beautiful Rosary in the world to cherish all my life—its lovely pearls are the hours I can spend with you—each one a heavenly joy—and if at the end I must always find a cross—I know that I shall also find your dear hand waiting, ready to give me the bread of life.

What a joy to have seen you for even such a little while in N. Y. One sweet long night in your arms and I can be contented for many weeks. What lovely memories I had after you were gone—I can still see you upon your arrival—cuddling your dear head on my breast and insisting you were "jealous"—Oh! My own dear little boy—never be that again. No baby in the world could ever replace you—that was just another way in which I hoped to find you most. But darling, in your dear man's arms I don't need anything more. The beautiful night is still fresh in my heart and I can finish the tour dreaming, remembering, and knowing that we shall soon be together again. What an empty world it is without you, but in my songs I can hold you in my arms and I will wait for you at home. Don't forget that secret you were supposed to tell me about.

How sweet are the reviews I am reading. The first two concerts have been wonderful. Keep it up, darling. Don't be lonely—and remember too—the telephone is always at hand.

Most of all the thing I want to thank you for during these past weeks is the great humility you have taught me.

"Jeanette says she cannot have her baby now, but I wouldn't trust her around the corner," wrote Sarah Tucker, now in her nineties and in rapidly failing health. "As soon as she is feeling stronger again—and also, I wouldn't trust Nelson either. Those darlings have reached the limit of their endurance, and I don't think they have any reasoning power any longer. If Nelson thinks Jeanette's happiness depends on a baby, he will lose his head again as sure as anything." In fact, Jeanette was ordered to have a complete physical, but she refused, telling her doctor, "I don't trust you. I'm afraid you just want to fix me so I can't ever have my baby." Even Blossom was worried, after learning from the doctor that "one more pregnancy could kill her." The man added that their unnatural relationship was not good for them "in a physical sense because of too much repressed emotion which can wreck the nervous system and has done so in both cases."

Blossom's comment to this was: "If it was left up to her she would just joyfully kill herself." Nelson told Blossom not to worry. "I know what's best for her and she will abide by my decision whether she likes it or not. There is not going to be another baby ever."

He was enjoying rave reviews during his tour, but attributed his success to Jeanette and the fact that "I never sing a concert without a wire, a phone call or a note in my dressing room before I go on. And I always call her afterwards to tell her how it went." The highlight of this tour for him was having dinner at the White House with President and Mrs. Truman and their daughter Margaret. "I think my little spouse had a finger in this," wrote Nelson. "They all talked about her constantly, and Margaret seems to fairly worship her. The President remarked that it was the ambition of her (Margaret's) life to sing on my program— so said of course that it would be an honor for me and perhaps it could be arranged this summer if he was willing. We left it at that but I know that would please Jeanette, as no one else has been able to arrange that—so it would be a feather in my cap. Margaret told me Jeanette had invited her as a house guest if she comes to Hollywood this summer. My little minx is always looking out for her husband's interests. Margaret, by the way, is a very charming girl."

Whatever Jeanette's hopes were for her reunion with Nelson, they were soon dashed. Ann Eddy suddenly decided to meet Nelson in Chicago and finish the tour with him. Her appearance had a disastrous effect on Nelson; he lost his voice in Davenport, Iowa, and battled a cold the rest of the tour. Returning home, Ann somehow learned about their rendezvous in Plattsburgh and discovered some love letters and "had a crazy fit." She screamed at Nelson and threatened to hurt Jeanette by destroying her beauty so he would never want any more "tender hours" with her. The next month Nelson battled a severe depression. After several nights of no sleep, he took a handful of sleeping pills to try and rest. Nelson wasn't accustomed to taking any medication and didn't realize he was overdosing, or perhaps he knew and simply didn't care. A few hours later Isabel received a frantic phone call from Ann. Nelson had locked himself in his room and she feared that he was unconscious. Since she couldn't get a response, Isabel rushed over to Ann's; they broke the door open and found Nelson "blue all over" and with "almost no pulse."

"I would have to say that Ann was very decent and seemed ready to help in any way," Isabel observed, once the doctor had been called. "And also, it was rather pitiful the way she just stood around and let me take over." When Nelson was out of danger, he went to his mother's to recuperate. Isabel was distraught at what she felt was a deliberate suicide attempt, even though Nelson promised her it would never happen again. Isabel feared that Ann would call Jeanette and "gleefully fill her in on the details," which prompted Nelson to tell Jeanette himself.

The subject of death, suicide and their wills was one they discussed frequently the summer of 1948. Jeanette felt very low at times but Nelson made her promise she would never take her life, nor would he. They decided, since their bodies were useless after death and their spirits would move on and take on new bodies, that when they died they should be cremated rather than interred. Jeanette was suffering from fear of the dark. The idea of being shut up in a coffin was abhorrent to her. Nelson reported that she often had nightmares about being in a coffin, unable to breathe. For a while she had trouble sleeping, even with him around, and he was forced to leave the lights on to calm her fears.

Nelson was unaware of what was triggering Jeanette's sudden obsession with death. She'd recently gone back to MGM to make a film, *Sun in the Morning*. Nelson had no reason to be jealous of her co-stars—they were teenaged Claude Jarman, Jr., of *The Yearling* fame, and Lassie. He felt she was making a mistake by doing this particular film, but she insisted it gave her something to do, and was less stressful than a concert tour. She was negotiating for them back at MGM, and to Nelson's delight, agreed to finally make a film with him after he finished his fall concert tour. During the filming, Jeanette had suffered a mild heart attack. Her old friend, still photographer Clarence Bull, was shooting her in a publicity sitting and suddenly she was unable to catch her breath and fainted. The frightened Bull had her taken to the hospital. The public version of the story was that Jeanette had had an allergic reaction to the flowers she was photographed with, but Bull later revealed that it was really a heart attack, and Jeanette had sworn him to secrecy. Nelson remained unaware of the heart attack, but was aware of her general fragility, describing her as "so delicate it seemed she'd easily break." In mid-June he returned to the Kraft Music Hall, this time with Dorothy Kirsten as co-star. He had Jeanette all to himself for her birthday and anniversary as Gene was in Hawaii working on a film.

Aunt Gert came for a visit while Jeanette was filming at MGM. Her comment was that Jeanette looked "utterly awful, and how the make-up department can make her presentable for a picture is absolutely beyond me. The circles under her

Jeanette's final film at MGM was to be a Lassie sequel with Elizabeth Taylor, who'd appeared in the 1943 classic, *Lassie Come Home*.

eyes are terrible and she is skinny as a rail." During "Aunt" Gert's stay at Isabel's, Jeanette spent one night in Nelson's bed. Isabel commented that when Jeanette couldn't be with Nelson, at least sleeping in his bed assured her of a good night's sleep.

"Now Jeanette is in solid at MGM and is well on her way to being queen of the lot again," wrote an insider. "They picked up her option on another pic to be made later this year . . . it will be with Nelson. Rumor has it [Joe] Pasternak is working on a pic for them—they won't solo star—they'll be part of a large cast, but it will give them an opportunity to prove they are top box office draws still. Then they can make another pic that will be like their best days . . . Two big shots [at the studio] were speculating on why MGM didn't make another Eddy-MacDonald pic. The one fellow said, 'The studio would like to, but you know Eddy is fairly well-to-do and he wants too much salary. He's getting $100,000 at Republic, you know.' . . . But after his sad experience at Republic I think Nelson has awakened to the fact that getting a big salary for a lousy pic cost him more in damage to his career in the long run than working for less to start with and working his way up into the big money again. Nelson is just now beginning to realize how far he's slipped, I think."

Gene returned from Hawaii and came to visit Jeanette on location in the Santa Cruz mountains. Naomi Gottlieb was a young woman on her honeymoon, staying in the same cabins as Jeanette and the *Sun in the Morning* crew. All the cabins had one double bed in them except for the honeymoon suite, which had an extra small room and bed. Naomi and her husband were surprised when the manager asked whether they would be agreeable to switching cabins with Jeanette, as her husband was coming to visit and she hadn't seen him in many weeks. Naomi agreed, but she couldn't understand why, after such a separation, the Raymonds needed a cabin with two separate beds.

During the summer, Nelson and Jeanette sang together at a party given by Artur Rubinstein, and they later had fun performing at Ringling Brothers' Circus premiere. On August 17 Jeanette sang again at the Hollywood Bowl; Nelson hid in the wings and listened, unobserved. The highlight of the evening was when a gust of wind blew Jeanette's dress up and her scarf around her head like a halo. The audience stamped and screamed its approval.

On the night of September 16, Dorothy Kirsten decided she was too ill to make the Kraft broadcast the next day, and Jeanette happily agreed to replace her. A program was hastily put together, and the next day at noon she and Nelson rehearsed it. The rehearsal tape has survived; both stars are playful and read their dialogue with exaggerated sweetness. But the highlight is Nelson whispering "Bravo! Bravo!" after Jeanette sings "Romance," and her giggling like a schoolgirl. During the actual broadcast, she was extremely nervous, and when Nelson asks her to sing "Romance," she sounds close to tears as she says, "There's no one I'd rather sing it for."

The studio audience at the broadcast was abuzz at their apparent closeness. "Jeanette bowed and smiled and blushed a little as she graciously acknowledged the very warm reception given her," noted one observer, "and all the while

Nelson stood beaming down upon her (with low-heeled sandals she looked very tiny beside him) and glancing out at the audience as though bursting with pride and happiness." The same source continued:

Obviously Jeanette felt a little uneasy having prepared for the show on such short notice, but Nelson slipped a reassuring arm around her waist as they went over to sit down, and he repeated the gesture many times during the program.

All through the program Nelson . . . no doubt well aware of Jeanette's nervousness, was at her elbow to lend a helping hand, pat her on the back for a job well done, explain some particular bit of business to her, or point out at which microphone they would work next. And when they worked together at the center microphone, he even took the cues from Producer Wilgus and gave them to Jeanette himself.

Jeanette sang "Romance" beautifully and at the end when, to achieve that fading effect, she backed slowly away from the microphone, Nelson came dashing up behind her and grabbed her by the waist to make sure she didn't crash into the row of chairs behind her.

At last the time came for the duet. [Robert] Armbruster started off with a tricky introduction—I don't think a single person in the audience could guess what the song was going to be. Nelson looked out at the audience, grinned an all-knowing grin, folded his arms, and calmly waited to see the audience's reaction. The instant Jeanette started the haunting strains of "Indian Love Call," the audience gave an ecstatic gasp of delight which made Nelson smile even more broadly. Then Nelson turned his attention to his music and after a few measures, he turned both his microphone and his music stand, the better to see Jeanette while they sang. At the same time she turned and watched him just as intently when he sang as he did her . . . They sang it magnificently . . . Each quickly anticipates the other's every move and responds sympathetically, resulting in a perfect blending of both voice and personality. Somehow Nelson seems to feel more at ease when working with Jeanette than any other co-star and she seems to inspire in him a degree of self-confidence that he never possesses when working alone or with others. With Jeanette he's completely at ease and wholly relaxed and his performance is always superlative. Individually Nelson and Jeanette are each superb artists in their own right, but together they form an incomparable team, magnificent in every respect—extravagant praise perhaps, but indicative of the effect these two have upon their admirers!

From another eyewitness report:

Everybody . . . came out of that broadcast raving about the effect she has on Nelson. He was an entirely different person that day. Just between you and me, I don't think he liked [Dorothy] Kirsten at all—she is too much the bold sort for him —he likes to do the pursuing of his women. Then too she is apparently quite a favorite with the Kraft people so poor Nelson was made to feel he was playing second fiddle to her . . . In the beginning Dorothy, in a rather queenly sort of way, went on the make for Nelson and he practically ran from her!—never saw him stand so far away from his leading lady! Dorothy soon gave up and from then on she and Nelson hardly looked at one another. His attempts to be playful and attentive were so phony anybody could have seen through them. And during the actual programs, neither he nor Dorothy hardly looked at one another while the other was performing.

What a different story the day Jeanette was on! He was the very soul of thoughtfulness and he looked at her with the most adoring gaze—never took his eyes off her the whole time and she the same with him. A couple of times when he was singing songs that seemed to have special significance to her I looked at her and she had the saddest look on her face, like he was cutting her heart out with a razor. [Others] made similar remarks to me so they must have observed the same thing.

Nelson completed his Kraft series in late September and left on tour. He had a falling out with Dr. Lippe, who usually helped him prepare his repertoire; Nelson refused to rehearse, saying he was only doing it for the money. Ann didn't accompany him on the tour, but Nelson discovered she'd sent a detective to follow him. Ann was aware that Nelson was sometimes unfaithful to Jeanette, and she wanted evidence of adultery either with Jeanette or anyone else. Ann informed Nelson that if she could get the goods on him enough to disgrace him completely she would finally divorce him. When her detective failed to unearth anything useful, Ann had Jeanette checked out and phoned places she'd been, asking for Nelson. Either Ann couldn't get enough evidence, or she was still determined to remain Mrs. Nelson Eddy. At the end of the tour, in late November, Ann played the loving wife, meeting him at the train with Eleanor Warren Griffin, Z. Wayne Griffin's wife. Nelson kissed Eleanor but gave Ann an impersonal hug.

On November 23, Nelson sang a concert at Hollywood High School; Jeanette and Gene were there, and Jeanette quietly went backstage after the program. Nelson was unusually jovial at this concert, and when he announced he was singing some of "our" songs, a cheer rose for Jeanette to join him onstage. She declined. Ted Paxson began the introduction to the next number, but Nelson just stood looking blank, his attention obviously still on Jeanette. A fan reported:

There was a split second of utter silence, and then Nelson, choking back a laugh, turned to Paxson and informed him "I haven't the faintest idea what you're playing!" Paxson looked up, a stunned expression on his face for an instant, and then he and Nelson burst out laughing and the audience gleefully joined in. The mixup completely convulsed Nelson, who had to turn his back to the audience and bent double with laughter, clung to the piano for dear life! Nelson laughed until he was red in the face, but when he recovered a bit of his breath, he looked at Paxson and then at the audience and remarked, "Ted has been with me twenty years now. I'm watching the boy. If he makes good, I'll put him on steady. But—" he turned sternly to Paxson, "you'll have to learn to play better introductions!" That started [everyone] off again and it seemed Nelson would never be able to regain his composure and go on with the song, but finally with great effort, he managed a degree of seriousness.

Nelson sang in Pasadena on the 30th; Jeanette wasn't there and the eagle-eyed fans noted the difference in Nelson—he seemed "slightly bored."

The Christmas season was upon them again, with the usual parties. The Eddys and the Raymonds seemed remarkably cozy this year. Ann Eddy even showed up at Jeanette's Christmas shindig, which was a disaster. She'd planned an afternoon garden party, even though the weather was unusually cold. One hundred and fifty guests huddled on the covered terrace when it suddenly started to rain, but then the wind came up and all the guests were drenched.

On December 28, a press preview was held for Jeanette's film, now retitled *The Sun Comes Up*. The Hollywood *Reporter* noted that the film was "the kind of homespun drama that will evoke few critical kudos, but it will satisfy where the motion pictures should—the audience. It is perfect family entertainment, and to insure marquee appeal, Metro has armed it with Technicolor, Lassie, and Jeanette MacDonald. The three make a most engaging combination."

Amazingly, the Eddys and the Raymonds "double-dated" over New Year's, staying at the Thunderbird Ranch near Palm Springs. Then Jeanette flew to San Francisco on January 11, 1949, for a hastily scheduled concert there on the thirteenth. On the twelfth she rushed off to meet Nelson for one night at Lake Tahoe, gave her concert on the thirteenth, then returned to Los Angeles. On the eighteenth, Nelson and Ann attended Atwater Kent's party. Theodor Uppman, one of the guests, noted that just after midnight Nelson kissed Ann on the cheek and wished her happy anniversary. It was in fact their tenth anniversary. Around 7:00 P.M. the next day, Jeanette and Gene arrived at the Eddys' home. Nelson poured a drink for Gene; Ann showed off her dress to Jeanette. Later in the evening, more friends arrived for an anniversary dinner party.

On January 22, Jeanette and Nelson apparently signed contracts with MGM to make one film together. Production would begin after Nelson's concert tour ended in early May.

The first quarter of the year was rocky for them. Jeanette did four radio performances with Gordon MacRae on the Railroad Hour. According to one of the show's writers, Jeanette wasn't singing well, and the chorus was beefed up to cover this. Jeanette repeatedly complained that the chorus was too loud, and couldn't understand why they weren't toned down. However, recordings of the performances show Jeanette was actually in fine voice, and the studio audiences found that she looked radiant. Nelson, meanwhile, was supposed to be preparing his new tour, but he instead spent more time with Jeanette. In a letter written to one of his fan clubs on January 31, 1949, he announced that he "went to the movies last night with Jeanette MacDonald." The film was a reissue of Gene's 1933 *Zoo in Budapest*. In February, one fan noted that Nelson had gained about twenty pounds and could barely button his jacket. Jeanette was going through her usual fears about agreeing to make a film with Nelson, though he persuaded her not to back out as she'd done in the past. The vehicle being prepared for them was called *Emissary from Brazil* or *His Excellency from Brazil*.

Nelson's tour began on March 1 in Ontario, California. He sang well, but afterwards he mentioned he was so scared and nervous he didn't think he was going to be able to get through the first number. The fans noted he had a large sheaf of notes and seemed completely unprepared for the concert. The tour was Nelson's most successful one since the war; at his Carnegie Hall Easter concert the place was completely sold out after one newspaper ad was run. Over $2,200 worth of mail orders had to be returned for lack of seats.

The Sun Comes Up was released in the spring of 1949 and did disappointing business. In April, MGM announced that the expected MacDonald-Eddy vehicle was now called *Nancy Goes to Rio*—but the stars were now José Iturbi and Ann Sothern.

What happened exactly is unknown, but Nelson and Jeanette had a major upset. Nelson returned to Los Angeles in May and Jeanette wrote that she and Gene had dinner with the Eddys the first night Nelson returned. However, she and Nelson were quarreling continually over the next few weeks. A different film project was being considered, but its title is unknown. Sybil Thomas noted that Nelson and Jeanette intended to finance their own films so they'd have more creative control, and had even formed their own company for this purpose. Decades later, Sybil didn't remember the exact name of the company, only that it was made up of their initials, and that she had become a shareholder at Nelson's request. A study of production companies at the time showed a "JEM" Productions, listed for one year only. Nelson approached the idea of producing with enthusiasm, but Jeanette had to be encouraged to make another film. There were several reasons. First, her health wasn't good and she'd been instructed by her doctor to retire. Although Jeanette had no intention of listening to her doctor, she was also worried that she looked her age while Nelson didn't. She wasn't sure how she'd photograph; during her last two films she wore special wigs that pulled back her skin and gave her an instant face lift.

But her main consideration was still their own personal relationship, which once again was on rocky ground. There were no more letters from Isabel to Sarah Tucker, as Mrs. Tucker was suffering from senility and would die in January of the following year, but according to the scanty documentation available from this period, their sex life was nearly nonexistent due to Nelson's insistence that Jeanette would "trick him" and get pregnant if she could. While Jeanette was forced to make do without intimacy, Nelson once again sought comfort elsewhere. He had two women in town he was seeing sporadically. One was a young, perky blonde named Inge who resembled June Allyson. She'd belonged to Jeanette's fan club, but met Nelson at the Herbert Wall studio where they both studied voice. Inge was inevitably curious about Jeanette; Nelson reassured her that they had once been lovers but were now only friends. The other woman was Maryon Murphy, wife of producer Ralph Murphy. Nelson had met her while at Republic studios, where her husband worked. Murphy was a sexy woman with a Tallulah Bankhead voice. They first met at a party; a year later Maryon happened to pass Nelson one day while driving; she tossed her phone number into Nelson's car and yelled, "Call me." He did; they became platonic friends for over two years. Now, suddenly, Nelson arrived at her home on Roxbury Drive with other ideas, and they began a long-term affair. Maryon was definitely in love with Nelson, but in retrospect her mother termed Nelson's feelings for her daughter as "purely sexual." What Nelson told Maryon about Jeanette is unknown; she later talked openly about her affair with Nelson but clammed up on the subject of Jeanette, saying coldly, "I do not discuss Miss MacDonald."

Jeanette resented these latest developments. Isabel warned her son to cease his "cheap love affairs," while Aunt Gert predicted "Jeanette may wash her hands of Nelson. There is nothing halfway about Jeanette; if she turns against him she will not want to know or let Isabel tell her anything more about Nelson whatever." Sybil Thomas lunched with Nelson and Jeanette at a restaurant and noted Jeanette's new abhorrence at his touch; his hands were constantly on her but she coldly pushed him away. Jeanette barely tolerated the situation, hoping that Nelson would calm down and perhaps change his tune once they were filming. They could look forward to months of togetherness. And after all, working together was what he'd claimed he'd wanted for them since they left MGM in 1942. They did begin using a rented house in Malibu as a new weekend rendezvous spot. But according to friends, the romantic hours were soured by their constant fighting, with one or the other walking out before the weekend was over. After one particularly ugly argument Jeanette suddenly groaned, "I can't take this anymore," and ran into the bathroom, slamming the door loudly behind her. Nelson started to walk out, but instinct made him hesitate. He walked into the bathroom and stopped in horror. She was standing at the sink, a razor blade poised at her wrist. Nelson stood frozen, then started to cry, frantically begging her not to do it. After a long moment of indecision she dropped the razor and fell into his arms.

Nelson felt "like a monster" for having driven her to the brink. He assured her that they could work out their differences, that any solution was better than suicide. For a time after this incident, things seemed to take a turn for the better. But then Jeanette's spirits sagged again. No matter how she tried to rationalize their situation, the insanity of it wore her down. She knew she could only blame herself; for the rest of her life she would curse her stupidity for marrying Gene and thus bringing about their present predicament.

Jeanette's emotional stability, clearly affected by her physical condition, was rapidly eroding. The few private moments she spent with Nelson now usually consisted of her crawling into his lap like a small child, clinging desperately to him as he stroked her hair and reassured her. She was now practically unable to sleep, even in his arms. One night he awoke after spending hours trying to get her to rest. She was not beside him. He found her sitting in a rocking chair near a window in the living room. Silent tears rolled down her cheeks. Nelson stood watching her, unnoticed. Despite his anguish at her suffering, he noted how the moonlight framed her "like a halo" and how exquisitely beautiful she was. The thought crossed his mind that he should capture this moment forever in a painting.

Nelson hoped that once they started working together she would snap out of her depression. He reassured her that she was up to filming, that she looked gorgeous and that he would do everything possible to make things easy for her on the set. Some filmed tests were made, but of what script, what scenes and where they were shot is unknown. One source suggested the footage was filmed at MGM in early July. But the outcome was disastrous. Jeanette overheard two bigwigs discussing how she photographed. They were concerned that she looked too old, and that Nelson should pick a younger co-star. For Jeanette this was the last straw. She informed the crew that she was quitting, packed her makeup kit and ran out. Nelson was quickly informed of her sudden outburst and tried to head her off, but she turned on him with years of pent-up rage and agony over their lives. "How you must hate me!" she screamed at him. After telling him she never wanted to see him again, she went home and collapsed with a nervous breakdown.

For days she was quite literally out of her head, and had to be sedated. What occurred thereafter is unclear; one nurse claimed in the 1970s that Gene had her taken to a mental hospital outside of Los Angeles county, but refused to name the hospital. When Jeanette was calmer she returned home, but any mention of Nelson or listening to his records set her off again, and she reportedly at one point attempted suicide by trying to drive her car off Bel Air Road. It was back to bed rest and sedation, and the house had to be purged of any reminders of Nelson that might upset her. The low point occurred when Blossom, visiting her sister and trying to get through to her, mentioned Nelson and watched Jeanette frowning, trying to remember who she was talking about.

Jeanette eventually recovered but she was a changed woman, which prompted some to wonder whether she'd had shock treatment. Her temperament seemed so different. In the months ahead, one of her friends was surprised when Jeanette blurted out that she was afraid Gene would have her "put away" if she stepped out of line.

Jeanette worked sporadically throughout the balance of 1949. In professional matters she was said to be irritable and dominating; in her private life she seemed sedate and content to be with Gene. During this period he took control of her life and her business affairs. There was no longer any talk of her making films, and she refused to discuss Nelson. In time she could hear his name without becoming hysterical, but after fifteen years of heartache, she considered Nelson Eddy a closed book. After so much pain it seemed impossible she could ever feel again.

As a fitting epilogue to this chapter in her life, Jeanette's mockery of a marriage was demonstrated when Gene Raymond was arrested yet again. "It was about the time of the annual Hollywood Christmas parade," remembered a retired Navy nurse. "I was in nursing school and my mother was dating a Hollywood undercover vice squad cop. One night he came home and told Mother and I: 'We did a bust tonight. We picked up a movie star, Gene Raymond. He was a solicitor for young men.' In other words, he was arrested for being a male pimp."

Jeanette faced the Christmas season of 1949 with the certainty that without exception, every area of her life had failed her. She was completely burned out, with nothing to show for her years of work and loyalty. But she was a fighter, and she somehow gathered the strength to begin a new life for herself.

26

End of an era

When Jeanette broke up with Nelson, he had no idea what had caused her sudden upset. Confident that she'd get over it in a day or two, as she always did, he waited for her phone call. When she didn't call, he called her and was told that she wouldn't speak with him. After a number of days he drove over to Twin Gables and banged on the door, insisting that he had to see her. When that didn't work, he parked his car by the house and waited, certain she would have to come out sometime.

By now he was frightened. He wrote letters but received no response. He could get no data from anyone—even Blossom wouldn't speak with him. Finally he decided that Jeanette meant what she said. She was through with him. With no warning or explanation, she had put him out of her life. He knew that he deserved it, but he couldn't understand how she'd stopped loving him after all these years

It took months before reality fully sank in. At any time he expected a letter or phone call, and he would have taken her back without recrimination He waited in vain. Nelson spent the summer doing another season of Kraft, then he left on another concert tour. He never hosted a radio show again and correctly sensed that the heyday of that medium was over. He felt that everything was falling apart in his life at once; though he still filled concert halls, clearly the new medium of choice was television. Nelson faced the fact he was a has-been in films and radio, and could only hope that he was not also washed-up in concerts.

He was home for the holiday season but Jeanette had gone to Europe with Gene to entertain soldiers. What began as a noble gesture on her part turned into a nightmare, demonstrating that her appeal to the general public had plunged too. One of the men in the company described his thrill at the idea of working with Jeanette MacDonald. But when he returned from the tour, he concluded that she was "a pain in the butt."

> First of all she ranted and raved at having to follow Whip Wilson, the Monogram cowboy actor, on the bill. Whip is a comparative newcomer, but he's rapidly gaining in popularity and he does a whip act that went over sensationally with the boys in service. Jeanette seemed to find it hard to compete with his act and consequently resented having to follow him on the bill. But the payoff came when Whip sang "The Lord's Prayer" at the Christmas shows. It was so impressive that Jeanette just couldn't top it so she simply demanded that he delete it from his act, or she wouldn't go on. So Whip was forced to bow to Prima Donna MacDonald, but not before he really put her in her place by quietly telling her that he considered it a great honor for one in her position to have to request him to omit material because she couldn't follow it! Poor Jeanette couldn't make any reply obviously but she sure did burn! Connie Bennett who headed the troupe (her husband is stationed over there you know) told Wilson that was the way to handle her.
>
> Jeanette did a lot of complaining about the food—she couldn't get her beloved Yami Yogurt. The worst incident of all, though, came during one of the holiday shows to which the servicemen's children were admitted. Knowing a cowboy was in the show, the kids of course all sat right down in front and they literally ate Whip up. When he finally left the stage they kept applauding and applauding. Then Jeanette came and started to sing, but the kids wanted more of Whip and were restless and noisy. Jeanette finally gave up trying to hold their attention and simply stopped singing and yelled for Gene (he emceed the show) to come out on the stage and "quiet those brats down." Gene managed to obtain a measure of silence, but the audience was so disgusted with Jeanette's display of temper that over half of them got up and walked out during her song.

During 1950 Nelson dated several women. He continued to see Maryon Murphy and Inge as well as others. In August he signed a new five-year contract with Columbia Records and kept busy recording for them. One album included duets sung with opera star Eleanor Steber. Steber was asked shortly before her death how she'd come to record with Nelson. "I picked him up in a bar," was her candid reply.

Over the next couple of years, Nelson and Jeanette ran into each other two or three times, usually at parties. In one instance, someone noted that they avoided each other and didn't speak. Other times they were with their spouses and other people and apparently forced to make small talk. Rumors were even printed that they were still planning to make a film together. Nelson was resigned to their separation, which would last nearly three years, but was still unable to purge Jeanette completely from his system. "She stopped loving me," he told one of his current flames. "After all these years, she stopped loving me." He rehashed the story of their romance. "We were so young and bright in those early days. Everything was new, falling in love for really the first time in our lives. Then my great love started to falter. She loved me, she loved me not. Talk about a yo-yo! I was like a puppy dog, I wouldn't let go. Whatever she did, I loved her. I would have gone through hell for her, and I did, often. But as long as I knew she loved me . . . Then the war came, and things were less bright. She was wrapped up in her marriage, I in mine. She'd changed, she was so fragile it seemed she'd easily break. I didn't care, I just loved her more. I would have gone on loving her till the day I died—" At this point in the story, Nelson would break down in tears. When he finally was able to continue he added, "The worst mistake I made was leaving Metro. I hated the place, hated the man. But everything I've touched since then has turned to shit. Pure shit." Three of Nelson's girlfriends from this period were asked whether Nelson would have left them and returned to Jeanette if she wanted Nelson back. Each girl grudgingly admitted the answer was yes.

Nelson made his first television appearances on the Allan Young Show, doing comedy and singing. He tried in vain to find a niche for himself in the new medium—starring in two pilots, and writing four sketches for yet another proposed series for himself, none of which was picked up.

■ During the spring of 1951 Nelson toured the Southwest, returning to the only medium that still truly wanted him: concerts. A candid of him sitting in his hotel room in Albuquerque shows him unsmiling, his face lined with unhappiness.

In early August he had a respite from Ann by flying to New York. He was scheduled to broadcast a Bell Telephone Hour live from Carnegie Hall on the thirtieth. While there he received a call from Luis Churchton, an old friend from his Philadelphia days. Churchton had lived abroad for many years, and dealt with imports and exports. Nelson was a pewter collector and Churchton occasionally bought pieces for him. Churchton was spending a week in New York with his fifteen-year-old daughter. After his wife's death, he'd turned over guardianship of the girl to his sister-in-law, and rarely saw her since he was out of the country so much. But now she was approaching her sixteenth birthday; he was in New York, so they did the town together.

Nelson was taken by the blonde, very shy girl who seemed so wise for her years. She'd lived a very sheltered and sterile existence with her aunt, didn't go the movies and had never heard of Nelson Eddy. This was a novelty to Nelson, and he suggested to Luis that he join them for sightseeing and shopping over the next few days. During the evenings they talked for hours in Nelson's hotel room, and Nelson updated Churchton on his breakup with Jeanette and the empty loneliness he'd lived with since. He couldn't speak of Jeanette without tears; the girl noticed this and was quietly sympathetic. Nelson found himself strangely drawn to her despite her age. Nelson, who was always impulsive in love, now asked Luis if he might take her away for a few days after the Carnegie Hall broadcast. Luis was continental, but after all, this *was* his daughter they were discussing. In the end, he agreed. Nelson arranged to spend a night or two at the home of his good friend Salvatore Baccaloni, then he chartered a yacht to sail down the coast to Virginia where he could find respite at his relatives' plantation. Baccaloni and Nelson's family were surprised and not a little disapproving of his latest amore, and repeatedly asked, "But what about the redhead?"

By the time they reached Richmond, Nelson had made some major decisions. He felt he'd found a second chance at love, and was determined not to blow it. Because of the girl's age, he knew they'd have to leave the country until he could obtain a divorce. He would cancel his fall concert tour and get out of an upcoming appearance on the Alan Young TV show by demanding so much money they'd have to drop him. His new plans included a move to Bogotá, Colombia, where he could earn money by touring South America. His family listened to these "plans" with open-mouthed amazement. They thought he'd completely lost his mind. Isabel was phoned and was urged to talk some sense into her son. Nelson tried to explain to her that he felt he was a desperate man given one last chance at life.

In the end, the matter was settled by the girl's guardian, who threatened to prosecute Nelson: first, he was a married man with a wife who refused to give him his freedom; second, Ann would nab him with a jailbait suit that would forever ruin his career.

Nelson returned to Los Angeles, extremely bitter. "Why, oh why didn't I divorce Ann years ago and let her do her worst?" Within months, he learned Churchton's daughter had died of a heart ailment.

Nelson survived this latest blow by throwing himself once again into his work. In October, he was off to Canada on another tour. December found him home again and deeply depressed. He made a rare visit to Sybil Thomas and, after updating her on his life, he casually asked for some cake and milk. She went to the kitchen, but something in his manner had disturbed her. She returned to the living room to see him going for her husband's loaded revolver. He was aiming it at his head by the time Sybil reached him. They fought for the gun; Nelson hit her, dropped the gun and walked out. Sybil wouldn't speak to him again for a very long time.

■Jeanette's last major radio show was a Screen Guild Theater *The Sun Comes Up* in March 1950. She, too, was in limbo and couldn't seem to muster the energy to rejuvenate her career. Friends continued to be amazed at her apparent apathy about her life and at her newfound submission to Gene's wishes. Miliza Korjus was present at a party during this period, at which Jeanette and Gene were also guests. After the dinner Gene, who'd had more than a few drinks, started talking about how *he* had made Jeanette a star, how *he* was responsible for her success. The other guests were embarrassed. Miliza was appalled at seeing Jeanette listening to all this, staring down at her lap, saying nothing. Finally someone told Gene to shut up. Miliza later commented that Jeanette took Gene's verbal abuse "as though she deserved it." Others made similar comments over the coming months after seeing Jeanette and Gene together.

One friend dared to ask Jeanette why she'd broken up with Nelson. To his horror, she said she didn't know and started to cry. Another friend recalled walking with Jeanette down Broadway in New York. One moment she was next to him, the next she was nowhere to be seen. The friend turned and saw her walking several paces behind him, with one foot in the gutter, muttering to herself. The same friend was later having tea with Jeanette and Gene in their New York apartment when Jeanette suffered yet another breakdown; she turned white and her hand shook as she stirred her tea endlessly and kept mumbling "Damnit, damnit, damnit." Under an alias, she was hospitalized for a few days suffering from "complete exhaustion."

In the fall of 1950 she started another concert tour, but physically she just wasn't up to it. One friend who saw her backstage in New York was appalled at her condition, and commented, "Jeanette looked utterly awful afterwards. I never saw her look like that. The minute she exhausts herself, she goes to pieces. She looked better in Albany than she did here; she had rested in New York several days before the concert. As usual the critics tore her to pieces and blamed her success on the movies, but nevertheless she was a terrific hit. They were even standing up in their seats and screaming at the top of their lungs and the house was packed to the rafters. Gene sat only a few rows in front of me. He left afterwards. They'd come in separate cars and Jeanette came with her own crowd. Gertrude Lawrence sat just a few seats from Gene and she attracted twice as much attention as Gene did. Gene has some sort of TV and radio thing going with Buddy Rogers; he is on TV tomorrow night."

Jeanette attempted suicide while in New York. She'd come back from a performance and was physically drained. She'd returned with Gene, but once in the hotel he left from a side exit to pursue his own interests, while she still had an escort with her, one of her gay friends. (Jackie Hoover, who as a young woman traveled with Jeanette as part of her entourage during a couple of tours, noted, "Jeanette always had gays hanging around her. I don't know where she got them, but they were always there.") In the lobby she was met by a group of reporters, one of whom was very well known. They wanted an interview, despite the late hour. She agreed to have the press come up to her suite with the stipulation that no photos with flash would be taken. Her eyes were strained from the lights on stage. If they respected her wishes, she'd consent to an interview.

Once upstairs, Jeanette patiently answered questions, then suddenly flashbulbs went off in her face. Jeanette tried to cover her eyes and cursed their treachery. The well-known reporter retorted, "I always heard you were a bitch," and packed up and left with the others. Jeanette grew hysterical. "Why did they have to do that? I tried to be nice to them." She became more and more inconsolable, sobbing. "He said they'd turn on me, they'll pretend to be nice to you, but one day they'll all turn on you." When the friend asked who the "he" was, she answered, "Nelson. He warned me some day this would happen. I never listened to him when I should have." She then started crying about her life and her lost love. Up until this time she had never even mentioned Nelson's name to this friend, or her film career. Both were taboo subjects. When the friend left Jeanette was still distraught, and finally took sleeping pills. It was up to her secretary to stay by her side and see her through it. Gene was registered in the same hotel, but a different room. Jeanette's next two concerts had to be canceled.

Jeanette's secretary lied magnificently for her for decades, but she revealed her true feelings when she confided to a friend that she hated both Nelson *and* Gene, and she wished that Jeanette would get rid of both of them. "They've managed to wreck Jeanette's life completely," said the secretary. "I've seen enough tears to float a battleship."

"I'm burnt out," Jeanette later admitted. "I worked long and hard and I've burnt myself out . . . I've given of myself until there's nothing left to give. And I've gotten nothing in return from anyone, except Nelson." Jeanette pulled herself together for her TV debut, appearing both on Toast of the Town and the Firestone Hour. She found live TV more nerve-wracking than radio, and felt that she would never find a niche in that medium.

After a rest, she regrouped her energies and decided that she and Gene should do a play together, an idea he'd been pushing for some time. They chose Molnar's *The Guardsman*, the old Lunt and Fontanne hit (which was also the plot of Nelson's film *The Chocolate Soldier*). The plan was to tour with the show around the East Coast, get the bugs worked out and then make a triumphant return to Broadway. But Jeanette made one fatal error with *The Guardsman*; she forgot that she and Gene had no chemistry together as actors. Their single film together, *Smilin' Through*, had not clicked with the audiences, nor would this latest project. Set designer Herbert Gahagan (cousin of Helen Gahagan Douglas) worked on *The Guardsman*. "Jeanette saw my work and liked it, and I was hired for the run. She was happy with the sets, but the show never made it to Broadway." He continued, "I thought she was a bitch. I didn't like her. She had a reputation for being temperamental, and I'm afraid I have to agree it was true. Part of it was that she took herself seriously. She had no sense of humor. She was a competent actress, not great, but she knew her strengths, and she knew how to market herself. You have to give her credit for that; she was a shrewd business-woman. But as a person I found her extremely selfish.

"It was her they came to see. She was the meal ticket. I remember when we did the set in Buffalo. She said, 'Gene, go out into the first row.' And he did and I was right there with him. And she said, 'Can you see it?' He said yes. She blasted, '*Are you sure?*' She was the balls in that outfit. That square jaw didn't permit anything else."

Gahagan was asked about Jeanette and Gene's personal relationship, and he retorted, "I don't gossip. When people ask me for interviews I talk until they start asking personal questions, then I tell them the interview is over.

"I would think you'd run across a lot of people who won't talk. For people like me, who worked backstage—these people paid our wages. You accepted these people for what they did and brought and gave in their work, not for what their personal habits were. It still holds true today, and it did way back in the twenties, when I first started."

Gahagan was pressed further and finally admitted that the MacDonald-Raymond marriage wasn't exactly what it was made out to be. "I couldn't swear on it on a stack of Bibles, since I certainly didn't sleep with him but—yes, it's true, [Gene] went for the guys. She didn't give a goddamn. She was wrapped up in the show, and her fans. That's what she lived for . . . Besides, the one she was really in love with was Nelson Eddy. They had married years ago but it didn't work out . . . It was the buzz-buzz among ourselves at the theater for awhile."

Jeanette was plagued with ill health during the run of the play, but in true trouper style continued to work. "I was there [in Columbus, Ohio] when she was throwing up all over backstage," said Jackie Hoover. "She kept leaving the stage. In the middle of something she'd just quietly, calmly walk off, throw up, then go back in there." Through the rest of 1950 and well into 1951, the Raymonds attempted to make a success with their play. The public drawn to the production was predominantly Jeanette's devout followers; the general public showed no interest in the show as it was. Jeanette even inserted a mini-concert into the show, which pleased her fans but still didn't make the play a hit. Finally she gave up, bitter with the knowledge that despite the years of personal sacrifice, now even her career had deserted her.

In 1952 Nelson again turned to religion in his search to give his life meaning. He did one lengthy concert tour, then he had months of time to re-evaluate his life. He was no longer involved in the Doreal studies, but turned to a new religious philosophy: Dianetics. A best-selling book written by L. Ron Hubbard was published in 1950; the basis for Hubbard's theories was that man was a spiritual being, not a body. A kind of counseling called "auditing" helped the person to remember painful or forgotten incidents in his life that had adversely affected him. Within two years Hubbard was publishing more books and articles on the subject, finding that by returning the person to earlier times— without the use of drugs or hypnosis—he was finding an astonishing number of people reporting past lives. Hubbard wrote that the controversy regarding past lives wasn't as important as the fact that these people dealing with the incidents they remembered got better afterwards. Nelson was introduced to Dianetics by Gloria Swanson, a friend and disciple of Hubbard's, and philosopher Will Durant, to whom the book *Dianetics: The Modern Science of Mental Health* was dedicated. Hubbard's past lives theories intrigued Nelson, and he delved into the early Dianetic auditing with his usual all-encompassing enthusiasm.

By fall 1952, Nelson had revitalized himself to such a degree that the results were dramatic; he was prepared to turn his life around and make a new professional start. Furthermore, within a matter of weeks he achieved something he'd once thought impossible, he and Jeanette were together again. The reconciliation took place on live television, in front of the entire nation.

■■■A new TV show had been launched during the fall 1952 season: "This Is Your Life," hosted by Ralph Edwards. Edwards specialized in tricking a celebrity into making an appearance on the show, then surprising him or her with friends and family and rehashing all his or her life achievements. Edwards was originally interested in featuring the team of MacDonald and Eddy on his show; he surprised other teams as well, such as Laurel and Hardy.

According to one source, Nelson was contacted about appearing on the show, which was surprising, considering Edwards's policy about tricking the guests. Sybil Thomas also verified that Nelson was contacted. She said he "told them where to go and hung up."

The next tactic was to do a show just on Jeanette and have Nelson make a guest appearance. Again, he wasn't interested. Now Blossom entered the picture. She'd learned about the proposed show from Gene, who was in cahoots on the "surprise." Blossom, certainly more gutsy and practical than her younger sister, had never completely understood the reasons behind Jeanette and Nelson's breakup. She'd never been able to get a straight answer from Jeanette, and only knew that afterwards Jeanette had suffered a breakdown and in some ways had never been the same. Neither had her career benefited from the professional dissolution. Blossom decided to confront Nelson and have it out with him herself. She asked him to meet her for lunch which, to her surprise, he agreed to do. At first she found him cool and aloof, unable to look her in the eye. She said, "Look, I don't know what happened to you two, but—" and went on to explain some of what had happened to Jeanette in the interim. Maybe the breakup had been her sister's fault, but she had suffered greatly, both emotionally and physically.

To Blossom's amazement, Nelson seemed unaware of the facts she was relating, especially the breakdown. The data she was relating seemed to answer some unspoken questions for him, and he warmed up a bit, though he was still more reserved and apathetic than Blossom had remembered. Blossom pointed out that since the show with Jeanette was a definite go, it would look very bad if Nelson didn't show up. To her relief, Nelson finally agreed to appear.

The air date was November 12, 1952. The night before, Jeanette gave a concert in Los Angeles. Nelson attended, but afterwards Nelson left without going backstage. The fans were curious as to why he wasn't letting Jeanette know he was there. The next day found Jeanette arriving at the El Capitan Theater in Hollywood, presumably to present Ralph Edwards with a plaque from the International Optimists Club. Nelson later related to Sybil Thomas that he'd refused to attend the rehearsal for the show, which caused a minor panic and resulted in a couple of back-up people being set up to appear in case Nelson reneged. One of those contacted was a woman from the MGM commissary, who was actually better friends with Nelson than Jeanette.

Nelson was extremely nervous when he arrived backstage for the show. He cursed and argued when they tried to make him up, and he was finally left alone to wonder whether he'd made a big mistake by agreeing to do this. Jeanette, meanwhile, wondered what was going on when the driver of her car was told to park the vehicle "right over there beside Nelson Eddy's." She made her entrance on live TV, presented Edwards with his plaque, then found out that "the surprise is on me!" She still had no real concept of what was going on until Edwards explained the format of the show to her. It took her meeting a guest or two from "out of her past" before she fully realized what might lie ahead with Nelson.

This Is Your Life captured, in a half-hour show, more insight about Jeanette, her relationships with Nelson, her husband and her sisters, than any single interview that had ever been given. Caught off-guard, her emotions were transparent as she gracefully struggled to get through what was evidently an emotional ordeal for her.

Among the surprise guests hauled on stage was Miss Edna Clear, Jeanette's seventh-grade English teacher, a soldier she danced with during the war, and Grace Newell, her voice teacher. The warmth and closeness between Jeanette and Blossom was obvious as Blossom explained to the audience how she got Jeanette her first job. Blossom seemed protective of her sister throughout the show. The appearance of Elsie, the third sister, elicited a different reaction from Jeanette; she wrinkled her nose and said, "Is she here too?" Amazed that her sister flew out from Philadelphia, she proclaimed, "This is the biggest surprise yet! It's a real family reunion!"

Gene Raymond was supposedly in New York, and a phone hook-up allowed Jeanette to speak with him. The irony of their marriage surfaced when he asked her to call him after the show. She quipped, "Will you be home?" As Ralph Edwards's mouth fell open, Gene told Jeanette, "There won't be any late date tonight. I'll wait for your call and make the date afterwards." Gene, of course, was backstage all the time. When he made his appearance Jeanette hugged him, laughing, "You lied to me." Then they sat on a couch, though not closely together.

Edwards mentioned Anna MacDonald's death in 1947, to which she replied "Uh huh," with no change of expression, no upset. Her response was also emotionless when Edwards asked her if she remembered her wedding date. The reverend who married them, another surprise guest, gushed on about how Jeanette and Gene "show in their life the philosophy of the holy bonds of matrimony." Jeanette was embarrassed and looked down at her lap.

The first time "your great co-star Nelson Eddy" was mentioned, Jeanette's smiling, social expression crumbled and her head instantly went down. The camera quickly cut to some photos from her films, but another time when Nelson and her films were mentioned, her head again went down. As Edwards went on and on about their films and her "song-filled life," she stared off, alternately worried, hopeful, scared. At one point she caught herself and gave Edwards a weak smile. When Edwards started to introduce "an old friend" she stiffened slightly and looked very intense, but it wasn't Nelson.

Then it happened. Edwards started to introduce another old friend; she stiffened again and bit her lip, her breathing changing noticeably. Nelson started singing off-stage, a song he'd performed at her wedding. At the sound of his voice her head dropped back, an expression of ecstasy on her face. After a moment she looked around, almost desperately, then tried to look nonchalant, but couldn't hold back the tears. She looked to Gene for assistance; he dutifully handed her a handkerchief. Nelson entered the stage. She bolted up from her seat and melted right into his arms. The difference between this body language and when she hugged Gene at his appearance was quite telling. When she finally nervously broke away, she stepped back and looked at Nelson adoringly. Her admiration was shared by the audience. Finally she sat down, with Nelson still holding her hand. They talked, still holding hands. Nelson lamely mumbled something about the memory with the "greatest warmth" of their professional relationship being when he sang at her wedding. He couldn't finish his prepared speech and trailed off uncertainly. Jeanette said, "What can I say, Nelson?" and then found the words to end this little conversation smoothly. Nelson caressed and kissed her hand, then backed off.

Gene, all this time, was the forgotten man. His reactions were also telling. At Jeanette's distress with Nelson singing, Gene's face hardened. He tried to look indifferent, but anger crossed his features more than once. He remained irritated by her emotional display, then looked resigned and reached for his handkerchief. When Nelson started his speech, saying "Jeanette—I may call you Jeanette, may I?" in a slightly sarcastic tone, Gene jumped in with, "That's all right, old man, I give you my permission." After the show, Ralph Edwards presented Jeanette with a gift, a Bulova diamond wristwatch. She started to show it to Gene, then

"This is Your Life," November 1952.

her head snapped over in Nelson's direction; she caught herself and turned back to Gene.

Afterwards there was a reception at the Bit of Sweden restaurant. The party finally dissolved. Blossom, keeping a close eye on Jeanette, watched as her sister's excitement suddenly deflated. Nelson had left with Ann, and Jeanette looked suddenly exhausted. Blossom walked her outside and they discovered that Nelson was still there, but Ann was gone. With a lame excuse, Blossom left the two of them together. "Whatever happened next," she said, "at least I'd tried."

Nelson drove Jeanette home via Mulholland Drive, a quiet, winding, star-lit lover's lane. He parked and they sat and talked. Or rather, Nelson talked. He blurted out many of the things that had happened to him personally and professionally. To his amazement, Jeanette sat quietly and listened. Usually she was such a chatterbox. Normally she might have reacted angrily at what he was saying. This time, however, she said, "I'm so sorry you've suffered. I wish there was some way I could help ease your pain."

Nelson later told Sybil, "If [during the TV program] she had greeted me socially like one of her old fans, that would have been it. But when I saw her reaction—" He added, "Then, later, when I talked to her, she had more warmth, more caring than I remembered. She was comfortable to be around." Jeanette also related details of their talk to Blossom. Curiously, there was no discussion of their feelings for each other; even after all this time, that was not in question. But their lives had changed, and as Nelson said, "We can never go back, but we can help each other go ahead, and share what we have left."

27

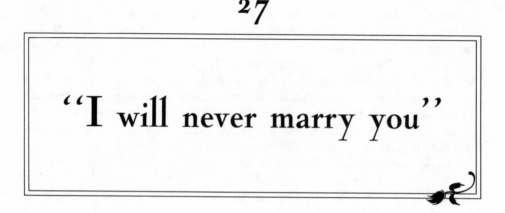

"**I will never marry you**"

After their talk on Mulholland Drive, Nelson drove Jeanette home. To her surprise, he did not call her during the coming days. She was the one who had to reach for him. When she phoned he was pleasant and talked of getting together, then dropped the ball again. It took Jeanette some time to realize that he meant what he said when he told her, "I'm afraid of getting hurt anymore. One can only suffer so much, then you either die or you learn not to feel." Their relationship might never have picked up again had it not been for Jeanette's efforts. She found ways to see him, and brought him little, lighthearted gifts that made him smile. Luckily, she was able to find an ally in Isabel Eddy. Isabel was thrilled to see Jeanette again. She and her son had not been getting along in recent years, and she greatly resented the mess her son had made of his life. Nelson had no patience with his mother's complaints, or her worries about his lifestyle, his drinking and his high blood pressure.

With Jeanette tentatively back in the picture, Isabel saw a ray of hope. Jeanette had always been the one person who could talk to Nelson. In the coming weeks, Isabel frequently invited Jeanette to her home so that just the three of them were together. Nelson began easing up, but still treated her like a platonic friend. Jeanette painfully recalled one instance when she arrived at Isabel's house to find Nelson at the piano, practicing some new songs. He frowned at seeing her, then greeted her cordially. All evening he was polite to her, but it broke her heart to see the difference in him. Finally Jeanette's patience won out. Their relationship became intimate again, and with this new turn of events their lives changed. Maryon Murphy reported that at this time Nelson stopped sleeping with her and they became "just friends." Another lover told a similar story. Nelson happily visited Sybil, telling her how he'd fallen in love with Jeanette all over again. He was excitedly looking at new avenues for their careers, and they were discussing doing a nightclub act together.

Sybil was horrified at this news; it was not yet fashionable for big stars to "demean themselves" by singing in nightclubs. Sybil thought it was degrading but Nelson didn't care. He had demanded and would receive big bucks, around $15,000 a week. Besides, what other medium was available to him? Concerts and radio were dead. He'd been unsuccessful in finding a niche in either TV or movies. And nightclubs would handle another problem; he and Jeanette could travel and be together for extended periods of time without being subjected to close scrutiny.

Jeanette still had concert commitments, so Nelson made his club debut solo. In mid-January 1953, he opened Tops in San Diego with a forty-five-minute show. It was a smash hit. *Variety* noted:

> Before Eddy had even started to sing, they liked him personally, as a warm human being—something he had never seemed to be in his long career in other mediums. The austerity had disappeared along with the stony-faced singing Mountie. He was, in truth, a "new" Nelson Eddy.
>
> Remarkably youthful, handsome baritone satirizes his own deadpan style . . . But his concert hall artistry is evident in such standards as "The Flea" and "Great Day," and a medley comprising "Rose Marie," "Indian Love Call," "Balalaika," "I Married an Angel," "Wanting You," "Sweet Mystery of Life" and "Stout-hearted Men"—the latter rocking the house as Eddy sings with a joshing smile . . . Eddy's longtime accompanist, Theodore Paxson, is at the piano.
>
> In sum, Eddy is a polished performer of surprising depth and feeling. What's more, he senses exactly what nitery freight-payers want; in this case, sincerity, sentiment, showmanship and a sterling voice. He has them all. This can't miss.

Nelson was booked into the Sahara Hotel in Las Vegas for four weeks starting April 7. During the interim he worked on improving his act, and told Jeanette he would definitely need a singing partner, as the fans wanted the songs from their films, especially the love duets. "I'm pretty good," he said, "but not enough to sing duets all by myself."

Jeanette decided to test the waters herself and opened in the spring at the Las Vegas Sands with a solo show. She had two rude awakenings. First, her devout fans had problems accepting her sitting on a piano, in black tights and slinky dress, belting out Sophie Tucker-like numbers. Interspersed with these songs, she sang two operatic arias as well. From all reports she was good, but her performance was out of character for her image. In addition, she did not like the nightclub atmosphere, "singing to a bunch of drunks," as Nelson put it. Neither did she have the sense of humor to verbally belittle her films, as Nelson did so successfully.

From the Sands Jeanette moved to the Sahara, where she added dancing to the program, but her nightclub days were numbered. Her health was too fragile to keep up with the grind. Her cousin Esther Shipp recalled coming to see Jeanette after a show. Jeanette staggered into her dressing room and collapsed into a chair, her arms flung out, her head falling back limply, gasping for breath.

Some weeks before Nelson opened in Las Vegas, it became apparent to him that he would not be teaming up with Jeanette. This was a crushing blow to him, for he felt that their relationship would falter if they went their separate ways professionally. But he could not force Jeanette. As further proof, she fell ill with a high fever. (She later suffered from hepatitis. It's unknown whether this earlier illness was a hepatitis attack or not.) Nelson nursed her through it; in her delirium her mind wandered and she talked as through it was 1935 and they were back at Tahoe filming *Rose Marie.*

To keep things going, Nelson hired a sexy young blonde singer, Gale Sherwood, to sing duets with him in Las Vegas. What he hoped would be a temporary hiring—"Maybe Jeanette will come around"—turned into a fourteen-year employment. At first Nelson still enjoyed solo billing, but Gale made a big impression on the audience, wearing a skimpy Indian maiden costume when they sang "Indian Love Call." Her participation in the show increased until Nelson eventually gave her equal status.

In January 1954, Jeanette tried to tackle nightclubs again, this time singing at the Coconut Grove in Los Angeles, but she felt the verdict was the same. "Miss MacDonald's vitality and ageless beauty are no small part of her glamour and she has plenty of glamour," noted the Hollywood *Citizen-News.* "Nevertheless the regular night owl clientele may put up strong resistance to her Grove engagement because it is dullishly routined."

She and Nelson looked for some other solution for being together. Nelson revamped his *Timothy Waits For Love* script as a TV movie for the two of them, and sketched out some other ideas for movie and/or TV spots. Later in 1954, they decided to do a joint singing tour in Australia. This news leaked out to his fans, and when it fell through, Nelson was irate with his fans, taking his frustration out on them. After these disappointments, Nelson gave up on their working together. Their relationship, as he'd foreseen, suffered. There were long separations as he traveled tirelessly around the country, singing in supper clubs, on tours that were sometimes months in duration. At some point he became physically involved with Gale Sherwood. Although Nelson would over the years publicly deny his affair with Gale, saying curtly, "I don't sleep with the help," he justified it to Jeanette by saying, "She's around and you're not." This brought new anguish to Jeanette, but she felt that there was nothing she could do about it. To keep her mind off her personal problems, she worked as much as possible in summer stock and did some scattered concerts. Once again, she gravitated to her fans for the affection she was not getting elsewhere. She desperately wanted the film role of Anna in *The King and I* but lost out, probably because she photo-graphed "too old."

She tried to spend more time with Nelson but complained to Blossom, "I'm just another mare in his stable." However, after spending a romantic weekend with Nelson she happily reported back to Blossom, "I'm the only mare he really wants." Their relationship had its ups and downs, as ever. Sybil Thomas reported that Nelson once came to see her, his arms covered with scratches. When she asked if "the redhead" was responsible, he grinned, "You should see her." He admitted that they fought, but that "it's good for her, it keeps her young." Another time Sybil asked Nelson if he was happy. He was silent for a moment and then said, "Things are different . . . but yes, I'm happy." Still another time Jeanette phoned Sybil, very upset, trying to find out where Nelson was. They'd had a fight and he hadn't called her in days. Sybil hadn't heard from him, nor would she have been likely to tell Jeanette if she had, as she considered herself Nelson's only true friend. Jeanette hung up in tears. The next time Sybil saw them together they were fine, as though nothing had occurred.

Sybil recalled it was either 1953 or 1954 when the three of them attended a Hollywood Bowl concert together. She was invited to go along as chaperon. Just as she was dressing, Nelson phoned to say the evening was off; Jeanette wasn't feeling well. Sybil hung up, silently cursing Jeanette. Twenty minutes later Nelson phoned to report that Jeanette was feeling better and they'd be by shortly to pick her up. Sybil finished dressing, still cursing Jeanette. Nelson knocked on Sybil's door. Jeanette remained in the car. Sybil found Jeanette sitting in the front seat, resting. Nelson ushered Sybil into the back seat. During the drive from Bel Air into Hollywood there was no conversation except for Jeanette sighing occasionally and Nelson anxiously asking, "Are you all right? Are you sure you're all right?" She'd reassure him and then they'd continue until the next sigh.

Once they arrived at the Bowl Jeanette was no livelier. All through the concert she sat sighing and leaning against Nelson. He continued asking if she was all right, until Sybil thought she'd scream if he asked her one more time. Sybil wondered why they'd even bothered to attend, since neither one seemed to hear a note of the music. Afterwards they started the long walk back to the car. Once out of the crowd's view, Nelson picked Jeanette up and carried her the rest of the way. On the drive back Jeanette fell asleep, her head on Nelson's shoulder. When they reached Sybil's residence, Nelson silently waved her out, so as not to disturb Jeanette. Sybil commented, in retelling the story, that she felt old watching them. She felt they had each been "beaten by life."

■ Around this time John Eddy re-entered his father's life. John had been raised in a happy household, but in his mid-teens wanted very much to meet his birth father. His "step-parents" contacted Nelson and he responded uncertainly, "Whatever's best for the kid." A meeting was set up the next time Nelson was to sing in Chicago. The concert was scheduled for October 31, 1949; the two met in the lobby of the Drake Hotel, embraced, and went off to have a talk. John attended his father's concert, saving the ticket stub in a scrapbook.

For the next few years John had no direct contact with Nelson, although his scrapbook contains at least one coded telegram from "Ann Eddy" to his step-parents with a message that makes no sense to the casual reader. In studying the scrapbook decades later, John recalled that his family never knew or communicated with Ann Eddy, but that Nelson had gone to great lengths to keep his connection with John's parents a secret.

John also spent time with his birth mother Maybelle Marsten and, after graduating high school, told her he wanted to be a singer like Nelson. At his urging, Maybelle phoned Nelson to ask for help with guidance, teachers, etc. Nelson angrily refused to help and tried to discourage Maybelle from allowing John to pursue a singing career. The two quarreled and finally Maybelle gave up. If John wanted to make it as a singer, it would be with no help from Nelson. John went with Maybelle on a vacation to Los Angeles, the only genuinely happy time he remembered with her. He has a single photograph of his parents together with him, also in his scrapbook.

Now, during Nelson's nightclub years, John became a part of his life. John lived for a time in the Las Vegas area, so whenever Nelson was there performing, John was a frequent visitor. He also visited for weeks at times when Nelson was in the Chicago or St. Louis areas. John traveled with the entourage for a while, becoming friends with Ted Paxson in particular. Decades later Paxson's sister-in-law remembered "Nelson's step-son John who used to tour with him," obviously confusing John with Sid Franklin, Jr., who was now married and raising his own family.

Even though still an outsider, John carefully observed his father and his life-style. Nelson was drinking, basically an unhappy man offstage, and "was more childish even at sixty than I ever was." John also observed Nelson's relationship with Gale, which he felt was born of convenience, a common occurrence in the nomadic lifestyle of nightclub performers. During the few intimate talks between father and son, John came to see the all-consuming effect Jeanette still had on Nelson. He concluded that Jeanette remained the great love of Nelson's life until his dying day.

John learned about two other girls whom Nelson had anonymously helped to raise, by providing money to their parents to help pay for survival and schooling. He didn't know the name of one of the girls, but the second one he knew as "Dorothy," a red-headed Southerner whom Nelson once wanted to adopt. She came from a large, poor family, and the story John heard was that her uncle was an electrician at MGM and was killed on one of the MacDonald-Eddy sets. Nelson took it upon himself to help raise the man's favorite niece, who had visited the *Sweethearts* set. The little girl claimed she'd grow up to be a famous singer just like Nelson, and she proved true to her word, though she made her fame in another type of singing. Her name was Dottie West.

John insisted that neither Dottie or the other girl were his half-sister, laughing, "Nelson didn't go around the country dropping sperm." He didn't exactly know the connection, but reported that this kind of help was typical from Nelson, who helped many people in his life but insisted on anonymity. John stresses the caring and generous side of his father, who made the special effort to meet and speak with people, whether it be a secretary or an important figure. Nelson did try to be a father figure to John. He bought him shares of stock in oil and in a new movie process he was investing in, similar to Todd-AO. The investments were not successful. Nelson also gave John his glass from the White House when he'd drunk with Harry Truman, some of his notes and scores from his nightclub routines, and other items. John has treasured these souvenirs over the years.

John met Ann Eddy only once, in Las Vegas. Nelson was appearing there and John was visiting. He was eating lunch in Foxy's deli with Ray Bolger when Nelson and Ann walked in. Nelson stopped dead in his tracks at seeing John, a look of horror crossing his face. Ann missed all this and walked right by. "I would have liked to think that my resemblance to Nelson would have given it away," John said, "but she was too absorbed with herself to notice the similarity." Seeing how flustered Nelson was, John smoothed things over by pretending to be a casual acquaintance.

John stayed in touch with Nelson sporadically over the years. He visited Nelson's home, but not while Ann was around. To keep his wife from becoming suspicious, Nelson insisted that John never call him at home; he should go through his secretary, Mildred Hudson, who would immediately let Nelson know of John's message and his whereabouts. Nelson then returned his call.

John never came out of the closet about his parentage because "I didn't think it would do my father any good, and I didn't need the money." Only in later years did he reluctantly speak to a few people because he was irritated by the way Nelson was being remembered and at the fact that Nelson's relationship with Jeanette was being loudly denied. He is wary of "those Nelson nuts finding me and banging on my door," and prefers not to talk about Nelson because "those people mean nothing in my life." Still, there is a touch of sad bitterness when he speaks of Nelson. Grateful as he is for the moments he shared with his father, he would have preferred to have a more meaningful role in Nelson's life.

During 1954–55 Nelson spent most of his time with Gale Sherwood, traveling on the road. According to opera star Robert Merrill, Nelson was in love with Gale and wanted to marry her. Harper McKay, a close confidant of Gale's, added that despite the physical relationship, Gale understood that marriage would never occur. "She was a realist," said McKay. "She realized what the situation was and just went with it. I never heard that Nelson wanted a divorce. I think he liked it the way it was. But that's just a supposition on my part. He was not a confiding kind of person. He'd tell a joke once in awhile. He was very private." Over the years, through his friendship with Gale and working as Nelson's arranger, McKay had an insider's view of their relationship. He described Nelson as jealous by nature; the times it was easy for McKay to give Gale

Nelson's nightclub act with singing partner Gale Sherwood.

a lift somewhere she tactfully declined; it was understood that "Nelson wouldn't like it." Nelson was also fussy about her appearance, said McKay. "At rehearsals she was always fully dressed, fully made up. On the road, any place, unless in very intimate circumstances, she was never any other way. She never showed up in jeans. That's the way he liked it." McKay remembered that Gale told him Nelson liked going to topless bars, and had taken her to a particular place he liked in New Orleans.

Jeanette, meanwhile, spent her idle hours in New York. She was bitter about Nelson and the few times she mentioned him to friends or fans, the comments were often derogatory. She usually changed the subject when his name was mentioned, nor would she talk about her film career. She remained in New York because even being in Los Angeles was abhorrent to her; Twin Gables was leased out, and Gene pursued his own interests. For all intents and purposes they were separated as well; during one year Jeanette claimed the only time she spent with Gene was at a press photo call to celebrate their anniversary. Her evenings were spent in her Park Avenue apartment playing cards with her secretary and a friend, often one of her protégées, Ann Torri; her voice teacher, Grace Newell; or any of the handful of gay escorts who were in her inner circle. She still suffered badly from insomnia, but her latest cure was to sleep in a completely darkened room. "Jeanette did a lot of busywork in the later years," said Blossom. "She was a jet setter, traveling a lot, but was in truth aimless and unsettled about herself. She would go through periods of doing nothing for days on end. She would get excited about doing a few concerts or a play, then the actual work would wear her out and she would quickly lose interest and only finish out the commitment because she felt she had to. The fact that her loyal fans kept coming to see her made her feel as though she was still in the game."

Nelson and Gale starred in a color television production of *The Desert Song* in 1955. Nelson's infatuation with Gale was evident when he wrote the show's producer, Max Liebman, with another idea for a TV project for them. Dated May 15, 1955, it read:

Dear Mr. Liebman,

My wheels are turning.

And an idea for a Spectacular has evolved.

Oh yes, there is a good part in it for me—wherein I can at last be my age and do a role that has long been an ambition of mine.

And a good part, too, for Gale Sherwood, wherein her loveliness and capabilities could be fully resolved.

It is "The Music Master." Remember? It is very strong. It was tremendously successful on the stage. David Warfield played in it for many years.

I have written a sort of treatment, adapting it more closely to your needs. I've made many cuts—and it's subject to many more.

Would you look it over?

Thank you, and all good wishes.

Liebman turned down the idea. Nelson had no luck selling any of his film or TV ideas. The only medium he could control was his nightclub act; he found he could write comedy as well if not better than the people he was paying. Pleased with all the money he was saving, he wrote all his own material from this point on.

By mid-1955, the situation changed yet again, and Nelson began meeting with Jeanette for intimate visits. One of their meeting places was an apartment in New York set up by Jeanette's good friend Irene Dunne. Gale also dated other men during the periods when she and Nelson were not working together.

One of Jeanette's escorts at this time was Samuel "Sunny" Griffin. Sunny was never told directly about the MacDonald-Eddy affair by Jeanette herself. Over the years he learned bits and pieces from Jeanette's associates and from Blossom, whom he also escorted on occasion. He finally became an insider when he moved for a while to New York, taking a makeup job at a mortuary. One day he received a phone call from Jeanette. She needed a giant favor from him; could they swap apartments for the weekend? Sunny agreed, thrilled that she would ask him. Jeanette asked him to pack a suitcase and take it with him on Friday to work. She had left plenty of food for him in the refrigerator. Finally, if Gene called looking for her, Sunny was to tell him she was at RCA, recording, no matter when he phoned. Sunny agreed.

Friday afternoon he arrived at Jeanette's apartment. To his surprise, the only food in the refrigerator was some moldy cheese and an old eggplant. He phoned Jeanette to complain, and to his surprise, she started reciting a good recipe for the eggplant. He told her he intended to go out to eat instead. That night, at two in the morning, he was awakened by a phone call from Gene who was, according to Sunny, "feeling no pain." Gene asked for "Bunco," his nickname for Jeanette. Sunny dutifully reported that she was at RCA, recording. Gene hung up, apparently satisfied. On Sunday, Jeanette phoned again to ask if she could keep the apartment another few days. Sunny agreed, but requested that she send over more clothes for the coming week. Jeanette apparently was calling from his bedroom because she asked him to direct her to the correct dresser drawers. He told her where to find an extra suitcase, and she in turn gave directions to someone else in the room. As Sunny continued ordering his clothes, Jeanette repeated his words to this other party. Sunny quickly learned who it was when the unmistakable voice of Nelson Eddy cursed, "Does he need his whole goddamned wardrobe?" Jeanette shushed him and Nelson continued grumbling. Finally Sunny finished and said, "Jeanette, please have *him* pack the clothes, you know how you just throw things into suitcases." To which Jeanette sweetly replied, "Him who?"

After this apartment swap, Jeanette said nothing directly about Nelson, but it was understood that Sunny now knew and was to keep it under wraps if he were to retain her trust and friendship. During the 1950s Sunny saw Jeanette about a dozen times. On one memorable occasion, Nelson had asked Sunny to bring a date and join them for the season opening at the Metropolitan Opera. Sunny had a friend whom he thought could be trusted. He briefed her on the evening, drilling into her that she wasn't to stare at them or be nervous, just to treat them like normal people. Nelson was late picking them up; he still had to get Jeanette. He reassured Sunny that his lateness was no problem as Jeanette herself was chronically late and probably hadn't started dressing yet. Nelson had barely stuck the key into the lock of Jeanette's apartment when she whipped the door open and started yelling at him for being late. She was not fully dressed, so Sunny wondered at the real cause of her rage. Nelson just grinned and ignored her, while Sunny's friend Claire stood in open-mouthed surprise. Jeanette kept yelling; Nelson didn't seem to understand her upset and just shrugged. This enraged her further; she threw an ashtray at him. Nelson finally started getting angry and yelled back at her while ducking flying objects. Sunny and Claire made a hasty exit. Once safely outside the apartment, Claire turned to Sunny and said, "I don't care if they *are* movie stars, they're nuts!"

The next day Sunny called Jeanette to find out how things ended up. Jeanette told him they'd "kissed and made up." He never did learn the cause of the upset.

Sunny was with them on other occasions when their tenderness together would have made their fans cheer. One such time was when they took the Keansburg ferry. "It was a very large ship," Sunny recalled.

> It would leave New York from the Battery about two o'clock in the afternoon, and it would leave Keansburg, New Jersey, at midnight. It only made one trip a day. It

was approximately a two-hour trip [over], and two and a half hours back because you were fighting the flow of the sea. They had a full orchestra and a ballroom on the ship. The orchestra leader was a monstrous man whose name was Arnold. He played beautiful piano.

The majority of people who went on this boat were elderly. When Arnold spotted Jeanette and Nelson he started playing and they danced. You should have seen them dance the "Blue Tango." It was the most hysterical, comical thing you ever saw. They couldn't tango worth a damn and they tried so hard.

The reason we'd come [to New Jersey] was to see Christine Jorgensen; he had become famous. Jeanette and Nelson wanted to see Jorgensen perform. We had plenty of time to have our dinner, see Jorgensen, and then Jeanette liked to play a gambling game which was legal at that time in Jersey called Keno. After Keno we reboarded the ship to come back to New York. Blossom was with us, and I danced with her.

It was a gorgeous night, clear sky, full moon and stars everywhere. All of a sudden Blossom said, "Where's Jeanette? Where's Nelson?" I said I didn't know, maybe they were up on deck. So we went on dancing. We could just about see the lower part of New York coming up on the horizon and Blossom said, "I think I'd better start looking for them." I said I would go up on deck. Down the center were two long rows of wooden benches; they came to a semi-triangle at the bow of the ship. There were people still sitting, hugging each other. At the front of the ship there's Jeanette and Nelson. He's laying with his head on her lap and she's just holding him and caressing him.

I went downstairs and said, "Well, they're all right but we'd better get them off the ship pretty quick because if we don't get them out of the circumstances they're in right now, it's going to be all over the pages tomorrow morning."

So Blossom and I went up. We made a quick movement and suddenly my head was laying on Jeanette's lap, and Nelson was laying on Blossom's, but we were about twenty-five feet apart. We got off okay.

Sunny observed Jeanette's feelings for Nelson as "sort of kittenish and school-girlish. She had read *Ivanhoe*, there was the man on the white charger. He came up, he was going to whip her off her feet and take her off to a blissful world. He was going with her to paradise.

"Jeanette was a little bit withdrawn, wasn't boisterous. She couldn't blurt it out, she would wring her hands and hold her breast, go through all these melodramatic things. She really was a wisp, a frail little woman who was afraid of her own shadow, extremely fearful of her success, overpowered by it . . . Nelson was a brash, brazen, forthright man. [He] didn't like to give autographs [on the street]. What Nelson liked was his public where they belonged, and that was in their seats, paying absolute attention to his performance."

What impressed Sunny the most was their spirituality. He described a party they attended at Kate Smith's. "Jeanette had called me to tell me Blossom was in town and Nelson was in town, and would I like to go get Blossom . . . And I went over and picked her up and we went down. The party broke up . . . we were all going down in the elevator and when we got out we started walking up

Park Avenue. We got up to Fifty-ninth Street and Nelson said, 'Let's go up Fifth Avenue.' [He] saw a horse-drawn carriage nearby, the kind that rides through Central Park, and he said to Jeanette, 'You know you rode the coach in *Maytime* and dreamt about me, let's ride a coach together and dream about each other.' "

Sunny added, "Their love wasn't just about jumping into the sack. [It was] a relationship where they've been together for years and years and she's still in awe of him. Now that kind of feeling she had for him was just beautiful."

Yet despite these intimate moments, they were apart more than together. Nelson had his hands full trying to keep Gale, Jeanette and Ann happy. Ann, who still resented Jeanette and still termed her "that woman," was now faced with another enemy, "that girl"—meaning Gale Sherwood. Although legend would have it that Ann and Gale got along quite well, Jon Eddy recalled that when Ann showed up to see Nelson perform she ordered Gale to be sent away before she would venture backstage to see her husband. Others remarked that Gale and even Ted Paxson meekly cleared the dressing room, or the hotel suite, whenever Ann appeared. But if Nelson kept up appearances, even with his wife in tow, it was to Gale's bed that he sneaked off in the dead of night when Ann was asleep.

Though Jeanette didn't figure prominently at this time, even she felt the effects of Ann's interference in Nelson's life, and her continuing refusal to give Nelson a divorce. Once Nelson was scheduled to meet Jeanette for a weekend in Washington, D.C., at an apartment they were borrowing. Jeanette waited excitedly for him until he phoned with bad news. Ann had unexpectedly flown into town and was "dogging his footsteps." Nelson couldn't take a chance on meeting Jeanette

Jeanette and Gene are here pictured with Vice-President Richard Nixon and his wife Pat . . .

. . . and with President Eisenhower at a fundraising dinner.

now. He'd keep in touch, maybe he'd be lucky and Ann would decide to leave, but for now, the rendezvous was off. Jeanette hung up, her face filled with pain, her eyes welling. "He can't come," she said, and sank into a chair, the life ebbed out of her. Occasionally Jeanette was spotted in the audience at Nelson's shows. In these instances Gale would quietly disappear afterwards and leave Nelson alone with Jeanette. But it was painful for Jeanette to watch Gale's familiarity with Nelson onstage and their inevitable kiss that brought cheers from the audience. To Jeanette it was obvious that they were lovers, and she was always worried that the audiences, usually made up of Nelson's old-time fans, noticed it as well. Jeanette felt inadequate around Gale for so many reasons; Gale was young, pretty, had a fresh, powerful voice and was very well endowed. Once at a dinner attended by the Raymonds, Eddys, and Gale, Jeanette wistfully made a comment about her lack of bust compared to Gale. Nelson embarrassed the group by piping up, "Oh, I've never found anything to complain about."

While in New York, Jeanette was surprised to receive a phone call from, of all people, Clark Gable. He asked to meet her for lunch, and named a time and place. Jeanette agreed, perplexed, wondering what Gable had to say to her after all these years. Gable's purpose in meeting was to apologize to her. He awkwardly admitted that he never used to like her, feeling years ago that she was fickle and playing with Nelson's emotions. He'd even turned Carole Lombard, then his girlfriend, against Jeanette by claiming that Jeanette had thrown herself at him. But over the years Gable was amazed to hear how she stuck by Nelson through thick and thin, and was still devoted to him. He had to admire her for that. Jeanette was deeply touched by Gable's words. They talked for awhile, comparing notes about how their lives had turned out. They parted friends, mending a twenty-year unspoken feud.

Nelson and Jeanette returned to Los Angeles in late 1955; he to sing at the Statler with Gale, she to do a new TV show, a half-hour comedy special written by Gene. Jeanette and Gene moved back to Twin Gables for the filming of the mildly amusing *Prima Donna* in which Jeanette played an opera singer who discovers a young singing talent. Twelve-year-old Al Caiazza played the boy. He told how he was chosen:

> There must have been five to six hundred boys lined up outside Hal Roach Studio. It was my turn to go in, and [Jeanette] said, "How old are you? What's your name?" I said my name was Alfred Caiazza. She said, "Okay, what do you want to sing?" I said, " 'Back to Sorrento.' " Now, there was no music. She believed if a voice was going to sound good you didn't need music behind it. So she said, "Go right ahead. Start any time you want." I must have sung maybe three or four lines and she said, "Stop!" And I said, "Did I do something wrong?" "No, I want you to

step aside. Would you just sit down right there?" And she told David Butler, the director, "Tell all the other boys to go home, and get his dad in here. He's my boy."

The half-hour show took two weeks to film. Caiazza remembered that Jeanette had some difficulty remembering her lines, but laughed it off and was in good humor throughout the shooting. Al was to be paid $500 for his work, but when his birthday fell during the filming, Jeanette had a cake brought out with an additional bonus check of another $500.

Al and his parents were invited to Twin Gables for dinner. Jeanette and Gene proved the perfect hosts. Jeanette gave them a tour of the grounds, and they were impressed with the hill of orange roses that Nelson had planted in the back. "Must have been a quarter of an acre of land just going down with nothing but different kinds of roses," recalled Caiazza. "Jeanette showed my mother all the different jewelry she had, and different things around her house. We went through every room in the house." But most surprising of all was a near life-size framed, colored photo hanging in the entrance of the house. "It was Nelson Eddy dressed in his Mountie uniform from *Rose Marie*," said Al. His father studied the huge photo and commented, "I wonder how Gene Raymond puts up living with *that*."

By early 1956, Nelson was guilt-ridden over how he was treating Jeanette. He felt they needed to work together and be together. On January 14, he handwrote a treatment called *Thinker for Hire* as a film for the two of them. He also penned a witty treatment for another film, *All Stars Don't Spangle*. In this story, he and Jeanette played over-the-hill movie stars who fight, take younger lovers, then happily reunite. A careful study of all Nelson's script ideas for them indicates this same theme in every story, although usually it was only Nelson's character who took the younger lover, then saw the folly of his ways. Also among Nelson's papers was found a list he'd compiled at this time regarding his professional goals for the coming year. One item listed was to make a record album with Jeanette.

Their relationship was heating up again, and Jeanette sought to provide romantic moments for Nelson that would keep him with her and away from Gale. Her tactics finally seemed to be working. Nelson, usually closemouthed about his personal life, sometimes revealed quite a lot after downing a few drinks. In November 1955, he'd sung at Blinstraub's in Boston. One evening he was at the bar with the hotel owner, and quite frankly admitted that he'd been in love with Jeanette for years and was still in love with her.

In December 1956, Nelson told interviewer Bob Thomas he'd always been ready to make a film with Jeanette, and was still searching for a good script. He explained that they didn't work together on television too often because "usually a show can afford one of us but not both.

"There have been some ugly rumors that I wouldn't consider a picture with Jeanette and she was hurt by them. I'd be glad to do a good picture with her. But the only things we've been offered were to be done on a shoestring in Mexico or England. We made some pretty fine pictures in our time. There's no sense in coming back to do a B musical at a time when there's no market for B musicals anyway.

"Jeanette and I . . . often would get around the piano and have some fun. It was out of such clowning that I developed the idea for my nightclub act."

In an effort to compete with Gale Sherwood, Jeanette kept quiet about her failing health. Had the arterial transplant procedure been developed in the 1950s she might have enjoyed a longer life with less suffering. Worried that Nelson might think her too old and undesirable and break with her completely, she insisted that no one tell Nelson the truth. Sunny Griffin recalled sometimes when they were walking together down the street, Jeanette would experience pains or numbness in her arms, and ask Sunny to beat or rub them to get the circulation moving again. Another time he was supposed to meet her to go shopping. When she didn't appear he went to her apartment and found her sitting slumped in a chair. He knew instantly something was very wrong; her face was red and feverish and her damp hair was frizzed around her face. She admitted to him that she'd suffered a heart attack, but didn't want anyone to know so she hadn't called a doctor. She managed a smile when he told her she looked like Elsa Lanchester in *The Bride of Frankenstein* and finally agreed to have him take her to a hospital. When they arrived Jeanette was wheeled inside on a stretcher with Sunny at her side; she pulled the sheet over her head so no one would recognize her, which garnered even more stares because it looked like Sunny was attempting to check a corpse in at the admitting desk. Finally Jeanette sat up, climbed off the gurney and told the admitting nurse she was leaving, there was nothing wrong with her; she'd just felt a little faint.

Jeanette still worked sporadically during this period. Jackie Hoover, who had stayed at her side during a straw-hat tour of *The King and I* in the Midwest, remarked that Jeanette had a doctor backstage who gave her injections several times during the performances. When Jeanette finally collapsed onstage the audience was told she'd fainted. The doctor diagnosed it as a heart attack, but Jackie wondered whether it might not have been a minor stroke; when Jeanette revived she was unable to speak for several minutes and was very disoriented. Amazingly, she pulled herself together and finished the performance.

During 1956 Jeanette and Nelson finally made their first television appearances together, on "Lux Video Theater," a variety show. The following year they recorded together for RCA for the first time since 1936. More TV appearances followed but Jeanette was frightened and nervous on live TV. Unbeknownst to Nelson, days before their appearance on "The Big Parade" Jeanette had suffered yet another heart attack. She was in no condition to perform but insisted on doing so. Just prior to their going on the air for "Ah, Sweet Mystery of Life," she turned white and started to faint. Nelson ran to her and somehow kept her on her feet, keeping constant eye contact with her and willing her to get

One of Nelson and Jeanette's rare TV appearances together.

through it. She didn't disappoint him and the audience cheered enthusiastically at seeing them together. But the few critics who really listened were appalled at how weak her singing voice was, and how Nelson kept slowing down the tempo so she could keep up.

Their old nemesis, Louis B. Mayer, died of leukemia on October 29, 1957. He'd fallen on hard times in his last years, living to see himself ousted from the studio he'd brought to power. Jeanette agreed to sing at his funeral, a decision that irritated Nelson. But he made up for it in his choice of wreaths. While Jeanette sent a large, lovely white one, Nelson chose a green one in the shape of a horseshoe. The handwritten note read: "Good luck on your new location."

Jeanette was finally hospitalized in December 1957, at Georgetown University Hospital for heart surgery. To put it simply, they opened her up, found that they couldn't help her and closed her up again. Her appendix was also taken out at this time, her nurse reported that "Jeanette was a very nice person and easy to nurse, but very meticulous. Jeanette had visits from Senators and many famous people, and Gene left her there and went on to New York. Enough said." She was left extremely weakened and discouraged that there was nothing medically to be done.

She was still recovering when Isabel Eddy died on December 20. Nelson was devastated by his mother's death, even though he had been on fairly cool terms with her during the last years. Jeanette was unable to attend the funeral, which upset Nelson even though he obviously understood the reason. Later Ann Eddy had to suffer the humiliation of calling on Jeanette and Gene for help; Nelson was crying at his mother's gravesite and wouldn't leave. With Gene's help Jeanette dragged herself from her sickbed to go to Nelson's rescue, waiting in the car while Gene went to get him.

Again Nelson threw himself into his work, reporting as scheduled to his next gig at the Royal York in Toronto. But with Isabel's passing Nelson was reminded of all his broken dreams of his life and hers, how she had loved Jeanette and called her "my daughter" up to the very end. This weighed heavily on Nelson's mind and no doubt contributed to his sudden decision to straighten out his life once and for all.

The year 1957 had seemed a hopeful year for them. Bill Thornton, the doorman at the Lenox apartments in Philadelphia (where Gertrude Evans still lived) remembered that Jeanette was staying with Nelson in his studio there. Their sudden renewed togetherness culminated in Nelson once again asking Ann for his freedom. Based on Jeanette's behind-the-scenes efforts, and after months of negotiating with lawyers, Ann Eddy finally did agree to a divorce. Jeanette promised to pay off Gene handsomely; all that was left now was for all the lawyers to work out the logistics. Jeanette was elated. At long last, after all the years of suffering, they were finally to win in the end. The unbelievable had occurred.

She and Nelson reported to the attorney's office in New York to sign the necessary papers. To her horror, Nelson balked after learning how much he was going to lose to Ann. After all these years of hard labor, he would be wiped out financially. He refused to sign. Jeanette argued with him, to no avail. "You wouldn't marry me when I first asked you to," he bitterly reminded her. "Now I'll never marry you." He stormed out of the office. Jeanette was left alone, in tears, echoes of the past ringing in her ears.

28

"All the years
we never had"

Jeanette never quite recovered from the shock of Nelson's final rejection. Their relationship was mostly off again for a long stretch of time. They had recorded a record album for RCA, *Favorites in Hi-Fi,* which was a best seller upon its release in 1958 and later went gold, but now they stopped working together. Nelson continued on the supper club circuit accompanied by Gale while Jeanette made a few scattered public performances before dropping out of the public eye. She toured briefly in a stage production of *Bittersweet* in 1959; one fan who saw her commented, "She was very beautiful still, and had been in good voice, but I was a little shocked at how tiny and frail she appeared to be." Jeanette's morale had plummeted to the point that, before going onstage one evening, she told a friend, "I hope I go out there and sing like I've never sung before, and then I hope I drop dead."

Charles Cagle, who worked with Jeanette in *Bittersweet* reflected, "Some of us thought Miss MacDonald as a bit standoffish, cold individual, but now that I look back on it, she just might have been insecure appearing in front of a live audience. She also appeared to me to have a much smaller voice (projection-wise) than she did in her pictures. She seemed rather fragile, and another actor and I would help her back up on her feet, as she had been kneeling beside her lover at the end of Act I. Another performance, she threw back her head while singing 'Ziguener' and her wig slipped back on her head an inch. She calmly turned around, pulled it back down, and continued the number."

Long-time friend Richard Sale noted a drastic change in Jeanette. "She'd had a wonderful sense of humor. Nelson had a good wit, but Jeanette tended to hide it. She was sassy, saucy and pert. I broke a tooth once and she sent me a whole new set of plastic teeth, all decayed. You know, that kind of humor. A lot of fun in the girl. Very Irish fun.

"She went downhill. It was very sad to see how she diminished away with that heart of hers. I remember seeing her the last time at Gail Patrick's. Gale had a party every year at Christmas. And we put those ornaments on the tree for all the years we'd been there. [Jeanette] was fine and happy to see us, but she was just melting away. This was the very late fifties. We weren't talking about it in those days; you just said, 'What's with Jeanette?'"

She'd started writing her autobiography and had told the truth, with the hopes that it would come out and explain to her fans why she and Nelson were divorcing and remarrying after all these years. Now, with the plans called off, she still wanted to finish the book. Nelson angrily told her to forget it and commented to an associate, "She lives in a dream world." After their latest quarrel over her book, Jeanette suffered a stroke. She and Gene set off to Europe presumably for a rest, but in actuality to consult some doctors.

With Jeanette gone Nelson suffered his old depression and guilt. What would turn out to be his will was written at this time. Jeanette, also feeling morose, recorded a tape for Nelson in which she thanked him for all the happy days she'd known in her life. She also mentioned that he shouldn't let Ann get him down, and that she would always love him. The tape never reached Nelson. When Jeanette asked him about it, weeks later, he confronted Ann and asked her what she'd done with it. Ann denied knowing anything about a tape. Nelson, furious, tore apart her rooms until he located it in a drawer. He cursed his wife, threatening to kill her if she ever intercepted his mail again.

The new decade found Nelson working as usual while Jeanette silently suffered. She'd given up trying to be an important part of Nelson's life and had busied herself with her autobiography—this time a less truthful version of her relationship to Nelson. First she hired a ghost-writer but she wasn't happy with the result; she later sued him. She struck out again on her own and found it purging to tell her story on paper, even if some of the vital details had to be altered.

She had returned to Los Angeles and was living again at Twin Gables, even though the house was up for sale. She stuck pretty much to home, and most of her friends never had any inkling of her private torments. Many of those who prided themselves on being long-time friends knew surprisingly little about her. To the very end they never believed that she had ever had an affair with Nelson or anyone else, believing her too "square," and too much in love with Gene. They never questioned Gene's frequent absences or even Jeanette's admission that hers was a marriage of "separation." Those who knew about Gene's alternate lifestyle, or his drinking, still adamantly defended this "happiest marriage in Hollywood." When Jeanette spoke of "my husband" they naturally assumed that she meant Gene. Yet, in an interview with Tony Thomas she almost gave herself away, having to think a long moment before stating which man she was talking about.

In a low moment, Jeanette sent Nelson a "goodbye love letter." Sunny Griffin, who was visiting Twin Gables briefly, managed to sneak a look at the letter before Jeanette mailed it. He didn't remember the words verbatim, but it went something like: "Dear Nelson, I'm aware of the great sacrifice you made in order to spend a few hours with me, and I know it was a tremendous burden on you to rearrange your schedule, but I'm deeply grateful that you were able to make the arrangements to be with me." Then the tone of the letter changed. "I feel that perhaps the final hour has come. But let me assure you that happiness lies there. I'm not afraid. I love you and I know you love me." The letter ended with this curious line: "Thank you for permitting me to love you."

Jeanette's "final hour" had not arrived, but the subject of death weighed heavily in her thoughts. She had told Sunny on several occasions, "If he goes first, promise me that you'll take care of me." What she meant, Sunny made clear, was that Sunny should kill her if anything were to happen to Nelson. Blossom also reported a similar request, saying incredulously, "She made me promise that if anything happened to Nelson before it happened to her, that I would chloroform her." Jeanette also made Blossom promise to take care of Nelson, if she went first. "It will kill him," she warned. "He will not outlive me by long."

Though unwilling to witness Jeanette's decline, Nelson was receptive enough to her to make an appearance when she asked for him. "I love her," he told Jack Parr on "The Tonight Show." "I think she loves me." He was the guest of honor at a welcome home party thrown by Jeanette, which was nearly ruined by Gene. Their old friend Sandy Reiss had come over early to help Jeanette with the hors d'oeuvres. Gene came in, drunk and swearing at Jeanette, and in his anger threw a platter of hors d'oeuvres at the wall. Jeanette yelled back at him that she was through, this was it, she was divorcing him. Gene suddenly sobered up, and in a "performance that would win an Academy Award" begged her not to divorce him. Jeanette finally told him to get out of her sight. Sandy helped her pick up the food. "Why don't you divorce him?" he asked. "I've tried," Jeanette sighed. "I've tried nine times."

Jeanette had pulled herself together and was all smiles by the time the guests arrived. She was positively radiant when Nelson came in. It had been months since they'd seen each other, and their relationship was all but platonic at this point. But now Nelson couldn't take his eyes off her and followed her around adoringly. Before long Jeanette had excused herself for a moment and went upstairs; Nelson waited a few minutes and then followed her. When they reappeared about twenty minutes later both were flushed and smiling, with no question as to what they'd been up to. Jeanette lived for these moments, as they were all too rare. Most of the time she was alone. Their old films were shown occasionally on TV; Jeanette would phone her friends and discuss them late into the night. To Sandy Reiss and a few select others she confided how lonely she was. Her life had dwindled down to battling her failing health, and waiting for the few moments of happiness Nelson granted her.

███ Nelson and Jeanette were both in Los Angeles in January 1962. Nelson recorded two albums for the Everest label, one solo (*Of Girls I Sing*) and a duet album with Gale. Jeanette had been ill for weeks, and wrote her fans, "What a nuisance sickness is!" Her timing, as it turned out, couldn't have been worse. According to a story told by Sybil Thomas, it was Jeanette's illness at this time— she was bedridden with a very high fever—that frustrated Nelson's plans for him and Jeanette to live together in Arizona.

Sybil had purchased a house in Scottsdale, Arizona. It's unclear whether this purchase came as a result of losing her home in the Bel Air fire of 1961; she was at that time remarried and her house was listed in the Los Angeles newspapers as one of the casualties. Whatever the case, Sybil offered Nelson first refusal on renting the Scottsdale house, since he had been mentioning for some time that he'd like to find a hideaway outside of the Los Angeles area for himself and Jeanette. Sybil couldn't believe he was serious about such an idea, nor did she believe his talk of retiring. In fact, he had a full very itinerary scheduled for the first half of 1962.

Nelson, however, was adamant that he wanted the Scottsdale house. He would move Jeanette there, then "make adjustments" to his own life and schedule. Possibly one factor in Nelson's decision was the fact that Jeanette and Gene were serious now about trying to sell Twin Gables, which had been for sale for a long time. In her generally weakened condition, it was too hard for Jeanette to maintain the house. Another factor might have been her medical problems and serious allergies, and Nelson apparently thought she'd do better in the Arizona climate.

Skeptical Sybil took the attitude that she'd believe this when it happened. And, like so many of Nelson's impulsive plans, it never did. Nelson named the date that he would take Jeanette to Scottsdale. That very day Sybil received a phone call from him; they had not left. Instead, Jeanette was very ill, apparently with hepatitis, with a fever so high the doctors didn't even want to move her to a hospital. Sybil said, "She always has some excuse, doesn't she?" and urged Nelson to get her out of there, or "You're never going to do this." Nelson said he knew, but she couldn't be moved.

By January 18, Nelson had left Los Angeles and was preparing to open his act in Salt Lake City. The plan to go away with Jeanette was discarded, for the time being. Sybil had told Nelson "It'll never happen," and he grudgingly admitted that maybe it wouldn't. Sybil leased the house to someone else. The emotional strain on Nelson was tremendous in these days, as evidenced by the photos taken of him. On January 12 Nelson reported that the cover shots for his Everest album "didn't turn out well" and had to be reshot. The portrait that did finally make the cover of *Of Girls I Sing* show a man with deep sadness in his eyes, despite the mild smile.

After Nelson's departure, Jeanette was melancholy. She admitted to being "very lonely, many times." She was unable to work, and this was devastating in itself. As much as she wanted Nelson around, she worried that retirement was not for him and that he would grow to resent her if he stopped his life to be with her. She thought that she was "too old and undesirable" for him and that she didn't deserve happiness. Still, the idea of their being together wasn't dropped totally and did represent a kind of hope for the future. During that year, the rumor of Jeanette and Gene separating was printed in a Boston newspaper, but as always, the rumor was disproved by the fact that no divorce ensued.

While Nelson was on the road, he and Jeanette stayed in constant phone communication. Nelson also tried to keep her spirits high by sending her little gifts. Once they were speaking long distance over the phone, and Jeanette asked what he was doing. Nelson said, "I'm eating an avocado salad." "Oh, how nice," Jeanette replied. A little while later, Jeanette's doorbell rang. Nelson had arranged for an avocado salad to be delivered to her.

Their phone bills were tremendous. Sometimes they literally talked for hours. Ted Paxson later complained that Jeanette phoned after Nelson was done working for the night, and needed his rest. Jeanette tried to keep in good spirits and not let Nelson know the true state of her health, but on a few occasions she phoned him, hysterical, frightened that she was dying. Nelson understandably had his hands full trying to calm her down. On at least one occasion, he flew back to Los Angeles from the Midwest to spend a few hours with her before flying back in time for that evening's first show. When Paxson spoke to him about the added strain such a lifestyle was putting on him physically, Nelson just shrugged it off. "It's my fault her life is this way," he said. Paxson told of one poignant incident when he awoke one morning to find Nelson in bed, holding the phone receiver to his ear, fast asleep. He'd been on the phone with Jeanette. When Paxson listened to see if the line was dead, he heard Jeanette's even breathing on the other end.

Later in 1962, Sybil Thomas received a phone call from Jeanette. It was always a surprise for Sybil to hear from her, since Sybil really only considered herself Nelson's friend. Sybil was well aware Jeanette's health was declining. Previously Nelson had asked Sybil to recommend a good nutritionist. He dragged Sybil along to see the nutritionist, explaining to the man that he had "a friend" who needed to be fattened up. She'd gotten so skinny that it was "kind of uncomfortable" for Nelson (he didn't specify *how* it was uncomfortable for him). Sybil sat listening to Nelson blushing and stammering about this "friend." When the nutritionist asked why this mysterious "she" couldn't come in himself, Nelson gave some lame excuse. He left the office with a hefty supply of vitamins and a recipe for an awful-tasting milkshake made with brewer's yeast.

Now Jeanette asked Sybil if she knew of a good heart specialist. Sybil gave her a name. Jeanette said she'd seen him. Sybil mentioned another one. Jeanette had seen this one, too. Sybil went through her phone book until she came up with a few more names. To her surprise, Jeanette claimed to know every one of them. Finally Sybil found a name new to her. Jeanette thanked her. There was a long silence. Then Sybil said, "Does Nelson know about this?" Jeanette said no, "and he doesn't want to know. So you must promise not to tell him." Sybil refused to promise. "He should be prepared, he should know. It's his right." Jeanette disagreed. "He doesn't want to know. I've tried to tell him, but he refuses to hear it." Sybil finally agreed to keep her mouth shut, at least for the time being.

Mid-year, Nelson was home for a short while between engagements. His first evening home he called Jeanette and asked her out for dinner. She turned him down, saying she wasn't feeling well, but that she would spend the following day with him. Nelson was disappointed and depressed. He phoned Ted Paxson and took him to dinner instead. He'd already made reservations at his and Jeanette's favorite Chinese restaurant. Nelson and Ted were eating when suddenly Nelson's attention was drawn to another table across the restaurant. Unbelievably, there was Jeanette eating with another man! Nelson saw red. He stomped over to her and loudly berated her. "So you're too sick to go out with me? Don't you ever tell me the truth? After all these years—" He made such a scene that Jeanette was reduced to tears, and a waiter hurried over to try and quiet him. Nelson told the waiter off in nasty terms and stormed out.

Late that night Sybil received an angry phone call from Nelson. He was ranting about Jeanette, how he should have "dumped her" years ago. It took Sybil some time to get a lucid response out of him as to what had occurred. His story didn't make sense to her; much as she disliked Jeanette, it didn't ring true that she was having an affair behind his back. Sybil finally asked Nelson to describe Jeanette's date. When he did, Sybil thought it sounded suspiciously like the heart specialist she'd recommended to Jeanette some time ago. Sybil scolded Nelson for jumping to conclusions and making such a public spectacle. Sybil finally hung up, satisfied that Nelson was now calmed down. She went to bed and was finally falling asleep when the phone rang again. It was now nearing dawn, and Nelson had not yet been to sleep. He'd thought of a way to get Jeanette to forgive him, but Sybil's help was needed to pull it off. He'd be right over to pick her up.

Together the two drove to Twin Gables. Sybil entered first; she found Jeanette sitting on a couch in the living room surrounded by a mound of soggy Kleenex. She had obviously been crying most of the night. Sybil greeted her and asked how she was doing. Jeanette went on about how she was totally friendless, how even Nelson hated her—and that she more than anyone knew how hard his heart could be when he felt betrayed. This was Sybil's cue. She said, "I thought you might be a bit down so I brought you something to cheer you up." She opened the front door and Nelson entered, balancing a tray in his hand with champagne and three glasses. Jeanette let out a shriek and ran into his arms. Somehow Nelson managed to catch her and still balance the tray. They made up with hugs and kisses, and Sybil excused herself to the kitchen to prepare some breakfast.

Afterwards, Jeanette said she had borrowed a print of *Sweethearts* and invited them both to watch it. Sybil didn't mind, but Nelson protested loudly. Quick as a flash, Jeanette whipped off his belt and said, "Now you'll have to stay." He still complained, so she next took off his shoes and socks, saying she didn't know how to run the "mean old projector." Nelson finally gave in, and they sat down to watch the film. They laughed at all the opening scenes, and Sybil got a first-hand account of various things that happened during the filming. During the "Pretty as a Picture" number Jeanette was sitting in Nelson's lap—just like in the movie —and they were "carrying on." Sybil figured she'd overstayed her welcome and slipped out unnoticed. As far as Sybil knew, Nelson never queried Jeanette as to why she was seeing this heart specialist.

Sybil saw them again some months later when she accompanied them to the Farmer's Market for some shopping. Jeanette bought strawberries and prattled on about how she and Allan Jones had filmed a scene eating strawberries in *The Firefly*. Sybil noted that Jeanette was on heavy medication and was practically staggering. (A woman who saw them there at the Farmer's Market decided that Jeanette must be drunk, she was so unsteady on her feet.) Sybil tried to draw Jeanette's condition to Nelson's attention, but he grinned happily and said, "Yes, isn't she beautiful? She's just as beautiful as the day I met her." Sybil gave up.

In June 1962, Jeanette attended a dinner given by her fan club members at the Luau restaurant, in celebration of her club's twenty-fifth anniversary. She was further drawn back into the limelight by the re-release of the MacDonald-Eddy films. The previous year MGM had experimented with running *Naughty Marietta* in Chicago. It did so well that now it was being reissued along with *Rose Marie*. By the end of the year, more of their films were being shown in limited run, and Jeanette made several personal appearances, introducing the films to the audience. Such events were tremendous morale boosters for her. She also granted a round of newspaper interviews, and her comments indicated her honest, straightforward appraisal of her life and career.

On her first film, *The Love Parade*: "It seemed a little naughty but is just silly now—I've seen it."

On her career: "I didn't hit my stride until I went from Paramount to Metro. I must have done seven or eight with Nelson; *Maytime* was the peak . . . I quit pictures in 1941 when the war broke out; Nelson made a few without me."

On her worst movies: "*The Vagabond King*, and three humdingers at Fox."

On her last film: "I played Lassie's mother."

On musicals using dubbed voices: "I do not approve of the dubbing-in of voices, having a voice that doesn't match at all. It has done more to hurt musicals than anything else."

On method acting: "Horrible!"

On the inevitable question—was she in love with Nelson? Why didn't she marry him? "If I had not met Gene just at that time, who knows?" Another time she said, "I like [Nelson] tremendously and always have. I always thought him better looking in person than on the screen."

On the afterlife: "A rather involved and complicated question which has so many ramifications that I would prefer not going into it. I simply believe Death is not final."

Jeanette appeared on January 22, 1963, at the Colorado Theater in Pasadena for a *Sweethearts* screening. After the movie, she received ten minutes of applause. She told the audience the applause reminded her of the movie premiere for *The Merry Widow*. She'd worn a big hat and an elaborate gown with a train. When she went on stage, the man behind her stepped on the train. She fell back into his arms and her hat flew off. Jeanette said she was pleased to see such a wonderful response to this type of picture. She emphasized that she hoped they would

Jeanette returned to MGM briefly for her last professional photo session, in conjunction with the re-issuing of the MacDonald-Eddy films.

attend other good movies, "not necessarily my films." She said she liked to come out of a movie feeling happy and refreshed, not ashamed to be a member of the human race.

On April 2, 1963, Jeanette made another appearance, this time at the Picwood Theater in Westwood, for *Maytime*. Again she addressed the audience.

> I must say, this is really a royal welcome. I couldn't be more flattered, having all of you come here tonight, and it really makes me feel good to know that you all have supported these pictures . . . that this is the kind of moving picture you all like . . . to feel good, even though maybe a little sad, when you leave the theater . . . and you do like the kind of music Nelson and I and some of the others have tried to offer you. And by your being here tonight you have certainly shown the kind of loyalty that makes me feel very good.
>
> As you know, most actresses and actors have a favorite role or picture that they particularly like, and I am quite frank to admit that my favorite picture and my favorite role was Marcia Mornay in *Maytime*. I think it's because one has a challenge at being an old woman, and a young girl, and a middle-aged woman. And I had the added advantage, of course, because I had also to age my voice and my singing voice as well. So it made it a double challenge for me . . .
>
> We all know that when you get rather elderly you slow down in your pace considerably, and of course, I've always been accused of running everywhere, never walking anywhere, so I never had walked very slowly. And so in order to make me seem to be walking a little bit more slowly they put lead in my heels. Now, if you've ever had lead in your heels, you know it does slow you down a bit—there's no question about that! But I used to have a great deal of fun walking to the set from my dressing room. Of course, ordinarily with these enormous costumes, some of them weighing forty-fifty pounds, they always sent a car for me to take me from my dressing room to the sound stage, which was really quite a walk . . . But on this occasion I thought, well, it would help me for one thing to get into the mood, and to also help me to slow down my pace, and so I preferred to walk from my dressing room to the sound stage. And on the way over I'd run into some young people, you see, and I'd go walking by and I'd say, "Good morning, there, young folks, how are you this morning?" And they'd say, "Who's that old gal?" Or I'd catch them looking at me, you see, and they'd say, "Who's she? Who's she? I've never seen her before." So, it was quite a kick to see people wonder who I was. Sort of tease them a little.
>
> Then, also, when we get on the set there is always a great deal of hilarity. Of course, there always is with music pictures, especially if it's a happy picture.

Jeanette then introduced Gene as "my better half," and he made a speech, too.

During 1963, Jeanette granted more interviews. She thought of "dusting off" her autobiography, she said, and publishing it as *The Second Coming of Jeanette MacDonald*. She added, "When I left the industry, let's face it, my time was out. But I think the public is ready for my kind of motion picture once again." And she was still hoping to work with Nelson. "I have two ideas for films that I would like to make. One, written by Arthur Cober, is a comedy with music. Once

Nelson and I were going to do it in England, but plans fell through. The other is a drama with music. Dewitt Bodeen wrote it. Most of the music we'll use is public domain." (Bodeen verified in an interview that he'd had meetings with Jeanette and Nelson regarding a film.) When asked what she'd been doing the last ten years she replied, "Nothing, really. Nelson went to Las Vegas. I tried it, but that sort of thing just isn't for me. So I stay here."

One reporter wrote that "Miss MacDonald has weathered the years better than her husband, who is wrinkled and pale," but noted Jeanette was very thin. "It is the hardest thing in the world to put on a pound," she admitted.

■■ Nelson experienced a strong surge in popularity in 1962. He toured his act through the Midwest states, Montreal, Juarez, Mexico and at long last, Australia. He'd talked of doing a tour there with Jeanette as long ago as 1953. Now he finally made it, but with Gale as his partner. They opened in early November at the Checquers Theatre Restaurant in Sydney. Nelson's show was booked until December 1, but it was such a rave success that the booking was extended to six weeks. It was standing room only at each performance, and Nelson broke all house attendance records. While in Australia he had bids to appear on TV and offers from other clubs outside of Sydney. A ten-week Australian tour was hastily booked for the fall of 1963.

In December, Nelson appeared on the popular Dinah Shore variety show, along with Milton Berle and current teen heart-throb Frankie Avalon. The critics were impressed; the New York *Daily News* reported, "There were only a few programs on the air last night worthy of notice. One of the exceptions was the color hours of Dinah Shore . . . Nelson Eddy still puts over with a bang the numbers he used to sing to Jeanette MacDonald. It was good to her him do such oldies as 'Rose Marie' and 'Rosalie' again." The Philadelphia *Inquirer* added, "The teaming of a couple of Philadelphians—Nelson Eddy and Frankie Avalon —provided an often lackluster Dinah Shore show with its brightest moments Friday. Booming-voiced Eddy and rock n' roller Avalon swapped suggestions on singing styles, then each took a crack at the other's specialty. Frankie was surprisingly audible in 'Mandalay' and Nelson a finger-snapping, shoulder-shaking fool in 'De De Dinah.' Eddy also relaxed to a degree in an exchange of insults with Milton Berle and triggered a colorful Northwest Mounted Police finale with a medley of operetta rousers. In fact, except for a dismaying discordant duet with Dinah, Eddy proved a most welcome new-old face and new-old voice."

■■ "After the Metro years, Jeanette never came back down to earth," Blossom said. "She just couldn't adjust to the real world. Nelson was the tie-in to all that she felt she had lost—beauty, fame, the admiration. She clung to him because of it. When Nelson first went to Australia, Jeanette got very thin and fragile. Every time he left town she stopped eating. Nelson used to call her 'my delicate angel.'

Once she told me they made love on the sofa at Twin Gables and he cried because she was so delicate. 'If only I could find a way to give you my strength,' he said. 'Promise me you won't slip away from me and leave me alone in this hell-on-earth existence.' " "They were always promising each other things," Blossom said wryly. "A book about Jeanette and Nelson should be called O Promise Me."

In 1963 Jeanette and Gene moved out of Twin Gables and into apartments 8C and 8D at the Wilshire Comstock, east building, with a connecting door between them. As Jeanette did her final packing, she tossed out many of her once-cherished possessions, and gave away many of her valuables, except for her fan collection. Many photos from her extensive still collection, private scrapbooks and appointment books were unceremoniously burned in the fireplace. Salvaged from this purge were some early photos of herself with Bob Ritchie. Jeanette studied them for a while, then put them aside, deciding she'd send them to Bob. From all accounts, she hated her new home, but her health was declining so rapidly, the idea of yet another move was unthinkable. Along with low blood pressure, frequent fainting spells, she'd also suffered at least one serious stroke, and her speech was temporarily affected. On June 10, she and Gene filmed an interview for the Canadian TV show Flashback, televised on June 23. Her speaking voice had deepened, and she stumbled over and slurred certain words. In October 1963, she did another interview, this time on the phone, with Ben Lyon. Her speaking voice was similarly deep.

Finally an arterial transplant was done. This was a new miracle surgery, performed by Dr. Michael DeBakey in Houston, Texas. DeBakey also operated on the Duke of Windsor the same year, and the surgery extended his life another decade. In Jeanette's case, she'd been living on borrowed time for so long that any relief in her condition was considered a success. But for Jeanette, the quality of her life was far more important a consideration than simply giving her a few more years of suffering. When the operation was deemed a success, Jeanette attempted to rekindle her career, claiming she still had a dream to make another film with Nelson. They were offered secondary roles in The Thrill of It All, but each turned it down. They were also offered roles on the Aaron Spelling TV show Burke's Law, playing a battling team of opera stars. According to a newspaper clipping, "[Spelling] has been landing a lot of stars for little money to do bit parts on this show, but Jeanette and Nelson responded with an abrupt no." Jeanette also talked of making a guest appearance with the San Francisco Opera for one or more performances of Flotow's Martha, but nothing came of it. Then she started work on a Broadway musical to star her and young Liza Minnelli as her daughter. The play was called A Little Night Music but was no relation to the work of the same name by Stephen Sondheim. Jeanette's role was a flashback, reminiscent of Maytime or Bittersweet, in which she recalls her sad love story. Her main song was "Wasn't It Romantic?," a take-off on "Isn't It Romantic?" According to one of the show's writers, the project got as far as having the music recorded, without the vocals. "Wasn't It Romantic?" was eventually recorded on an excellent Michael Feinstein album.

Jeanette's final professional dream was to play the Mother Abbess in the film version of *The Sound of Music.* It was a cameo role, but she could sing "Climb Every Mountain," a song she loved.

In November 1963, Nelson was off to Australia for his second tour. However, according to the press, he was having problems with his vocal cords and suddenly canceled the rest of the tour, returning home. There seems no doubt that he was ill, but what is surprising was that this occurred the very week that Jeanette checked into the Houston Methodist Hospital for an extended stay. Furthermore, just before he left Australia, he told a fan who asked about Jeanette, "I'm very worried—we are very concerned about her health." According to one Houston resident, Nelson visited Jeanette, causing a furor in the hospital, with the whole place abuzz that "Nelson Eddy is on the floor visiting Jeanette Mac-Donald."

A curious letter was sent to her fan club by Jeanette, or by her secretary on her behalf, at this time. It read, in part, "I have recently had very nice conversations with Ann Eddy. She apparently is well, though of course she misses Nelson since he is away so much of the time. She gets awfully lonesome, I am sure. I read her a letter I had had from Nelson after he had learned of my surgery. Very cute, but I have a heck of a time understanding his handwriting. He is a good guy, let's face it, and I have always been very fond of him, as you all know." Ann Eddy herself notified Nelson that "your girlfriend" was hospitalized in November. Jeanette at first had hoped to keep the news from him, figuring to be released and back at home by the time his Australian tour was over. To her dismay, the hospital "visit" dragged on through December and into January 1964. She developed pleurisy along with her other problems, which required her to remain flat on her back for an extended time. Blossom came to visit her sister, and a Texan fan took a snapshot of them together.

Jeanette finally returned home, but was shortly after admitted into UCLA medical center. Nelson was distraught at her failure to bounce back as she'd always done before; after visiting her on one occasion in the hospital, he collapsed. Throughout 1964 Jeanette battled in vain to regain her health. The periodic letters to her fan club demonstrate her losing fight:

February 14, 1964: "I do not know how many of you may or may not have read of my recent expedition to the hospital in Houston, Texas, where I underwent major surgery, but I am happy to report that I am home again, and gaining my strength slowly but surely.

May 19, 1964: "I have simply been trying to get well, and this isn't easy as one would think. I suppose patience plays a large part of any recuperation—something which I ain't got!"

August 13, 1964: "It has been such a long time since I have written to you, but I am sure you will forgive me, knowing how difficult it is for me to get up enough energy to dictate to Emily. . . . It is a long pull getting back my strength, but I am feeling better each day."

November 16, 1964: "Now the invitations are coming in thick and fast to attend cocktail parties, Egg Nog and Christmas parties, etc. Maybe I am becoming an old fogy, but the truth of the matter is I couldn't care less, and I really don't feel like parties, when my main objective right now is to get completely well."

A major factor in her struggle was the emptiness of her personal life. Nelson was on the road much of the time and saw her infrequently. One time he showed up for a visit and found her administering medication to herself. Minutes later Sybil Thomas received a frantic phone call from Nelson: "My God, she's on morphine!" In the background Jeanette was sobbing and arguing that she was in terrible pain, and Nelson shouted at her while trying to ask Sybil what he should do. Nelson ended up paying for a Chinese herb specialist to get Jeanette off her various medications. Both he and the doctor stayed, and Nelson held Jeanette's hand through the next few painful days until she was better. Nelson later reported it had cost him a small fortune, but it was worth every cent to see Jeanette better.

Nelson finally realized that without him around, Jeanette would surely die. It was something he had tried not to face, but now, suddenly, after years of carefully staying away from her, he suddenly jumped into action. Sybil's house was up for lease again; Nelson informed her that he was taking it and that he would finally make the break from Ann, divorce or no divorce. "After all, we're in our sixties now, who will care if we run off together?"

Miliza Korjus, who visited Jeanette in her last year, reported that Jeanette spoke vaguely about some plans concerning Nelson. Jeanette insisted on taking a walk with Miliza; the "walk" consisted of their going outside the apartment building and walking up and down a small stretch of Wilshire Boulevard. This was all Jeanette could manage, but it seemed to do her good.

Unknown to many, Nelson had also taken an apartment at the Wilshire Comstock, but it was rarely used until after his death, when Ann Eddy made it her residence.

Nelson had for some time been diverting funds from his bank accounts with Ann; he informed Jeanette that this was the money they would live on when they made the break. But when Nelson went to the bank to draw out the funds, he discovered the money was gone. Somehow his wife had gotten to it. Nelson was devastated. He had worked and slaved all his life, and for what? All the millions he'd made had gone to supporting others; his wife, his parents, Ted Paxson, Gale Sherwood. He had virtually nothing to show for his efforts. "Nelson aged overnight," claimed Jon Eddy. "He looked small and shrunken." Nelson finally pulled himself together and began to plan anew, now diverting funds out of California altogether, where Ann could never get to them. Jon Eddy was under the impression that Ted Paxson was put in charge of these funds, should anything happen to Nelson.

Now Nelson was faced with telling Jeanette that their plans would be once again postponed. She tried not to show her disappointment to Nelson, but she'd lived so long on hope and sheer will that this seemed the last straw. Quietly, the dream was fading away.

★ ★ ★

Sybil saw Jeanette only twice that year. Once was in a jewelry shop in Beverly Hills. Jeanette was there alone, and didn't look well. She leaned against the counter, as if to hold herself up. She looked faded—her hair *was* faded—and her vitality was gone. She seemed so alien to the Jeanette she knew that Sybil wasn't even sure if it was her. She said "Jeanette?" in a questioning voice. Jeanette turned to look at her, hurt showing in her eyes because Sybil hadn't recognized her immediately. Sybil made some excuses about not having her glasses, but it didn't wash. Then Gene and Jeanette's secretary entered the shop and escorted Jeanette out. Jeanette wordlessly turned back to look at Sybil, a helpless, lonely look in her eyes that Sybil couldn't forget.

Some weeks later Sybil was at a party that was attended by both Nelson and Jeanette. Sybil was amazed at the change in Jeanette. "Even her hair looked brighter." Sybil carefully scrutinized Jeanette. Her eyes were too bright, which indicated that she was on some heavy medication. One hand stayed in her lap at dinner and Nelson cut her food for her. She also didn't talk much, just sat quietly most of the evening, just watching the goings-on. But at one point, Nelson made her dance with him. He did most of the dancing, literally holding her up and keeping a tight grip on her. The way they looked at each other belied the years; it was that timeless look that had never changed. The bottom line for Jeanette and the hardest part of her convalescence was that she was constantly alone. She still had her secretary and her cook who worked for her and Gene, but stayed in the second bedroom in her apartment. Otherwise she had very little contact with the outside world. Gene was working in TV, stage and film; comments made by Jeanette in her fan publications indicated his disappointment about his career attempts not taking off, being severely edited out of films, etc. In the fall of 1964 Blossom started work on her own very successful TV show, "The Addams Family," in which she played Grandmama, undergoing a four-hour makeup job each day she worked. She wrote at least one unproduced script for the show, in which her supporting role was beefed up. Jeanette was thrilled at Blossom's success and her finally reaching stardom so late in life. Blossom's life had until recently had its share of upsets as well. She had separated from her husband (they never divorced) before his death in 1960. Then she herself had suffered a mild stroke and Jeanette had nursed her back to health. Now Blossom was reciprocating, giving encouragement to Jeanette. Jeanette faithfully watched "The Addams Family" each week. For herself, she abhorred the illness that had reduced her to lonely idleness.

She was cheered by a brief visit from Nelson before he left again for Australia, and everyone was ordered to stay away from her apartment while he was there. He came early in the day and left late at night. Jeanette never revealed all that occurred, but she did confide that he'd told her what she wanted to hear; that he would finish all his obligations, and then he'd be with her forever. When Blossom entered her sister's bedroom that night, she found Jeanette dressed in a robe, looking surprisingly beautiful and young, staring teary-eyed out the window. Nelson was gone but his pipe was on her nightstand. Jeanette turned to her sister and said with great poignancy, "Tonight makes up for all the years we never had."

29

The song is ended

With the final days of 1964, Jeanette's suffering increased. "Haven't I been punished enough?" she asked her sister. She relived the failures of her life, the damage she'd done to others, and talked of the only blissful days she remembered —being with Nelson at Lake Tahoe in 1935. When Blossom was later asked what caused her sister's death, she answered, "Guilt." Blossom was present while her sister was writing a last letter to Nelson, which he was to read after her death. She tore up several versions, and cried, "How do I say farewell to him? He's my life, my strength. Anything that was good in me was because of him. All I did was to torture him, and ruin his life. I never deserved his love."

"She knew she was dying, she didn't care," said Phyllis Woodbury, a psychic whom Jeanette had consulted some time earlier in New York. "The suffering got to her, and she didn't want to live anymore." Jeanette poured out her heart to Woodbury, telling her she and Nelson had been in love all their lives, and had married the wrong people. Woodbury clarified, "The karmic law was difficult for both of them. They fell in love and they never knew they loved each other so much. So it was hard for them to maintain a balance in their own personal lives." She continued,

> She wanted to know how her life was going to end . . . She said, "Don't be afraid to tell me anything." And I said, "I like to tell everything, whether it's good, bad, or indifferent, so you know how to protect yourself." And I said, "My dear,

A grieving Nelson is escorted to Jeanette's funeral by his wife Ann and Gale Sherwood, January 18, 1965. Behind them throng thousands of mourning fans.

you've been very spiritual on all levels. You'll be with God, and with anything and everything you've missed in this particular life. Both of you will be together, you'll be with each other, and there'll be no interference."

I think it did [make her feel better]. Right after that, I don't know when it was, she passed on. I guess the idea knowing that someone understood her and gave her hope— She said that the love was strong and good, and it hurt her to know that she had to suffer.

Part of Jeanette's anguish stemmed from the fact that Nelson was rarely there, and his blind refusal to see that she was dying. Phyllis Woodbury tried to clarify this:

There's a difference between male and female. A female can do many things and contend with it, but a male, if he's not working, his whole world is shattered. So he had to work, no matter what the opinions may be of others.

She didn't want him to know [she was dying]. You see, he didn't do anything about his situation [with Ann]. Maybe he didn't deserve to be there. And also, she wanted to spare him the pain. That's all.

In Jeanette's final weeks, there were few visitors. Vivien Leigh was told Jeanette was "too ill" to see her. Others were told she wasn't quite lucid. But the facts speak strongly of neglect. All the telephones were removed from the apartment except for one in the living room, and Nelson and others were told she had to rest. Nelson even mentioned to a friend that his phone calls to Jeanette were being diverted to Gene's apartment. Blossom was unable to see her sister during the daytime hours due to her work schedule; she came early in the morning, when Jeanette was asleep, and late at night, when she was asleep. A depressed Blossom often reported her sister's condition to Mrs. Cameron, her next-door neighbor. They lived at the top of a long, lonely driveway, and when Blossom came home late at night Mrs. Cameron would have a bowl of hot chili waiting for her.

A woman in Jeanette's weakened condition needed a full-time nurse, but it is clear that she did not have one. The only claim made against Jeanette's estate was a private duty nurse for the last two days of her life in the Houston hospital. The secretary and cook were not much in evidence either, and a year after Jeanette's death, the cook suffered a nervous breakdown. Richard Wells, who drove the woman to the hospital, related on tape a chilling account of her self-professed guilt over Jeanette's final days, including this admission, "I helped kill Jeanette."

To the end Nelson always saw Jeanette as beautiful. As late as September 30, 1964, he told an interviewer: "She's still very much alive and very beautiful, and very attractive." On December 21, Nelson came to see Jeanette only to learn that she was being rushed to UCLA with abdominal adhesions. Nelson had a previous agreement with the hospital that he could sign any release forms needed for Jeanette, but no one at the hospital seemed to know anything about it. Nelson, hysterical and angry, spent much of the evening going in and out of gay and straight bars on Santa Monica Boulevard, searching for Gene Raymond. A leading actor of the 1950s verified Nelson's actions that night, asserting, "It's true that Nelson Eddy was going in and out of bars, looking for Gene Raymond. I was in one of the bars when he came in searching for him."

Gene was finally located, the surgery was performed and Jeanette remained hospitalized for ten days. In early January she went home and Nelson returned to work, figuring she was in good hands. Even now he was unwilling to face her impending death. He refused to know she was that ill; nor did she make the effort to enlighten him. They last spoke about a week before her death. Blossom had come to visit her sister during the daytime. To her horror, she found Jeanette attempting to get to the phone in the living room. She was nearly incoherent, but Blossom was finally able to understand that Jeanette had to call Nelson, to prove that Gene was wrong about Nelson, and that he still loved her. Blossom, unable to verbally describe that scene years later due to a stroke, pantomimed her sister dragging herself to the phone, and her distraught frame of mind. Blossom dialed for her sister. Once Nelson came on the line, Jeanette suddenly "came to life," talking cheerfully and not telling Nelson how bad off she was. She told him she loved him and would see him soon. When she finally hung up, Blossom grabbed the phone, determined to phone Nelson back and insist that he come at once. Jeanette stopped her, warning her it would only upset him. To the end of her days, Blossom blamed herself for not calling Nelson back. When Nelson later talked to the press about that last phone conversation, he admitted that he and Jeanette had talked only about getting together for dinner.

Blossom helped her sister back to bed, amazed at her sudden serenity and declaration that she could wait just a little longer to have Nelson with her always. Then Blossom went to the kitchen to prepare something to eat. She found the cupboards basically empty except for a can of tomato soup. The lack of any food in the house didn't alert Blossom, who apparently thought outside food was being brought in. She made her sister the soup, and sat with her until she finally fell back to sleep.

On January 12, 1965, Jeanette returned to Houston on a commercial plane. Friends were later unbelieving that Gene hadn't chartered a private carrier, as Jeanette was "in very bad heart failure" upon arrival, according to her doctor, Michael DeBakey. She was so emaciated she was too weak for any surgery. DeBakey put her on intravenous feeding in the hopes that she could be stabilized enough to survive.

The doorman at the Wilshire Comstock later revealed that there was a great deal he could tell about Jeanette's final days and her trip to Houston. After much hedging, he admitted only that Gene had phoned him and asked him to drive them to the airport. Jeanette had to be carried downstairs; she was incoherent and the man confided confidentially, "She thought I was Nelson."

Despite DeBakey's attempt to rally Jeanette, it was too little, too late. She died at 4:32 P.M., on January 14, 1965. The press claimed a beautiful death scene with Gene at her side and her last words being "I love you." However, later accounts cast doubt that Gene was even there, and Sybil Thomas, upon hearing that Jeanette had asked for her feet to be rubbed, asserted "She must have thought he was Nelson. Nelson was the only one who rubbed her feet." Jeanette's last struggle was anything but pleasant, as attested to by Bill Tuttle, who did her makeup for the funeral. He confirmed that she was "very blue" and that he had to do the makeup twice to try to cover it for the funeral. In his opinion, having an open casket at the funeral was a distasteful move.

Ann's son claims that Nelson was in his workshop at home when the phone call came; however, Nelson had checked into his hotel in Anaheim, California, where he was scheduled to open the following evening. Some of his groupies ate breakfast in a coffee shop with him, and eavesdropped on him, Gale, and Ted Paxson as they rehearsed during the afternoon.

The press found Nelson immediately. "The networks were there and I was crying," he later said. He seemed bewildered and disbelieving in a televised interview that night. "She was stunning and startlingly beautiful," he said of the first time he met her. "She would take your breath away." He was able to tell a funny story about *Sweethearts* and the supposed MacDonald-Eddy feud. "There never was anything to it," he said, but when the interviewer pressed him, as an ex-newspaperman, to write the lead for this story, Nelson grew suddenly bitter. "From my point of view it would be very difficult to write a lead because I'm—I —hardly know what to say myself, much less put it in writing for—uh—uh— public consumption."

The interviewer pressed him, and Nelson finally became agitated. "Don't ask me to do that! You write a story and I'll write a head—maybe— But—uh, I don't know, it was a shocking thing to learn the way I did, so suddenly. I—I—I —was so upset, I was so put out. And then people started calling from—from all over—uh, New York, Chicago, San Francisco, London—They want a statement. Why, a statement was the—would—it's a very hard thing to make, you see. You don't make statements—You just kind of bite your lips and say I'm sorry—(voice breaks)—I—can't believe it, and you kind of stutter—I'm still stuttering—I still don't—(starts to cry)—I—I—still—can't—believe it."

Mercifully, the interview was ended.

Nelson had been scheduled to open the following night in Anaheim. "I canceled the show," he said later, "then decided that was wrong." He felt Jeanette would want him to go on, and he did. The audience felt his devastation, listened to his unsteady voice, and witnessed his eyes repeatedly filling throughout the first night's show—and indeed, throughout the week. Certain songs he couldn't bring himself to sing, but somehow he managed to keep himself together onstage.

When Jeanette's body was returned to Los Angeles, Nelson was granted all the private time he needed with her. At the mortuary he took the emerald engagement ring he'd bought her in 1935 and slipped it back on her finger. It sickened him to see how large it was on her, and he fell to his knees, crying and asking her forgiveness. Then he berated her for leaving him, hating her for deserting him. Finally he begged her to take him with her, to help him die. As the minutes passed and he wasn't struck down at her feet, he finally realized his "punishment" was to go on living. He stumbled out of the mortuary and was met by curious reporters. One of them was an ABC news anchor, who studied Nelson and then motioned the others not to bother him. "Leave the man to his grief," the newscaster said. "There's no story here."

███ Over the next few days Nelson had little time for private grief. He was always on display, if not singing, with Jeanette's friends and family. A small gathering was held at Jeanette's apartment, and Nelson attended with Ann. One of the people there noted that some of Jeanette's things had already been removed from the apartment.

Jeanette's funeral at Forest Lawn Glendale on January 18 was, according to Nelson, "a circus." Her singing voice boomed out of loudspeakers strategically placed from the chapel. People filed past the open casket; many were stunned at Jeanette's emaciated appearance and the orange "Harpo Marx" wig, and felt it cruel that Gene had decided on an open casket. One person watched Gene during the proceedings and commented sarcastically, "At last he's the star."

Nelson made one private trip to Jeanette's apartment, where he found a letter she had left for him, secreted in a hidden drawer in her desk. In the letter she proclaimed her love for him, and advised him to be grateful she wasn't suffering any longer. In the coming days Nelson learned just a little of what Jeanette had endured, and he turned on Gene and her secretary, blaming them for deserting her when she needed them the most. After all the years of her faithfully supporting them, the least they could have done was to take care of her.

Nelson never socialized with Jeanette's family or associates again. He saw Blossom one final time and broke down, sobbing, "I didn't know she was so sick." Blossom was angry with him; she never forgave him for what she felt was his shortcoming in not being with Jeanette when she needed him. Over the next months, Nelson turned to various friends in dealing with his grief. They reported that he alternately loved and hated Jeanette. To some he cursed the day he'd met her, hating himself for never getting over her, for not being more promiscuous and sleeping with enough women to drive her out of his mind. He proclaimed his unwavering love for her over the years "a sickness." Then, at other times, he hated himself for his weaknesses, for not divorcing Ann years earlier, for allowing the decades of hellish existence that had driven Jeanette to an early grave. Finally he dealt with his feelings in the only way he could keep his sanity—he tried to close the book on Jeanette forever. "Miss MacDonald was a period of my life that was wonderful," he said in an interview, and then went on to make clear that that part of his life was over. He did, however, keep a framed picture of Jeanette as the Merry Widow on his night table in the house he shared with Ann.

Jon Eddy saw Nelson only once after Jeanette's death. He attempted to talk to Nelson about her, thinking that maybe Nelson could confide in him and perhaps in this way establish a closer relationship between his father and son. But Jon finally gave up, claiming Nelson's attitude was "as if she never existed."

The proof of Nelson's feelings, buried or not, were expressed in his own scrapbooks. After his mother's death, his secretary had taken over the task of pasting in his clippings and reviews, and Nelson often annotated them. The front page of each scrapbook was saved for a very special photo or clipping. In the scrapbook dealing with the 1960s, Nelson used for a front piece the record cover of himself and Jeanette in their *Favorites in Hi-Fi* album. He then devoted a total of fourteen pages in this scrapbook to Jeanette's obituaries, which he personally labeled and dated. Across one write-up of the funeral he wrote: "shared headlines with Johnson Inaugural," as if comforted by the fact that her funeral coverage was as newsworthy as the swearing-in of a President. In another clipping he underlined a few lines from a Milwaukee paper, in which Jeanette was praised for holding the all-time record for paid concert attendance at a music-under-the-stars concert. The quote that Nelson underlined was an apt tribute: "None of the famous who have come this way has an equal gift for projecting personality . . . none has such a knack of counterfeiting intimacy . . . and generally convincing the listeners that the songs being sung so affectionately carry a special dedication."

In the end, Nelson offered his own tribute to Jeanette when he told a reporter: "She was the greatest woman movie singer who ever lived."

Nelson receives the news of Jeanette's death, January 14, 1965.

30

"I've Tried So Hard"

Nelson returned to work with a vengeance, ignoring his own weakening health. He came from long-lived stock, and from all accounts should have lived well into his eighties or nineties. But the tremendous stress he lived with, the lonely and unhappy circumstances of his personal life, and the self-destructive side to his nature all worked against him. On stage he was still dynamic and energetic, occasionally performing as many as three shows a day. His voice seemed untouched by time; frequently he'd push aside the microphone and belt out an old standard like "Shenandoah," which brought the house down. The hundreds of fan write-ups and the favorable critical reviews attest to his tremendous success in the nightclub field. He was praised for being courteous and caring to his faithful fans; his whole life was preparing for and performing his act.

He still had his share of fanatics, reminiscent of the Hollywood days. At one performance in Anaheim, California, in November 1965, a woman barged onto the stage and insisted she was going to sing a duet with the great Nelson Eddy. Nelson tried to calm her down, asking what she wanted to sing with him. When the woman replied, "You name it!" he turned to the orchestra and said, "Okay, play a chorus of 'You Name It.'" A policeman and the theater manager came on stage to take the woman away, but soft-hearted Nelson protested "No, wait, let her go, fellas." The woman was released, but after the show she hounded him at the stage door, and Nelson had to call the security guards.

Although his fans were grateful to see Nelson in person, the majority of them still disliked seeing him mocking himself and his films. Many felt uneasy about the casual nightclub atmosphere; occasionally there were loud drunk people interrupting the show, or someone yelling "Fix the mike!" or "The orchestra is too loud!" One wonders whether a purist like Nelson ever got used to the insulting rudeness of the nightclub audience.

Offstage, or out of the public eye, Nelson wilted. One fan described seeing him at the Valley Music Theater in Los Angeles when he wasn't catering to the fans. Her close-up scrutiny revealed that his skin was pasty, his pallor bad; he was unsmiling and looked miserable. The fan attempted to get his autograph but was intercepted by Gale Sherwood, who warned her off by telling her that Nelson wasn't well. Reports from other fans noted similar things; he seemed lifeless offstage and didn't look well. Most people were unaware that he'd had at least one stroke—in 1963 (he was hospitalized, but the excuse was pneumonia). Nelson did little to protect his health though he claimed, "I don't smoke anymore. I quit two years ago. I decided that anybody who tries to sing and smoke at my age is a damn fool."

Nelson had problems with his throat and Jon Eddy, who was well versed in nutrition, suggested a course of vitamin supplements to help. Nelson, who had been so adamant about consulting a nutritionist on Jeanette's behalf, just shrugged, disinterested. He argued that he ate his "three squares a day," but in reality he didn't eat well and drank more heavily than before.

A month after Jeanette's death Nelson was onstage in Toronto despite being in constant pain due to a back problem. He informed Toronto radio listeners that after the engagement he was returning to Los Angeles for disk surgery. In mid-March he had a hernia operation.

Though he could still be jovial around his fans, especially when he was being photographed with a drink in his hand, there was a darker side to Nelson. Filmed interviews showed a pained look crossing his face when, inevitably, Jeanette's name is mentioned. His many interviews in the last years of his life reveal a lonely person who is clearly not at peace with himself or his life. One of the greatest areas of resentment was money; he had made millions but had little to show for it in his old age. A 1966 clipping from Vancouver pasted in his scrapbook read: "The Stadium Show, presented free, cost the PNE $80,000 to produce. Much of this went to the three name stars, Nelson Eddy, Frank Sinatra, Jr., and Frank 'Crazy Guggenheim' Fontaine." Nelson angrily noted in the margin of this paragraph: "Ha! RCMP Ride cost $25,000."

Nelson never hid his bitterness over money, but the unanswered question is what happened to it all.

Nelson told baritone Robert Merrill that he'd made five million dollars from his sixteen films, "when taxes were only fleabites," and that in the 1940s he commanded $10,000 a concert and $5,000 a week radio. Merrill, for one, was at a loss to understand why Nelson now felt he had to continue working, except that he didn't want to be home with his wife, and preferred to travel with Gale Sherwood. Still, Merrill was appalled at the lifestyle Nelson had chosen for himself. "To lay out a tour of clubs, you often break a long trip with stopovers that are not up to your usual standard," Merrill said. "I saw him when he appeared in St. Louis; he and Miss Sherwood were playing in a downtown hotel. The nightclub was dowdy, the air was stale, and the customers noisy." During the show Nelson sang "Rose Marie," but later confided to Merrill: "God, how I hate that song! I personify a wonderful, nostalgic era for so many people—all they want from me is 'Short'nin' Bread' and 'Ah, Sweet Mystery of life.' I'm trapped in their thirties!"

In an interview from July, 1964, Nelson said bluntly, "I'm poison in California. Hollywood is everything there. I'm just a broken-down actor to them." In the margin of this article Nelson angrily wrote: "A lady-*rat*."

From August, 1964: "People have been telling me for the last 25 I'm too old. It doesn't bother me. I'm doing what I like most to do, and that's night club acts before a live audience. I've always been controlled before by agents, managers and producers, and now I'm doing the controlling. If I don't like something in my act, I put something else in and that's that."

From Australia, fall of 1964: "I look all dark, creased and seamy—about 83. But I'm only 63. A lot of talent but I'm not as pretty as I used to be. People still ask what happened to Nelson Eddy. Well, I have news for them, he grew up.

"I'm indestructible. I can claim this. I've been singing professionally before the public since 1918. A lot of singers wear out long before then. I haven't so at least I'm hardy . . .

"Now I just want to do the best for people as long as I can. I have to fulfil my destiny. If I don't do that I'll be a shirker and I'll be damned if I'll be a shirker. Retirement? I don't know what you're talking about.

"I've got the most loyal bunch of fans, you know. They're everywhere and I had a whole lot of fan letters waiting for me again this time. I get presents, too. A woman I've never heard of has knitted me the most beautiful sweater. Look at these cufflinks. A fan sent them to me last time I was here. I don't know if they're valuable but I know they're beautiful cufflinks and I appreciate the gift. I've had a fan club for 29 years now and it's more than 20 years since I made a picture.

"I earn quite a lot of money but my expenses are enormous. Fifty percent of my earnings go to pay commissions and the salaries of my partner, Miss Gale Sherwood, and my musical director. Fifty percent of what I have left goes in taxes. Other expenses come out of the rest and we go first class all the way. . . . I'm not rich, not like some old film stars. Not like Harold Lloyd, for instance. I think he's just about got all the money there is.

"I think I'm wonderful because I've tried so hard."

From Toronto, February 1965: "Toronto people used to resent Gale. These society people would call out during the show: get rid of that dame, she's no MacDonald. They hated her because she had left Canada, and also because they remembered Miss MacDonald. I thought we'd get cheers in her own country and we got boos.

"First of all, I couldn't afford Miss MacDonald, and she didn't like the night-club business, anyway. She was always very religious and didn't like drinking.

And besides that, I think Gale does our kind of show better . . . Miss MacDonald never said an unkind word about Gale; in fact, they got along quite well."

From Ohio, October 1965: "I have many acquaintances, but I feel most people only make three or four friends in a lifetime. I found that out twenty years ago when I lost my big popularity."

From Australia, February 1967: "I'll be singing a serious song and someone will call out: Sing 'Rose Marie.' I used to get upset, but I don't anymore. I just sing 'Rose Marie.' " When asked how many times he'd sung that song in his lifetime, Nelson estimated 6,000 or 7,000 times.

Regarding Jeanette's funeral: "The publicity people turned it into a circus. They piped her old songs over loudspeakers and upset me, although possibly some people got a lot of pleasure from hearing them . . . When I go it will be in a private ceremony.

"At the end of my life, when they come to write down my occupation I hope they'll describe me as 'concert performer,' not 'film star.' "

■ Nelson was determined to keep working at a killing pace, although his health was suffering. At times it seemed that no amount of keeping busy would obliterate his despair, which was transparent to those who really scrutinized him. Two Australian interviewers used similar adjectives in describing Nelson: "bitter," "lonely," "sad," "a broken man, beaten by life." A third interviewer, Charles Higham (later a best-selling author), termed Nelson "a kvetch," a Yiddish word meaning someone who complains. According to Higham, Nelson seemed very ungrateful, complaining about his film career, Louis B. Mayer and even Gale Sherwood, with whom Nelson was upset because she was seeing other men. The only person Nelson didn't complain about, said Higham, was Jeanette MacDonald; he only had good things to say about her.

Nelson made three half-hearted suicide attempts after Jeanette's death. The first was driving his car off a road; the car was damaged but miraculously he escaped injury. The next incident took place in a hotel room; Nelson stood at a bathroom mirror shaving and impulsively decided to cut his throat. He held the razor to his throat for a long time, trying to get the courage to go through with it. Vanity finally prevented him; he could anticipate the press making a big deal about how he'd cut "Nelson Eddy's golden throat." Angrily he nicked his wrist instead, but barely enough to even draw blood. In disgust at his weakness, he threw the razor down. The final attempt was in New York. He'd had a few drinks and decided to jump out his hotel room window. Once again, he couldn't do it, and he collapsed on the bed and cried. His life, toward the end, seemed curiously empty. He described himself as an old cornstalk waving in the wind.

For the first time in over a decade, Nelson returned to his spiritual search. In 1966 he spoke with a Dianetics counselor about receiving some help dealing with his life. Nelson considered this, then turned down the counseling. He said he was no longer interested in fixing up this lifetime, but he would do it "next trip," meaning his next lifetime.

He did try to establish communication with Jeanette, certain as he was that she was watching over him. Once Ted Paxson found him sitting in a darkened room, his head bowed. Nelson told Ted "We're just being together. Sometimes she's so close I can smell her perfume and feel her hot breath on my ear." Another time he described the Jeanette he saw: young, beautiful, wearing the yellow dress and sun hat she'd worn for an early studio picnic they attended together.

In early 1967 Nelson was off to Australia for his fourth tour there. One reviewer wrote of him and Gale, "They are a strange pair—she's a vivacious, sparkling young woman and he's a slightly portly, tired old man. But the Adelaide public is just loving them and clamoring for more."

Returning to the United States, Nelson was off to Florida for a stint in Miami. On March 5 he granted a poolside interview at his hotel to several members of the press. "I'm working harder than I ever have in my life," he said. "I love it. I hope to keep on going till I drop." One of the photographers there wore a toupee. Somehow the men got to playing with it and tossing it to each other. Nelson caught the wig and stuck it on his head, slightly askew, as a joke. His photo was snapped, and it was this ridiculous shot that made the front pages of newspapers all over the world the next day.

That night Nelson was singing before a crowd of 400 people when he suddenly said to the audience, "Would you bear with me a minute? I can't seem to get the words out." He started another song but seemed to lose his memory, and turned to Ted Paxson. "Would you play 'Dardenella'? Maybe I'll get the words back." Then he said, "My face is getting numb. Is there a doctor here?" He collapsed, and was caught by the others as he fell. They managed to get him into a chair in the hotel hallway. By the time he was rushed to the hospital, he was unable to speak and his right side was paralyzed. He died at 7:30 the next morning, March 6. Ann Eddy was contacted but remained in Los Angeles, and the body was flown home. The private funeral was held three days later. Nelson was buried next to his mother Isabel in a modest grave at Hollywood Memorial Park, adjacent to Paramount Studios. One of Nelson's friends, Z. Wayne Griffin, eulogized him as "A simple and straightforward man, yet one of the most delicate, sensitive and complex natures I have known."

A newspaper photographer caught a candid shot of Gene Raymond greeting Ann Eddy at the funeral. To the astonishment of those standing nearby, Ann was overheard telling Gene, "Now they can sing together forever."

Sweethearts

Epilogue

Jeanette MacDonald and Nelson Eddy were two of the most influential singers of the twentieth century. They inspired several generations of young people to pursue musical or entertainment careers, including stars like Mario Lanza, Joan Sutherland, Beverly Sills, Carol Burnett and Betty White, just to name a few of the better-known celebrities.

Blossom MacDonald Rock suffered a stroke in 1966 and recovered at the Motion Picture Country Home in Woodland Hills, California. She continued to live there in The Lodge (a retirement hotel setup) until her death on January 14, 1978, exactly thirteen years to the day after Jeanette's death.

Elsie MacDonald Scheiter, the oldest MacDonald sister, died in 1970 in Philadelphia.

Jeanette's estate, though considerable, was depleted fairly rapidly. In 1974 Gene Raymond remarried. His wife, Nelson Ada Hees (known as "Nels" for short), was a rich Canadian heiress. After their marriage Gene gave up his apartment at the Wilshire Comstock and moved into his wife's Pacific Palisades home. At this writing he is still living.

Nelson also left most of his money to his spouse. Friends and fans were appalled to learn that his estate was valued at about one-half million dollars. The question of where Nelson's money disappeared has never been satisfactorily answered.

Ann Eddy moved out of the Eddys' last home, 166 Ashdale Place, into an apartment on Doheny Drive. She then moved into an apartment Nelson had kept at the Wilshire Comstock, where she lived for a number of years. She moved once more, down the street on Wilshire, before settling into a nursing home. As long as she was mobile, she continued to visit Nelson's grave regularly. The cemetery attendants were not fond of her, complaining that she was ill-tempered and often hit them with her cane. She died of old age on August 28, 1987. Before her death she sold off most of Nelson's paintings and sculptures. She was buried next to Nelson, but no headstone was laid for over a year. A cemetery representative explained the apparent oversight, claiming, "The family hasn't bothered to pay for it." Eventually a stone was laid, calling Ann "Beloved Wife."

Theodore Paxson retired, though he occasionally accompanied singers until his death in 1979. Except for a brief five-minute interview in the mid-1970s, he was never known to speak publicly about Nelson's private life.

Gale Sherwood attempted a career of her own, singing in musical comedy, with Liberace, and on cruise ships. She finally retired, married an Eastern Airlines pilot, and has lived happily out of the limelight.

John Eddy inherited more than simply good looks from his father. He has a beautiful, large, ringing voice and has sung professionally. He has a caring, dynamic personality, and once ran, albeit unsuccessfully, for public office.

Jon is currently divorced, and at this writing has two children and two grandchildren. After much soul-searching, he made the decision to go public about his identity and has been giving concerts all over the country, showcasing upcoming singers as Nelson once did. Jon is constantly amazed at the numbers and the love of MacDonald/Eddy fans, young and old.

In 1984, a furor broke out in the city of San Francisco over Jeanette's rendition of the song "San Francisco." For many decades that song had been the official song of the city. Then, in 1969, the Board of Supervisors voted to change it to Tony Bennett's recording of "I Left My Heart in San Francisco." According to music historian Bob Grimes, they wanted a city song that was "snappy and unoffending that would lure the mindless to San Francisco. They were afraid of [Jeanette's song], afraid to promote anything attached to the earthquake because it might scare off tourists." In 1984, San Franciscan columnist Warren Hinckle started a new crusade to change the city song back to "San Francisco." Public response was tremendous, with letters and newspaper articles and editorials filling the city's papers for weeks. Due to public pressure, the Board of Supervisors was forced to take a new vote. On the fateful day, over 5,000 people gathered outside of the City Hall on May 3, 1984, to cheer for the song Jeanette had immortalized. The Board had no other choice but to vote for "San Francisco" as the official song of that city. As a consolation prize, "I Left My Heart" was made the city ballad.

After years of arguments from MGM that there was no interest in the Mac-Donald-Eddy films, MGM library owner Ted Turner took a chance and in conjunction with MGM Video, released all of the MacDonald–Eddy films on video. To everyone's surprise—except, of course, their devoted fans—the films sold well and have continued to sell through the years. Through video, an entire new generation is discovering the artistry and charm of Jeanette MacDonald and Nelson Eddy, who sang together, always out of love.

Source Notes

Sources for this book include many interviews, most of which from the mid 1970s on were audio or videotaped. Other sources were written affidavits, hundreds of letters from family, fans and friends, and written eyewitness accounts of radio shows or other events. One of the major sources was over a thousand pages of letters representing Isabel Eddy's correspondence with Sarah Tucker. The handwritten letters I was lucky enough to see were dated from 1945 to 1950, and averaged at least one letter a week—sometimes more. The originals have survived with postmarked envelopes intact. In some cases, typewritten attachments were sent along with the letters, including Isabel's unfinished and unpublished memoirs. In the notations below, "IL" indicates the source is the "Isabel letters." "AL" stands for "anonymous letter," in which the author's name is being withheld.

CHAPTER 1

"Three whole days and nights . . ." IL, 2/4/46

CHAPTER 2

"She was stunning . . ." TV interview with Nelson, 1/14/65
Frank Lloyd party, Isabel Eddy's unpublished memoirs
Wilbur Evans date, interview with Susan Foster
Malcolm Poindexter, Jr. data, interview with the author
"Captain Bud" data, interview with Jean Warren
Robert Eddy quote, interview with the author, 1994
November 21 concert, interviews with Marie Collick, Isabel Eddy memoirs

Doris Kenyon party, interviews with Marie Collick, Sybil Thomas to Diane Goodrich
Jeanette meets Isabel Eddy, Isabel Eddy's memoirs

CHAPTER 3

"He was the first thing . . ." IL, 7/22/45
"Did someone tell you . . ." Isabel Eddy memoirs
Santa Barbara concert, NC, videotaped interviews with Marie Collick and Sunny Griffin, also Diane Goodrich
"I don't care what she did . . ." interview with Marie Collick
Studio picnic, interviews with Marie Collick, Sandy Reiss, Diane Goodrich

CHAPTER 4

Background information on Nelson's childhood is culled from interviews, articles and clippings throughout his scrapbooks (housed at USC) and other sources, plus the court transcript of the testimonies given by Isabel Eddy and her mother Caroline Kendrick during Isabel's divorce proceedings against William Eddy.

Mary Smith data, Marie Collick, Diane Goodrich
Malcolm Poindexter quotes, Jean Warren interview with Poindexter, 1990

CHAPTER 5

Opera reviews and Nelson interviews are from his scrapbooks and other clipping sources.

Maybelle Marsten information, interviews with Jean Warren, Sarah Smith, Elsa Dik Glass, Jon Eddy
Malcolm Poindexter quotes, Jean Warren interview, 1990
Rose Bampton quotes, interview with author, 1989
Helen Jepson quotes, interview with author, 1989
Nelson's sudden wealth, interview with Marie Collick

CHAPTER 6

Background data and quotes were taken from early newspaper clippings, plus interviews with Jeanette's sister, Blossom Rock; her cousins Esther Shipp and Katherine Pickens; Esther Shipp's written correspondences with their other first cousins, such as Charles Wright, who verified/corrected data printed in other books or newspaper interviews; Joan Bice; plus 1880, 1900, 1910 census (which verifies Jeanette's 1903 birthdate). Daniel MacDonald's obituary claimed he died on July 31, 1924, but his death certificate states it was 4:30 AM on August 1st.

Irving Stone episode, unpublished Bill Bass manuscript
Irving Caesar quotes, unpublished Bill Bass manuscript

CHAPTER 7

Much of the data came from published interviews, plus Jeanette's letters to Bob Ritchie, which were written as frequently as two or three times a week.

Nat Finston quotes, unpublished Bill Bass manuscript
John Engstead quotes, unpublished Bill Bass manuscript
Miles Krueger quotes, interview with author, 9/9/82
Rouben Mamoulian quotes, Photoplay magazine, 6/40, plus author's interview, 1972.
Myrna Loy quotes, *Being and Becoming* by Myrna Loy, p. 72
"Chevalier says he can't . . .", *Marlene Dietrich* by Maria Riva, p. 264.
Truely McGee quotes, interview with Judy Burns and T. A. Long, 10/6/81

CHAPTER 8

Details of the filming of *Naughty Marietta* came from interviews with Fred Phillips, Marie
    Collick, Florence Thomas, Diane Goodrich, Ken Hollywood, transcripts of phone
    conversations with Sybil Thomas, *Van Dyke and the Mythical City of Hollywood* newspa-
    per interviews and articles and comments made by other studio co-workers, in the
    commissary, make-up and wardrobe departments.

Their first sexual encounter and its aftermath, told by Nelson to Sandy Reiss, verified by
    Blossom Rock and Isabel Eddy's memoirs
Sandy Reiss quotes, video interviews and written affidavit of 7/24/81
"My shy little maiden . . ." IL, 2/2/46
"I thought I had never seen . . ." Ibid.
Sybil Thomas quotes, transcripts from phone conversations with Diane Goodrich, 1977
Washington D.C. premiere, *Van Dyke and the Mythical City of Hollywood* plus newspaper
    accounts
"Never to be forgotten weekend," Isabel's memoirs

CHAPTER 9

Background on *Rose Marie* came from clippings and articles, and interviews with Mary
    Sale, Richard Sale, Fred Phillips, William Tuttle, Iron Eyes Cody, June Swift, Ruth
    Van Dyke, Diane Goodrich, Blossom Rock, *Van Dyke and the Mythical City of Holly-
    wood* and Jeanette's letters to Bob Ritchie.

"I knew when I met Nelson . . ." IL, 5/28/45
"You know, if I could ever live . . ." IL, 5/21/45
Twenty-seven-hour marathon, Frank Laric interview with Inge

CHAPTER 10

Reviews and written interviews from clippings and articles, also interview with Woody
    Van Dyke III, and Jeanette's letters to Bob Ritchie.

Noble "Kid" Chissell quotes, from published interview in *Mac/Eddy Today,* Issue #5
Anita Loos quote, *Anita Loos* by Gary Carey, p. 165
Louella Parsons luncheon, interviews with Marie Collick, Sandy Reiss
Nelson's manic attack, Jeanette to Blossom Rock, interview with Charles Russell plus
    other members of MGM make-up department

CHAPTER 11

Concert and film reviews from newspaper clippings and articles; on-the-set incidents reported by studio co-workers.
Helen Ferguson data, author's interview with Frank Lieberman, 1974
Francis X. Bushman quote, *The Ragman's Son* by Kirk Douglas
Luise Rainer quote, TV interview on AMC
Betty Jaynes quotes, interview with author, 6/18/83
"You've had three or four . . ." Marie Collick interview with author
Mae Mann episode, newspaper and magazine articles written by Mae Mann, also interview with Elsa Dik Glass

CHAPTER 12

Jeanette's wedding was covered by newspapers all over the world.
Reviews and filming schedules from newspapers and clippings.
Noble "Kid" Chissell quotes, from published interview in *Mac/Eddy Today*, Issue #5
Nelson and Allan Jones feud, interviews and statements made by Marie Collick, Sybil Thomas, Sandy Reiss, Allan Jones, Bob Connolly
"I found him with his head on his desk . . ." IL, 12/31/45

CHAPTER 13

Gene Raymond background from articles and interviews
Richard Halverson quotes, interview with the author, 6/20/90
"Always I will remember . . ." IL, 5/21/45
Eleanor Powell reminiscences, interview with the author, 1977
"She may be Gene's wife . . ." Isabel Eddy's memoirs
"I've had about a dozen . . ." Ibid.
Locked car incident, Marie Collick interview
"My baby's arms . . ." Isabel Eddy's memoirs
"When I kissed her . . ." Ibid.
"Do you love your husband . . ." IL, 6/12/45
Eva Justice quotes, interview with author, 10/21/84 and 1993

CHAPTER 14

Background for this chapter came from newspaper articles and clippings, interviews with Betty Jaynes, Mickey Knazik, Isabel Eddy memoirs, Sybil Thomas phone conversations with Diane Goodrich

Data re: Stonyvale and Mariposa houses, interviews with 1980s tenants and neighbors; data re: Mists from Isabel Eddy's letters
Betty Jaynes quotes, 6/18/83
Miliza Korjus quotes, interview with author, 1978

CHAPTER 15

Data regarding *Sweethearts* from interviews with Florence Thomas, William Tuttle, Diane Goodrich, Marie Collick, Sybil Thomas, Blossom Rock, Mickey Knazik and other studio employees. William Tuttle was interviewed by Judy Burns, but was reluctant to speak due to his friendship with Gene Raymond.

Stonyvale photos, interview with Sylvia Collender, 1985
Herbert Gahagan quotes, interviews with the author, 1987
Frank Laric quotes, interviews with the author, various dates

CHAPTER 16

Nelson's marriage, excerpts from Isabel Eddy's memoirs, interviews and comments made by Nelson and Jeanette to Sandy Reiss, Marie Collick, Diane Goodrich, Ted Paxson, Sunny Griffin and others.
"On the long trail of life . . ." IL, 5/28/45
"Darling, the hardest . . ." Isabel Eddy memoirs

CHAPTER 17

Miliza Korjus quote, interview 1977
"Sing even if you don't mean it . . ." Isabel Eddy memoirs
"One does not hurt a woman . . ." Ibid.
"Oh Nelson, it hurts so . . ." IL, 1/9/46
Poppy Delmando, interview with T. A. Long, 10/6/81

CHAPTER 18

"I have loved Nelson . . ." IL, 7/29/45
Shirley Temple quote from her autobiography
Ann Eddy background, IL, other correspondence and eyewitness comments
"I went to him as quickly as possible . . ." Isabel Eddy memoirs
Risë Stevens quotes, interview with the author, 9/17/82
Irving Jones data, letter to author, 11/29/92
Risë Stevens "affair," eyewitness reports, plus several IL, especially 6/5/45

CHAPTER 19

Anita Loos quotes, *Anita Loos* by Gary Carey, pp. 197–98
Ann Eddy "pregnancy," IL, 7/4/45
Frank Laric quote, interview with author
Harper McKay quote, interview with author, 1992
"Tired, very pretty," Bobbie Nelson to Eleanor Hagemann, 8/18/42
Ann at Old Gold radio shows, 9/6/42

CHAPTER 20

Journey for Margaret background, author's interview with Margaret O'Brien, 1978, plus *Van Dyke and the Mythical City of Hollywood*
Woody Van Dyke's death, IL, 6/4/45, interview with Shirley Johnson
"Over and over they sang it," eyewitness account, 11/3/43
Ann Eddy suicide attempt, IL, 5/28/45
"Perhaps some day we will see . . ." IL, 1/26/46
Susanna Foster quote, interview with author, 1982

Bernard Brown quote, interview with author, 1977
Philadelphia rendezvous, Katherine Pickens, IL
"Old friend" quote, *Mac/Eddy Today,* Issue #12
Rose Bampton quote, interview with author
Gene arrest in England, letter from Joe Sampson, plus two English sources
"I kissed her and tried to tell her . . ." IL, 2/16/45
Shelley Winters quote from her autobiography, *Shelley*

Data regarding Nelson's war work was brought to my attention by Judy Burns and T. A. Long, and verified by Frank Laric, Lawrence Tibbett, Jr., Diane Goodrich, John Pickard, Sunny Griffin and English sources.

CHAPTER 21

Letters containing eyewitness accounts were utilized for details of radio broadcasts. In some instances these letters were published in the fan club journals, but I was lucky enough to obtain other letters, shown only to a privileged few, which contained omitted facts not deemed suitable for the general fan club public.

"I have just received . . ." IL, 5/28/45
Kansas City rendezvous, IL, 1/26/46
Susanna Foster quote, interview with author
Mike Todd incident, IL, 5/28/45
The new "nightie," IL, 11/26/46
"Is this going on . . ." IL, 5/28/45
Christmas 1944 recordings, IL, 5/21/45
Robert Merrill quote, from *Between Acts*
"All my life . . ." IL, 1/26/46

CHAPTER 22

Eyewitness accounts of radio shows and backstage at the concerts were obtained in the manner noted for Chapter 21.

List of confidants, IL, 11/26/45
East Wind details, interview with Dewitt Bodeen, October 1981
"They have been singing their throats out . . ." IL, 7/29/45
"My baby . . ." IL, 9/16/45
"My dear . . ." Ibid.
John Brownlee incident, IL, 8/28/45
"If I get sick . . ." Ibid.
"The living room walls . . ." IL, 9/16/45
"I had never felt so lonely . . ." IL, 2/16/46
John Wyman letter, IL, 1/18/46
His concert gift to Jeanette, IL, 10/20/45
"Someday soon I hope . . .", IL, 2/8/46
"I am alone here . . .", IL, 11/10/45
"Nelson was broiling a steak . . ." IL, 2/21/46

Helen Ferguson dinner, IL, 6/4/47
Christmas 1945, IL, 2/8/46

CHAPTER 23

Data regarding events leading up to Nelson's pneumonia came from anonymous letters
    and eyewitness accounts.
"On the plane bound from home—" IL, 3/15/46
Movie theater incident, eyewitness account
"Jeanette has listened . . ." IL, 5/7/46
Sweethearts broadcast, eyewitness account
"As you read this . . ." IL, 5/21/46
"Oh no, darling . . ." IL, 2/21/46
Hedda Hopper incident, IL, 4/21/46
Norma Nelson episode, interviews with the author, 1978
"I tried so hard . . ." IL, 6/6/46
"A woman wants security . . ." IL, 6/22/46
"Calling Nelson Eddy . . ." Hollywood *Reporter,* 8/21/46
Jeanette's arrival in England, newspaper article
Jeanette's miscarriage, IL, 3/30/47
Home recordings, IL, 10/26/46
Atwater Kent auditions, eyewitness account
Herbert Wall Studio incident, interview with Frank Laric

CHAPTER 24

"My own—" IL, 8/11/47
Farmer's market incident, AL
Christmas broadcast, AL
Chase and Sanborn show, AL
"It was the way . . ." AL
Maggie Tyte concert, AL
Later in February . . . , IL, 5/21/47
"I have nothing left . . ." IL, 6/4/47
Nelson threw himself into religion . . . IL, several letters, 1947
"I was utterly adrift . . ." IL, 5/1/47
"Darling, marriage is not . . ." IL, 5/2/47
"My dearest—", IL, 7/21/47
Jeanette's weekend at Isabel's, IL, 5/21/47
She fainted at home, Ibid.
Gene had awakened . . . Ibid.
Nelson received yet another call . . . , IL, 7/1/47
"What a child he would grow up to be . . ." IL, 7/14/47
Fans who drove by Nelson's home, AL
John Charles Thomas concert, AL
Anna MacDonald's death; letters by Jeanette; IL, 6/4/46, 6/14/47
Atwater Kent auditions, AL, 7/28/47
"Jeanette settled a large sum . . ." IL, 9/19/47
"I have not and never shall be . . ." IL, 8/5/47

"I could break down that . . ." ibid.
She worked herself into hysterics . . . IL, 7/14/47
"He doesn't make love to me . . ." IL, 9/19/47
Screen Guild broadcast, AL, 6/29/47
"I wish I could put down . . ." IL, 11/10/47

CHAPTER 25

"We are so grateful . . ." IL, 12/1/47
Three Daring Daughters preview, AL, 7/16/47
Birth control, IL, 10/23/47
Spanish girl, AL, 9/22/47
Mexican girl, AL, 10/27/47
"Nelson definitely does not ogle . . ." AL
Santa Monica beach, Marie Collick interview
Nelson dedicating "The Lost Chord," IL, 10/6/47
"I've never seen his face . . ." ? 10/27/47
Nelson and Jeanette's anniversary, IL, 10/6/47
"I have no pity for Ann . . ." Ibid.
Nelson and Ann at movie theater, AL, 7/28/47
Jeanette's pregnancy, IL, 1/21/48 and 2/6/48
"Nelson seems like a nice fellow . . ." AL, 11/21/47
Nelson stared out window, AL, 10/27/47
"Nelson can be the soul of cooperation . . ." AL, 11/3/47
"She is worried about me . . ." IL, 8/5/47
"Now he's completely crazy . . ." Ibid.
Atwater Kent party, five old-fashioneds, AL, 10/27/47, and Theodor Uppman, 8/3/91
    interview
Hollywood Story, Richard Sale interview with author
Sweethearts broadcast, AL, 1/31/47
Jeanette's miscarriage, IL, 1/23/48, 2/6/48, 4/20/48
"For awhile there . . ." IL, 2/6/48
Christmas eve party, Ibid.
The night of the 30th, AL, 2/17/48
"My whole life is yours . . ." IL, 2/6/48
"These have been days of pain . . ." Ibid.
"How shall I tell you . . ." IL, 5/4/48
Plattsburg rendezvous, IL, 5/14/48
"I have been so happy . . ." IL, 4/22/48
"Jeanette says she cannot have her baby . . ." IL, 2/6/48
"I don't trust you . . ." IL, 4/20/48
"If it was left up to her . . ." IL, 2/6/48
"I never sing a concert . . ." IL, 1/21/48
White House dinner, IL, 5/4/48
Ann Eddy shows up on tour, IL, 4/20/48
The next month was hell, IL, 6/11/48
Nelson's "suicide" attempt, IL, 6/21/48
Jeanette's heart attack, author's interview with Clarence Bull, 1971
"Jeanette looked utterly awful . . ." IL, 7/13/48

"Now Jeanette is in solid at MGM . . ." AL, 9/16/48

Gene in Hawaii, Hollywood *Citizen-News,* 6/19/48

Naomi Gottlieb data, letter to author, 1992

Kraft Music Hall write-up, eyewitness account

"Everybody came out at that broadcast . . ." AL, 11/30/48

He had a falling out with Lippe, IL, 12/5/48

She'd sent a detective . . . IL, 10/3/48

Nelson's LA concert, AL, 11/26/48

Nelson's Pasadena concert, AL

Jeanette's Christmas party, AL

Atwater Kent party, interview with Theodor Uppman, 8/3/91

Anniversary party, Ibid., AL, 1/20/49, AL

Ontario concert, AL, 4/6/49

Carnegie Hall, Los Angeles *Examiner,* 4/5/49

Affair with Inge, interview with Frank Laric

Maryon Murphy affair, interview with Maryon Murphy

Gene Raymond arrest, interview with P.H., 7/21/93

Data on the filmed test and Jeanette's subsequent breakdown came from Sybil Thomas, Marie Collick, Blossom Rock and others.

CHAPTER 26

Information for this chapter came from interviews with Marie Collick, Maryon Murphy, Frank Laric, Diane Goodrich and others, also from viewing "This is Your Life."

CHAPTER 27

This chapter includes data from Sandy Reiss, Theodore Paxson, Esther Shipp, Marie Collick, Harper McKay, Diane Goodrich, Jon Eddy and Sunny Griffin.

Bob Hope radio show, eyewitness account

Nelson's letter to Max Liebman, from the Nelson Eddy collection at USC

Al Caiazza quotes from interviews with the author

"All Stars Don't Spangle," entire text reproduced in *Mac/Eddy Today,* Issue #50

Two unfinished poems, handwritten sheets form Nelson's collection at USC

Nelson at Blinstaub's, author's interview with Bette Wilmot, 3/14/91

Jackie Hoover data, interviews with the author

Jeanette's hospitalization, letter to author, 1/20/94

Nelson at Isabel's grave, interviews with Marie Collick, Diane Goodrich

Bill Thornton data from Elsa Dik Glass

Divorce fiasco, data from Marie Collick and Sybil Thomas via Diane Goodrich

CHAPTER 28

Important data came from Sandy Reiss, Miliza Korjus, Sunny Griffin, Theodore Paxson, Blossom Rock and Richard Wells

"Some of us thought . . ." letter from Charles Cogle to author, 9/9/92

Richard Sales quotes, interview with author

Dick Weston quotes, letter to author, 1982

"I'm very worried," letter from Peggy Phillips to author, 1983

CHAPTER 29

Data came from Phyllis Woodbury, Richard Wells, Susan Nelson, Marie Collick, Blossom Rock, Diane Goodrich, plus anonymous sources.

CHAPTER 30

Nelson is quoted from various interviews. Author's interviews included Charles Higham, Sandy Reiss, Sunny Griffin, Jon Eddy, Theodore Paxson, Frank Laric, Maryon Murphy, Diane Goodrich.

The baptismal record that proves absolutely that Jeannette Anna McDonald was born on June 18, 1903.

Filmography

THE LOVE PARADE (Paramount, 1929).

Executive producer, Adolph Zukor. Produced and directed by Ernst Lubitsch. Screenplay by Ernest Vadja and Guy Bolton.

Songs: "Dream Lover," "My Love Parade," "March of the Grenadiers," "Anything to Please the Queen," "Let's Be Common," "Paris Stays the Same," "Nobody's Using It Now," "Ooo La La," "The Queen is Always Right."

Cast: Maurice Chevalier, Jeanette MacDonald, Lupino Lane, Lillian Roth, Virginia Bruce, Jean Harlow (as an extra).

THE VAGABOND KING (Paramount, 1930).

Produced by Adolph Zukor, Directed by Ludwig Berger. Screenplay by Herman Mankiewicz, based on the Play *If I Were King*. Filmed in Technicolor. Music by Rudolph Friml.

Songs: "Huguette Waltz," "Love for Sale," "Love Me Tonight," "Only a Rose," "Some Day," "Song of the Vagabonds," "If I Were King."

Cast: Dennis King, Jeanette MacDonald, Lillian Roth, Warner Oland.

PARAMOUNT ON PARADE (Paramount, 1930).

This was an all-star revue featuring most of the Paramount stars of the day. Some sequences were filmed in Technicolor, and several directors were involved. Jeanette was completely cut out of the American version, though in the Spanish version she served as

Mistress of Ceremonies, and sang one number with David Newell while floating in a gondola along the Grand Canal.

LET'S GO NATIVE (Paramount, 1930).

Executive producer, Adolph Zukor. Produced and directed by Leo McCarey. Screenplay by George Marion, Jr. and Percy Heath. Music and lyrics by George Marion, Jr. and Richard Whiting.

Songs: "I've Got a Yen For You," "It Seems to Be Spring," "Let's Go Native," "My Mad Moment," "Don't I Do," "Pampa Rose," "Joe Jazz."

Cast: Jeanette MacDonald, Jack Oakie, James Hall, Skeets Gallagher, Kay Francis.

·MONTE CARLO (Paramount, 1930).

Produced by Adolph Zukor. Associate producer and director, Ernst Lubitsch. Screenplay by Ernest Vajda, from the play *The Blue Coast* by Leon Xanrof and Jules Chancel. Music by Richard Whiting and Frank Harling.

Songs: "Give Me A Moment Please," "Beyond the Blue Horizon," "This is Something New to Me," "Women Just Women," "I'm a Simple-Hearted Man," "She'll Love Me and Like It," "Whatever it Is, It's Grand," "Always in All Ways," "Trimmin' the Women," "Day of Days."

Cast: Jack Buchanan, Jeanette MacDonald, Zasu Pitts

THE LOTTERY BRIDE (UA, 1930).

Produced by Arthur Hammerstein. Directed by Paul Stein. Original story by Herbert Stothart. Musical conductor, Herbert Stothart. Music by Carter Desmond, Howard Dietz and Arthur Schwartz. Finale filmed in Technicolor.

Songs: "You're an Angel," "I'll Follow the Trail," "My Northern Light."

Cast: Jeanette MacDonald, John Garrick, Joe E. Brown, Zasu Pitts, Robert Chisolm.

OH, FOR A MAN (Fox 1930).

Executive producer, William Fox. Associate producer and director, Hamilton McFadden. Screenplay by Lynn Starling and Philip Klein, based on *Stolen Thunder* by Mary F. Watkins. Music by William Kernell.

Songs: "On a Summer Night," "I'm Just Nuts About You"; and Jeanette sings Wagner's "Liebestod" from *Tristan and Isolde*.

Cast: Jeanette MacDonald, Reginald Denny, Marjorie White, Alison Skipworth, Bela Lugosi.

DON'T BET ON WOMEN (Fox, 1930).

Produced by William Fox. Directed by William K. Howard. Screenplay by Lynn Starling and Leon Gordon, based on the story *All Women Are Bad* by William Anthony McGuire. No songs.

Cast: Edmund Lowe, Jeanette MacDonald, Roland Young, Una Merkel.

ANNABELLE'S AFFAIRS (Fox, 1931).

Executive producer, William Fox. Associate producer, William Goetz. Directed by Alfred Werker. Screenplay by Leon Gordon, based on the play *Good Gracious Anabelle* by Clare Kummer. Music by James Hanley.

Song: "If Someone Should Kiss You."

Cast: Victor McLaglen, Jeanette MacDonald, Roland Young, Joyce Compton, Sally Blane.

ONE HOUR WITH YOU (Paramount, 1932).

Produced and directed by Ernst Lubitsch and George Cukor. Screenplay by Samson Raphaelson. Music by Oscar Straus, lyrics by Leo Robin. This was a remake of Lubitsch's 1924 film *The Marriage Circle*.

Songs: "One Hour with You," "Oh, That Mitzi," "We Will Always Be Sweethearts," "What Would You Do," "Three Times a Day," "What a Thing Like a Wedding Ring Can Do."

Cast: Maurice Chevalier, Jeanette MacDonald, Genvieve Tobin, Charles Ruggles, Roland Young.

LOVE ME TONIGHT (Paramount, 1932).

Produced and directed by Rouben Mamoulian. Screenplay by Samuel Hoffenstein, Waldemar Young and George Marion, Jr. Music by Richard Rodgers, lyrics by Lorenz Hart.

Songs: "Isn't It Romantic," "Mimi," "Love Me Tonight," "Poor Apache," "Lover," "The Song of Paree," "How Are You," "A Woman Needs Something Like That," "The Son of a Gun is Nothing But a Tailor."

Cast: Maurice Chevalier, Jeanette MacDonald, Charles Ruggles, Myrna Loy, Charles Butterworth, C. Aubrey Smith.

BROADWAY TO HOLLYWOOD (MGM, 1933).

Associate producer Harry Rapf. Directed by Willard Mack. Screenplay by Willard Mack and Edgar Allan Woolf.

Cast: Alice Brady, Frank Morgan, Mickey Rooney, Jackie Cooper. Nelson had a walk-on role and sang one number, "In the Garden of My Heart," music by Ernest Ball, lyrics by Carol Roma.

DANCING LADY (MGM, 1933).

Produced by David O. Selznick. Directed by Robert Z. Leonard. Screenplay by Allen Rivkin and P. J. Wolfson.

Cast: Joan Crawford, Clark Gable, Franchot Tone. Among the performers who had walk-on roles were Fred Astaire, The Three Stooges and Nelson, who sang "Rhythm of the Day," music by Richard Rodgers, lyrics by Lorenz Hart.

THE CAT AND THE FIDDLE (MGM, 1933).

Produced by Bernard Hyman. Directed by William K. Howard. Screenplay by Sam and Bella Spewack; based on the Jerome Kern-Otto Harbach musical play. Musical director, Herbert Stothart.

Songs: "The Night Was Made for Love," "Try to Forget," "She Didn't Say Yes," "One Moment Alone," "A New Love is Old," "I Watched the Love Parade," "Poor Pierrot."

Cast: Ramon Novarro, Jeanette MacDonald, Frank Morgan, Charles Butterworth, Vivenne Segal.

STUDENT TOUR (MGM, 1934).

Produced by Monta Bell. Directed by Charles Reisner. Screenplay by Ralph Spence and Phillip Dunne.

Cast: Jimmy Durante, Charles Butterworth, Maxine Doyle, Phil Regan, Betty Grable. Nelson played himself and had a few lines of dialogue, and sang "The Carlo," music and lyrics by Nacio Herb Brown and Arthur Freed.

THE MERRY WIDOW (MGM, 1934).

Executive producer, Irving Thalberg. Produced and directed by Ernst Lubitsch. Screenplay by Ernest Vajda and Samson Raphaelson, based on Franz Lehar's operetta *The Merry Widow*. Musical director, Herbert Stothart.

Songs: "Girls, Girls, Girls," "Maxim's," "Vilia," "Tonight Will Teach Me to Forget," "The Merry Widow Waltz."

Cast: Maurice Chevalier, Jeanette MacDonald, Edward Everett Horton, Una Merkel, Herman Bing.

NAUGHTY MARIETTA (MGM, 1935).

Produced by Hunt Stromberg. Directed by W. S. Van Dyke II. Screenplay by John Lee Mahin, Frances Goodrich and Albert Hackett. Music by Victor Herbert, lyrics by Rida Johnson Young and Gus Kahn.

Songs: "Chansonette," "Antoinette and Anatole," "Tramp, Tramp, Tramp," "Owl and the Bobcat," " 'Neath the Southern Moon," "Italian Street Song," "I'm Falling in Love with Someone," "Ah, Sweet Mystery of Life."

Cast: Jeanette MacDonald, Nelson Eddy, Frank Morgan, Elsa Lanchester, Douglas Dumbrille, Cecilia Parker.

ROSE MARIE (MGM, 1936).

Produced by Hunt Stromberg. Directed by W. S. Van Dyke II. Screenplay by Frances Goodrich, Albert Hackett and Alice Duer Miller, based on the operetta with music by Rudolph Friml and Herbert Stothart. Musical director, Herbert Stothart.

Songs: "Rose Marie," "Song of the Mounties," "Indian Love Call," "Totem Tom Tom," "Pardon Me Madame," "Just for You," "Dinah," "Some of These Days," Jeanette sings operatic excerpts from Gounod's *Roméo and Juliette* and Puccini's *Tosca*.

Cast: Jeanette MacDonald, Nelson Eddy, Reginald Owen, Una O'Connor, George Regis, James Stewart, Allan Jones, Gilda Gray, David Niven, Alan Mowbray, Herman Bing.

SAN FRANCISCO (MGM, 1936).

Produced by John Emerson and Bernard H. Hyman. Directed by W. S. Van Dyke II. Screenplay by Anita Loos. Musical director, Herbert Stothart. Costumes by Adrian.

Songs: "San Francisco" and "The One Love" by Gus Kahn, Bronislau Kaper and Walter Jurmann. "Would You" by Nacio Herb Brown and Arthur Freed.

Cast: Clark Gable, Jeanette MacDonald, Spencer Tracy, Jack Holt, Jessie Ralph, Ted Healy.

MAYTIME (MGM, 1937).

Produced by Hunt Stromberg. Directed by Robert Z. Leonard. Screenplay by Noel Langley, based on the Sigmund Romberg operetta. Additional songs by Chet Forrest, Bob Wright, and Herbert Stothart. Musical director, Herbert Stothart. Gowns by Adrian.

Songs: "Will You Remember," "Virginia Ham and Eggs," "Student Drinking Song," "Carry Me Back to Old Virginny," "Les Filles de Cadiz," Page's Aria from *Les Huguenots* by Meyerbeer, "Czaritza," based on Tchaikovsky's Fifth Symphony.

THE FIREFLY (MGM, 1937).

Produced by Hunt Stromberg. Directed by Robert Z. Leonard. Screenplay by Frances Goodrich and Albert Hackett, based on the Rudolph Friml operetta. Musical director, Herbert Stothart. Dances by Albertina Rasch. Gowns by Adrian. Filmed in sepia.

Songs: "Love is Like a Firefly," "He Who Loves and Runs Away," "When a Maid Comes Knocking at Your Heart," "A Woman's Kiss," "When the Wine is Full of Fire," "Sympathy," "Giannina Mia," "Donkey Serenade."

Cast: Jeanette MacDonald, Allan Jones, Warren William, Douglas Dumbrille.

ROSALIE (MGM, 1937).

Produced and written by William Anthony McGuire. Directed by W. S. Van Dyke II. Musical director, Herbert Stothart. Dances by Albertina Rasch. Music by Cole Porter.

Songs: "Rosalie," "In the Still of the Night," "Who Knows," "Why Should I Care," "I've Got a Strange New Rhythm in My Heart," "Spring Love is in the Air," "To Love or Not to Love," "It's All Over But the Shouting," "I Know It's Not Meant to Be," "Oh, Brave Old Army Team," "Close."

Cast: Nelson Eddy, Eleanor Powell, Ilona Massey, Ray Bolger, Frank Morgan, Edna May Oliver.

GIRL OF THE GOLDEN WEST (MGM, 1938).

Produced by William Anthony McGuire. Directed by Robert Z. Leonard. Screenplay by Isabel Dawn and Boyce DeGaw, based on the David Belasco play. Musical director, Herbert Stothart. Songs by Sigmund Romberg and Gus Kahn. Dances by Albertina Rasch. Gowns by Adrian. Filmed in sepia.

Songs: "Soldiers of Fortune," "Shadows on the Moon," "Gentle Wind in the Trees," "Seniorita," "Mariache," "Sun Up to Sun Down," "The West Ain't Wild Anymore," "Obey Your Heart."

Cast: Jeanette MacDonald, Nelson Eddy, Walter Pidgeon, Leo Carrillo, Buddy Ebsen, Priscilla Lawson, H. B. Warner, Jeanne Ellis, Bill Cody, Jr.

SWEETHEARTS (MGM, 1938).

Produced by Hunt Stromberg. Directed by W. S. Van Dyke II. Screenplay by Dorothy Parker and Alan Campbell, based on the Victor Herbert operetta. Musical director, Herbert Stothart. Dances by Albertina Rasch. Gowns by Adrian. Filmed in Technicolor.

Songs: "Wooden Shoes," "For Ev'ry Lover Must Meet His Fate," "Sweethearts," "Pretty as a Picture," "The Game of Love," "Mademoiselle on Parade," "Summer Serenade," "On Parade," "Little Grey Home in the West."

Cast: Jeanette MacDonald, Nelson Eddy, Frank Morgan, Ray Bolger, Florence Rice, Mischa Auer, Terry Kilburn, Betty Jaynes, Douglas McPhail, Kathleen Lockhart, Gene Lockhart, Reginald Gardiner, Herman Bing, Dalies Frantz.

LET FREEDOM RING (MGM, 1939).

Produced by Harry Rapf. Directed by Jack Conway. Screenplay by Ben Hecht. Filmed in sepia.

Songs: "Dusty Road," Drigo's "Love Serenade," "Home Sweet Home," "When Irish Eyes Are Smiling," "America," "Pat Sez He," "Where Else But Here."

Cast: Nelson Eddy, Virginia Bruce, Lionel Barrymore, Edward Arnold, Victor McLaglen, Charles Butterworth, H. B. Warner.

BROADWAY SERENADE (MGM, 1939).

Produced and directed by Robert Z. Leonard. Screenplay by Charles Lederer. Songs by Herbert Stothart, Edward Ward, Bob Wright, Chet Forrest, Gus Kahn. Gowns by Adrian. Finale sequence staged by Busby Berkeley.

Songs: "For Every Lonely Heart," "Rhapsody," "Flying High," "One Look at You," "Time Changes Everything," "No Time to Argue," "Ridin' on a Rainbow," "Un Bel Di" from *Madame Butterfly*.

Cast: Jeanette MacDonald, Lew Ayres, Ian Hunter, Frank Morgan, Rita Johnson, Virginia Grey.

BALALAIKA (MGM, 1939).

Produced by Lawrence Weingarten. Directed by Reinhold Schunzel. Screenplay by Leon Gordon, Charles Bennett and Jacques Deval. Musical director, Herbert Stothart.

Songs: "At the Balalaika," "Tanya," "Ride, Cossack, Ride," "Volga Boatman," "The Magic of Your Love," "Silent Night," "My Heart is a Gypsy," vocal selections set to *Scheherezade* and Bizet's *Carmen,* including the "Toreador Song."

Cast: Nelson Eddy, Ilona Massey, Charles Ruggles, Frank Morgan, C. Aubrey Smith, Joyce Compton, Dalies Franz.

NEW MOON (MGM, 1940).

Produced and directed by Robert Z. Leonard. Screenplay by Jacques Deval and Robert Arthur, based on the Sigmund Romberg operetta. Musical director, Herbert Stothart. Gowns by Adrian.

Songs: "Lover, Come Back to Me," "Wanting You," "Softly as in a Morning Sunrise," "Stouthearted Men," "One Kiss," "Marianne."

Cast: Jeanette MacDonald, Nelson Eddy, Mary Boland, George Zucco, H. B. Warner.

BITTERSWEET (MGM, 1940).

Produced by Victor Saville. Directed by W. S. Van Dyke II. Screenplay by Lesser Samuels, based on the Noel Coward play. Musical director, Herbert Stothart. Gowns by Adrian. Filmed in Technicolor.

Songs: "Ziguener," "If You Could Only Come with Me," "Kiss Me," "I'll See You Again," "Dear Little Cafe," "What is Love," "Ladies of the Town," "Tokay," "Love in Any Language."

Cast: Jeanette MacDonald, Nelson Eddy, George Sanders, Ian Hunter, Edward Ashley, Lynne Carver, Diana Lewis, Veda Ann Borg, Herman Bing.

SMILIN' THROUGH (MGM, 1941).

Produced by Victor Saville. Directed by Frank Borzage. Screenplay by Donald Ogden Stewart and John Balderston, from the play by Jane Cowl and Jane Murfin. Musical director, Herbert Stothart. Gowns by Adrian. Filmed in Technicolor.

Songs: "Smilin' Through," "Just a Little Love, a Little Kiss," Bizet's "Ouvre Ton Coeur," "The Kerry Dance," "Hope and Glory," "Drink to Me Only with Thine Eyes."

Cast: Jeanette MacDonald, Brian Aherne, Gene Raymond, Ian Hunter.

THE CHOCOLATE SOLDIER (MGM, 1941).

Produced by Victor Saville. Directed by Roy Del Ruth. Screenplay by Keith Winter and Leonard Lee, based on the Molnar play *The Guardsman*. Musical director, Herbert Stothart.

Songs: "While My Lady Sleeps," "Song of the Flea," "Evening Star," "My Hero," "Thank the Lord the War is Over," "Sympathy," "The Chocolate Soldier," "Forgive," "Ti-Ra-La-La."

Cast: Nelson Eddy, Risë Stevens, Nigel Bruce, Florence Bates.

I MARRIED AN ANGEL (MGM, 1942).

Produced by Hunt Stromberg. Directed by W.S. Van Dyke II. Screenplay by Anita Loos; based on the play by Vaszary Jones.

Songs: "I Married An Angel," "Spring is Here," "I'll Tell the Man in the Street," "A Twinkle in Your Eye."

Cast: Jeanette MacDonald, Nelson Eddy, Edward Everett Horton, Binnie Barnes, Reginald Owen, Douglas Dumbrille, Mona Marris, Leonid Kinsky, Anne Jeffreys, Janis Carter.

CAIRO (MGM, 1942).

Produced by MGM. Directed by W. S. Van Dyke II. Screenplay by John McClain.

Songs: "The Maid from Cadiz," "Buds Won't Bud," "A Woman Without a Man," "Keep the Light Burning Bright in the Harbor," "Cairo."

Cast: Jeanette MacDonald, Robert Young, Ethel Waters, Reginald Owen, Lionel Atwill, Mona Barrie, Dooley Wilson.

The Phantom of the Opera (Universal, 1943).

Produced by George Waggner. Directed by Arthur Lubin. Filmed in Technicolor.
Songs: "Lullaby of the Bells." Nelson sings the drinking song from *Martha* and two operatic scenes based on themes by Chopin and Tchaikovsky's Fourth Symphony.
Cast: Nelson Eddy, Susanna Foster, Claude Rains, Edgar Barrier, Leo Carrillo, Jane Farrar.

Knickerbocker Holiday (UA, 1944).

Produced and directed by Harry Joe Brown. Based on the Maxwell Anderson play.
Songs: "September Song," "Sing Out," "Let's Make Tomorrow Today," "Love Has Made This Such a Lovely Day," "Zuyder Zee," "The Jail Song," "One More Smile," "Be Not Hasty, Gentle Maiden."
Cast: Nelson Eddy, Charles Coburn, Constance Dowling, Shelley Winters, Otto Krueger.

Follow the Boys (Universal, 1944).

Produced by Charles K. Feldman. Directed by Eddie Sutherland. Jeanette played herself in an all-star revue, singing two numbers, "Beyond the Blue Horizon" and "I'll See You In My Dreams."

Make Mine Music (Walt Disney, 1946).

Similar to *Fantasia* in style, this film consisted of ten musical/animated segments. Nelson's ten-minute sequence about Willie, "The Whale Who Wanted to Sing at the Met" was the most popular portion of the film, and has been released by Disney Video as a short subject.

Northwest Outpost (Republic, 1947).

Produced by Herbert J. Yates. Directed by Allan Dwan. Screenplay by Elizabeth Meehan and Richard Sale. Music by Rudolph Friml.
Songs: "One More Mile to Go," "Raindrops on a Drum," "Love is the Time," "Nearer and Dearer," "Tell Me With Your Eyes," "Russian Easter Hymn," "Weary."
Cast: Nelson Eddy, Ilona Massey, Joseph Schildkraut, Elsa Lanchester, American G.I. chorus.

Three Daring Daughters (MGM, 1948).

Produced by Joe Pasternak. Directed by Fred M. Wilcox. Screenplay by Albert Mannheimer, Frederick Kohner, Sonja Levien and John Meehan. Gowns by Irene. Filmed in Technicolor.
Songs: "The Dickey Bird Song," "Route 66," "You Made Me Love You," "Sweethearts," Grieg's "Springtide."
Cast: Jeanette MacDonald, Jose Iturbi, Jane Powell, Ann E. Todd, Elinor Donahue, Edward Arnold, Moyna MacGill.

THE SUN COMES UP (MGM, 1949).

Produced by Robert Sisk. Directed by Richard Thorpe. Screenplay by William Ludwig and Margaret Fitts; based on the novel *Mountain Prelude* by Marjorie Kinnan Rawlings. Music by André Previn. Gowns by Irene. Filmed in Technicolor.

Songs: "Un Bel Di" from *Madame Butterfly,* "Songs My Mother Taught Me," "Tes Jolies Yeux," "Cousin Ebenezer," "Romance."

Cast: Jeanette MacDonald, Claude Jarman, Jr., Lassie, Lloyd Nolan, Percy Kilbride, Margaret Hamilton.

Selected References

Books

Cannom, Robert C., *Van Dyke and the Mythical City of Hollywood,* Murray & Gee, Inc., 1948

Carey, Gary, *Anita Loos,* New York, Alfred A. Knopf, 1988

Castanza, Philip, *The Films of Jeanette MacDonald and Nelson Eddy,* Citadel Press, 1978

Chevalier, Maurice, *I Remember It Well,* New York, Macmillan Co., 1970

————, *With Love,* Boston, Little Brown & Company, 1960

Cooper, Jackie, *Please Don't Shoot My Dog,* New York, William Morrow & Co., 1981

Goodrich, Diane and Sharon Rich, *Farewell to Dreams,* Jeanette MacDonald/Nelson Eddy Friendship Club, 1979.

Higham, Charles, *Charles Laughton,* New York, Doubleday, 1976

Kotsilibas, James and Myrna Loy, *Myrna Loy, Being and Becoming,* New York, Alfred A. Knopf, 1987

Kiner, Larry, *Nelson Eddy: a bio-discography,* Scarecrow Press, 1992

Knowles, Eleanor, *The Films of Jeanette MacDonald and Nelson Eddy,* A. S. Barnes & Co., 1975

Lanchester, Elsa, *Elsa Lanchester Herself,* New York, St. Martin's Press, 1983

Merrill, Robert, *Between Acts,* New York, McGraw Hill, 1976

————, *Once More From the Beginning,* New York, MacMillan, 1965

Parish, James Robert, *The Jeanette MacDonald Story,* Mason Charter, 1976

Rich, Sharon, *Jeanette MacDonald: A Pictorial Treasury,* Times Mirror, 1973

Riva, Maria, *Marlene Dietrich,* New York, Alfred A. Knopf, 1993

Stack, Robert, *Straight Shooting,* New York, Macmillan Co., 1980

Winters, Shelley, *Shelley,* New York, William Morrow & Co., 1980

Periodicals

Magazine sources included The Hollywood Reporter, Variety and fan club publications from all the Nelson Eddy and Jeanette MacDonald clubs from 1935 through 1967. Also invaluable was *Mac/Eddy Today,* the magazine published by the Mac/Eddy Club, 101 Cedar Lane, Teaneck NJ 07666. Newspaper clippings and reviews were collected from major newspapers around the world, as well as Nelson's scrapbooks housed at USC.

A Note to Collectors

All of the eight MacDonald-Eddy films together have been released on video, also all of their solo MGM films, plus Nelson's *Phantom of the Opera.* Any of these can be ordered through a video store. For those collecting tapes/CDs, or who want a complete list of all Nelson's radio shows and recordings, the best reference book is the Larry Kiner bio-discography mentioned above. It's not available through stores, but ordering information can be obtained from the Mac/Eddy Club noted above.

NOTE: All the photos in this book are from the author's personal collection.

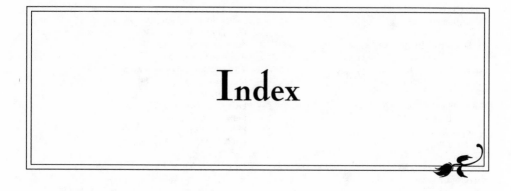

Index